Musical Exoticism

A Japanese geisha, a Middle Eastern caravan, a Hungarian-"Gypsy" fiddler, Carmen flinging a rose at Don José, Josephine Baker singing "Petite Tonkinoise" – portrayals of people and places that are considered somehow "exotic" have been ubiquitous from 1700 to today, whether in opera, Broadway musicals, instrumental music, film scores, or in jazz and popular song. Often these portrayals are highly stereotypical but also powerful, indelible, and touching – or troubling. *Musical Exoticism* surveys the vast and varied repertoire of Western musical works that evoke exotic locales. It relates trends in musical exoticism to other trends in music, such as program music and avant-garde experimentation, as well as to broader historical developments, such as nationalism and empire. Ralph P. Locke traces the history of exotic depiction from the Baroque era onward, and illustrates its phases through close study of numerous exotic works, including operas by Handel and Rameau, Mozart's *Rondo alla turca*, Rimsky-Korsakov's *Sheherazade*, Debussy's *Pagodes*, Puccini's *Madama Butterfly*, Bernstein's *West Side Story*, and the culture-bridging opera *Marco Polo* by Chinese-born composer Tan Dun.

RALPH P. LOCKE is Professor of Musicology at Eastman School of Music, University of Rochester. He is a five-time winner of the ASCAP-Deems Taylor Award for Excellence in Writing about Music, and in 2006 he won the H. Colin Slim Award from the American Musicological Society. His previous books are *Music, Musicians, and the Saint-Simonians* (1986), and (as contributing co-editor) *Cultivating Music in America: Women Patrons and Activists since 1860* (1997), and his essays have appeared in many journals and books including *Journal of the American Musicological Society*, *Cambridge Opera Journal*, and *19th-Century Music*. He is the founding editor of the award-winning book series Eastman Studies in Music.

Musical Exoticism
Images and Reflections
———

RALPH P. LOCKE

Eastman School of Music (University of Rochester)

CAMBRIDGE UNIVERSITY PRESS
Cambridge, New York, Melbourne, Madrid, Cape Town,
Singapore, São Paulo, Delhi, Tokyo, Mexico City

Cambridge University Press
The Edinburgh Building, Cambridge CB2 8RU, UK

Published in the United States of America by Cambridge University Press, New York

www.cambridge.org
Information on this title: www.cambridge.org/9780521349550

© Ralph P. Locke 2009

This publication is in copyright. Subject to statutory exception
and to the provisions of relevant collective licensing agreements,
no reproduction of any part may take place without the written
permission of Cambridge University Press.

First published 2009
3rd printing 2011
First paperback edition 2011

A catalogue record for this publication is available from the British Library

ISBN 978-0-521-87793-0 Hardback
ISBN 978-0-521-34955-0 Paperback

Cambridge University Press has no responsibility for the persistence or
accuracy of URLs for external or third-party internet websites referred to in
this publication, and does not guarantee that any content on such websites is,
or will remain, accurate or appropriate.

For Lona, with love and thanks

Contents

Figures [*page* x]
Musical examples [xii]
Acknowledgments [xiv]
Notes to the reader [xvii]

Introduction [1]

PART I [13]

1 Music, the world, and the critic [15]
   Stylistic listening and worldly criticism [15]
   Works, values, and scholars [19]

2 Questions of value [25]
   "Exotic": high praise or curse word? [25]
   Edward Said's *Orientalism* and other ideological critiques [34]
   Applying Orientalist critiques to music [36]
   Beauty and beastliness [38]

3 Exoticism with and without exotic style [43]
   Existing definitions [44]
   A broader definition [46]
   The "Exotic-Style Only" Paradigm [48]
   The "All the Music in Full Context" Paradigm [59]
   The then/now binarism [64]
   Four other binarisms [66]
      Self/Other
      Nearness/distance
      The real/the fictive
      Musical/extramusical signs and indicators

4 Who is "Us"? The national and/as the exotic, and the treatment of stereotypes [72]

National style or exoticism? [72]
How works handle stereotypes and binarisms [79]

PART II [85]

5 Baroque portrayals of despots: ancient Babylon, Incan Peru [87]
Handel's Eastern dramas [89]
Belshazzar, semi-comic Babylonian tyrant [90]
Empire and virtue [96]
Les Indes galantes: encyclopedic world tour [97]
Rameau's Huascar: corrupt ruler and anticolonial terrorist [100]

6 A world of exotic styles, 1750–1880 [106]
Eighteenth-century ethnicities [108]
Delightful and vicious Turks: Molière/Lully, Favart, Gluck, Mozart [110]
The Turkish style [114]
Mozart's *alla turca* non-rondo [123]
The proliferation of exotic and national dialects [126]
Liszt's gifts: Gypsy "opium" and the national rhapsody [135]

7 Exotic operas and two Spanish Gypsies [150]
Regions on the nineteenth-century musical stage [150]
The Roma (Gypsies) in life and image [154]
"Abietta zingara" [156]
Gypsy characters and poor Andalusians [160]
The Gypsy Carmen's non-Gypsyish lament [169]

8 Imperialism and "the exotic Orient" [175]
Multiple empires, multiple Orients [176]
Silence over the imperial encounter [178]
The paradigmatic Oriental-opera plot [180]
Fragile women, fatal women, and the pentatonic [184]
Men: the forceful and the gentle [192]
Rituals, priests, and crowds [196]
Madama Butterfly: an opera of, and against, empire [202]

9 Exoticism in a modernist age (c. 1890–1960) [214]
The turn against Overt Exoticism [214]
Submerged Exoticisms: (1) the arabesque [217]
Submerged Exoticisms: (2) bold harmonic procedures [222]
Transcultural Composing [228]

Pagodes: Javanese pentatonicism Trans(culturally)figured [233]
Are Submerged and Transcultural approaches exotic? [236]
Overt Exoticism in concert music and opera [244]
   Composers from a minority group or "peripheral" culture [244]
   Non-modernists [248]
   The Soviet era through the 1950s [250]
Overt Exoticism in popular genres [251]
   Light orchestral music and jazz [251]
   Popular song: America and France [254]
   Operetta and musical [260]
   Film music [263]
West Side Story and exotic Otherness [268]

10 Exoticism in a global age (*c.* 1960 to today) [276]
   New compositions [278]
      Composers from beyond "the Western mainstream" [279]
      The later Soviet era, the State of Israel [282]
      Composers in the West [284]
      Takemitsu and Tan Dun [293]
   Exotic varieties of jazz [299]
   With technological assistance from … [300]
   Elfin kingdom and other movie realms [301]
   Pop exotica [304]

11 Epilogue: exotic works of the past, today [312]
   Performing exotic works [312]
   The afterlife of exotic stage works [317]
   Pondering exotic works as they are [325]

Notes [328]
Bibliography [369]
Index [407]

Figures

Figure 3.1 Stylistic features within Western music that suggest an exotic locale or culture. [*pages* 51–54]
Figure 5.1 Rembrandt, *Belshazzar's Feast* (*c.* 1635). [91]
Figure 5.2 Rameau, *Les Indes galantes* (1735–36): the Incan tyrant Huascar lording it over Phani. [101]
Figure 6.1 Early eighteenth-century Turkish painting of a Janissary military band. [115]
Figure 6.2 Turkish musicians with *dümbelek, miskal, ney, tambur,* and *ayakh keman* (ink drawing, *c.* 1750). [117]
Figure 6.3 Component traits of the *alla turca* style, *c.* 1750–1830. [118–21]
Figure 6.4 Portrait of the masterful Rom ("Gypsy") fiddler János Bihari by János Donát (1820). [138]
Figure 6.5 Concordance of six Hungarian Rhapsodies by Liszt. [142]
Figure 7.1 Magda Spiegel as Verdi's Azucena, in Gypsy costume (*c.* 1920). [158]
Figure 7.2 Emma Calvé in Carmen's Card Aria (1893). [173]
Figure 8.1 In Bizet's *Les pêcheurs de perles*, Nadir recognizes the Brahmin priestess Leïla. [193]
Figure 8.2 In *Madama Butterfly*, Leontyne Price, as Cio-Cio-San, bids her bridesmaids modestly bow. [199]
Figure 8.3 The Bonze and the wedding guests curse Cio-Cio-San (Yoko Watanabe). [207]
Figure 9.1 Debussy and Zohra ben Brahim, the Algerian mistress of his writer-friend Pierre Louÿs. [219]
Figure 9.2 Arabeques from fifteenth-century Cairo, as analyzed in Riegl's *Stilfragen* (1893). [220]
Figure 9.3 Michel Fokine's ballet *Sheherazade*. [224]
Figure 9.4 Costume design by Léon Bakst for the Blue Sultana in Fokine's *Sheherazade*. [225]

Figure 9.5	Javanese dancers at the 1889 Paris World's Fair. [230]
Figure 9.6	Gamelan at the Javanese *kampong* at the 1889 Paris World's Fair. [231]
Figure 9.7	Partch's *The Delusion of the Fury* (1965–66). [240]
Figure 9.8	Young musicians playing Harry Partch's instruments, including the Gourd Tree. [241]
Figure 9.9	French bandleader Ray Ventura, with his "Collégiens" (college boys) in "Chinese" costumes. [258]
Figure 9.10	Caricature of performers in the Black Birds revue in Paris's Moulin Rouge nightclub (1929). [258]
Figure 9.11	A page from the Erdmann-Becce *General Handbook of Film Music* (1927). [265]
Figure 9.12	Anita and Bernardo show the native-born New Yorkers how to do the mambo with passion and style. [272]
Figure 9.13	Anita is taunted and physically threatened by the Jets. [274]
Figure 10.1	"Music of the Spheres," watercolor by Bernard Xolotl and Barbara Falconer. [286]
Figure 10.2	Steve Reich and Musicians playing Reich's *Music for 18 Instruments*. [287]
Figure 10.3	Scene from Tan Dun's opera *Marco Polo* (1996). [296]
Figure 11.1	Carmen (mezzo-soprano Miao Qing) sings the Seguidilla to Don José (tenor Lin Jin Yuan) in Beijing (1982). [318]
Figure 11.2	American mezzo-soprano Marianne Cornetti as Verdi's Azucena (2006). [321]

Musical examples

Example 3.1 Rimsky-Korsakov, *Sheherazade*: theme representing Sheherazade herself. [*page* 60]
Example 5.1 Handel, Belshazzar's aria "Let the deep bowl thy praise confess." [93]
Example 5.2 Rameau, "Les sauvages" for harpsichord. [99]
Example 5.3 Rameau, *Les Indes galantes*, deuxième entrée: *Les Incas du Pérou*, "Obéissons sans balancer." [102]
Example 6.1 Mozart, Piano Sonata in A Major, K331, movement 3, "Alla turca," mm. 1–8. [124]
Example 6.2 Liszt, Hungarian Rhapsody No. 14, mm. 243–56. [147]
Example 7.1 Verdi, *Il trovatore*, Act 2: Azucena's "Stride la vampa," opening. [159]
Example 7.2 Bizet, *Carmen*, Act 3: Carmen's Card Aria, opening. [171]
Example 8.1 Puccini, *Turandot*, Act 3: Liù's "Tu che di gel sei cinta." [190]
Example 8.2 Puccini, *Turandot*, Act 1: the "Mo-Li-Hua" tune. [191]
Example 8.3 Puccini, *Turandot*, Act 1: Liù's "Signore, ascolta!" [191]
Example 8.4 Bizet, *Les pêcheurs de perles*, Nadir's Act 1 aria "Je crois entendre encore." [195]
Example 8.5 Bizet's "Temple Duet" and Puccini's "O Kami!" chorus compared. [197]
Example 8.6 Puccini, *Madama Butterfly*, Act 1: arrival of "the happiest girl in Japan" and her friends. [209]
Example 8.7 Puccini, *Madama Butterfly*, Act 1: procession of the wedding guests, with pile-up resulting in three measures on an eleventh chord. [211]
Example 8.8 Puccini, *Madama Butterfly*, Act 2, scene 2: trio for Suzuki, Pinkerton, and Sharpless. [212]
Example 9.1 Debussy, *Prélude à l'Après-midi d'un faune*, mm. 1–4. [218]

Example 9.2   Debussy, *Prélude à l'Après-midi d'un faune*, mm. 61–62, winds playing the "Sheherazade" figure.   [221]
Example 9.3   Debussy, *Pagodes*, mm. 33–36.   [235]
Example 9.4   Chausson, *Poème* for violin and orchestra, at rehearsal no. 18.   [235]
Example 9.5   Bernstein, *West Side Story*: Maria and Tony's *cha-cha-chá*, mm. 5–10.   [270]

Acknowledgments

Music has long evoked exotic places, peoples, and ways of life. Exploring the vast repertoire of exotic evocations, and its contexts and implications, has been a decades-long trip for me. The journey picked up speed in graduate school at the University of Chicago, thanks to, among others, Philip Gossett, Robert B. Marshall, the late Leonard B. Meyer, H. Colin Slim (visiting for a year), Rose Rosengard Subotnik, and the late Hans Lenneberg (all in the Department of Music) and (in the Department of History) Keith M. Baker and the late Leonard Krieger. A nice push forward was provided by some eye-opening pages in a book by the late Georg Knepler, by stimulating encounters with Knepler in (then-)East Berlin and, a few years later, by extensive discussions with Amnon Shiloah, the late Alexander Ringer, and the late Dorothy V. Hagan.

I am enormously grateful to a number of scholars who have read chapter drafts in their areas of special expertise or who, over the years, have batted ideas back and forth with me or shown me their own work-in-progress. At the risk of forgetting some major debt of mine in this regard, I should mention Naomi André, Ayden Adler, Daniel Albright, Nasser Al-Taee, Arved Ashby, Jean-Rerre Bartoli Jonathan Bellman, Thomas Betzwieser, Gurminder Kaur Bhogal, Olivia A. Bloechl, Bruce Alan Brown, David Claman, Catherine Cole, Jeremy Day-O'Connell, Yayoi Uno Everett, Annegret Fauser, Andreas Gieger, Jeremy Grimshaw, Arthur Groos, Ellen T. Harris, Rebecca Harris-Warrick, Karen Henson, Steven Huebner, Mary Hunter, Francesco Izzo, Sylvia Kahan, Tamara Levitz, Shay Loya, Claire Mabilat, Hugh Macdonald, Catherine Mayes, David R. Nicholls, David Patterson, James Parakilas, Michael V. Pisani, Michael Puri, David Rosen, Julian Rushton, Martin Scherzinger, Emanuele Senici, Ronit Seter, W. Anthony Sheppard, Mary Ann Smart, Jürgen Thym, Kate van Orden, Elizabeth Wells, Amanda Eubanks Winkler, Lesley A. Wright, Stephen Zank, and Bennett Zon.

Other scholars, as well as librarians, composers, performing musicians, and other friends, have encouraged or provided materials, reproached or goaded, discussed specific musical passages with me, or helped with translations from such languages as Hungarian and Japanese. Particularly supportive were Celia Applegate, Mieke Bal, Jonathan Baldo, Ryan Raul Bañagale, the late

M. Elizabeth C. Bartlet, Daniel Beaumont, Michael Beckerman, Ali Behdad, M. Jennifer Bloxam, Philip Bohlman, Frederick N. Bohrer, Paul Bové, the late Philip Brett, the late Barry Brook, Paul A. Bushkovitch, Bernard Camier, Lorenzo Candelaria, Philip Carli, Theo Cateforis, Lori Dabbagh, James Deaville, Fabrizio Della Seta, Pascal Denécheau (who made available a crucial manuscript source for Rameau's *Les Indes galantes*), Deniz Ertan, Angela Escott, Lisa Feuerzeig, Phil Ford, Roger Freitas, Alain Frogley, Andy Fry, Albrecht Gaub, Andreas Gieger, Louise Goldberg, Sumanth Gopinath, Philip Gossett, Saed Haddad, George Haggerty, Wayne Heisler, Denis Herlin, Berthold Hoeckner, T. Emil Homerin, Sion E. Honea, Nadine Hubbs, Mary Hunter, Gabriela Ilnitchi, Arnold Jacobshagen, Hervé Lacombe, Rob Lancefield, Steven Laitz, Kenneth Langevin, the late François Lesure, David B. Levy, R. Allen Lott, Kathryn Lowerre, Patrick Macey, Jürgen Maehder, Stephen C. Meyer, Balázs Mikusi, Barbara A. Milewski, Michael Miller, Giuseppe Montemagno, Michela Niccolai, Roger Parker, Pierluigi Petrobelli, David Pollack, Pierpaolo Polzonetti, Walid Raad, Ellen Rosand, Joan Shelley Rubin, Carlos Sanchez-Gutierrez, Grace Seiberling, Edwin Seroussi, Sharon Shafrir, Christie and Suresh Sunderrajan, Ted Swedenburg, Timothy D. Taylor, David Temperley, Judith Tick, Michael Walter, William A. Weber, Gretchen Wheelock, Janet Wolff, Stephen Zank, Neal Zaslaw, Ricardo Zohn-Muldoon – and, over the years, a host of splendid librarians at the Eastman School's Sibley Music Library, most notably Linda Blair, Alice Carli, Matthew Colbert, David Peter Coppen, Mary Wallace Davidson, James Farrington, Louise Goldberg, E. Sion Honea, Robert Iannapollo, Gerald Szymanski, the late Ruth Watanabe, and (the Library's current director) Daniel Zager. Scott Perkins prepared the musical examples insightfully. Numerous individuals and institutions assisted in locating illustrations: particularly helpful were Danlee Mitchell and Jon Szanto (of the Harry Partch Archive), the great French singer Line Renaud (and her staff at the Archives Loulou Gasté), Steve Reich, and Bernard Xolotl. I have attempted to locate the original of all illustrations and to contact the appropriate rights-holders; I will gladly incorporate any corrections or additional information into future printings of the book.

I am grateful to faculty members and students at a number of institutions – including Cornell University, The Catholic University of America, St. Mary's College (University of Maryland), Smith College, Syracuse University, Williams College, University of Buffalo, and University of North Carolina (Chapel Hill) – who invited me to present my findings and enriched my thinking by their lively reactions.

Other graduate students (and a few undergraduates), mainly at the Eastman School of Music and at the University of Rochester's College of Arts and

Sciences, also explored these issues with me, and offered insights – and certainly much encouragement – that no doubt echo in this book. Some of them have, in the meantime, gone on to offer distinguished scholarship in this or other areas. I particularly mention (besides a few named earlier) Sylvia Alajaji, Andrew Allen, Tekla Babelak (at Cornell), Tyler Cassidy-Heacock, Lars Christensen (at University of Minnesota), Michael Dodds, Caroline Ehman, Joshua Fein, Kimberly Hannon, Robert Haskins, Katherine Hutchings, Cara Johnson, Amy Kintner, Cindy L. Kim, Zhichun Lin (at Ohio State University), Marie Sumner Lott, Emily Mills, Matthew Morrow, Jo Nardolillo, Martin Nedbal, Jonathan Paget, Stephen Rice, Marjorie Roth, Tanya Sermer, Alexander Stefaniak, Kira Thurman, and Sarah Weiss.

Repeated support for research and conference travel came from the University of Rochester's Susan B. Anthony Institute for Gender and Women's Studies and from the Eastman School of Music. A greatly welcome year of writing was enabled by a fellowship from the National Endowment for the Humanities, generously supplemented by the University of Rochester and, again, the Eastman School of Music. I cannot thank enough four successive heads of Eastman – Robert N. Freeman, James Undercofler, Jamal Rossi, and Douglas Lowry – for their unfailing assistance and encouragement.

Portions of Chapters 1 and 3 appeared in my article "Exoticism and Orientalism in Music: Problems for the Worldly Critic." (Full citations are given in the Bibliography.) Materials in various parts of the book, notably Chapters 3, 5, 7, and 8 (including discussions of *Belshazzar*, *Les Indes galantes*, *Carmen*, and *Madama Butterfly*), appeared in somewhat different form in "A Broader View of Musical Exoticism." Certain discussions of other musical works – for example, various "Oriental" operas and *West Side Story* – first appeared in other articles of mine, as the endnotes indicate. The discussions of most other works were newly written for the present book. The entire project was set in motion by my writing, within a frustratingly tight word limit, the entries on "exoticism" and "Orientalism" – topics that had never before been treated by a music encyclopedia – for the 2001 edition of *Grove Dictionary of Music and Musicians*. I hope that the late Stanley Sadie, farsighted editor of *Grove* at the time, will look down with pleasure at what has come of that commission.

I remain deeply indebted to my parents, Doris Locke Dranetz and the late Merle I. Locke.

Most of all, I would like to thank this book's dedicatee, my wife Lona M. Farhi, and our daughters, Marti and Susannah, for making the past several decades so wondrous.

Notes to the reader

The first time I mention a work whose title is not in English (e.g., Mozart's *Entführung aus dem Serail*), I generally give the original title as well as a translation. I do not, however, do this when it would be cumbersome, as in the discussions of numerous oft-performed operas in Chapters 7 and 8. A work's date is usually given at its initial mention or at the start of an extended discussion. Dates indicate when a piece was completed, published, or (in the case of an opera or oratorio) first performed.

Basic facts about certain musical works have been checked against the entries in *Grove Music Online*, ed. Laura Macy (accessed on a continuing basis during the years 2001–8 at www.grovemusic.com), which incorporates *The New Grove Dictionary of Opera* and other *New Grove* reference works.

I freely refer to the notes in a scale as (for example) "step 6," "the sixth degree," "$\hat{6}$," or simply "6." Sometimes, when the music is heavily colored by common-practice tonality, I refer to $\hat{1}$ as "tonic," $\hat{4}$ as "subdominant," and $\hat{5}$ as "dominant." I occasionally use certain standard Western names for scales (or pitch collections) that are used in one or another folk or non-Western musical culture. I do so for convenience ("Mixolydian" instantly translates for many music lovers as "major with lowered seventh degree") and also to suggest the tendency of Western composers and listeners to hear unfamiliar musical traditions through the scrim of Western art-music practices.

Certain types of ethnic/national terms, though potentially ambiguous, are used so frequently here that to put quotation marks around them every time would be distracting. When I refer to "elements of Mozart's Turkish style," for example, the reader should recall that the style was largely invented by Westerners and had little – though not quite nothing – to do with actual musical traditions of Turkey. A mention of "Oriental operas," likewise, does not indicate, say, the traditional genre of Beijing opera (Peking opera) but, rather, Western operas – especially in the eighteenth century – that were set in a half-imagined version of some land in "the East," such as Turkey, India, or China.

The style that has long been known as "Hungarian-Gypsy" (and that is familiar from Liszt's Hungarian Rhapsodies and Brahms's Hungarian

Dances) derives from the music that fiddlers in Hungary, most of them Roma, played for their non-Rom listeners (e.g., Magyars, Germans, and Slavs). Some of the tunes that the fiddlers and their bands played were composed by Hungarians, others by the fiddlers themselves. Either way, the tunes largely belonged to established Hungarian dance-genres (such as *verbunkos* and *csárdás*). Since these tunes did not derive primarily from the indigenous musical traditions of the Rom community, I have maintained the traditional phrase "Hungarian-Gypsy" (rather than, for example, "Hungarian-Romani"). When a Rom musician played for Hungarians, he did so in the role of a Gypsy (*cigány*). I discuss this problem of nomenclature further in the third section of Chapter 6.

I make a somewhat analogous distinction regarding the Spanish Roma (Chapter 7). Consistent with standard practice among students of literary images of the *gitana* and *gitano*, I call Spanish-Rom operatic characters "Gypsies." The word should suggest that these imagined creations – notably Verdi's Azucena and Bizet's Carmen – have a life of their own and may bear little resemblance to actual Roma in Spanish society. Nobody, I hope, would think it an improvement to call Azucena a "crazed old Rom woman," nor to write "the Rom cigarette-factory worker Carmen who seduces the Spanish soldier Don José."

I occasionally refer to "exotic musical works" or, for example, "Debussy's exotic (or, sometimes, exoticist) works." I do not believe, as such simple labeling might inadvertently suggest, that exoticism inheres entirely in the pitches, rhythms, and timbres of a musical work. But to restate my position (see Introduction and Chapter 3) at every such juncture struck me as unnecessarily distracting. The same is true of the more specific categories that I develop in Chapter 9: Overt Exoticism, Submerged Exoticism, and Transcultural Composing. At times I put a given work into one of these categories, but this is shorthand and should always be understood as indicating that (1) the composer evidently (or indeed explicitly) intended to evoke the exotic locale in question (or at least the musical practices of that locale) and/or (2) performers, listeners, critics, and scholars have perceived the work as evoking that exotic locale (and/or those musical practices).

Translations from critical and scholarly writings in foreign languages are my own unless otherwise indicated.

Introduction

Exoticism in music is a quality that links a work to some especially fascinating, attractive, or fearsome place: to an Elsewhere and, usually, to its inhabitants and their supposed inclinations and ways. My aim is to establish some clear guidelines about what musical exoticism is (and is not), how it functions (from the composer's point of view, the performer's, and the listener's), and what broader cultural work it carries out. By "cultural work," I am thinking of, for example, the ways in which a song, instrumental piece, or opera may reflect and reinforce Eurocentric prejudices regarding distant and different peoples; or the opposite: challenge those prejudices. (Perhaps I should say West-centric prejudices, thereby including America as part of the "center.") I focus my primary attention on what is often called Western classical music. To a lesser extent, I also consider certain streams of cultural life that tend to make less ambitious aesthetic claims, such as popular song, the Broadway musical, and film music. Within these latter "streams," I focus on instances that have attained a relatively stable version that the reader can get to know: a frequently revived Broadway musical, a successful film (with its more or less effective musical score), or the most widely available recording of a certain popular song.

Exotic and exoticism have many meanings. Those most relevant to the present study have to do with "coming from (or referring to, or evoking) a place other than here." This basic core of meaning follows logically from the etymological root "exo-" ("outside of" or "away from"). I shall return to the implications of the phrase "musical exoticism" at the end of this Introduction and shall propose a new definition of it in Chapter 3.

There have been occasional calls for a comprehensive study of exoticism in Western music.[1] The repertoire that would need to be covered, however, is vast. Composers have evoked a near-endless variety of distant and disparate worlds and peoples: Incas of Peru, Scottish bards, Tyrolean villagers, the Hungarian Roma ("Gypsies"), characters from the ancient and biblical Middle East, pashas and casbah dancers (standing for a Middle East of more recent vintage), sub-Saharan Africans (including, in two notable cases, Madagascans),[2] Chinese princesses – and, of course, one

Japanese geisha, Puccini's Cio-Cio-San (*Madama Butterfly*), whose suicide is bewept, in production after production, by opera lovers around the world.

Like *Madama Butterfly*, many exotic works are permanent items in the concert and opera repertoire. Put another way, exoticism has been a recurrent, defining force in the growth and elaboration of Western art music and its canon of performed works. Yet the exotic aspects of many patently exotic (or, one might say, exoticist) works have often been insufficiently examined, as has the relationship between those exotic aspects and such matters as the work's style and structure; its reception by audiences at the time the work was first performed; its dependence on works (exotic and not) of earlier composers; and its influence on works (exotic and not) of later ones.

Broader issues and developments may likewise bear on an exotic work and its meanings in its own day. These include the structures of musical life, general social and cultural contexts, and what, at the time, was known – or believed to be true – about the region being portrayed, including its musical practices.[3] Then there are the new meanings that accrue to a work over time.

How to structure a book on a topic that has so many different facets, none of which it has the space to treat comprehensively?

The four chapters that make up Part I explore, in essayistic fashion, various terms, concepts, and themes relating to the problem of musical exoticism. Chapters 1 and 2 lay the conceptual groundwork for Chapter 3, in which I define musical exoticism afresh and propose a broader-than-usual methodology for studying it. Chapter 4 expands on some particular complications, such as the (perhaps counterintuitive) overlap between musical exoticism and musical nationalism. Chapters 5–10 then illustrate how exoticism has manifested itself (whether overtly or not) across the past three centuries in various genres and works central to Western music. These chapters also suggest at times how musical exoticism has contributed to the definition, growth, and elaboration of the larger enterprise of Western music, and thereby to Westerners' sense of who they are and of their relationship to the rest of the world. The Epilogue (Chapter 11) focuses on the enriching and sometimes problematic place of exotic musical works – including many from decades or even centuries past – in today's musical life.

Throughout, it is my contention that music critics and musicologists have adopted too exclusively what I call the "Exotic Style Only" Paradigm of musical exoticism, which regards established stylistic codes as the main or even sole factor in the process of exotic portrayal. Some of the most sophisticated studies of musical exoticism or of particular exotic works – as well as many textbooks and shelves' worth of concert- and opera-program notes – state or imply that the "Exotic Style Only" Paradigm tells the whole story of how exoticism can be conveyed in a musical work. (In Figure 3.1, I lay out the main types of codes or features that the "Exotic Style Only" Paradigm isolates as markers of the exotic in Western music.)

As I have come to see it, musical exoticism is not "contained in" specific devices. Rather, it arises through an interaction between a work, in *all* its aspects, and the listener. I therefore have developed a broader approach, which I half-humorously call the "All the Music in Full Context" Paradigm. This more inclusive Paradigm accords well with the insights of various theorists and aestheticians who, in recent decades, have emphasized that the reception (in its fullest sense) of works of literature and visual art is inevitably mediated by a variety of clues. In exotic musical works, some clues are musico-stylistic (whether recognizably exotic – and thus fitting the "Exotic Style Only" Paradigm – or not). Other clues, especially in genres such as opera, are verbal and visual. In addition, exotic musical works are, like all art works, mediated by cultural preconceptions that may be less concrete than the various clues just mentioned but no less real. Responses to exotic works with a substantial musical component are – like all forms of knowledge (taking that word in the broad sense) – "situated": that is, they are shaped by such basic factors as social and cultural context, community values, and the experiences and attitudes of the individual listener. Although some aspects of the works and their meanings are relatively fixed, others are constantly open to negotiation. These "images" of Elsewhere – these often-distorted "reflections" of reality (I highlight the terms from this book's subtitle) – call forth ever-new "reflections" in the other sense of that word: reactions, commentaries, statements of value, and decisions about which exotic works to maintain in the repertoire and how to perform them.

It may help to lay out the structure of the book in somewhat more detail. Chapter 1 (the beginning of Part I) broadly explores music's relationship to culture and history, and concludes with a brief glance at existing accounts of musical exoticism. Chapter 2 examines how exoticism has been regarded by prominent composers and critics, including Wagner, Debussy, Schoenberg, Heinrich Schenker, Steve Reich, and Richard Taruskin. It also considers applications of the much-debated term "Orientalism" to music. "Orientalism" has for more than a century been understood by literary and art historians as indicating the variants of (literary and artistic) exoticism that deal with "the East": the Arab world, Turkey, Persia and other countries of Central Asia, the Indian subcontinent (with its vast Hindu and Muslim populations), and all of East and Southeast Asia. But, ever since Edward W. Said's 1978 book *Orientalism*, the term has been understood by historians and cultural critics as indicating a much more "real-world" phenomenon: the ideologically supported system by which the West, for centuries, dominated large parts of the non-Western world (especially the Middle East, India, and East and Southeast Asia). I felt the need to sort out the ways in which this heavily political (and sometimes politicized) use of the term Orientalism has and has not proven helpful for discussions of exoticism in music. The chapter concludes by raising some ethical questions about the condescending and sometimes defamatory ethno-cultural stereotypes upon which so many musical representations of the Other rely.

Chapter 3 presents a new, broader way of studying and thinking about exotic works: the aforementioned "All the Music in Full Context" Paradigm. I define this new paradigm as extremely broad and as incorporating the prevailing "Exotic Style Only" Paradigm. Had I proposed the new paradigm as a non-overlapping alternative or complement (say, the "Non-Exotic Style Only" Paradigm), I would have created the problem of policing the boundary between exotic and non-exotic style. I believe that such policing is pointless. There is no boundary. As we shall see repeatedly in the case studies of Chapters 5–10, exoticness often depends not just on the musical notes but also on their context as well as on other factors, such as the particulars of a given performance and the musical and cultural preparation of a given listener.

Chapter 4 explores the inherent overlaps – and disparities – between and among such categories as musical exoticism (including its Middle Eastern and other "Oriental" variants), musical nationalism (e.g., a Russian composer consciously trying, on a given occasion, to sound Russian), and various longstanding and arguably non-representational uses of national styles (as in Bach's Italian Concerto for harpsichord). The chapter concludes by exploring more extensively than did Chapter 2 the question of (often noxious) stereotypes.

Chapters 5–10 – which make up the bulk of Part II – survey some major developments in musical exoticism in rough chronological order from 1700 to the present. They also pause for discussion of significant representative works. The proportion between these two methods of organization varies from chapter to chapter. In Chapter 5, two extended case studies (Handel's *Belshazzar* and the portrayal of the Incan priest Huascar in Rameau's *Les Indes galantes*) are introduced and linked by briefer summaries of relevant trends in musico-exotic portrayal at the time. A somewhat similar structure prevails in Chapter 6 (the two works are Mozart's "Rondo alla turca" and Liszt's Hungarian Rhapsody No. 14, the latter giving evidence of a complex relationship between "Hungarian-Gypsy" exoticism and Hungarian nationalism) and in Chapter 7 (focusing on "Spanish-Gypsy" characters in Verdi's *Il trovatore* and Bizet's *Carmen*). Chapter 8 explores – in varying degrees of detail – operatic works set in "the Orient" by eight composers. It focuses particularly on neglected or misunderstood aspects of Puccini's *Madama Butterfly*. Chapters 9 and 10 discuss the (evidently, or at least arguably) exotic explorations and experiments of an even greater number of composers than does Chapter 8. But they, too, pause at times to consider in somewhat more detail a few works that prove to be particularly rich or complex, notably (in Chapter 9) Debussy's *Pagodes* and *Prélude à l'Après-midi d'un faune*, Bernstein's *West Side Story*, and the famous *chanson* "Petite Tonkinoise," as sung by Josephine Baker; and (in Chapter 10) two works by Tan Dun: *Symphony 1997: Heaven, Earth, Mankind* and *Marco Polo*.

I have just said that the works discussed in Part II are representative. Perhaps a better word would be "indicative." The two works in Chapter 5 – by Handel and Rameau – are unique creations and cannot fully stand for other works about non-Western tyrants, much less for works built upon very different (yet unquestionably exotic) plots.[4] Nonetheless, the figure of the tyrant has long been so central to Western conceptions of non-Western regions that it seemed to me important to explore its musical manifestations, especially since Baroque-era Oriental-tyrant operas and oratorios have often been omitted from, or minimized in, previous accounts of musical exoticism.

Chapters 6, 7, and 8, taken together, consider certain peoples that were conjured up with particular frequency by European culture during the long nineteenth century (c. 1780–1915): the Roma of Hungary and Spain, and the inhabitants of various regions regarded as Oriental, including ancient Egypt; the Arab world (as described in the *Thousand and One Nights*); the Ottoman Empire; legendary China and India; and current-day Japan. (Consistent with the practice among social and cultural historians, I use the word "Gypsies" to indicate fictional and stereotypical images of the Roma. As with terms such as "Oriental" and "Turkish style," the word will generally appear without quotation marks except when there is some risk of ambiguity.[5]) The specific Gypsy and (broadly) "Eastern" works to be explored are among the best-known and most indelible in the repertoire. I have welcomed the opportunity to discuss their exotic portrayals in some detail.[6] The resulting panorama would have been somewhat different if more of the works chosen for discussion had focused on certain other peoples: for example, Scots, Tyroleans, Poles, Russians, Native Americans, African-Americans, sub-Saharan Africans, or peoples from various Latin American countries. The reader is directed, in the notes and Bibliography, to excellent studies that can round out the picture.[7]

Chapters 9 and 10 (dealing with the long twentieth century) take a somewhat different approach, and for a reason. Whereas there is probably general consensus that the works discussed in Chapters 5–8 are indeed exotic portrayals, beginning around 1900 – in works such as *Prélude à l'Après-midi d'un faune* and *Pagodes* – the problem of musical exoticism becomes drastically more complex. The Western musical world's interest in and contact with other cultures increased greatly, with the predictable result that composers, to a much greater extent than before 1900, incorporated aspects from far-flung musical traditions in their works. What is less predictable is that they now did so in works of many kinds, not just ones that set out to portray or represent a distant people. And the same occurs with musical materials (e.g., the octatonic scale) that had been invented by previous Western musicians and associated with exotic realms: they become more broadly diffused in Western musical language. Thus, whereas, in Chapters 5–8, we often see exoticism carried out through non-exotic means, in Chapters 9–10 we encounter something of the opposite: non-exotic (or arguably non-exotic) pieces that use musical materials borrowed from distant countries or at least (if invented, not borrowed) long linked with the exotic.

In an attempt to suggest this blurring boundary between exotic and non-exotic and the resulting variety of approaches to the problem of representing distant cultures (and/or of borrowing from them), I propose near the beginning of Chapter 9 three new categories: Overt Exoticism (which roughly amounts to what the previous chapters have simply called "musical exoticism"), Submerged Exoticism, and Transcultural Composing. These categories suggest the range of options for composing music in an increasingly globalized world. They also indicate some ways in which unfamiliar, even initially off-putting musical materials and conceptions gradually reshaped mainstream musical vocabulary and other compositional practices in the West. Nonetheless, once I have established these categories in the first half of Chapter 9, I feel no need to keep mentioning them in the remainder of that chapter nor in Chapter 10 (dealing with 1960 to today). Instead, I mostly allow them to linger in the reader's mind as a grid of possibilities against which he or she may wish to evaluate the numerous instances of musical exoticism that we encounter in the past century-plus.

Chapters 9 and 10 raise another new complication: who is a Westerner? I draw attention to some composers who were born and trained in countries distant from New York, Paris, or Berlin: for example, in Brazil, Egypt, Iran, the Tatar Soviet Republic, Japan, and China. The output of many of these composers posed (or poses) interesting questions of cultural identity when heard in North America and Europe (often as a result of the composer's settling in a major Western metropolis or visiting it frequently). I also discuss more countries or regions than in earlier chapters (including some – such as Brazil – that are Western yet often regarded as exotic/peripheral in North America and Europe) and more genres and streams of music-making, including popular song and film music. Even so, no claim is made toward comprehensiveness. As in Chapters 5–8, the notes and Bibliography will guide interested readers to fine studies on topics that are here treated briefly (such as the Asian roots of American experimentalists Cowell and Cage).

The works explored at some length in Chapters 5–10 come from many different genres: piano works, orchestral works, a sacred dramatic oratorio, a Broadway musical, some French and American popular songs, some film scores, and operas of several distinct varieties. All these works are also unusually communicative, demonstrably long-lived, and available on one or more excellent recordings or (for stage works) video recordings.[8] Some have been discussed extensively (if not always adequately) by scholars and critics as instances of musical exoticism: for example, *Les Indes galantes*, "Rondo alla turca," *Carmen*, *Madama Butterfly*, and *Pagodes*. Others have been much more briefly examined (if at all) in this regard: for example, *Belshazzar*, *West Side Story*, and the *chanson* "Petite Tonkinoise."

Some people express surprise when I suggest that a work such as *West Side Story* can be interestingly linked to the concept of musical exoticism. What is exotic, these people argue, must be far away from "here," whereas Puerto Ricans in Manhattan are, of course, just around the corner (from the presumed audience members, and also from the Jets, the non-exotic half of the show's cast). But "internal Others" – including Puerto Ricans in the USA during the 1950s and, a century earlier, Rom fiddlers in the Austro-Hungarian Empire – have been exoticized (by the society's dominant population) no less than cultures that lie across an ocean. In addition, a work that evokes the composer's homeland and its music – a Chopin mazurka, Albéniz's piano suite *Ibéria*, or Takemitsu's *November Steps* for *biwa*, *shakuhachi*, and orchestra – can easily gain in exotic fascination when performed abroad.

Certain case studies in Chapters 5–10 echo each other. Recurring musical treatment of New World "natives," the Roma (Hungarian and Spanish), and peoples of the Middle East (ancient and current-day) and of East Asia (again, ancient/legendary and recent) permits the positing of comparisons and contrasts. Sometimes the influence of one repertoire item (e.g., Mozart's "Rondo alla turca") is noted. Sometimes an issue will recur in discussion of two very different works: for example, do *West Side Story* and Tan Dun's *Marco Polo* both envision – indeed, enact in some ways – an end to musical exoticism? Most of all, the reader will sense my abiding concern to distinguish – explicitly or implicitly – between cases that can be largely encompassed by the "Exotic Style Only" Paradigm (the "Rondo alla turca" being one such case) and cases that need the broader "All the Music in Full Context" Paradigm to do them justice (such as various Baroque-era dramatic works, or long stretches of *Carmen* and *Madama Butterfly*).

The Epilogue (Chapter 11) discusses why and how works that are colored to some degree by musical exoticism matter to musicians and audiences today – and sometimes trouble them. Among other things, it explores the ways in which certain operas have been reconfigured in different recent productions, and how they might profitably be reconfigured in the future, not just on stage but also in the mind of the thoughtful audience member.

Before closing this Introduction, I would like to raise several distinctions – familiar and unfamiliar – that underlie the entire book, and to offer several other preparatory comments that are crucial to understanding what musical exoticism is and how it functions in Western culture (or what we might call globalized post-industrial culture, in order to bring into consideration the musical publics of, say, Tokyo, Singapore, Mumbai, and Tehran).[9]

The first two distinctions are familiar and intertwined. Scholars and critics have regularly distinguished between, on the one hand, exotic styles that are closely derived from musical practices of the society being portrayed and, on the other, styles that are meant to register as exotic but have, in fact, been largely invented by Western musicians. Related to this first familiar distinction is a second: between, on the one hand, cultures whose musical traditions are (or were, at the time) relatively familiar to Western composers and audiences and, on the other, cultures whose musical traditions are not (were not) and so cannot (could not) be reliably alluded to. For example, the music-making of the Rom ("Gypsy") fiddle bands became familiar to Western composers and audiences earlier than did many other "foreign" musics. Also, this "Gypsy" music was particularly easy for Westerners to understand and assimilate because, over the centuries, it had absorbed much from its interactions with various European musical traditions. By contrast, East Asian and sub-Saharan musics were largely unknown during the nineteenth and early twentieth centuries, even in Paris, never mind in somewhat less cosmopolitan cities, such as Milan or Munich. Composers have thus been forced (or, in a sense, freed) to invent musical materials that could somehow be perceived as acceptably Other. True, Puccini, when preparing to compose *Turandot*, ended up transcribing Chinese tunes played by a music box, including the recurring Mo-Li-Hua tune ("Jasmine Flower"). But this hardly amounts to a rich encounter with a living tradition.[10] Equally typical in *Turandot* is Liù's aria "Tu che di gel sei cinta," for which the composer simply invented a tune that, to his ear, had what he called a "Chinese flavor" (*sapore cinese*). Most listeners and critics would have had trouble – and would have trouble today – distinguishing the echoes of "the real thing" in this opera from moments marked by a pseudo-Chinese spice.

When I say that the Chineseness of Liù's aria is "pseudo" (implying fake, manufactured), I do not mean that the effect is not beautiful or dramatically apposite. I wish to distance myself from the tendency to suggest that invented exoticisms are somehow invalid in music, as if the composer were too lazy or too culturally narrow to offer the listener something more authentic. We should remember that invented exoticisms are central to exoticist traditions in other arts. Frederick N. Bohrer offers a valuable observation regarding the many paintings that attempted to open a window on one famously hidden-away aspect of the Islamic Middle East: the harem:

Nineteenth-century Western exoticism is replete with such almost completely imaginary representations as the eroticized harem and the odalisque ... [that scarcely resemble] anything in contemporary Eastern realities ... Such images ... largely imitate each other in their putative reference to Eastern practice, but they [nonetheless] belong just as much to the exoticist corpus. They refer to the East without precisely imitating anything of it.[11]

Bohrer's remark may remind us of what the philosopher and cultural theoretician Michel Foucault calls the "archeological" nature of all cultural (including political) discourse. A given generation of writers relies on the writings of the generation or two that came before it (what we might call, taking Foucault's "archeological" image literally, the stratum just below). The writers rework and transform for their own purposes what they find written. They do so with (most often) the professed and sincere aim of discovering a solid, durable image that closely matches reality (or, in Foucault's term, an image that "deciphers" reality). But what they produce may instead meet an unspoken societal goal of which the writer or artist is barely aware: *inventing* a version of reality. This version of reality may be, on the surface, consolingly "continuous" (which, for Foucault, means, among other things, internally consistent). Yet, at a deeper level, it may function to "exclude" from general awareness any phenomena that are felt (at that time and place) to be too threatening or "discontinuous." Particularly forbidden to delineate, often, is the repressive power of the society in which the writer lives and operates.[12]

Educated people know that discursive statements and representations are largely invented by people (at a certain point in time and space) and ought always to be treated with skepticism. Few would confidently turn to centuries-old history books, physics treatises, or medical advice. But literature and the arts are different. Even though we know that their images of some real-world locale are primarily imagined, we feel no cause to demean the work that contains them since, after all, accuracy is not the point. The wording in the previous sentence points to a tautology: "images" (that word, again, from the book's subtitle) are frankly "imagined." But, unlike a tautology in logical argument, which invalidates the claims being made, this tautology of the imagined image is fundamental to literature and the arts and is inherently productive. Art often flourishes, perhaps flourishes best, when freed from the expectation that it closely reproduce reality (that it "decipher" it) in a documentary manner or, as art historians might say, in a photo-realist one.

Another distinction is much less familiar in discussions of exotic musical works but no less crucial: the distinction between, on the one hand, music whose style itself is understood as exotic, in that it reflects another culture's *music* (or at least reflects the perception of that music by the composer and his/her audience); and, on the other, music that portrays the other *culture* itself (as a whole). Representing (however inaccurately) a culture's *music* is, essentially, the core of the "Exotic Style Only" Paradigm. Representing (however inaccurately) the *culture as a whole* expands the scope to include much that the "Exotic Style Only" Paradigm leaves out of consideration. This is what makes the "All the Music in Full Context" Paradigm adequate to a wider range of works and musical passages. A composer of an exotic work often characterizes a place, culture, people – however half-imaginary – with all the stylistic tools in his/her *regular* (non-exotic) compositional kit, or else with a combination of exotic tools and non-exotic ones.

The process of using regular, non-exotic musical means to portray an exotic culture is particularly apparent in opera:

- Handel, in *Tamerlano* (1724), portrays the Tatar tyrant Tamburlaine (Timur-Leng) as monstrously vicious, yet does so with little or no recourse to stylistic devices or mannerisms intended to resemble those of actual Eastern literary or musical traditions.

- Saint-Saëns, in *Samson et Dalila* (1875), emphasizes Delilah's Eastern seductiveness in her first and third arias without making them sound remotely foreign (whereas the famous Bacchanale, in the opera's final act, does mark the Philistines, her people, as indelibly Other – and specifically Middle Eastern).
- Puccini, in *Madama Butterfly* (1904–6), indicates, through various musical devices, Cio-Cio-San's delicacy and smallness even when he is not reinforcing the point with Japanese-sounding pentatonic writing.

None of this is to gainsay the important and widespread use of styles coded as coming "from" Elsewhere. Such uses necessarily remain an active component in the present book. Though exotic styles have been too exclusively emphasized by scholars until now, they nonetheless need to be examined still more thoroughly, not least with regard to how they function in a given piece and also with regard to the cultural work that they do. In short, the "Exotic Style Only" Paradigm still has much to contribute – and especially from the early twentieth century onward, as various non-Western musics became (and continue to become) more widely known. Still, even in recent works, the "Exotic Style Only" Paradigm must often yield to the broader "All the Music in Full Context" Paradigm.

This book examines from an unaccustomed angle (namely, portrayals of the exotic) some episodes or instances in the past three centuries of Western music. I hope this angle may bring freshness to the view of the musical past as a whole. The book also runs up against some questions that are not easily answered, such as whether a given musical influence or borrowing (e.g., from Hungarian-Gypsy style) is exotic, and to whom. But, then, as I said earlier, exoticism does not inhere totally in musical works, as some kind of sedimented, irreducible "content." The exotic traits that a musical community (performers, listeners, critics) perceive as being "in" a work are the product of a relational process between that community and the work.[13]

Listeners are not blank slates. They have been trained, some more completely than others, to receive works in certain ways. Every community has its "technologies" of listening (to use a current term from cultural theory) that large parts of the population have mastered. Within the world of Western-style concert music and opera, the written word can play a major role in these technologies of listening, often by disseminating superficial "analyses" of works, hoary biographical anecdotes about composers, and – crucial for the repertoires under study here – stereotyped images of national and ethnic groups.[14] For example, the names and verbal appendages affixed by many nineteenth-century composers to certain purely instrumental works are manifestations of an urge to guide the process of listening and set the terms of the discourse that would soon surround the work.[15] When Tchaikovsky labeled one of his major orchestral pieces *Romeo and Juliet*, he could be confident that most people in the audience would know the plot of Shakespeare's play and keep it in mind while listening. Similarly, most classical-music listeners across nearly two centuries – and around the world – have associated Chopin with a few facts about Polish nationalism: for example, that it involved a yearning to free the country from oppressive Russian control and to establish an independent cultural identity for Poles within Europe. This knowledge (however incomplete) conditioned the ways that they responded to various strikingly folklike or exotic – some writers even say "Oriental" – features in the mazurkas.[16]

If a purely instrumental work can tap into a listener's prior knowledge, a vocal or dramatic work can do so far more concretely and diversely. In the case of *Madama Butterfly*, we audience members come armed with relevant "information" about the Japanese. In the course of the opera, we "learn" yet more.[17] We see that Cio-Cio-San is a geisha, are reminded – by Pinkerton – that Japanese women are small (doll-like, etc.), and hear Butterfly express her vulnerability. She compares herself fearfully to butterflies that Westerners collect, kill with a pin, and display. She asks to be loved with "a very little love" rather than a massive, possessive one that might prove her undoing. All this predisposes the operagoer to hear certain exoticizing messages about her in the music, even during long stretches when Puccini has not used Japanese-sounding procedures.

Frederick Bohrer, the art historian whom I quoted earlier regarding images of the harem, nicely stresses the role of the viewer (or, for us, listener) and his or her cultural preparation, in determining how exoticism is received. His words might helpfully be heard as an undertone to the rest of the present book:

The construct of the exotic is never unmediated, but rather always forged in connection with the concerns of the observer. Though ever resistant in some degree to the Western observer's acquaintance, the exotic object is inevitably construed from the observer's language [taking "language" in the broadest sense, i.e., conceptual framework]. Thus reception is not merely a useful methodology in the study of exoticism. Rather exoticism, in a fundamental sense, *is* reception.[18]

PART I

1 | Music, the world, and the critic

Stylistic listening and worldly criticism

Exotic musical works raise important basic questions about the relationship between art and society. This is especially true if one accepts that such works, indeed all cultural products, are "enmeshed" in their time and place. The literary and cultural critic Edward W. Said put this general principle well in a 1983 essay on what he called "worldliness" in criticism:

> Worldliness does not come and go ... Texts [including musical scores and performances] have ways of existing that even in their most rarefied form are always enmeshed in circumstance, time, place, and society.[1]

Such a quest forces us to consider social contexts that often go unremarked in standard critical and historical writing about literature and the arts. As Said explained, "A text's being in the world ... is a more complicated matter than the private process of reading" because it involves two separate and in some cases almost incommensurable terms – text and world – as well as the "interplay, the constitutive interaction," between them.[2] Furthermore, the work of the critic adds yet a third entity that then interacts with the first two. (In the performing arts, I would add, an insightful – or, for that matter, obtuse – performance adds a fourth ingredient to the mix.)

Edward Said's call for a "worldly criticism" may thus be phrased as a series of related questions:

- How intricately does a text enmesh with – how deeply does it incorporate – the worldly?
- How does such enmeshment/worldliness vary with different works and different "recipients" (readers, audiences)?
- How does the work change with the passage of time, as critics, listeners, and performers interact with it, and as composers and other creative artists respond (in new works) to the work's original text and to the overtones that it has acquired through decades of cultural interaction? Does all this cultural interaction with the work preserve or distort it, enrich or impoverish?

Such questions can be posed straightforwardly in regard to many (most?) instances of verbal and visual expression: books, comic strips, photographs, television shows, and so on. But they turn instantly problematic when addressed to almost any music – particularly to instrumental music, and most particularly to certain instrumental traditions within Western art music, notably sonata, string quartet (and other chamber music), and symphony.[3] (The special complications – and advantages – of opera and other "mixed" genres for conveying the exotic will be noted shortly.) Indeed, the question of whether, how much, and *how* instrumental repertoires engage in representing anything "extramusical" – anything outside of "the music itself" – has been a central, perpetually vexing one throughout the history of Western musical aesthetics.[4] Much twentieth-century musical criticism, especially of the more academic variety, has skirted the problem entirely by abandoning criticism (as that term was previously understood). It has become, instead, "musical analysis": a type of scholarly research that focuses on a work's internal structure and other elements that are (or at least are often described as being) relatively independent of context and social function and therefore, by definition, highly "autonomous."

But, as musicologist Rose Rosengard Subotnik reminds us, this principled emphasis on autonomy and structure (even when the concept of structure is taken in a richly "replete" sense, as Subotnik calls it, rather than a pedantically narrow one) has led many critics and scholars to ignore any elements of a work that are not explicitly laid out in the printed notes of the score. Among the crucial elements whose discussion tends to be endlessly deferred are stylistic background, extramusical associations, societal function/context, and the performer's creative insights.[5] This autonomist position – and all that bracketing – has been rightly faulted by various music scholars, most notably Richard Taruskin.[6]

The emphasis (by both Subotnik and Taruskin) on elements beyond structure raises a natural worry: how inclusive can we expect our understanding of a given musical work to become? Or to put it in terms of direct relevance to the present study:

- Given the many possible meanings and extramusical contexts that may be plausibly linked to a given musical text, which are the ones that are most appropriate, productive, and revealing?

This question cannot be easily brushed aside. Music is a form of expression that, by contrast to the visual and the verbal, is far less obviously redolent of the larger world of people and things. Words comprise the medium in which we most often articulate meanings and contexts – and the medium in which the critic or scholar (the third entity in Said's scheme mentioned earlier) operates. To be sure, music often allies itself in various ways with the visual and the verbal: for example, in instrumental works (such as symphonic poems) that carry descriptive titles and in vocal and dramatic works.[7] But this alliance does not resolve the problem of evaluating music's relationship to its contexts. It merely shifts it to a different conceptual level.[8]

In order to "get a handle" on the problem of music and its contexts, it makes sense to choose a repertoire in which extramusical meaning or reference is strikingly foregrounded. The present book explores one repertoire (some of it much-loved) that has needed more systematic attention: musical works from Europe and America that were/are patently inspired by and evocative of exotic places. It also draws attention briefly (in parts of Chapters 9 and 10) to the special, varied situations embodied – whether eagerly (Piazzolla, Tan Dun) or a bit reluctantly (Takemitsu) – by certain composers who come from a location or ethnic group long considered exotic by many Europeans and North Americans.

Because most of my examples come from Western art music, or "classical music," they raise with particular acuteness the problem of music's relationship to its contexts. Works of Western art music tend to present themselves as aesthetically elaborate, demanding, and gratifying.[9] And they succeed, if one can judge success by the devotion of generations of listeners of quite diverse geographic, ethnic, and class backgrounds. You do not have to be Russian to love Tchaikovsky.

Certain works, however, are at once widely loved and demonstrably drenched in social meanings. In some cases, these meanings, though broadly shared at the moment of composition and first performance, may today seem racist or, in some other way, socially regressive. Such works are in particular need of a critical approach that we might call "multivoiced." The present book, especially in certain of the longer case studies (e.g., Handel, Liszt, Puccini, Bernstein), sketches some ways in which Western art music may be approached through a criticism that is open to divergent points of view and sensitive to the interactions and cross-currents between different layers of social and cultural analysis. In *Culture and Imperialism*, Said repeatedly uses "contrapuntal" – a similar term – as a way of directing attention to major societal contexts and forces that shaped works of literature that are set in (or allude to) colonized locales (e.g., Kipling's *Kim*, in British India).[10] One often-relevant societal context is the colonial system itself and its military, commercial, educational, and other branches. Another could be the growing native resistance to that system. This is not to suggest that the colonialist (and anti-colonialist) contexts of a work such as *Aida* (1871) or *Madama Butterfly* (1904–6) encompass or define the entire work. As Said often notes in his writings, one crucial facet or strand in a "contrapuntal" critical approach involves attending to the artistic power and subtlety of what we tend to think of as "the work itself" (questions of genre, style, internal coherence, departures from convention, and so on). In *Culture and Imperialism*, he warns that Jane Austen's *Mansfield Park*, a novel with occasional but resonant references to the Caribbean slave trade, is "rich in ... aesthetic intellectual complexity" and should not be treated as if it were a crudely "jingoistic ditty" in support of empire.[11]

Submitting musical works to any kind of social analysis, much less a carefully contrapuntal one as I have just advocated, is no simple task. It is, of course, famously difficult for the sonatas, symphonies, string quartets, and other "abstract" works referred to earlier. The works to be sorted and examined in this book – whether briefly or in detail – have the advantage (for the contrapuntal critic) that they are, for the most part, not primarily abstract but, rather, self-evidently "about" some other place and people. We discern this from their titles and from other clues. But, as soon as this simple statement is made, a troubling doubt may arise:

- To what extent do such works offer representations at all?

After all, the portrayal of a (real) geographical and ethnic location in a work of fiction (for example) was not, when that work was first released into the world, taken as necessarily "true" – i.e., as a reliable representation of that location – even by those who consumed it.

This frank sense of exoticism's untruth is abundantly clear in an eloquent two sentences from the memoirs of John Henry Newman (1801–90), the distinguished Victorian-era theologian:

[As a schoolchild,] I used to wish the Arabian Tales were true: my imagination ran on unknown influences, on magical powers, and talismans. I thought life might be a dream, or I an Angel, and all this world a deception, my fellow-angels by a playful device concealing themselves from me, and deceiving me with the semblance of a material world.[12]

The stories that enchanted Newman in his childhood and that he considered frankly imaginary were those of the *Thousand and One Nights* (the so-called *Arabian Nights*), which he surely knew through one or another of several widely available translations and adaptations. In the *Nights*, fictiveness is a crucial and overt structural premise of the telling. For example, a character in one tale might pause to tell a lengthy tale of his own. Yet anyone with a modicum of literacy also knew that this body of tales came from a very concrete geo-cultural region – the largely Islamic world extending from North Africa to Persia – and reflected aspects of daily life and culture there.[13]

Works, values, and scholars

Exotic musical works are similar, in this respect, to the *Nights* tales. For centuries now, many Westerners – writers, businesspeople, governmental officials, and average citizens – have had their conceptions of Middle Easterners shaped in part by certain musical works that they heard on the parlor piano – notably Mozart's insistent, pounding, quirky "Rondo alla turca" (from the Sonata in A, K331, 1781–83) – or in the concert hall or opera house – notably Saint-Saëns's lascivious and sacrilegious "Bacchanale" (which comprises the main ballet number in his opera *Samson et Dalila*, 1877). Travelers to North Africa actually commented that they were reminded of Félicien David's then-popular secular oratorio *Le désert* (1844) as they traveled around the country.[14] *The Mikado* (1885) and *Madama Butterfly* (1904–6) have no doubt performed a similar function as components and shapers of "knowledge" of Japan for many in the West.

Unfortunately, most cultural historians writing on Western views of these regions mention musical works briefly, if at all. Musicologists, too, have dealt with the musical evocation of Elsewhere less extensively than the topic deserves. Until the 1990s, broad-based studies of the topic were almost nonexistent. One 1977 monograph, by Peter Gradenwitz, did profess to be a "cultural history" of musical exchanges between "Orient and Occident." It touched on a number of fascinating moments and instances but was shallow in its research and undiscriminating in its critical stance.[15] Fortunately, a number of insightful studies of musical exoticism have been produced in the past few decades. But these have limited themselves to works that evoke one or a few particular region(s) or culture(s), such as Spain, the Hungarian Roma (Gypsies), the Middle East, or Japan; or to works written in a certain genre, time period, and/or country.[16]

In any case, nearly all of these studies, however broad or narrow, focus on what is sometimes called the "musical encounter" between the West and the Rest – and, more specifically, on the question:

- How much did the music of the country being portrayed influence the Western musical work in question?

Key words in the resulting studies tend to include not only "influence" but also "borrowing" and (recently and with possible moral disapproval) "appropriation." These studies rarely give sustained attention to more general questions, such as:

- How is the unfamiliar region portrayed, even when so-called "authentic" materials and styles are not being imitated or even hinted at?

In other words, basic questions about what literary critics and art historians describe as "representation of the Other" have been reduced, in musicological discourse, to the more concrete problem of how specific items of music – transcribed tunes, characteristic scales, instrumental timbres, accompanimental drumbeat and dance rhythms – are transferred to – or distorted or freely reimagined in – a Western context. This tendency (which I call the "Exotic Style Only" Paradigm of musical exoticism) attained a kind of coronation in a 1983 conference on "exoticism and local color in the operas of Puccini." At that conference, the term "exoticism" was understood by the participants as meaning something like "varieties of local color (including stylistic devices) that indicate exotic regions." One participant even presented a paper about "non-exotic exoticism," a delightfully paradoxical term by which he meant the application of (normally) exotic style-traits to dramatic situations that are not exotic (e.g., pentatonic phrases in *Tosca*).[17] Few if any speakers so much as hinted at the opposite possibility: works (and moments in works) that portray exotic locales, cultures, and individuals but *without* using exotic stylistic devices. This opposite possibility could just as plausibly be termed "non-exotic exoticism." Its largely unrecognized importance in the history of Western musical representations of the Other is a major theme of the present book.

The explanation for the self-imposed constraints within studies of musical exoticism until now is four-pronged. First, anyone undertaking a serious study of how "the Other" has been represented in Western music during the past several centuries needs to be willing – in the interests of historical accuracy – to examine a large number of works, some well known, others nearly forgotten, in order to be able to sense which ones might be typical or, in some other way, revealing. But our field, though long eager to catalogue and explore the smallest surviving scrap of Medieval and Renaissance music, has, until recently, been less willing to explore forgotten works from later eras that were manifestly important at the time. These might include once-major items in the operatic repertoire – such as Campra's *L'Europe galante* of 1697 (perhaps translatable as "Courtly Behavior across Europe") and Meyerbeer's *Il crociato in Egitto* of 1824 (The Crusader in Egypt) – but also once-beloved bits of early twentieth-century popular culture, such as a particularly exquisite *chanson coloniale*: Josephine Baker's 1935 recording of "Sous le ciel d'Afrique."[18]

Second, exotic efforts, forgotten or still-familiar, often carry a special stigma that trio sonatas or sacred works do not: their eager recourse to ethnic/racial stereotyping in text and/or musical style can eventually render them uncomfortable and embarrassing, hence unperformable and – in scholarly and critical discourse – either unmentionable or else matter for automatic disparagement (see Chapter 2).

The third consideration requires more extensive discussion here because it is wide-ranging, having to do with the special place of instrumental music within musicology and musical criticism, generally. Since around the middle of the nineteenth century, writers on Western art music have tended to adopt a sharply hierarchized value system that varies depending on the era under discussion. This value system places religious music at the top of the heap when discussing the half-millennium from Gregorian chant to Bach. Thereafter, it places instrumental works (most often German and Austrian ones) at the top: the symphonies, string quartets, and piano sonatas of Haydn, Mozart, and Beethoven; symphonies and chamber works of Brahms; and whatever post-1900 works the given writer feels have best carried on this admirable tradition. The art songs of such composers as Schubert and Debussy are among the few exceptions to the (supposed) preeminence of instrumental music since 1750. This value system more or less reifies the aesthetic preferences of the various eras in question. Philosophers and critics, throughout the Renaissance and Baroque (i.e., during much of what historians today call the Early Modern Era), placed greatest value on church music, then shifted that honor to instrumental music once the greatness of Beethoven's contributions became widely accepted and his works began to serve as exemplars for young composers. A notable exception has normally been made for the operas of two composers from the German-speaking realm – Mozart and Wagner – whereas Verdi, Bizet, and other master opera composers could not, until very recently, be mentioned in the same breath as Bach, Beethoven, and Brahms.[19]

Related to the historians' (and, even more, music theorists') preference for instrumental music written in the past few centuries is the longstanding tendency to view the history of Western art music as a quasi-triumphal procession of unified "style periods," each vaguely embodying the spirit of its age and, after exhausting itself, being replaced by a new style and spirit that offers fresh aesthetic challenges. The period style is seen as inhering in "purely musical" elements of compositional language, and these are understood – at least from the eighteenth century onward – as presenting themselves most overtly and intensely in the instrumental realm, where they are not constrained by extramusical considerations (such as a preexisting narrative plot) nor by widely shared cultural assumptions (such as, of obvious interest to the present book, national and ethnic stereotypes).[20]

The "Exotic Style Only" Paradigm of musical exoticism is particularly well suited to dealing with exotically colored instrumental works, in which there are usually no clues to the work's intended ethnic reference other than the notes and other markings in the score and perhaps a brief title. Mozart's keyboard "Rondo alla turca" again comes to mind, as do important works by several generations of French composers, including Lalo's *Symphonie espagnole* (Spanish Symphony – actually a five-movement concerto – for violin and orchestra, 1874) and Debussy's *Pagodes* (Pagodas, 1903). But attempts at quoting, adapting, or even inventing foreign styles were and remain only one drawer that the exotic composer may choose to open in his or her toolkit. In this regard, the exotic (or, we might say, exoticist) composer is often closely analogous to the nationalist one. Richard Taruskin notes that such composers as Wagner, Verdi, Debussy, and Bartók all, at times, asserted their own country's values and identity, but not necessarily by quoting folk songs and dances. "Folklorism or vernacularism ... was only a superficial and dispensable marker of nationalism."[21]

A paradigm is needed that is not opposed to the "Exotic Style Only" Paradigm but, rather, contains everything addressed by it and much more besides. This broader Paradigm has been anticipated by various scholars and critics in studies of individual works, but has never been brought to explicit, elaborated statement. It can deal more effectively with the wide range of musical genres that freely invoke extramusical reality (or, we might add, extramusical fantasy) – and invoke that reality (fantasy) in ways that are striking and eminently discussable. The genres in question include such major ones as symphonic poem, program symphony, art song, descriptive/ "characteristic" piano piece, opera, dramatic oratorio, and (often overlooked by music historians) ballet scores and film music.

Such genres, when they attempt the portrayal of a culture regarded as exotic, sometimes use the distinctive "borrowed"/invented styles that the "Exotic Style Only" Paradigm addresses so well. But sometimes they (instead or also) tap a wide range of prevailing (but *not* exotically tinged) musical styles of the day: styles that have been well honed – in tens of thousands of non-exotic instrumental or operatic works – to convey emotional tones (tenderness or terror), character traits (seductiveness, submissiveness), and behaviors (rage, reproach, rejoicing). These non-exotic styles serve the portrayal of an exotic place or people because of the context in which they are placed. This "All the Music in Full Context"

Paradigm is proposed in Chapter 3 and is then exemplified in the case studies of Part II.

The fourth and final reason why musicologists have tended not to give adequate consideration to exotic portrayals in music has to do with the problem of subtexts. Musicology has a longstanding formalist/structural/autonomist bias traceable back to Hanslick and other nineteenth-century idealists but particularly pervasive in the Cold War era of the 1950s–80s. As a result, musicologists tended until around 1990 to shy away from ideological and other deeply social readings – that is, from ferreting out (or, a horrifying word to some musicologists of that era, speculating about) certain meanings that lie behind Western society's musical practices and beneath a given work's surface.[22] This was the case even for exotically tinged repertoires that have been much studied in other (supposedly more "objective") respects. For example, the chaconne and sarabande, two of the most important dances in French music of the seventeenth and early eighteenth centuries, were originally from South America and had reached Europe by way of Spain. The stylistic and formal properties of these dances, and the ways that these properties were exploited and extended by J. S. Bach, have generated a long and closely documented scholarly literature. Only in recent decades, by contrast, have scholars explored the exotically freighted associations – with Spaniards (if perhaps no longer with the natives of America) and with carnal relations – that those dances carried when, for example, used in French operas of the same era.[23]

For all four reasons discussed in this section, the interaction between Western exotic musical efforts (on the one hand) and the cultural values, concerns, and prejudices of their day (on the other) has been treated spottily. Only two books on musical exoticism have thus far attempted to range widely across centuries, countries, and genres and also to come to terms with basic issues about how music, in itself and in context, "represents."

The first of these books is edited by Jonathan Bellman and entitled *The Exotic in Western Music*. Bellman's volume has the advantage of being divided into, for the most part, chapters of the "region-being-portrayed" type: Spain, Hungary (and its Rom fiddlers), Central Asia (in Russian music), Indonesian influence in Debussy and Britten, American jazz as exotic (to Europeans), and so on.[24] But this structural decision carries a concomitant disadvantage, for it leaves the chapter authors little opportunity for comparisons and contrasts between "regions portrayed" and also (except in Bellman's five-page preface) for larger speculations.[25] Furthermore, certain of the chapters in *The Exotic in Western Music* continue the longstanding musicological practice of viewing musical exoticism as inhering in concrete stylistic "borrowings" and other "influences" from the music of the culture being portrayed. That is, they work, productively, within the "Exotic Style Only" Paradigm.

Timothy D. Taylor's recent *Beyond Exoticism: Western Music and the World* is almost a counterpart to Bellman's. It sets out to dig deep into the cultural and historical roots of "representation of the Other" by emphasizing broad trends across the past five centuries of world history: colonialism, imperialism, and globalization. The result is a refreshing, challenging look at trends and pieces that have tended to be regarded through the exclusively aesthetic/technical lens of non-Western stylistic "borrowings" or "influences" – or else have scarcely been examined at all, such as television ads using non-Western music.

The first part of Taylor's book discusses some musical works from the seventeenth and eighteenth centuries (e.g., by Lawes, Purcell, Rameau, and Mozart) and from the beginning of the twentieth (Ives, Ravel, Cowell) that reflect increasing awareness of distant territories or peoples. The second and longer part deals with the impact of globalization, since 1980, on pop music and on music in television advertising. Unfortunately, Taylor omits the massive nineteenth- and early twentieth-century exotic repertoire (including Gypsy-style works by Liszt, and operas by Verdi, Bizet, and Puccini that are set in Spain, Ceylon, Japan, or China) as well as concert music and opera from the mid-twentieth century onward (e.g., by Britten, Messiaen, Hovhaness, Reich). A few Asian-style works of Debussy are mentioned but not studied. Nonetheless, throughout the book, Taylor lays out helpful principles for thinking about the connections between musical products and the colonialist and imperialist projects – principles that can be applied to the eras and repertoires that he omits. A more serious limitation is that Taylor's otherwise insightful discussions focus almost entirely on (in his words) "musical signs signifying nonwestern Others."[26] In short, they (like most of the chapters in *The Exotic in Western Music*) are framed within the "Exotic Style Only" Paradigm.

The chapters ahead attempt to build upon Taylor's *Beyond Exoticism*, on the Bellman-edited *Exotic in Western Music*, and also upon studies of selected portions of the exotic repertoire.[27] The book also draws on detailed studies of individual works by critics and specialist scholars. The dual aim throughout is to explore some crucial and neglected issues associated with musical exoticism and to stimulate fresh thinking about a number of works that are central to Western musical life and often rife with complex and contradictory social meanings.

2 | Questions of value

"Exotic": high praise or curse word?

Musical works evoking exotic places and peoples have long been subjected to extreme and injudicious assessments. Composers, critics, and scholars have tended to brand musical exoticism as either healthful and invigorating or decadent and noxious. The nature and intensity of the opinionizing varies: fewer nasty things and more celebratory ones are said, not surprisingly, about Mozart's *Die Entführung aus dem Serail* (Abduction from the Harem, 1782) than about Albert Ketèlbey's *In a Persian Market* (1920). Either way, though, exotic works stimulate reactions. At the end of the previous chapter, I dealt with some prominent attempts at tracking the *existence* of musical exoticism in many genres and across several centuries. In the present chapter, I would like to focus on the prevailing *attitudes towards* such portrayals.

For several centuries now, the prevailing tone in writings about exoticism in music and other creative realms has been distinctly positive. It is primarily the listener – or the listener's representative, the critic – whose delight is recorded in glowing terms. Dozens of reviewers of early productions of Verdi's *Aida* (first performed in 1871) expressed special admiration for the chants of the ancient Egyptian priests and the dances of the priestesses and the Moorish slave boys: "The new [musical] expression [in this work is] faithful to the local color – so much so that the … pharaohs of the great dynasties seem to have been truly brought back to life."[1] Even some works that are today nearly forgotten once captured the imagination of audiences. The scholar and critic Julien Tiersot summarized faithfully in 1889 the excitement that several generations of music lovers in France (and indeed across Europe and North America) had experienced at encountering *Le désert* (1844) by Félicien David: "This music, whose character was so novel for its time, transported its French listeners into an unknown world that was full of attractions [*séductions*] and charms – but, most of all, a world that was alive."[2]

These two quotations form a complementary pair. In one, the pharaohs and their minions are magically brought to life in the opera house of a modern European (or European-dominated) city, be it Cairo (in the 1870s), Milan, Paris, or London. In the other, the listeners are the ones who are carried, in spirit, to a locale and way of life far from their own. The specific direction of the metaphorical travel hardly matters. Two places – or places and times, in the case of *Aida* – have been brought into imaginative contact.

Sometimes the praise of exotic works has focused, not on the listener's experience, but on the composer's. Writers have tended to hail any composer's search for inspiration and challenge in the musical products and procedures of distant cultures. Peter Gradenwitz's *Zwischen Orient und Okzident* adopts a consistently laudatory tone about what the West has made of its musical contacts with the East. More recent commentators, such as Mervyn Cooke, join this chorus of approval for composers' explorations of non-Western materials. In his concluding page, Cooke focuses strongly on the composer as primary agent:

> On a purely musical level ... the most satisfying experiments with gamelan material have been achieved by composers who perceived in Indonesian music elements already inherent in their compositional thinking ... The gamelan acted as a catalyst [for Debussy and Britten] by throwing up fortuitous musical parallels that focused their attention on more radical aspects of their old style.[3]

Such an exclusive emphasis on the composer's creative needs risks minimizing the role (and artistry) of the foreign music in question.

Some scholars have praised exoticism – in literature and the arts, generally – as a crucial element in human development. According to Pierre Leprohon (in the *Enciclopedia dello spettacolo*, a comprehensive reference work on theater, opera, and film), *esotismo* can help an individual – the creative artist but also a member of the audience – to achieve liberation from the constraints of his or her own culture and upbringing:

> The expression, from the Greek *exotikos*, indicates an innate tendency of the human mind to escape from the circle of one's own traditions by a yearning for contact ... with remote environments [*ambienti*] and things.[4]

That was in 1957. But, over thirty-five years later, a prominent opera scholar, Gilles de Van, could still regard exoticism as a metaphor for the psychological truism that an individual must explore the broader world in order to achieve personal autonomy and adulthood:

> Exoticism is ... the attraction for a civilization – manners, social behavior, clothing – foreign to our own, far from us in time or space ... The psychic foundation of all forms of exoticism ... [is] the need to leave home.[5]

Negative evaluations, too, have been heard across many generations and have taken a variety of forms. One "family" of objections – already frequent in the mid- and late nineteenth century – focused primarily on whether a given work borrows from, or *should* borrow from, native musical styles, and how this should best be done. (Two other families of objections began to crop up in the mid- and late twentieth century, respectively, and will be dealt with at the end of the present section and in the following one.) To be sure, use of distinctively exotic styles and materials is, as the present book's distinction between the "Exotic Style Only" Paradigm and the "All the Music in Full Context" Paradigm indicates, one of many ways in which music can contribute to the representation of another place or culture. Nonetheless, it has been extensively treated as if it were the one central, defining feature in musical exoticism, and negative comments about musical exoticism have often focused upon it. I would like to spend some time with instances of this first family of negative evaluation that occur in essays by five distinguished composers (Wagner, Debussy, Schoenberg, Reich, Boulez), by an early twentieth-century music theorist (Heinrich Schenker), and by a late twentieth-century music historian (Carl Dahlhaus).

Several of the quotations that I am about to discuss refer in whole or part to works that employ tunes or other musical materials from the composer's own native land or other European lands. (Such compositions are sometimes described by music historians as "nationalist," "folkloristic," or – Richard Taruskin's recent word – "vernacularist.") But this is natural, given that the categories of "nationalist"/folk-inspired music, on the one hand, and "exotic" music, on the other, display certain inherent similarities:

- Both types of pieces – nationalist/folkloristic ones and exotic ones – tend to isolate melodies, rhythms, and sonorities that are considered "typical" or somehow characteristic of the home or distant people and that are usually also considered somehow pure, simple, and natural. The pieces enrich those musical materials harmonically, develop them motivically, and so on, in order that the resulting musical whole be acceptable within the parameters of Western art music.[6]
- When folk- or nationally tinged works of Chopin, Tchaikovsky, Grieg, or Albéniz are performed elsewhere than in the composer's native land, they are often received – that is, they function in musical life – as exotic, much the way that "truly" exotic pieces do (such as Rimsky-Korsakov's *Capriccio espagnol*, 1887, or Debussy's *Pagodes*, 1903).
- Numerous pieces are neither purely national nor purely exotic, even apart from the question of how they are received abroad. A European

composer (or one from North America) may use a European national style that is different from his or her own, yet the exotic charge of the piece is often less intense than it is in, say, Mozart's "Rondo alla turca" or the East Asian "Laideronnette" movement from Ravel's *Ma Mère l'Oye* (Mother Goose, 1910–11). Examples of this in-between category include operatic cabalettas in polonaise or bolero rhythm by Verdi ("Di quella pira," from *Il trovatore*, 1853) or Ambroise Thomas ("Je suis Titania," from *Mignon*, 1866); Édouard Lalo's violin concertos on Norwegian and Russian themes (1878 and 1879); and the effervescent rural-Italian *Grande tarantelle* for piano and orchestra (1858–64) by New Orleans-born, Paris-trained composer Louis Moreau Gottschalk.[7]

The first of our quotations about folk and exotic styles comes from an essay of 1879 by Richard Wagner. We shall focus on its polemical thrust, but it is also utterly typical of its era in espousing two ideals that may sound antithetical but were often closely intertwined: artistic originality, and a seamless connection between a composer and his own national tradition.

Wagner laments that German composers of his day dabble in a range of foreign styles as if unable to find their own voice and that of Germany as a whole. (In context, the "we" clearly excludes Wagner himself.)

> We [modern-day German composers of large-scale instrumental works] brood, we even rave ... We are brisk, sturdy, blunt, Hungarian, or Scottish – which, unfortunately, for others [who have to listen], means boring.[8]

Wagner packs a lot of disdain into a few words. "Scottish" is a clear attack on Felix Mendelssohn for his overture *The Hebrides* (1829–32) and his Symphony No. 3, "Scottish" (1842). Mendelssohn was a favorite target of Wagner's because of his Jewish family origins and his comfort at working within existing artistic traditions that Wagner was determined to replace with his new blend of opera, symphony, and national epic.

The code word "Hungarian" aims at another composer: Johannes Brahms, who published two enormously successful sets of dances in the Hungarian-Gypsy manner (1868–80; see Chapter 6). Several of Brahms's most widely performed works – notably the G-Minor Piano Quartet (1861), Piano Quintet (1861–64), and Violin Concerto (1878) – have final movements in this same Hungarian-Gypsy style. Wagner castigated Brahms, in another essay of the same year (and, again, without deigning to name him), as a "Jewish leader [i.e., conductor] of a *csárdás* band."[9] Brahms was often regarded at the time, and not least by Wagner himself, as Wagner's polar opposite: that is, as a post-Mendelssohnian upholder of "pure" Classic traditions in symphonic and chamber works. Brahms was not of Jewish origin, but facts never posed an obstacle to Wagner the essayist. The pithy phrase in question ("Jewish leader ...") not only castigates Brahms's use of Hungarian-Gypsy motives as inauthentic. It also reinforces a widespread antisemitic stereotype: the cosmopolitan Jew who makes a comfy living at someone else's expense (in this case by having his band members play dance tunes that belong more properly to, Wagner is implying, the Hungarians and the Roma).[10]

Wagner reveals his closed-mindedness most clearly when, at the end of the sentence, he dismisses Scottish- and Hungarian-style works as "boring" (*langweilig*). Though Wagner here claims to speak objectively and on behalf of Mendelssohn's and Brahms's tormented audiences, he is clearly motivated by ill will and speaking only for himself. The various Hungarian-style pieces by Brahms mentioned above are famously tuneful and varied; few concertgoers would describe them as boring. The same applies to the Hungarian-Gypsy works of Franz Liszt (who grew up in Hungary but whose parents were Germans, not Magyars). Liszt's Hungarian Rhapsody No. 2 has long been one of the most widely enjoyed – and endlessly adapted – pieces in the whole classical repertoire. Bugs Bunny played the work with delight and many a virtuosic flourish in the memorable Warner Bros. cartoon entitled *Rhapsody Rabbit* (1946).[11]

Claude Debussy (writing in 1901) made some of the same points as Wagner but, in addition, posited an inherent incompatibility between folk tune and symphonic art:

The new Russian school tried to rejuvenate the symphony by borrowing ideas from "folk themes" ... Soon the fashion of the folk theme extended across the whole musical world. People went digging in the most obscure provinces, from East to West. And they tore naïve tunes out of aging peasant mouths – tunes that were then quite perplexed to find themselves dressed up in harmonies of lace-like intricacy.[12]

In 1947, the high-modernist composer Arnold Schoenberg asserted, much like Debussy, this supposed incompatibility of the folk-like and the artistic, but he emphasized technical considerations. Many European and Russian folk songs, he opined, are "perfect" and thus too complete in themselves to allow for elaborate thematic and motivic development. They are also too "primitive" in their implied "harmonic progression" to offer much interest when submitted to "contrapuntal combinations."[13]

These quotations from Wagner, Debussy, and Schoenberg focus primarily (though, in Debussy's case, not solely) on folk traditions from within Europe. Other instances of what I have called the first family of objections to exoticism and national styles in music focus instead on borrowings from beyond the West and sometimes reveal, in the process, a subtle condescension. Or not so subtle. The music theorist Heinrich Schenker declared around 1910 that "Arabic, Japanese, and Turkish songs" can be compared to "the babbling of a child." These non-Western melodies, "often original [and charming] only because of their imperfections and awkwardness," have nothing to contribute to "a more advanced art" such as has been achieved by "the [European] masters."[14] Likewise, Schoenberg proposed – again emphasizing technical considerations – that, because certain non-Western traditions are "based on extraordinary or exotic scales," they display "more characteristics [than European folk song], and perhaps even too many ... It is ... impossible to derive [a harmonic accompaniment] logically or naturally from these [unstable, shifting] scales."[15]

More recently, composer-conductor Pierre Boulez has echoed Schoenberg's objection that the great non-Western art-music traditions are too "perfect" in themselves to be useful to a Western composer. And he goes further, arguing that they are doomed:

The music of Asia and India is to be admired because it has reached a stage of perfection, and it is this stage of perfection that interests me. But otherwise the music is dead ... The influence is on my spirit and not on my work. The [three] main points [of affinity for me] are as follows: the time structure, the conception of time being different; the idea of anonymity; [and] the idea of a work of art not being admired as a masterpiece but as an element of spiritual life ... There is no sense in trying to build specimens of Oriental music into contemporary music; no influence is good except when it is transcended.[16]

By contrast, Steve Reich would never give non-Western musical traditions the left-handed compliment of having attained perfection. After all, he once studied drumming in Ghana and steeped himself in the gamelan traditions of Indonesia. Nonetheless, he, too – perhaps precisely because he knows how vital and ever-changing those indigenous traditions can be – evidences a distaste for Western musicians' using almost any kind of easily perceivable "local color," which he castigates as merely decorative:

The least interesting form of influence ... is that of imitating the *sound* of non-Western music. This can be done by using non-Western instruments in one's own music (sitars in the rock band), or using one's own instruments to sound like non-Western ones (singing "Indian style" melodies over electronic drones). This method is the simplest and most superficial way of dealing with non-Western music, since the general sound of these musics can be absorbed in a few minutes of listening without further study. Imitating the sound of non-Western music leads to "exotic music" – what used to be called "Chinoiserie."

Alternately, one can create a music with one's own sound that is constructed in the light of one's knowledge of non-Western *structures* ... This is a more genuine and interesting form of influence, because while listening one is not necessarily aware of some non-Western music being imitated. Instead of imitation, the influence of non-Western musical structures on the thinking of a Western composer is likely to produce something genuinely new.[17]

Reich's discussion (from 1973) might seem to bypass a primary concern of this book, namely how the West portrays unfamiliar societies in musical works and whether it ought to do so at all. Instead, it focuses on a narrower topic: the aspects of a non-Western or folk tradition that a composer of high aspirations should and should not borrow (or assimilate). But the sharply dichotomous wording ("superficial imitation" vs. "genuine influence") gives his statement – which otherwise resembles in basic spirit the statements by Wagner, Debussy, Schoenberg, Schenker, and Boulez – an additional spin, a frankly ethical one, that brings it particularly close to our present discussion.

Reich's ethical considerations become explicit in a more recent essay (1988). He recalls that, when he brought back some iron bells from Ghana, his first inclination was to file them down so that their pitches would correspond to the equal-tempered scale of the Western instruments in his ensemble. "The more I thought about this, the more it began to seem like a kind of musical rape." Instead, he set the bells aside and taught some Ghanaian patterns of interlocking rhythms to his glockenspiel players.[18]

Prominent music historians have shared the wariness or even hostility toward musical exoticism displayed by these six renowned figures. In his widely cited study of nineteenth-century music, Dahlhaus minimizes the specificity of various national and exotic stylistic colorations in Western art music. His aim is to show that such exoticisms have little to do with the music of the country in question. "It is no easy matter to see a definitive distinction" between an Arab-style piece by Bizet and a Norwegian-style piece by Grieg. But Dahlhaus's point is undermined by his own Bizet and Grieg excerpts, which are wildly different in style and do in fact reflect selected aspects of the musical culture in question.[19]

Dahlhaus's particular objection (like others in the first family of objections) has been heard recurrently over several centuries. The complaint can take two opposite forms, together constituting a double-bind for any composer who might be tempted to evoke another region or culture. (1) A composer can be damned for *not* using styles typical of (or thought typical of) the locale. For example, if a character (or the chorus) in an exotic opera does not "sound foreign" (in musical style), some complain that the composer has neglected the ethnic/national element of the characterization.

An early critic of Boieldieu's opera *Le calife de Bagdad* (The Caliph of Baghdad, 1800) regretted that the "author" (perhaps primarily the librettist but also, the context implies, the composer as well) had not done enough to "transport our imaginations to the locations where he has set the scene."[20] (2) A composer can be damned for almost the opposite: not using ethnic styles faithfully enough. Observers often object that elements of exotic or other "local color" are standardized, hence insufficiently true to actual folk practice. Raymond Monelle has recently dismissed the "clichés" and "mannerism[s]" (such as "snap rhythms" and "the habit of slipping down a whole tone for the second line of a tune") that were disproportionately represented in collections of real and purported Scottish tunes for the parlor and that, consequently, were adopted by composers when writing in supposedly Scottish manner.[21]

A constructive response to objections such as Monelle's would be that Western art music is not folk music. It has its own aesthetic aims and parameters. Two of the most basic of these are:

- the concept of a relatively fixed musical "work" (the composer sets down in the score the desired pitches and rhythms, unlike folk-music traditions, which usually leave much more to the improvising performer); and
- the establishing of coded styles – what Leonard Ratner and others have called topics (or *topoi*) – that, by their very stereotyped nature, can then be skillfully invoked, altered, contrasted, and combined.[22]

It is thus not productive to dismiss a work – Rossini's *La donna del lago* (1819, after Sir Walter Scott's poem *The Lady of the Lake*), Brahms's "Edward" Ballade (1854), or Bruch's *Scottish Fantasia* (1880) – as being unimaginative or ill-researched simply because it makes use of Scottish clichés. It can, however, be quite productive to consider:

- the extent and nature of the borrowing (the degree of verisimilitude), i.e., what the well-known exotic clichés or "topics" have chosen from the native style and then highlighted, distorted, or recontextualized; and
- how imaginatively the clichés are used and to what expressive – and, in some cases, arguably ideological – end.

So much for the first of our three families of objections: ones based upon a composer's use or avoidance of exotic or more local "folk" styles. Objections have tended to proliferate on two other bases as well. One is the dismay with which serious artists and scholars, since the early twentieth century, have viewed the increasing proliferation of relatively formulaic exotic effects in the arts and entertainment industry. (The other will be given its own, separate section in a moment.)

This distressed response to what one might call "trickle-down," "commercialized," or "middlebrow and lowbrow" exoticism cries out at one point from the *esotismo* entry in the *Enciclopedia dello spettacolo*. Shortly after the confident definition cited earlier (exoticism as an innate human tendency), the author suddenly cautions – in the hushed tone of a worried mental-health professional – that the urge toward the exotic can turn from a "legitimate need" into "vice, decadence, and, finally, flight from what is familiar and known, and from oneself."[23] At first glance, the wording may remind one of certain literary characters – Michel in Gide's *L'immoraliste* or Sebastian Flyte in Evelyn Waugh's *Brideshead Revisited* – who fall from grace and social responsibility into a slough of self-indulgence, often in Algeria or Morocco.

What the entry in the *Enciclopedia dello spettacolo* has in mind, though, is not carefully ironic or disturbingly truthful portrayals such as Gide's and Waugh's but slick, commercial fare: what it bluntly calls *falso esotismo*. The article inveighs against "certain old American [film] productions, of which *The Sheik* (1921), with Rudolph Valentino, is utterly typical." "European directors [are] more scrupulous," it adds, for they place "actors and technical staff in authentic locales when making feature films."

The example chosen to represent *falso esotismo* is unfortunate. One suspects that *The Sheik* was at least somewhat kitsch-y from the time it was first shown on the silent screen. Its obvious falseness – perhaps pointed up at the time by the amused pianist or organist accompanying it – is part of both its playful vitality and its ability to unsettle the most cynical watcher. Parodies of Valentino's over-the-top portrayal started early, as if to contain the threat of the actor's animal vigor and ambiguous sexuality.

The encyclopedia entry might have done better to mention the thoughtless or even outright vicious portrayals of African "witch doctors" and scheming Chinese opium dealers in hundreds of run-of-the-mill adventure films. The theater pianist or (after the introduction of sound film) on-track studio orchestra generally reinforced the effect of such film portrayals by utterly stereotypical musical devices reeking of supposed "local color." Those films are now barely watchable, not because the portrayals in them are any less true than Valentino's sheik (they hardly could be), nor because they are nastier (though they generally are), but because they are unimaginative and clunkily predictable.

Edward Said's *Orientalism* and other ideological critiques

The last family of objections to exoticism in music and other creative spheres is related to this call, in the *Enciclopedia*, for authentic (documentary-realistic) portrayal. But it comes from a very different quarter: the intersecting worlds of politics, political science, area studies (e.g., schools or departments of African or Asian studies), and certain recent trends in literary and cultural criticism. In particular, it draws upon reactions, across all of these fields, to one of the most momentous developments in world history during the past two centuries: the decolonization of territories that had long been ruled by the European powers (notably England and France, but also Portugal, Belgium, and the Netherlands, and, in earlier centuries, Spain).

In the middle decades of the twentieth century, this collapse of empire was encouraged and sympathetically analyzed by such powerful writers as Frantz Fanon and Bryan S. Turner. Edward Said's *Orientalism* (1978) broadened the critique to include not just the concrete institutions and procedures of imperialism – asymmetrical tariff laws, schools taught in the language of the colonizer, military suppression of uprisings – but also the many kinds of writings that coincided with, and often supported or enabled, those more practical efforts of the imperial powers.

Said's *Orientalism* focuses its attention almost exclusively on non-fiction writings (e.g., travelers' and governmental reports) and, as Said himself admitted, gives less attention to exotic portrayals in literature and the arts than they deserve.[24] In his later study *Culture and Imperialism*, Said finally did some public struggling with the issue of how political ideology and cultural stereotypes function within major works of the creative imagination. There he repeatedly expresses admiration for certain novels by Jane Austen, Rudyard Kipling, and Joseph Conrad that are related to empire and colonialism – and also, in a pathbreaking chapter, admiration for Verdi's *Aida*. At the same time, he offers trenchant comments on the ways in which the works reflect the myths that empire generated for its self-justification. Sometimes – as with Austen's *Mansfield Park* – he guides the reader to passages that seem to convey glimmerings of doubt about current-day imperial policies, or at least – itself a big leap forward – some minimal effort at "historical honesty."[25] Other times, as with *Aida*, he points out (more in line with passages in *Orientalism*) that aesthetic pleasure, subtle workmanship, complex structuring – in short, artistry – could serve in part to "occlude" (veil from sight for the European reader or audience member) the functioning of empire. What makes a work such as *Aida* effective and gratifying is also what "permits the conqueror" – in the work's own day – "not to look into the truth of the violence he does."[26]

Despite Said's frequent warnings that very different approaches are necessary when dealing with non-fiction accounts and with high-level literary and artistic production, critics and scholars began to use the words "Orientalism" and "Orientalist" extensively in specific relation to literature and the arts. "Orientalism" thus came to be widely accepted (at least in academia and, to some extent, journalism) as a more sharply disapproving substitute for the word "exoticism." By today, this negative meaning is widely taken for granted. Foreign-affairs journalist Ian Buruma and philosopher Avishai Margalit can thus invert the word to produce "Occidentalism," by which they mean hatred of the West, whether in post-Meiji Japan, in radical-Islamist circles today, or among anti-globalization activists within the West itself.[27]

Some people writing in the immediate wake of Said's book restricted their use of the term "Orientalism" to the Middle East. Others extended it to South and East Asia. Either way, conferences and books proliferated, reporting on the ways that prejudicial attitudes show up in Western portrayals – including artistic ones – of the location in question.[28] In the process, the organizers and speakers often ignored Said's point that writings could be Orientalist in function – could be part and parcel of the large project of Western domination – even without distorting or slanting the representation of the dominated place and people. The supposedly "Saidian" views were, in one sense, broader than what Said himself had in mind (because they extended further afield geographically) but, in another sense, narrower, in that they focused almost exclusively on the West's supposed need to vilify the East at every step on the way to dominating it.

Objections to Said's book – and/or to this geographically broader but more consistently negative use of the term "Orientalism," which quickly became accepted as *his* position – have likewise been numerous and heated. They have come from different ideological and aesthetic camps. And they have often ignored Said's own sharp delineation between mainstream responses to "the Orient" (whether bureaucratic or casual) and creative ones. John M. MacKenzie, a noted historian of the British Empire and of English popular culture, wrote a book whose chapters defend, in turn, each of the arts – even the Middle Eastern designs of English train stations – from Said's supposed attack.[29]

Other critics, such as Homi Bhabha, stressed – as Said sometimes did not take pains to do – how inadequate Orientalist and other stereotypes were and are as descriptions of a region's actual inhabitants, and their lives:

The stereotype ... must be anxiously repeated ... as if the essential duplicity of the Asiatic or the bestial sexual licence of the African ... can never really, in discourse, be proved.[30]

Cultural anthropologist James Clifford twitted Said for essentializing the West and selecting his evidence.[31] Lisa Lowe made some of the same points as Clifford but in greater detail. Lowe demonstrated that Orientalist attitudes were not as monolithic as Said implied but, rather, varied over time and from one imperialist power to another (e.g., England or France).[32] Ania Loomba and others objected that Said's account – by attending only to the actions of Europeans – missed the opportunity to draw attention to the ways in which the populations of colonized and other non-Western territories responded to and, in time, obstructed imperial power.[33]

Along the way, some commentators have brought attention to unusually open-minded European visitors who were neglected by Said. In particular, they argue that certain women, such as Lady Mary Wortley Montagu (*Turkish Letters*, 1717–18), responded in more individual, "less preconditioned" ways. Explanations include the marginal status of European women in the imperial enterprise and the growing awareness (among many European women at the time) of parallels between the enslavement and exploitation by Europeans of populations overseas and, back at home, the hegemony of men over women.[34]

Most relevant for the present study, certain scholars have begun to develop Said's own point that his book's reliance on texts claiming to be objective reportage or political argument leaves almost unexplored the rich literary works that evoke the region – and that do so for a wide range of ideological and artistic purposes.[35] For example, although various Eastern traditions – Hindu *satih* (suttee), the Muslim harem – were widely viewed by Westerners around 1800 as cruel, Marilyn Butler has recently made clear that, in many English poems and tales from around 1793 to 1820, the attacks on such Eastern traditions were often aimed (on a deeper level) at "institutionalized religion" as a whole or, indeed, at one wing of Christianity in particular: the Catholic Church, viewed by "[many] English liberals (including Byron and Shelley) ... as the leading counter-revolutionary force in postwar Europe."[36]

Applying Orientalist critiques to music

Inspired in part by these new scholarly concerns and cross-currents, scholars and critics have begun to examine musical works from around 1700 onward for their echoes of imperialist practices or, more generally, of an increasing global awareness.[37] Some recent music critics and scholars have wielded the term "Orientalism" in either Said's sense or the more extreme sense(s) propounded by certain of his followers. Matthew Head entitles his book *Orientalism, Masquerade and Mozart's Turkish Music*, appropriately enough, given that the works in question (notably the "Rondo alla turca" and *Die Entführung aus dem Serail*) evoke the Ottoman Empire. Israeli-born musicologist Ronit Seter frankly names Orientalism as one of several "Western maladies" introduced into the young state of Israel by European Jews who had settled the land over the previous decades. Seter notes that, when Salim Al-Nur, an "exquisite" master musician from Baghdad, fled to Israel to escape persecution, he was denied esteem, or even much of a hearing, because Iraqi music "was considered the music of the Other, or worse, the music of the [Arab] Enemy."[38] W. Anthony Sheppard stretches "Orientalism" very plausibly to Japan, when explaining how certain conventions of *nōh* drama are extracted and manipulated in Benjamin Britten's *Curlew River* (1964) and other twentieth-century operas and oratorios.[39]

In the past two decades, the term has been invoked in connection to a wide range of locales. Susan McClary claims to find Orientalist attitudes in the way that the title character is portrayed in Bizet's *Carmen*. The discussion would have been more nuanced if McClary had made some distinction between that opera's nervy Gypsy heroine and the more pliable, doe-eyed Turkish-harem seductresses of so many other art works of the day.[40] Lawrence Kramer proposes that Orientalism can be felt, or sniffed out, in Ravel's *Daphnis et Chloé* (1912), even though the ballet's setting is essentially that of the mythical Arcadia of ancient Greece.[41] George Lipsitz pushes the term further still from any kind of East. He writes that alternative pop artist David Byrne, by inserting into one of his songs the voice of Cuban-born singer Celia Cruz, was invoking "primitivism, exoticism, Orientalism." "[Cruz] is an all-purpose 'other' summoned up to symbolize Byrne's delight in musical difference on the west side of Manhattan."[42] Lipsitz even finds Orientalism in the somewhat condescending attraction that the protagonist in a Willa Cather novel feels toward the Bohemian- and Norwegian-American "hired girls" in Nebraska.[43]

In short, despite its origins, "Orientalism" has become a term that can refer to any world population – including Caribbeans and blond Scandinavian-Americans – that differs from whatever a work of art constructs as its mainstream European or white-American persona or viewpoint. And, with rare exceptions (Kramer), it accuses the West of intolerance (condescension, etc.) toward whatever ethnic Other is in question.

Naturally enough, then, "Orientalism" has also become for some music critics and scholars – just as for literary critics and such – a curse word, a sharply disapproving substitute for a word – "exotic" – that had so long been used in a (now-considered-naïve?) spirit of delighted endorsement. When ethnomusicologist Mark Slobin wants to group together Western marginalizations of all musical traditions other than the Bach-to-Ligeti lineage, "Orientalism" is the word he chooses, clearly regarding it as today's synonym for "Eurocentrism" or simple "classical-music snobbery."[44]

One can thus understand why writers who deal with musical works that openly borrow musical devices and other cultural *topoi* from the Middle East or from East or South Asia sometimes leap to the defense. Often, as in the Boulez and Reich quotations earlier, the saving distinction is one between superficial and structural – or, in the following comments from a book review (by S. Andrew Granade, a specialist on the music-theater works of Harry Partch), between ornamental/quaint and conceptual/deep:

> An Orientalist critique [of Benjamin Britten's *Death in Venice*, with its borrowings from Balinese gamelan, or of *Curlew River*] has merit. But Partch especially was not after an ornamental overlay of quaint exotic sounds or forms. His employment of exotic models sprang from a conceptual framework and originated in a deep respect for the theater of other countries and cultures. Partch simply used those models as inspiration for crafting his unique vision, one that was distinctly American. As he stated in the preface to *Delusion of the Fury*, the first act of which is based on two separate Noh plays, "Act I is actually a development of my own style in dramatic music, particularly as evidenced in *Oedipus* and *Revelation [in the Courthouse Square]*. If for no other reason than the music, its *daimon* is American" … In order to fully understand the implications of this type of conceptual exoticism, new language and new tropes [other than "cultural imperialism"] need to be developed.[45]

In this passage, Granade protects Partch's Asian-inspired works from ideological attack by offering works by Britten as more appropriate targets. But, even if we do conclude that these works by Britten, and maybe by Partch, reflect Orientalist attitudes and "cultural imperialism," in what manner does this invalidate them, and to whom? This brings me to the last of my introductory reflections, which reaches far beyond the specifically exotic repertoires that this book explores.

Beauty and beastliness

Cultural imperialism – or any other ideology or political trend that a given individual today finds repellent – can be condemned in the realm of politics but, I would propose, can and should be allowed to find expression in art, especially when the work in question is, in some sense, worthy enough (as, musicians and audiences agree, *Madama Butterfly* and Britten's *Death in Venice* clearly are). By this, I do not mean that standard-repertoire operas – and avant-garde experiments such as Partch's *Delusion of the Fury* – are more accurate or respectful than bits of tasty treacle such as Ketèlbey's *In a Persian Market*, a work that was probably accepted by many as enjoyable but somewhat silly *falso esotismo* from the start.

Rather, I propose that we accept that each of these exotically inspired works – the Puccini, the Britten, the Partch, the Ketèlbey – is rooted in a unique mixture of fragmentary and often distorted impressions of, and perhaps even defamatory stereotypes of, the culture (and, when relevant, musical traditions) in question. The difference in effect and value lies partly in the particular images that make up the mix in one work rather than another. But it also lies in the greater ambition and skill on the part of some creators (composer, librettist, *et al.*) than others. The result, in a great exoticist work, is a more intense and artistically persuasive enactment of the stereotypes and (partial, distorted) impressions that it engages. Or, to be more fair, an enactment of the stereotypes, an undermining of them, or sometimes a bit of each of these (see the various case studies in Chapters 5–10). To paraphrase Said's remark about Jane Austen (see Chapter 1 above), Puccini should not be discussed as if he were Ketèlbey.

What makes many art works great and durable, and meaningful to many different kinds of listeners and viewers, is in part that they so successfully convey the prevailing ideology of their day. They convey a sense of that ideology and the feelings that drove it, even to audiences in very different societies (or to later generations) who may not endorse the ideology in question – audiences who may, left to their own devices, barely be able to conceive of it. *Madama Butterfly* can give a fuller and more powerful sense of Western cultural-racial ideology than can a Ketèlbey orchestral bauble. By this I mean that Puccini's opera replays the ideology in all its richness, reveals more of its internal consistencies and (deeply human) inconsistencies. Furthermore, the ideological resonances in such a work can become richer as a listener studies the work more closely and learns more about its cultural and social contexts.

This position is similar to one taken at times by Susan McClary and Richard Taruskin.[46] Taruskin has recently proposed that the politically or ethically troubling aspects of a work (for example, the "disquieting [proto-fascistic] political implications" of Stravinsky's portrayal of rigid Russian-peasant social conventions in *Les noces*) should not cause us to close our ears: "The way [this work's] beauty coexist[s] with unbeautiful implications create[s] a compelling tension that [is] worth exploring."[47] Taruskin is not, as some might think, proposing a strict division between work and (disposable) context. Quite the contrary, as he has shown elsewhere, the "unbeautiful" ideological implications of *Les noces* are part of what led Stravinsky to use certain style features in the work. It is enriching for us to know more about what Stravinsky and his contemporaries would have read into those style features, and to ponder possibly analogous implications in other repertoires, including ones of our own day.

But what if those implications are not merely "unbeautiful" but, say, offensive to one or another national or ethnic group? I draw the word "offensive" into this discussion intentionally because it tends to be invoked in two very different ways nowadays that I feel should not be – as they often are – conflated:

(1) to label and proscribe speech and other acts that are defamatory, threatening, and thus profoundly uncivil; but also
(2) to suppress actions, verbal statements, and art works that express views or touch upon issues that are currently unpopular with, or feared by, a given group or partisan cohort (or government), i.e., are considered "politically incorrect," immoral, or subversive.

How seriously (how prescriptively) should society as a whole take the accusation that a work of art offends an individual or group? As recent legal cases – and uproars in the media and sometimes in the streets – demonstrate, there is no international consensus about where to draw the line between, on the one hand, actionable "hate speech" or racist provocation (the famous Danish cartoons of 2005 criticizing radical Islam?) and, on the other, thoughtful commentary on, playful banter about, or cultural/creative "borrowing" from one or another ethnic or other social group.

In the arts, too, offensiveness, like exoticism and so many other kinds of meaning, is in the eye of the beholder. The degree of offensiveness that a person or group feels when encountering a work or even simply hearing or reading about it – the degree to which he or she feels offended, or feels that his or her group is being defamed – may be in proportion to how intensely he or she was affected by the particular oppressive values or crimes against humanity that have come to be associated (rightly or wrongly) with the work and various of its manifest features.[48] For example, music of the courts of Louis XIV and his several predecessors does not distress many listeners nowadays, no doubt because we would have to work hard (as we listen for minutes on end) to keep associating the gracious musical sounds of a gavotte or musette with the crushing social realities of the monarchical system: abusive taxation, religious intolerance, government-organized massacres of Protestants, and so on.

Maybe the question of recentness and personal relevance explains why nobody to my knowledge has suggested that Lully *opéras-ballets* be suppressed. Nor, as Charles Rosen pointedly notes, has anybody proposed that the words be altered in performances of Counter-Reformation works, such as one particular motet by the great sixteenth-century composer Orlando di Lasso, which praises (with some verbal wit) the Archbishop of Canterbury for having Protestants burned at the stake.[49] The centuries-long fratricidal hatred of Catholics and Protestants is something that most people nowadays seem to be able to relegate to history.

In any case, we should recall that many instances of musical exoticism are not tied so directly, or solely, or even at all, to systematic hatred nor to events of great beastliness. Handel's various Eastern tyrants may reflect the aims of British imperialism (which was widely viewed by English people, at the time, as an expansive, patriotic endeavor). But those stage tyrants may, at least as much, also have been intended as metaphors for political and religious struggles internal to Britain (see Chapter 5). And at least as often, in the present book, the norm is a work such as Rimsky-Korsakov's *Capriccio espagnol*: a celebration of a different and attractive musical and ethnic culture, a vision of an entrancing world far from "here." Rimsky-Korsakov seems to have felt, like Glinka before him, a kinship between Russia and Spain, two lands at the (supposed) margins of Europe. If we can delight today that various Others – including former subjects of empire – are "writing back" to the Western metropolis,[50] maybe we can enjoy what resulted when a composer from the (Eastern) margin, over a hundred years ago, "wrote back" to the self-proclaimed center of the musical world, i.e., Western Europe – and not least to Germany, where various pieces by Rimsky-Korsakov and his fellow Russians were first published.

Kwame Anthony Appiah, in a recent and thoughtful short book, offers wise words on the positive values – the necessity, the inevitability – of cultural contact and mingling in past centuries and, increasingly, in the present day:

Conversations across boundaries can be fraught, all the more so as the world grows smaller and the stakes grow larger. It's therefore worth remembering that they can also be a pleasure. What academics sometimes dub "cultural otherness" should prompt neither piety nor consternation ... The way of segregation and seclusion has always been anomalous in our perpetually voyaging species. Cosmopolitanism isn't hard work; repudiating it is.[51]

If Appiah's point holds for actual human conversations and encounters, how much more true is it of art works that permit people in one locale to summon up some version or vision – some image, however stereotyped, distorted, or utterly fantastical – of another locale and to reflect upon it. A recent book by two authors, one Japanese, the other American, documents, more thoroughly and accurately than ever before, the early twentieth-century attempts of Japanese dancer and choreographer Michio Ito at creating works inspired by Japanese traditions, in conjunction with the poet-playwright William Butler Yeats (*At the Hawk's Well*, 1916) and with such composers as the Englishman Gustav Holst, the American Charles Griffes, and Ito's (Western-trained) countryman Kósçak (Kosaku) Yamada. The authors speak admiringly of the result: a "rich interplay between Japanese and Western cultures," a "flexible melding of East and West that lay at the heart of [Ito's] own modernism, and perhaps of modernism itself," even while admitting that, for Yeats at least, the whole project of creating an English-language *nōh* drama was something of a "scholarly parlor game."[52]

Any such attempt to reach across cultural boundaries through art, or to use artistic means – whether (as the "All the Music in Full Context" Paradigm allows) exotic or not – in order to comment on life beyond those boundaries is fraught with risks, no matter what the nationality/ethnicity of the creative artist or artists who undertake it. The resulting images (to refer again to this book's subtitle) may be marked forever by the contending motivations that brought that work into being. But the fraught-ness itself can, as Taruskin points out, give such works, such images, a "compelling tension," make them fascinating, and offer occasion for ... reflection.

3 | Exoticism with and without exotic style

What kind of "-ism" is exoticism? The word relates, etymologically, to places or settings "away from" some vantage point considered normative, most often that of the observer. Like so many "-isms" (idealism, Romanticism), it can be broad and relatively abstract: an ideology; a diverse collection of prejudices and "facts"; an intellectual tendency. Or, it can be broad and concrete: a cultural trend with rich and varied manifestations.

In the visual arts and literature, exoticism is generally sought in a work's subject matter and in the evident messages (mood, etc.) that the work's creator was attempting to convey – but not necessarily in the work's style. For example, nineteenth-century French Orientalist paintings (of, say, a harem scene or a grizzled North African pirate with curved dagger) rely upon standard up-to-date Western techniques, such as the modeling of three-dimensional form through perspective, color, and shadow. Indeed, Delacroix, though a prolific producer of images of the Middle East, frankly admitted to finding non-European art flat and uninvolving.[1] (Attitudes changed later in the nineteenth century and early twentieth, with Manet, Gauguin, Picasso, and Matisse.[2])

Within the musical realm, by contrast, exoticism has often been treated less as a broad mindset or artistic approach and more as a lexicon of specific stylistic devices that the composer – and presumably many listeners – associated, rightly or wrongly, with the distant country or people in question. We sometimes even use the word in the plural, saying that a piece makes great or little use of the various prevailing "exoticisms" of the era.[3] "An exoticism," in this sense, is something small-scale and countable: a single exotic-sounding style trait or, at most, a coherent collection of traits indicating one particular exotic locale and culture. A recent scholar calls the *alla turca* style, used by Mozart in his famous "Rondo," "the first recognizable exoticism in [Western] music," a phrase that may give the erroneous impression that exoticism – in the broader sense – was not already at work in music during the decades or even centuries before Mozart.[4]

I do not mean to belittle the quasi-empirical approach of hunting for stylistic exoticisms. Quite the contrary, I will spend some time in this chapter drawing attention to this approach and laying out its explicit or implicit lexicon of devices. I will dub it, for polemical and practical purposes, the "Exotic Style Only" Paradigm (of musical exoticism). But I will also go on to propose a more encompassing definition of musical exoticism that enables us to deal with a wider range of instances of musical portrayals of "the exotic," including works from before Mozart – and also works (such as *Madama Butterfly*) that engage almost continuously in exotic portrayal, even during passages that make little or no use of musical "exoticisms" in the narrow, countable sense.

Existing definitions

Currently circulating definitions, such as the ones found in music dictionaries, encyclopedias, and critical writings, often center on issues of musical style. Perhaps they have been influenced by a similar tendency in art history. According to the noted art historian Enrico Crispolti,

"Exoticism" may be defined as the imitation of elements in alien cultures that differ from native traditions.[5]

("Elements," a vague enough word, can include both kinds of visual exoticism mentioned above: Delacroix's way of portraying Eastern subject matter without altering his usual Western techniques; and the indebtedness of later artists to the flatness of Japanese wood-block prints or the angularity and generalized features of African masks.)

Definitions of musical exoticism have surely also been shaped by a general tendency within music scholarship to privilege explanations that grow out of what is regarded as the ultimate empirical evidence: the notes of the score, "the music itself." This is a corollary of the tendency to conceive of music history primarily in terms of styles and genres – often embodied in a small number of masterworks – rather than in terms of institutions, functions, meanings, and performative (and listening) practices.[6]

The tendency to see exoticism as embodied in specific musical materials (or stylistic markers) is particularly clear in a recent, thoughtful series of articles on musical exoticism by the French musicologist Jean-Pierre Bartoli:

In the artistic domain [generally], "exoticism" indicates a combination of procedures that evoke cultural and geographical Otherness [*altérité*]. Most often, such a combination makes use of meaning-units [*unités significatives*] that seem not to belong to the idiomatic artistic language but, rather, seem borrowed from a foreign artistic language.[7]

Bartoli goes on to demonstrate a corollary of this principle: certain "meaning-units" that are standard options within the foreign artistic (or, more specifically, musical) tradition but happen to be shared by Western styles are chosen less often as markers of the exotic. A tune that does come from the region in question but uses what, to Western ears, might sound a lot like the C-major scale may not feel unfamiliar enough to merit its being incorporated into an exotic piece.[8]

Bartoli often writes as if the musical "procedures" and "units" that are selected and combined by the exotic composer operate in a purely musical context. He makes little or no mention of non-musical elements (such as an exotic opera's plot, sets, and costumes), even though these have often been what motivated the composer to copy or create distinctive musical elements and have then served as the framework within which the performer and listener "reads" the musical codes.[9] Most basically, Bartoli sees the "units" as either selective "borrowings" (*emprunts*) – in other words, what Crispolti calls "imitations" – from the music of the region or else as invented devices that give the impression of standing in for the foreign music (in more or less the same way that selective "borrowings" do, except with less documentary verisimilitude).

Whatever one calls it, the close copying (or attempted or apparent copying) of a foreign style undoubtedly comprises, for many scholars, the core – or even the near-entirety – of the exoticizing process. Jonathan Bellman invokes the familiar musicological concept of stylistic "borrowing" to launch his richly suggestive introduction to the 1998 essay-collection *The Exotic in Western Music*.

Musical exoticism ... may be defined as the borrowing or use of musical materials that evoke distant locales or alien frames of reference ... Characteristic and easily recognized musical gestures from the alien culture are assimilated into a more familiar style, giving it an exotic color and suggestiveness.[10]

These foreign gestures comprise what Bellman calls the "nuts and bolts level" at which exoticism (*always*, he implies) works in music.[11]

Thomas Betzwieser, in the authoritative encyclopedia *Die Musik in Geschichte und Gegenwart*, expresses the same point of view even more plainly, using another favorite musicological term: "influence." Like Bartoli, he starts by addressing exoticism in the arts, generally. "The chief characteristic [of exoticism in art] consists of the influence of foreign, especially non-European elements upon European art." In musical works, Betzwieser continues, these foreign elements are of three distinct kinds. (1) All exotic works make "use of 'exotic' musical material." Operas, in addition, make use of (2) plots and characters that are similarly marked as exotic and (3) production aspects (sets, costumes), likewise marked.[12] What is true for opera, Betzwieser implies, is also true for genres and art forms that are closely analogous, such as dance works, Broadway musicals, and films.

Thus, in this standard view, the exotic in music comes "from the alien culture" (Bellman) – or at least is fashioned to sound as if it might easily have come from it – and consists of "non-European elements" (Betzwieser) or ones that could credibly be heard as such. I would agree that emphasizing concrete details of style and the authenticity of the borrowings is important and often utterly crucial. But by emphasizing the principle of stylistic codes (or by discussing it and almost nothing else, as Bartoli does), we end up giving too little attention to broader and equally crucial principles. The quotation above from Bellman hints at this, by referring to "evok[ing]" and "suggestiveness." These resonant words suggest that we might profitably consider the non-musical elements in an exotic work (e.g., genre, work title, an opera's plot) or, at a deeper level, the cultural values (including ethnic stereotypes) that shaped a work's composition and that continue thereafter to shape its performance and reception in successive generations. Such a broader area of focus is perhaps reflected also in Betzwieser's quick shift from "foreign" and "non-European" to "'exotic' musical material" (with scare quotes around the crucial word). We need to pay attention to what the chosen musical materials were intended to signify, in context, and what they have meant to audiences and critics over the years.

Furthermore, we need to have a working definition of musical exoticism that does not exclude works that unquestionably evoke a foreign place or people despite using few stylistic markers of "Otherness" or none at all – works such as Rossini's *Italiana in Algeri* (The Italian Woman in Algiers, 1813), which sounds obviously Middle Eastern in just one number for chorus. Steven Huebner has put the matter plainly with specific regard to operatic portrayals of the Middle East or Orient (taking the latter term broadly enough to include the Gypsy woman Carmen):

Some of the best writing on this subject ... [falls into] a kind of reductionism ... "Orientalism" appears to exist for [critics such as Herbert] Lindenberger only in music with an oriental color, even though the signs and topics of common-practice tonal syntax can project equally well a stand toward a passive [or seductive or nasty] East that might also be called orientalist.[13]

A broader definition

In short, we need a broader approach. I therefore propose the following new definition of musical exoticism. It forms the starting point for our remaining deliberations in this chapter and the rest of the book. Or starting points, for its five distinct aspects encompass various considerations that previous definitions have generally not addressed, such as the functions that musical exoticism can carry out within the culture that produces it.

- Musical exoticism is the process of evoking in or through music – whether that music is "exotic-sounding" or not – a place, people, or social milieu that is not entirely imaginary and that differs profoundly from the home country or culture in attitudes, customs, and morals. (The setting can also be removed in time, as we shall discuss.) More precisely, it is the process of evoking a place (people, social milieu) that is *perceived* as different from home by the people who created the exoticist cultural product and by the people who receive it.
- Beneath the surface, the place (people, social milieu) that is being evoked may be perceived as resembling home in certain ways.
- The differences and resemblances between Here and There may carry a variety of emotional charges: they may register as consoling, may trouble a listener's complacency, and so on.
- Whereas the differences between Here and There were generally conscious on the part of the creator(s) of the exotic musical work and readily apparent to listeners of the day, the *resemblances* may have been relatively conscious *or quite unconscious* and readily apparent *or not readily apparent*. For example, they may not have been mentioned by critics at the time of the work's first appearance.
- In any case, if the work continues to be performed over many years, such broader cultural resonances – the perceived differences from *and* resemblances to the home culture – are likely to fade and be replaced by others, given that listeners may now be living in new and different cultural situations and may thus bring different values and expectations to the work.

This new definition, multifaceted though it is, remains woefully incomplete. For one thing, it does not even raise a crucial question: "How do musical elements, in an exotic work, interact with non-musical ones?" For another, the clause "whether 'exotic-sounding' or not" skirts the no-less-crucial question, "How much and in what ways does the resulting music sound like the music of the region or culture in question – or at least plausibly evoke it for a listener who has never encountered the musical tradition in question?" My definition does not rely upon the presence of exotically coded musical styles – the very "figures," "elements," "meaning-units," or "nuts and bolts" that previous definitions have understood to be (in the language of logic) a sufficient indicator of musical exoticism and (according to Bartoli, at least) a necessary one as well.[14]

Still, my definition explicitly includes the possible use of such coded styles. It needs to, given that so many exotic works rely upon them. Indeed, as we shall see, the adoption of musical styles from cultures perceived as Other became so widespread in the twentieth century that some observers began to prefer not to consider it exotic at all but instead simply an aspect of intercultural sharing, with no larger "representational" function. In their view, the musical aspects of the distant culture are being represented (adapted, etc.) but no other aspects. (See Chapters 9–10.)

By keeping the various options open – exoticism that makes extensive use, little use, or no use of exotic style – the definition sets us on the path toward formulating a broader paradigm (or method of approach) for musical exoticism than the one that has prevailed for several centuries and that still shapes much thinking and commentary today. This new, broader paradigm deserves explicit presentation in the present chapter, as I shall be applying and testing it repeatedly in Part II of the book. First, though, we should discuss in some detail the paradigm that is currently in place.

The "Exotic Style Only" Paradigm

Given that most prior studies of musical exoticism have been based on narrowly focused definitions, it comes as no surprise that they have adopted a variety of correspondingly "narrow-bore" approaches. (I mean this term descriptively, not judgmentally. A narrow approach, after all, has a chance at digging deep, and a broad one may easily become superficial.) These determinedly narrow approaches, taken together, comprise what I call the "Exotic Style Only" Paradigm of musical exoticism (or Exotic-Style Paradigm, for short).

The Exotic-Style Paradigm assumes that music is, by compositional intent, exotic – and that it registers as exotic to the listener – if (and, often, only if) it incorporates specific musical signifiers of Otherness. In recent years, these signifiers have sometimes been described as analogous to visual or verbal markers (such as have been codified by semioticians and narrativity theorists). Tara Browner, for example, has proposed applying the threefold terminology of Peircean semiotics – symbol, index, icon – to compositions (e.g., by Arthur Farwell) that in some way "appropriate" (her word) musical traditions of Native Americans.[15] Michael Pisani, studying that same repertoire in greater detail, finds particularly helpful

Browner's distinction between works, passages, or devices that, in "indexical" manner, attempt to "approximate native sounds" and ones that, in "iconic" manner, use actual "materials from native music." A "symbol" (or "symbolic" representation) in that repertoire would be one that is merely "native-inspired" and – through verbal or visual cues – alludes to customs of the exotic people even though the music does not sound "Indian-like" or, in any other way, unusual.[16]

Bartoli finds these kinds of distinctions – based on the level of resemblance to actual musical practices of the culture that is deemed exotic – largely irrelevant:

Exoticism in art arrays itself along a continuum that runs from the most realistic possible borrowing of actual figures [drawn from music of the foreign culture] to the totally fantastic [*onirique*] construction of imaginary exotic figures. Nonetheless, despite what one might think, the question of the [degree of] veracity of the borrowing has no bearing on how one gauges the effectiveness of the communication established between the creator and his public. The question … is: What is the most persuasive at a given moment.[17]

There is no way to say who is right on this matter: Browner (and Pisani) or Bartoli. Different listeners will possess more or less familiarity with the styles of this or that region or culture – as will different composers. Thus the distinction between relatively concrete and faithful borrowings and utterly imaginary inventions may be, Bartoli notwithstanding, a real and important one to some listeners. And, as those listeners learn more, they may make finer discriminations about what they hear, what it might have meant at the time it was composed, and what it might mean now.[18]

All commentators on musical exoticism would agree, however, that these various "nuts and bolts" of musical exoticism range widely, from drones and "primitive" harmonies to foreign or at least unusual-sounding tunes and rhythms. Just how various they are has, admittedly, not always been appreciated. For example, when, in an important statement from 1980, the distinguished and influential music historian Carl Dahlhaus lists the most important musical indicators of the exotic, the concrete instances that he names have only to do with pitch. He names static open-fifth pedals and several different gapped and modal scales that result in melodic and harmonic styles drastically different from those prevailing under functional tonality.[19] Dahlhaus was here no doubt following the all-too-standard twentieth-century habit (typical of those who, like Dahlhaus, were heavily shaped by Schoenberg's version of modernism) of focusing on the parameter of pitch – rather than, say, rhythm or instrumental timbre – as the primary means of identifying what is important or "progressive" in music.[20] (Manifestations of pitch include, for example, harmony, part-writing, and dissonance treatment.)

Fortunately, Dahlhaus opens a window, almost in spite of himself, to a broader horizon of exotic traits by briefly mentioning three principles that push beyond pitch: (1) the principle of excessive or seemingly endless repetition; (2) the principle of exotic styles "negating" whatever is normative in European art music at the time; and (3) the principle of using dance rhythms that listeners at the time would have recognized as typical of the country or people being evoked.[21]

I would like to expand on Dahlhaus's reluctant hint and lay out, in Figure 3.1, the main types or families of stylistic features that have occurred within Western musical exoticism over several centuries. Many of these go beyond questions of pitch content to include rhythm, phrase structure, vocal production, and instrumental timbre, as well as "purely musical" gestures that can advance (or meaningfully disrupt) the musical argument.[22] This list can serve as a rough but relatively comprehensive typology within which the reader may place the numerous, more specific stylistic usages to be encountered in later chapters.[23]

Many style features in the various categories of Figure 3.1 carry exotic connotations when and only when other style traits are also present. Indeed, some are worded in ways that indicate that they are inherently "compound." That is, they involve several different style parameters that, through combination and overlap, create a clear meaning. Take, for example, the long violin solos mentioned as one instance of style feature 10. In Rimsky-Korsakov's *Capriccio espagnol* and *Sheherazade*, and in the episode within the last movement of Mozart's Violin Concerto No. 5 in A major that has resulted in the work's nickname of "Turkish," a violin solo will register as frankly exotic thanks to the unusual figurations that it incorporates, the scales and harmonic devices that it uses, and the title or nickname of the piece. By contrast, in hundreds of violin concertos, a long violin solo is just a long violin solo.

Various of the individual musical features in Figure 3.1 were and/or are believed to be typical of one or another region or people. For example, a highly stereotyped drumbeat pattern of four equally spaced beats – LOUD soft soft soft – repeated again and again is still thought by many to represent Native Americans, though music lovers in the late eighteenth century might more likely have associated the same four-beat pattern with Turks (see Chapter 6). Similarly, skittering around the major-pentatonic scale (such as is generated by playing a number of black notes of the piano quickly

Exoticism with and without exotic style

(1) **Modes and harmonies** that were considered non-normative in the era and place where the work was composed. This category of features is vast and varied. In the art music of the eighteenth and early nineteenth centuries, and in many film scores, popular songs, and Broadway shows of the twentieth and twenty-first centuries, the norm consisted/consists of what music theorists call "functional tonality" or the major-minor tonal system. One should immediately note that, from around 1850 onward, many art-music composers began to enrich the major and minor modes, break down the distinction between them, and create or elaborate new modes (e.g., Aeolian, whole-tone, and octatonic) and harmonic practices (bitonal, atonal, dodecaphonic). Some film composers have followed suit. But, even in the contexts of more "extended" and alternative harmonic practices, the basic "tool" defined in the first sentence remained (and remains) available for evoking the exotic, namely using modes and harmonies different from whatever was (or is) the prevailing norm in the given work – or in other works in that genre at that time and place. (For simplicity's sake, style features nos. 2–6 are worded with regard to the basic major-minor tonal system.)

(2) One sub-category of style feature no. 1: pentatonic (e.g., black-key) and other so-called **"gapped" scales**, with their strong implications of simplicity and, hence, of stable, unchanging sociocultural conditions.

(3) Another sub-category of style feature no. 1 (and almost the opposite in means and effect from no. 2): **intense chromaticism** and constantly **shifting harmonies**, which may move purposefully toward a goal, slither sinuously, or yank about jerkily.

(4) Somewhat in between style features 2 and 3: **modes and scales with chromatically "altered" notes**; and **whole-tone** and **octatonic** scales. In the first of these possibilities, the chromatic alterations may include such things as the lowering of the second scalar degree (e.g., D♭ in the C-major or C-minor scale), raising of the fourth (F♯), and a fluctuating treatment – sometimes natural, sometimes

flatted – of the sixth (A) and seventh (B). The second possibility, whole-tone writing, is valued in part because it tends to deprive the listener of a home tonality. All the notes being the same distance apart, the listener cannot determine – without other factors, such as a long-held pedal tone in the accompaniment – which note in the scale is "home." The third possibility, octatonic writing, is somewhat similar to whole-tone in that it constructs its scales systematically, except that their notes are, in alternation, a whole step and a half step apart (see Chapter 9). Again, a sense of "tonic," if the composer desires it, needs to be achieved by a pedal or other means.

(5) Related to style feature no. 2 above: **bare textures**, such as unharmonized unisons or octaves, parallel fourths or fifths, and drones (pedal points – whether tonic or open-fifth); and **static harmonies** (often based on a single chord; or employing two chords in lengthy, perhaps slowish oscillation).

(6) The opposite of style feature no. 5 (and related to style features nos. 3 and 4 above): **complex and inherently undefined chords** (sometimes described as "magical" or "mystical") that, because they can resolve in several ways, operate in unpredictable ways; or chords that are cacophonous or cluster-like.

(7) Distinctive repeated **rhythmic or melodic patterns**, sometimes deriving from dances of the country or group being portrayed; or repeated (ostinato) rhythms – for example in an instrumental accompaniment – that are not distinctive (not inherently marked as to origin) but nonetheless suggest either Otherness (by their rigid insistence) or rural-ness (by their resemblance, general or specific, to the recurring patterns of folk dance). Certain exotic styles make use of rhythmic complexities considered characteristic of the location (e.g., the polyrhythms of Caribbean, sub-Saharan African, Middle Eastern, and Indonesian musical traditions).

(8) Opera arias – or melodies in instrumental works – that are more like **simple songs**, hence are presumably more typical of simple folk, whether in rural locations of the home

country or in places far away. Sometimes opera arias of this sort are flagged by a genre designation such as Romance. (This is not to say that all arias called "Romance" are exotic.)

(9) Vocal passages that evoke ritualistic (and incomprehensible) chanting by means of extended melismas on "Ah!" or nonsense syllables in free rhythm. Or (as in the case of despotic legalistic decrees) by declamation in a monotone and to a rigid, undifferentiated rhythm. Also various **"cries"** – such as the riveting "Aoua!" in Ravel's *Chansons madécasses* – or other musical highlighting of **unusual words** that are supposedly typical or indicative of the culture in question. Yet another possibility: use of **local linguistic variants** that are understood as bizarre or peculiar, such as the *lingua franca* in various Turkish and other Middle Eastern works of the late seventeenth and eighteenth centuries.

(10) **Instrumental lines** that are the presumed equivalent of the melismas common in many traditional vocal styles (e.g., *rāga*-based singing in India) and also in many traditional instrumental styles (*vīnā* playing). These instrumental lines may take the form of extended "arabesque"-style wind or violin solos that are perceived as being "arabesque"-like, not only by their curling shape but because they make heavy use of unbroken chains of escape-note figures such as are indeed found in much Middle Eastern music.

(11) **Departures from normative types of continuity** or compositional patterning and forward flow. These departures may include "asymmetrical" phrase structure, "rhapsodic" melodic motion, sudden pauses or long notes (or quick notes), and intentionally "excessive" repetition (of, for example, short melodic fragments using a few notes close together; or of accompanimental rhythms, as noted in style feature no. 7 above).

(12) **Quick ornaments** used obtrusively or over-predictably, and presumably intended to be perceived as decorative encrustation – or as dissonant, nerve-jangling annoyance – rather than as organically integrated design. The

"arabesque" solos mentioned in style feature no. 10 above are based on this principle of ornament (but repeat the ornamental feature many times in quick succession).

(13) **Foreign musical instruments**, or Western ones that are used in ways that make them sound foreign, for example xylophone, which, played pentatonically, can signify East and Southeast Asia; or specific piano figurations that evoke a Spanish guitar or Hungarian (or Hungarian-Gypsy) cimbalom. Also, instruments that are used in a context that is unusual for them. Particularly valuable for a composer in these various regards are woodwind instruments, such as flute, oboe, or (more striking because it is rarely used in Western art music) English horn, especially when any of these is given an extensive solo of an "arabesque" or a "melancholy-minor" type. Likewise valuable are unpitched percussion instruments, such as tom-tom, conga, and darabukka (to mention three relatively culture-specific options) but also the more generic ones: tambourine, bass drum, triangle, gong, and small bells.

(14) **Highly distinctive instrumental techniques** (and also techniques that are more usual – such as portamento, pizzicato, or double stops – but used in an unusual context). Also, emphatically regular (stomping, relentless) performance of repeated rhythms. Or the opposite: flexible, floating, "timeless" rendition of vocal melismas or instrumental solos (see style features nos. 9, 10, and 13 above).

(15) Distinctive uses of **vocal range and tessitura** (e.g., the "sultry" – to use a standard, freighted term – mezzo-soprano voice), and unusual styles of vocal production ("darkened" sound, throbbing vibrato, lack of vibrato, etc.).

Figure 3.1 Stylistic features within Western music that are often employed (especially in combination) to suggest an exotic locale or culture

upward and downward several times, starting and ending on F♯) could, in the early twentieth century, be predictably heard by the ignorant Western ear, and still often is so heard today, as authentically Chinese or Japanese (or at least "close enough" to be a clear marker of one, the other, or both).[24]

In the Native American and Chinese/Japanese cases, a feature of the music of the region or culture has been extracted, simplified, and generalized. Browner and Pisani tend, therefore, to consider such exotic markers indexical rather than iconic. But, as Bartoli might note, the marker makes its effect because its signification is familiar to and accepted by composer and audience alike even though it lacks detailed resemblance to the music of the people (purportedly) being depicted.

In contrast, certain other individual features (such as the xylophone mentioned in style feature no. 13) could/can carry widely differing associations, depending on which other elements are/were simultaneously present. The question of combining the elements is crucial. Many of these features are so malleable in themselves that they only take on exotic coloration when joined to one or several others. Bartoli makes this crucial point with regard to the augmented-second interval. When harmonized according to the rules of tonal harmony, it functions as a syntactically normal part of music in the minor mode (as in Mozart's Keyboard Sonata in F Major, K 533/494, movement 1, m. 86). Yet, when it is heard with a pounding rhythm and unchanging, drone-based harmonies, it becomes a crystal-clear announcement that we are now "in" the Middle East.[25]

Not all of the style features in Figure 3.1, however, combine with ease. Some are near opposites. For example, style feature no. 8 – use of simple, folklike/"primitive" songs – tends to be incompatible with certain aspects of style features nos. 3, 6, and 11, such as intensely mobile harmony, weird chords, and highly irregular phrase structure. In any case, the associations that such elements carry can fade or shift across the decades and centuries and can vary with listeners of different origins and musical backgrounds.

Many of these stylistic indicators deserve to be elaborated upon at length. For example, one might submit the various possibilities within a single style factor to extensive taxonomical categorizing. Particularly rich would be no. 1: the modes/scales – and, by implication, the resulting harmonies – employed in varying types of exotic portrayal. In close second place might be no. 7: dance rhythms.

The "Exotic Style Only" Paradigm, with its focus on traits of the types seen in Figure 3.1, often proves adequate, even enlightening. Especially in the case of purely instrumental works, a wide range of devices that are foreign-sounding – that is, conventionally identifiable with distant/different regions and peoples – have manifestly comprised, for several centuries now, the essential Exotic Composers' Toolkit. The list of beloved (and, in some cases, much-studied) works that use tools from this kit include such hardy exemplars as Mozart's "Rondo alla turca";[26] Debussy's Spanish-influenced works, such as *Ibéria* and *Soirée dans Grenade*; and the latter's gamelan-influenced ones, such as *Pagodes*.

In the four pieces just named, the national/ethnic "location" is quite specific. But I stress that the musical materials in Figure 3.1 are often used in such a way as to be "foreign-sounding" in the broad sense. That is, they sound as if they were the kind of music that is made somewhere else, but they do not conjure up one particular locale. Furthermore, as Mary Hunter has pointed out, many exotic pieces offer not an echo of the *materials* that were objectively used (or reported to be used) in the given foreign music but a "translation" (her word) of the *impression* that Westerners had of that music. Thus, a composer might provide a Turkish character in an opera with music whose features matched his or her own reaction to Turkish music, i.e., features that were considered (within the context of their era) violently noisy or formally or tonally incoherent.[27]

It is revealing that nearly all the devices arrayed in Figure 3.1 are embodied in the "purely" musical markings in a score: the notated pitches, rhythms, and instrumental timbres. (In such a context, "purely" proves a helpfully loaded word, as I shall explain in a moment.) For example, a writer might refer to "the hypnotically undulating chromatic line in triplet rhythm in the flute's low register" – summarizing what s/he is hearing in the music and seeing in the score – and might add further technical details, such as upper-neighbor notes in the melody or an open-fifth drone in the accompaniment. And all of this the music lover can confirm or challenge for him- or herself by the same process of listening (and/or looking at the score).

Writers who emphasize the score's written-down musical instructions, sometimes to the exclusion of all other considerations, may well feel that they are evincing devotion to "hard" musical data and avoiding (as I said earlier) "speculation." In so doing, they are falling in line with musicology's longstanding and, as has been argued, sometimes pseudoscientific attraction to the empirically verifiable.[28]

This just-the-notes approach – the Exotic-Style Paradigm, in other words – tends to work, as I said, "purely." It is biased in favor of instrumental music because the latter is more completely embodied in musical notation than is a compound genre such as song, opera, or film. The bias in this approach relates to a deeper-rooted tendency, not just in musicology but in the world of high-art music in the West, generally. I am referring to the tendency of professional musicians, critics, and music lovers alike to valorize (as being "purer," more "abstract") those musical genres and repertoires that involve only instruments and are not somehow sullied by words or "extra-musical" message or references.[29]

Exoticism with and without exotic style

The tendency to limit the study of exoticism to instrumental works is not total. The Exotic-Style Paradigm has proven quite apt for studying certain moments in operas set in some real or half-imagined Elsewhere. These moments are particularly frequent in scene-setting numbers, such as choruses, ballets, and ceremonial processions, all laden with extramusical markers of Otherness. Scholars have successfully demonstrated that Puccini incorporated tunes from Japan and China, respectively, in *Madama Butterfly* (1904–6) and *Turandot* (1926).[30] Among the ablest early handlers of the technique were Gluck – in French operas written for Vienna and (later) for Paris – and Mozart. The latter, in *Die Entführung aus dem Serail* (1782), based certain numbers for Osmin and for the chorus on so-called "Turkish" musical style features that he knew would be recognized with delight, and found humorous, by the "Viennese gentlemen" (his phrase) who would be in the audience.[31]

But the Exotic-Style Paradigm proves incapable of dealing with many musical numbers in these same three operas – indeed, in most stage works "about" exotic places. Julian Smith, one of the world's authorities on *Madama Butterfly*, lays out a clear plan for exploring exoticism in that opera. Five of his six categories involve ways in which Puccini uses or imitates Japanese music, and the sixth involves ways in which Puccini uses the singing voices "in a manner suggestive of Japanese people" – i.e., their (supposed or perceived) ways of speaking.[32] These six categories of Japanisms do, admittedly, cover large stretches of this particular opera (see Chapter 8), but they also leave equally large stretches out of account.

It sometimes seems easier for scholars and other commentators to ponder how exotic sounds function in patently non-exotic works than to ponder the reverse: how a patently exoticizing work functions when it is not sounding exotic. For example, Richard Langham Smith, in support of his call for "an exhaustive study" of "exoticism in music," notes that attention needs to be paid to the occasions where black-note pentatonicism, "meandering heterophony[, ... and other] oriental techniques were used by Debussy in pieces which had nothing whatever to do with the Orient."[33] As so often, music scholars, trained to think of music history as the history of musical style, group together pieces that have musico-technical features in common (in this case, features that are considered reliable markers of the "exotic"), and give less attention (if any) to pieces – or extended passages in pieces – that are exotic in intent but do not embody that intent in sonic codes. Raymond Monelle, working within the same paradigm, dismisses "the Turkish topic" in music as a "passing fashion" of the years 1760–1830, and not at all a "major cultural theme," unlike the three (undoubtedly major) musical topics – that is, style markers of extramusical reality – that his book treats: hunting calls, military marches, and indicators of the "pastoral" (rural life and music-making).[34] But surely Europe's tense interactions with, and its concomitant obsessions with, the Ottoman Empire amounted to a "major [European] cultural theme" during the very centuries that Monelle's book most heavily explores (the seventeenth through nineteenth) – not to mention Europe's fascination and engagement with other regions, such as the Americas, sub-Saharan Africa, the Indian subcontinent, and East Asia.

This primary scholarly focus on what "sounds exotic" has an intriguing parallel to traditions of musical inquiry into other important trends and genres in Western art music: for example, program music (instrumental works with descriptive titles or more extensive prefaces) and non-theatrical vocal works that feature a particularly tight relationship between text and music (such as sixteenth-century Italian madrigals or nineteenth-century German art songs). The conventional first line of approach in dealing with such repertoires is to look for some fairly evident relationship between the musical notes and the intended extramusical image. Familiar examples include music evocative of flowing water (a motion image that, in nature, also carries certain associated sounds); music evocative of bird call (a purely auditory image); or conventionalized melodic figures, such as drooping pairs of notes indicating sadness (a semi-auditory image deriving, presumably, from sighing and/or physical collapse).[35]

But music, once it is given a text to comment on and support, commands a much wider range of expressive devices than this. In Schubert's "Gretchen am Spinnrade," the motion of the spinning wheel (in the pianist's right-hand part) is indeed mimetic yet it is also expressive (of Gretchen's recurring obsession with the handsome, newly young Faust).[36] Besides, many aspects of the song's music – the shifts of harmony, the surges and eventual exhausted collapse in the melodic line – help convey the successive moods of the poem's protagonist *without* so concretely mimicking sounds or physical actions.

Before leaving the Exotic-Style Paradigm, I want to stress again that I in no way disparage it. Quite the contrary, I would insist that its findings have not been given sufficient attention. Many revelations by scholars working within this paradigm have not found their deserved way into standard writings on the works in question. For example, most music lovers have no way of knowing that Rameau's often-revived *Les Indes galantes* (1735–36) adapts a "Turkish" (and, indeed, unusual) tune from a work by Campra (*L'Europe galante*, 1697), or that Mahler may have intended passages of heterophony in *Das Lied von der Erde* (1909) as markers of Chineseness.

(Mahler may have learned about heterophonic procedures in traditional Chinese music from his friend, the Viennese musicologist Guido Adler.)[37] Also, new results of the Exotic-Style Paradigm are reaching publication all the time – though, likewise, often in specialized studies whose findings will unfortunately not go on to be incorporated into CD booklet essays, music-encyclopedia articles, or other writings intended for a broad readership.[38]

Because there is a natural tendency for specific exotic stylistic conventions to lose their meaning over time, scholars have had quite a job to do in recent decades, helping us hear what it is that sounds (or at least might have been intended to sound) Italian or Scottish in Mendelssohn's symphonies that bear those nicknames; what the various (real or supposed) Gypsy traits are in the Hungarian Rhapsodies of Liszt; or which once-well-known Japanese tunes lie a bit buried – and might not be caught by later generations – in the orchestral texture of *Madama Butterfly*. I wonder how many operagoers today can recognize Puccini's quoted chunks from *Sakura*, once an internationally beloved – or, in Korea, I am told, hated – symbol of Japan.

There are also ramifications here for performance and interpretation. A pianist who understands the figurations in Liszt's Hungarian Rhapsodies that were intended to evoke, respectively, the cimbalom (a hammered dulcimer that makes heavy use of tremolo figuration) and semi-improvised violin solos and who is familiar with nineteenth-century stereotypes of Roma (drunken males, brazenly seductive females) will feel invited to vary the tempo and other aspects of her or his playing so as to "enact" various aspects of the scene more concretely. A Hungarian Rhapsody is not just one more virtuosic showpiece, to be played in more or less strict tempo, as written.

Still, the Exotic-Style Paradigm – for all its explanatory power – does not suffice to do justice to all works that evoke exotic locales, especially ones containing long stretches of music that, taken in isolation, would not strike most listeners as exotic- or even unusual-sounding.

The "All the Music in Full Context" Paradigm

We need a paradigm that can respond to a wider range of musical evocations of exotic regions and peoples. These evocations include certain more or less programmatic pieces for solo instrument or orchestra that do not consistently (if at all) use musical features that are marked as ethnic or Other.

An interesting case is Rimsky-Korsakov's symphonic suite *Sheherazade* (1888). Some seasoned concertgoers might, at first, recall *Sheherazade* as being exotic through and through. This certainly seems plausible, given that

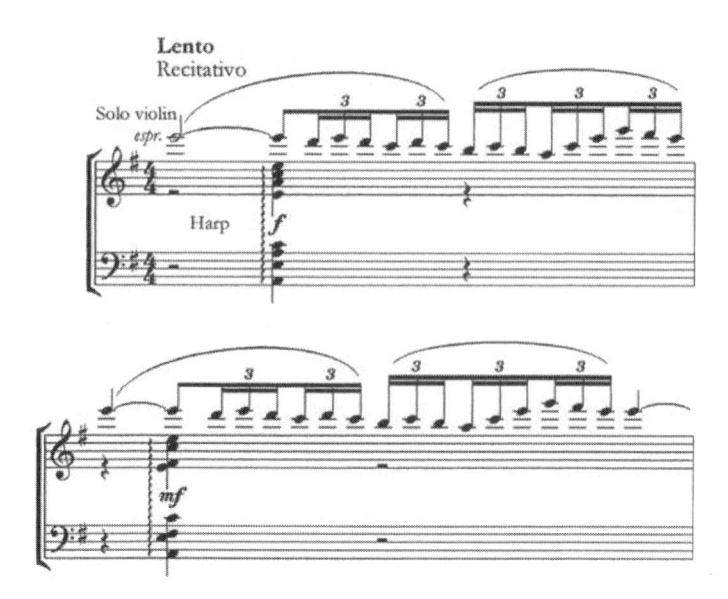

Example 3.1 Rimsky-Korsakov, *Sheherazade*, symphonic suite for orchestra, Op. 35, the theme representing Sheherazade herself, mm. 14–15.

the work is frankly based on tales from the *Thousand and One Nights* (or *Arabian Nights*).[39] It also employs, in many of its sections, stylistic devices that were recognizable markers of Middle Easternness at the time (and, for many listeners, remain so today). In particular, the recurring violin solo – which, by all accounts, represents Sheherazade herself – begins with a memorable sad and stepwise-descending melody (Ex. 3.1), in which each main note alternates with its upper neighbor in triplets, resulting in the very kind of decorative, curvaceous line that, in writings about this and other works, was (and still is) often described as "arabesque."

But a look at the score of *Sheherazade* quickly reveals that certain passages are not in any way marked as Middle Eastern. Yet these passages, too, help to retell certain Arab legends and to sketch certain scenes deemed "typical" of the region: Sinbad's ship roving the sea, a tender episode between a young prince and princess, the bustling activity at an outdoor market. We know that the recurring theme that opens the piece (in unharmonized unisons) represents Sultan Shahriar because of the composer's plot summary published at the head of the score and because the theme is stern and threatening, though not notably exotic in style.[40]

Likewise, in the work's second seascape – the section of movement 4 in which "the Ship Breaks against a Cliff That Is Surmounted by a Bronze

Horseman" – the rising sequences, rapid scales upward and down, and unsettled harmonies are similar to those used in musical sea-storms that "occur" in other climes (e.g., along the Norwegian coast, in the case of Wagner's *Der fliegende Holländer*, The Flying Dutchman, 1843). Yet concert-hall audiences and CD listeners perceive Rimsky-Korsakov's brief but violent sea scene as part of an exotic narrative, i.e., as one in a string of Arabian Nights tales.[41] They do so because they hear it *in the context of* the composer's plot summary, the colorful titles of the four movements, and the many sections of the work that do sound "Middle Eastern." And, no doubt, because many of them are conditioned by the experience of attending, and hearing excerpts from, exotic operas.

Art song is another such area, though one to which the present book will give far too little attention (as is unfortunately true of art song in music-historical writings, generally). Many important Lieder by Schubert and other nineteenth-century composers use poems inspired by, or based on, poetic texts from Persia and elsewhere in the Middle East, yet the music of the songs makes no gesture toward the musical traditions of the region. Indeed, David Gramit argues intriguingly that "songs like 'Du liebst mich nicht' [and 'Dass sie hier gewesen,' both to texts of Friedrich Rückert] ... are able to participate all the more fully in the shaping of images of the Orient because they could not be dismissed as replications of familiar and trivialized fashions [of musical Orientalism]."[42]

The richest harvest of the "All the Music in Full Context" Paradigm will come from operas and other dramatic works. These genres tend to work very differently than do purely instrumental ones. In opera and dramatic oratorio, music is heard within the powerfully controlling yet also liberating frame of plot and sung words. To these verbal and musical elements, opera adds a rich array of primarily visual ones: costumes, sets, stage movement, dance, lighting. Opera – and, again, analogous genres (such as film, with its varied camera angles and types of cutting and montage) – thus makes available to the composer – or, better, to the compositional team, including the librettist, scriptwriter, or other provider of plot structure and words – a larger and more varied Exotic Toolkit than the one that is available to composers of instrumental music. Furthermore, because opera's Exotic Toolkit works in ways that are often less immediately evident to the listener, it can work more powerfully.

Yet, despite this famously wide range of possibilities for representing the exotic Other in dramatic works (whether for concert hall, stage, or, more recently, film), the existing scholarly and critical literature on the exotic in dramatic music tends to linger on only those few moments in a given work that happen to fit comfortably the Exotic-Style Paradigm, i.e., those scenes or passages that sound non-Western. And the literature tends to leave unmentioned the many Baroque-era operas and dramatic oratorios that focus on despicable Eastern tyrants, or else excludes them explicitly from consideration simply because they rarely if ever invoke exotic styles.[43] The result is a kind of blindness to the complex fascinations of Baroque-era exoticism. The inadequacy of this scholarly and critical response is all the more apparent now that many exotic operas and dramatic oratorios of the Baroque era, such as Handel's *opera seria*s *Tamerlano* and *Giulio Cesare* and his dramatic oratorio *Belshazzar* are becoming part, again, of the lived reality of modern musical life, in productions by imaginative stage directors (e.g., Jonathan Miller) and with exciting and artful singers (e.g., countertenor Brian Asawa).

I do not mean to suggest that the "All the Music in Full Context" Paradigm is an entirely unprecedented discovery of my own. We noticed hints of it in certain phrases of Bellman's and Betzwieser's definitions above. Mary Hunter points out that the violent and irrational aspects of the (largely invented) "alla turca" styles also seem to symbolize – in many of the works that use it – the (perceived) violent and unpredictable behaviors of the region's male inhabitants.[44] We will encounter other such remarks, but applied to individual works, in Part II, for example, Winton Dean on *Belshazzar* and Cuthbert Girdlestone on Rameau's *Les Indes galantes*. But, again, the insightful remarks of specialists seem not to have been incorporated into general discussions of musical exoticism, nor into writings about the works in question for a broad audience. And some such remarks (though not Hunter's) stop short of exploring, even in basic ways, the very connection that they posit.

A more encompassing view – what I call the "All the Music in Full Context" Paradigm (or, for short, Full-Context Paradigm) – thus deserves to be laid out in plain words. And, though it can happily call upon previous specialized studies, this broader approach will also quickly notice many other instances and aspects that have escaped discussion entirely. As I mentioned, many of these will be from opera or other narrative/dramatic genres. For a composer working within such genres, explicit musical codes are but one tool among many. An opera (or oratorio, Broadway musical, or film) that is set in an exotic locale may engage almost any stylistic and formal resource in order to convey exotically shaded portrayals of vicious warlords, seductive females, or other accepted exotic types. Similarly, such a work may use a wide range of musical (and other) materials to construct situations and moods (e.g., menacing or idyllic) that were understood at the time as characteristic of the place or people in question. The "All the Music in Full-Context" Paradigm, unlike the currently prevailing one, has the freedom to consider all of these different types of means and materials.

How this operates will not surprise students of opera, film music, or song, since it is simply a special case of the more general ways that music functions in dramatic and other overtly representational genres. The words and visual elements in an opera, oratorio, or film "place" the character or group in a given Elsewhere. The music then marks the character or group indelibly (on its own, or at least more indelibly than the words and action could do without music's boost) as "barbarous," "seductive," or whatever. And the audience melds the two forms of information into an indissoluble whole. "This unfamiliar Elsewhere [Japan, North Africa, etc.]," they sense, "is a place of barbarity" (or seduction, etc.). Were one to hear the music on its own, it might not convey any immediate geographic or ethnic overtones. In context, the audience accepts it as consistent with the exotic setting and with the exotic character's or group's apparent proclivities.

Music in operas and dramatic oratorios thus helps "characterize" (to use a term that is standard in discussions of opera and art song) the exotic entity being represented, just as it so often does when the representation involves madness, or women, or other conditions, groups, or individuals that have long been viewed as Other, i.e., as departing in some basic way from the heroic, masculine norm.

I spoke a moment ago of music that is not exotic-sounding but is nonetheless consistent with the emotional tone of a given exotic setting or situation. Actually, I would push the argument even further. The music in certain exotic portrayals may, at times, not even be notably consistent with the exotic people's quality or characteristics (as defined by the words and dramatic action). The music in question is simply good, effective, even (many would agree) "great" music that does not register as notably *in*consistent with – in other words, it does not conspicuously contradict – the quality or mood defined by those words and actions. The composer puts into gear all the usual ways and means of compositional excellence – melodic and harmonic coherence, subtle variation in phrase structure, orchestration that is delicate or forceful, and so on – to keep us listening and watching, and to help us feel involved in the proceedings.

An extreme instance might be the artful melismatic vocal writing in certain eighteenth- and early nineteenth-century works that are set in this or that Elsewhere. If we were to examine such *fioritura* in isolation, on the page, we might be tempted to term it a "purely musical" device and to describe it as a horizontal play of pitches and rhythms, enlivened perhaps by the thrill and risk of live performance but not "indicating" anything more specific. We might even have difficulty differentiating it, in purely technical terms, from florid passages in certain sonatas for melody instrument and keyboard (or continuo). Within an operatic aria, though, such singing is more productively regarded as a generic emblem of feeling (and/or of physical movement) that takes on the coloration of the words and dramatic situation into which it is placed. One and the same melismatic passage may tell as vengeful in a given context and as some other highly charged sentiment – for example, desirous or determined – in another.[45]

"Illogical!": such is the usual objection of those who insist that art must consist of a line-up of one-to-one semiotic indicators that need no context to do their work. But audiences regularly experience this kind of "illogical," context-dependent artistic truth in the opera house, concert hall (for oratorio), and movie theater.[46]

The then/now binarism

Once one accepts that the notes of the score do not always exhaust the matter, a host of other considerations arise. The first of these has to do with the possibly relevant binarism of **then and now**. The Full-Context Paradigm is broad in methodology. But is it broad enough to include distance-in-time? The Middle Ages? The various ancient worlds (the Holy Land, the Greeks, the Romans)? In what sense might certain of these be exotic, and to whom?

The visual arts offer some helpful parallels. One art historian, Frederick N. Bohrer, has persuasively argued the case for "antiquity as a [possible] site of Exoticism."[47] My definition of musical exoticism does not mention time as a factor but also does not exclude it. The definition therefore allows that *selected* evocations of the ancient (including biblical) world *may* be considered exotic. Plausible instances include Mendelssohn's "War March of the [Ancient Judaean] Priests" (from his incidental music to Racine's *Athalie*, 1845), Massenet's opera *Hérodiade* (1881), and Ravel's ballet *Daphnis et Chloë* (1912).

But Bohrer's carefully shaded findings (in regard to visual depictions of ancient cultures) should warn us against a tendency to subsume all operas set in, say, ancient and medieval Rome and all the characters in them – for example, Handel's *Giulio Cesare* (1724; notably its title character, Julius Caesar) or Mozart's *Idomeneo* (1781) – into the category of the exotic. Romans were often viewed as the immediate forebears of "the West" and praised for holding values and behaviors dear to modern-day readers and audience. I would argue that, to the extent that Julius Caesar was not perceived as differing profoundly from current-day Westerners (hence not felt as essentially Other), his Roman world, and most musical evocations of that world were not, in any significant sense, exotic.

Interestingly, the fascination with the Middle Ages, though a period closer to us than Roman antiquity, often embodies a search for an exotic alternative, for a world different in feeling or values. Not always, of course. Some medieval archaisms seem primarily to focus on "way back then": for example chivalric style conventions in Brahms, or Debussy's evocation of Catholic sacred music in *La cathédrale engloutie*.[48] But other medieval archaisms add an aura of "other place or land" to that of "other era," as in the case of two "Scottish" pieces: Mendelssohn's "Hebrides" Overture and Brahms's "Edward" Ballade for piano in D Minor (Op. 10, no. 1).[49] And, in recent decades, "way back then" really has become almost "another country" – an imagined, yearned-for realm of feeling. I am thinking of the wildfire success of CDs of Gregorian chant in the early 1990s, marketed as entertainment at once escapist and restorative, the musical equivalent of a good backrub at an island getaway.[50] Thus is the asceticism of a thousand years ago reconfigured to meet the psychological needs of today's harried consumers.

In any case, as the Scottish examples of Mendelssohn and Brahms suggest, distance in time often comes combined with distance in place and culture, giving the listener (operagoer, etc.) a sense of being doubly transported out of the familiar. We are transported not to ancient Rome – too much like "the here and now" – but to ancient Egypt or legendary imperial China. True, numerous operas involve Charlemagne's knights, a patent symbol of the Christian West. But the works present them less often in a purely Frankish context than – as in various tales of Roland and Tancred – on the battlefield against the conniving and sorcery-assisted Saracens (i.e., Muslims in Spain or in the Holy Land).

The inclusion of temporal displacement as a possible factor swells the number of exotic portrayals that might be discussed and increases the complexity of discussing them. How does one begin to make sense of such a vast and varied repertoire? The Full-Context Paradigm, like my definition from which it derives, does not offer a single obvious way. But the usual scholarly and critical sorting-rules would seem likely to prove profitable. One might, for example, group pieces by

- chronology and style (e.g., Baroque or Romantic);
- genre (e.g., opera, ballet, or instrumental dance and rhapsody);

- the "nation being evoked" (e.g., pieces "about" – or in the style of – Spain or Hungary); or
- the "nation doing the evoking" (works composed in, say, France for primarily French consumption, as opposed to ones composed in Italy or Russia).[51]

Many of the case studies in Part II will exercise this option, focusing on one or more of the four guiding principles just listed.

Sorting can have disadvantages, though. It separates works (or trends) that share common features or that, if they were juxtaposed, would more readily reveal their distinctive (contrasting) features. In the remainder of this chapter, I explore four binarisms that are inherent in nearly *any* musical repertoire that observers would recognize as carrying out an exoticizing project. These binarisms signify four creative tensions and enabling dichotomies that – like the **then and now** binarism already discussed but even more so – are inherent in the process of musical exoticism.

Four other binarisms

The most crucial of these four additional binarisms is the distinction between the "home" culture and places portrayed as "Elsewhere" – in other words, the dichotomy between **Self and Other**. Within Western art music, the normative pattern assigns to the West the role of exoticizer. The role of the exoticized thereby falls to some contrasting region: for example, China or sub-Saharan Africa. But we should not forget that exoticizing tendencies exist in many musical cultures. Some of these might be considered "reverse exoticisms" (by people in North America or Europe). In the rock music and rap of certain European and non-Western countries, the United States and its heavily African-American inner cities have arguably become the Other whose vitality, energy, and style (as "known" mostly through recordings, movies, and music videos) are envied, imitated, and elaborated in accordance with local interests and traditions. How much do people in France, Algeria, or the Philippines, for example, know and understand the (largely African-American) cultural context of the musical styles and genres that they are absorbing and adapting?[52] How much do they need to know? Might these peoples' own search for expressive authenticity rely to some extent on a relative *lack* of knowledge about the original contexts of what they are imitating (and creatively reworking), just as ignorance of the realities of Spain has probably contributed to the popularity and persuasiveness of *Carmen* north of the Pyrenees (and in Chicago, Warsaw, and Tokyo)? Is not a largely ignorant exoticism at work among Japanese youths who augment their affection for hip-hop music and clothing by donning blackface?[53] The same binarism of home and elsewhere becomes interesting and problematic (in a different way) in certain works written by composers who have a foot in both East and West, such as Tan Dun (see Chapter 10).

A second crucial binarism has to do with **nearness and distance**. My definition earlier in the chapter merely specifies that a work is exotic if it evokes a locale (people, social milieu) that is felt to be very *different*. Some may think it odd that the definition does not prescribe or presume that the locale be geographically *distant*. I would argue that a work may be situated relatively close to the city or country in which the composer and intended listeners are located and yet qualify as exotic. For example, numerous French comic operas take place in some (often unspecified) rural French village, even though (or precisely because) the opera was composed for Paris, where peasants were thought simple-minded, good-hearted, and more or less amusing. Model instances of this type of portrayal of (nearby) rural life include the pathbreaking comic opera *Le devin du village* (The Village Soothsayer, 1752), with words and music by the philosopher Jean-Jacques Rousseau, and numerous operas from the several decades thereafter, including Monsigny's *Rose et Colas* (1764).

More recent examples might include Gounod's gentle opera *Mireille* (1864, set in Provence) and – a non-operatic instance – the four sets of *Chants de l'Auvergne* (1923–30) that Joseph Canteloube arranged for voice and orchestra, selections from which have been recorded by singers as contrasting as Victoria de los Angeles and Barbra Streisand. Clearly related to the same tradition are instrumental movements marked "musette" (the French word for bagpipe), such as those found in French Baroque music, the *Little Notebook for Anna Magdalena Bach* (BWV Anh. 126), and, much later, Schoenberg's Piano Suite (1921).

What is true of French villages, with their bagpipes, also applies, in some degree, to Bohemian villages (Smetana's *The Bartered Bride*, 1866–70) and German ones (comic operas of Suppé and Lortzing, such as the latter's *Der Waffenschmied*, 1846).[54] But often the locale is quite far away, as in Rameau's aforementioned operatic extravaganza *Les Indes galantes* and Mozart's "Rondo alla turca" for keyboard. Finally, mixing near and far are groups often portrayed as "internal exotics," such as the Roma (in works set in Hungary or Spain), Jews (in many European countries, two instances being Halévy's *La juive*, 1835, and "'Samuel' Goldenberg and 'Schmuyle'," from Musorgsky's *Pictures at an Exhibition*, 1874), and – within a North American context – native ("Indian") tribes or, as in *Porgy and Bess* (1935), African-Americans on the South Carolina coast.

Still, substantial geographical distance-and-difference is a frequent and, in a sense, convenient marker of the cultural distance that is central to an exotic musical work. A location that is not just "far away" but often also distinct in climate, topography, and natural resources is a prime feature of most of the works discussed in the present book. As a result, the location is also lower – or perceived as lower – in economic, social, and cultural development. Combined with the **Self/Other** binarism (of which it is, in a sense, a subcategory), the **near/far** binarism often ends up being reinforced by cultural factors having little or nothing inherently to do with location (e.g., gender).[55]

A third crucial binary distinction implicit within my definition touches on **the real and the fictive**: an exotic locale must be "not entirely imaginary." The word "exoticism," as its etymology suggests, could easily refer to a non-existent realm.[56] The word "exotic" thus defines Elsewhere in terms of what it is not. "Exotic" – "not here" – and "utopian" – literally, "no place" – are thus closely linked concepts, though one should also quickly note that exotic locales often turn out to be, instead, distopian: "bad place."

Fully imaginary settings – ones far from any social reality – could, in theory, be a locus for exotic yearnings. Yet one has to strain to think of a successful opera, oratorio, or symphonic poem that features talking animals, non-Earthlings, or other fantasy creatures: the musical equivalent of, say, TV's *Star Trek* or the vast literature of fable and fairy tale. Karl Birger Blomdahl's once-newsworthy science-fiction opera *Aniara* comes to mind (1959, subtitled "A Revue about Man in Time and Space"). In Wagner's *Ring* cycle, a bird and a dragon do briefly sing, but the various Norse gods – the opera's main characters – are, despite their supernatural powers, all too human in their impulses, much like, say, the Queen of the Night in Mozart's magic-filled *Die Zauberflöte* (1790). The Greek divinities, in certain stage works by Cavalli or by Offenbach, are likewise selfish, craven, and so on. The title character in Rameau's opera *Platée* (1745) is a grotesquely ugly water nymph (sung by a high tenor), delighted to believe that Jupiter is smitten with her. Only one repertoire item, Janáček's *The Cunning Little Vixen* (1924), is populated by beasts of the forests, with their species-specific ways of moving about and behaving. Yet, these singing animals, too, prove to be emblematic of human concerns, not in the least far-fetched. In any case, none of the works just mentioned would probably strike most listeners and critics as invoking "the exotic."

This is no inconsistency. As Gilles de Van has explained, a "mixture of realism and hallucination [*onirisme*]" is always strikingly present in exotic representations. The exotic arises in the interactive middle field between what he calls "knowledge" of another place (the kind of knowledge that is served by anthropology and related studies) and, at the other extreme, myth or, as he puts it, "fairy tale" (which would occur "were [the artist's/reader's/listener's] desire to invent its own representation" without reference to an Other). In order for exoticism to be born, there needs to be "a meeting between the objectivity of knowledge (however approximate)" and "*la subjectivité d'une interprétation intéressée*": that is, an interpretative field that reads those bits of "knowledge" in accordance with the artist's/reader's/listener's own needs.[57]

All of this suggests that exoticism arises, for both the makers and users of art, as soon as a work plays upon what we know (or "know") about some real yet distinctively "Other" place and the people that inhabit it. Thus a crucial tension is at work in the phenomenon of musical exoticism: the tension between a real location and an imagined one. We (including composer, librettist, and performers) set up a screen of human believability – anchored by concrete references to a place that really exists (or once existed) – on which we can then project our wildest scenarios, however atypical they may be of, or even how impossible they would be in, the real location in question. We set our exotic works – at least our successful, cherished ones – in places that we are able to locate on a map and learn about in a history book. Then the fantasy can begin, as it has begun with the Baghdad of the *Thousand and One Nights* for millions of Western readers over the past three hundred years.

A fourth and final binary distinction briefly arose in the discussion (earlier in this chapter) of the Exotic-Style and Full-Context Paradigms: **musical and extramusical signs**. I realize that I may have given the false impression that exotically tinged instrumental music is utterly devoid of verbal clues. There are such silent cases, of course. Bizet simply labels "Adagio" the oboe melody that opens the slow movement of his Symphony in C (1855), yet critics agree that the melody is quintessentially "Middle Eastern" in style. We might call this a case of implicit evocation. In many exotic instrumental works, however, the exotic intent is not entirely implicit but is confirmed by verbal indications. The verbal clues may be few and brief: a specifying title and/or a suggestive performance marking. Nonetheless, they may suggest (or may have suggested, for the composer's contemporaries) a whole range of exotic associations, as in Liszt's nineteen Hungarian (i.e., Gypsy-style) Rhapsodies. Similarly, several Vivaldi concertos (e.g., the

Concerto in G Major for Strings and Continuo, RV 151) bear such subtitles as *alla rustica*: "in rustic style." Any further details or richer associations are left by Vivaldi (as by Liszt) to the imagination of the listener.

And also to the imagination of the performer. A title or other verbal indication, such as *alla rustica* or (in Liszt's or other composers' Gypsy works) *all'ongherese* or *alla zingarese*, can easily suggest not just a composed style but also a way of playing. We have already noted some aspects of an appropriate Hungarian-Gypsy manner for pianists. String players (in Liszt's own orchestrated versions of his Hungarian Rhapsodies) might justifiably indulge in slashing bow strokes, and the conductor might call for impulsive shifts in tempo – all to convey the supposed propensity of the Roma for unpredictable passion and arbitrary, defiant, or devious behavior.

The intended character of the music in an exotic work – and a performance manner appropriate to that character – may at times be further suggested by a performance direction in the score, such as *allegro feroce* – fast and wild – or (in rustic/pastoral works) *adagio piacevole* – slow and peaceful. Somewhat frustratingly, the directions in many of Vivaldi's rustic pieces – in accordance with general Baroque-era practice – comprise little more than conventional indications of speed or basic mood. But the style-sensitive performer of a piece labeled *alla rustica* may take that simple but resonant phrase as permission to add unnotated touches of peasant inelegance (as imagined by city folk). S/he may, for example, emphasize the downbeat accents so as to imply cheerful bumptiousness or even boorishness.

Vocal works (as discussed earlier in this chapter) usually contain not one or two brief verbal indicators of a work's location but many extensive ones. That is, an exotic-vocal work offers not only a suggestive title and the usual range of performing indications, but also a sung text that can go on for a few lines or dozens of pages. This text may be of real literary merit. One thinks of the Persian-inspired poems of Rückert and Goethe that were set as art songs by Schubert and Wolf. In addition, opera – and sometimes oratorio – gives the listener a good deal more that is concretely extramusical to respond to: a plot, extensive dialogue or narration (whether spoken or sung), and names for certain characters. Exotic instances range from Schumann's oratorio *Das Paradies und die Peri* (Paradise and the Peri, 1843), based on Thomas Moore's tale of the diaphanous Peri ("fairy," in Persian mythology) and her desperate quest, to Rossini's *Italiana in Algeri* (1813), in which several mostly well-intentioned Italian characters are set adrift among unsavory, sometimes buffoonish Easterners with such names as Mustafà Bey and Haly (an Italian spelling of Ali). To these largely verbal indicators, opera and somewhat analogous genres (Broadway musical, film) add a number of specific and crucial visual ones (stage sets, etc., as noted earlier) that derive directly from the plot and libretto. All of these factors deserve to be named and described, studied separately and together, weighed and probed, from the viewpoint of how they help construct the image of an exotic land or people.

4 | Who is "Us"? The national and/as the exotic, and the treatment of stereotypes

In the trends and case studies of Chapters 5–11, two challenging questions will arise again and again:

- How might one distinguish between, on the one hand, musical works that demonstrably represent or portray the exotic, and, on the other, works (e.g., by Bach or, some would argue, by Steve Reich) that use foreign styles *without* conveying an exotic charge?
- In what ways do exotic musical works reinforce, engage creatively with, or possibly even undermine the binaristic categories proposed in Chapter 3, especially one frequent manifestation of the Self/Other split: ethnic/cultural stereotypes, some of which are now recognized as misleading or even noxious?

These questions are so basic that they deserve concentrated discussion. The present chapter explores them, referring most often to pieces that will not be encountered in Chapters 5–11 (some of them in genres that are not treated extensively in those chapters, such as symphony and comic opera). As in the end of the previous chapter, the discussion here frequently cuts across two of the guiding principles of Chapters 5–11: chronology and genre.

National style or exoticism?

The first of the indented questions above asks, "When does a work merely use a specific national style and when does it cross the line into evoking a distinctively 'exotic' region or culture?" Consider various "Italian" works by non-Italians. The *Capriccio italien* (1880) of Tchaikovsky and *Aus Italien* (1886) of Richard Strauss are clearly exoticist since they make overt use of folk-like tunes such as a tourist might have expected to hear in the streets of Naples. In the Strauss work, one of the tunes is the well-known Neapolitan song "Funiculi, funiculà." It is not a folk song – produced and honed over generations by anonymous musicians – but a commercial popular song composed and published by an identifiable individual, Luigi Denza (1846–1922). Still, Strauss assumed it was a folk song, as have most performers and listeners since his day. In the concert hall, or on CD today, this is all that matters. In a court of law – as Strauss soon learned to his sorrow – definitions of intellectual property hold sway. (Denza sued Strauss's publisher for copyright infringement, and Strauss was forced to pay damages.)

A striking contrast comes from Italian aspects of the music of J. S. Bach. His concertos (many of them written around 1720) adopt certain melodic and structural procedures typical of works by his great contemporary Antonio Vivaldi and other prominent Italians. Bach even frankly entitled one piece (for solo keyboard) "Concerto in the Italian Manner" (1735). Yet these various concertos do not portray or represent Italian scenes, Italian life, or Italian folk-music traditions. They are simply up-to-date examples of good – which, at the time, meant Italian – concerto writing. Something similar can be said of the incorporation of Italianate (Rossinian) structural conventions and stylistic mannerisms in the operas that Auber and Meyerbeer composed in the mid-nineteenth century for Paris, even if the plot unfolds in Nordic lands or on Hindu Madagascar. These composers were adopting (and, as so often, adapting) fashionably up-to-date and cosmopolitan procedures for putting an effective opera together.

Somewhere between these two extremes (Strauss's use of a folk-like tune, and Bach's, Auber's, and Meyerbeer's absorption of Italian compositional conventions), I would place three symphonic finales based on the lively Italian folk dance known as the saltarello (from the verb *saltare*: "to jump"). The one in Mendelssohn's "Italian" Symphony (1833) clearly crosses the border toward exoticist territory. That is, we are expected to think of Italy as a locale in which the dancing is understood as "taking place" (a phrase that nicely reminds us that, as I argued in regard to my definition in Chapter 3, exotic things happen in a real or imagined-as-real *place*). The same may be said of two saltarello-like finales that Mendelssohn's own finale seems to have inspired: one in Saint-Saëns's Symphony No. 2 in A Minor, Op. 55 (1859), the other in Lalo's Symphony in G Minor (1886). Furthermore, these two symphonies, taken as wholes, inevitably evoked yet another country for many listeners of the day: Germany. (French music critics often described Germany and Austria – admiringly or enviously – as "the land of the symphony.") German features in French symphonies were heard as more distinctively non-French than were Italian features in French operas.[1] The composer Auber's words of welcome for Charles Gounod's Symphony No. 1 (1855) reveal a deep anxiety toward the German lands: "It would be a happiness and a glory for France to be able to point to a music so sensible [*si sage*], so pure, and so inspired as counterpart to the divagations [i.e., endless digressions] of what is called the modern German School."[2]

Clearly, the discussion has become rather subjective when we find ourselves trying to compare the Italianate elements in French operas and the possible Germanness of French symphonies modeled on German ones. The distinction between the two large categories in the previous paragraphs – (1) works that were intended to be heard as exotic, and generally are, and (2) works that are merely influenced by, or even "written in," a distinctive foreign style – is, inevitably, not a clear one. I find it helpful to think of the first category – works that are exotic (or exoticist) – as manifesting what one might call the will to represent or, returning to the language of my definition in the Chapter 3, the will to evoke. I admit, though, that the distinction is inherently problematic. What evidence can we take as indicating the presence of such a "will"?

Clearly, one can seek evidence of the "will to represent" in extramusical clues.[3] Some of these clues are more or less "official," more or less part of the work itself or the way that it was consciously framed by the composer and his/her co-creators: such clues as sung text, a title (printed above the music), costumes, or choreography. Other clues are more circumstantial though not necessarily any less revealing, such as contemporary reviews in the public press, or remarks in letters by the composer or those close to him/her.

These various kinds of evidence make indisputably clear that the odd recurring heaviness in a certain dance in Act 3 of Tchaikovsky's *Swan Lake* is not only a compositionally fresh experiment in alternating between forward motion and sudden halts but also an attempt at writing a somewhat stiff, haughty dance perceived as coming from a particular exotic land, namely Hungary. The decisive clue to the latter is the word "Csárdás" above the printed music. Of course, in a staged, danced performance of the ballet, additional clues would be offered in the choreography (e.g., heel-clicking) and costumes (e.g., high boots). But it is worth remembering that many more people nowadays encounter the music of *Swan Lake* (or at least certain beloved excerpts) on recordings/radio or in concert than in a danced performance and so must respond mainly or solely to its aural features. In the theater and concert hall, the program book might list the various numbers of the ballet, or even include a detailed synopsis, or it might not. Similarly, CD booklets do not always explain what a *csárdás* is. In any case, concertgoers may not read the entire program book, just as CD listeners do not always extract the annoyingly packaged booklets. As for classical-station radio announcers, they almost never share much information – sometimes not even the names of movements – before playing a piece.

The *csárdás* in *Swan Lake* is at least hiding in plain sight. In the case of Dvořák's Symphony No. 9 (subtitled "From the New World"), direct evidence is available, but of more recondite sorts: letters, newspaper interviews with the composer, and early reviews. Various scholars, notably Michael Beckerman, have gathered and evaluated enough of this evidence to prove, with some assurance, that parts of the symphony evoke Native American customs described in Longfellow's *The Song of Hiawatha*: a passage in the slow movement was originally intended to portray the solemn homeward procession after Minnehaha's funeral in the forest, and the opening of the scherzo was conceived as a stomping, whirling dance for the warrior Pau-Puk-Keewis.[4]

But surely just as important as verbal labels and historical documentation are the collective perceptions of stylistically informed listeners, then and since. There are no external clues from Chopin about the Polishness of the long first section of the Nocturne in G Minor, Op. 15, no. 3 (1833), yet Polish it certainly sounds, as if it were a mazurka that had been accidentally mislabeled. For more than a century, critics and scholars, including recently Jeffrey Kallberg, have noted the Polishness of this nocturne.[5] Listeners familiar with nineteenth-century repertoires and styles respond similarly to this work. And the clincher, perhaps, is that pianists, responding to features in the written notes, employ certain distinctive rhythmic freedoms that have long been part of the tradition for performing mazurkas, quite unlike those that are understood as being appropriate to nocturnes.[6] Pianists, and listeners, know a mazurka, regardless of the label on the container.

The music of Chopin raises another aspect of the problem of delimiting the exotic: how to distinguish between the evocation of a different place and the evocation of a part of one's own homeland. Here, too, there is no sharp line. The rural villages of Poland must have seemed exotic indeed to the highly refined Chopin. After all, his father was a Frenchman who was more or less stranded in Warsaw. Though young Fryderyk, on a summer vacation in the countryside, listened intently to some folk musicians – singers and players – and even joined in on the double bass, he received the bulk of his musical training through years of study with conservatory pedagogues in Warsaw. Indeed, there is evidence that Chopin's concept of the mazurka was shaped far more by published salon mazurkas (and folk-inspired theater music) from a generation or two before him than by direct exposure to folk culture.[7]

Nonetheless – and as early as 1829, when he left Warsaw permanently for Vienna and then Paris – Chopin does seem to have considered the music of rural Poland and its echoes in the salon music of his predecessors as something very much his own and as an appropriate way to present himself publicly. Some of his earliest compositions, and some of the earliest that he published, were mazurkas (e.g., the two mazurkas of 1826, and the sets published in the early 1830s as Op 6, Op. 7, and Op. 17). Various Polish dance types show up in his most "public" works, namely in the finales of the two concertos and in three of his four other pieces for piano and orchestra.[8] Also, he treated that rural style as something that he could alter at will and incorporate into his highly personal manner. Yet the process of incorporating-and-altering seems largely similar in various encounters that we would tend to consider exotic rather than national(ist): for example, Saint-Saëns's encounters – fifty years after Chopin's mazurkas – with traditional Algerian and Egyptian musical styles and fragments; and, another few decades later, Ravel's encounters with blues and jazz.

James Parakilas offers some challenging thoughts about different varieties of "Spanish" exotica. He notes that Russian composers – Glinka (*Jota aragonesa*, 1845), Rimsky-Korsakov (*Capriccio espagnol*, 1887), and Tchaikovsky (*The Nutcracker*'s "Spanish Dance," 1892), to which I might add Shostakovich (*Spanish Songs*, Op. 100, 1956) – have been drawn to Spanish music and imagery partly because they identify with a country that, like Russia itself, was often perceived as being located on the geographical and cultural outer edge of Europe. The Spanish composer Albéniz had immensely greater familiarity with the folk music of various regions in Spain than did the Russians. Yet, in a way, he exploited Spanish materials and compositional procedures with similarly forthright exoticist intent in *Ibéria* (1906–8), a mammoth series of pieces that was first published in Paris and whose twelve substantial movements evoke Spanish locales and even an event as specific as the famous Corpus Christi Day procession in Seville. One might say that Albéniz engages in the process of rendering himself and his native land exotic – engages, that is, in "autoexoticizing" (to borrow Parakilas's term regarding a later composer, Manuel de Falla).[9] By building up the Spanishness of his compositional persona, Albéniz helped make his music sound different from what he and others would have recognized as the European mainstream.

Albéniz seems to have sensed that he would cut a sharper profile in Paris by sounding Spanish than by trying to compete with Franck, Fauré, or Debussy at their own game. There is a clear parallel here with Dvořák: the latter's folk-tinged works created for the composer what Michael Beckerman describes as a personal "niche" in the "ecosystem" of the European musical world, which was already filled to surfeit with extremely demanding works by Brahms and Wagner. Beckerman jokes that Dvořák, in effect, responded to an implied advertisement from the music-publishing and symphony-orchestra industry: "Hear, hear! We have an opening in the composers' pantheon for an ethnic lyricist."[10]

The strategy remains effective today for works from a variety of locales. The Argentinian composer Astor Piazzolla caused great excitement within the "classical" and crossover worlds in the 1990s, thanks to his many pieces that rework elements from the rich and varied local traditions of the tango. Polish composer Henryk Górecki exerted a stunning impact with a single work, his Symphony No. 3 ("Symphony of Sorrowful Songs," 1976). When listeners outside of Poland became aware of it in 1992, it sounded like nothing else around. A recording of the work on the Nonesuch label moved into the Top 20 on the pop-music charts in the UK and was much heard on US radio as well. (The Elektra/Nonesuch record firm facilitated this by releasing part of the symphony as a single.) The "sorrow" in the symphony's title refers to the historical sufferings and deep traditional spirituality of the composer's native Poland. This reference is carried out less through distinctive Polishisms in the music than through the folk texts (sung by its female soloist); a near-quotation of Chopin's harmonically ambiguous Mazurka in A minor, Op. 17, no. 4 (1833), at the beginning and end of movement 3; and the general religious tone of much of the music, clearly suggesting the centuries-old link between the Polish people and the Catholic Church. In particular, the massive canon for the string orchestra that frames the soprano's lament to her dying son in movement 1 may, in context, be perceived as deeply Catholic, not least because the instrumental lines move in determinedly stepwise fashion, like so much Gregorian chant.

Works by such composers as Albéniz, Dvořák, Piazzolla, and Górecki perform, in the composer's own country, what music history books would call "nationalism"; in the broader cosmopolis, they function (instead or as well) as an exotic product. The case of Dvořák's *Moravian Duets*, as described by Beckerman, is particularly clear:

Both the Czech patriot in Prague and the German music teacher in Leipzig bought Dvořák's *Moravian Duets* because they were "good music," but on another level the patriots probably purchased their sets because the music was about "themselves," while the teachers paid their thalers precisely because it was somehow about strangers.[11]

Beckerman makes the whole process seem innocent and win/win. But, notes Richard Taruskin, there is often a price to be paid. This "colonialist nationalism," which allows composers from culturally marginal countries to be welcomed in a country that deems itself the center, ends up becoming "a double bind":

Dvořák's Bohemianisms were at once the vehicle of his international appeal and the eventual guarantee of his secondary status vis-à-vis natural-born universals like Brahms. Without the native costume, a "peripheral" composer would never achieve even secondary canonical rank, but with it he could never achieve more.[12]

We might expand a bit on this double bind, as it applies to Piazzolla, who continues to be one of the hotter commodities on today's "classical" music market. How devoted would performers and record companies have been to Piazzolla's later works if he had suddenly traded his tango-inflected style for that of the cosmopolitan modernist mainstream? Conversely, can the work of a composer who has spent decades exploring the tango ever be considered important within standard music histories and critical surveys?[13] Even one of Piazzolla's biggest supporters these days, Latvian-born violinist Gidon Kremer, admits to "find[ing] it irritating ... that Astor Piazzolla is automatically equated with the Tango – to me he is much bigger than that."[14] Ironically, this protest occurs in notes to a compact disc that consists of nothing but performances by Kremer (and friends) of tango-based pieces, including several "tango songs," and is entitled – and why not? – *El tango*.

The double bind is at work in many corners of Western musical life, including opera. Is it coincidental that, of all Pietro Mascagni's fifteen operas, the one that has lodged itself in the repertoire is *Cavalleria rusticana*, which trades rather heavy-handedly in stereotypes about violent, emotionally destructive townspeople in the composer's native Italy? The stereotyping starts with the sarcasm of the title. "Rustic chivalry" amounts here to deceit, marital infidelity, jealousy, gossip-mongering, and murder. What can one possibly expect, the work declares, shaking its head ruefully, of crude Sicilian villagers? This, too, is autoexoticism, by someone who is still today taken as a "native informant."

Cavalleria rusticana – though much loved by singers and audiences alike – has been doomed to second- or even third-rate status by the arbiters of taste and historical significance. To be sure, music-history textbooks generally make at least brief mention of the work, presenting it – accurately enough – as an instance of operatic *verismo*, which was a major late nineteenth-century operatic trend toward gutsy "real life" plots, orchestral music reflecting the (often) lower-class characters' passionate impulses, and naturalistic (i.e., speech-inflected) sung dialogue. Rarely do these books relate it to other trends in which it participates just as clearly: exoticism, and explorations of that ever-related development, cultural nationalism (which those same books do not hesitate to notice in works by various Russians and Spaniards, by Grieg, or, in Germany and France, by Wagner and d'Indy). As so often, context determines discourse, and discourse shapes how we listen, respond, and evaluate. Mascagni was an Italian composing operas – within the Italian operatic mainstream – about Italians. (Provincial Italians, to be sure.) As a result, the opera's exoticizing attitude goes unremarked. This is not to say that the attitude goes unfelt. *Cavalleria rusticana* does its work faithfully and reliably in opera houses around the world.

One notable Sicilian is proud of the way that *Cavalleria* portrays the island and its inhabitants. Tenor Marcello Giordani spoke to the *New York Times* of the work, and of Sicily, in bragging tones:

Different peoples ... have settled there: Arabs, Greeks, Normans, the Swedes. That has made us different from others. We exaggerate, we overdo ... We cry, we fight, sometimes for nothing. We don't have the middle of the line. We're on the edge.[15]

How works handle stereotypes and binarisms

Whether composed by individuals who (like Mascagni or Piazzolla) come from the territory in question or, more often, by outsiders, exotic (or taken-as-exotic) musical works are often obsessed in some way with the split – often viewed rather stereotypically – between the Western/European/metropolitan Self and some kind of Eastern/primitive/rural Other. This is particularly evident in operas (and analogous genres, such as dramatic oratorio and film), whereas one is perpetually on more shifting ground when trying to read the meanings in (or read meanings into?) instrumental works. Therefore, it is with exotic operas that we shall remain to the end of the chapter. (We shall explore the special problems of instrumental pieces – and examine some significant cases – in Chapters 6, 9, and 10.)

The split between the West and the Other is sometimes presented in operas in ways that, to later generations, seem ludicrous. In part, this is because an opera libretto tends toward the telegraphic; as a result, it simplifies and intensifies concepts and contrasts, making them seem – if examined in the cold light of day – almost childishly naive, if not frankly polemical (e.g., patriotic), prejudicial, or defamatory. Concepts that are perfectly respectable in novels, spoken drama, poetry, or philosophical and religious writings – righteous anger, heroic determination, faithful devotion – may seem laughably absurd in libretto language.

The immediate result, for purposes of the present study, is that the operatic repertoire, over the past two or three decades, has been full of works that reenact – in music as well as words – more or less standardized, sometimes stereotypical visions of what distant and fabled lands look like and of how the inhabitants there think and act. (Over a hundred alone have focused on Cleopatra.)

It may be helpful to think a little more explicitly about the exotic works that have more or less "become lost" over time, the stereotypes that abound in them, and why anybody was attracted to them in the past or might be today. Comic operas tend to delight in stereotypes. Two examples illustrate very different approaches:

- *1001 Nacht* (The Thousand and One Nights), an operetta of 1906, was freely based on music by Johann Strauss, Jr. (Strauss had died seven years earlier; the music comes primarily from his early opera *Indigo und die vierzig Räuber*.) A lighthearted confection, it went on to hold the boards in German-speaking theaters for several decades (including repeated productions at the Bregenz Festival featuring such famed singers as tenor Helge Rosvaenge) but has slipped from view in recent decades. The work bases much of its repetitious humor on fairly simple notions, such as that Middle Easterners are uncultured (they prefer camels, of all things, to railroads) and are irrepressibly, and cutely, polygamous.[16] The very disparity between, on the one hand, a plot set in the Middle East and, on the other, Strauss's standard-issue Viennese waltzes and galops lends an element of farce from the start.
- Offenbach likewise strove for a literally "dis-Orienting" effect in his operettas set in distant places. *Ba-Ta-Clan* (1855), a one-act work, was notably successful in its day.[17] Its libretto twits the Chinese emperors for their supposed numerous grisly ways of executing enemies (stabbing, dismemberment, impalement) and praises the pleasures of the Parisian boulevards. The four characters – silly folks all – gradually reveal to each other, one by one, that they are French, and they end up heading home, except for the chief of the imperial guard, who was born to a Parisian laundress but maintains his Chinese disguise so that he can ascend the throne. The opera's music parodies, by turns, opéra-comique, Donizettian tragic opera, and French grand opera. At the climax of a ridiculous uprising of conspirators, the Lutheran chorale tune "Ein' feste Burg ist unser Gott" rings out much as it did in a similar (but grimly serious) situation in Meyerbeer's *Les huguenots* (1836).

The Strauss-derived work, though modest in its demands, is rarely performed today. The Offenbach does get mounted occasionally, but primarily by student opera workshops and smaller opera companies.

By contrast, numerous other heavily exotic works – such as Mozart's *Die Entführung aus dem Serail*, Bizet's *Les pêcheurs de perles*, Verdi's *Aida*,

Strauss's *Salome*, and Puccini's *Turandot* – are staples in the international opera-house repertoire and well known through multiple recordings. Surely, one reason for this is that the representations of exotic places that they offer are – in the cumulative opinion of generations of performers, operagoers, and critics – more imaginative, powerful, affecting, and nuanced than those of the aforementioned Johann Strauss(-derived) and Offenbach works.

What makes a work more or less powerful and more or less nuanced often has to do with its handling of stereotypes. Some works embody, more or less straightforwardly, stereotypes (and hence cultural values) that strike many of us today as noxious or oppressive.[18] Historical awareness can help us gain some distance from these stereotypes, however alluringly they are presented. Michael V. Pisani, at the end of a book that has brought the reader into contact with a wide array of musical and music-reinforced portrayals of Native Americans – some directly denigrating, others filled with condescending "admiration" – concludes:

Censoring a stereotype – even one based in sound – does not make it disappear. But putting a frame around it, consciously acknowledging its borders, and addressing its history at least helps us understand why such stereotypes exist in the first place, and perhaps even to recognize, when we next encounter them, their effects on us and on society as a whole.[19]

As a guide when one is approaching the vast and varied repertoire of works based on ethnic or exotic stereotypes – including sentimental parlor songs and slick, formulaic film scores – Pisani's double principle of "putting a frame around [the work]" and noticing (interrogating) our own response to the work's various messages may be impossible to better.

But the case can be made that certain deeper or more complex works – and Pisani's book treats some of those as well – do not simply reenact stereotypes but reinterpret or subvert them. Some of the works mentioned two paragraphs back (by Mozart, *et al.*) give a timeworn convention a new twist; they allow a given character to shift back and forth between two sides of a dichotomy basic to the plot (notably the Self/Other binarism, so crucial in the formation and maintenance of racial/ethnic stereotypes).[20] Or they align several different stereotypes in such a way that the stereotypes at times reinforce each other, at times conflict and thereby throw each other into relief. Deconstructing the binarisms in these ways may allow for critique of the stereotypes themselves. The critic does not need to put a frame around such a work and name its ideology, in order to be able to reflect upon it: the work itself engages in critical work from which we might learn something.

For example, the emphasis on extravagant luxury and overweening power in certain "Middle Eastern" operas – *Aida*, *Samson et Dalila* – can implicate the Europe of Verdi's and Saint-Saëns's day.[21]

Indeed, an exotic work may suggest many kinds of issues beyond those associated with the locale that is signaled by its libretto, sets, and costumes. The key to this lies in the broad concept of the "Other" (discussed in a subsection of Chapter 3). The Other is primarily understood in the present book the way it is understood in much cultural and critical theory dealing with Western culture: as referring to geographical, ethnic, racial, and religious difference from the West. But the concept of the Other derives ultimately from more basic philosophical principles, pondered over millennia, of how the individual subject ("I," or the Self) conceives of, and relates to, another individual ("you," the Other).[22] The terms Self and Other thus lend themselves well to describing relationships (within an art work) that involve another binary category, perhaps the most basic one in human life: gender.

By "gender" I mean a broad category of patterns involving the roles and expectations, the enticing opportunities and oppressive restrictions, that a given society permits and/or enforces. Most often, in literary works (hence also in operas and dramatic oratorios), the basic category of Other applies to women. This is especially true in genres and traditions in which the normative agent is the male hero. "Other" can also apply to men who neglect their national-patriotic duties, or homosexual males – indeed, to any individual or group understood as not inviting identification on the part of the viewer.[23] One of most fascinating, and sometimes questionable, features in an exotic work involves the ways in which the ethnic-racial-religious binarism of Self/Other partly does and partly does not map onto a Self/Other binarism of gender. The male protagonists in *Aida* and *Samson et Dalila* are clearly symbols of Us (see Chapter 8), but they become partly Other by yielding to the attractions of a female representative of Them – that is, by (in Rudyard Kipling's famous term) "going native." In the process, these Us-men put their own lives in danger, and they also complicate an audience member's response to their predicament and choices.

The various binarisms of Self and Other in a work are most easily demonstrable in operas and other musicodramatic works at what we might call the foundational or plot-premise level, where they are conveyed through prose summary, set design, costuming, and stage movement. The binarisms can be supported but also undermined by the specific artfulnesses available within music theater: artfulnesses in the libretto – including shifts of tone and topic, a character's declarations and poetic flights, and his/her loaded words and no less powerful silences – but also, of course, artfulnesses in the music – including vocal lines and orchestral passages that may be resplendent or touching, mystery-laden or spine-chilling – all inflected by the technical command and fresh creative nuances of the particular production and performers.[24]

The rather hierarchized outline just set forth – a hierarchy moving upward from plot summary and stage sets to imaged verse, shimmering or passionate music, and dramatic accomplishment – may seem to slight the importance of that first, "prosaic" level (including highly conventionalized visual markers), subordinating it to the more "poetic" or "artistic" ones. My intention is quite the opposite. I feel it crucial to start out by establishing that the basic givens in an exotic work (the premise of an instrumental piece, plot of an opera) were often shaped by – and, in turn, convey to the audience – an ideologically driven view of the exotic region in question, of "proper" gender roles, and so on. The poetry, music, and performance decisions may intensify, complicate, and even, at times, contradict these basic conceptions, but they never completely efface them.

This point is often neglected. Musicologists regularly approach the problem of what is exotic in a work by going right to the notes of the score, identifying the one or two most overtly foreign-sounding numbers (often ballets or choruses, in the case of an exotic opera), and noting the use, in those few numbers, of unusual melodic touches or orchestrational devices – or else declaring a work non-exotic if it lacks such codes or signs.[25] Such a search for exotic sounds is an important and inviting task for scholar or critic, but it remains a severely limited one, precisely because it scrutinizes the upper, "poetic" commentaries but shortchanges the foundational givens upon which they comment. It is as if, in regard to Leonardo da Vinci's painting of *The Last Supper*, one were to seek out a religious message in the brushstrokes and color alone without first discussing the painting's formal composition (how the figures, objects, architectural space, and landscape relate to each other) and its use of iconography (including the identity of the two men who reach for the same piece of bread: Jesus, centrally placed; and, in the shadow, the dark-haired Judas Iscariot, clutching a bag of coins).

An exclusive focus on musical style tends to echo an unspoken ideology of formalism. The too-common assumption is that somehow the pitches and rhythms in a piece will convey to a listener all the necessary data or messages, whether s/he is or is not familiar with the work's social and cultural contexts.[26]

In a frankly anti-formalist spirit, I urge attention, on the journey in Chapters 5–11, to one of the chief "contextual" aspects of exotic musical works (and especially exotic operas, oratorios, musicals, film scores, and the like), an aspect that composers, impresarios, singers, contemporary critics, and audience members through the years – if sometimes not scholars – have always understood to be essential, even preconditional, for understanding a work: its premise (often a brief but immensely resonant title, as in Mozart's "Rondo alla turca") or (in an opera or analogous work) its plot, action, and sung words. This premise or (in opera) this plot-plus frames the musical devices employed and gives us big clues about how to hear them, what they "mean." It can also stir our broader range of associations and meanings – some of which could not have been known to the composer and his or her original listeners – thereby making the work more durably enjoyable, continuingly relevant, and perhaps, by the very strength of its musical imagination, healthily problematic.

PART II

5 | Baroque portrayals of despots: ancient Babylon, Incan Peru

It is often claimed that there were very few significant exotic musical portrayals until the mid-eighteenth-century vogue of *alla turca* operas. But exoticism had already played a major role in various musical genres for several centuries. Scholars have noted an intriguing parallel, on a basic conceptual level, between, on the one hand, the exploration of the globe and the discovery of numerous previously unknown lands, creatures, and cultures; and, on the other, the move from a small number of church modes to the tonal system, which permitted all twelve notes of the chromatic scale to function as a home "key." (Johann David Heinichen was one of the first to connect the keys in a closed circle, in 1711, thereby permitting them to be, one might say, "circumnavigated" in concept and practice.[1]) More concretely, portrayals of distant Others were numerous in the Age of Exploration (i.e., the sixteenth, seventeenth, and early eighteenth centuries). Court ballets (called "masques" in England) regularly involved stately visits from dancers costumed as Chinese, Scandinavians, or Aztec warriors – not to speak of supernatural characters (witches, for example), who bear a certain similarity to exotic characters in that they come from a (truly extreme) Elsewhere.[2] Venetian operas similarly included danced *intermezzi* between the acts or even within an act. These *intermezzi* featured dancers representing countries far and near – whether ancient Egyptians, Chinese courtiers, or more or less present-day Turks or Germans – and often did so with little regard to the setting and time period of the opera.[3] Much the same occurred in the French *opéras-ballets* of Lully and his followers.

In addition, certain types of dances from a wide range of countries – or written in the supposed style of those countries – circulated in lute or harpsichord arrangements that were used for performance at home or court. "During the 17th and 18th centuries," notes Rogério Budasz, "many dances of African influence appeared almost simultaneously in different points of the so-called Atlantic triangle, a region that comprised coastal cities of the Congo-Angola, Iberian Peninsula and Latin America." They were apparently disseminated, and to some extent arose, through the contacts between sailors, dockworkers, slaves from Africa, and "free people of color." Budasz transcribes an *arromba* ("forced entry" in Portuguese) that is strikingly dissonant and full of intense strumming. According to the seventeenth-century Brazilian poet Gregório de Mattos, the dance involved only hands and feet – "never moving one's arse [*o cu*]."[4]

Among the widely used foreign dances-types were the sarabande and chaconne (probably from, respectively, Central and South America) and – foreign to the Continent, anyway – the lively English jig (which became the gigue). Often, the features of the steps and music of a dance-type from (or associated with) a given country confirmed or enriched prevailing impressions of that country when performed elsewhere.[5] A recent study by Rose A. Pruiksma focuses on the undertones of cultural Otherness that the chaconne, in particular, conveyed in seventeenth-century France. In Lully's ballets and *comédies-ballets* (the latter to texts by Molière), the dance was often assigned to Mediterranean characters and was explicitly danced in honor of conjugal love:

> The chaconne, as an Hispanic export [that may have still carried associations with South America], allowed for the presence of the necessary physical side of love on the stage at the same time that it kept that carnality slightly apart from the character of the true Frenchman.[6]

Perhaps the richest and most extended exotic portrayals in music before 1750 occurred in Italian and French opera (and related genres, such as the *opéra-ballet*) and in English dramatic oratorio. Hundreds of such works involved, or even centered on, ancient Eastern tyrants (as known from the Bible or Greek history) or indigenous New World ones. These works included operas composed by such major figures as Lully and Handel and several of Handel's dramatic oratorios. Two authorities on pre-1800 musical exoticism, Miriam K. Whaples and Thomas Betzwieser, exclude such operas and dramatic oratorios from consideration, for the primary reason that the music almost never sounds (nor apparently was intended to sound) non-European and thus is not open to exploration using what I call the "Exotic Style Only" Paradigm (see Chapter 3).[7] One prominent Baroque-opera scholar (Silke Leopold) frankly states that "operatic plots from the Islamic cultural region only find significant [*grösseres*] interest in the second half of the eighteenth century," without so much as mentioning an example from the first half of the century (e.g., Handel's superb operas *Rinaldo*, *Tamerlano*, and *Radamisto*, the latter featuring a tyrannical and brutish king of Armenia named Tiridate).[8] Another opera scholar (Gilles de Van) pushes the date of onset even later, stating that "the great age of exoticism in the operatic domain" began in the early nineteenth century, when locations became more geographically specific through theatrical and musical *couleur locale* and the characters were now "marked by their place of origin." That last phrase gives the unfortunate impression that, in Baroque-era works, Eastern monarchs (kings and queens of Babylonia, Persia, and India) and native leaders of New World peoples (notably Montezuma, who was rendered operatically by such prominent composers as Purcell, Vivaldi, and Graun) were in no way marked as being different from the Western characters with whom they were coming into contact (ancient Greeks and Romans, sixteenth-century Spaniards).[9]

This widespread view hobbles any just appreciation of the multiple ways in which the West viewed the East, and New World "natives," in various musical genres during the crucial centuries and decades before Mozart. We shall examine the depth, power, and variety of two such portrayals: one in a Handel oratorio, the other in a Rameau *opéra-ballet*.

Handel's Eastern dramas

Baroque-era portrayals of the non-European Other were, in no matter what genre, almost always set in the distant past. It may be best to start by glancing briefly at how this played out in opera, the genre that set many of the norms for Handel's dramatic oratorios, generally, and thus for the "Eastern" oratorio upon which we shall be focusing, *Belshazzar*.

Early eighteenth-century operas were often based on military and political struggles between, on the one hand, a Greek or Roman emperor or military commander, such as Alexander the Great, and, on the other, the ruler of an "Eastern" land: Egypt, Byzantium, Persia, India, and the (today Turkish) regions of Pontus and Capadocia.[10] Handel's first Italian opera, *Rinaldo* (1711), moved this West–East conflict into the Middle Ages, pitting Crusader knights against Argante, a Muslim king (and relentless womanizer) who rules over Jerusalem. A later Handel opera, *Tamerlano* (1725), varies the pattern further by making both of its most extensively developed characters Muslim. But, in other respects, *Tamerlano* follows normal Baroque procedures for portrayals of exotic characters, such as freely adapting historical data (facts mixed with legends) about how the vicious Turko-Mongolian conqueror Tamburlaine (1336–1405; also known as Tamerlane or Timur) cruelly mistreated the conquered Ottoman sultan Beyazid I (1354–1403).

Tamerlano maintains a grimmer tone than any other opera by Handel. Near the end, Bajazete (i.e., Beyazid) dies, in a protracted and deeply moving scene. Tamerlano is thus prevented from carrying out his plan of causing Bajazete's daughter Asteria to be raped by slaves while her father watched.

Nonetheless, much in the opera is, again, typical. We are repeatedly led to view Tamerlano's viciousness through the eyes of the put-upon Asteria and the Christian characters Andronico and Irene. And, in the work's final moments, Tamerlano relents. He permits each of the characters to marry the individual that he or she truly loves, and – surely a welcome relief to the audience in Handel's day – he installs Andronico, rather than a Muslim like himself, on the throne of Byzantium. (The historical Tamerlane did nothing of the kind.)

Sacred oratorio likewise often pitted various stand-ins of West and East against each other: ancient Hebrews against Assyrians, Philistines, or Persians; or, if set several centuries later, Christian saints against Syrians or other Eastern pagans. Handel's oratorio *Belshazzar* of 1745, though only mildly successful during the composer's lifetime, is a splendid example. *Belshazzar* centers on the morally depraved king of Babylon and his hatred of the Jews, who are, as in many other oratorios, presented as forerunners of Christians.[11] Some recent commentators have focused on internal features of the work. Particularly intriguing is the balance of tragic and comic aspects in the portrayal of the title figure, as seen in the libretto (by Charles Jennens) and in the musical means that Handel mobilized in setting it.[12] Other commentators have worked more contextually, assessing the ways in which the work echoes contemporary debates about the legitimacy of the Whig government and its suppression of all things Catholic.[13]

By contrast, a third aspect – one that, like the second, emphasizes context – has been barely considered: how *Belshazzar* reflects European attitudes toward the Middle East of more recent eras and of Handel's day, and how it reflects such basic facts as the burgeoning British imperial adventures in India and other regions then regarded as exotic. This exotic/imperial aspect proves to be not unrelated to the two better-studied aspects: comic-tragic balance, and commentary on political and religious tensions within England.

Belshazzar, semi-comic Babylonian tyrant

One perceptive literary historian, Peter Bachmann, has demonstrated that various verbal details in Handel's operas and oratorios about Eastern monarchs echo early eighteenth-century attitudes toward non-European rulers of more recent centuries and the luxury in which they dwelled. Bachmann even notes certain aspects of the libretto for Handel's oratorio *Solomon*, a work that few listeners today would immediately relate to the world of Ottoman sultans.[14]

Figure 5.1 In the Rembrandt painting of *Belshazzar's Feast* (*c.* 1635), the ancient Babylonian tyrant is given an elaborate turban that draws a parallel to more recent Arab sultans. (© The National Gallery, London.)

Handel specialists, too, have made scattered remarks pointing in that direction, and with specific regard to *Belshazzar*. Winton Dean notes that Jennens's libretto presents the Babylonian tyrant's court as "a riot of oriental colour – wives, concubines, astrologers, and all."[15] Dean might have stated more explicitly why those images in the oratorio would have been perceived as "Oriental": they correspond to details in the *Thousand and One Nights* (or *Arabian Nights*). This collection had become widely known in the early 1700s through the famous French translation of Galland and its English adaptations. But the trend was established well before Galland. Rembrandt's painting of *Belshazzar's Feast* (*c.* 1635 – Fig. 5.1) already equates the Babylonian monarch, through turban and other details, with Middle Eastern rulers of the painter's own day.

Dean rightly observes that Belshazzar is portrayed for us (in advance of our meeting him) as a "sottish self-indulgent tyrant," and that the portrayal occurs in notes as well as words. Gobryas, whose son was one of Belshazzar's recent victims, decries the tyrant in a memorable aria: "Behold the monstrous human beast / Wallowing in excessive feast! / ... Self-degraded to a swine, / ... grov'ling on the ground." Handel's music for the opening words nicely conveys what Dean calls the tyrant's "swaggering gait."[16] Particularly striking, and relevant to the "All the Music in Full Context" Paradigm, are the coloratura passages. The more or less generic up-and-down alternations take on specific associations because they are sung to the repeated word "wallowing." One thus easily imagines the "self-degraded" Belshazzar flopping around in mud, this way and that.

Equally vivid and even more plainly linked to then-prevailing images of the Middle East is Handel's setting of the passage in Act 2 in which the cruel, cowardly despot urges his courtiers to join him in drinking wine served in vessels that his nation's troops had stolen from Solomon's great Temple (Ex. 5.1). The words with which Belshazzar calls for more drink verge on the blasphemous. The Babylonian king here imagines himself becoming godlike – not by engaging in virtuous behavior (along the lines of a proper *imitatio dei*) but by indulging to excess in fermented beverage:

Another bowl! – 'tis gen'rous wine,
Exalts the human to divine.

Handel's rising vocal scale on "Exalts ... " audibly mimics Belshazzar's claim of rising to godhood. The effect is, one scholar notes, "buffoonish."[17]

Handel sets Belshazzar's opening words in this aria ("Another bowl!") as a spirited arpeggiated drinking call, stating it four times.[18] Each time, he echoes it in the oboes. These short instrumental interpolations allow the listener to imagine appropriate stage action: Belshazzar grabbing and swigging one cup after another. On a 1976 recording, conductor Nikolaus Harnoncourt adds dramatically effective little pauses to emphasize this stage business further. (Tenor Robert Tear, during the fourth and final rendering of "Another bowl," introduces a wonderfully smeary portamento, suggesting that Belshazzar has become totally soused.[19]) The aforementioned melismatic passage (rising to a long-held G on "ex*alts*") is another of those instances that are "read" in context as revealing a character's merit (or lack of merit). Belshazzar here shows how caught up he is in drunken grandiosity. (The tenor can feel free to fling out that high note.) And how determined a foe to the (incipient) West and its religious traditions.

This whole episode (including Gobryas's description in advance) links Belshazzar to the stereotypical image of a Middle Eastern sultan enjoying a selfish life of opulence, sensuality, and unbounded personal pleasure – and

Example 5.1 Handel, *Belshazzar*, Act 2, Belshazzar's aria "Let the deep bowl thy praise confess" (passage beginning "Another bowl!").

also, at times, engaging in hostile acts against Europe and Europeans (or proto-Europeans, in this case, namely the Jews).[20]

Why did Jennens and Handel portray in semi-comic fashion the behavior of a vicious Middle Eastern pagan clearly intent on destroying the believers in Jehovah? English theatrical tradition, in the early eighteenth century, continued to permit and even encourage the mixing of theatrical modes, at a time when the opposite – an increasingly sharp distinction between serious and playful – was becoming normative both in French spoken theater (Corneille's tragedies vs. Molière's comedies) and in musical genres for the Italian and French stage (*opera seria* vs. the vernacular comic operas in 1680s Bologna; or Lully's late operatic tragedies vs. the lighthearted ballets of Campra).

But equally important were certain beliefs (or ideals) about behavior that were central to court culture during what historians nowadays call the Early Modern Era (*c.* 1500–1800). Profound character flaws, such as King Belshazzar reveals in the oratorio, were felt to be unacceptable among members of the ruling classes of any well-ordered society. A society's leaders most often came from a background of wealth, privilege, and leisure and were understood as bearing attendant responsibilities (such as military leadership). Aristotle, centuries earlier, had laid out a number of basic guidelines in his *Nicomachean Ethics*: a true aristocrat or leader must, for example, display emotional self-control (be slow to anger) and act with appropriate generosity in a given circumstance.[21]

That, at least, was the ideal. In fact, as historical sociologist Norbert Elias has made clear, aristocrats often engaged in "prestige consumption," which required one "to make the cost of maintaining one's household ... match ... the status one possesses or aspires to." As a result, noble families – more often than members of the bourgeois and professional classes – regularly "ruined themselves" through costly rivalry.[22] Even traits that might seem to resemble those urged by Aristotle, such as self-restraint in expressing one's reactions to others, took on a highly functional, strategic sheen in the courtly world. The "constant masking of momentary emotional impulses" was less an ethically principled virtue than "a means of social survival and success" and, in time, became "an integral feature of [each aristocrat's] personality structure."[23]

Operas and dramatic oratorios (such as *Belshazzar*) were struts in the ideological support system of court society. This was the case even in England, where traditional social structures were being challenged, in part, by growing middle-class entrepreneurship. Musicodramatic works therefore continued to praise and promote – straightforwardly and moralistically – duty, noble self-sacrifice, and other professed ideals.

According to this same, long-traditional line of thought, people from the lower social orders could hardly be expected to engage in such virtuous behaviors, given their lack of education and also the pressures with which they had daily to contend in order to feed their families.[24] Aristotle's treatise makes the point explicit: whereas privilege, wealth, and reputation "bring great expectations with them," the limited "circumstances" of the poor person do not "merit or require" such traits as openhanded generosity.[25] In seventeenth- and eighteenth-century opera, middle- and lower-class characters – regular folk – prove Aristotle's point again and again. They stumble or lurch (often comically) into arrant selfishness, drunken excess, erratic behavior, sloth, and blind rage.

Eastern tyrants in operas of this era, not surprisingly, show some of the same tendencies, precisely because they are emblematic of a part of the world that is portrayed as ignoring or rejecting cherished tenets of Western society, such as the rational philosophy and (partly) democratic politics of ancient Greece and the moral imperatives of the Old and New Testament (e.g., universal compassion). The result is often not comic. A powerful tyrant can do vast harm by a simple whim. Still, it was easy and apparently tempting for librettist, composer, and presumably performer to give the portrayal of ignoble traits – especially excessive self-indulgence – a slight nudge toward ridicule and satire. Belshazzar's drinking scene makes the point that a person who is devoid of self-restraint and respect for others, and sacrilegious to boot, is unworthy of leading a great nation.

The scene also had a specific, timely political message. As Jennens later wrote to a friend, he had had a "farther aim" in proposing a Belshazzar libretto to Handel. Jennens was clearly referring to his own confirmed opposition to the corrupt Whig government of the Hanoverian king, George II. (Jennens propounded, in numerous brochures, the Non-Juror position: that England bring back the Stuarts, though not Catholicism.[26])

But an endotic explanation should not end the discussion of this exotic characterization. Jennens chose to make the religio-political point by engaging the available stereotypes of overprivileged, dissolute Eastern monarchs. In the process, he disseminated and (through Handel's genius) reinforced those stereotypes.

Jennens's particular current-day political take on Belshazzar – as symbolizing the worst aspects of Whigdom – gradually faded for audiences and commentators and so needed, in the late twentieth century, to be patiently reconstructed by devoted scholars. By contrast, the reading of Belshazzar as a typically self-centered and pleasure-crazed Eastern ruler remains potent as ever for performers and audiences, embodied as it is more or less directly in words and notes – even though those notes do not (as the Exotic-Style Paradigm would require) sound "Eastern."

Empire and virtue

The portrait of the dissolute Belshazzar is made so telling by the presence of a foil, a "Glorious Prince" (as the chorus calls him): King Cyrus of Persia. It was unusual to assign the role of good ruler to an Eastern monarch, but the Old Testament had prepared the way by making Cyrus a blessed figure – indeed, "anointed" – for doing the Lord's work of reestablishing the Hebrew people in their ancestral homeland and encouraging the rebuilding of the Temple in Jerusalem.[27] Throughout Handel's oratorio, the libretto establishes a contrast between bad and good imperial rule. In the very first vocal number of the work, Belshazzar's mother resignedly proposes a cyclical pattern of rise and fall: every "human empire, / ... Arriv'd to full maturity ... / o'erleaps all bounds, / Robs, ravages and wastes the frighted world" and then withers in "pride, luxury, corruption, perfidy." At the end of the next scene, the Persian chorus stresses, less fatalistically, that imperial rulers can flourish if they conduct themselves virtuously: "All empires upon God depend; / Begun by his command, at his command they end. / ... Look up to Him in all your ways" (i.e., in everything you do). Cyrus, in the course of overrunning Belshazzar's palace, acts in accord with various noble virtues extolled by Judaeo-Christian tradition. For example, though he has no hesitation in slaying Belshazzar and members of the court – Cyrus's basic job as the story's hero – he admirably spares the lives of all innocents: "To tyrants only I'm a foe, / To virtue and her friends, a friend."

Thus we are only a little surprised when, at the end of the oratorio, Cyrus not only frees the Jews to return to their homeland and vows to rebuild the Temple in Jerusalem but – taking an unlikely step for which there is no evidence in either the biblical narrative or historical accounts – accepts the "God of Israel" ("thus prostrate I confess"). Cyrus even vows to be God's "shepherd" to the peoples of the world. The choice of a word with New Testament overtones was surely not accidental.

By all these means, the oratorio's Cyrus demonstrated his wisdom to the work's original audiences and his close identity with whomever those listeners – depending on whether they were pro-Whig or pro-Stuart – took to be the rightful king of England and head of its proper national church.[28] Cyrus's words must also have reminded them that England's God-given role was to propagate Christianity throughout the "kingdoms of the earth" and to ensure its own freedom of navigation and commerce. The desired end-result of such uniformly beneficent world rule is told by the Persians (in an expanded version, from 1751, of their chorus that ends Act 2). Under princes as good as Cyrus, the "earth" would be "like heav'n," and "subjection" would be "free, unforc'd": "Obedience is the child of love."

By Handel's day, Britain was already well on its way toward ruling the waves and holding the world in a subjection that was, however, far from "unforc'd." Britain owned much of North America and, in recent decades, had acquired merchant monopolies from the Mughals in such cities as Madras, Bombay, and Calcutta (i.e., Chennai, Mumbai, and Kolkata). Over the next 250 years, this dream of happy empire would be challenged – by England's own colonists in North America in 1776, by the native populations of India in 1857 and the 1940s – until it has become, today, almost blotted out of many people's memory.[29] But, in 1745, such a dream was coming to be widely shared by English people of many social classes and was receiving support, in literature and the arts, through the frequently repeated narrative of a good empire's freeing a foreign land from its unjust, greedy native ruler.[30] Indeed, Ellen Harris has noted intriguing connections between the overseas commercial interests of the investors in Handel's opera house and the geographic locations of the operas performed in it.[31]

The dream of empire would continue to be promoted over the next century and more, with increasing explicitness and patriotically and religiously bolstered vociferousness, and would continue to be commodified in works of mystery and delight.[32] Handel's (and Jennens's) King Belshazzar stands as a prototype of the exotic tyrant from whom Britain, France, and successive world powers would claim to free the burdened, benighted natives of various territories. King Cyrus – though, unusually, an Eastern ruler himself – is the Eastern tyrant's prototypical Western (here proto-Western) counterpart: a shining leader who does the necessary work of subjugating populations, in the name of the true Lord and other values sometimes blandly or manipulatively (then and today) vaunted as universal, such as freedom, democracy, the needs of commerce, and the rule of law.

Les Indes galantes: encyclopedic world tour

Belshazzar, typical of many Baroque-era exotic (and non-exotic) portrayals, focuses at length on a single story from the ancient past. Rameau's *Les Indes galantes* (1735, revised 1736), by contrast, portrays, in succession, four different foreign peoples – three of them in relatively recent encounters with Westerners.

Les Indes, to a text by Louis Fuzelier, was no doubt inspired by several famous recent *opéras-ballets* that were set in Venice and other favored travel destinations.[33] But *Les Indes* went far beyond them in musicodramatic ambition and in its introducing of moral lessons. Virtue is sometimes embodied in the European characters, other times in one or more foreign characters (in accordance with the Enlightenment notion of the noble savage). The work's systematic and thoughtfully nuanced world tour seems to breathe the same air as that archetypal Enlightenment effort, the *Encyclopédie* of Diderot and d'Alembert (which would be published, after years of preparation, in 1751–80).

Rameau's remarkable travelogue-in-music consists of a prologue and four entirely independent acts, called *entrées*, set in, respectively, Turkey, Peru, Persia, and the unspoiled North American woodlands. The first *entrée* – *Le Turc généreux* (The Generous Turk) – is built upon a plot that was already decades old: a European woman has been shipwrecked or captured by pirates, and is now a captive in the harem of a great sultan. Her European lover arrives, and either he steals her back or (as in this case) the sultan turns magnanimous and lets the couple go free. The second *entrée*, to which we shall return, features a tale of Peru under the *conquistadores*. The third *entrée* – *Les fleurs: Fête persane* (The Persian Flower Festival) – offers a lighthearted farce involving only locals, the central figure being a prince who disguises himself as a woman in order to find out if his beloved Fatima really loves him. Some audience members in 1735 objected to the indignity of the gender disguise. As a result, for performances a year later, Fuzelier and Rameau substantially rewrote the words and music of this *entrée*.

The final, North American *entrée* (written for the 1736 performances) gives the local woman – Zima – a choice of several lovers: a jealous and possessive Spaniard named Don Alvar; a flighty and faithless Frenchman, Damon; and – her eventual and wise choice – a fellow native named Adario. This *entrée* contains one of the most widely known numbers from *Les Indes*: the celebratory chorus of the "savages," "Forêts paisibles" ("Peaceful forests").[34]

In this "American Indian" chorus Rameau was plainly eager to give an appropriate musical profile to a distant people.[35] He based "Forêts paisibles" on a harpsichord piece, *Les sauvages*, that he had composed in 1728 with the intention of (as he put it) "characteriz[ing]" a dance performance that he had witnessed on a Paris stage by two members of a Native North American tribe who had been transported from "Louisiana" (i.e., the vast French territories extending up the Mississippi into Canada).[36]

Example 5.2 Rameau, "Les sauvages," harpsichord piece (published 1728), which was later arranged by Rameau for voices and orchestra and inserted into the new *entrée* "Les sauvages" that ends his 1736 revision of *Les Indes galantes*.

Rameau's word "characterized" can be taken several different ways. The energetic arpeggiated thrusts assigned first to the right hand, then to the left (Ex. 5.2), can be understood as mimicking what Rameau had seen at the performance. As the *Mercure de France* reported at the time, the two visitors from across the Atlantic had mimed and danced a number of scenes: forming an alliance (by passing the peace-pipe), launching battle against an enemy tribe, experiencing the horrors of war, and rejoicing with a dance of victory. Similarly, the underlying rhythm of long-short-short (half and two quarters, or half and four eighths) may conceivably echo what Rameau had heard: some foot-stomping, and the drum-beating with which (as the *Mercure* reported) one of the dancers accompanied the other's hunt for the enemy.

Miriam Whaples, in the spirit of the Full-Context Paradigm, proposes a less literal reading: "Rameau was characterizing not the actual performance that he had seen [and the drum-beating] so much as a real or imagined nobility of bearing, a natural dignity, a quality of soul."[37] In any case, as Catherine Cole has recently stressed, what is truly significant about the whole *entrée* is not this one possible case of "native sounds in a French score" but Fuzelier's and Rameau's decision to put "good savages" at the center of the action throughout the *entrée* instead of confining them to a decorative *divertissement*. "Rameau crafts a complex yet easily audible semiotics made up of instrumentation, mode, and harmony that constructs cultural difference very effectively … by manipulating the conventions at his disposal."[38]

Rameau's Huascar: corrupt ruler and anticolonial terrorist

This utterly revolutionary project of portraying a contemporary society of Others is carried out even more dramatically in the second *entrée*, *Les Incas du Pérou*, and, again, mostly without recourse to exotic-sounding materials. To be sure, *Les Incas* contains several major numbers that display ancient-"weird" features, notably the orchestral march and dances for the Incas' Festival of the Sun, and – to bring the *entrée* to an impressive end – the orchestral portrayal, supported by onstage mechanical contrivances, of a volcano erupting. But equally striking is what occurs in the sections that do not sound in any way foreign, such as the first section of this *entrée*. The Rameau authority Sylvie Bouissou dismisses these opening pages as comparatively "weak."[39] Less colorful they surely are. Yet, I would argue, Fuzelier and Rameau accomplish something crucial here: letting us see and hear the central character of the *entrée* – the Incan high priest Huascar – as he attempts to manipulate the Incan maiden Phani into marrying him.

Several moments in this section are particularly revealing of Huascar's qualities (positive and negative) and, by extension, those of the non-Western tradition that he represents. The first of these is a short but trenchant *air* that (as Girdlestone put it in his famous book on Rameau) conveys the Incan priest's "blustering and domineering character."[40] Through short scalar fragments and largish leaps, and of course through the words, Huascar tells Phani that "we" – in other words, she – must obey the will of heaven *sans balancer* (that is, without thinking for herself – see Figure 5.2).

Obéissons sans balancer	Let us obey without hesitation
Lorsque le ciel commande!	When heaven commands!
Nous ne pouvons trop nous presser	We cannot hasten quickly enough
D'accorder ce qu'il nous demande;	To comply with what it [heaven] asks of us.
Y réfléchir, c'est l'offenser.	To [pause and] reflect upon it [the request] is to offend it [heaven].

The imitative texture of this aria seems to symbolize, in context, the very act of blind obedience that Huascar is demanding of Phani. At times Huascar "obeys" one of the two instrumental lines, at times one of those instrumental

Figure 5.2 Rameau, *Les Indes galantes* (1735–36): Huascar (Bernard Delétré) lording it over a momentarily cowed Phani (Isabelle Poulenard), in the work's second *entrée*, *Les Incas du Pérou*. From a 1991 production by L'Opéra de Montepellier. (©Michel Szabo / Les Arts Florissants.)

lines echoes him (Ex. 5.3), and the resulting somewhat mechanical quality feels (in the context of Huascar's rhetorical onslaught) coercive – quite the opposite of the considered weighing of evidence for and against various arguments that was so central to Enlightenment thought. This is a clear instance of exotic portrayal without exotic style, the very type of passage that, like those discussed above from *Belshazzar*, can be encompassed by the Full-Context Paradigm but not by the Exotic-Style Paradigm.[41]

Huascar here shows himself to be an unworthy ruler, abusing his religious authority for purely personal gain. His intended conquest of Phani is equivalent to what, in other such tyrant figures, takes the form of greed or of lust for power. Eastern and New World tyrants tend to display other

Example 5.3 Rameau, *Les Indes galantes*, deuxième entrée: *Les Incas du Pérou*, "Obéissons sans balancer." (The version here is based primarily on Paris Opéra ms. A.132.a, plus the edition – published c. 1740 – of the music of *Les Indes* "arranged into four large concerts." Clefs and time signatures have been modernized.)

deplorable behaviors as well, such as blind rage, erratic behavior, or excessive interest in the charms of the opposite sex – as well as, in the case of Muslims, drunken excess (which is often presented as a hypocritical flouting of the Qur'anic strictures against imbibing alcohol). The people of the exotic country in question are rarely shown as resenting the tyrant's oppressive rule. This suggests that they have little sense of the virtues that are appropriate for a king (or, by extension, for his subjects: themselves). Admittedly, the Incas, in honoring the Sun, praise the power of nature's light and also evince their own collective social dignity.[42] But they give no hint of envisioning a truly beneficent social structure, an en*light*ened (rational, moderate) despotism, rather than the Incas' current be*night*ed one.

One Inca, Phani, proves an exception. She thereby suggests the potential in her people as a whole. Phani may be a simple maiden, but her way of responding to Huascar's threats (soon after Ex. 5.3) demonstrates her intuitive grasp of Enlightenment rationality as well as the healthy influence of her Spanish soldier-boyfriend Carlos. Phani observes coolly – her music here is relatively unruffled – that people who "speak in the name of the gods" are often guilty of "imposture." Huascar parries with claims that are yet more emphatic and egocentric, and with excitable, angular melody: "What a heinous insult to the Gods and to me!" ("Pour les Dieux et pour moi, quelle coupable injure!"). Fuzelier, in his preface to the libretto, worded Phani's accusation more bluntly: Huascar typifies "imposture hidden under the sacred cloak of religion" – presumably meaning "any religion." The librettist thereby made as clear as he could, without risking censorship (or worse) from the government and the Catholic Church, that Huascar, though presented within the drama as a "pagan sacrificer" (Fuzelier's term), could also stand for any prominent member of a clerical hierarchy – including, presumably, a bishop or a pope – who abuses religious authority for selfish ends.[43]

In the final phase of the exchange with Phani, Huascar reveals that he knows that she loves a Spanish soldier. He even tries invoking a native patriotism to win Phani away from his European rival.

C'est l'or qu'avec empressement,	It is gold that these barbarians devour – eagerly,
Sans jamais s'assouvir, ces barbares dévorent.	Without ever being sated.
L'or qui de nos autels ne fait que l'ornement	Gold, which is mere ornament on our altars,
Est le seul Dieu que nos tyrans adorent.	Is the only God that these men who tyrannize us adore.[44]

Huascar's castigating words here are utterly remarkable, revealing a native nobility that even eighteenth-century Parisian courtiers might cautiously admire. The Spanish conquerors, the Incan priest accuses, are "barbarians" motivated, not by belief in one God and in salvation through Christ (as they claim), but by greed.[45]

Minutes earlier, Phani had warned Carlos that the "barbarous" Incas might do him harm if he tried to have her flee with him. Here, by contrast, Huascar applies the word *barbares* to the (supposedly civilized) Europeans. Rameau places its accented second syllable on an eloquently intense high F. And he brings Huascar's prosecuting statement to a forceful close with what is, within the context of Rameauian recitative, a most emphatic cadence: two successive falling fifths in the voice part, over the strong progression I^6–ii^6–I^6_4–V^7–I. On one recording, the singer Bernard Delétré adds a derisive portamento to connect the two opening words "C'est l'or."[46] This may serve as a reminder of how a skillful performer can carry out the implications of a musicodramatic work. And, in the case of an exotic work, how that same performer can intensify the exoticness, by means that are inherently neutral (ethnically unmarked) and would have served quite different purposes in other contexts.

Huascar's tirade about the Spaniards' thirst for gold thus shows him as an aggrieved, untiring, and increasingly persuasive representative of a colonized people: an agitator against the oppressor. The nobility of Huascar's political stance, however, is corrupted by his "furious love" (as he puts it).[47] Huascar eventually rolls a boulder into a volcano, in order to make it erupt. (His plan is that this will scare Phani into running to safety with him.) Enlightenment writers would have not hesitated to call this an act of "terror" typical of despotic governments.[48] Huascar is here attempting to exploit the ignorance of Phani and the other Peruvians by appealing to their fear of Divine retribution. Furthermore, he is strikingly juxtaposed with the rational man of science (Carlos), who, before the cataclysm begins, appears and explains Huascar's heinous act to Phani.

The Incan maiden, her eyes now open, rejects Huascar one last time. The evildoer recognizes – in accordance with the standard Enlightenment plot of "the tyrant corrected" – that he has betrayed the ethical injunctions of his own religion. Or, as Enlightenment thinkers might have said, the ethical injunctions of all religion, all proper philosophy. Catherine Cole notes a likely endotic message that is yet more specific than the one discussed earlier regarding Huascar's claim to know the gods' will. Huascar's manipulative use of his scientific knowledge, Cole points out, "perfectly illustrates the Enlightenment stereotype of a corrupt priest, a clergyman who manipulates his people by abusing their credulous 'superstition' concerning the natural environment."[49]

Thanks to Carlos's alertness and scientific savvy, the natives and the Spaniards now run clear of the cascading lava, while the orchestra plays an extended passage that is heard (in context) as rumbling, surging, and violent – and not at all as Incan. (A volcano has no ethnic identity.) Huascar sacrifices himself under the molten flow, thereby restoring, it is implied, the social order. One final time in this *entrée*, the portrayal of the doings, and undoing, of a mostly nefarious – but also briefly admirable – exotic leader has been deepened and intensified by music that the "Exotic Style Only" Paradigm cannot encompass but the "All the Music in Full Context" Paradigm can.

How did people read Huascar in 1736, or decades later, when that particular *entrée* was still being performed, almost on the eve of the French Revolution? Did the audience see him only as an Incan tyrant, or did they see him the way that many in Handel's London audience presumably saw Belshazzar: as – to follow Fuzelier's hint – an instance of a broader category, namely the unworthy ruler of a potentially noble and humane people (in which case, that people could potentially be understood as Us, not Them)? To what extent did the audience members reflect on the justice of his (musically assisted) rage against the destruction wreaked by the Spanish "barbarians"? On the one hand, we risk engaging in ventriloquism – anachronism, or, as some call it, presentism – if we assert that the audience "must surely have noticed" meanings that, though not manifest on the surface of the work, strike us as self-evident today. On the other, we engage in twenty-first-century smugness if we insist that various of these readings could not possibly have occurred to people of an earlier era.

Finally, should we nowadays update or "relocate" *Les Indes* in some way? After all, the sociocultural situation in which we find ourselves is vastly different from that of Early Modern France, which was experiencing the heady excitement of getting to know, and beginning to claim and settle, large swaths of the Western hemisphere. We shall consider this problem in a general way, and also with regard to *Les Indes*, in Chapter 11.

6 | A world of exotic styles, 1750–1880

The two Baroque-era works from the 1730s–40s discussed in the preceding chapter carry out their exotic portrayals in a manner largely typical for their day: they employ dramatic (verbal and scenic) devices that register as overtly exotic but musical devices that – either for the most part (Rameau's *Les Indes galantes*) or entirely (Handel's *Belshazzar*) – do not.

In the subsequent century and a half – across the eras of Mozart, Beethoven, Rossini, Berlioz, Liszt, Brahms, and Tchaikovsky – a whole range of musical styles arose that were understood by anyone familiar with the conventions of Western classical music as indicating this or that locale. The composers using these styles came from, or were active in, many different places. In *España* (1883), the French composer Emmanuel Chabrier conveyed his fascination with the music he had heard – and eagerly transcribed – in a *café cantante* in Seville.[1] Nikolai Rimsky-Korsakov, a Russian, evoked in *Sheherazade* (1888) the legendary Middle East. And, as early as 1849, Louis Moreau Gottschalk's *La bamboula, danse de nègres* (Bamboula, Dance of the Negroes) conveyed African-American traditions through the ears of a New Orleans-born composer whose mother was a French-speaking Louisianan and whose father was a London-born Jew. When *La bamboula* was published, the twenty-year-old was already actively concertizing in Paris. He spent some of his later years giving concert tours of his music in the Caribbean and Brazil. (Indeed, a rich topic deserving exploration is the way in which European styles redolent of exotic places – or, more generally, European portrayals of such places – were perceived in various colonized non-European locales.[2])

No lexicon of ethnic/national styles – that is, of styles that were perceived as exotic by many culturally educated Europeans – was written down at the time, much less published. Nor has such a lexicon been compiled since then by scholars, though certain dialects (e.g., *alla turca*, Polish, Hungarian-Gypsy, and Andalusian) have been studied in detail. Nonetheless, a set of symbolic equivalences clearly existed in the minds of composers, performers, and listeners alike. And the equivalences were disseminated, enriched, and altered by the continuing production of musical works written in the foreign (or supposed-foreign) style in question.

Certain of these national/regional/exotic styles were inherited from the Baroque era. Leonard Ratner, in his pathbreaking study of mid- to late eighteenth-century stylistic *topoi* (or, as he calls them, "topics"), includes some *topoi* that carried national, regional-ethnic, or exotic associations, such as *contredanse* (derived from the English country dance), French overture, polonaise, sarabande, siciliano, Swabian allemande, and Turkish (Janissary) style.[3] Transcriptions of folk tunes were published in increasing numbers, starting in the late eighteenth century and continuing into the nineteenth. From these, too, many a composer extracted stylistic features typical (or thought to be typical) of a given people or region.

The result was a kind of lexicon – widely understood, yet never written down – of exotic and national styles.[4] This informal lexicon arose in close parallel with certain new or newly important instrumental genres during the early to mid-nineteenth century, notably (for orchestra) the opera overture, concert overture, and symphonic poem and (for piano) the character piece, fantasy, and rhapsody. One early practice was to devote a single movement in a concerto, symphony, or sonata – often a finale – to national or exotic material, as Mozart did in the case of the "Rondo alla turca" (the finale of the Sonata in A Major, K331) and the Fifth Concerto ("Turkish") for Violin and Orchestra, K219.

How this lexicon of exotic and national styles developed and functioned in such genres is matter for the present chapter. We shall note a number of stylistic options that were used for portraying the exotic in instrumental works, look more closely at two such exotic style dialects – the *alla turca* style and (more obviously overlapping with the category of "national") the Hungarian-Gypsy style – and explore how they are manifested in, respectively, Mozart's aforementioned "Rondo alla turca" and Liszt's Hungarian Rhapsody No. 14. These two pieces – and some others that we will encounter more briefly – give a sense of how exoticism worked in instrumental genres, especially in the hands of a master composer. We shall also give some attention to eighteenth-century "Turkish" operas and their dramatic application of the style that Mozart used in his "Rondo alla turca."

One might suppose that the pieces of music in this chapter would be easier to discuss than were the Handel and the Rameau works in Chapter 5, precisely because they plainly set out to sound exotic and therefore are more or less fully containable within the well-established Exotic-Style Paradigm.[5] But these works have tricky aspects of their own. For one thing, because the works are (in most cases) purely instrumental, an attempt at discussing them is harder to present in non-technical language than is the case with works that have a substantial verbal, dramatic, or visual component. Nonetheless, I will try to use plain words as much as possible.

The other difficulty has to do with meanings. The meanings that the pieces in this chapter carried were shaped and colored by widespread attitudes and familiar images that are often partially or wholly lost to performers and listeners today. Whereas, in operas (for example), the necessary images and other elements of cultural "framing" were/are supplied directly, an instrumental piece such as Liszt's Hungarian Rhapsody No. 14 may have as part of its cultural background certain preconceptions – even prejudices – about the cultural-ethnic group in question (the Eastern European Roma). Many of these preconceptions are today considered noxious or insulting. Historical distance, though, should enable us to observe such attitudes as they were held by people in the past and to recognize how those attitudes were embodied and made deliciously palatable – or resisted, or appropriated for new purposes – in the musical works.[6]

Eighteenth-century ethnicities

The fact that a style (or "topic") was associated with one locale did not automatically make it exotic to listeners in another. This was particularly true in the seventeenth and eighteenth centuries (i.e., toward the end of what historians call the Early Modern Era). As we noted in Chapter 4, certain styles that were much practiced in each of the countries perceived as the "center" of the European musical world – notably France, Italy, and Germany – were recognized as freely available for adoption by a composer in the other two countries, or indeed anywhere else, such as England, Scandinavia, Spain, Poland, or the various colonized territories of the Western hemisphere. French-style dance suites, Italianate concertos and sonatas, Italian-style (Catholic) church music, German-style (Lutheran) church music – none of these probably counted as exotic in intent and effect when adopted elsewhere. A composer who used one of them was simply partaking of one prevailing option within current Western art-music (and sacred-music) traditions.

Certain specific musical dialects did carry a strong association with places perceived as lying far from the centers of cultural life. For example, the early eighteenth century saw a flourishing of "pastoral"-style pieces (in, say, Corelli's Christmas Concerto) that referred to New Testament shepherds – ancient Middle Easterners, in a sense – viewing the Christ child in the manger. From the sixteenth century onward (as noted in Chapter 5), French and German music lovers enjoyed various foreign dances, such as chaconnes and sarabandes. Neapolitans, in the late sixteenth century, enjoyed vocal pieces known as *moresche* and *todesche*: satirical, sometimes scatalogical portrayals of North African "Moors" and German soldiers – two populations that were considered funny and (we might or might not be surprised to learn) lecherous.[7]

By the early eighteenth century, styles began to proliferate that were strikingly different from the prevailing musical languages of Western Europe and that were specifically localized. Germany's neighbor Poland was an obvious source. Georg Philipp Telemann composed several vibrant Polish-style pieces, and even Johann Sebastian Bach wrote a (milder) *polacca* in the finale to his First Brandenburg Concerto (*c*. 1717).[8] A so-called Turkish style shows up in French and German operas in the middle of the century and also in instrumental works. (More on this in a moment.) A third prominent musical "location" was Scotland. Scottish tunes abound in the publications of late eighteenth-century English musicians around 1770, as in Robert Bremner's book for beginning keyboard players.[9] The piano accompaniment that the publishers added under these Scottish tunes often relies upon drones, in imitation of bagpipes.[10] Not surprisingly, England also experienced a vogue for tunes (real or supposed) from one of its most significant overseas territories, India.[11]

The fascination with an increasing range of ethnic and regional musical traditions received encouragement and quasi-official cultural approbation through the writings of Johann Gottfried Herder (1744–1803). One of the forefathers of folklore studies and of cultural anthropology, Herder urged scholars in his own day to collect the songs that were still being sung, and the stories that were still being told, in the various rural areas of Europe. He argued that, in each such body of folklore was to be found the collective soul of the local populace.[12] Herder's emphasis on cultural specificity led naturally to the conclusion – though he did not express it quite in these terms – that a local tradition is, by definition, not exotic to someone who grew up in that region whereas analogous traditions from almost any other place may well be perceived as exotic by that person.

By Herder's day, people, increasingly concentrated in cities, were losing touch with their country's own rural folk-music traditions. Still, they could read about them, and about the equivalent folk-music traditions of neighboring lands. They could also encounter them by traveling. Telemann lived for a time on an estate in Sorau (now Zary, Poland) while in the service of Count Erdmann. Late in life, in an autobiographical entry for a music encyclopedia, he recalled with evident pleasure the inspiration for his Polish-style pieces:

An observant person could pick up enough ideas from [these Polish bands] in a week to last a lifetime ... In short, this music contains much valuable material, if it is properly treated ... In time, I wrote various grand concertos and trios in this manner which I clothed in Italian dress, with divers[e] adagios and allegros.[13]

Such words signal a new appreciation of the usefulness, to musical art, of local dialects. But this appreciation did not dissolve crucial distinctions between what composers did and what "the folk" did. Quite the contrary (as Matthew Gelbart has recently explained), the discovery of Europe's folk-music traditions in the eighteenth and early nineteenth centuries – starting with Scottish songs – "spark[ed] the polarization of folk and art [music]" throughout the Western world.[14] For our purposes, what is at least as crucial is that many of these traditions – even when watered down – struck composers and their listeners as exotic indeed.

Delightful and vicious Turks: Molière/Lully, Favart, Gluck, Mozart

In the end, it was not Polish, Scottish, or Indian music but Turkish music – more accurately: a limited, distorted, even somewhat fantastical Western version thereof – that would set the model for how a sense of ethnic Otherness might be conveyed and incorporated within Western art-music genres. As Jonathan Bellman notes, *alla turca* was "the first codified expression of the strange and exotic" in Western music and was also "largely burlesque" in tone.[15] We shall see, in the section after this one, the particular features that enabled it to comment on – and call briefly into question – the age's prevailing insistence on decorum and noble gracefulness.[16] First, though, we should deal with the broader issue of how Turks were portrayed in eighteenth-century musical works (especially opera) – whether with or without use of the Turkish style.

Throughout much of the sixteenth and seventeenth centuries, the Ottomans had contended with Venice for control of various Mediterranean islands and ports. They also held large swaths of Europe, from Greece northward to the Balkans and sometimes beyond. In 1683, they laid siege to Vienna (as they had once before, in 1529), but were driven back into southeastern Europe, this time definitively, by Habsburg, Polish, and other forces.

Europeans were understandably fascinated by, yet fearful of, the Turks and their sultan. This obsession with a nearby powerful enemy led to a rage for paintings (by Europeans) of splendid but fiercely guarded Ottoman palaces or of Turkish emissaries in turbans and voluminous robes and for theatrical and other literary works (again, by Europeans) that featured Turkish characters. These Turkish portrayals sometimes carried a second, metaphorical layer of meaning, commenting on societal arrangements *within* the writer's native land. In his widely read essay-collection *Les lettres persanes* (1721), Montesquieu employed an imaginary Turkish visitor as a mouthpiece for his own devastating critique of French government and society. The obsession found a twofold echo in eighteenth-century music: "Turkish" instrumental pieces (to be discussed in the section after this one) and "Turkish" stage works, including operas.

The single most influential Baroque-era Turkish musical theatre work – what Thomas Betzwieser calls the "flint" that sparked the trend – was a lengthy scene within the 1670 *comédie-ballet* by the playwright Molière and the composer Jean-Baptiste Lully entitled *Le bourgeois gentilhomme* (The Bourgeois Who Believed He Was a Gentleman).[17] The scene (Act 4, scene 5) contains no Turkish characters. Rather, a pack of French nobles make fun of the pretentious main character, Monsieur Jourdain, by masquerading as Turks and raising him to the (supposed) esteemed Turkish rank of a Mamamouchi. Many spoken exchanges are carried out in *lingua franca*.[18] For the costumed pseudo-Turks, the composer Lully provided a wonderfully awkward, heavy-footed Turkish March and a literally monotonous chant to the repeated word "Allah."[19] The French courtiers who have donned the Turkish costumes clearly view the Middle East as a hopelessly deficient place, and we may surmise that the audience (and Lully) shared this view.[20]

We have seen (in Chapter 5) that tyrants of ancient and primitive non-Western countries were considered eminently fit for *tragédie lyrique* and *opera seria*, where they often served as a foil to the Western hero. Contemporary-era Turks mostly appeared, instead, in operatic genres that were more or less comic. Some of these Turkish operas relied upon tales found in the *Thousand and One Nights*; others, upon newspaper headlines. The abduction of Europeans by Barbary pirates – a matter of real and recurrent concern – formed the premise for numerous works, two early instances being Rameau's *Le Turc généreux* (see Chapter 5) and an intriguing English work of 1741, *The Happy Captive*. In the latter, the Turks imbibe alcoholic beverages (which, as librettists and audiences alike knew, the Qur'an calls "Satan's handiwork" and an "abomination"). The music, startlingly dissonant for its era, makes the drinkers seem truly out of control.[21]

Various eighteenth-century Turkish operas were based on some version of a plot premise that was quite different in tone: women in a Turkish harem contend with each other, usually in arias, to gain the special favor of the sultan. (The women may include, in an overlapping with the "Turkish

Captivity" plot, some from Europe.) Particularly influential was Favart's *Soliman II, ou Les trois sultanes* (1761, consisting of much spoken dialogue, with short sung numbers composed by Paul-César Gibert). This Favart libretto maintained a life of its own – through translation and adaptation, with new music – in France and other European countries.[22]

One wonders whether the theatergoers of the day took these exotic plot elements as a mix of direct reportage and fairy tale or, perhaps more intriguingly, as Montesquieu-like commentary on situations and political arrangements within Europe itself. How much (in other words) did the exotic surface disguise "endotic" concerns, some of which might not have been safe to speak aloud? Fortunately, in the case of one Middle Eastern opera by Christoph Willibald Gluck (best known today for his *Orfeo ed Euridice*), a politicized reading survives from an eyewitness.

The work in question, *La rencontre imprévue, ou Les pèlerins de la Mecque* (The Unforeseen Encounter; or, The Mecca Pilgrims), was the most extended French comic opera that Gluck composed for Vienna. (The composer later moved to Paris and focused more exclusively on tragic works.) *La rencontre* received its premiere in 1764, though its libretto is based on one that had been written in 1726.[23] Despite the reference to Mecca in its title, the work is set in Cairo. Early on in *La rencontre*, we witness the machinations of a wandering dervish. More accurately, he is a fake-dervish who brazenly takes alms from passersby. To a confederate, he confesses that he himself does not understand the nonsensical pseudo-blessings he utters ("Castagno, castagna, pistafanache," etc.) and that he only cries out Allah's name in order to stimulate donations. In addition, the librettist (the Viennese court poet Louis Hurtaut Dancourt) gave the mendacious mendicant a drinking song and some related dialogue that together make clear that he enjoys good wine – despite the strictures against it in the Qur'an – and, worse, that he does so in a spirit of intolerance and greedy selfishness:

Quel dommage que les Francs puissent en boire. Un breuvage aussi savoureux devrait être réservé pour les enfants du Prophète.

[What a shame that the Franks [i.e., Europeans] can drink some of this. Such a tasty brew should be kept for the children of the Prophet.]

All the while, as the sly oaf makes even clearer in another song, the "stupid people here" whom he has defrauded think him a model of probity and severe self-denial.

Count Karl von Zinzendorf left his impressions of one of the first performances of *La rencontre*. Zinzendorf was a Protestant diplomat who had settled permanently in Vienna and was in the process of converting (under pressure) to Catholicism. In his diary, he noted that the portrayal of the fake-dervish was "a quite biting satire on the [Catholic] monks,"[24] i.e., individuals who (in many people's view) lived a life without toil at the expense of their credulous co-religionists. In addition, as the Count surely knew, monks and the Catholic clergy generally – as well as the many church-run schools – were able to flourish in such countries as France and the Holy Roman Empire because of government protection and even direct funding. An attack on "the monks" (through the camouflage of a Cairo dervish) could thus be read also as simultaneously criticizing European governments.

Turkish exoticism gradually spread to more and more prestigious stages across Europe. (We can safely take "Turkish" in a broad sense, as people did at the time, to include the North African regions that were Ottoman-controlled.) In 1783, Grétry's *La caravane du Caire* (The Cairo Caravan) would bring the Islamic Middle East, and an *opéra-comique* bounciness, onto the stage of the otherwise, by that date, rather stodgily sober Paris Opéra. Meanwhile, as a result of various diplomatic and military engagements between the Ottomans and Austria-Hungary, a spate of German works had continued to spin more variations on the Turkish Captivity/Generous Sultan theme, culminating in Mozart's youthful marvel *Die Entführung aus dem Serail* (The Abduction from the Harem, 1782).[25]

Mozart's work features what is perhaps the most memorable and disturbing portrayal of a non-European individual, *as* a non-European, to survive into today's operatic repertoire. Osmin is the overseer of Pasha Selim's estate, and he is presented as conniving, hypocritical (about, again, the Qur'anic prohibition on drinking wine), full of hatred toward Christians, and a near-rapist (in his scene with Blonde, the captive Englishwoman who, however, outwits him – to the delight of audiences then and now). These traits are emphasized in highly distinctive music, including some passages inspired by the singer for whom the role was written (who was capable of plunging into a very low register for comic effect) and other passages indebted to the frantic poundings of the *alla turca* style.

The Turkish style also marks the opening and closing sections of the work's overture, as well as two choruses for the Turkish women and men.[26] Again, did people take this music, these characterizations, as some kind of "window" onto another civilization? A comment made in 1840, two generations after Mozart's day, by an astute observer – the Russian, but German-trained, music enthusiast and amateur scholar Aleksandr Ulibichev (Oulibicheff) – suggests that many of them probably did:

The Persians and the Turks would not recognize themselves in these Choruses of Janissaries, but we Europeans recognize them perfectly ... Mozart [here] introduces frequent prolonged unisons and a few of the modulations most characteristic of primitive song. Minor and major alternate continually, with [a resulting alternation between] a sort of savage jubilation and a joyousness that borders on melancholy, which come totally from the Orient.[27]

Even today, the Turkish music in *Die Entführung* can startle a listener – especially when it is reinforced by numerous percussion instruments (left unnotated by Mozart, in accordance with the practice of the day), as is aggressively realized in the recording conducted by Nikolaus Harnoncourt.[28]

The Turkish style

Though the Turkish style became well known in the latter decades of the eighteenth century through its use in certain operas of the sorts just discussed, significant elements of it had also been circulating for decades or even centuries in purely instrumental numbers associated in some way with the Middle East, most notably in seventeenth-century Hungarian lute pieces labeled "Törökös" (Turkish).[29] A *Marche des janissaires* (the Janissaries were the Ottoman army's elite corps) survives in several seventeenth- and early eighteenth-century manuscripts for keyboard and was, Thomas Betzwieser reveals, inserted into Campra's much-performed opera-ballet *L'Europe galante* (in its *entrée* about Turkey).[30] A dance called *La Turque* (or *Contredanse turque*) crops up in various eighteenth-century manuscripts and was published around 1750 in one of the *concertos comiques* of Michel Corrette. Another Corrette piece, a *Concerto turc*, was performed in 1742 in Paris, in honor of the Turkish ambassador Zaid Effendi, and in 1758 at Vienna's Burgtheater, for the Turkish consul Resmi Achmet. One also finds various published Greek and Cypriot dances that seem stylistically congruent with these explicitly "Turkish" numbers – not surprisingly, given that Greece and Cyprus were Ottoman-controlled.[31]

Thanks to these Turkish-style keyboard and orchestral pieces, and thanks to the aforementioned operas, ballets, and other stage works that made occasional use of similar styles, the music-loving public throughout the Western world acquired a recognizable sonic image of the Middle East. This Turkish (or *alla turca* or Janissary) style was a complex of generally noisy sonic materials derived, in large part, from the military music of Janissary troops (see Fig. 6.1) or, rather, from Western impressions and distant memories thereof. The style (to be described in Figure 6.3 below)

Figure 6.1. Early eighteenth-century painting of a *mehter* (Janissary military or ceremonial band) by the Turkish miniaturist Abdülcelil Levni (late seventeenth century–1732). Levni served as court painter to Sultan Ahmed III. The painting shown here is part of his famous illustrated manuscript entitled *Surname-i Vehbi* (The [Illustrated Festival] Book of [the Poet Hüseyn] Vehbi). Three musicians riding camels play pairs of kettledrums (*kös*) with two heavy-headed beaters. On horseback, twenty other musicians play the trumpet (*boru*), cymbals (*zil*), and – with a curved beater in one hand and a light stick in the other – cylindrical drum (*davul*). European memories of the loud, highly rhythmic music of bands such as the one depicted here remained strong for more than a century after the lengthy but ultimately unsuccessful Ottoman siege of Vienna in 1683. (By permission of the Topkapı Museum, Istanbul.)

quickly found a home in comic operas (particularly German and Austrian), where it most frequently occurred in conjunction with portrayals of male Islamic power. Some of these portrayals were noble and frightening. Pasha Selim in Mozart's *Die Entführung aus dem Serail*, chillingly, speaks all of his lines, as if he is so powerful that he can refuse to sing like the rest of the characters. More often the portrayals were ridiculous, though with an undertone of menace: platoons of waddling Turkish guards in puffy trousers, conniving merchants, and lascivious government officials (such as Osmin).[32]

Another intriguing Mozart case is Monostatos, in *Die Zauberflöte*. This somewhat puzzling character is repeatedly called a "Moor" and "black," and he calls himself "ugly" (*häßlich*).[33] But "black" could, for northerners, simply mean "darker than us," and "Moor" generally meant Arab. The opera is set in a highly imaginary version of Egypt, mixing pharaonic and Muslim characteristics and adding a male protagonist who wears a splendid *javonischen* hunting costume. (Scholars take the word in the original printed libretto as a misprint for either "Japanese" or "Javanese.") The fact that the Moor has been put in charge of the abducted Pamina makes him, in effect, a harem guard. In his one aria, he announces that he will force himself on the sleeping Pamina ("A white woman has captured me ... I must kiss her"), and he tells the moon to close its eyes if it is distressed by what it is about to see. The orchestra's part in the aria is performed in a sneaky *pianissimo*. It abounds in Turkish-style figurations (such as are discussed below) and features relentless rapid forward motion – suggesting Monostatos's unbridled lust – and a nearly continuous, fidgety part for flute (in high register) and piccolo playing in unison. Monastatos's singing part is written for what is sometimes called a "character-tenor": a voice-type that, though not conventionally full or beautiful, is well suited to spitting out quickly the humorously repulsive words.[34]

Most of all, the Turkish style was associated with certain percussion instruments: cymbals and large drum (see Figs. 6.1 and 6.2), both of which were commonly used by the Janissary bands, but also triangle, which perhaps was inspired by the Turkish *çağana*, a crescent-shaped rattle with small bells. (Western adaptations of the *çağana*, but using a long pole, acquired a variety of names, including Turkish crescent, jingling johnny, and *chapeau chinois* – literally, "Chinese hat."[35]) Janissary bands also contained loud wind instruments – notably the *zurna* (an instrument similar to the Western oboe but with a fuller, more cutting sound) and the *boru* (trumpet). This may explain composers' frequent recourse to loud dynamic levels or, in pieces for or with orchestra, uninhibited use of wind instruments, from the piccolo down to the trombone.

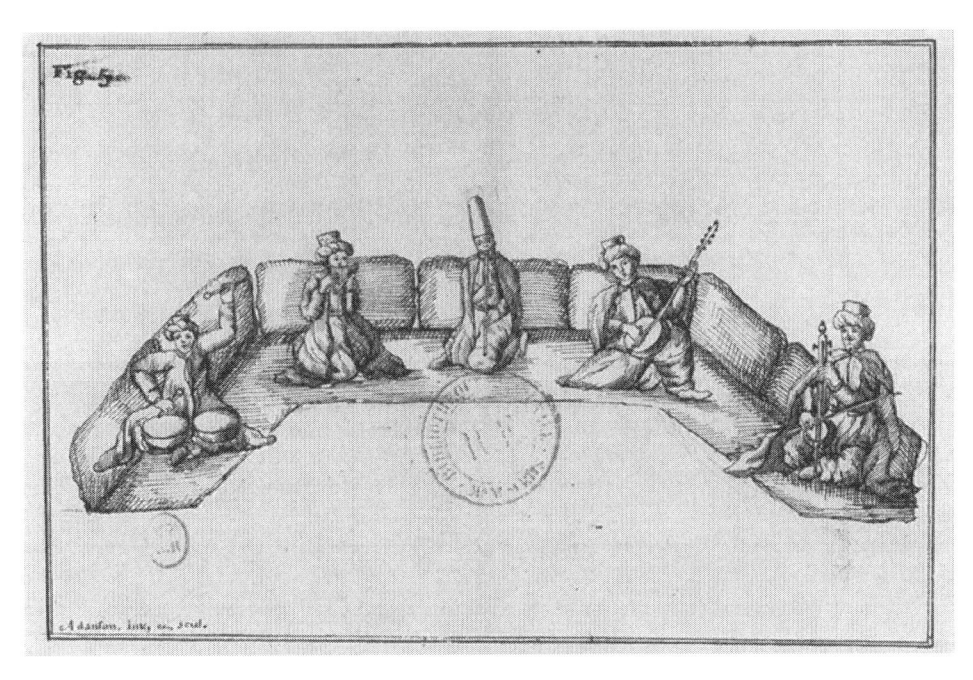

Figure 6.2 Turkish musicians with *dümbelek*, *miskal*, *ney*, *tambur*, and *ayakh keman*. Ink drawing, c. 1750, by Jean-Baptiste Adanson (see Neubauer, *Essai*, 4–6).

No doubt because the style was so limited, it was never applied to many numbers in a single opera. Nonetheless, a single chorus or march, or even a few distinctive phrases in the overture, could guide audience reaction to other elements in a "Turkish" opera (including the solo female characters, even though they almost never sing music of Orientalized hue).[36]

Despite its narrow range of moods, the Turkish style drew upon a surprisingly large number of stylistic traits. These were combined and elaborated with great sophistication in several instrumental works by Mozart. The scintillating set of variations for piano K455 (1784), based on the song of Gluck's fake-dervish discussed earlier, makes much play with certain features of *alla turca* style: unison, octave, and broken-octave textures as well as, in the right hand, quick on-beat decorative turns.[37] The last movement of the Violin Concerto in A Major, K219 (1775), consists of an elegant French-style minuet that is, however, interrupted by a wild Turkish (or, as several scholars suggest, an alternatingly Hungarian-Gypsy and Turkish) interlude. At one point, the players in the orchestra are instructed to play *col legno*: that is, with the bow upside down, wood rapping percussively against string. The minuet then returns to end the piece. The stylistic juxtaposition gives a somewhat humorous impression, as if two cultural worlds were colliding and yet each stubbornly refused to let itself be altered by the experience or even to admit awareness of the other's existence.[38] *Alla turca* also occurs in numerous other pieces of the Classic era, sometimes glancingly (as in the last movement of Mozart's Serenade in B-flat Major for thirteen wind instruments, K361), and sometimes blatantly, as in the Turkish March from Beethoven's incidental music to the pageant *Die Ruinen von Athen* (The Ruins of Athens, 1811).[39]

The more strictly stylistic features of *alla turca* touch upon all of the usual components that go into musical composition: melody, harmony, rhythm, harmonic rhythm, phrase structure, texture, orchestration, and so on. I would propose that *alla turca*, in many ways, set the pattern – in part because of the impact of Mozart's pieces in the style – for exotic "dialects" in Western music and the stylistic experimentation that often went along with them. For that reason, its features are worth listing in detail. I present them more completely than has been done by previous scholars.[40] The interested reader may wish to compare Figure 6.3 with the list of broadly exotic stylistic features in Figure 3.1. Though no attempt is made here to follow the same sequence of parameters, the many parallels will be evident.

(1) Preference for **keys with few flats or sharps**. (These keys were presumably viewed at the time as "simple.") Most notable are **A minor** and its two most closely related major keys: A major and C major; less often, B-flat major, G minor, or G major.[41]

(2) **Simple harmonic vocabulary** with primarily root-position chords and relatively **little harmonic change** (if harmony is present at all).

(3) A seemingly opposed tendency: **sudden shifting from one tonal area to another**. This is particularly striking when the keys are distant from each other, such as modulations by a third, or differ in mode (or both: A minor to F major, for the middle section of the first Janissary chorus in *Entführung*).

(4) **Duple meter**, especially 2/4, less often 4/4 and *alla breve* (marked the usual way: ₵). This predominance of duple meter may relate to military traditions, such as the "quick march," but the downbeat here is frequently given

heavy emphasis. Intended may be the extreme disparity between loud and soft beats in Middle Eastern drumming. These alternating low and high sounds, onomatopoeically called *dum* and *tek* by Turkish musicians, are produced by very different effects, for example, by a large stick (*dum*) vs. a brush or switch (*tek*), or by the heel of the hand in the center of the drumhead vs. tapping of the fingers along the rim.[42]

(5) **Repeated notes (or thirds)** in melodies; and repeated notes (or thirds or chords) in accompanimental patterns. Also, at a higher structural level, almost incessantly **repeated brief rhythmic figures** in the accompaniment, such as a bass line in broken octaves.[43]

(6) **Specific repeated rhythmic patterns** in the accompaniment, arguably equivalent to some of the simpler of the dozens of rhythmic modes that are used in Middle Eastern music and known in Turkish as *usul* (in Arabic, *darb*). Previous scholars have denied or minimized this particular borrowing, but it is surely not by chance that so many prominent examples of *alla turca* music employ some version of one basic rhythmic pattern: | Long Long | short short Long |.[44]

(7) **Unison textures** (or extensive doubling at the octave), sometimes over a pedal accompaniment, with a resulting limited participation of harmony in the writing. Related but less extreme textures include: (a) use of "forbidden" **parallel octaves**; also (b) not-forbidden but extensive (excessive?) parallel part-writing, for example, **doubling** the main part at the third, sixth, or octave over many beats or measures.

(8) Extensive use, in the melody, of a scalar descending line decorated with **neighbor notes** or **escape notes**.[45] Sometimes the undecorated descending scale is played simultaneously in another instrumental part, producing a heterophonic effect.

(9) In the melodic line, **long note-values at the beginning of a phrase**, followed by shorter ones.

(10) Frequent turns, short trills, and other **quick melodic decorations**, especially acciaccaturas and the like (which

land on the beat, creating little bursts of dissonance with the other parts).

(11) **Melodic motion** that either moves **rapidly stepwise up and down** (often within a narrow distance, such as a third) or else **"hops" back and forth between two notes** that lie a third, a fourth, or sometimes a fifth apart.

(12) **Loud playing** and (in orchestral works) **full instrumentation**, using such instruments as horns, trumpets, trombones (decades before the latter were put to regular use in purely symphonic music, notably by Beethoven), and timpani. Sometimes the loud playing is pointedly juxtaposed with passages that are softer and/or less (or not at all) "Turkish" in style.

(13) **Percussion instruments**: especially bass drum, cymbals, and triangle. Some keyboard instruments were outfitted with "Janissary" devices that (when engaged) rattled and banged in ways that mimic these percussion instruments.

(14) **Modal touches in the melodic line**, especially the raised fourth degree. The raised fourth served as an apparent allusion to the Lydian mode or to various non-Western scales that had been published in scientific and travel books over the past century or so. In the first Janissary chorus of *Entführung*, Mozart further activated this astonishing fourth degree by doubling it at the lower third, all over a tonic pedal. The result is a II^7 chord which subverts the sense of tonal clarity by moving directly back to the tonic chord ($D^7 \rightarrow C$) instead of functioning the way it "should" in tonal harmony (namely as a secondary dominant resolving to a G-major chord).

(15) **Phraseological inanity or impulsivity**, seen in such things as: (a) stubborn repetition of short phrases or motives, and heavy-footed or abrupt endings of phrases (e.g., closing every phrase with a long note and then a rest); (b) literal sequential repetition (upwards or downwards) of a single motive or phrase, sometimes for a total of three or more statements; or (c) the sudden intrusion of a phrase with an odd number of measures (especially coming after a series of highly regular phrases).

(16) **Simplicity of phrase structure and form**. Many "Turkish" numbers (for example, Turkish-style movements, or passages, in instrumental works such as Mozart's sonata and violin concerto) are constructed of a chain of short, independent statements using regular balanced phrases (the opposite of style feature 15!) and build larger sections by use of simple additive forms such as ABA and rondo (ABACABA).

(17) Other features that somehow **"characterize" the area and its inhabitants** when used in this context. For example, **quick patter** in numbers for a comic bass character who is a Turk – especially when European characters in the same opera do not sing this way – can be read as a commentary on the perceived garrulousness (i.e., lack of reasonableness) not just of the one individual but of Middle Easterners, generally. Similarly, an aria whose **structure seems intentionally confused or irresolute** might normally imply all-purpose comic confusion but, in Turkish operas, can be read as implying a more specific or inherent limitation of Turks and their leaders.[46]

Figure 6.3 Component traits of the *alla turca* style (or "topic"), c. 1750–1830.

It should be stressed that none of these features is (in the logician's sense) a "necessary" marker of Middle Easternness. That is to say, no one of them is so absolutely essential that it will be found in every musical work invoking the Middle East. A few of them do border on being "sufficient." For example, the escape-note descent (feature 8 above) is so specific and stands in such sharp contrast to prevailing Western styles that it must have signaled Middle Easternness rather reliably to listeners at the time. Mozart admitted that the Turkish devices were well understood by his audience. He wrote to his father that he intentionally incorporated them into *Entführung* because "those Viennese gentlemen" liked hearing them and would expect them – and find them comical – in an opera set in Turkey.[47]

The greater majority of the features in Figure 6.3 are neither necessary indicators nor sufficient ones. Duple meter (style feature 4) is encountered throughout much European music of that era. It cannot therefore specify, by itself, an exotic location, much less comment on it. Nor can unison and other thin textures, heavy downbeats, on-beat ornaments, phrases of odd length, or the use of ABA and other simple forms. Similarly, cymbals and drums found their way in the eighteenth century into European military music (thanks, originally, to contact with the Ottomans) and, by the late 1790s, into symphonic music. This makes it hard to judge whether or not one is hearing a shadow of the "Turkish threat" in certain movements that employ a military-style march (often complete with cymbals and either bass drum or timpani). The most heavily debated such instance is the tenor-and-men's-chorus passage in B-flat from the finale of Beethoven's Ninth Symphony; another instance is the Haydn Symphony No. 100 in G Major (1793–94, nicknamed the "Military"). Still, when several of the features in Figure 6.3 are used simultaneously, or in close succession, the total package could (and can) suffice to suggest the Middle East to any listener familiar with the standard options within Western music of the late eighteenth and early nineteenth centuries.

Part of what makes many features in Figure 6.3 so effective at rendering a sense of Turkishness (for listeners at the time) was, remarks Mary Hunter, that they function, not so much as "an imitation of an original" but rather "as a translation of a [widely held] *perception* of Turkish music." And also as a translation of a broader perception of Turks and their doings. That is, the (perceived) incoherence and eruptiveness of Turkish music (e.g., feature 15) was consistent with the (supposed) irrational and incontinent behavior of Turkish men in other (non-musical) aspects of their lives, as attested in the widespread accounts (some accurate, others legendary) of their torturing Christians and commanding obedience from multiple wives.[48]

Few of the markers of Turkishness in Figure 6.3 had direct analogues within the actual music of the region at the time. Cymbals and drums did. Unbroken (unvaried) successions of parallel thirds did not, except as an instance of "translating a perception of deficiency," in Hunter's sense (parallel thirds being, within Western music, a "primitive" and unvaried form of harmonic writing). But *alla turca* conventions may be more indebted to Middle Eastern music than we know. Though the transcribed sources for authentic Janissary and other traditional musics of the region from that era are frustratingly few, some of these do show suggestive points of similarity.[49] No less intriguingly, so do some of the aforementioned "Turkish" tunes preserved in old Hungarian lute books. One is struck, especially, by the "hopping-thirds" figure and – less surprisingly because it is ubiquitous in Middle Eastern music even today – the escape-note descent.[50]

One cannot help noticing that, when items on this list do find a rough equivalent within Middle Eastern traditions, the latter is often only the simplest of a number of authentic possibilities within the tradition. For example, take the occasional preference for balanced phrases in 2/4 meter (features 4 and 16).

Descriptions of Middle Eastern music across the centuries have attested the presence of music that (in Western terms) displays these tendencies, particularly in relatively simple folk traditions (e.g., songs of the Bedouins) or in concluding, somewhat up-tempo or dancelike sections of longer instrumental performances (after a freer, more improvisatory opening and perhaps several intervening sections). By contrast, *alla turca* style appears blissfully unaware of more complex and extended rhythmic-structural options within Middle Eastern traditions, such as *usul* patterns of eleven or thirty-one beats.

What nearly all of the items in the list *do* indicate – as Mary Hunter's principle of "translating a perception of deficiency" makes clear – is an intention on the composer's part to deprive the music of the structural and stylistic features typical of Western art music. In particular, the composer avoided those features that tended to be accorded high aesthetic value and intellectual status, such as flexible phrase structure, smooth and goal-oriented modulation techniques, full four-part writing (with the voices moving and resolving in ways prescribed by composition treatises), and clear large-scale formal shaping.

Mozart's *alla turca* non-rondo

One of the best-known pieces of Western classical music is a movement by Mozart, generally known as the "Turkish Rondo" (or "Rondo alla turca," Ex. 6.1) that ends his Piano Sonata in A Major K331 (*c.* 1778 or 1783).[51] Eric Rice has persuasively demonstrated that this Turkish Rondo "may have the strongest relationship with *mehter* [actual music of the Janissary troops] of any 'Turkish' composition in the Western repertory."[52] (Perhaps Mozart had direct or indirect knowledge of certain published travelers' reports, or perhaps he simply agglomerated many of the features that he had encountered in earlier "Turkish" pieces, such as Gluck's overture to *La rencontre imprévue*.) Not surprisingly, the movement features many characteristics from Figure 6.3, some of them repeated to the point of saturation. The *usul* described above (in feature 6) as | Long Long | short short Long | is heard throughout the movement in the bass. In the A section alone, it occurs six times (mm. 1–8, 17–24), and its latter half (short short Long) is heard four times more (in mm. 9–16), transformed into comically striding octave leaps. Melody and harmony are similarly unnuanced or, in a sense, mechanical. In the opening melody, motives are often presented several times – in rising sequence or at the same pitch level – over a single harmony (e.g., the tonic chord in mm. 1–4). This procedure sometimes creates piquant dissonances, as in mm. 5–8: the "passing" thirds in the right hand against the hammering

Example 6.1 Mozart, Piano Sonata in A Major, K331, movement 3, "Alla turca," mm. 1–8.

dominant chords in the left. And that same right-hand passage is decorated by overly insistent double grace-notes (feature 10).

At the same time, many aspects of this movement are normatively Western. The melody's opening four-measure phrase, once one removes the five-times-repeated turn figure (Figure 6.3, feature 10), turns out to be structured by a bold arpeggiated ascent that spans more than an octave, a particularly attention-grabbing, goal-directed melodic pattern that was central to instrumental art music in the Haydn-Mozart era and that sometimes is known today in music histories as the Mannheim Rocket.[53] Furthermore, mm. 8–12 (the passage before the "rounding," i.e., before the return of the opening material) is built upon a brief modulatory progression that is identical to one that is stated (or implied) at that same structural point in numerous eighteenth-century European minor-mode dances and songs.[54]

The mixing of Western and (supposedly) Eastern aesthetic preferences is evident in the accepted name of this Mozart movement: Turkish Rondo. In the late eighteenth century, the concluding movement of a multi-movement instrumental work was most often some kind of rondo, a type of movement related to various European dances, notably the English country dance (known on the Continent as *contredanse*). The name Turkish Rondo is thus, in itself, a bit of a tease. Rondos were not traditionally Turkish, any more than Sauerbraten was part of Turkish cuisine, or the Petrarchan sonnet a Turkish literary genre.

Revealingly, though, the first published version of Mozart's sonata (the autograph is mostly lost) does not use the term "Rondo" at all. The movement is simply entitled "Alla Turca," and the tempo and/or character are indicated as Allegretto (i.e., somewhat fast or cheerful). The movement is, I would say, no rondo at all. Its form has generally been diagrammed as

A B C B A B' coda

Scholars have puzzled about why there are only two statements of A, since rondos always have at least three statements of the basic "rondo theme." One scholar expresses his consternation a bit differently, pondering why there are three thematic statements (B C B) in the "first episode" between the two A's.[55]

The movement is better seen as a ternary form (what is often called ABA form; to avoid confusion here, I shall call it XYX) that has been enriched – or imperiled – by repeated insertion of an eight-measure **Refrain** (the B in the diagram above) at the end of each of the three sections. In other words, the C in the diagram above is really the Y section of an XYX, and the form should be understood as

X Refrain Y Refrain X Refrain' coda

The **Refrain** section screams out deficiency, slamming at the third degree of the scale (C♯) on four of the eight downbeats. Furthermore, this **Refrain** is a mere eight measures long. By contrast, X and Y – i.e., A and C in the first of the two diagrams above – are both in 24-measure rounded-binary form, like thousands of European folk and dance tunes of the era and thousands also of folk-influenced minuets and rondo themes in symphonies, sonatas, and quartets and other chamber works. Both times that this **Refrain** (i.e., B) arrives, it is as if, after a solo by a *zurna* or some other Turkish instrument over steady drumbeats, the whole Janissary ensemble were suddenly joining in with a noisy passage of comment or contrast. (The big rolled chords seem ungainly by intent.) Indeed, a short, loud refrain was a common option in *mehter* music and other traditional Turkish genres of the day.[56]

Mozart chose the sequence of keys across this movement for drastic and repeated contrast between minor and major modes (a supposedly Eastern feature, included as features 1 and 3 in Fig. 6.3). The two X sections are in A minor (Mozart's favorite key for *alla turca* pieces), the three **Refrains** are in A major (parallel major to the main key), and Y is in F-sharp minor (relative minor of A major, the key that has just preceded it). Most strikingly, the **coda** resolves the tension between major and the two kinds of minor by restoring the key of A major. This simultaneously closes the circle of the whole sonata (since A major was the key of the first movement) and averts the disturbing possibility of concluding in the minor mode a sonata that began in the major. In his Turkish opera *Die Entführung aus dem Serail*, Mozart had dared to end an aria for Osmin not just in the minor but in a different key entirely than the one in which the aria had begun. As he explained to his father in a letter, this was justified by Osmin's "towering rage [which] oversteps all the bounds of order, moderation, and propriety."[57] In this keyboard sonata, though, there was no such dramatic justification, and Mozart chose to restore a sense of order through the coda's key. At the same time, he challenged that very sense of order through the coda's material, which is even more insistent and jangly, now featuring acciaccaturas and repeated notes in both hands. By the time we finish listening to this movement, we are exhausted and exhilarated – and perhaps stunned at the sharp contrast between the (persuasively purveyed) gracelessness throughout this (non-)rondo and the suppleness and delicacy of most of the sonata's first movement and all of its middle movement (a Menuetto and Trio).

The renown of this movement by Mozart no doubt contributed greatly to the continuing vogue for Turkish style for several decades. Beethoven's "Turkish March" (from the incidental music to *Die Ruinen von Athen*, 1811) seems to have directly copied Mozart's *usul* and his recurring jangly grace notes. Although the Turkish style is sometimes described as a "passing fashion" and is said to have stopped around 1830,[58] aspects of it continued to crop up in other exotic portrayals, such as the Gypsies' music in Verdi's *Il trovatore* (see Chapter 7), the "Indian March" from *L'Africaine*, and the dance of the Moorish slave-boys in *Aida*. It is more accurate to say that, by the end of the nineteenth century, Turkish style had become only one in a large number of widely understood – sometimes contrasting, sometimes overlapping – ethnic and exotic musical dialects or markers. In the remainder of this chapter, we shall briefly explore this broadening of the (understood, unpublished) exotic lexicon and then look, in particular, at the remarkable style that was and still is – however accurately or inaccurately – associated with the Hungarian Roma (or Gypsies).

The proliferation of exotic and national dialects

Over the course of the nineteenth century, many different national styles were used by composers. People across Europe came to associate them near-automatically with the particular locale. These styles were often based on folk-dance types, such as the Spanish bolero, the Italian tarantella and saltarello, and the German waltz (literally: turning-dance). The barcarolle – long associated with Venetian gondoliers – could become, in Auber's much-performed *La muette de Portici* (The Mute Girl of Portici, 1828), a marker of Italian fishermen in Naples.[59] In Act 1 of Auber's even longer-lived comic opera *Fra Diavolo* (1830), a barcarolle, "Le gondolier fidèle," is sung by an Italian bandit in order to make himself seem an innocent music-loving local to the English Lord Cockburn when he is, in fact, attempting to ingratiate himself with Lady Cockburn and steal her diamond locket. Another Italian feature here is that the bandit accompanies his own singing by playing the mandolin. (The instrument is in fact rendered orchestrally by pizzicato strings. Mozart had portrayed the Spanish guitar in this same manner in *Le nozze di Figaro*. As so often, a device that is nearly place-neutral, namely pizzicato, acquires cultural specificity, and exotic resonance, from the operatic context into which it has been inserted.) Scotland was often represented by bagpipe-type drones, pentatonic melody, and reverse dotted rhythms (i.e., the shorter note is on the beat, producing what is sometimes called the "Scotch snap" and indeed is typical of certain Scottish dances, such as the strathspey).[60] American blackface minstrelsy was indicated, as in Gottschalk's remarkable *Le banjo: Grotesque fantaisie* (1855), by syncopated melodies and textures reminiscent of banjo strumming and picking. Russia could be signaled by chant style and choral harmonies redolent of those of the Orthodox Church. Japan and China were often evoked by pentatonic melodies that (unlike pentatonic melodies signifying Scotland) made use of "chattering" rhythms based on rapid notes of equal duration. And the Middle East was regularly announced by florid melodies (assigned to the oboe or English horn) that were full of augmented seconds and supported by drones (either on degree 1 or on the $\hat{1}$–$\hat{5}$ open fifth) that were rhythmicized using drumbeat patterns supposedly typical of the region. These and many other identifiable "national" dialects were surely felt as exotic by many European (and, in time, American) listeners. For each dialect, one could potentially draw up a detailed list (analogous to Fig. 6.3) of features that readily signaled the locale, especially when several of the features occurred at the same time.

The nineteenth century was, of course, an era of vast economic and industrial expansion in Europe and North America. One of the chief factors in the growing industrial and consumer sectors was the principle of standardization of parts and models (styles of looms, furniture, carriages, umbrellas, silk scarves, and so on). The creators of cultural products, too, seem to have quickly adopted this rationalized approach to generating and then meeting consumer demands. There was little advantage to offering the purchaser a multiplicity of choices, most of which would be quickly rejected. Milking – reprinting, arranging, etc. – an item that had become a public favorite, especially one marked by distinctive stylistic features, was surely a more reliable investment. From the hundreds or thousands of songs published in early nineteenth-century Spain in a wide range of folk and popular styles, pan-European musical life selected only a few for repeated performance and publication – notably Manuel García's songs "Cuerpo bueno, alma divina," and "El contrabandista," and Sebastián Iradier's "La paloma" and "El arreglito." (Bizet freely adapted the first and last of these in Carmen. Liszt wrote a piano piece on "El contrabandista." And "La paloma" has remained an international "standard" up to our own day.[61]) The appeal, in each case, is easy to understand. All four songs are musically attractive and memorable. All contain emphatic Hispanicisms, such as flamenco-like vocal cadenzas, and harmony built on a guitar-derived alternation of the chords V and ♭VI.[62] And, in each song, the words are redolent of images of Spanish life that were thought to be typical (such as smugglers, a woman teasing her passionate lover, and a sailor regretfully leaving Havana and the native Cuban woman he had met there).[63]

The highly selective process of defining a given region, nation, or ethnic group with a few scraps of tune and/or other stylistic features – especially ones that could be straightforwardly conveyed in Western notation – permitted composers and audiences to accumulate an understood (if, as noted earlier, never written-down) "lexicon" of exotic and national styles. These standardized indicators of place could be precise but also narrow. In the case of Norway, as Carl Dahlhaus points out, Grieg's somewhat idiosyncratic version of (half-invented) Norwegian-folk style came to "mean" Norway to most listeners, even though it reflected certain specific aspects of Norwegian traditional (folk) music-making but not other, arguably more significant ones.[64]

One of the insufficiently reported stories about the development of Western art music is its constant self-renewal through contact with nearby folk-music traditions, with ethnic dances from so-called "peripheral" areas of Europe – the (more or less Polish) polonaise, the (originally Bohemian) polka, the (Spanish) bolero – and, increasingly, with non-Western traditions.[65] Tunes in various of these folk and non-Western traditions often use pentatonic or other scales that would be described (by observers steeped in Western art music) as "gapped" or "incomplete." The usual major and minor scales contain seven notes (such as the rising major scale, which, in the version starting on C, runs C–D–E–F–G–A–B and then starts again on the C that is an octave higher than the first C), and the full chromatic scale contains twelve notes (C–C♯–D, and so on). So-called gapped scales contain (most often) only five. The term "gapped" (i.e., incomplete) is blatantly Eurocentric. From the viewpoint of players of a five-note gamelan, or pentatonic instruments in Japan or China, nothing is missing. When, as often in East Asian traditions, additional notes are added by a voice or wind or string instrument, those new notes tend to be understood not as expanding to six or seven the five conceptually foundational pitches but as decorative auxiliaries to them. (Ethnomusicologists sometimes call such additional pitches *pien* tones – from Chinese music theory – or changing tones.) Particularly frequent in music cultures around the world (Andean, Celtic, sub-Saharan, East and Southeast Asian) are pentatonic collections that Westerners would hear and describe as more or less equivalent to the major triad plus degrees 2 and 6: for example, C–D–E–G–A. (The latter five-note collection can be transposed to begin on other notes of the piano – such as all the black notes, starting at F♯. See Chapter 8.)

In most folk and other oral-tradition contexts, pentatonic melodies – whether of this "black-note" or other kinds – are accompanied (if at all) by long-held drone notes, or else several varied versions of the melody are sung or played at the same time (a process known as heterophony). By contrast, the traditions of Western composition have long ordained that a melody be accompanied by chords. Composers and arrangers in the late 1700s and early 1800s often added standard functional chords to pentatonic folk or folk-like melodies, resulting in such then-piquant sonorities as the added-sixth and dominant-ninth chords. Instances appear in minuets and German dances of Haydn and Mozart and more emphatically, a few decades later, in the Viennese waltzes of Joseph Lanner and Johann Strauss, Jr.[66] A notable exception was the Abbé Vogler, an intrepid musical explorer, who composed a quirky piano piece entirely out of the five black-note pitches and named it *Pente chordium* (literally: Five Strings).

By the mid- and late nineteenth century, musicians and early folk-music collectors and arrangers often debated such questions as whether, in adding a piano accompaniment to a pentatonic or other gapped-scale melody (e.g., Scottish, Native American, "Hindostannie," or Javanese), a Western composer should restrict him- or herself to the notes of the pentatonic set or should feel free to bring in all seven notes of the diatonic scale (or even all twelve notes of the full chromatic scale), thereby making possible a rich and tonally "functional" harmonic language typical of the compositional style prevailing in Europe and North America at the time.[67]

Sometimes a composer employed several of these solutions in a single work. Dvořák opens his Symphony No. 9 ("From the New World," 1893) with a melody based on a somewhat unusual "gapped scale." The four-pitch collection – E–G–B–C – is not anhemitonic, B and C being a half-step apart. Furthermore, Dvořák harmonizes the melody with the only two triads that can be made out of those same four pitches (E minor and C major, which are, in the work's home tonality, i and VI). But the first movement goes on to develop this four-pitch tune, extending and inverting its intervals, and supporting these new versions with a wide range of harmonic resources.

Certain genres and performance media lent themselves particularly well to an array of exotic and other ethnic styles. Opera is the most obvious (see Chapters 7–8), as it had the ability to tell stories set in this or that distant locale. But ballet should not be forgotten (as it tends to be, in music-history books). Whole evening-length ballets were now built around plots set in exotic locales. Prominent instances are *La source*, set in Central Asia and based on music by Delibes and Minkus (1866); and two ballets with music by Minkus alone: *Don Quixote* (1869) and *La bayadère* (1877), both composed for St. Petersburg, Russia, but set in, respectively, Spain and India. A famous, extended dream scene from *La bayadère*, "The Kingdom of the Shades," occurs in Hindu heaven (or – in some productions – in a mountainous location that is equivalent to heaven come down to earth). The music is unremarkable in any way. For *Don Quixote*, Minkus added some Spanish tinges to his habitual blandness. Perhaps in part for that reason, the ballet entered the Russian repertoire, stayed there, and, by the late twentieth century, had been taken up – in whole or part – by numerous companies in Europe, America, and Japan. Other late nineteenth-century ballets contained *divertissements* within them, in which characters on stage, just as if this were an opera, are entertained by dancers – that is, by dancers playing dancers – from a variety of distant lands (and, in some cases, from the local countryside). For example, Tchaikovsky's ballet *The Nutcracker* is set in Germany, and its *divertissement* contains dances from Arabia and China, plus a Russian *trepak*.[68]

Sometimes the characters in an opera or ballet are not so much entertained by the *divertissement* as unnerved by it. In the third movement of the spectral Walpurgisnacht ballet in Gounod's opera *Faust*, female Nubian slaves "drink Cleopatra's poison from chalices of gold."[69] Again and again the music's phrases end after the downbeat – a feature that Berlioz once described as characteristically Middle Eastern[70] – and the largely tonal harmonic language is colored by modal surprises: G minor with an occasional lowered second degree, then B-flat major with a lowered sixth degree. Exotic styles found their way into "purely" instrumental works as well, as in the Middle Eastern-style tune of the slow movement of Bizet's Symphony in C or (as we shall discuss below) the Hungarian-Gypsy finales by Brahms and others.

The relatively sudden expansion of the musically exotic, over the course of the nineteenth century, was surely encouraged by the success of the immediately preceding *alla turca* vogue (and the eventual desire to provide alternatives to it). It also responded to a number of more general and interrelated trends within musical composition and reception:

- An increased exploitation of **characteristic styles** (or "topics"), such as pastoral, military, and sacred/learned traits, and traits associated specifically with distant places and their inhabitants.[71]
- An increased production of **programmatic works**: instrumental pieces that make an overt attempt to portray, depict, or narrate. Program music had already been practiced by certain earlier composers (e.g., Kuhnau's six multi-movement biblical sonatas for keyboard, 1700), was actively championed by such Haydn-era symphonists as Dittersdorf, deepened and enriched by Beethoven (notably in Symphony No. 6, "Pastoral," 1808), and, during the 1830s–50s, further elaborated and publicly promoted by Berlioz and Liszt.[72]
- The expanded use of musical **"local color"** in opera (such as the recurring appearance of a Lutheran chorale in Meyerbeer's *Les Huguenots*, 1836) as well as in other works of stage and spectacle. These works included ballets (as already discussed), spoken plays with extensive incidental music, melodramas (in which the instrumental music was particularly extensive and sometimes also underscored scenes of action and pantomime), the dioramas of Daguerre, and *tableaux vivants* (posed scenes with costumes and sets, accompanied by readings and/or music).[73]
- Cheaper and more widespread **dissemination of published music**, and increasingly international performance possibilities, thanks to the growing number of symphony orchestras, opera companies, choral societies, and – in the home – pianos. Whereas Rameau surely did not plan for *Les Indes galantes* (1735–36) to reach a pan-European audience (though bits of it eventually did), Chopin, in the 1830s–40s, took pains to ensure that his works – including the often exotic-sounding mazurkas – be published simultaneously in Paris, London, and, for Central and Eastern Europe, Leipzig or Vienna.[74] Editions of

Chopin's works soon were imported into (and, in time, published directly in) cities across the Atlantic, such as Boston, New Orleans, and Buenos Aires.

- Numerous published collections of **folk songs** of various traditional cultures, and published descriptions, often detailed, of those cultures' music-making practices.[75] The region under study might be geographically close to the collector (e.g., Lvov and Prach's collection of Russian folk songs, 1809) or far away (Guillaume Villoteau's study of muezzin chants and other specimens of Egyptian music, 1809–12). Either way, the materials could become fodder for exotic musical projects by composers living elsewhere. Beethoven incorporated traditional Russian melodies from the Lvov and Prach anthology in his "Rasumovsky" String Quartets, Op. 59 (1805–6). The use of "folk tunes" (or "national melodies," as they were often called) was particularly encouraged by Georg Joseph Vogler (the "Abbé" Vogler), who taught both Carl Maria von Weber and Giacomo Meyerbeer, and who once improvised at length upon an "African" (presumably North African) theme in the presence of a fascinated Beethoven.[76]

- Increased **contact with the actual music-making of various distant lands**. As early as 1838, a troupe of dancers and musicians from India gave eight weeks of public performances in Paris. Berlioz heard a Chinese ensemble at the London World's Fair of 1851. He later recalled the singing as resembling the sound of "dogs yawning, or cats coughing up a fish bone" and joked that the "instruments of music" were closer to "instruments of torture."[77] Something like the full panoply of world musics – groups from French villages, Romania, Tunisia, Vietnam, even sub-Saharan Africa – reached Paris (and listeners from many lands) at the 1889 World's Fair. It was here that Debussy heard and saw a Javanese gamelan perform and came away forever changed. Four years later, America held an enormous, city-sized fair (the World Columbian Exhibition, situated on the southern edge of Chicago) that overflowed with presentations from around the globe, including a much-noted novelty: Middle Eastern belly dancing.

These various musical trends during the late eighteenth century and the first half of the nineteenth, and especially the last two trends – scholarly efforts at documenting and preserving various unfamiliar musical traditions, and increased public exposure to such traditions – arose in close parallel to broader political and cultural developments. These included:

- the further spread of Europe's empires;[78]
- increasing access, through translations and scholarly studies, to literary, philosophical, and other traditions of distant cultures;
- poems, novels, plays – and a seemingly endless stream of paintings – inspired by Spaniards, Roma (Gypsies), Middle Eastern Muslims, and other distant and/or different peoples;
- the rise of political and cultural nationalism, manifested concretely in the creation of nation-states across Europe (e.g., Italy and Germany) and in the growing resistance to colonial and imperial control (e.g., revolutions in North America, Haiti, and South America; Greece's struggle for independence from the Ottoman Empire; and, in India, the Rebellion of 1857 against the British East India Company).

To return to the more specifically musical realm, the widespread surge of nationalism (just mentioned) was reflected in an important trend that would turn out to be acutely relevant to the phenomenon of musical exoticism:

- Increased efforts at writing **works that consciously refer to a nation or ethnic/cultural group**. Verdi's operas of the 1840s made a forthright case for Italian independence from the Austro-Hungarian Empire. Wagner's Ring cycle (1848–74), was based on the legends of the Nordic gods. Around 1870, for many composers in countries considered somehow culturally "peripheral" (Spain, Russia, the Scandinavian countries), the search for a distinctive national cultural identity or profile was a powerful motivator, and it shaped their musical output. That search was already in progress earlier, and in works of composers at the supposed cultural "center." For example, in *Der Freischütz* (1821), Carl Maria von Weber consciously strove to establish a model for serious German-language opera. The work itself – though set in a neighboring region (Bohemia) – transparently attempts to reflect various aspects of German village life from Weber's day or shortly before: hunting contests, male choral-singing traditions, wedding customs, and so on.[79]

To be sure, defining and valuing the musical culture of one's own nation or group may at first sound like the polar opposite of musical exoticism. But, with the increasingly wide dissemination of musical works in the nineteenth century, works crossed borders and found acceptance with players and audiences of very different backgrounds. What spoke of "home" to a work's original audience spoke of "elsewhere" to audiences in other lands.

For example, Spanish songs (mentioned earlier) were much performed in Paris. Their recurring images of Spanish bandits, coquettish Spanish females, and the like – reinforced by distinctive syncopations, melismas, and modal features derived from Spanish folk music – helped engrave deeper in the French mind many already prevailing stereotypes of life on the Iberian Peninsula. Likewise, Chopin's mazurkas conveyed a special fascination to listeners far from Chopin's native land. One recent scholar notes that, though scholars may disagree whether "[Chopin's] Lydian fourths, drone fifths, dance rhythms, and occasional pentatonicism" derive from Polish folk traditions, these features "delimit the beginnings of exoticism *cum* nationalism."[80] People outside Poland were often struck by the strange and foreign (hence exotic) features of Chopin's works in Polish style: Schumann invoked the ancient Sarmatians of Iran (who were sometimes viewed as forebears of the Poles); Maurice Bourges, the Alhambra and its "delicious caprices of Arab genius."[81] True, many outsiders (including Schumann) heard these pieces primarily in relationship to Russia's oppression of Polish aspirations for political and cultural independence. But, then, East Europe itself – and its internal struggles – must often have seemed exotic and nearly incomprehensible to many Parisians or Londoners.[82]

I should stress that many nineteenth-century exotic works, or long passages in those works, did not sound exotic. Operas often marked foreignness in the words and visual/dramatic features but restricted musical codes of Otherness to an occasional chorus or dance number. We shall explore this phenomenon – which is, of course, one that the Full-Context Paradigm can address and the Exotic-Style Paradigm cannot – in Chapters 7 and 8, with regard to operas with Spanish Gypsy characters and to operas set in some part of "the East."

Some English and American parlor songs and French *romances* and *mélodies* used stylistic markers of place.[83] German art songs (Lieder) almost consistently did not, even when songs were based on poems that incorporated Persian or Turkish references and images. For example, Heine wrote a much-loved (and often-set) poem about a snow-covered fir tree, on a mountain in "the North," that yearns for a sad, mournful palm tree in the sun-baked "Orient" (*Morgenland*, a term suggesting Arabia and the biblical terrains). Composers such as Schubert and Liszt treated such poems as semi-philosophical ruminations about matters perceived as at once universal and highly individual: in this case, the male's yearning for the unreachable female. Despite the avoidance of exotic style, the very intensity of the feelings and situations depicted in the words often bring the composer to employ some of his or her most extreme musical devices, such as highly chromatic harmony and ambiguous modulations.[84] With regard to Schubert's song "Du liebst mich nicht" (1822), based on a Middle Eastern-style poem of 1821 by August von Platen, David Gramit concludes:

Self-evidently "other" in its poetic language [including reference to a typically "Eastern" flower, the jasmine] yet evoking a familiar (if extreme) emotional experience, "Du liebst mich nicht" could open through its associations with the exotic the possibility of an *unthinkable* but musically *representable* alternative to conventional existence to those, like Schubert and many others within his culture, for whom this kind of alternative had intense appeal.[85]

German poets and composers were also attracted to the Persian poetic form of the *ghazāl*, with its seemingly constraining – or wittily playful – use of internal rhymes and sometimes near-obsessive repetition of a refrain word (or end-rhyme). In the Schubert song just discussed, the despairing title phrase – "Du liebst mich nicht" – is stated at the end of six of the ten lines. One of Brahms's most famous songs, "Wie bist du, meine Königin," is based on a German reworking of a text by the fourteenth-century Persian poet Hafiz. The word "wonnevoll!" (blissful) recurs five times, with changing meaning and syntactical function, and its melodic contour gets picked up again and again by the piano, too.[86] This repeated welling up, reinforced by the Eastern origin of the poem's form, must have evoked for many of Brahms's listeners the image of the Middle East as a space of limitless pleasure. Thus, paradoxically, the Eastern poetic constraint of word repetition became a symbol of freedom from the tensions and disappointments of life in the West.

Liszt's gifts: Gypsy "opium" and the national rhapsody

I wish, in the remainder of this chapter, to linger on works that *were* written in plainly exotic styles – and, particularly, on instrumental works. The vast repertoire of instrumental pieces in a national or exotic style is impossible to explore in a relatively small space. We have already encountered, in Chapter 4, the "Italian" Symphony of Mendelssohn and certain self-consciously Norwegian-style pieces by Edvard Grieg. Michael Pisani has recently drawn attention to a surprisingly large number of nineteenth-century "war dances," written in the (supposed) musical manner of this or that Native American tribe or simply of "American Indians," generally. The composers include Americans and Britons, understandably, but also the Italian-born opera composer Gaspare Spontini and the Danish dance composer Hans Christian Lumbye (in an 1860 ballet that is set on a ship and entitled *Fjernt fra Danmark* – Far from Denmark).[87]

Among the richest and most durable of the century's many national/exoticist works are the Hungarian Rhapsodies of Franz Liszt. These works attained enormous popularity – and were plainly considered exotic – outside of Hungary, whereas to Hungarians they were and remain among the enduring monuments of Hungarian musical nationalism.[88] More crucially for our purposes, the Rhapsodies challenge the very distinction between nationalism and exoticism because they derive largely from the musical practices of an "internal outsider" population: the Roma who had long been resident in Hungarian territory. As we shall see, Liszt used the word "exotic" to describe the resonances – even for himself and for other Hungarians – of the heavily improvised musical tradition of the "Gypsy music" bands that he preserved, reworked, and embellished in these Rhapsodies. Nonetheless, he proudly insisted on the title "Hungarian Rhapsodies," rather than, say, "Gypsy Rhapsodies," for he loved to twit Hungarians that their most vital and characteristic national music was not fully Hungarian (Magyar) but rather of mixed ethnic origin, and that the Hungarians had for centuries paid Rom musicians to play in this style for them. As we shall see, the adjective "Hungarian" – and Liszt's lengthy published explanations of it – led to predictable misunderstandings and accusations.

The Roma are a people, or complex of ethnic groups, that most likely originated in northern India. They made their way westward over an extended time, reaching various European countries by the fifteenth or sixteenth centuries. Perhaps because many Roma had come by way of the Ottoman Empire, they were long thought to have originated in Egypt.[89] This led to their being called *égyptiens* (in sixteenth-century French writings), Gypsies, or *gitanos*. (The last of these remains the most commonly used Spanish term even today.) Other terms frequently used in the eighteenth and nineteenth centuries include the French word *bohémiens* – because the Roma reached Western Europe by way of Eastern Europe – and the German word *Zigeuner*, which derives from a Byzantine-Greek term for a people in Asia Minor. Whereas in many countries, such as Austria and Russia, the Roma were subject to official persecution and at times expulsion, they were treated somewhat more tolerantly in certain areas of Eastern Europe that are today part of Hungary, Slovakia, or Romania.[90] In certain of the latter territories, Roma were regularly hired, even adulated, for their music-making.

I henceforth use the phrase "Hungarian-Gypsy music" to refer to the kinds of music that bands made up primarily of Rom musicians played for the Magyar magnates and other non-Rom listeners. The phrase is problematic because it includes the word "Gypsy," which many Roma today consider pejorative.[91] (Some Roma have recently reclaimed it, in ways roughly analogous to the affirmative use of "queer" by some gays and lesbians and "Indian" by some Native Americans.[92])

Unfortunately, the obvious alternatives to the phrase "Hungarian-Gypsy music" have their own disadvantages. The phrase "*verbunkos* music" (preferred by some Hungarian scholars) risks naming a varied repertoire for one particular dance type. More problematically still, it renders invisible the many Rom performers who were largely responsible for developing the style in question and who even composed some of its most beloved tunes (though the latter were often in established Hungarian dance-tune genres, such as *verbunkos* and *csárdás*). Other alternative phrases to "Hungarian-Gypsy music" that might at first seem logical, such as "Rom (or Romani) band music," have rarely if ever been used by scholars, and for good reason. The music that the fiddlers, cimbalom players, and other musicians played incorporated musical elements from a variety of Eastern European cultures (Magyar, Slav, Austro-German, and so on). Presumably it also incorporated features from centuries-old Rom musical traditions, but what those features could have been is something of a puzzle. The songs that the Hungarian Roma have long performed when they are amongst themselves display little of the luxuriant embellishment typical of the Hungarian-Gypsy-music bands and also make little use of the so-called Gypsy interval of the augmented second. More surprisingly still (to outsiders), the singer of the Rom songs tends not to be accompanied by instruments at all. Instead, other singers – most often several males – clap their hands, snap their fingers, and sing nonsense syllables (or, to use the ethnomusicological term, vocables) in a guttural fashion that is often very approximate in pitch, as if taking the place of a loosely strung double-bass.[93]

For all these reasons, the phrase "Hungarian-Gypsy music" will have an important function in the present chapter.[94] I would particularly stress two advantages of the phrase: its inclusion of the word "Gypsy" reminds us – as "*verbunkos*" does not – that Roma were centrally involved in composing and performing this music; and the same word, by its very datedness, also reminds us that a Rom musician, in making this music for his non-Rom employers and listeners, was engaging in one of the few wage-earning activities available to him: performing a type of music that was at once his own and not his own. In playing this music, he was not, for an hour or two, Rom; he was a representative of a half-real, half-imagined people called, by Hungarians, *cigányok* and, by foreigners, "the Hungarian Gypsies." (Henceforth, the terms "Gypsies" and Hungarian-"Gypsy" music will not generally be set off by quotation marks.)

Was Hungarian-Gypsy music exotic to its listeners, in Hungary and beyond? Franz Liszt himself (as we shall see) did term the music "exotic." Such a statement is significant coming from someone particularly attuned to questions of national identity and culture-crossing. Born in 1811 to

Figure 6.4 Portrait of the masterful Rom ("Gypsy") fiddler János Bihari by János Donát (1820). The museum-style stone pilaster upon which his violin is displayed carries the words "BIHARI a Magyar Cziganyok Közt Orpheus": "BIHARI: Orpheus among the Hungarian Gypsies." (Reproduced by permission of the Hungarian National Museum, which acquired the portrait in 1851.)

German-speaking parents in a largely Hungarian town (Doborján, known in German as Raiding), the precocious musician relocated to Vienna at age eleven for better musical training, and then to Paris at age twelve. By the mid-1830s, when Liszt was in his twenties, he was already well on his way to becoming the most renowned traveling virtuoso pianist of his age and had become enmeshed in the French literary, artistic, and political scene. Yet Liszt was also, especially from his thirties onward, a proud Hungarian nationalist, as well as – he saw no conflict in this – a proponent of the bands playing Hungarian-Gypsy music.

Liszt pointedly called Hungarian-Gypsy music "exotic." In 1859, now living in Weimar, Germany, he published a 300-page book (in French, soon translated into German and Hungarian) that he meant to serve as an explanatory preface to his first fifteen Hungarian Rhapsodies: *On the Gypsies and Their Music in Hungary*. The lengthy sections on the history and culture of the Roma were written primarily by Princess Carolyne von Sayn-Wittgenstein (Liszt's primary mistress during the second half of his life).[95] The more concretely musical sections can be attributed, in substance if not in every detail of wording, to Liszt. And they display, as do many of his letters, his close knowledge of and enthusiasm for the bands that he had heard from childhood years onward – and, not least, for the great Rom fiddler János Bihari (Fig. 6.4).[96]

Liszt uses the word "exotic" in the course of grumpy remarks about a composition by Schubert that was, until Liszt composed the Rhapsodies, the most extended exercise in Hungarian-Gypsy style by any composer. Schubert composed this (too-modestly titled) *Divertissement à l'hongroise* (for piano four-hands, 1824) after returning from a stay at the Hungarian summer estate of Johann Karl Esterházy in Zseliz (today Želiezovce in Slovakia). Schubert, complains Liszt, flattened out the dissonances, sudden modulations, and other distinctive features of Hungarian-Gypsy music. He "did not recognize [in the Gypsy motives] an art different from every other, constructed upon another foundation and structured on different principles." In short, Schubert should have "look[ed] upon these productions as exotic plants, as specimens [*échantillons*] revealing the unfamiliar flora of a zone as yet unexplored. He did not go to the trouble of penetrating sufficiently [the music's] spirit and its intimate meaning."[97]

Liszt idolized Schubert. He even freely adapted this very *Divertissement* for piano solo (entitling it *Mélodies hongroises, d'après Schubert*, 1838–39).[98] Nonetheless, Liszt could not help concluding that Schubert "imagined that he was giving [the Gypsy fragments] some value by trimming them up according to our rules and methods."[99] The alternative method (as Liszt proposes) would be to appreciate these *plantes exotiques* for their unique and unfamiliar properties. Liszt thus presents himself as the musical equivalent of a botanist. After all, plants are, by definition, exotic if they flourish in other environments than those that prevail "here" at home. And their value is inherent, needing to be neither earned nor argued.

By the standards of the day, Liszt was a relatively objective observer of the Gypsy musical tradition. His handwritten transcriptions – some of them apparently made immediately upon hearing a performance by a fiddler or band specializing in Hungarian-Gypsy music – are quite detailed. Certain of them (or, indeed, certain passages in the Hungarian Rhapsodies) provide the earliest evidence for one or another tune. (Critics have long assumed that Liszt invented many tunes in the Rhapsodies. But field transcriptions by respected folklorists of the era keep turning up, confirming the origins of one tune after another in the performed repertoire of the fiddlers and bands.[100])

Though Liszt's "field" transcriptions of the fiddlers' tunes were proto-scholarly, his attitude toward their music-making, as a whole, was by no means disinterested. Quite the contrary, he was the most visible and enthusiastic booster of what he and most other non-Rom called "the Gypsy bands." In 1846, one such band (from Sziget) was brought to play for him, at his specific request, while he was staying at Klausenburg (Kolozsvár; today Cluj, in Romania). Count Sándor Teleki later recalled: "Liszt's eyes were burning during the playing; he snapped his fingers and shouted to the music. Then, while everyone was dancing, Liszt sat down at the piano and composed his First Hungarian Rhapsody" (i.e., Hungarian Rhapsody No. 14 – on numbering, see Fig. 6.5 below).[101] (More likely, as Zoltán Gárdonyi argues, Liszt improvised on one particular tune that later appeared in that Rhapsody, namely the *Koltói csárdás* – discussed further below.[102]) Liszt was so obsessed with the music-making of "the Gypsy fiddlers" that he once described it as "a kind of opium, of which I am sometimes in great need." He jokingly dubbed himself "the first Gypsy in the Kingdom of Hungary."[103]

As the latter phrase suggests, Liszt identified with the fiddlers.[104] Just as Bihari and the others improvised upon a wide range of musical styles and materials, so Liszt loved to sit at the piano and meditate on one or several tunes or motives by other composers. Most of his compositions up to the mid-1850s – and a good many of them during the rest of his career – are not wholly original creations but arrangements, "paraphrases," fantasies, and the like. Furthermore, Liszt's book often presents the fiddle-wielding leader of a Hungarian-Gypsy band as a suffering and unappreciated artist, like Beethoven.[105] Or like himself: his letters and published essays, especially in his early years, are filled with complaints about traveling around to play in private homes for people who want only simple tunes and flashy playing and who make him enter the house by the servant door.[106]

Soon after the book appeared, various professional Hungarian songwriters and musically literate members of the Austro-Hungarian gentry spoke up forcefully, laying claim to authorship of certain tunes and sometimes devaluing entirely the contributions of the (largely Rom) musicians who played Hungarian-Gypsy music. Liszt wrote a letter focusing only on the broader point, saying that many tunes played by the bands are known to have been composed by specific Rom musicians. To claim all the music of the Hungarian-Gypsy bands as the cultural property of Hungarians is to "steal from those we have *patronized*," i.e., those that we have, for hundreds of years, paid to make music for us.[107] (Here Liszt includes himself as part of the greater-Hungarian "us," dissolving the then-fraught distinction between German-speakers and Magyars.) In his book, though not in this letter, Liszt attacked the specific claims as well, pointing out that the Hungarian tune-composers in question – he did not deny that there were some – were simply adopting a musical style that had already "reached its zenith" under the fingers of far more numerous Rom virtuoso fiddler-composers.[108] At the same time, though, Liszt made a token gesture to the Magyar magnates that was, in a way, more insulting to the Roma than anything else in his book. He claimed that the Roma were incapable of being "receptive" to the genius of a great player of Hungarian-Gypsy music (such as Bihari) and hence of "stimulating him" to achieve his fullest art. A Rom "[spends] his whole life obeying blindly his primary impulses … The Hungarians were the intelligent listeners without whom the Gypsy art would have died off entirely."[109]

Liszt seems to have found in the freshness of the best Hungarian-Gypsy music a fruitful challenge to what he called (in that passage on Schubert) "our [standard European] rules and methods." As Shay Loya has demonstrated in detail, the "exotic" ways in which the bands and their fiddlers put notes together would help Liszt in some of his most daring compositional exploits, including ones in which the Hungarian-Gypsy influence is neither indicated in the title (e.g., works on sacred Latin texts) nor immediately obvious to the ear.[110]

Liszt knew what he was talking about. He had heard Hungarian-Gypsy bands from childhood on, not least while studying in Vienna. His interest grew more sustained in the mid-1840s, when he was in his mid-thirties. Over the next few years, he transcribed, arranged, and combined dozens of fragments of this music, and published the results in several sets, the largest two of which he entitled *Magyar dallok* and *Magyar rapszódiák* ("Hungarian Melodies" and "Hungarian Rhapsodies").

These early workings-up of the Hungarian-Gypsy melodies sold few copies, but Liszt kept playing them, reshaping and refining their component parts, and recombining them for greater effect and coherence. In 1851–53, he published the definitive results: fifteen Hungarian Rhapsodies. (Four more followed later in life.) Six became so beloved that Liszt adapted them for orchestra (with help from Franz Doppler), sometimes expanding or tightening them. Since the equivalence between the two numberings is not always stated on recordings or in other sources, it is shown for convenience in Figure 6.5.[111]

A few of the Hungarian Rhapsodies maintain a single character more or less throughout: for example, No. 15 (the Rákóczi March, first stated in brash, unconventional harmonies) and No. 5 (a stirring funeral march, with a recurring consolatory episode in the major mode). More often a piece arrays tune after tune, perhaps lingering for a few varied statements of one

Versions for orchestra and for piano four-hands (pub. 1874–75)	Based on piano original (pub. 1851–53)
1 in F minor	14 in F minor
2 in D minor	2 in C-sharp minor
3 in D major	6 in D-flat major
4 in D minor	12 in C-sharp minor
5 in E minor, Héroïde-élégiaque	5 in E minor, Héroïde-élégiaque
6 in D major, "Carnival in Pesth"	9 in E-flat major, "Carnival in Pesth"

Figure 6.5 Concordance of the orchestral and piano versions of six of the Hungarian Rhapsodies by Liszt.

but then moving smartly to the next. No. 2, which follows this plan, is the best known, no doubt because the tunes – and Liszt's ways of elaborating upon them – are so captivating.

The Hungarian-Gypsy style had been anticipated in certain works by Haydn, Beethoven, Hummel, Weber, and (as mentioned) Schubert.[112] It was already becoming one of the standard folk or exotic styles in which to write up-tempo rondo-type finales, very much analogous to the *alla turca* finales of Mozart and Beethoven discussed earlier. Weber, for example, wrote an Andante and Hungarian Rondo in C minor, Op. 35, for bassoon and orchestra (1815).[113] But, thanks to Liszt's Rhapsodies, the Hungarian-Gypsy style now became, along with the Andalusian style, one of the most widely known non-Western "dialects" within Western music.

The Hungarian-Gypsy musical dialect that Liszt purveyed in the Rhapsodies is, as he himself noted, internally consistent.[114] For example, several tunes are marked by distinctive syncopated rhythms, such as |♪ ♩ ♪| (as in the up-tempo conclusion of Hungarian Rhapsody No. 6). Many tunes use distinctive scales that resist "normal" harmonization, such as one that Shay Loya has helpfully termed "*verbunkos*-minor," with an augmented second between scale degrees 3 and 4 and between 6 and 7: C–D–E♭–F♯–G–A♭–B–C. (The other main Hungarian-Gypsy scale, *kalindra*, uses the same intervals but starting on what is G in the scale just given, hence producing augmented seconds between 2 and 3 and between 6 and 7.[115]) Many of the tunes end with one of several equally distinctive melodic-rhythmic cadential patterns. These *bokázó* cadences often give the impression of firmly "closing off" a phrase, much the way that the steps of various Hungarian folk dances, notably the *csárdás*, end a section with a sharp clicking of the heels.[116]

Liszt wrote some explicit instructions into the scores of the Hungarian Rhapsodies. The declamatory passage at the beginning of No. 7, in D minor, is "to be performed in the [alternately] defiant and pensive Gypsy style." The pianist is thereby told to apply everything that s/he knows about the Hungarian-Gypsy performance manner. For example, s/he may wish to race ahead on the fast flourishes and then stretch out the main melodic note. Furthermore, performers may profitably carry this clue from No. 7 over to passages that are analogous, such as the opening of the aforementioned Hungarian Rhapsody No. 2, marked *Lento a capriccio* ("slow and following one's own whim"). Hungarian Rhapsody No. 7, after the alternatingly defiant and pensive opening just discussed, gains the extra indication *a capriccio* in m. 9 and, to drive the point home further, *capricciosamente* in m. 15. Liszt clearly sensed that players shaped by the increasingly regimented, metronome-guided musical culture of the nineteenth century would need encouragement toward emulating the freedom and willfulness of the soloists in Hungarian-Gypsy bands.[117]

Liszt, believing that the culture of the Hungarian Roma was not well enough understood, concluded that this culture needed to be "heard" through his Rhapsodies – and through the book that he and Princess Carolyne put together. The book is filled with passage after passage describing, in vivid exoticizing manner, the lives and performances of the Romani, based in part on Liszt's own observations from childhood onward. These "bohémiens" are presented as utterly different from regular Europeans, whether of town or farm. They embody contrasts and paradoxes beyond telling: chapter titles include "Nature for the Gypsies," "The Laziness of the Gypsies," and "The Industriousness of the Gypsies."[118] "Les bohémiens," according to Liszt's book, indulge in pleasures to an almost dangerous extreme. For them, perpetual music-making and dancing are means to delirium and exhaustion, as are equally unabating sex and drink:

[When I was a young pupil of Czerny,] I was pursued in my daydreams by these bronzed faces, which ... seemed to me as if they had become prematurely withered; partly by the inclemency of the seasons, but also by the unregulated – or rather galvanizing – emotions of their disordered life ... The Gypsy's life is a closely woven tissue of pleasures and sufferings that follow closely one upon the other without break or repose, and are at once caused and consoled by four elements of sensuality and exaltation [*de volupté et de vertige*]: love, song, dance, and drink. Four chasms of perdition these may well be; but still, four glittering stars: four fountains – bitter in flavor – whose very approach excites thirst; [fountains] in which the lips bathe with delight, and which, once tasted, make one love falling into ruin [*aimer l'anéantissement*].[119]

The specific shape that Liszt gave Hungarian Rhapsody No. 2 and most of the other fourteen helps explain his adoption of the term "rhapsody." Etymologically, a rhapsody is a piece (or, in ancient Greece, a recitation) "stitched together" from various "odes" (songs, or excerpts from epic poetry). Liszt selected the Hungarian-Gypsy tunes and "stitched" them together in ways that reflected the flow of a typical Hungarian-Gypsy performance of his day. The latter might begin with slow, heavily improvised passages in free rhythm – perhaps conveying a mournful or meditative mood – that alternated with lyrical or melancholy melodies. These melodies were sometimes repeated many times, each time differently embellished. Sooner or later, the performance would move to a second, culminating phase, in which one or several uptempo tunes were likewise repeated with increasingly elaborate ornamentation and at an increasingly frantic tempo:

During the tempestuous finale [of one Gypsy performance during my second return to Hungary], it was as if every possible sound or tone was tumbling down together like mountain crests that fall with a frightful uproar in sheets of sand mixed with rocks and stones. One felt uncertain whether the whole [aural] edifice, which seemed to shift under these sudden displacements of sonorous currents and vibrations, might not fall upon our heads. Such was the crushing nature of the instrumentation of [the fiddler's quasi-]concerto, which all the conservatories of the world would surely have condemned, and which even I, for once, found (as people say) a bit "daring"![120]

These two large phases in a Hungarian-Gypsy performance were called *lassú* (or *lassan*) and *friss* (or *friska*), terms that Liszt wrote into the published score of No. 2 at the appropriate spots.

Typical is Hungarian Rhapsody No. 14, which, clocking in at about twelve minutes, is one of the longest and most eventful. It also has the special advantage of being easily available in one form or another. In addition to the definitive piano-solo version of 1853 and Liszt's orchestral and four-hand versions (which, as noted above, are designated "No. 1"), one can encounter most of its material, in more or less the same sequence, in the Fantasia on Hungarian Folk Melodies for Piano and Orchestra (often known simply as "Hungarian Fantasia" – 1849–52, pub. 1864).

Hungarian Rhapsody No. 14 faithfully follows the basic pattern of slow-to-fast (*lassú* to *friss*), but the gradual speed-up is pleasantly interrupted by various digressive changes of mood along the way. The opening theme, in the style of a funeral march (*Lento, quasi marcia funebre*), is marked by a syncopated, symmetrical rhythm typical of various Hungarian-Gypsy and other Eastern European dances: | ♩. ♪ | ♪ ♩. |.[121] Each phrase ends with a heavy-footed cadential pattern of three long chords, presumably linked also to a typical sequence of dance steps. The theme is accompanied by extensive open-fifth tremolos that evoke the cimbalom.[122] (The cimbalom is a type of hammered dulcimer widely used in Eastern Europe. It consists of dozens of strings, arranged somewhat like the strings inside a piano, only much smaller. The player strikes the strings with small hammer-headed wooden sticks.)

At m. 25, the opening theme returns with a double surprise: it is in the major mode and is played in bold chords by the two hands (*Allegro eroico*). The listener now realizes that this heroic version is the tune's primary version, which the funeral-march version was "anticipating." By this progression from mourning to valor, Liszt perhaps intended an unspoken program: Hungarian national pride and vitality arising out of the ashes of defeat and subjugation. Liszt was soon to become known (somewhat controversially) for what is now called "thematic transformation," the process by which a work takes a single theme through several distinct changes of mood or aspect. Notable examples include his Piano Sonata in B Minor (1853); his operatic fantasies (many from the 1840s) on themes from the great operas of, say, Mozart or Bellini; and his thirteen symphonic poems (mainly from the 1850s, the same era that produced the Hungarian Rhapsodies and the book about them). This passage in Hungarian Rhapsody No. 14 demonstrates that Liszt considered Hungarian-Gypsy materials to be no less worthy of being regarded from different angles and in different lights than widely loved opera arias, or motives and melodies of his own invention.

The *Poco allegretto (a capriccio)*, mm. 77–120, offers a livelier but quietly questioning tune that keeps getting interrupted by slow reminiscences of the work's opening, as if a fiddler or cimbalom-player were bittersweetly alternating a brisk new theme with fragments of a melancholy one played earlier. The downshifting causes the highly rhythmical cadence, when it does arrive (*Allegro*), to sound all the more crisp and spritely.

At m. 121 an enchanting minor-mode dotted-figure tune arrives, expressly marked "in Gypsy style" (*Allegretto alla zingarese, dolce con grazia*). One noted Hungarian authority points out that the tune "corresponds to the character of the passage marked *Figura* in the fast, closing section of a Hungarian recruiting-dance composition" (i.e., a *Verbunkos* – the term derives from the German word for military recruitment: *Werbung*).[123] Liszt executes several variations upon this *zingarese* theme: first simply up an octave, then in smooth rather than dotted rhythm – with a regular alternation between the melody note and a repeated note on the dominant, as if the fiddler's bow were jumping back and forth between two strings – and eventually over quick three-note turns. This sequence of variations corresponds closely to Liszt's description of the true masters of the Hungarian-Gypsy fiddle style:

Having syncopated their theme to give it a slight swinging effect, [they then] restore it to the normal measure as if preparing to lead the stars of the skies in dancing [*mener la danse des astres*]; after which it casts sparks in every direction by clusters of small trills, which give it a *mordante* [biting quality], ... and suddenly changes into a sprightly hobgoblin, nibbling at the ear with his steely, shrill fast notes.[124]

In the midst of these variations, Liszt takes a break to bring in a melody that will never be heard again. Marked *Allegro vivace*, it begins – rather than ends – with three stomping chords. We presumably imagine the chords as being played by the whole Gypsy band, to which the "soloist" giddily responds.[125] The first half of the piece comes to a grand conclusion with a more "composerly" treatment of bits of the *zingarese* theme (one suddenly encounters much modulating, though also the indication *quasi zimbalo* – "like a cimbalom"), a *fortissimo* statement of the piece's main theme, and a breathtaking cadenza.

The second, more "up-tempo" half of the piece, marked *Vivace assai* (i.e., the *friss* section), likewise presents several tunes, but now all in the same tempo and with nary a backwards glance to earlier material. Liszt interpolates a few short cadenzas as well as white-key glissando passages whose recurring use of B♮ startle the ear in the context of so much F-major music. The three tunes in this *Vivace assai* might seem unrelated to each other. For example, the first has a unique texture that suggests that the tune is being pecked out with alternating cimbalom hammers. (Liszt, in his sketchbook of Hungarian and Hungarian-Gypsy tunes, calls this tune the *Koltói csárdás*.) Despite their differences, though, the tunes link up very persuasively.[126]

Liszt the composer takes charge more obviously in the next section, which tosses fragments of the tunes into distant keys (e.g., D-flat major) and also gets faster, leading to an *Allegro brioso* coda in strict rhythm.[127] At the very end, the coda remembers to "mention" again, repeatedly, the dotted figure that has recurred – straight and reversed, notated in various ways (e.g., as a grace note) – at various points throughout the work.

The alert reader may begin to suspect that to speak of the "tunes" in this piece (as is nearly always done, and as I have done above) is misleading. Most centuries-old non-Western musical traditions – for example, those of Japan or North Africa – are based upon the principle of an instrumental melody (or singing voice) moving over a drone, drumbeat rhythm, or rhythmicized drone – and/or the principle of several voices or melody

Example 6.2 Liszt, Hungarian Rhapsody No. 14, mm. 243–56.

instruments performing slightly different versions of the same materials, resulting in what ethnomusicologists (as noted earlier) call heterophony. Hungarian-Gypsy music was quite different, having already, in Liszt's day, absorbed central features of Western music, such as accompanimental harmonies and even a sometimes-independent bass line; the ensembles had also expanded to include, when available, additional violins, a double-bass, one or more wind instruments, and the most distinctive instrument of Hungarian and Hungarian-Gypsy musical culture, the cimbalom.

Liszt was clearly fascinated by the freshness of the resulting simultaneous combinations that Hungarian-Gypsy ensembles of this type produced, such as the way that the melody might, to Western ears, clash with one or more of the accompanying parts. The third (*sfogato*) tune of the *Vivace assai* section (Ex. 6.2) is in D major but turns to A minor at the end, except that the accompaniment insists on A major. Furthermore, the suddenness of the arrival leaves the ear unsure whether it is hearing a full cadence in A minor-major or a half-cadence in D minor-major.[128] One finds similarly powerful moments of ambiguity in certain Hungarian-Gypsy-influenced Brahms movements as well, such as the Scherzo of the Piano Quintet.[129] Such underminings and blurrings of tonal function would become central to Liszt's more experimental works in his later years.[130]

Another "folk" touch occurs in certain of Liszt's Hungarian-Gypsy pieces: the top and bottom musical "voices" (melody and bass) join for several beats at the unison or octave, as if mimicking folk heterophony. The resulting parallel and direct octaves in the *eroico* main theme and in the theme that launches the *Vivace assai* of Hungarian Rhapsody No. 14 might have enraged any proper harmony teacher. Except that harmony teachers – like critics and music historians – rarely took Liszt's Hungarian pieces seriously enough to get upset about them. How artistic, they seem to have reasoned, could a work be that granted the performer such a large creative role and that reveled in the thrills that he or she could evoke in an adoring audience?

Performers and listeners, though, knew better, and took Liszt's Hungarian Rhapsodies to their heart, along with much other subsequent Hungarian- and Hungarian-Gypsy-inspired music, from the Hungarian Dances of Brahms (a North German) to virtuoso violin pieces by Spaniard Pablo de Sarasate (*Zigeunerweisen*, 1878), by Naples-born Vittorio Monti (*Czardas*, c. 1904), and by the great Romanian violinist of Rom extraction Grigoraş Dinicu (*Hora staccato*, 1906, best known in an arrangement by concert violinist Jascha Heifetz). To help listeners "know" how this music reflected the exotic lifestyle and passions of the Roma, journalists and program-note writers summarized, or copied verbatim, pithy phrases from Liszt's book or other questionably reliable writings of the time.[131] In the late 1950s, the jacket note for an American LP entitled "Gypsy!" was still recycling the old images: "horse-stealing," "audacious knavery," "the tawny skin of their beautiful women," and – as instruction for what to think about when listening in one's North American living room – "flaming, heel-stamping music which reflects the emotions of an extremely hot-blooded and passionate folk, and which stirs in the non-gypsy listener a half-acknowledged wish to follow the Romany Road to adventure."[132] A notable recent study of the Brahms Hungarian Dances still speaks of Gypsy-style works from Liszt to Ravel (*Tzigane*, 1924) as expressing "the simultaneous plight and glory of the Gypsy."[133] In addition, the Liszt Rhapsodies were sometimes described as reflecting the vastness of the Hungarian steppes (the *puszta*) or various supposed qualities of the Magyars, such as their primitiveness (based on now largely disputed theories that they derived from the Huns, Scythians, or Turks) and their boldness in battle, across the centuries, against the Ottoman Empire and against Austria.[134]

Over the next few generations, many composers emulated Liszt, producing works entitled Rhapsody (or Fantasy or Capriccio) plus an exotic/ethnic qualifier. Although some of these offspring – such as the two Enesco *Romanian Rhapsodies* (1901) and Hubert Bath's *Cornish Rhapsody* (for piano and orchestra, written for the British film *Love Story*, 1944) – were conceived in a spirit of cultural nationalism or regional pride, they also arguably registered as exotic when performed elsewhere.[135] Some rhapsodies carried overt exotic connotations from the outset: Lalo's *Rapsodie norvégienne* (Norwegian Rhapsody, 1879), Saint-Saëns's "Rhapsodie mauresque" (Moorish Rhapsody, the second movement of his *Suite algérienne*, 1880), Rimsky-Korsakov's *Capriccio espagnol* (Spanish Capriccio, 1887), and two once-popular French rhapsodies inspired by overseas territories: the *Rapsodie cambodgienne* of L. A. Bourgault-Ducoudray (1882) and the *Rapsodie malgache* of Raymond Loucheur (1945, commissioned by the French Radio to commemorate the fiftieth anniversary of the French annexation of Madagascar). Gershwin's *Rhapsody in Blue* (1924) could just as easily have been called *Rhapsody of Harlem*, given its echoes of blues, syncopated popular dances, and the instrumentation and performance style of Lenox Avenue-style jazz bands.

Colorful and effective works such as these paid a heartfelt and grateful tribute to Liszt, the bold musician who recognized that, in music, "exotic plants" – styles and traditions that were based on principles different from the norm, from "our [standard European] rules and methods" – could convey a magic and meaning of their own. Such exotic/ethnic rhapsodies have brought zest, variety, and challenge to music in the parlor or the concert stage. But they have also done more specific "cultural work" than this. They have brought (and still bring) to audible expression qualities that listeners once attributed (and perhaps still attribute) to the more or less exotic locale or people named in the title.

7 | Exotic operas and two Spanish Gypsies

Regions on the nineteenth-century musical stage

Certain of the same regions that were increasingly embodied in stylistic dialects (see Chapter 6) also became favored exotic settings for operas, ballets, and spoken plays with incidental music. The present chapter is devoted primarily to a study of two operas, *Il trovatore* and *Carmen*, set in one of those favored locations, Spain. Both operas are particularly interesting to us as the ethnic group they portray – the Gypsies or Roma – was the primary "internal Other" within Spain and was considered intensely exotic by most Europeans and Americans.

By way of introduction, we should at least glance at the wider range of locales chosen for many stage works at the time. How many? It depends if one counts all works that were composed, works that were performed with some success, or only the few works repeatedly performed throughout the Western world. Nonetheless, it is probably safe to say that, besides Spain, two other regions or geo-cultural settings were chosen for the stage particularly often during this time period: the world of the Eastern European Gypsies (which we encountered in the context of instrumental music in Chapter 6 and whose stage manifestations include the Viennese operetta *Der Zigeunerbaron* – The Gypsy Baron, 1885 – of Johann Strauss, Jr.) and what we might call "the greater Middle East." Middle Eastern works used stories from the Bible (e.g., Saint-Saëns's *Samson et Dalila*, 1875) or from the *Thousand and One Nights* (Peter Cornelius's *Der Barbier von Bagdad*, 1858), but that did not prevent them from introducing various bits of dramatic and musical color that were thought to be typical of a region that (most people supposed) had barely changed over the millennia.

Also popular as operatic locales were the "Orient" in the present-day English-language sense – East and South Asia, as in Delibes's *Lakmé*, Puccini's two great Asian masterworks, *Madama Butterfly* and *Turandot*, and, to name one comic opera of many, Gilbert and Sullivan's *The Mikado*. European regions considered "peripheral" seem to have had the double advantage of being just distant enough to be somewhat intriguing: Scotland, the Alps, or Eastern Europe in its non-Gypsy aspect (e.g., a Polish village, in a work composed for Paris or London).[1] Scotland and England from centuries earlier had the particular advantage of helping continental librettists deal with political and social issues – such as despotism – without running afoul of the local censors.[2] North and South America appeared on stage far less often.[3]

Sub-Saharan Africa seems to have been considered a problematic or unappealing choice for serious (or even comic) stage works. David Rosen has noted that, in productions of *Un ballo in maschera* (1859, set in colonial Boston), Ulrica was generally portrayed, not as "a fortune-teller of Negro race" – to quote the libretto – but a Gypsy one. (Her music, though, is more similar to that of the prophetic witches in Verdi's *Macbeth* than to that of two true Verdian Gypsies: Azucena and – in *La forza del destino* – Preziosilla.[4]) Perhaps portrayal of very dark skin was becoming unshakably associated with blackface minstrelsy, a form of relatively lowbrow entertainment that, from the 1830s on, gained an increasingly widespread presence not just in North America but also in Europe because of tours by groups using the famous name Christy's Minstrels.[5] In 1890, George Bernard Shaw, reviewing a London performance of *Aida*, protested that the baritone playing Amonasro, the Ethiopian (i.e., Nubian) warrior-king, behaved like a "bedlamite [i.e., crazed] Christy minstrel." Shaw's dismissive words suggest that almost any effort at portraying a truly dark-skinned character, especially one behaving in agitated or ignoble manner – was hard for sophisticated theatergoers to take seriously and risked sinking the whole work.[6]

In many exotic operas from the first half of the nineteenth century, especially ones that had patently high aesthetic aims and were based on the Bible or ancient history (e.g., Rossini's *Mosè in Egitto*, 1818, and *Le siège de Corinthe*, 1826), Western composers did little to indicate, in musical terms, the specific geographical and temporal location. For example, Verdi's earlyish opera *Alzira* (1845) is set in Peru during its conquest by Spain yet little in it besides the first section of its overture indulges in stylistic Otherness.[7] In Voltaire's play *Alzire* (1732), the native warrior Zamore had been, as Julian Budden notes, a classic case of "the noble savage, inflexible in his loves and hates, yet capable of disinterested generosity." Verdi and his librettist Cammarano turned him into a standard *primo ottocento* hotheaded tenor, constant in his devotion to one woman. Only one flicker remains of Voltaire's portrayal: the opera's Zamoro acts with unexpected kindness toward the father of his (Spanish) rival-in-love.

As the nineteenth century advanced, composers increasingly used specific documentable aspects of the traditional music of distant locales to expand and refresh their own musical language. The secular oratorio *Le désert* by Félicien David was enormously popular in many countries of Europe and even in North America for several decades after its premiere in 1844. Spoken verses tell of a caravan moving through an Arabian desert, and David's music brings the scene vividly to life, especially in those numbers that incorporate musical elements that he had observed during the two years that he had lived and traveled in Egypt, Syria, and Turkey.[8] These elements include song and dance tunes, drumbeat rhythms, instrumental effects (an oboe substitutes for a *zurna*), and a cadenza sung with microtonal inflections. The "Danse des almées" (Dance of the Dancing-Women) around the evening campfire is an early instance of the ripely exoticized and eroticized Orient – whether Middle or Far East – that would become normative in late nineteenth-century operas by Saint-Saëns, Massenet, and Puccini.

As for Russian composers, they relished the opportunity of invoking a wide range of, to them, exotic styles, from Spanish and Polish (the latter in Act 3 of the 1872 version of Musorgsky's *Boris Godunov*) to Middle Eastern and Central Asian. Often they made use of intriguing invented scales and harmonies (e.g., octatonic) that bore no relationship to the actual music of the region in question (see Chapter 9). Indeed, as Simon Morrison argues, sometimes exotic and otherwise unusual harmonic procedures are incorporated so pervasively in a Russian work that they dwarf the more conventionally exotic colorations of passages assigned to this or that foreign character. For example, in Rimsky-Korsakov's fantasy-rich *Sadko*, "the music assigned to the [Viking, Venetian, and Hindu] traders sounds less exotic than that assigned to the underwater kingdom" into which the Russian hero Sadko descends (in order to return to the surface, triumphant). Morrison notes further: "The Enlightened cosmopolitanism of the opera resides in the notion that, once the protagonist recognizes his own foreignness [by going into the watery depths, not by contact with the foreign traders], he can [return to the world and] reside with others."[9]

A more straightforward "Eastern" exoticism in Russian music is found in Borodin's dance music (for orchestra with chorus) in the scene among the Polovetsians, in *Prince Igor* (1869–97). Borodin himself was partially of Georgian origin and made unusual efforts to get to know music of the region – or of other non-European regions that he may have considered somehow analogous.[10] Perhaps for that reason, these "Polovetsian Dances" retain a special place in the repertoire of musical exoticism, being an unusually vivid portrayal of contrasting moods, by turns violent, languorous, and exultant.

Most examples of operatic Otherness were not nearly as grounded in the actual music of foreign locales as were David's *Le désert* and Borodin's "Polovetsian Dances." Bizet's *Les pêcheurs de perles* (1863) has a libretto that anchors the work in local details about pearl fishing and in prayers to Brahma and "fair Siva" (one of them by a kneeling chorus), but the exotic passages in the music are not particularly Eastern/Oriental-sounding (much less specifically Ceylonese) but, rather, fantastic: for example, the obsessively rhythmic choral dance at the start of Act 2, with two piccolos buzzing trills in thirds. Thirds are a Western feature, but the high-pitched trills nonetheless tell of a realm of delightful weirdness.

Sometimes the chosen setting created problems, but also opportunities. In Verdi's aforementioned *Aida* (1870–71), the music for the ancient Egyptian priests and priestesses, and for a night scene by the Nile, show the composer moving into previously uncharted stylistic territory, including experimental uses of modal harmonies and static textures – what Dahlhaus calls "sheets of sound": *Klangflächen*.[11] Because no notated ancient-Egyptian music survives, Verdi was deprived of aural stimulus but, on the positive side, was also free of stylistic constraints.

In a few cases, the librettists or censors shifted the setting to some other part of the world while a work was in the course of being put together. In 1843, Meyerbeer completed a version of an opera entitled *L'Africaine* (The African Woman). Its last two acts were set on the Niger River, in West Africa. In the early 1850s, he and the librettist Scribe revised it thoroughly. They changed the Europeans from Spaniards to Portuguese (and consequently renamed the work *Vasco da Gama*), and they moved the final acts to India. After Meyerbeer's death, the work was readied for performance by the musicologist and composer Fétis, who split the difference: Vasco da Gama remained, but Sélika – the "African woman" in the now-restored title – was made queen of Madagascar. Since Madagascar lies off the coast of Africa, in the Indian Ocean, Fétis must have calculated that this would be the perfect location for a work about an African queen in which multiple references were made in the text to the Indian gods Brahma, Vishnu, and Siva. Operagoers, far from objecting, have been thrilled by the work, which was much performed for several decades and was famously revived (in the 1970s) with Shirley Verrett and Plácido Domingo.

At the same time, the very intense focus on Otherness in works such as *L'Africaine* – the overwhelming impressiveness, combined, in many cases, with the inherent falseness (if one insists that "truth" resides only in reliable representation) – tended to call forth objections and cynical jibes. Offenbach – born in Germany but long resident in Paris – set many of his satirical *opéras-bouffes* in a supposed exotic locale, precisely in order to poke fun at the supposed high-minded (but sometimes merely exploitive) foreign settings of French grand opera. One stage direction encapsulates the critique: *Les brigands* (1869) is set "on the border between Spain and Italy," even though the two countries do not touch. Or maybe there *is* a border – rather wide and deep – between Spain and Italy. It is called France. Opera's eternally sought Elsewhere was often simply Nowhere, or else – like it or not – Here.

Such a conclusion, presented comically in the Offenbach, creates deeper implications for nineteenth-century serious operas than might appear on the surface. These implications become evident when one turns to operas about Gypsies. Gypsies – mainstream European representations of the people who more often call themselves Roma – have long been granted an almost mythical presence within the European imagination. Spanish Gypsies, in particular, are central to the experience of opera lovers. Bizet's Carmen is the most renowned, but a close runner-up is surely Verdi's Azucena, the central character (many have argued) of Verdi's *Il trovatore*.[12] We might even think of Azucena as the operatic "mother" of Carmen. Verdi's three most popular middle-period operas – *Rigoletto*, *Il trovatore*, and *La traviata* – were among Bizet's favorites in the Italian repertoire. He praised them for their "flashes of genius." And *Il trovatore*, in particular, was surely in his mind when he wrote, in an article, that the best of Verdi's works are "vigorously alive, kneaded of gold, mud, gall, and blood."[13]

What, then, do the Gypsies in these two operas – Azucena and Carmen but also various secondary characters – tell us about themselves, through their words and actions, and the various types of music assigned to them? How specifically Spanish or Spanish-Gypsy are they? Do they present any features that link them to Gypsies elsewhere, or to other exotics, such as Middle Easterners? Are they really Us? The remainder of the present chapter attempts to suggest some answers to these questions by looking, first, at widespread images of Spanish Gypsies and, then, at various aspects of, and moments in, *Il trovatore* and *Carmen*.

The Roma (Gypsies) in life and image

European Gypsies are now generally called Roma and include the Sinti and other sub-groups. The Roma in Spain, though, are more often referred to – including by themselves – as *gitanos*, the Spanish etymological equivalent of "Gypsies" (see Chapter 6). In Verdi's *Il trovatore* (1853), the Gypsies are generally referred to by the standard Italian terms *zingari* and *zingarelle*. Each act of this opera bears a title, and the one for Act 2 – in which we meet Azucena – is the Spanish word for a female Gypsy, "La gitana."

The Roma (or Romani people) of Spain arrived, to a large extent, during the so-called Golden Age of Spain, when the Muslims ruled the Iberian Peninsula. For centuries after the Christian "Reconquista" (1492), the Roma in Spain often lived under fear of expulsion. Their children were sometimes taken away and raised as Christians in orphanages. Rom men were long excluded from government service and trade guilds and were often conscripted to row the nation's galleys. Roma ended up as wanderers within Spanish society, traveling from village to village. They repaired items of metal, told fortunes, and sang and danced. In time, they ended up speaking a version of Spanish (called *caló*) that was laced with Romani words. And their musical traditions became one of the primary bases of the performance art that, by the mid-nineteenth century, was known as flamenco.

In addition, a whole raft of stereotypes – some perhaps innocuous or even "admiring," others plainly pernicious – grew up around the *gitanos*, such as that they preferred their life of perpetual wandering for its "freedom," disdained material possessions, but also, though outwardly cheerful, were untrustworthy and violence-prone (as one could purportedly sense in their music-making and dancing). Many Spaniards believed that the *gitanos* stole Christian babies and could lay a curse on someone with an evil stare. More generally, the very fact that the *gitanos* regularly interacted with the larger society – and, in some cases, could pass for Spaniards – no doubt made them appear more threatening than if they had lived entirely apart, speaking little or no Spanish.[14] Yet, though unique in many ways, the Roma of Spain were (and remain today) an instance also of a more basic and familiar phenomenon that has occurred and continues to occur in many countries: an impoverished and, to some extent, culturally distinct ethnic immigrant population.

The international literary and artistic world, including the world of opera, seems to have half-recognized this. Obsessed with the Spanish Gypsies for several centuries now, creative artists and nattering journalists alike have often let the Roma (from Spain or elsewhere), "stand for" other marginalized groups. The concept of the Gypsy or (in French) *bohémien* became a widely resonant metaphor. Poor students and artists, though neither truly oppressed nor set apart ethnically, were described as living "like Gypsies" if they avoided fixed employment and moved from one cheap apartment to another.[15] The laconic title of Puccini's opera *La bohème* – based on Henri

Murger's novel *Scènes de la vie de bohème* – is always left untranslated. Its import might be rendered as "Life in That Part of Paris Where Young People Who Should Know Better and Are Lucky Enough to Have Decent Prospects in Life Choose Instead (the Sweet, Idealistic Fools!) to Live like Gypsies."

"Abietta zingara"

Verdi based *Il trovatore* on the most successful Spanish play of the Romantic era, *El trovador* (1836) by Antonio García Gutiérrez. The libretto (primarily by Salvatore Cammarano) reproduces nearly all of the stereotypes, positive and negative, mentioned above. For example, Azucena tries to deflect the Count's questions by claiming – in the third person – that a Gypsy wanders without plan: "The sky is her roof / And the world, her country." The libretto also reflects certain historical realities, most basically the status of the *gitanos* as Spain's internal Other. Seen against the opera's ethnic norm – its Us, namely the Count, Leonora, and the Spanish soldiers – the Gypsies are at once Them and part of the opera's Us. "They" speak "our" language (Spanish, represented in the opera by Italian), and live and work in "our" vicinity.

Il trovatore is set in the early fifteenth century, a time when (historians tell us) significant numbers of Roma arrived in Spain. We quickly see that the native aristocrats are in near-constant battle with each other over control of land and castles, and ready to duel over a particularly desirable young gentlewoman. Gypsy smiths provide the needed swords and armor. Indeed, at the beginning of Act 2, the Gypsy men sing the famous "Anvil Chorus" while hammering red-hot metal. (The Gypsy women join the cheerful refrain.) The Anvil Chorus amounts to one of the few portrayals of physical labor in nineteenth-century opera. Julian Budden notes that its tune is "primitive, demotic" and lacks evident exotic traits.[16] The net result echoes an unusually sympathetic view – and a not inaccurate one, as noted above – of Roma as hard workers.

By contrast, the orchestral introduction to this Anvil Chorus marks the Gypsies as different from the rest of the opera's characters. It is studded with features from the *alla turca* style, such as sudden shifts of key and mode, and downbeat trills followed by repeated upward leaps of a fourth (see Fig. 6.3, features 3, 10, and 11).[17] These features are consistent with the aura of Easternness that surrounded the Roma throughout Europe. In other words, there seems to be no particular desire here to match any known (or imagined) features of actual Spanish or Spanish-Gypsy (e.g., flamenco) music-making. "Oriental" touches draw the crucial line of ethnic division.

In the generation or two before Verdi, Italian opera had engaged very little in exotic, national, or other local-color effects. There are the barest hints of Scotch-snap rhythms – or of any other marker of place – in Rossini's *La donna del lago*, based on Sir Walter Scott's *The Lady of the Lake*. There are none at all – and certainly no bagpipe drones – in Donizetti's *Lucia di Lammermoor*, likewise set in Scotland. But certain French grand and comic operas from the same era by Auber and Meyerbeer had given prominent space to such aurally localizing devices. One suspects that Verdi was emulating them when he launched the Anvil Chorus, and thus Act 2, with vibrant, jagged "Eastern" devices in the orchestra.

The listener already encounters musical portrayals of Gypsies at the beginning of the first act. There, Ferrando, an aged officer in the army of Count di Luna, tells the soldiers a chilling story about Azucena's mother. He reports that, years ago, the old Gypsy laid a curse upon the Count's baby brother. The baby became ill, so, at the command of the two boys' father, Azucena's mother was burned at the stake. And Azucena then stole the baby and burned it on the same pyre. The music to which Ferrando sings the crucial words about Azucena's mother – "Abbietta zingara, fosca vegliarda" (despicable Gypsy woman, dark-complexioned old crone) – anticipates the "Eastern" style of Azucena, including use of minor mode and on-beat flourishes.[18] Similarly, the orchestra's mysteriously oscillating, proto-Musorgskian representation of the old Gypsy's "damned soul" wandering the earth at night will be given again, but in a brighter, "daytime" version, by the Gypsies in the unharmonized tune that they sing as part of the introduction to the Anvil Chorus proper.

Azucena (Fig. 7.1) is one of Verdi's most memorable creations. Rigoletto, the hunchbacked title figure in Verdi's immediately preceding opera (1851), was physically and spiritually deformed, and a lurching limp can be heard, at times, in music associated with him. Azucena is not misshapen but *turpe* (foul, disgusting) and presumably also, like her mother, *fosca* (dark) – hence, in the eyes of the Count and Ferrando (whose words these are), menacing, untrustworthy, and hell-bound. We observers might, more objectively, suggest that Azucena – very much like Rigoletto – is morally twisted by her outsider status and by the trauma that she experienced many years earlier.

Azucena's monomania is audible in "Stride la vampa!" (Ex. 7.1), the famous aria that follows the Anvil Chorus and that makes more insistent the various features that, by this point, the listener has been prepared to

Figure 7.1 Renowned Prague-born alto Magda Spiegel as Verdi's Azucena, in full-fringed Gypsy costume and somewhat dark face makeup. Anonymous photo, c. 1920. (By permission of the Frauen-Kultur-Archiv, Heinrich-Heine-Universität Düsseldorf.)

accept as Gypsy-like. The decorative flourishes are now dotted, making them angular and weird, and they occur again and again, indicating how obsessed Azucena is by the memory of her mother's death and by her mother's final plea of "Avenge me!" Also, the vocal line – here and throughout the role – requires great fullness at the lower end, quite unusual for a leading female role in those days. Azucena's age, ugliness, wild hair, and dark skin and her desperate brooding on revenge – understood as a "darkness" in her soul – are thus emphasized by the aural means of chest resonance.[19]

Next we learn that Ferrando's account in Act 1 lacked one crucial detail. On that fateful day, Azucena, in her crazed state, had thrown her own baby

Example 7.1 Verdi, *Il trovatore*, Act 2: Azucena's "Stride la vampa," opening.

son onto the fire, not (as she had intended) the Count's. Thereafter, she had raised the Count's son as her own (calling him Manrico). Her music, from this point onward to the end of the opera, makes no use of exotic style. But it traverses a wide range of moods as Azucena rages, lies (to Manrico and, later, the Count), pleads, despairs, and, finally, drifts off into nostalgic visions of her distant mountain home ("Ai nostri monti"). We understand all these mental states, and not least Azucena's final illusion of being back in Biscay (or, in Spanish, Vizcaya) with Manrico, as manifestations of the aggrieved consciousness of Gypsies, who are ever-rejected by conventional Western society.

And we come to empathize. After all, Azucena's mother had done nothing more than glare at the baby and tell his horoscope. A mid-nineteenth-century operagoer of even modestly liberal or rationalistic inclinations may well have wondered, "Which is worse, really: to give the 'evil eye' and mumble some words, or to *believe* – as did the old Count – that a person can kill with a glance or a word and therefore should be put to death?" And an operagoer of opposite inclinations – one who did harbor such superstitions – might feel some kind of relief to hear those officially disavowed notions uttered on stage yet safely displaced to fifteenth-century Spain.

"Ai nostri monti," the tune to which Azucena yearns for home in Act 4, is as different from her "Stride la vampa" of Act 2 as one might imagine. Sweetly folklike in tone – rather like two hymns to the peacefulness of rural France in Verdi's next opera, *La traviata* (Germont's "Di Provenza il mar" and Alfredo's "Parigi, o cara") – it indicates her desire to flee the vicious power games of the Spanish aristocrats. Exhausted and weakened but unable to sleep, Azucena is, in effect, singing a lullaby to herself, with soothing responses from Manrico that are made even more touching by the fact that he knows he is about to be executed by the Count. We cannot help but hear such a desire for escape, and (on Manrico's part) for an end to his parent's travails, as a universal trait – especially since the music is innocent in manner and devoid of specific local color.

Interestingly, *Il trovatore* was "a particular favorite" opera of the novelist James Joyce.[20] An avid and accomplished singer, he frequently sang this Azucena-Manrico duet with the editor and translator Maria Jolas in Paris in the 1920s–30s.[21] One wonders if Joyce associated it with his own lingering attachment to his parents back in Ireland, whom he had abandoned long ago for a cosmopolitan life on the Continent.[22] Azucena's song of loss and dislocation has spoken to many across the years, partly because the tune registers as familiar (even the first time one hears it) and partly because many people empathize with Azucena because of her mistreatment by mainstream society.

At the same time, opera lovers have probably been pleased to note that they themselves have not become as warped as Azucena. The empathy we feel for *la gitana* is complicated by what one keen observer has called her insistence on carrying to its completion the implacable "logic" of the "cycle of violence" that the old Count had set in motion.[23] When given one last chance to save Manrico – the creature who, she has insisted, is her "only hope" in life – Azucena does not reveal until too late the information that might have saved him. "He was your brother!" she cries to the Count a moment after the axe falls. With this heartless past tense, Azucena fulfills her mother's dying wish and attains peace of mind – a reminder that the will for revenge (among the Gypsies? in any group?) can be even stronger than maternal love.

Gypsy characters and poor Andalusians

Bizet's *Carmen* avoids some of the by-then hoary stereotypes of Gypsies, such as the death stare. The emphasis is on two other stereotypes: the criminal activities of Gypsy men (here, smuggling) and the beauty and audacity, the "sexual availability and wantonness," of the Gypsy women.[24]

Musically, the opera's title character follows the basic pattern set by Azucena and many other exotic characters in opera. She starts out by singing (and, in her case, sometimes dancing to) exotic music and, from the middle of Act 2 onward, expresses herself musically in more "universal" ways. But this shift makes a very different impression in *Carmen* than it does in *Il trovatore*. For one thing, there are simply more exotic numbers in the work – as one would expect of a French opera of that era – than the few in *Il trovatore*. Just as importantly, Bizet's opera is set further to the south, in Andalusia, though it also includes some major characters from Navarra, aptly described by Parakilas as one of "the northernmost, least Moorish, hence most 'European' part[s] of Spain."[25] This regional diversity allows the Andalusians (who are described as dark in color) to be treated as exotic within the context of the work, though still less exotic than the (even darker) Gypsies. And it raises plentiful questions of how we are to read the (variously) Spanish-sounding styles that we hear at many points in the work.

One still sometimes reads today that Bizet's *Carmen* makes no use of Spanish music.[26] Scholars have established, though, that some of the most Hispanic-sounding numbers in the opera are indeed modeled on specific Spanish performance traditions and on folk-style pieces by professionally trained Spanish composers.[27]

The denials of Spanishness in *Carmen* seem to arise from the mistaken assumption that an opera, if it is truly responsive to its locale, exhibits local color (or, in exotic works, exotic color) in its musical style, from beginning to end. Such an assumption derives from a simplistic understanding of "realism": a late nineteenth-century aesthetic trend, of which *Carmen* was, in other respects, a prominent manifestation. There is no inherent reason to expect that a French opera of the 1870s, set in Spain, will be drenched in Spanish musical idioms. True, Paris-based opera composers before Bizet – Auber, Meyerbeer, Halévy – had all introduced "typical"-sounding music into *certain* numbers of an opera, creating a musical correlative to the increasingly detailed sets, costumes, and staged numbers (e.g., rituals and local or ethnic celebrations). But not even Meyerbeer would have thought to make all or even half of the music in a work for the theater "sound like" a given country's music.

The principles of musical exoticism that we have established in Chapter 3 should lead us to expect the opposite. In *Carmen*, Spain will be presented as relatively unmarked, equivalent to Us, whereas the Gypsies, and most notably Carmen herself, will be set apart through musical and other means as Them, the Other (though an internal Other, with certain resulting complications). That is what we have seen in *Il trovatore* (with the Gypsy music of Act 2), and we see it in *Carmen* as well, but with the additional complication (noted earlier) of an Us/Them divide between northern and southern Spaniards.

The emphasis on racial disparity and incompatibility, Parakilas adds, is found in many art works of the later nineteenth century – that is, from the years when the colonial and imperialist enterprise was at its height. In *Carmen*, Delibes's *Lakmé*, and other works, we sense a "turning of artistic focus to something new," namely the unsettling awareness of "the frustrations that power [over other individuals or groups] cannot cure, not only in colonial enterprises, but in social experience generally."[28]

The means by which these frustrations are made manifest in *Carmen* include Spanish-sounding gestures but also (consistent with the Full-Context Paradigm) a variety of other, more generic (not place- or ethnic-oriented) operatic procedures and stylistic resources. The clear Exotic-Style Paradigm cases include some Spanish-style numbers sung by Carmen (about which more later) and the tightly wound entr'acte to Act 4, which is based directly on a well-known song in Andalusian style composed by the renowned operatic tenor Manuel García.[29]

One other Exotic-Style Paradigm case is the memorable minor-mode theme first heard over tremolo accompaniment at the conclusion of the otherwise joyous Prelude. This theme recurs at decisive moments throughout the work, but always only in the orchestra. It seems to signal different aspects of the story: Carmen herself (a speeded-up version when she first steps onto stage), her deleterious effect on Don José, and her eventual death at his hand. From the last of these derives the theme's nickname, "Fate."[30]

This slow, downward-spiraling theme includes three consecutively lower statements of the augmented second, the melodic interval that was and is one of Western music's most unmistakable markers of Easternness, Spanishness, and Gypsyness.[31] As a result, the theme does not conform to any standard Western scale since its pitches, if one were to line them up from bottom to top (or, following the melody's own primary thrust, from top to bottom), would include both a major and minor third degree. Additional dissonance and ambiguity are added by the slithering chromatic tremolos in the accompaniment. All in all, the "Fate" theme is surely part of what audiences and critics, expecting more stable and harmonious chordal progressions, objected to in 1875.[32]

Once the curtain rises, we need the (broader) Full-Context Paradigm of musical exoticism if we are to grasp the full range of ethnic portrayals.

Various of the Spanish characters – let us save the Gypsies for the moment – are portrayed in ways that set them apart from the Parisian or cosmopolitan (urban) norm. Don José, in particular, is as irascible and (in the last act) as unhinged a tenor hero as French opera of the era offers. His passionate excess would make him a caricature of Spanishness, were the portrayal not carried out in such idiosyncratic, realistic-feeling detail.

For example, in Don José's first scene (spoken dialogue, with Zuniga), we learn that he was forced to leave his native Navarra and his intended career as a priest because he had pummeled another man in a fistfight after they had played a very competitive game of *pelota*.[33] (Much background information is lost when the passages of spoken dialogue are drastically cut or else – as they were in most performances and recordings outside of France until the 1970s – replaced by the compressed recitatives that Ernest Guiraud composed shortly after Bizet's death to enable the work to be performed in opera houses that required operas to be sung from beginning to end.) Later in the opera, Don José becomes jealous and resentful when Carmen rejects him out of boredom, and he turns murderously insane when she takes up with the bullfighter Escamillo.

Though Don José is pointedly presented in Act 1 as a northern Spaniard (in order to heighten the contrast with Carmen), his behavior in Acts 3 and 4 fits a longstanding stereotype of Spanish males, generally, as menacingly possessive. We encountered an early example in Don Alvar, the Spaniard who "loves too much," in Rameau's *Les Indes galantes* (Chapter 5). As with so many cultural stereotypes, the point is not to argue that the stereotype is utterly false. Sociologists might (or might not) be able to ascertain whether there is a statistically greater tendency for males in Spain than elsewhere in Europe to be possessive, or whether they carry out their possessiveness in certain culturally distinct ways. But Mérimée and the opera's collaborators have embodied this tendency in a vivid literary/operatic character, who has then, over time, become a prominent symbol of "Spanish maleness" to the world at large. The result "Other-izes" a distant country's population (or at least the male half of it) and, perhaps more to the point, excuses (or critiques perhaps too obliquely) similar behaviors in people "here" at home, far from the Mediterranean.

One brief passage in the Séguedille duet-scene shows, in words and music, Don José attempting to acquire Carmen by the force of his passion. Carmen, acquisitive in her own, flightier way, has just fed him an offer of (temporary) companionship, to a surging melodic line typical of the grand-opera style of Gounod. Earlier in the act, Don José slid comfortably into this very style when singing a duet with his hometown girlfriend Micaëla. Now, in response, Don José does not ask Carmen, "Will you keep your promise?" Rather, he insists to her that she will or must do so: "If I give in to you, ... you will keep your promise! If I love you, Carmen, you will love me!" As if he has taken the tasty "bait" (the image is Susan McClary's), Don José sings this demand to the Gounodesque melody that Carmen has just offered. He then tries to overpower her by extending the melody one scale-step higher, loudly hitting a high A♯ (the leading-tone of the currently prevailing tonality, B major) on the second syllable of her name: "Ah! si je t'aime, Car*men*, Carmen, tu m'aimeras!"[34] Carmen responds by offering an utterly ambiguous "Oui," which Don José seems to think means "Yes, I'll love you" but in fact promises no more than "We'll go dancing."[35]

In this opera, the women of Spain come in two varieties. Micaëla is virtuous, devoted, quick-witted, and brave, a less droopy version of the typical middle-class girl (or proper farm-family girl) of so many nineteenth-century novels and plays. She was created by the librettists, no doubt to set in relief the two eruptive central characters. And, like Don José, she comes from Basque territory in the north of Spain (Navarra).[36] The rest of the women are either Gypsies (*bohémiennes*) or lower-class Andalusians. Carmen is, of course, one of the former, as are her two female buddies-in-smuggling, Frasquita and Mercédès.[37]

It is less clear whether the women who work in the tobacco factory include any Gypsies (other than Carmen). In spoken dialogue, Don José tells Lieutenant Zuniga (who is new to Seville) that these are local Andalusian women, and that they are always teasing, never talking sense. Don José adds that they are off having their midday meal (and, one presumes, siesta) and that, when they return, there will be "quite a crowd to watch them pass by." Moments later, the women come strolling back. The young men and the soldiers observe aloud (in a sung passage to be discussed below) that the women are "impudent" and "coquettish" in manner, are smoking cigarettes held "between the edges of their teeth," and, crucially, are "brown."

Translators have often, and plausibly, rendered the latter adjective as "brunette" or "dark-haired." At the English National Opera, though, the relevant phrase, *brunes cigarières*, is sung as "dusky little beauties."[38] The latter rendering conveys better that the women are naturally dark-complexioned, or else tanned from outdoor work and from traveling by foot or on horseback. Still, darkened skin does not mean that the women are Gypsies. When, later in Act 1, the libretto wants to point out the physical traits of Gypsies, it includes more than skin tone. Don José tells Carmen (in spoken dialogue) that he knows she is a Gypsy from her "coloring" (*teint*) but also from "everything" about her, including her "eyes and mouth."[39] Therefore, even if one imagines that at least a few of the 300 women working in the factory (besides Carmen) are Gypsies, the bulk of them are, as Don José has told Zuniga, true Andalusians.[40] A critic who hated the work at its first performance (Oscar Comettant) described the chorus as "Andalusian women with tanned chest [*au sein bruni*], such as can only be found – or so I would like to believe – in the taverns of Seville and Grenada."[41]

Whatever the ethnicity of the women, the scene stages an episode of exotic tourism in an unusually literal sense. Soldiers from across Spain as well as young local men from various social classes – stand-ins for the French spectators in the opera's audience – look the lower-class females up and down. The young men openly confess that they have come here to "lie in wait" for the women, almost as if to entrap them: the verb *guetter* is normally used more for sentinels, spies, or highway robbers.

Some remarkable changes in the music and sung text here help direct the audience's gaze toward the incoming *cigarières*. First, the young men (a group of choral tenors) who are waiting for the "brown" women sing softly and "lightly," as if whispering confidentially. Their tune is bright, in 2/4 meter, squarely phrased, and marked Allegretto. The women then enter, to new and slower music (Andantino 6/8) over a long-held dominant pedal. The melody here, assigned to the orchestra, is not Spanish-sounding but something more specifically appropriate: smooth and sinuous, as if reflecting the beauty and lazily graceful movements of these sauntering *femmes de Séville*.

Above this orchestral tissue, the soldiers (a group of choral baritones) are suddenly reduced to a dazed state, from which they (to the aforementioned words about the women's impudent manner) manage to rouse themselves just enough to emit slow repeated pitches: eleven spellbound Bs, then twelve A-sharps, finally relaxing helplessly into an A. In the instrumental codetta, the bass line finally slides up and down, and up and down again, chromatically, between the fifth and sixth degrees of the scale (B–C–C♯–C♮) – a frequent mid-nineteenth-century symbol of yearning and sexual desire.[42]

The women then begin to sing their own version of the orchestra's slowly rising melody, with some delectable overlapping between sopranos and altos, while the cellos and basses create an airy pulsation under the tune by plucking a single note on each (slow) beat. This music marks the women as peacefully sensual, much in the manner of other outdoor mood-pieces for women in French opera, including ones in *Les huguenots* and *Don Carlos* (Act 2 in both cases), plus, eight years after *Carmen*, the Flower Duet in *Lakmé*. The words that the *cigarières* sing are all about how the smoke, in the air, rises (like, of course, the melody) and how it makes one light-headed and cheers one's spirits. The vocal phrases are artfully extended – seven measures, then again seven – to add to the sense of timeless wafting.

In the middle section of their number, the women finally reveal themselves as the teasers that Don José described. They declare more quickly, jumpily – in a minor-mode pout – that men's words of love are like smoke. The young men (tenors) accuse the women of cruelly ignoring their pleas, but the women merely repeat their gibe, and the *cigarières* then return to singing calmly about the smoke curling upwards from their cigarettes.[43]

The women's dismissal of men's protestations of love is based upon once-widespread images of courtship rituals in Spain. A typical example is *El arreglito* (1857), the song by Sebastián Iradier whose music (though not words) Bizet used as the basis for Carmen's Habanera (i.e., the number that immediately follows this chorus). In Iradier's song, Pepito pleads with Chinita, and she (until the end, when she capitulates) sports with him, declaring that all men are liars:

Ch.: [...] yo veo con gran pesar	Ch.: [...] I see with great regret
Que todo es guasa, música celestial.	That all [men's talk of love] is teasing, and music of the spheres.

The French translation that was published under the vocal line (along with the Spanish) is even more sarcastic, no doubt reflecting a French tendency to displace coquetry to "that country" beyond the Pyrenees.

P.: Chinita mia, danse avec moi,	P.: My darling, dance with me,
Ne sais-tu pas que je me meurs pour toi?	Don't you know that I'm dying away for you?
Ch.: Pepito mio, mourir pour moi! Le beau discours, je n'en crois rien, ma foi!	Ch.: My Pepito, dying because of me! Such fancy talk, I don't believe a word of it![44]

So much for regular Spaniards, especially lower-class females native to the area around Seville. What of the Gypsies, who in the opera are even more exotic than the Andalusians? Some of the music associated with them is not ethnically marked. The Act 2 Quintet – in the course of which Carmen refuses to join the latest smuggling trip because she is awaiting Don José – is in standard *opéra-comique* or even Offenbachian *opéra-bouffe* style, which has the effect of endearing the characters to us, as if they were a familiar set of French servants or tradespeople. Much the same is true of the carefree Gypsy ensemble in Act 3 ("Quant au douanier"), in which the three women promise to distract the customs agent, by any means necessary, so the contraband goods can go through. In both numbers, the Gypsy characters, interacting only with each other, seem to feel no need to put on Gypsy or Spanish airs, musically or otherwise.

A more complex representation of the Gypsy smugglers occurs in the number that begins Act 3. Parakilas, after admitting that exotic style is absent here as well, helpfully asks what *is* in the number and comes up with a likely dramaturgical explanation:

> ["Ecoute, compagnon"] is no Gypsy dance; it is all business, all discipline ... This music can be heard as a grim musical joke on Don José, showing that for him there is no escape from the soldier's life, no escape from his culture and the rule of force that it has imposed on other cultures.[45]

Parakilas's reading seems all the more persuasive when one notices that the minor-mode march tune resembles Gounod's famous *Funeral March of a Marionette* (1872 for piano, orchestrated 1878), down to the mechanically recurring little decorative figures in the melody (on beat 2 in the Gounod; on the downbeat here).[46]

However discouraging to Don José, the number encourages the audience to feel some empathy with these social outsiders. The upward-plodding thirds in the low strings and (midway through the number) the unsettling, labyrinthine chromatic modulation from A-flat major back to C minor tell us – in tandem with the words – that these bandits are hard workers (like the anvil-smiters in *Trovatore*), pooling their efforts toward a common goal in spite of rugged terrain and harsh weather – which, they note, might cause one to lose one's footing or one's way – and armed government agents lying in ambush. Bizet's mix of conventional and modernistic (for his day) Western musical procedures portrays Gypsy bandits as neither comic nor threatening but somehow admirable – and courageous under threat.

Carmen differs from the rest of the Gypsies in her musical behavior. She *is* regularly assigned, or otherwise associated with, exotic music of three different kinds: Spanish, Cuban, and flamenco (Spanish-Gypsy). The aforementioned Fate theme (with the three Gypsyish augmented seconds) is an obvious case: after the Prelude, it is heard only when Carmen appears on stage or is being mentioned. Five of her other solos are frankly Spanish or Spanish-Gypsy in genre and style, and in all of these she is singing what we might call a "stage song" or, to use the language of film criticism, a diegetic number: a song that other characters on stage know is a song. (Stage songs are thus set apart from the more usual kinds of operatic expression, which often function more like inner thoughts that the audience is being allowed to "hear.")

Carmen's five Spanish-style numbers are:

- the Habanera, which is based on Iradier's aforementioned Cuban-style song "El arreglito" ("Habanera" simply means "song [or dance] from Havana");
- the taunting song – "Tra la la, coupe-moi, brûle-moi" – that Carmen sings "impertinently" (Bizet's own instruction) to Lieutenant Zuniga;
- the Séguedille (briefly discussed above);
- the "Chanson bohème," a flamenco-like number sung and danced with Frasquita and Mercédès at the beginning of Act 2; and
- the seductively wordless song (accompanied by pizzicato strings) that Carmen sings when dancing and playing the castanets for Don José alone in the middle of Act 2.

Carmen's willingness to engage in song at a moment's notice echoes stereotypes of the Gypsy as carefree and fun-loving. It also presents her as manipulating the feelings of her onstage audience – the other characters – through song and dance. Parakilas notes:

An audience hearing Carmen sing her Gypsy music [including flamenco- and other Spanish-sounding numbers] cannot tell what it represents about her, whether it is her Gypsy nature, or the image she wants others to have of her, or the nature that a Spanish soldier ascribes to her because it answers to his dream of escape from the bonds of European life.[47]

In Acts 3 and 4, Carmen ceases to manipulate Don José, instead treating him with total honesty, which, it turns out, he cannot handle. She also no longer sings exotic numbers.[48] The sudden shift away from explicitly exotic numbers is thus, as Parakilas notes, "a matter of dramatic structure, not simply of local color."[49]

True, there is (in Act 2) one Spanish number sung by a non-Gypsy: the bolero-like opening section of Escamillo's Toreador Song ("Votre toast"). But this, too, is a case of a character dressing himself up to play a public role and announcing "who I am" in a bragging aria whose dramatic function somewhat resembles that of a stage song. Bizet even tells the baritone to sing the lines "fatuously."

In short, all five Spanish, Gypsy, or Cuban-sounding vocal numbers in the opera, except for Escamillo's "Votre toast," come from the mouth of our Gypsy (anti-)heroine early in the opera. One assumes that Carmen is choosing to present herself in various musical languages that the Spaniards to whom she is singing can understand and enjoy. As for the three numbers that are specifically Spanish (without an admixture of Gypsy or Cuban), perhaps Carmen can sing them because (consistent with the special place of the Roma in Spanish society) she *is* a sort of Spaniard, a slippery crosser of boundaries, part of the opera's Us as well as part of its own local Them.[50]

The remaining two numbers hint at yet other aspects of Carmen. The Habanera, given its Cuban origin and its remarkable African-derived syncopations, must have linked Carmen in the minds of many operagoers with even darker-skinned people than herself: a nearly unique case of sub-Saharan Africa finding some resonance (even if by way of the Caribbean) in a major nineteenth-century repertoire work. As for the Act 2 "Chanson bohème," it gives Carmen and her female Gypsy friends a chance to present themselves in a flamenco performance of song and dance, for an onstage audience of Spanish soldiers (including Zuniga). Two guitarists strum away, and the tempo increases toward the end, as in flamenco performances in Bizet's day (and our own): Andantino, Animato, Plus vite (faster), and a breathtaking final Presto. At its end, even the endlessly energetic Carmen "falls down, panting, onto a bench."

The Gypsy Carmen's non-Gypsyish lament

Carmen's so-called Card Aria is strikingly different from all five of these Spanish (and Cuban and flamenco) numbers. This aria is a musical soliloquy inserted into the middle of the Act 3 Trio (after a first section sung by Frasquita and Mercédès). It conveys aspects of Carmen's Gypsy-ness through specific musical and musico-textual details, but these are not style markers of the sort that the Exotic-Style Paradigm recognizes. Perhaps for this reason, the Card Aria has rarely been examined in any detail.[51] The explanatory power of the Full-Context Paradigm helps do justice to this remarkable piece of characterization, which the Bizet authority Hervé Lacombe suggestively calls "the black pearl" of the score.[52]

It may seem risky to explore the meanings of Carmen's various musical styles. With the possible exception of Mozart's Don Giovanni, she is the most vivid instance of an opera character who engages in different musical manners with different individuals or groups. Nonetheless, the Card Trio – as those commentators who have spent any time with it agree – does show us, more directly than any other moment in the opera, Carmen without guile. Frasquita and then Mercédès have just playfully told their own respective fortunes with a deck of cards. Carmen takes the deck, starts turning cards over, and is stunned by what they predict: death for herself and then for Don

José. The number, as various critics – including Nietzsche and Adorno – have noted, gives voice to Carmen's deepest concerns through words and music.[53] Whereas so often Carmen performs for one person or a crowd, this time she is alone with her thoughts.

The Card Aria differs drastically from Carmen's sexy numbers early in the opera, and differs just as much from the life-affirming anthem of personal *liberté* under an "open sky" that Carmen leads – to non-exotic music, as if speaking the hidden feelings of the city dwellers in the audience – at the end of Act 2. Here we encounter a gloomier stereotype of the Gypsy: superstitious, irrational, and oppressed by fear of fate.[54] The stereotype is deepened by the music that Bizet assigns the orchestra, which, as Lesley Wright observes, "with its repeated tones, minor modality, and low[-]pitched heavy brass chords, specifically the funereal trombones, evokes the mode of expression used by the oracles of death in French operatic history."[55]

Above this throbbing, Carmen slowly unfurls a vocal melody uniquely appropriate to the dramatic situation and – despite its lack of Gypsy coloration – appropriate also to her ethnic identity. This melody states an unusually extended rhythmic pattern – four measures – six times in a row (and the beginning of a seventh), heedless of shifts in the melody's pitches and swerves in the orchestral harmonies (Ex. 7.2). This long, rigid rhythmic pattern derives its uniqueness from four factors. (1) It uses almost nothing but eighth notes rather than – as is more usual in music of this opera and of the era, generally – a syntactically structured mixture of long and short notes. (2) The music's regular four-measure pace stands in incongruous tension with the unusual poetic structure, each quatrain being constructed of thirteen- and six-syllable lines in alternation (or, in French terminology, feminine alexandrines and hemistiches), as in the first quatrain:

En vain pour éviter les réponses amères,	In vain do you shuffle the cards
En vain tu mêleras,	In an attempt at avoiding results that are distressing;
Cela ne sert à rien, les cartes sont sincères	It serves no purpose, for the cards are truthful
Et ne mentiront pas.	And do not lie.

(3) The four-measure rhythmic pattern extends beyond the downbeat, and Bizet adds a sorrowful appoggiatura-and-release to several of the half- and full cadences, such as the rich, if diatonic, pileup of E, F, and A♭ (resolving to G) on "et ne men*tiront* pas." (4) The final *e*'s in words such as réponses

Example 7.2 Bizet, *Carmen*, Act 3: Carmen's Card Aria, opening.

and cartes (in the strophe reproduced above, and circled in Ex. 7.2) are not mute, as in spoken French, but are given the same stress and held for the same length as the other syllables.

Bizet marks the music "simplement, très également" (simply, very evenly). The whole three-minute aria (except as it nears the end) must, Bizet requests, be performed in a more or less unrelenting tread, without highly personal or spontaneous-sounding application of rubato. Bizet does mark important changes in dynamics, but these are presumably meant to occur in a state of tension with the unyielding rhythm. Carmen is trapped by the implacable pulsing in her brain. She struggles with the confining fatalism of her (ultimately non-European, "primitive") culture but is unable to break free of it. In effect, she sings her own funeral march.

The rigid rhythm causes several instances of "wrong" accentuation, including two in the second line of the aria's final quatrain.

Mais si tu dois mourir, si le mot redoutable
    Est écrit **par** le sort,
	But if you must die, if the
	    terrible word
	    Is written by fate,

Recommence vingt fois... la carte impitoyable
    Répétera: la mort!
	You can start again twenty
	    times, but the pitiless card
	    Will repeat: "Death!"

Carmen is not to be understood as mangling the Spanish language (here represented, of course, by French). Misaccentuation was an integral feature of much nineteenth-century French opera, especially the comic varieties, where it often added a silly or carefree gloss to the goings-on. Indeed, in other numbers in *Carmen* itself, accents can occur on weak syllables, and to potentially good effect. In the Séguedille, an alert singer can show Carmen's self-deprecating humor by enjoying the bumps in "Il **n'est** que bri**ga**dier / Mais **c'est** assez **pour** une bo**hé**mienne" (He's only a corporal, but that's good enough for a Gypsy woman). The grim relentlessness of the Card Aria, by contrast, renders this same kind of unnatural declamation constricting, even dehumanizing.

In the remaining minute or so of her aria, Carmen breaks briefly from the confines of her repeated four-measure pattern. She ascends to a (mezzo's) high F, *fortissimo*, and achieves one precious measure of rhythmic freedom. (Bizet tells the orchestra to adjust to the singer's rhythm here.) During this passage of climax and release, Carmen starts freely repeating, to increasingly intense music, words that themselves involve the verb "repeat" – "the pitiless card will repeat: 'Death!'" As a result, Carmen seems to be coming under the hypnotic spell of that card of doom.

One recurring trait of the wording also helps us see ourselves in the despairing Carmen. Bizet apparently wrote the text of the Card Aria himself, following the verse meter and number of lines (and a few words) of the blander version that had been provided for him by Meilhac and Halévy. Among other things, he replaced the librettists' first- and occasional third-person constructions with the second-person singular, *tu*. What results, notes Lacombe, is "a process of doubling. It is as if, from this point on, [Carmen], having attained tragic wisdom, were watching herself act" (and, indeed addressing herself).[56]

All these different aspects of the Card Aria converge to make a single basic point: a musical number in an opera (or dramatic oratorio) can convey ethnic or exotic characterization without ethnic or exotic style. In this particular case, I would go so far as to suggest that, paradoxical though it

Figure 7.2 Emma Calvé in Carmen's Card Aria, as photographed in a studio in New York, 1893. (From the Raymond Mander and Joe Mitchenson Theatre Collection.)

may seem, Carmen comes across in this aria as more deeply "a Gypsy" than in her patently Gypsy numbers earlier in the opera.

This is not to deny that Carmen here also becomes an object for empathetic identification for "us" (non-Gypsies and non-Spaniards), precisely by the avoidance of musical Gypsyisms or Hispanicisms. Lacombe terms the effect of this aria "cathartic," by analogy to ancient tragedy. "For an instant, the performance ... when it reaches this point of tragic experience, binds the spectator to, and then releases him [or her] from, the anguish of death."[57] Even Susan McClary, who helpfully stresses the core tension of supposed "civilized" and "Gypsy" values elsewhere in this work, concludes that Carmen, by making no use of "her characteristic gypsy discourse" in this aria, shows herself to possess "'universal' subjectivity," to be "just like everyone else."[58]

But Carmen is primarily, in this aria (as elsewhere), presented as *not* being "just like everyone else." I suspect that many of us in the audience find ourselves able to empathize readily with this searing portrayal of a person facing her own death sentence precisely because we know that the singer up there on stage is (within the context of the plot and costumes) one of "those Gypsies": superstitious creatures who react passively to Fate (as we more "rational" beings supposedly do not). We thus may permit ourselves to recognize the deep human truths in Carmen's song, instead of resisting them as we might have, had she looked just a bit more like us and behaved more the way we (think we) do. And all of this is achieved precisely through the avoidance of musical Gypsyisms or Hispanicisms.

Two great Carmens of the early twentieth century left photographic evidence – studio photos but taken in costume – that surely reveal how this moment was often staged. Both Emma Calvé and Rosa Ponselle stare out at the audience, the former more childlike, the latter more worldly. Calvé (Fig. 7.2) points at the accusatory cards, like a stunned sybil; Ponselle tilts her set of cards toward us, in horror, as if to enlist our corroboration.[59] Neither bit of stage business is indicated in the libretto, yet either one can add another layer of complexity to the exotic characterization. Is Carmen – superstitious Gypsy that she is – showing us what she ignorantly accepts as her own unavoidable fate? Or is she more coolly reminding us, like an experienced and all-knowing Gypsy fortuneteller, of the doom that awaits each of *us*?

8 | Imperialism and "the exotic Orient"

During the nineteenth and early twentieth centuries, Britain, France, and other Western countries extended their control over the resources of ever larger portions of the earth's surface. Sometimes they filled the (perceived) empty spaces with colonists. Other times they satisfied themselves with securing the river and coastal waterways that were necessary for trade to grow unhindered. Always, they increased their dominion over native human populations.

Contact with distant regions and cultures gradually introduced the West to previously unsuspected cultural patterns and to "exotic" products ranging from fabrics to foodstuffs. It also clarified Westerners' sense of themselves, and sometimes complicated it. An English or French person, for example, was someone who (among other things) had certain political rights that distant natives did not. He or she could visit the colonies, read about them, or perhaps send money to establish missions and clinics.[1] Yet, at the same time, increased knowledge of different ways of life could threaten a Westerner's settled belief that only Europe (and its offshoots in the Americas) possessed values that were admirable and expressive traditions worthy of being called "culture."[2]

Among the values that (as gradually became evident) were not at all unique to the West was a desire for independence and self-determination. Resistance to imperial and colonial domination flared up sporadically but powerfully throughout the nineteenth century, notably in India (a revolt in 1857, often called the "Indian Mutiny" in English newspapers and textbooks), Jamaica, Egypt, and Indonesia.[3] These uprisings often had the immediate effect of intensifying the determination of the government and population in the imperial home country to send more military troops so as to defend the nation's honor and to force the indigenous people to accept the benefits of Europe's civilizing mission.[4] Nonetheless, such resistance would culminate in the dismantling of empire in the course of the twentieth century (see Chapters 9 and 10).

Music and the arts come into this complex story in a variety of ways. Whole books have been written, or remain to be written, on the ways in which "native" musics were described to audiences back in the Western homeland, and on the uses to which Western music was put in colonial homes, schools, and missionary institutions.[5] Given the aims of the present book, the more immediate question for this chapter is: How did Western musical works – especially operas – reflect, and participate in, the representation of distant and exotic-seeming regions? In particular, how was the "East" or "Orient" portrayed, both on its own and in relationship to the imperial West? A related question – how literally, or metaphorically, did people take these portrayals at the time? – will be raised briefly at several points (as it was in Chapters 5 and 7).

Multiple empires, multiple Orients

By the early nineteenth century, the Western hemisphere had already been conquered and settled by Europeans, and the colonists themselves – or, in Saint-Domingue (Haïti), the former slaves, freed in the wake of the French Revolution – were beginning to shake off the yoke of control by an overseas power.[6] As a result, literary and operatic topics involving the European conquest of the Americas, though greatly favored during the seventeenth through early nineteenth centuries, gradually came to be regarded as outmoded.[7] By 1888, one writer could opine that the Aztecs were not suitable matter for a new opera because they had become "parlor-clock material": that is, overly familiar motifs in bourgeois home decor.[8]

The most extensive territory-grabbing now took place in sub-Saharan Africa and in what was known as "the East."[9] But, whereas "black Africa" found relatively little immediate echo in Western musical life, "the East" or "the Orient" (including, as we shall see, North Africa) quickly became the distant region of predilection for literature and the arts during the nineteenth century.[10]

Imperial control over "the East" – as over other territories – involved competition and also collaboration. The major powers competed for markets, raw materials, cheap labor, speedy ocean travel, and strategic military advantages, but they also kept competition from escalating into war by dividing up the globe into accepted "spheres of influence." The Netherlands declared Indonesia a colony in 1798 (after two centuries of commercial activity there). France, in the space of a half-century (1830–84), established sovereignty over Morocco, Algeria, and Tunisia, as well as Indochina.[11] Britain secured – through a variety of legal and military means – Egypt and most of the Arabian Peninsula, consolidated its hold on India (including what is now Pakistan), and established crucial treaty ports, leased-territories, and other forms of "informal empire" in China and elsewhere.[12] Russia increased its hegemony over extensive formerly Ottoman territories, sometimes for the purpose of (or under the guise of) protecting fellow Eastern Orthodox Christians. The relatively young United States likewise became a major player in the (broadly defined) "Orient," starting with crucial naval victories over pirates who operated out of ports in North Africa (1815) and continuing with the forcible "opening" of Japan to world trade by Commodore Perry in 1853.[13]

The crucial phrase "the Orient" deserves a brief discussion. Today it is often used as a (non-scholarly) designation for East Asia.[14] In the nineteenth and early twentieth centuries, though, "the Orient" often designated a portion of the globe much closer to Europe: North Africa and the Arabian Peninsula, with the possible addition of Persia and India. But "Orient" and its derivative terms were also sometimes used to refer to an even more immense swath of terrain combining these two meanings and thus reaching from Morocco, at the western end, all the way east – more or less along the Silk Road – to China and Japan.[15] This capacious sense of "Orient," "Orientalism," and so on is the one primarily adopted in the present chapter. I hope thereby to suggest how little the European imagination tended to differentiate between various cultures that, to us today, may appear quite disparate.

I also want to stress that "Orientalism" and "Orientalist" are used, in this chapter, as relatively neutral labels, much as they have regularly been used since the mid-nineteenth century in the world of visual art. "Orientalist" is not construed here – in the manner of much recent cultural criticism – as automatically implying that the works in question systematically denigrate the regions and peoples that they portray. But neither are these nineteenth-century Orientalist musical works construed, in advance, as inherently incapable of denigrating places, peoples, and ways of life.[16] The present chapter is interested in noting evidence of Western attitudes toward "the exotic East" in specific works (here operas, mostly). It prefers, though, not to take as a given that those attitudes were omnipresent, straightforward in function, or monolithic.

To adopt a broad use of the term "the Orient," as I do in this chapter, is admittedly problematic. Not least, it bundles together various societies and locales that long carried divergent images in the Western mind. For example, one thinks of certain almost polar-opposite stereotypes: Japanese personal modesty, emotional repression, and obedient self-control (including a rigid code of honor that could lead to suicide-on-command); and, in sharp contrast, Middle Eastern impulsiveness, the institution of the harem, philosophical reflection (by famous caliphs and poets, real or fictional), vengeful blood lust, religious fanaticism, and slow treks on camelback across a silent desert.[17] Nonetheless, by lumping these diverse (real or half-imagined) countries and regions together, one notices certain common features that were often assigned to them indiscriminately in the Western mind – and thus in Western musical culture – during the century and more under discussion.

The chapter focuses primarily on opera, the "high art" genre in which musical portrayals of the Orient (the reader should henceforth imagine scare quotes around "Orient") have been more numerous, lasting, and influential than any other. I take my examples mainly from operas that are patently serious in aspiration.[18] I explore some archetypal plot structures and characters around which their libretti tend to be constructed, and examine how the archetypes are reinforced, or sometimes undercut, through music. I conclude with a somewhat more detailed look at one opera in which Orientalist conventions, and some of those specific stereotypes of "the Japanese," mentioned above, are, by turns (or at one and the same time), manifested, critiqued, and subverted: Puccini's *Madama Butterfly*.

Of particular interest will be the question of whether the music in a given work or passage is adequately explained by the Exotic-Style Paradigm or requires the broader Full-Context Paradigm. That is, does the music respond to the plot's setting mainly through accepted stylistic signifiers of Elsewhere, or does it engage (instead, or as well) a wide range of tools of the opera composer's trade *not* associated with an Elsewhere?

Silence over the imperial encounter

First off, it is striking to notice one thing that nineteenth- and early twentieth-century Oriental operas almost never do: directly portray recent or current imperial and colonial encounters carried out by the composer's own country.[19]

Some operas (and works in related genres) from this period portrayed encounters from the days of the explorers, that is, from a few centuries earlier. Examples include Spontini's *Fernand Cortez* (1809, rev. 1817); Félicien David's *Christophe Colomb* (1847; a secular oratorio with spoken narration); and the vigorous and still stageworthy *Il guarany* by Carlos Gomes (1870; the work is based on a dynastic struggle between Spaniards and Portuguese in early seventeenth-century Brazil).[20] Meyerbeer created the most lasting such opera: *L'Africaine* (1865).[21] In all these cases, the displacement is not just temporal but spatial: the imperial power is some other European country, not that of the composer nor of the audience for which the opera was composed.[22]

Paintings, novels, poems, and spoken plays of the day often employed the same strategy of setting an exotic story several centuries back, or even a millennium or two; or else they avoided questions of time-period by portraying the distant locale as unchanging (before it came into contact with Westerners), legendary, or even fantastic. Perhaps writers and artists preferred not to raise matters of public contentiousness, or feared that well-known subject matter might impede the "willing suspension of disbelief" – the phrase is Coleridge's (1817) – that was widely considered essential (in those pre-Brechtian days) to apprehending any work of art. In opera, the strategy of muting any connections to the day's headlines seems to have succeeded. Karen Henson studied a mountain of French published reviews of late nineteenth-century exotic operas but found "not ... a single reference to France's colonial projects and conquests."[23]

To be sure, this silence is not as unusual as one might think: nineteenth-century critics and other observers almost never made explicit connections between plots of serious operas (the satirical operettas of Offenbach are another matter) and the political tensions of the day.[24] Nevertheless, certain parallels seem obvious to us now. For example, all the characters in Massenet's *Le roi de Lahore* (1877) are Indian Hindus, whose territory is under apparently unmotivated attack from "Mohammedans." The Hindu priest Timour urges King Alim to send troops to repel those who, "in the name of Mohammed, whom they call the Prophet," are burning towns and fields as they march toward the city:

Le sultan Mahmoud vient pour combattre nos dieux! ...	Sultan Mahmud comes to fight our gods...
Rassemble ton armée, [ô roi,] marche vers le désert,	Rally your soldiers, [oh, King,] and march towards the desert,
et que devant tes pas, ainsi qu'une fumée,	So that, before you even reach them, the enemy
s'efface l'ennemi menaçant notre sol.	That threatens our land will disperse like a wisp of smoke.

France had conquered large coastal areas of Algeria in the early 1830s–40s and, ever since, had tried to contain uprisings of "Mohammedans," notably a revolt in Kabylia (a mountainous region in the north) in 1871, just a few years before Massenet and his librettist began planning their opera.

Admittedly, the situations are not fully analogous: in Algeria, the Muslims (whether Arab or Berber) were the natives and the French the foreign invaders. Still, the logic of imperialism granted the French – like the British in India and elsewhere – a "civilizing mission" on this and other non-Christian terrains. Any native resistance was therefore an attack on France itself.[25]

The fact that those marauding Muslims we hear about in *Le roi de Lahore* never appear onstage – or even sing from offstage – demands an explanation. Perhaps this strategic absence allowed operagoers to recall with some satisfaction various French victories over North Africans – and without the discomfort of seeing the Hindus (stand-ins for the French) being attacked, or even audibly (musically) challenged, by the Muslims. The end of the opera may have gone further in this direction, suggesting the vast military superiority of the French in North Africa. One character simply reports to the others that "the Sultan's men ... are heading back to the desert." Thus is the crisis averted, without the forces of (Hindu) order having to shed Muslim blood.

The case is similar with Verdi's *Aida*. On the one hand, French, Italian, and English reviews of the opera's early productions accepted, with rare exceptions (such as two reviews by George Bernard Shaw), the opera's premised time and place as parameters within which to discuss the work.[26] On the other, people at the time were surely capable of drawing – or at least sensing – parallels between the actions of ancient empires (in an opera) and the actions of the European powers. In this case, we have two revelatory bits of evidence from the composer himself. (1) In 1871, while completing the opera, Verdi instructed the librettist, Ghislanzoni, to base some lines for the Egyptian priests in the Act 2 Triumphal Scene on the telegrams that the King of Prussia had recently sent, attributing to God the recent triumph of Prussia's troops over those of France. (2) In an interview conducted late in his life, Verdi decried the British subjugation of Egypt and India and the Italian attempts at gaining a foothold in the Horn of Africa. He even drew an analogy between native resistance in India and the ideals of the Italian *Risorgimento*, ideals that – though he did not make the point explicit to the interviewer – had plainly found an echo in *Aida*, namely in the portrayal of Amonasro, the king of oppressed Nubia (called Ethiopia in the opera).[27]

The paradigmatic Oriental-opera plot

As I argued at the end of Chapter 4, any attempt at defining exoticism solely in terms of non-Western style traits tends to align itself, if not always explicitly, with the formalism that dominated twentieth-century writings in music aesthetics, history, and criticism (as in some influential books by Stravinsky).[28] A formalist view of musical art tends to focus more or less exclusively on musical form and style. It works on the assumption that the pitches and rhythms in a work of music (in our case, an exotic work) somehow convey to a listener all the necessary data or messages, whether s/he is or is not familiar with the work's social and cultural contexts. An anti-formalist aesthetics, by contrast, insists that pitches and rhythms are always heard in a concrete (if not necessarily stable) context. In an opera, the context for the notes – a pervasive, often persuasive one – is of course the plot and all that it entails (sets, costumes, sung words, stage action). I therefore start this chapter's examination of Orientalist operas in a frankly anti-formalist spirit. I discuss their plots.

Or, rather, their *plot* (in the singular). I venture that a single paradigmatic plot drives many nineteenth- and early twentieth-century Orientalist operas, including both canonical and forgotten ones.[29] As noted earlier, I am here using the word "Orientalist" in a primarily descriptive sense, the way that art historians do with regard to the thousands of paintings with Turkish, Arab, Persian, Indian, and East Asian subject matter by Ingres, Delacroix, Gérôme, Alma-Tadema, and Redon (and, later, Picasso and Matisse). But this does not mean that we should blind ourselves to evidence of ideological subtexts. The paradigmatic plot is loaded with messages about Them, and especially about the ways that They contrast with Us.

The plot can be schematized as follows. I choose words that neither avoid nor disguise but, to the contrary, faithfully echo certain cultural preconceptions of the time, including attitudes toward gender and race that may strike us today as crude or oppressive:

Young, tolerant, brave, possibly naive or selfish, white-European tenor-hero intrudes (at risk of disloyalty to his own people and to colonialist ethic, with which he is identified) into mysterious, brown- or (less often) black-skinned colonized territory represented by female dancers of irresistible allure and by deeply affectionate, sensitive lyric soprano, thereby incurring wrath of brutal, intransigent priest or tribal chieftain (bass or sometimes baritone) and latter's blindly obedient chorus of male savages.

This plot essentially transposes into the cultural and artistic language of the day a travel narrative that was standard during the age of empire: what Patrick Brantlinger calls a "non-fictional quest romance," in which a Westerner – often in sub-Saharan Africa – struggles his way "through enchanted or bedeviled lands toward a goal, ostensibly the discovery of the Nile's sources or the conversion of the cannibals."[30] In operas of the period, this basic story is generally given dramatic shape by means of the then-normative romantic triangle, in which two powerful males vie for a valued female.[31] And, again and again, the story gets located, not in sub-Saharan Africa, but in some version of "the East."

The standard Oriental-opera plot, or a substantial portion of it, provides the basic structure for such still-durable works as Meyerbeer's *L'Africaine* (set on "a [Hindu] island in the Indian Ocean" near the coast of Africa), Verdi's *Aida*, Saint-Saëns's *Samson et Dalila*, Delibes's *Lakmé*, and (substituting distinctive facial features for darker-than-European skin color) Puccini's *Madama Butterfly*.

An archetypal plot is not a rigid template. Each of the five Oriental operas just named contains a unique combination of elements, giving it a profile and tone of its own and thereby enabling it to gain and hold a place in the repertoire. The female protagonists in *Aida*, *Lakmé*, and *Madama Butterfly* are sensitive and (vocally) high-floating sopranos. They also display some traits of the *femme fragile*, a character-type that became ever more prominent in painting and literature across the nineteenth century, from the title figure in Edgar Allan Poe's tale *Ligeia* (1838) to paintings by Dante Gabriel Rossetti, to the female protagonist of Maeterlinck's play *Pelléas et Mélisande* (1892) and Debussy's operatic setting of it (1902).[32] Saint-Saëns's Dalila and Meyerbeer's Sélika (the queen of a Hindu, hence "Eastern," people, in *L'Africaine*) were cast as mezzo-sopranos, in accordance with a mid-nineteenth-century practice for "dark" females.[33] These two characters are also (and not unrelatedly) rather fearsome individuals, close to the *femme fatale* stereotype that, like the *femme fragile*, came to increasing prominence as the century progressed. (The prominence of both female types – *fragile* and *fatale* – has been plausibly explained as a reaction to the increasing visibility and power of women in European and American social and cultural life.)[34] *Samson et Dalila* has no other female characters (besides the women in the chorus). *L'Africaine* does have a role for lyric soprano, but it is assigned to the Portuguese woman Inès, to whom the tenor hero – cured of his exotic infatuation – finally returns.

Act 1 of *Samson et Dalila* presents two varieties of *femme fatale*. The Philistine priestesses are given a soft, flowing choral paean to springtime and a delicately voluptuous dance. These women thus represent a gentle variety of *femme fatale*, seducing – through fine-spun grace, and almost inadvertently – the Hebrew (hence proto-Western) males on stage, who are stunned to silence by this display of aural and visual exquisiteness. By contrast, the deep-voiced Dalila brings her proto-Western male low through determined sexual chicanery, in a manner familiar from current-day paintings of ancient Middle-Eastern females such as Judith, Cleopatra, Salome – and Delilah herself.[35] Dalila's characterization is made unusually rich, though, by her evident attraction to the very man she is trying to undo.[36] (We shall return to the women characters in more detail below.)

Other crucial aspects of the paradigmatic plot are followed more straightforwardly in both *L'Africaine* and *Samson et Dalila*, notably the vengefulness of the local males against the interloping tenor who represents (in one way or another) the West. Indeed, of the five Orientalist operas mentioned above, it is not these two – despite their mezzos – but *Aida* that is the most idiosyncratic. Verdi's Egyptian opera – his only work besides *Nabucco* to be set in ancient times – mixes elements of the plot sketched above with elements from several other plot and character archetypes and (lightly disguised) current-day agendas. As Edward Said was the first to make clear, these agendas included the military exploits (in dark-skinned Sudan) of Khedive Ismail, the Egyptian ruler who commissioned *Aida* from Verdi for the recently built Cairo opera house.[37]

To be sure, certain Orientalist operas of the nineteenth and early twentieth centuries do not fit this archetype, notably many operas entirely peopled by Easterners. Even so, certain scene-types from the paradigmatic plot occur in Oriental operas that are *not* premised upon a (proto-)Western incursion into the East. Act 3 of the aforementioned *Le roi de Lahore*, for example, consists entirely of an extended scene of Eastern ceremoniality (about which more below).

The same is true of certain character-types. Bizet's *Les pêcheurs de perles* (The Pearl Fishers, 1863) is set in a storybook Ceylon of no particular century, perhaps at a time so long ago that "the West" did not yet, in any significant sense, exist. Nonetheless, Nadir finds himself in much the same risky position as the tenor heroes of the five East–West operas mentioned above. He has traveled some distance to reach this modest seaside village. He becomes clandestinely involved (or, more accurately, reinvolved) with an affectionate, sensitive soprano heroine (lyric-coloratura, in this case). And he thereby angers the village's autocratic leaders and their armed minions.

Similarly, Puccini's *Turandot* tells of a tenor's quest for a soprano who is (by her own choice, in this case) off-limits to him. In so doing, Calàf runs the risk of losing his head to the local executioner's axe. Furthermore, though this opera offers a somewhat exceptional dramatic-soprano heroine – similar in some ways to the mezzos in *Samson* and *L'Africaine* – it counterbalances her with an equally or even more fully "Oriental" lyric soprano, namely the young slave Liù.

James Parakilas has recently traced intriguing connections between the archetypal plot (in its various manifestations) and various stages in the development of imperialist-era ideologies. He notes a shift from what he calls "Age of Discovery" operas (such as *Fernand Cortez* and *L'Africaine*) to operas that treat the theme that he calls "the Soldier and the Exotic."[38] The "Age of Discovery" operas allow for the possibility of a mutual love relationship between the Western male and the female whom he meets in the new territory, especially if the female is willing to accept the Westerner's religion. The "Soldier and the Exotic" operas are, instead, premised upon an inherent incompatibility between Western soldier and female Exotic – an incompatibility that is largely congruent with the increasing racialism in social thought at the time, as seen in the writings of Ernest Renan or Count Gobineau.[39]

Now that we have been introduced to some of the standard characters in Oriental (or some might call them Orientalist) operas and have seen how they interact with the single most frequently recurring plot scheme, we can turn to their manifestations in a number of specific works. This requires looking at the characters' concrete words and actions (in the libretto) and the music that is associated with each character (whether sung by him/her or played in the orchestra).[40]

It may be best to start by looking more closely at the women characters, then (in two subsequent sections) examine male characters and crowds. The chapter closes with a discussion of three ensembles in *Madama Butterfly*.

Fragile women, fatal women, and the pentatonic

Even though the paradigmatic plot is structured around the quest of a Western male, the motivating object of desire is always a woman. Four of the five operas cited earlier as manifesting the paradigmatic plot carry as their entire title the exotic woman's name (or descriptor, in the case of *L'Africaine*). Even the one exception, *Samson et Dalila*, was originally entitled (in the manuscript, and at the opera's world premiere, in Weimar) *Dalila*.[41] How does the libretto (at a more detailed level than just plot) help define these title characters and other prominent female roles? How is this further specified and elaborated – intensified, possibly resisted – by the music, whether through accepted stylistic signifiers of Elsewhere – as prescribed in the Exotic Style Paradigm – or by a more varied range of devices – as allowed by the broader Full-Context Paradigm?

We have noted that the portrayals of Oriental women in opera can vary widely. Their diverse features show up not just in vocal type (some are bright sopranos, others resonant mezzos) and basic events of plot but, more trenchantly, in their musical numbers. Dalila seduces Samson with luscious, looping melodic figures in Act 1. And she dominates him in an Act 2 love duet that amounts to a (largely mendacious) "love" aria for her, with little more than short, helpless exclamations from him.[42] By contrast, Aida is a primarily helpless figure in the opera that bears her name: at the beginning of Act 3 – on the banks of the Nile, at night – she gives vent to her despair and lonely sorrow against a musical backdrop of nature sounds and the piping of a distant flute.

Aida's Nile Scene aligns the "weak" or subordinate terms of a number of characteristically Romantic binary oppositions: woman rather than man; nature rather than societal conventions and structures; feelings of the heart rather than denial of feelings in the interest of some "higher" ideal, such as patriotism; passivity and helplessness rather than active solution-seeking; and the exotic and/or primitive in contrast to the technologically advanced and powerful. (In this opera, power is of course embodied in imperial Egypt's overwhelming armies and intimidating hierarchy of priests and oppressive laws.[43])

Equally representative, and equally distinctive, is the title character of *Lakmé*. (Her name is presumably a simplification of Lakshmi.) At the command of her father Nilakantha, who is a Brahmin high priest and the head of the local anti-colonial resistance, Lakmé sings a glittering "Bell Song" to a crowd of English tourists. (Nilakantha hopes that Lakmé's singing will eventually draw her secret English lover, the soldier Gérald, out of the crowd, and it eventually does.) Lakmé commands the attention of the onstage listeners – and simultaneously exposes her own vulnerability – by means of modal, unaccompanied, and coloratura vocalises that are impersonal in effect, rather than expressive. The fast section (about the little magic bell) is particularly mechanical in its angular leaps and odd resulting harmonies.[44]

These three operatic women could easily define a continuum running between the aforementioned categories of *femme fatale* and *femme fragile*. As we noted, Dalila is one of the ultimate models of the woman seeking the (proto-)Western man's downfall. Lakmé is her opposite: a type that has been called "marionette victim."[45] In the end, the English soldier Gérald cannot break with England and his regiment. Lakmé ends up committing suicide by chewing the hallucinogenic and ultimately poisonous *datura* (jimsonweed or thorn-apple).[46] Aida holds a fascinating middle position between Dalila and Lakmé. A princess yet also a captive, she cannot let her powerful and just desires be known, much less act on them. The role thereby gives many options for a soprano to mix and vary the shades of submission, despair, loving devotion, and strength (including a brief rebellious outburst in Act 1, and successful manipulation of Radames in Act 3).[47]

Despite the vast differences between these and other operatic portrayals of Oriental females, we can also see in them some parallel to Orientalist paintings of the day, which tend likewise to construct Eastern woman as object of desire, as a sensual creature who – however innocently or craftily – beckons. Not just Aida but Dalila, Lakmé, and Cio-Cio-San, too, are associated with nature's irresistible attractions for the duty-bound male. Dalila awaits her love-thirsty tenor, Samson, in a hideaway abounding in creepers and other plant life. Gérald, ready for adventure, first encounters Lakmé in a beautiful floral garden, on whose pond the audience has previously seen Lakmé and her maid Nélika gliding in a boat and singing the magically graceful (and not at all foreign-sounding) Flower Duet. And Cio-Cio-San and Suzuki, in Puccini's *Madama Butterfly*, will twenty years later have a (similarly non-exotic-sounding) Flower Duet of their own.

Cio-Cio-San is perhaps the most complete, most famous embodiment of the archetypally beautiful, loving, gentle, submissive Oriental female.[48] Yet she displays certain qualities that are almost the opposite of this archetype, making her one of the most richly realized characters in the operatic repertoire. Some of Cio-Cio-San's most idiosyncratic qualities come to the fore after Pinkerton abandons her. The relationship at the core of the usual Oriental plot now flips: Pinkerton becomes the distant object of desire, the representative of an attractive Other world for the character who henceforth takes center stage. So deep is this Oriental woman's devotion, so intense her desire to believe in the absent Pinkerton and all he stands for, that we come to see her situation largely through her eyes. We understand her choices and perhaps admire them, despite the expressions of doubt and despair from Cio-Cio-San's maid Suzuki and the bursts of outright ridicule from the matchmaker Goro and from Cio-Cio-San's tiresome suitor Prince Yamadori.

Cio-Cio-San's sincerity and largeness of spirit are already vividly apparent in the middle of Act 1, when she first confesses her devotion to Pinkerton. The music begins with tightly constrained declamation and stark parallel harmonies (at "Ieri son salita": "Yesterday I went up to the Mission church") of a sort that Puccini repeatedly associated with

Cio-Cio-San's sad family history or her other disappointments.[49] It then blossoms into a rapturous melody, the beginning of which ("Io seguo il mio destino": "I follow my destiny") had first been heard, as orchestral commentary, right after Cio-Cio-San's entrance with her friends.[50] Though the melody freely incorporates certain pentatonic features, it is harmonized in Puccini's lushest manner. The whole thirty-two-measure passage (from "Ieri son salita" onward) enacts the very transformation of which Cio-Cio-San is singing: the process of turning from an Easterner into a Westerner, even to the extent of her adopting Pinkerton's religion so that they can worship together "in the same little church."[51] It is revealing that, in their only love duet (at the end of Act 1), Cio-Cio-San expresses herself in more expansive melodic structures – suggestive of a deeper stratum of emotional involvement – than those that Pinkerton keeps falling back on.[52]

Once Pinkerton returns to the United States, Cio-Cio-San's behavior becomes more erratic. On the one hand, she condescendingly lectures Suzuki (early in Act 2) that, unlike the "lazy, potbellied gods" of Japanese tradition, "the American God" answers pleas quickly. And she goads Yamadori about his supposed willingness to die for her love, then "triumphantly" (according to the stage directions) acts out a little playlet demonstrating how American courts protect the rights of married women. On the other hand, Cio-Cio-San takes on ever more aspects of the good-hearted but sickly or neurasthenic *femme fragile*. Already in Act 1, she weeps when her family and community have rejected her and left the premises, and "covers her ears" so as not to hear the distant echo of their shouting. In Act 2, her mood alternates rapidly between elation and despair. She nervously interrupts the consul Sharpless several times when he is attempting to reveal to her that Pinkerton will never return.

Cio-Cio-San knows what Sharpless will say. She has already heard Suzuki's prediction at the beginning of the act. Also, a certain melancholy was apparent in the opening measures of her famous aria "Un bel dì," sung only minutes before Sharpless arrives. "One fine day ... the ship appears," soar the words, but the melody sinks inexorably, as if chained to the descending bass line in the orchestra and to the parallel chords that get dragged down with it. This music returns twice more in the aria, the last time by the orchestra *fff largamente*, as Butterfly breaks off singing – after a high B♭ on "I wait for him" – and (the stage directions tell us) embraces her maid in sadness. Overcome by her (spoken) yearning and (unspoken) despair, she lets the orchestra – representing her soul or inner thoughts – finish the aria for her. This *farfalla* senses that she has no freedom to fly. The dreaded fate of which she spoke in her duet with Pinkerton – that she will be sacrificed, much the way that, in the West, a butterfly often gets pinned by "a man's hand" to a wooden board – is now inexorably arriving.

Susan McClary has recently compared Butterfly's full-voiced high B♭ to the triumphant cry by a Verdian tenor.[53] (A classic instance that comes to mind is Manrico's "All'armi!" that ends Act 3 of *Il trovatore*.) But surely the sense of triumph is somewhat undercut by the fact that Cio-Cio-San breaks off singing before the music ends and without cadencing to the tonic. (That B♭ is the third degree of the prevailing key.) As Steven Huebner has noted, her "immutability" – that is, her exceeding (and, finally, fatal) devotion to Pinkerton – is further emphasized when the peroration from "Un bel dì" reappears (again, in the orchestra) as Sharpless departs after he has "brutally" (as he himself expresses it) delivered the news to her.[54]

Later in the act, after Cio-Cio-San has spied Pinkerton's boat arriving in the harbor, her vocal line enacts a fully satisfying cadence. The orchestra immediately bursts forth with a version of the first-act love theme, now enriched by repeated upward-thrusting arpeggios that echo the opening of the *Star-Spangled Banner* (which had been prominently quoted moments earlier). Even otherwise well-trained audiences tend to break into applause here, perhaps out of a desperate desire to have Pinkerton, just this once, return to this woman who loves him – more than he deserves – and to his blond-haired child.

Cio-Cio-San is a particularly rich case of a "weak" yet, in the end, also strong (steadfast, according to her own lights) Oriental woman. The slave Liù in Puccini's *Turandot* (1926) shows fewer contrasting facets than Butterfly: no nervous pseudo-gaiety, no sarcasm or playacting. But she displays an almost superhuman willingness to give her life, for love of the heedless tenor who (she recalls) once smiled at her in the palace. This devotion – devotion to an ideal, we might say, in Romantic-era language – is embodied in Liù's delicately floating, arching vocal lines, and (at the end of her first aria, "Signore, ascolta") long-held soft high notes.

Liù's aria gives us the occasion to broach the fraught question of exotic style. (We shall examine *Madama Butterfly* in this respect at the end of the chapter.) Though several actual Chinese melodies are quoted extensively elsewhere in the opera, Liù's music here is freshly invented by Puccini. Nonetheless, her entire vocal part in this number (except for two grace notes) is confined to what is sometimes called the "major pentatonic mode." This mode, so characteristic of Chinese music, we can (approximately) represent on the piano with the notes C–D–E–G–A. Since Westerners often perceive these notes as the C-major scale without degrees 4 and 7 (F and B), they are sometimes described as the "major-pentatonic" scale.[55]

This pentatonic scale or mode can be transposed so as to begin on any pitch. Conveniently, for purposes of demonstration, the version beginning on F♯ is identical to the black keys on the piano: F♯–G♯–A♯–C♯–D♯. For that reason, writers often refer to it as "black-note pentatonicism," regardless of what note a given instance is built upon (e.g., C, as earlier in the paragraph). This scale is often described as "anhemitonic," because no two notes in it are a half-step (semitone/hemitone) apart, unlike, say, in the *in* pentatonic scale that is widely used in Japanese traditional music.

Peter Schatt argues that Liù is trapped in her pentatonicism and that, later in the opera, her growing independence and courage in Act 3 are seen in her vocal lines – now fully diatonic – and their harmonically sophisticated accompaniment.[56] The point is a solid one, and it fits well with the now widely accepted argument (presented by William Ashbrook and Harold Powers) that the various sections of *Turandot* are written in one or another of four largely distinct musical "colors" or styles (*tinte*, in Italian).[57] Of these four, the two most important are the aforementioned major-pentatonic mode, and the rich blending of diatonic and chromatic that was so typical of Western art music in Puccini's day.[58] The former patently represents the East, so the latter, presumably, represents the subjective complexity of the Western artistic persona. There are no Western characters as such in the opera, and the latter style (Puccini's standard one) is invoked for Timur, Calàf (the stand-in for the West, since he comes from somewhere outside of China), and, at many moments, Turandot herself. We may conclude that the composer has contrived to make us sympathize with these Easterners by showing that they think and feel in a style normally associated with "us."

To describe the various *tinte* as entirely separate does not do justice to Puccini's subtle way of blending elements of one *tinta* into another. In Liù's aforementioned "Tu che di gel sei cinta" (Act 3), which Schatt describes as diatonic (hence non-Chinese), brief pentatonic figures still occur, such as the melodic drop from scale-degree 5 to 4 to 1 early in the song (at "fiamma vinta" – Ex. 8.1).[59] In some non-exotic operas, or in an instrumental piece, the listener might not consider this cadential figure pentatonic at all, depending on the harmonic context. (More on harmony in a moment.) But, by this point in the opera, Puccini has often problematized gapped-scale music ("gapped," again, according to Western expectations) by setting it in firm opposition to more fully diatonic and chromatic music. As a result, we continue to hear Liù's three-note drop here, 5–4–1, as a reminder of her own special nature – which is also her extreme Orientalness.

Example 8.1 Puccini, *Turandot*, Act 3: Liù's "Tu che di gel sei cinta." Exx. 8.1–8.3 are reprinted by kind permission of G. Ricordi and Co. © 1929, renewed 1954, G. Ricordi and Co.

Still, Schatt and others are right to assert that Liù's musical identity – hence her dramatic profile – was established in the first of her three arias: the aforementioned "Signore, ascolta!" Ashbrook and Powers straightforwardly refer to this memorable solo as "Liù's sweetly pathetic pentatonic aria."[60] Their description makes sense as far as the vocal line is concerned, but one must also pay attention to harmony. As Ashbrook and Powers are the first to admit in regard to other passages in *Turandot*, Puccini often harmonizes pentatonic melodies in non-pentatonic fashion. For example, the important and recurring traditional "Mo-Li-Hua" tune ("Jasmine Flower") is almost entirely pentatonic – not surprisingly, given that Puccini transcribed it from a Chinese music box.[61] More precisely, the tune uses the major-pentatonic mode mentioned above (this time transposed to begin on E♭). Yet, at its first and fullest statement (rehearsal no. 19), the melody is supported in the orchestra by the tonic chord I (i.e., E-flat major) alternating with ♭VII (D-flat major) or v^7 (B-flat-minor seventh), and the latter two chords necessarily introduce notes foreign to the melody (i.e., degrees ♭7 and 4, see Ex. 8.2).[62]

The same is true for "Signore, ascolta!" Puccini builds his orchestral accompaniment with clear diatonic progressions that introduce the very tones so scrupulously avoided by the voice, namely degrees 4 and 7. Note the structural chord-progression IV–V–I in mm. 5–6 of the aria – Ex. 8.3. Is "Signore, ascolta!" a "pentatonic aria" at all? The answer depends on how capable a given listener is of hearing a vocal line separately from its harmonization.

Perhaps Puccini avoided pentatonic harmonization in "Signore, ascolta!" in order to generate a feeling of tension and then release – and, for that purpose, modulation to the dominant (or some other key) was helpful. Liù is in a state of crisis and near-despair here, confessing her long-unspoken love yet sensing all the while that the Prince will pursue his seemingly fatal fantasy of winning the hand of the icy, vindictive Princess Turandot. In this sense, Puccini's harmonization de-Orientalizes Liù, makes her not a

Imperialism and "the exotic Orient"   191

Example 8.2 Puccini, *Turandot*, Act 1: first (and only complete) setting of the "Mo-Li-Hua" tune.

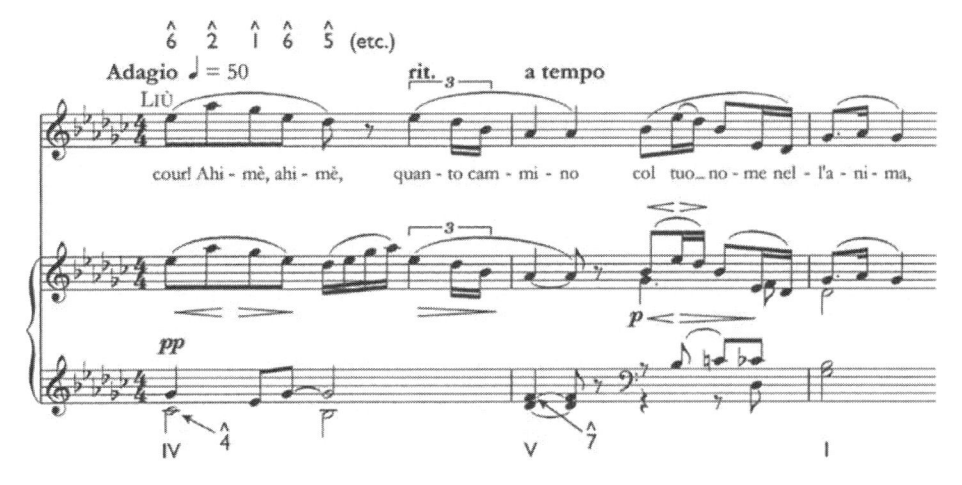

Example 8.3 Puccini, *Turandot*, Act 1: Liù's "Signore, ascolta!"

representative of a specific foreign locality but a "universal human" with whom "we" Westerners can all, presumably, identify.

In treating Liù in this way, Puccini was following a long-established operatic tradition, and one that was not restricted to exotic characters. As Carl Dahlhaus points out, nineteenth-century composers often evinced sincere respect for their lower-class heroes and heroines (e.g., peasants) by letting them sing, not (as we might expect) in some watered-down folk-song style, but in the elevated and emotionally varied, or even heroic, musical language of grand opera long associated with Roman emperors and other noble Westerners.[63]

Men: the forceful and the gentle

When we turn to portrayals of Oriental men, we find much reinforcing of the longstanding masculine images (authority, militarism, etc.) cited earlier in regard to the Nile Scene in *Aida*. Although Calàf, in *Turandot*, is only "sort of" a Westerner, he is nonetheless largely typical of the heroes of Orientalist operas, including Vasco da Gama, Radames, and Samson. Calàf is a powerful royal prince, in exile now because his father was recently deposed from the throne. He proves stubborn and fearless in his warrior-like intention to "conquer" the Chinese imperial princess with whom he is smitten. "Nessun dorma," his world-renowned aria from the last act, ends with a memorable (and challenging) leap to a high B on "Vincerò! "vincerò!"

Nadir, the tenor in *Les pêcheurs de perles*, is quite without Western connotations, yet he is likewise a searcher after *la femme orientale*. What truly distinguishes him from the four other searchers just mentioned is that he is no assertive warrior. In earlier days, Nadir and his friend Zurga had traveled together across their island home (Ceylon). In Kandy, they had encountered Leïla (the opera's soprano heroine) in a temple.[64] Both were instantly captivated by her beauty, but it was Nadir who then followed her from place to place, listening, under cover of darkness, to her magical singing. When the opera opens, Nadir has arrived at an unnamed beachside village on the very day (by chance, arrangement, or instinct) when Leïla is arriving "from far away." Leïla's duty is to chant to Brahma atop a high rock, thereby warding off evil spirits and ensuring success for the annual harvesting of pearls by the town's divers. The graceful, liquid-voiced beauty, who, as she will soon admit, has continued to "adore" Nadir, glimpses him upon her arrival. After night falls, she stands on her rock and surreptitiously draws him close with a most appealing waltz-aria, "Dans le ciel sans voile" (Fig. 8.1).

Imperialism and "the exotic Orient" 193

Figure 8.1 In the end of Act 1 of Bizet's *Les pêcheurs de perles*, set in Ceylon (Sri Lanka), Nadir recognizes the Brahmin priestess Leïla, despite her long veil, by her singing. (Illustration from *Il teatro illustrato*, April 1886, published on the occasion of a production at La Scala, Milan.)

Nadir is almost an *homme fragile*. Puppy-like in his willingness to trail after the elusive *bien-aimée*, he is reduced to near-stupor by any reminder of her physical and vocal beauty. He resembles not so much the typical operatic hero as he does certain dreamy aristocratic rulers in the *Thousand and One Nights*, including Harun Al-Rashid of Baghdad, the fifth Abassid caliph (*c.* 763–809), renowned for his scholarly and poetic efforts.[65] Being "an Oriental," Nadir can participate – more than most tenor heroes of Orientalist operas, because they are Westerners – in the foreign-fantastic sound world that is a fresh and inventive feature of many numbers in this opera. Nadir is somewhat feminized by his association with Oriental style, and this further emphasizes his lack of manly swagger. Both aspects – his Easternness and his dreaminess – are on full display in his fragrant Act 1 *romance* "Je crois entendre encore," one of the most beloved tenor arias in all opera.

"Je crois" opens with a recurring phrase for English horn that focuses on the note E in the context of a scale that otherwise implies A minor. But, if one thinks of E (not A) as the tonic note, then the first three notes moving upward from that E imply Phrygian mode, a mode that was already relatively unusual in Gregorian chant and Renaissance polyphony and, by the eighteenth and nineteenth centuries, had become almost unknown except in music-history books. Phrygian mode lowers not just the third degree (G, in this case) but also the second (F). (If transposed to C, the mode would begin C–D♭–E♭–F–G.)

Nadir's opening melodic phrase (which recurs three times more) emphasizes the same Phrygian-sounding group of pitches E–F–G, and his final note in the aria is, surprisingly, not the tonic note A but, again, E. Bizet's decision not to resolve the E in the voice creates an open-ended effect that matches the stage action, in which Nadir drifts off to sleep, murmuring of past joys with Leïla: "O doux souvenir" ("Oh, the tender memory" – Ex. 8.4).[66] Here, even more than in Liù's "Signore, ascolta" from *Turandot*, the listener is guided to hearing the singer's modal line as at least partly independent of its tonally clarifying accompaniment. We might also note that, whereas Liù's pentatonicism is easily encompassed by the Exotic-Style Paradigm, Nadir's Phrygian vocal line seems more problematic – and thus calls for the Full-Context Paradigm – because a Phrygian vocal line would not have been thought either *inherently* or *conventionally* Eastern (much less specifically Ceylonese) at the time. Rather, a pre-modern Western device here *takes on* connotations of Easternness because of the way it is framed by plot, sets, costumes, and the Eastern associations of the tenor's name. (History's most renowned Nadir, 1688–1747, was shah of Iran.)

Example 8.4 Bizet, *Les pêcheurs de perles*, Nadir's Act 1 aria "Je crois entendre encore," concluding measure, in Bizet's authorized version, in which the tenor trails off on E, the Phrygian tonic (or is it the dominant in A minor?).

The poetically reflective, sensually overwhelmed Nadir continues a long-standing *opéra-comique* and *opéra-lyrique* tradition in which the male protagonist is a light, lyrical tenor. Gérald in *Lakmé* is another such lyric-tenor role.[67] More often, in operas (whether grand or light), the Oriental males are the bad guys – the local heavies – and are well suited to being sung by another staple element in nineteenth-century opera houses: baritones and basses equipped with baleful voice, emphatic declamation, and commanding, threatening stage manner. Of course, there are heavies also in operas set in the West, and at least a few are as unredeemedly nasty as the worst Oriental males. The demise of Scarpia, in Puccini's *Tosca*, generally brings a sigh of relief and maybe even a stifled cheer from audience members. But nastiness in a Western male is generally presented as an exception, or as tied to a particularly noxious social institution from the past (as in the case of the Grand Inquisitor, in Verdi's *Don Carlos*).

Eastern heavies represent their whole society's (supposedly) more or less eternal and accepted cultural values. Among the normative obsessions of opera's Oriental males are war, religious ritual, oppressive legalism, and a hatred of foreigners and intruders – or some combination of these, as in the cases of Nourabad (*Les pêcheurs de perles*), Ramfis (*Aida*), and Nilakantha (*Lakmé*).[68] All three men are not only priests. They also have power to arrest, punish, or – in Nilakantha's case, with the sweet-voiced Gérald as his intended victim – assassinate.

Rituals, priests, and crowds

The coercive power of these Oriental priests/leaders is almost always portrayed as being endorsed or tacitly accepted by the populace.[69] As a result, the most prominent dramatized markers of an Eastern society – the markers felt to be peculiarly representative of that society – are its rituals and processions. Those societal displays often carry a charge that is almost unknown in analogous operatic scenes set in the West: erotic delight or (its near opposite) eruptive and personally vindictive violence.

The first of these – a sensual eroticism – occurs somewhat less often, but treasurably. Eroticism mingles with mysterious ceremoniality in various dances of priestesses in French exotic operas (e.g., in Act 1 of *Samson et Dalila*) and in Massenet's *Le roi de Lahore*, whose Act 3 is set entirely in a Frenchman's vision of Hindu heaven. It includes a danced *divertissement* of celestial nymphs (no doubt clad in gauzy fabrics), in which a modally ambiguous "Hindic melody," played by the flute without accompaniment, is followed by five variations making heavy use of the changing-background technique familiar from many nineteenth-century Russian pieces (such as Glinka's influential *Kamarinskaya* for orchestra, 1848). The remainder of the act is colored periodically by melodic use of a solo saxophone. Though the saxophone was an utterly European instrument – invented in the 1840s by the Belgian manufacturer Adolphe Sax – it was apparently still considered new and weird enough to lend a strange glow to the proceedings, most effectively in the ritualistic exchanges between the spirit of the recently deceased King Alim and the god Indra.[70]

The same mix of the gently erotic and the gravely ceremonial prevails in one of the best-loved numbers in all opera: the so-called "Temple Duet" for tenor and baritone from, again, *Les pêcheurs de perles*. The two singers are Nadir and his friend Zurga. The latter – the opera's baritone role – is, by this point in the story, the secular and military leader of the village in Ceylon where the action takes place. Like many operatic baritones, he is riven by conflicting feelings, largely because he wishes to remain a true friend to Nadir even though they both love the same woman. (The village's religious leader Nourabad – the bass role – is more consistent in his motivations and actions. In one nighttime scene, he commands a predictable chorus of threatening, torch-carrying guards.) Nadir and Zurga launch their duet by recalling the beautiful, veiled priestess whom they saw years earlier as she walked through a crowded temple in Kandy. Bizet's orchestra illustrates the memory by a refrain (see Ex. 8.5, topmost and bottommost staves) whose stately pace suggests a religious procession.

The melody of the refrain is first stated in the flute over rising arpeggios in the harp. This instrumental combination was one of the standard French-operatic markers of ancient or exotic religiosity. Bizet increases the smoothness by using the tonic chord as upbeat to a weak downbeat chord: I | iii vi | II. In addition, the use of mainly root-position chords produces or implies

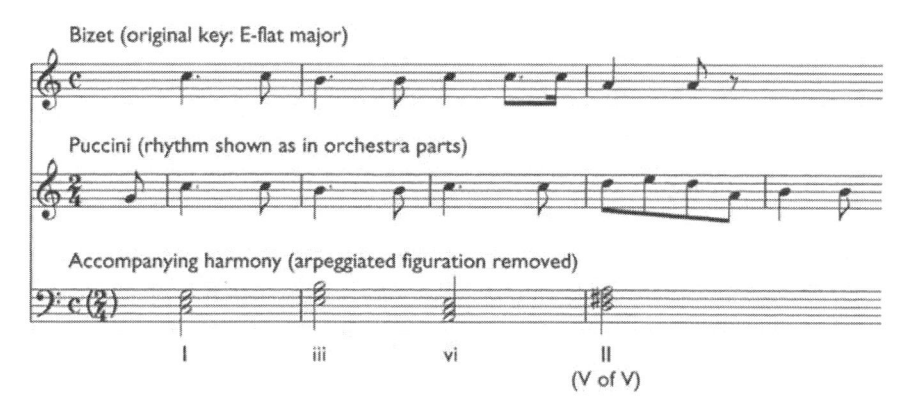

Example 8.5 Melodic lines from Bizet's "Temple Duet" and Puccini's "O Kami!" chorus, over the (arpeggiated) harmonic progression that accompanies both.

chains of parallel fifths and octaves. The resulting unschooled thinness of texture reminds us, repeatedly, that we are in a primitive, non-Western locale.[71] True, the passage sounds nothing at all like music of the Indian subcontinent. As in Nadir's aria, Bizet here revives some nearly forgotten Western practices of previous centuries. Yet, in context, the music's lulling mood comports well with mental images that audience members would have had back then – and still have today – of Hindu temples filled with colorful flowers, wafting incense, and glittering portraits of various divine emanations.[72]

Although we are looking at this example primarily for its representation of maleness and religion, we might also note how it leads the viewer to share Nadir and Zurga's fascination with that standard icon of desire, the exotic female body hidden from male view. During the narrative passages (while flute and harp are playing the stately Temple tune for the first time), Nadir and Zurga shift to using present tense, as if suddenly transported back to the moment they are recalling. They seem to see again how the crowd in the temple falls to the ground and stares at the priestess, how she reaches her arms out toward the two men, and how her veil lifts (*se soulève*–it literally "raises itself") to reveal a dreamlike vision of loveliness. The men mention only the priestess's face, but the fact that the veil is (they say) "long" suggests strongly that its mysterious lifting reveals – in their joint reverie – more of her to them.[73] As Karen Henson notes, Bizet's canny decision to progress from a purely instrumental statement (with simultaneous sung commentary) to a direct vocal statement *by* the two men – "Oui, c'est elle, / C'est la déesse" – "conveys an almost palpable sense of the [remembered] heroine coming gradually into view."[74]

Opera often condemns Eastern religion.[75] In Meyerbeer's *L'Africaine*, the primitive and authoritarian rule of the priests of Brahma is well limned in the famous "Marche indienne" at the beginning of Act 4 (soon after Vasco da Gama has reached shore). Its opening section consists of nothing but a minor-mode melody stated in unison by the lower strings and lower winds over cymbals and bass drum. The melody is more or less *alla turca* in style, with a pounding beat, eerie trills, and, in its second phrase, two pitches that are repeated four times in a row in an angular dotted rhythm, clearly marking the Madagascan Hindus as uncivilized.

Often the high priest – whether he is or is not also the community's leader – displays a fanatical rigidity and intolerance. In Act 1 of *Madama Butterfly*, the Bonze (a Buddhist monk), who is also one of Cio-Cio-San's uncles, interrupts the wedding festivities to curse the bride for abandoning the religion of her family and ancestors (Fig. 8.3). Over a harsh motive dissonantly bearing down on a melodic tritone, he repeatedly booms

Imperialism and "the exotic Orient" 199

Figure 8.2 After Cio-Cio-San and her chorus of kimono-clad bridesmaids have come gently up the hill to the house with rice-paper walls, Cio-Cio-San bids them all modestly bow. A solemn Cio-Cio-San (Leontyne Price, in a production from 1962) conveys some anxiety about the future. (Photo by Louis Mélançon, by permission of the Metropolitan Opera.)

Cio-Cio-San's name in denunciatory fashion and does not respond (musically or textually) to the interjections of the other characters on stage.

The Bonze's entrance interrupts the lovely, thrice-stated choral prayer honoring the happy couple ("O Kami! O Kami!"), making him seem that much more insensitive by contrast. All of Cio-Cio-San's wedding guests, including her mother, take his side, literally. They move to the back of the stage with him – as if drawn by a magnet – and, "stretching their arms out towards Butterfly" in a gesture of renunciation and horror, join him in cursing her.

We might pause to note the music of the "O Kami" prayer that the chorus was singing before the Bonze entered. This gentle ceremonial moment resembles closely the recurring passage from Bizet's Temple Duet in its melody (rhythm and pitch), its rising harp arpeggios, and its unusual striding or "oscillating," root-position harmonic progression (see Ex. 8.5, middle and bottom staves).[76] Is this a case of direct influence, whether conscious or unconscious? The question is hard to answer. *Les pêcheurs de perles* was well known in Italy by Puccini's day (in Italian translation), but resemblances of this sort between passages written by two or more different composers to invoke Eastern rituals occur throughout the repertoire.[77] Orientalist composers often relied for stylistic guidance on elements from previous Orientalist compositions, more than on what was known of the actual music of the region. In Foucault's terminology, we might speak here of the "archeology" – in Said's terminology, the "textuality" – of the operatic Orient. As we dig through the repertoire, we encounter layer upon layer of "texts" (musical, verbal, or both), with each layer referring back to one or more of the previous ones for its representational authority.[78]

The rigidity and repressive power of Oriental society, conveyed so powerfully by the scene with the Bonze, similarly pervades the ritualistic exchanges in Act 2 between Princess Turandot's decrepit yet still dignified father (Emperor Altoum) and her determined suitor (Calàf). Here the "major-pentatonic" mode (discussed earlier, in regard to Liù) is applied in a tightly constrained fashion, making it seem symbolic of a soulless despotic system to whose cruel, legalistic dictates even the monarch himself must bend. Singing mostly without accompaniment, the Emperor declares himself unwilling to see the Prince risk his life. The orchestra proposes a crushing penalty after each of the Emperor's three warnings. The Prince insists resolutely each time (and without accompaniment) on undergoing the test of the three riddles. And the orchestra echoes him with stiff, unharmonized statements of his request tune. The last of these statements uses a rather mechanical and repeated triplet diminution that is surely meant to evoke – in a stereotypically simplified fashion – the variation procedures that were (and are) typical of Chinese music for instruments such as the *ch'in* and *pipa*.

Such stiffness here symbolizes a lack of flexibility and of spiritual growth – characteristically "Eastern" limitations that can already be seen, *in nuce*, in certain eighteenth-century works. In the last minutes of Mozart's *Die Entführung aus dem Serail*, Osmin, who is the overseer of the sultan's estates and also an Islamic fanatic (see Chapter 6) – once again, a male figure blending temporal and religious power – finishes his final violent outburst and then is immediately put in his place by the European characters. "Nichts ist so häßlich wie die Rache" ("Nothing is so ugly as vengefulness"), they intone in reproving and self-congratulatory manner before resuming their cheerful *vaudeville* finale. The same point gets made more emphatically and grimly in late nineteenth-century works. In *Samson et Dalila*, Abimélech damns himself in the audience's eyes not just by his taunts against the God of Israel and his impulsive use of the dagger against God's chosen one, Samson, but also by the ungainliness of his melodic lines, nastily doubled by the orchestra, with no harmonization whatsoever.[79]

To be sure, the punitive priests and other authority figures in Oriental operas need not be interpreted only in a literal way. Arguably, they may also be commenting on religious intolerance, generally, or on the frequent alliance between religion and noxious social custom or political oppressiveness. Such features can be seen more straightforwardly (i.e., without the distancing of Eastern disguise) in various operas that portray the Catholic clergy and church-entangled government officials as harsh or corrupt. Yet even those cases generally project such tensions back a century (Puccini's *Tosca*, 1900, set in the Napoleonic era) or several centuries (Verdi's *Don Carlos*, 1867, set around 1560). Would all operagoers have made the imaginative leap from Then to Now or (in the case of exotic works) from There to Here? Perhaps not. But one may propose that nasty portrayals of Eastern authorities served to deflect attention away from intolerance and abuses in religious institutions closer to home, and from those institutions' trusted, honored representatives.

The viciousness that we repeatedly find in the portrayals of the leaders of Oriental peoples is, not surprisingly, often echoed in the portrayal of the people itself: the Eastern crowd. To be sure, there are many instances of "lovely" choral ensembles in these Oriental operas, one being the aforementioned "O Kami!" wedding chorus in *Butterfly* (Ex. 8.5, middle and bottom staves). But equally revealing (and more closely analogous to Osmin, Abimélech, and Nilakantha) are the many instances of the opposite tendency: the supposed inclination of Eastern crowds towards violence.

Mass hysteria fills the stage in "Ungi, arrotta," the choral scene from Act 1 of *Turandot* in which the local men and women alike urge the executioner's men to "turn the grindstone" until the "blade spurts fire and blood." One wonders how Puccini and his librettists would have treated such a moment if the plot of this opera had been set in Spain, England, France, or Germany – countries that had their own history of state- and church-led public executions (e.g., burning of heretics). Would they have indulged so heavily in gruesome verbal and visual imagery, barbaric rhythmic pounding, and ghastly bitonal dissonance? If so, would audiences and critics have welcomed the work quite so willingly?[80] Or *were* thoughtful audience members able to see past the Chinese costumes and face makeup to some enduring truths about the behavior of a crowd and how easily it can be manipulated?

In fairness, Orientalist stereotypes of the crowd (however one reads them, or may have read them a century ago) are not always as pervasive and extreme as they are in *Turandot*. When the male chorus in *Aida* cries out for war against Ethiopia ("Guerra! guerra!"), the result is not much different from what the composer had previously provided for stories located closer to home (e.g., the heated calls from the anti-patrician crowd in *Simon Boccanegra*, 1857, rev. 1881). Indeed, when this same "Guerra! guerra!" returns at the end of the scene, it takes on another aspect. Aida's voice now soars in distress *over* it – to words of her own ("Deggio amarlo?": "Must I love him?") – yet in a sense also *with* it, as if the music were now reflecting the exalted and tangled emotions of all the participants in this tragedy-in-the-making. In other words, the first "Guerra! guerra!" is what we might call "music of character": music that "belongs" to someone onstage, namely, in this case, the multiheaded character known as the chorus. Its restatement (with Aida and the other characters singing, too) is suddenly "music of situation." This shift in musicodramatic function makes the question "What individual or group is the music representing?" harder to resolve (in regard to the restatement), but also, curiously, less troubling. The listener focuses now on dramatic events and the characters' surging feelings – even though those characters' feelings actually differ – and may no longer feel called upon, as s/he did in the first statement (for chorus, without the solo roles), or in the "executioner" scene of Turandot, to associate the music with a particular character or group on stage.

Madama Butterfly: an opera of, and against, empire

Madama Butterfly is a work that displays a wide range of musicodramatic devices: specific stylistic borrowings from (or imagined echoes of) the music of Japan but also more standard musicodramatic devices that characterize emotions or actions and reveal the relationships between individuals and groups. These devices – all of them acceptable within the Full-Context

Paradigm – interact with each other in order to convey various attitudes toward "the Orient" and toward Western (and specifically American) imperialism as it manifested itself in regard to Japan.

We have already sketched some of *Butterfly*'s more "prosaic" aspects, most basically its structural dependence on the standard Oriental-opera plot, whereby the Western tenor – here foolhardy rather than heroic – penetrates the hidden Eastern world and captures, and/or is captivated by, a beautiful native woman despite fearsome thunderings from the local chief or religious leader. We have looked at the wedding chorus and observed a number of moments involving Butterfly herself that reveal some facets of her character that are archetypally Oriental and others that are more particular to her.

As we leaf through the rest of Puccini's score, we immediately encounter many passages that are amenable to an analysis within the confines of the Exotic-Style Paradigm. The work is rightly renowned for its imaginative and varied use of musical materials that were once, and largely still are, redolent of the place being depicted. Puccini authority Michele Girardi counts ten preexisting Japanese melodies that Puccini knew (e.g., from recordings or published transcriptions) and that are used entire or in large and mostly recognizable chunks. Girardi calculates that some 25 per cent of the measures in Act 1 use one or another of these more-or-less authentic melodies.[81] Two of these melodies are famous from other contexts and are, no doubt for that reason, heard at moments in which Japanese characters engage in formal presentations. The folk song "Sakura" (Cherry Blossom) – widely known, even today – is heard when Cio-Cio-San shows Pinkerton the various objects that she keeps in the sleeves of her robe, including what he takes to be silly dolls but are, she quietly explains, the souls of her ancestors. "Myasama" (or "Tonyare-bushi"), used in Gilbert and Sullivan's *The Mikado* (1885) for the choral hymn in praise of the title character, is here associated primarily with the wealthy Prince Yamadori, when he visits in Act 2 to repeat his dubious offer of lifelong devotion.

Many equally vivid passages are built upon melodies that Puccini composed in what he took to be Japanese style. (Sometimes he incorporated short fragments from yet other Japanese tunes to which he had been introduced.) Melodies from this latter group, Girardi calculates, show up in another 20 per cent of the measures in Act 1. Certain of them use the standard major-pentatonic scale discussed earlier, a scale that closely approximates certain scales that are widely found in musical traditions of East Asia, including China, Thailand, and Indonesia. But Japan is well known for having certain distinctive scales that cannot be expressed, even approximately, on the black keys of the piano. One of these – the *in* scale (or mode) – was already becoming a favorite marker of Japan in Puccini's day.[82]

Puccini also favors the use of the whole-tone scale (e.g., C–D–E–F♯–G♯–A♯ [or B♭]–C), a scale that resists harmonization within the Western major–minor system.[83] Though this scale is not characteristic of Japanese music, Puccini often uses it with parallel chords, in parallel thirds with scary trills (e.g., for the aforementioned Bonze's Curse – the scene shown in Figure 8.3), or with no harmonization at all. All of this combines to suggest the inability of Japan to be readily absorbed into Western ways of thinking and feeling. A memorable whole-tone phrase occurs (unharmonized) in the famous aria "Un bel dì" when Cio-Cio-San imagines Pinkerton's coming back "up the hill" ("S'avvia per la collina").[84] That phrase will return twice (still unharmonized) in the opera's final minutes, with dramatic irony: first, when Butterfly says that Pinkerton should come "up the hill" for his child and then – in an intense, faster version – when he does come running up the hill, frantically calling out Butterfly's name.[85]

Other musical devices in *Butterfly* (rhythmic, harmonic, orchestrational) likewise differ substantially from those that prevail in Puccini's operas – or those of his predecessors and contemporaries – that are set in the West. They thus seem intended as further markers of Japaneseness:

- Several themes heard in the first few scenes employ rhythms that are rapid and bustling or mechanically repeated, in some cases explicitly mimicking mindless chatter. At those moments, the characters in question seem doll-like and comical: the marriage-broker Goro, the house-servant Suzuki (when first introduced to Pinkerton), and Butterfly's family members.
- The frequent use of chords moving in lockstep with the voice suggests – in context, though not of course inherently – that Japanese music lacks an understanding of harmony and also, symbolically, that Japanese society is largely undifferentiated and has not yet developed a proper concept of "voices," i.e., of individual personal identities.[86]
- The orchestration, especially in Act 1, offers a variety of alternately luminous and brittle colorations, such as flute and piccolo, played staccato, plus harp and glockenspiel.[87] These are clearly intended to approximate the sounds of Japanese music, with its many high-pitched instruments (e.g., *shamisen*, *koto*, and *shō*) and bells and gongs – or at least the impression that such sounds often made on Westerners.[88]

Less often noted are moments that characterize Japan and its people – or that map out the power relations between the Americans and the

Japanese – through music that, observers would generally agree, was *not* meant to strike the ear as Other-sounding.[89] For these, the (more inclusive) Full-Context Paradigm is needed.

Let us start by exploring further some facets of Cio-Cio-San that were only briefly touched upon earlier in this chapter. These features are presented not solely as personal idiosyncrasies but also as characteristic aspects of her Japaneseness, as can be seen by the fact that Suzuki, Goro, and Yamadori share some (though not all) of them. Two of these are striking: her smallness and fragility (or seeming fragility) and her impulsive and naively "childlike" quality (the adjective is recurringly indicated in the stage directions).[90] These characteristics distinguish her from her beloved American naval officer, Lieutenant B. F. Pinkerton, who is nonchalant, condescending, callous, and even – as critics have repeatedly noted – loutishly prone to ridicule Japanese customs.[91] The two other American characters plainly come from the same universe as Pinkerton: the world-weary Sharpless and the poised, perhaps chilly Kate Pinkerton.

Cio-Cio-San's "Japanese" fragility and childlike traits distinguish her from heroines of other Puccini operas, notably the fiery-tempered Tosca, the sturdy Wild West saloon-keeper Minnie (in *La fanciulla del West*), and – an Eastern instance – the Chinese "ice princess" Turandot. None of these three Puccini women has Cio-Cio-San's habit – we therefore take it to be typically Japanese – of offering endless solicitous compliments and artifice-laden, hyperbolic statements, bursts of poetic imagery, or repeated exclamations.[92] None has such a trustingly literal way of thinking. We are startled, in particular, to "hear" in the orchestra's woodwinds the robins whose springtime nesting, Pinkerton told her, would coincide with his return. Julian Smith insists that "the question of birds in *Madama Butterfly* ... is not anything to do with exoticism but is as natural a sound as the church bells in *Tosca*."[93] But surely, once one defines exoticism broadly enough to include the portrayal of how an Oriental or other exotic character thinks, feels, and acts, then these invisible twittering redbreasts do seem a manifestation of Cio-Cio-San's astonishing (exotic) naiveté.

And none of the Puccini heroines just mentioned – whether Oriental or Western – is given anything that remotely resembles the "Flower Duet" (sung by Cio-Cio-San and her maid Suzuki before they begin their vigil), a swooning waltz that marks Cio-Cio-San's last moment of romantic illusion before being forced to confront the truth that Pinkerton has betrayed her. Real-life Asians in the late nineteenth century did not sing waltzes as they scattered flower petals. Nor was Puccini's "Flower Duet" intended to register to the listener, on a conscious level, *as* a ballroom dance from Vienna or

Paris. But the power of a flowing waltz to suggest a character's openness to amorous affection must have been too much for the composer to resist at this point, and audiences do not resist it, either.[94] (Puccini and his librettists may have had in mind the gentle 6/8-meter barcarolle that Delibes wrote for the equivalent Flower Duet in the widely performed *Lakmé* of twenty years earlier.) Puccini's Flower Duet characterizes as tender, gracious, and yielding *this* Japanese woman, her supportive female servant, and, by extension, Japanese women generally. It also portrays them as at least partly adaptable to Western customs. Because the portrayal occurs in music and without quite drawing our attention to it, it operates more powerfully than did Cio-Cio-San's (musically unremarkable) offer of American cigarettes to Sharpless minutes earlier.[95]

Before we leave Cio-Cio-San, we might well point out a revealing exception to the "Japaneseness" that we have emphasized thus far. Though her fragility distinguishes her from the three Puccini heroines mentioned earlier (Tosca, Minnie, and Turandot), it does not distinguish her from the other, more gentle female in *Turandot*, Liù (likewise discussed earlier), nor from the Parisian seamstress Mimì in *La bohème* (1896). The resemblance to Mimì reminds us of why an exotic character such as Cio-Cio-San speaks to the listener, why she does not seem *entirely* alien but someone with whom we in the audience can identify across the chasm of culture.

Does Cio-Cio-San's fragility turn her into a victim – and thereby all Asian women as well? Susan McClary is frankly troubled by this possibility and hesitantly proposes an against-the-grain reading that might show how this opera "empowers women and condemns imperialism." She quickly adds, though, that she has "difficulty imagining that Puccini in 1904 had this kind of cultural critique in mind as he penned his score."[96] Furthermore, McClary herself halfway dismisses this reading. She calls it "politically correct" and suggests that it would be good mainly for bolstering the career of an upwardly mobile academic.[97] McClary's first instinct is more solid than she suspects. "Devastating attacks on patriarchy and imperialism" (her phrase) are clearly what Puccini and his librettists had in mind, *in part*.[98] Certain portions of the work dramatize effectively the principle – much heard today – of respecting the worth and potential of a person whose cultural situation is very different from one's own.[99]

Still, *Madama Butterfly* is complex and contradictory. McClary's initial proposal *and* her ensuing doubt are each justified by certain aspects of the work that have long deserved closer attention. In particular, three ensembles show how diversely and – can we say this without implying some kind of artistic failure? – inconsistently Puccini and his librettists portrayed Japan,

Figure 8.3 The Bonze (Jean-Louis Soumagnas) curses Cio-Cio-San (Yoko Watanabe), and her relatives and the other wedding guests join him: "Hou! Cio-Cio-San!" From a 1982 touring production by L'Opéra du Rhin. (Photo by Alain Kaiser, used by permission.)

its people, and its new and often fraught relationship to the imperial West. All three carry out their vivid portrayals without using the musical markers of Japan found in many other places in the score.

The first appearance of Butterfly and her friends in Act 1 is visually spectacular.[100] Dozens of kimonos and "brightly colored parasols" gracefully move up the hill (or across a curved bridge, in some productions) to attend the wedding ceremony in Butterfly's garden (Fig. 8.2).[101] The music is harmonically rich (including augmented triads) and ripely orchestrated. But it is not at all Asian-sounding. This has led the scholar-conductor Julian Smith to comment that "exoticism is [suddenly] discarded" here. "[In] what in theory one might have expected to be the exotic opportunity *par excellence* ... Japan is forgotten for a moment."[102]

Quite the contrary, in this timeless-feeling moment, the "exotic opportunity *par excellence*" is fully exploited. As the Full-Context Paradigm makes clear, exoticism – that is, representation of an exotic land and its people – does not require the presence of exotic-sounding musical style. The librettists and Puccini here produce – even without any musical signifiers of Japaneseness – an unsurpassed scopic and aural emphasis on Oriental (East

Asian) feminine beauty and grace. This occurs at the level both of the group and – as the voice of the "happiest girl in Japan" soars above the chorus – of the individual (Ex. 8.6). The resulting, memorable moment can be regarded as the most oppressive in the work – the most quintessentially Orientalist, in the denigratory sense. All Asian womanhood, practically, is reduced to a vision of loveliness for the delectation of the Western gazer.

Viewed another way, though, this idyllic scene of young Japanese women arriving *en masse* also quivers with what William Ashbrook has called "bitter irony." The scene is launched immediately after Pinkerton's triumphant words (and music) announcing to Sharpless his plan to marry one day "a true, American wife."[103] The sequence of musicalized events – Pinkerton's heartless vow, Butterfly's floating entrance and graceful landing – surely castigates Pinkerton's selfishness and hypocrisy. By extension, it also castigates the imperial system that has brought Pinkerton to this distant land with dollars enough to turn things to his advantage.

By contrast, the ensemble that soon follows cannot remotely be read as engaging in a "cultural critique" of imperialism. Butterfly's wedding guests look Pinkerton over and make various admiring or skeptical comments to each other, sometimes at the same time or in canon. The resulting verbal gabble puts the audience in somewhat the same position as Pinkerton, who has already made various jokes about the incomprehensibility of Japanese customs. The overload of instant opinions from this diverse Japanese throng is echoed in the harmonic language here, which several times engages in unusual levels of dissonance: for example, three full measures built on an eleventh chord.[104]

It might seem odd of Puccini to use the most advanced (i.e., Debussyan) harmonic tools to describe a supposedly backward Eastern society. But that eleventh chord – in this particular context – results from the rather mechanical process of a pileup. (The "processional" melody is stated at rising pitch levels over a static open-fifth pedal in the low instruments.) The device suggests a race of automatons, who are unable to react to a newcomer with anything other than superficial conventionality and jealous lies. (The first sopranos and the Cousin: "[Goro] also offered him to me, but I answered, 'I don't want him!'" – Ex. 8.7.)

This scene also lays the groundwork for another ensemble which is yet more negatively skewed (discussed earlier and illustrated in Fig. 8.3). The rigidly traditional Bonze enters, cursing Cio-Cio-San for having abandoned her people's religion. We – now well prepared – accept as natural the guests' unanimous alignment with the intolerant priest as he curses the fifteen-year-old. Whereas his harshly dissonant, hence threatening, music relies on

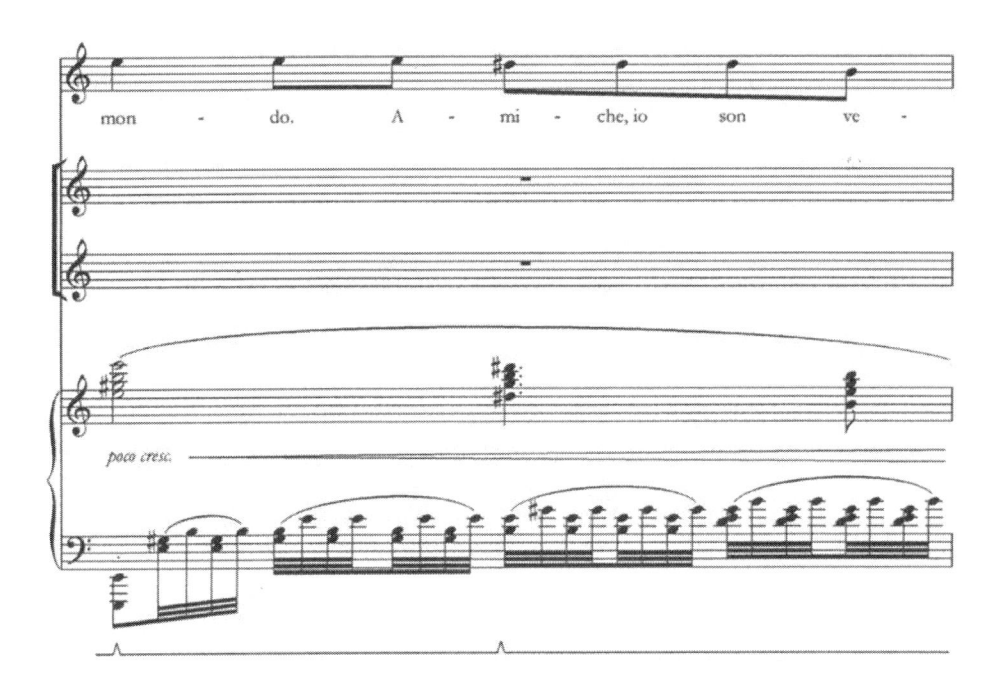

Example 8.6 Puccini, *Madama Butterfly*, Act 1: arrival of "the happiest girl in Japan" and her friends.

[Example 8.6 (cont.)]

Example 8.6 (cont.)

all-purpose operatic signifiers, the horror of the wedding guests is marked as audibly Japanese ("Hou! Hou!").

The very last ensemble in the opera is as empathetic with Cio-Cio-San and her people as the "wedding guests" ensemble was condescending. It also amounts to a ruefully realistic commentary on the imperial stance of many American soldiers, businessmen, and diplomats toward the "exotic" peoples – as they clearly often viewed them – whose territories they were increasingly entering and, with diverse intents, attempting to exploit.[105] In this powerful trio, the American consul Sharpless pleads with Cio-Cio-San's maid Suzuki to persuade Cio-Cio-San to give up her child to the "motherly care" of Kate Pinkerton so as to "safeguard the child's future." Meanwhile, Pinkerton wanders around the little house, commenting on what he is reencountering after an absence of three years: flowers, the bedroom, a statue of the Buddha, a photograph of Pinkerton himself. The three characters' words, if one merely reads them in the libretto, suggest a discussion between the baritone and mezzo, with Pinkerton muttering asides and "becoming more and more

Example 8.7 Puccini, *Madama Butterfly*, Act 1: procession of the wedding guests, with pile-up resulting in three measures on an eleventh chord.

agitated." Suzuki twice expresses her horror to Sharpless: "And you want me to ask a mother to…." (She cannot bring herself to utter the obvious last words.)

The music enacts a very different scenario, reflecting (but, I would argue, not identifying with) the power relations of imperialism. Throughout the thirty slow (*largo*) measures of the trio, the orchestra plays a surging and ever-unfurling melody that was first heard when the two men arrived at the house. Sharpless and Pinkerton take turns doubling the orchestra's melody. Beginning softly and *dolce*, they gradually build to an immense climax, at which the tenor holds a four-beat-long high B♭. The baritone finally joins him on his own equally intense high F. It is not Pinkerton (as his words might suggest) but Suzuki who is, throughout most of the trio, reduced to muttering. Her protesting words are mostly set as recitative-like interjections, and they seem to bounce ineffectually off the seamless wall of male legato singing (Ex. 8.8).

Example 8.8 Puccini, *Madama Butterfly*, Act 2, scene 2: trio for Suzuki, Pinkerton, and Sharpless.

The whole number is underpinned by a striding bass line that is often doubled by Sharpless when Pinkerton (as in most of Ex. 8.8) takes the main melody. Pinkerton and Sharpless could easily perform their parts (without Suzuki) as a satisfying duet. Suzuki gives the effect of trying to get their attention while the men, focusing on their respective intense feelings, sing away. Sharpless's words are, in his own eyes, reasonable ones, rather like those of another figure of authority, Germont *père* in Verdi's *La traviata*. But those words are also – again, like Germont's – cruel, for they do not take into consideration Cio-Cio-San's feelings, nor anticipate that giving up her child will lead her to suicide. Pinkerton's behavior seems equally heartless. He is here taking selfish refuge in his pain, just as he has acted selfishly throughout the opera.

One imagines that the two American men think their cultural values superior to those of the Japanese. Pinkerton had ridiculed the Bonze in Act 1. Yet here the men prove themselves to be as deaf to a Japanese woman's entreaty – as unlistening – as was the Bonze on that former occasion.

After we have experienced a performance of this trio, we may not find so implausible McClary's tentative claim that *Madama Butterfly* engages in a critique of imperialism and Western cultural superiority. Certainly, few listeners would endorse Mosco Carner's gripe that "this trio represents a concession on the part of the dramatist to the musicians [i.e., the composer and his singers], for the dramatic situation hardly warrants it." The stage direction at the end of this trio is eloquent: Suzuki, still resisting Sharpless's instruction that she go talk with Kate Pinkerton in the garden, has to be "thrust" (*spinta*) there by him. The historically determined powerlessness of the non-Western, exotic Other is vividly realized in this trio and in the peremptory shove from Sharpless that ends it. And the portrayal is (in accordance with the Full-Context Paradigm) carried out by means that – were one to close one's eyes and listen only to the music and not the words – might not seem exotic/Oriental at all.

9 | Exoticism in a modernist age (c. 1890–1960)

By the turn of the twentieth century, Western composers were using not one but three distinct types of musical exoticism. The most basic and continuing type of musical exoticism is the one that consists of explicit portrayals of unfamiliar places and peoples. I propose, at this point (because of this proliferation of approaches), to give it a more specific name, Overt Exoticism. Overt Exoticism is most often what writers have in mind when they discuss the phenomenon of musical exoticism, and it is largely what we have been talking about in the essays of Chapters 1–4 and in the historical chapters up to this point. In the present chapter, we shall continue to focus primarily on Overt Exoticism – namely in the "long" half-century 1890–1960. First, though, we shall explore the two other types of musical exoticism prominent in this period, types that had great and lasting significance for the development of musical art generally during the Debussy era and would continue to do so for generations after. I call them Submerged Exoticism and Transcultural Composing. Whether they indeed amount to types of exoticism at all – or are something else entirely – will be discussed along the way.

In addition to noting these three basic tendencies or approaches, the chapter will pause at times to explore how exoticism functioned in the output (and careers) of a number of very disparate composers, some of whom (such as Villa-Lobos and Hovhaness) were clearly aware of their special place as semi-exotic figures within the world of Western art music. Particular attention will be paid to a classic instance of Overt Exoticism (or is it, rather, an instance of Transcultural Composing?) for piano solo, Debussy's *Pagodes*; some frankly Overt-Exotic popular songs from France and America; and a work rarely mentioned in regard to exoticism: Leonard Bernstein's durable Broadway hit, *West Side Story*. For these, and for other works discussed more briefly, one or both of the Paradigms defined in Chapter 3 (Exotic-Style and Full-Context) will continue to find helpful application.

The turn against Overt Exoticism

Around 1900 or a bit before, some of the most skillful and adventurous composers of concert and stage works were beginning to hold Overt

Exoticism in disdain. Two broad trends in the history of the West relate indirectly to this shift in attitude:

- **Unease about empire.** Europeans could easily look askance at overseas rule and commercial control when, as in *Madama Butterfly*, the imperialists in question were Americans. But, by the early twentieth century, broad doubts were emerging about the efforts of the major European powers themselves, notably Britain and France, at "civilizing" the "inferior races" of Africa, South Asia, and other distant regions.[1] The turn of attitude against empire was particularly prevalent among artists and intellectuals who thought themselves sensitive and cosmopolitan; it stands in sharp contrast to the vociferously pro-empire sentiments that largely continued among political leaders and the working and middle classes.[2] In 1907, Saint-Saëns, who had, over many winters, spent months in North Africa, commented in a letter: "Wherever Europe gains a foothold it destroys the land and creates ugliness and misery."[3] A distaste for certain aspects of imperial domination did not necessarily entail an opposition to exoticism in the arts. Quite the contrary, it could go hand in hand with a respect for and interest in learning from foreign cultures (within the limits of what was possible at the time). Saint-Saëns himself showed this in the Bacchanale from *Samson et Dalila* (1877); the *Suite algérienne* for orchestra, Op. 60 (1880); and also later works such as the second movement, "Vision congolaise" (Vision of the Congo) from his *Triptyque*, Op. 136, for violin and piano (1912).
- **Access to distant lands and their cultural products.** During the decades around the turn of the century, travel by train and ship became swifter and safer. Western-style amenities increased along with the numbers of European (and American) military, commercial, and tourist visitors and residents. This reduced the mystery and aura that had initially surrounded locales as diverse as Havana and Marrakesh, Bombay and Tokyo, and that had made musical works that were in some way "about" them so exciting. Experts in comparative musicology and (its successor field) ethnomusicology published some of the first even semi-reliable transcriptions and descriptive accounts of the musics of many important world cultures. The successive advances in sound-recording technology during the first half of the twentieth century gradually made a significant library of aural samples available, albeit primarily to scholars rather than to the general public. Meanwhile, journalists and travel writers helped give some sense of the performative and cultural contexts of music-making abroad. (More systematic scholarly attention to the place of

music-making in communal life would come in the 1960s, when ethnomusicology, to a large extent, took the "anthropological turn.") All this increased contact and knowledge made it easier for composers to write works reflecting at least a few musical features of the culture in question. At the same time, it gradually revealed, to those who were interested enough to notice, the inherent artificiality and inauthenticity of many standard exotic codes.

Even more powerfully and directly, two broad aesthetic trends redirected composers, especially those of an exploratory or modernist bent, away from Overt Exoticism:

- **Quest for originality.** Though the early modernists (if we take that term in its original sense, referring to such turn-of-the-century composers as Debussy, Strauss, Mahler, and Scriabin) rejected many aspects of Romanticism, they continued to embrace wholeheartedly its tenet that art, to be great, needs to be original, and expressive of the artist's psychological makeup.[4] Around 1900, many people in the musical community who considered themselves serious and demanding were coming to view musical exoticism (and also musical nationalism, its seeming opposite) as less original, fresh, and surprising than it had seemed in earlier decades.[5] The very success and proliferation of the exotic in musical life surely played a part in this. Numerous exotic (and national/exotic) works, whether for keyboard, orchestra, or the stage, were now standard items in the repertoire and had made various exotic compositional devices overly familiar.[6] The proliferation of exoticism in lower-status streams of cultural life such as parlor song, operetta, and, in England, Arabian Nights "pantomimes" for the Christmas season, encouraged the impression that the exoticist project – at least when carried out in straightforward, Overt manner – was inherently cheap and formulaic.[7]
- **Rejection of realistic representation.** Several successive or overlapping trends in literature and visual art – Pre-Raphaelitism, Symbolism, Primitivism, Fauvism, Cubism – cast a shadow over aesthetic principles that had, for centuries, been fundamental within Western culture. No longer was art conceived of in accordance with Aristotelian principles, namely as a direct and reliable "mirroring" of real situations in the past or present, and as an occasion for conveying moral messages about human activity (e.g., good government or choosing virtue). Instead, pushing the principle of Romantic subjectivity to new heights of intensity, artists sought out realms of strangeness as analogues to the dream world – the

desires and fears – of the creative mind. The African masks that appear in Picasso's *Les demoiselles d'Avignon* (1907) and in paintings by Ernst-Ludwig Kirchner (*Berlin Street Scene*, 1913) and Paul Klee functioned less as an image of life on African soil than as a shocking way to re-envision the West and as challenge to the techniques and aesthetic presuppositions of academic Realism and of the sometimes facile prettiness of (once-daring) Impressionism.[8]

Within the musical realm, these two broad aesthetic trends found expression in the harsh attitude toward Overt Exotic representation (and toward frankly exotic styles) that we encountered in Chapter 2 in writings of Debussy, Schenker, and Schoenberg. It can be sensed, equally, in the many musical works – by Debussy, Stravinsky, Messiaen, and others – that engage far more often in Submerged and Transcultural approaches to musical exoticism than in Overt ones.

Let us begin with Submerged Exoticism. By this term, I mean the tendency (in the late nineteenth and early twentieth centuries) for general musical style to incorporate distinctive scales, harmonies, orchestral colors, and other features that had previously been associated with exotic realms. I call it Submerged rather than, say, Absorbed because I want to stress that the exotic aura that had long surrounded these musical materials – even when it was not avowed at the surface level of the work – lingered for many listeners, and perhaps for the composer as well. I would imagine that an Absorbed Exoticism – if such a thing exists – has shed its exotic aura entirely. (A linguistic analogy to Absorbed Exoticism might be the dead metaphor: when we hear of "windfall profits," we do not think of apples hitting the ground.) I shall return to this problem – the possible loss of the exotic aura – in discussing Transcultural Composing. First, I focus on two prominent techniques–exoticism*s* in the narrow, countable sense (see Chapter 3) – that became typical of Submerged Exoticism around the turn of the twentieth century: (1) "arabesque" melodic figures and (2) unusual scales – especially whole-tone and octatonic – and their associated harmonies.

Submerged Exoticisms: (1) the arabesque

The concept of arabesque is crucial to understanding many works from the decades around 1900 and especially those of Debussy. By his day, the word had accumulated multiple associations. "Arabesque" derived, originally, from an art-historical term for the geometric shapes, tendril-like lines, and highly patterned calligraphy in decorative art of the Islamic Middle

Très modéré ♩. = 44

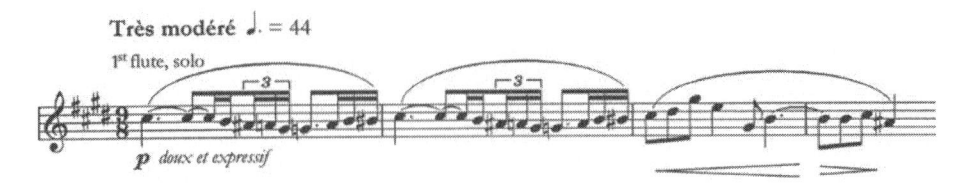

Example 9.1 Debussy, *Prélude à l'Après-midi d'un faune*, mm. 1–4.

East, such as one finds on the walls of the Alhambra. In the course of the late eighteenth and nineteenth centuries, "arabesque" had also acquired a broader meaning in European aesthetics. For Kant, it meant a form of artistic expression that stirred a purposeless sense of pleasure. Through Kant's influence, arabesque went on to become, as one scholar has recently noted, "a paradigm of aesthetic autonomy."[9] Schumann presumably had this sense in mind when giving his exquisite but utterly non-exotic Op. 18 piano piece (1839) the title *Arabeske*. Later in the nineteenth century, the term "arabesque" was put into broader circulation in France by writers associated with the Symbolist movement, notably Stéphane Mallarmé, and it found practical embodiment in the work of artists and decorators associated with Art Nouveau and Jugendstil (Figs. 9.1 and 9.2).[10] Debussy, who knew Mallarmé and others in that world, used "arabesque" in several different ways: for example, to indicate the curvaceous, overlapping lines in the music of Lasso, Palestrina, and J. S. Bach.[11]

But it is in regard to his own pathbreaking work *Prélude à l'Après-midi d'un faune* (1894, for orchestra) that one sees most clearly the lingering exotic overtones of the term for Debussy. The poem of Mallarmé upon which Debussy based the work takes place among the mythological shepherds and nymphs, fauns and satyrs of ancient Greece – a world that had long been considered half-Eastern, akin in certain ways to the polytheistic cultures of ancient Mesopotamia and to the (more recent) Islamic Middle East.[12] Shortly before the first performance of Debussy's *Faune*, the composer wrote to Stéphane Mallarmé: "[Would you] be so kind as to encourage with your presence the arabesques that – I have been led to believe, perhaps through an excess of pride – were dictated to me by the Flute of your Faun?"[13] Nine years later, Debussy reused the term with regard to the work.[14] Another year later (in 1914), he described his *Faune* one more time, in an interview. Although he now did not use the word "arabesque," his phrases point to some of the features that had clearly been in his mind on those previous occasions. He explained that the music is "undulating, soothing [or rocking: *berceuse*], and full of curved lines."[15] In addition,

Figure 9.1 Debussy and Zohra ben Brahim, the Algerian mistress of his writer-friend Pierre Louÿs, in Louÿs's dining room in 1897. Debussy relaxes in a bentwood rocking chair, perhaps manufactured by the Austrian firm of Thonet. The William Morris wallpaper is influenced by the stylized floral motifs of Turkish and Persian enamelware. The photo (taken by Louÿs) is from the photo album of composer Francis Poulenc, whose handwritten caption identifies the woman as "sister of the little Arab thief in [André Gide's novel] *L'immoraliste*." Zohra's traits are echoed in those of the character Aracoeli (in Louÿs's novel *Psyché*) and in several poems in Louÿs's collection *Chansons de Bilitis*. The collection was a source for three works by Debussy: the *Trois chansons de Bilitis* for voice and piano (1897–98); the incidental music, for two flutes, two harps, and celesta, for a public reading of twelve of Louÿs's *Chansons de Bilitis* (1901); and the *Six épigraphes antiques* (1914, freely based on the incidental music) for piano four-hands or for piano solo. (By permission of the Bibliothèque Nationale de France.)

notes Caroline Potter, Debussy seems to have considered lines arabesque-like if they were "continuously evolving," "grow[ing] organically rather than being divided into periodic phrases."[16] Gurminder Kaur Bhogal adds other musical parameters, notably "irregular rhythm and dissonant metre."[17]

Sensuality, curvaceousness, rhythmic and metrical fluidity, and a continuous spun-out quality are indeed what we find in the music of *Faune*. The piece begins with a shapely unaccompanied flute solo whose rhythms and pitches are unpredictable enough to make it sound quasi-improvised.[18] William Austin keenly notes the resemblance between Example 9.1 and a famous moment in Saint-Saëns's exotic opera *Samson et Dalila*: the

220　　　Musical Exoticism: Images and Reflections

Figure 9.2 Arabeques from an early fifteenth-century Cairo manuscript, as copied and analyzed in fig. 139 of Riegl's famous *Stilfragen* (1893).

downward flowing refrain "Ah, reviens" from Dalila's Act 2 aria "Mon coeur s'ouvre à ta voix."[19]

The opening melody of *Faune* returns repeatedly throughout the piece, always subtly altered, often reharmonized or further extended, yet mostly starting on the same pitch (C♯), and almost always assigned to the flute. This perhaps recalls the way that (as many writers had described) an instrumentalist from a folk or non-Western tradition might play a short or narrow-range melody repeatedly yet with constant changes. In a similar spirit (though without explicit mention of repetition), Debussy gave the following words (in 1900) to his fictional mouthpiece, Monsieur Croche: "My favorite music is those few notes that an Egyptian shepherd plays on his flute: he joins in with the landscape around him and hears harmonies that are not found in those treatises of yours."[20] We shall return in the next section to the implied "harmonies" – i.e., the pitch content – of the Faun's flute solo.

A more plainly Middle Eastern-sounding "arabesque" is what Austin calls *Faune*'s "flowing motif" (m. 28).[21] The line descends (as it did in the

Exoticism in a modernist age (c. 1890–1960) 221

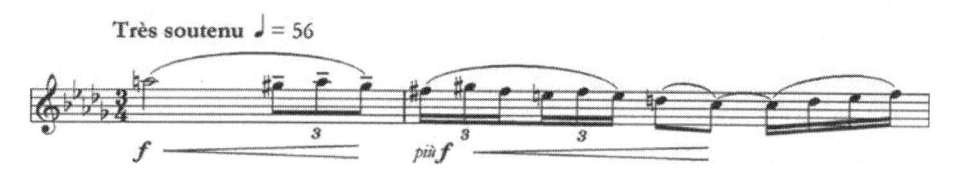

Example 9.2 Debussy, *Prélude à l'Après-midi d'un faune*, mm. 61–62, winds in unison playing the "Sheherazade" figure.

opening), but each step is now decorated with a triplet figure involving the upper-neighbor note, a variation procedure typical of much Middle Eastern music.[22] At m. 61, near the emotional climax of the work, Debussy precedes the "flowing motif" with a long note.[23] The result (Ex. 9.2) closely resembles in rhythm and contour (though not in harmony) one of the most famous exotic themes in the repertoire, the violin solo in Rimsky-Korsakov's *Sheherazade* (1888) that portrays the skillful tale-spinner herself (Ex. 3.1).

Arabesque is at work prominently in numerous other pieces by Debussy. In some, the exotic connection is explicit. The *Épigraphes antiques* for piano four-hands (1914) are freely based on short pieces for chamber ensemble that Debussy composed in 1901 to serve as interludes between recited poems (written by his friend Pierre Louÿs, who took the photo reproduced as Fig. 9.1). The poems are filled with sensuous images of the Eastern Mediterranean: a naked young woman with freely floating black curls; Egyptian courtesans squatting on yellow mats; a dancer playing the crotales and smiling over her shoulder as she "quivers" her "convulsive, muscled rump"; and verses written in the sand during a morning rain-shower.[24] In *La mer* (1905), by contrast, the title and movement headings do not suggest any sea in particular. Nonetheless, the "Sheherazade" descending-triplet figure just discussed (Exx. 3.1, 9.2) occurs soon into the first movement (on a flute line, m. 74, that repeatedly rises and descends, like a gentle ocean wave). A related figure shows up repeatedly in the second movement; at m. 12 it is played by the English horn, an instrument that had often been a marker of exotic regions, as in Borodin's *In [the Steppes of] Central Asia*.

Arabesque contributed to important structural aspects of Debussy's works as well. An elaborate, flexible melody lends itself to being accompanied by relatively static harmonies that will neither distract the ear nor impose a heavy metrical beat. As a result, notes Boyd Pomeroy, Debussy tended to "chain" several statements of an arabesque melody together, in a relatively non-goal-directed manner, over a tonally static accompaniment. The result was a "novel and distinctly twentieth-century approach to form generation."[25] In the process – and depending on a variety of factors, such as the background of a given listener – the exotic aspect of arabesque melody in a given piece can go beyond Submerged to what (as mentioned earlier) we might call totally Absorbed.

At times, though, the pitch content of these harmonically static passages may sharply remind the listener consciously or unconsciously of Middle Eastern or other non-Western regions. A remarkable twelve-measure-long passage in the first movement of *La mer* is built entirely on a fluttering "black-note" D♭-pentatonic ostinato figure, over which the high winds present a melody using that same pentatonic set (and harmonized in parallel fifths, mm. 33–34). In this case, listeners familiar with musical traditions of Japan, China, Southeast Asia, or India – or with Western conventions for representing those regions musically – will sense one or more likely sources of inspiration here.[26] (The front cover of the published score gives a hint, too. Following Debussy's specifications, the publisher based the design on a famous woodblock print of a massive, foaming ocean billow by the Japanese artist Hokusai.[27]) Similarly, very near the end of the second movement, a slow arpeggio in the harp spells out the same black-note pentatonic set, though over an open fifth using notes pungently dissonant with those of the arpeggio. (We shall return to black-note pentatonicism in the section on Transcultural Composing.)

Submerged Exoticisms: (2) bold harmonic procedures

As a fledgling composer, Debussy had already been fascinated by a variety of national and exotic styles, notably Spanish, Slavic, and Middle Eastern. He later recalled that, when attending a performance of Lalo's heavily Middle Eastern-style ballet *Namouna* (a work from 1882), he became so "noisy in my enthusiasm" that he was led out the door by the director of the opera house.[28] Set on Corfu (in the Ionian Sea), *Namouna* presents the story of an Arab female slave who is fought over by two men (one the head of a pirate fleet). The ballet contains dances for Moroccan slaves, a delightfully drowsy "Siesta" movement, and a Cigarette Waltz whose music seems partly modeled on the seductive dance for Anitra (daughter of a Bedouin chief) in Grieg's incidental music for Ibsen's play *Peer Gynt* (1875).[29]

But the most lasting faraway influence upon Debussy – and perhaps on Western European music of his era, generally – came from Russia. In the late nineteenth and early twentieth centuries, Westerners gradually gained exposure to Russian music through concerts featuring instrumental pieces – some drawn from operas – and also through published scores. As early as 1874, the Paris Conservatoire Library received a shipment of twenty-seven

Russian scores, among them Glinka's opera *Ruslan and Lyudmila* (1842), Rimsky-Korsakov's tone poem *Sadko* (1869), and Musorgsky's opera *Boris Godunov* (1869–72).[30] The young Debussy spent the summer of 1880 in Switzerland, southern France, and Italy in the employ of the Russian noblewoman Nadezhda von Meck (best known to history as Tchaikovsky's patron). Debussy and Mme von Meck played works of Glinka and Tchaikovsky together in arrangements for piano four-hands.[31] The impact of Russia on Western European composers increased yet more in the early decades of the twentieth century, when some of Russia's leading composers (including Prokofiev, Stravinsky, and, for periods, Rachmaninoff) settled in Paris and the impresario Serge Diaghilev organized a widely hailed and socially fashionable series of ballet and opera performances in Paris (1909–29) focusing heavily on Russian works, many of them set in the Middle East, Central Asia, or India (Figs. 9.3–9.4).

Russia had a complex relationship to the concept of exoticism. Its empire expanded to the south and east during the nineteenth and early twentieth centuries. (It was thus, as Taruskin notes, a contiguous empire, like those of Austria and Turkey, and very unlike the overseas empires of Britain or France.[32]) As a result, Russia was often regarded by Europeans (and by certain Westernizers within Russia itself) as somehow "Eastern": uncultured, backward, incomprehensible, or even frankly dangerous or unstable.[33] Many Russians were fascinated with the largely Islamic territories over which their army was gaining sway.[34] Russian literature regularly presented these territories as realms of folk tale, magic, evildoing, and (for males) available female sexual partners.[35] Some particularly reactionary Russians (especially ones who emigrated to Western Europe in response to the revolutions of 1905 and 1917) argued that the entire Russian-controlled land mass was a single "Eurasian" unit. They regularly claimed the steppes and mountain villages of Central Asia as central to greater-Russian identity. This entailed a certain degree of empathic identification with Georgians, Kazakhs, and other peoples who spoke Caucasian or Turkic languages and lived primarily as herders or subsistence farmers (or even as nomads). It also often entailed an interest in these peoples' diverse traditional musics, which (as the Eurasianists pointed out) had more in common with those of Arabia, Persia, or even East Asia than with those of Europe. All this, according to the Eurasianist thesis, marked greater-Russia with typically non-Western features, such as collective group "spontaneity" (rather than individualistic, decadent "culture").[36]

Greater-Russian images of this sort filtered into many prominent Diaghilev productions, including four from the 1909–10 seasons: *L'oiseau*

Figure 9.3 A moment from Michel Fokine's ballet *Shéhérazade*, as shown in a photograph included in the official program book (Souvenir, 1916) of the performances by Diaghilev's Ballets Russes at New York's Metropolitan Opera House and on the subsequent tour of other American cities. Zobéïde (Flore Revalles) is here possessively embraced by what the program book calls one of the harem's "stalwart negro slaves" (Adolf Bolm, in dark makeup and body stocking, and with stereotypically bulging eyes). The music for Fokine's ballet (first performed in 1910) used Rimsky-Korsakov's beloved orchestral suite, but ignored the descriptive titles of its movements. Instead, the action was based on the opening tale from the *Thousand and One Nights*, about Sultan Shahriar's favorite wife, who, during her husband's hunting trips, would repeatedly engage in sex with the dark-skinned slave Mas'ud. The program book informed the audience that, when the "voluptuous orgy ... reaches its maddest height," the Sultan, "a sinister tragedian of silence, returns unexpectedly" and slays all but Zobéïde, who "stabs herself at his feet."

Figure 9.4 Costume design by Léon Bakst for the Blue Sultana in Fokine's *Shéhérazade*, as reproduced in the same program book of 1916.

de feu (The Firebird, to a score commissioned from Igor Stravinsky), *Shéhérazade* (to Rimsky-Korsakov's four-movement symphonic suite), *Les orientales*, and *Cléopâtre* (the latter two using compilations of pieces by several Russian composers). Such images shaped with particular intensity a Diaghilev production from the 1913 season: *Le sacre du printemps: Tableaux de la Russie païenne* (The Rite of Spring: Pictures of Pagan Russia, 1913, again with music by Stravinsky). And the Eurasian thesis found a different sort of expression in a subsequent work by Stravinsky that is filled with pentatonic and other gapped-scale melodies of narrow range: *Les noces* (The Peasant Wedding, 1913–23).[37]

The three exotic/pagan/peasant Stravinsky works just mentioned also reflected and extended the longstanding Russian interest in musical experimentation.[38] Glinka (in the 1840s) and then Rimsky-Korsakov and composers in the latter's orbit (notably the young Stravinsky) had been fascinated with a wide range of unusual scales and the harmonic devices that could be derived from them.[39] They seem to have been inspired directly or indirectly by certain tonally exploratory passages in works of such composers as Beethoven, Schubert, and Liszt. Two scales (or pitch collections) proved particularly important and influential:

- **The whole-tone scale.** This was often generated by sequencing, or sometimes repeated modulating, at the distance of a major third; or by juxtaposing two augmented triads that are a whole step apart. The resulting scale consists of only six notes rather than (as in the usual major and minor scales) seven.
- **The octatonic scale.** This was often generated by sequencing, or sometimes repeated modulating, at the distance of a minor third (or of a tritone, i.e., two minor thirds); or by juxtaposing two diminished-seventh chords a half-step apart. The resulting scale consists of eight notes rather than (again) seven.

Russian composers from Glinka to Stravinsky made striking recourse to these scales when evoking evil Eastern sorcerers – Chernomor in *Ruslan and Lyudmila* (whole-tone), Kashchei the Immortal in *Firebird* (octatonic) – or supernatural phenomena more generally.[40]

These features – primitivism (and Eurasianism), exoticism, and musical experimentalism – combined in powerful ways that nobody would have predicted. A notable example of the obsessively systematic use of the octatonic scale is Rimsky-Korsakov's opera *The Golden Cockerel* (1909), which is set in a magical Arabian kingdom. The preference for fantastic, exotic plots over historical ones was, notes Richard Taruskin, a response to increased censorship during the years after the assassination (in 1881) of the liberal tsar Alexander II.[41] Russian composers often associated supposed traits of "Easterners" (in the Caucasus region, say) with specific musical features other than scales: the opulence of tribal chieftains and their retinue, with glittering and colorful orchestration; warlike violence, with pounding, syncopated rhythms; and sexual longing and lassitude, with long-held pedal tones and the somewhat slithery chromatic fragment 5–5♯–6–6♭–5.[42] Such style traits show up prominently in Borodin's *In [the Steppes of] Central Asia*, in the Polovetsian March and Polovetsian Dances from that same composer's *Prince Igor*, and in Rimsky-Korsakov's Symphony No. 2, "Antar" (based on tales about a sixth-century Arab poet and military leader).

In 1889, all four Borodin and Rimsky-Korsakov works just mentioned were performed (under Rimsky-Korsakov's baton) at the Exposition Universelle in Paris. "Among the musicians applauding enthusiastically," notes Annegret Fauser, "were Alfred Bruneau, Claude Debussy, Gabriel Fauré, André Messager, and [music critic and scholar] Julien Tiersot."[43] One reviewer specifically commented that the two concerts "charmed and astonished our Western ears."[44] The unspoken corollary was that Russian ears were somehow Eastern (perhaps inherently or by an influence from Central Asia). Even a piece that was based on the Song of the Volga Boatmen and that therefore, from a Russian point of view, was the opposite of exotic could be praised by a French critic in terms familiar from many descriptions of desert and jungle locales: "the strangest rhythms," "effects of extraordinary violence and extraordinary vividness," and "an expressive and tender melancholy."[45]

Octatonic procedures, often coupled with pounding and asymmetrical rhythms and brash orchestral colors, quickly became widespread in many works of Western European composers, even when the work has no Eastern (or even Russian) associations. Ravel reached for them when writing his early *Shéhérazade* overture but also *Rapsodie espagnole* and *Daphnis et Chloé*, as well as a number of important works with no ethnic/exotic associations whatever.[46] The same group of procedures became widely known (and imitated) thanks to Stravinsky's three ballets for Diaghilev: *Firebird*, with its aforementioned Eastern sorcerer; *Petrushka*, which includes, along with its many Russian characters, a "Moor" (i.e., dark-skinned Muslim) and a wizard-like Asian puppet-master; and *Le sacre du printemps*, whose music and choreography portrayed prehistoric Russia in so plainly threatening – indeed, primitive – a manner that the cultured Parisians who attended the premiere broke out into a (rather primitive) riot.[47] *Le sacre*, in particular, became a primary model for numerous works on the borderline between primitivism and exoticism for generations to come. For example, Prokofiev's *Scythian Suite* (1918) is drawn from his (unperformed) ballet *Ala and Lolli*. The ballet was loosely based on tales of the Scythians, ancient Iranian horse-riding warriors who have sometimes been described as the ancestors of the Russians. Particularly harsh and angular is movement 2, in which Chuzhbog (the "enemy god," associated with darkness and reptiles) does a violent dance before attempting to abduct the heroine, Ala.[48]

Whole-tone procedures became a particular obsession of Debussy (whereas Ravel largely avoided them).[49] Some heavily whole-tone pieces – such as *Voiles* and *Cloches à travers les feuilles* – give no unmistakable outward indication of Elsewhereness. (In the first of these pieces, the *voiles* could be veils on women in Algiers or, equally well, sails on boats in a French port. In the second, the *cloches* – church bells – whose chiming we are hearing through leafy trees are presumably in rural France.) The titles of other such whole-tone-drenched pieces suggest places that are somehow "special" yet still undefined: for example, "Fêtes" (Festivals, the second of the three *Nocturnes* for orchestra) and the expansive piano piece *L'isle joyeuse* (The Joyful Island).[50] One more glance at *Faune* can demonstrate how whole-tone writing can be incorporated and what effect it can make. The opening flute solo (Ex. 9.1 above) feels like a whole-tone fragment that has been enriched by a few chromatic passing notes. Measure 32 brings four whole-tone flourishes, two in the clarinet and two in the flute. These four flourishes, and Example 9.1, amount to arabesques, and "modernist" – or Russian-influenced – ones. In them, Easternness is at once present and hidden: half-Submerged, we might say.

Transcultural Composing

The discussion of musical exoticism becomes more varied and complex as we move to consider pieces composed (and often read) in a frank spirit of transculturalism. By Transcultural Composing I mean the practice of composing for Western contexts – for example, a piano recital or a wind-ensemble concert – a work that incorporates certain stylistic and formal conventions of another culture's music, often a music that has a quite different context (e.g., a village celebration or religiously inflected ritual). Pieces typical of Transcultural Composing blend, interweave, or merge musical elements that the composer (and audience) would recognize as being "our own" with those of the distant Other culture (or several distant Other cultures).

Earlier in this book, we encountered several intentional and at least somewhat informed efforts at such stylistic replication (though at that point we simply called them instances of exoticism). Mozart's "Rondo alla turca," we may recall, repeats a standard (if simple) Turkish *usul* drum rhythm again and again in the left-hand accompaniment; and Liszt's Hungarian Rhapsody No. 14 incorporates melodies, instrumental sonorities, and harmonic practices that Liszt encountered in "Gypsy" music of the day. Nonetheless, and for reasons noted earlier, it was in the early twentieth century that Transcultural Composing suddenly became a more widely practiced and accepted compositional option and one that might or might not (depending on many factors) deserve to be distinguished from exoticism. Prominent instances include pieces in Indonesian style, such as Debussy's *Pagodes* and Ravel's *Laideronnette, impératrice des pagodes*; and pieces in Spanish style, such as Debussy's *Soirée dans Grenade* and *Ibéria* and Ravel's *Rapsodie espagnole* and *Boléro*.[51] Are such works not just Transcultural but also exotic (in the sense defined in Chapter 3)? That is, do they portray a locale and its population? Or do they merely absorb and incorporate (or give the impression of incorporating) the musical sounds that those people make? For the moment, I prefer to leave such questions open, which is why I have proposed the phrase "Transcultural Composing" rather than, say, "Purely Musical Exoticism."[52]

Like Submerged (and half-Submerged, and Absorbed), the term Transcultural is not standard within musicology. It derives from "transculturation," a concept that social scientists – concerned to remain "value-free," i.e., disinterested – have devised for discussing the process by which cultures draw from and influence each other. Along with related concepts – for example, colonial encounter, cultural transfer, and syncretism – transculturation has been eagerly taken up by literary historians and ethnomusicologists.[53] (The term "multicultural" has more broadly political-ideological implications. For example, multicultural curricula in America's public schools encourage exposure to and tolerance of ethnic difference.)

Recent writers addressing the influence of non-Western music on Western art music employ other terms that overlap significantly with my use of "transcultural": "transethnic," "intercultural," "hybrid."[54] I follow Shay Loya in adopting "transcultural" because of his persuasive application of it to the Liszt Hungarian(-"Gypsy") Rhapsodies.[55] Loya finds the concept attractive because it permits a range of possible relationships – including some degree of reciprocity – between the two cultures in question. He helpfully contrasts it to other terms often used by scholars for Western compositions based on non-Western or internal-minority (e.g., Romani/"Gypsy") musical traditions, terms such as "Orientalism" and "cultural appropriation." Such terms seem to Loya fraught with predetermined aesthetic and political value judgments. At the very least, they have acquired so many meanings by now that they are easily misunderstood.[56]

Certain commentators have described this or that instance of Transcultural Composing as if it amounted to a complete and faithful rendition, only minimally adapted, of a distant musical tradition. In 1947, Wilfrid Mellers dismissed certain pieces from the height of Debussy's

230   Musical Exoticism: Images and Reflections

Figure 9.5 The performances at the Javanese *kampong* at the 1889 Paris World's Fair were witnessed with astonishment and delight by Debussy and hundreds of thousands of other visitors from across Europe and around the world. Above: four graceful *tandak* (courtly dancers, sent by the prince of Surakarta), named Seriem, Soekia, Taminah, and Wakiem. (By permission of the Société de Géographie and Bibliothèque Nationale de France.)

career – including *Pagodes* and the heavily Andalusian *Soirée dans Grenade* – as "too much like the raw material out of which art might be made, so passively sensory as to be hardly worth calling art at all."[57] In 1983, Richard Freed described *Pagodes* as "a more or less direct representation of [the gamelan's] sounds in keyboard terms."[58]

Freed's phrase "in keyboard terms" hints at a crucial feature of *Pagodes* that Mellers sought to deny: the work's artistry. Debussy, as his own writings and those of his friends attest, had listened intently to, and watched, Javanese gamelan and dance performances at the 1889 Exposition Universelle in Paris (see Figs. 9.5–9.6).[59] His enthusiasm was boundless, and he used the subtle sounds and shifting textures that he had heard in the *kampong javanais* to point up limitations in Western music. (The

Figure 9.6 Likewise photographed at the Javanese *kampong* at the 1889 Paris World's Fair, the two-dozen-strong gamelan included performers on the *kendang* (barrel drum) and *bonang* (sets of six cradled kettle or pot gongs). (By permission of the Société de Géographie and Bibliothèque Nationale de France.)

polyphony in Palestrina suddenly seemed like "child's play"; Western percussion instruments, like "the barbarous noise at a fairground circus.")[60] The piano is in some ways apt for rendering the sounds of a gamelan. A piano note, played staccato, resembles somewhat a note struck on the gamelan's tuned percussion instruments (and then, usually, damped with the player's other hand). Also, the sustaining (right) pedal on the piano permits separate pitches to blend in a way analogous to the long, slow die-off of the sound of the gamelan's gong.[61]

But to transcribe an actual gamelan performance for piano would have been impossible since this would have required suppressing or drastically altering some of the primary features of Indonesian music-making.[62] A gamelan is an ensemble, containing multiple instruments (sometimes a few, other times a dozen or more). Although all the instruments in any one gamelan are tuned to a single scale, the scale's five (or sometimes seven) notes rarely correspond to any one collection of five (or seven) notes on the piano. They may not exactly match the notes of the gamelan in a neighboring village, even one supposedly tuned to the same mode. Furthermore, the slight but significant differences between the tunings of the various instruments in a single gamelan (often not so slight in Bali) create rapid throbbing "beats." The resulting aural shimmer is much prized by local musicians and their audiences, whereas pianos are carefully tuned to minimize audible "beats" between the two or three strings that are tuned to a single note.[63] Still, critics such as Mellers and Freed are right in a way: a piece such as *Pagodes* gives the impression – to Western concertgoers – of being an intensely observed, though drastically condensed, reenactment of a performance from a highly developed foreign musical culture.[64]

François Lesure puts an even more positive, almost ethical spin on the Transcultural aspect of pieces such as *Soirée* and *Pagodes*:

[Debussy] disdained the amusing [*risible*] attempt at escape-through-sound that is called "exoticism." He was one of the first to admit [as even possible] a conversation [*communicabilité*] between musical cultures and to take an interest in what other musics could bring to the West, thanks to a broadened conception of musical time.[65]

In order to praise the Transcultural Composing that occurs in pieces such as *Pagodes*, Lesure denigrates exoticism, implying that it is hopelessly superficial if not entirely fabricated. Even if Lesure had accepted a less dismissive definition of exoticism (such as the one offered in Chapter 3), he might have still considered a piece such as *Pagodes* to be something very different: an instance of musician-to-musician sharing that somehow transcends or happily ignores all other (non-aural) aspects of the two cultures.

There are two obvious yet little-noted reasons why Transcultural pieces of the early twentieth century may strike observers (such as Mellers, Freed, and Lesure) as not obviously exotic(izing) in the manner of so many works from the previous century and more:

(1) Whereas the exotic regions and peoples that had been regularly alluded to by Mozart, Liszt, Verdi, or Bizet were few (e.g., Spaniards, "Gypsies," Eastern Europeans, and the Middle East), more and more cultures were now becoming known in the West. Information about the musics of these widespread cultures was potentially accessible to the determined seeker. Unfortunately, it tended to be hidden away in scholarly monographs or (for field recordings) in museums and archives. A composer could not count on audience members' knowing much about any relatively unfamiliar musical tradition (that is, other than

Hungarian-Gypsy, Spanish, and so on) that his or her piece was seeking to echo.

(2) On a non-musical level, most world cultures were quite unfamiliar, being geographically more distant from Europe, as in the case of East Asia, and/or inaccessible, as in the case of most of sub-Saharan Africa. They were also harder to understand, because they were culturally more different from the West than groups within Europe (e.g., the Roma) or the Middle East. (For example, Hindu and Shintoist religious texts do not overlap with the Bible as the Koran does.)

We may note a curious flip-flop in many critical and scholarly writings about works that engage in Transcultural Composing. The presence of exotic style elements has long been the primary factor by which writers determine whether a work between the years 1750 and 1900 engaged in the process of exoticizing a foreign culture. The absence of exotic (or foreign-sounding) style – a feature of almost all exoticizing works from before the *alla turca* craze – has tended to rule out a work from being considered as engaging in exoticism.[66] But suddenly, at the point when numerous composers do become deeply responsive to foreign styles – namely in the first half of the twentieth century – critics (and, subsequently, historians) tend to view this responsiveness as a marker of honest intercultural exchange, presumably free from the taint of Western dominance or condescension. A writer, such as Lesure (cited above), may consider a nineteenth-century work exotic(izing) – and, often, may object to it – because it contains just a hint of foreign (or imagined-as-foreign) music. Yet the same writer may rule out exoticism – and breathe a sigh of relief – when a work (from the twentieth century) actually contains more extensive (and/or more accurate) foreign elements. A double standard seems at work here. What Debussy and subsequent composers do tends to be regarded as well intentioned and admirable, whereas what Liszt (in the Hungarian Rhapsodies) and Delibes (in *Lakmé*) did several generations earlier – though perhaps, in technical terms, not always so dissimilar – is rejected as artistically trivial and culturally exploitive.[67]

Pagodes: Javanese pentatonicism Trans(culturally)figured

How Transcultural Composing operates – and whether we should regard as exotic(izing) a piece that engages in Transcultural Composing – can be better understood by looking at Debussy's *Pagodes* (c. 1903).

The radical modernity of Debussy's *Pagodes* is that it uses "black-note" pentatonicism more consistently in both melody and accompaniment than did any previous piece.[68] Eventual competitors would come some years later: Casella's "Canone (sui tasti neri)," from *11 Pezzi infantili* (1921), McPhee's *Tabuh-Tabuhan* (1936), Bartók's "The Isle of Bali" (from *Mikrokosmos*, 1926–39, bk. 4), and various works of Lou Harrison.

Pagodes is built on the tonic note B, so the pentatonic scale in question is B–C♯–D♯–F♯–G♯, which I shall represent by the step-numbers 1 2 3 5 6.[69] Time and again, Debussy undermines tonal solidity by not using melodic combinations involving steps 1 or 6 (e.g., 1–2–3–5 nor 6–1–2–3), since these would have suggested, respectively, B major and G-sharp minor. More generally, Debussy emphasizes the intervals of the second and fourth in the pentatonic set, such as the two-note melodic fragments 2–3, 5–6, and 2–5 rather than thirds and fifths (which, again, more readily suggest tonal triads).[70]

Other features could likewise have come directly from Debussy's memory of performances in the various Southeast Asian pavilions of the 1889 World's Fair (or that of 1900, which he probably also attended). A number of the melodic shapes that he introduces use only four of the five notes in the black-note pentatonic mode, as was (and remains) typical of many gamelan performances. Several passages involve an intricate layering of melodic phrases and figurations in different rhythmic values, and most of these are wholly or primarily pentatonic. For example, the main tune of m. 3, largely using sixteenth notes, returns in m. 7 with a smooth eighth-note countermelody beneath and then in m. 11 returns again, transformed rhythmically into triplets, over a stolid countermelody mostly in quarter notes. One astonishing passage, mm. 23–26, lays three different half-measure phrases over each other (two at a time) in several different ways and in several different octaves. This reflects a standard feature of gamelan music: instruments that are of different sizes – and hence are pitched in different octaves (as a Westerner would say) – play the same core melody in similar or different ways, often at the same time (resulting in what scholars call heterophony). Often Debussy reflects the standard gamelan habit of making musical lines more active the higher they are in pitch. Consistent with this principle, the numerous long-held left-hand notes (or, in mm. 19–26, low octaves) recall the recurring resonant notes struck on the gamelan's gong, though without the structural function of the gong tone (to signal the end of an extended rhythmic cycle).[71]

The prevailing pentatonicism in *Pagodes* is fascinatingly enriched by the selective admixture of non-pentatonic language. The passage leading up to

Example 9.3 Debussy, *Pagodes*, mm. 33–36.

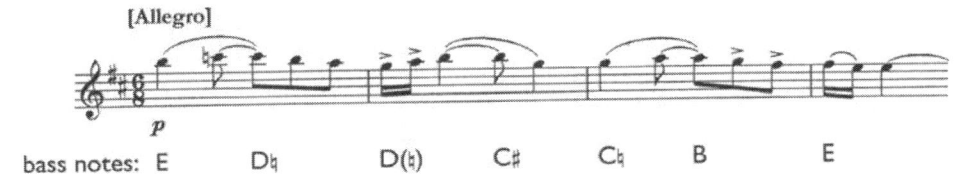

Example 9.4 Chausson, Poème for violin and orchestra, Op. 25, at rehearsal no. 18. The bass line is as shown in letters below the solo violin part.

the eighth-note countermelody mentioned above adds a "foreign" A♮. The resulting V^7 chord leads the ear to hear the passage at m. 7 in a kind of E major. By a curious inversion of cultural perspective, the A♮ – though "foreign" to the pentatonic context thus far established – renders the passage more tonally functional, hence less foreign-sounding (in the more usual sense).

The complexity of Debussy's artistry quickly reasserts itself, for that countermelody built upon the home note of E is itself intruded upon by a foreign note, A♯, making us feel that the melody is either in an unusual mode (Lydian, i.e., with raised fourth degree) or is actually not "in E" at all but in a variety of G-sharp minor. To further complicate matters, m. 7 is still underpinned by the open fifth (B–F♯) that we have been hearing since the beginning of the piece.[72]

At m. 33 a contrasting middle section begins with a yearning melody built mainly of notes from the whole-tone scale (Ex. 9.3). Debussy alerts the ear by beginning the melody with a note (E♯) that is foreign to the B-pentatonic mode that we have been hearing until now. In contour and rhythm, however, the melody bears a surprising resemblance to the recurring melody in a major French work from just a few years earlier, the *Poème* for violin and orchestra of Ernest Chausson (Ex. 9.4). Debussy gives the Chausson-like melody his own stamp, through the whole-tone inflection, and simultaneously creates a quietly jarring minor second (against the E♯) by introducing an F♯ in the accompaniment.[73]

Elsewhere in the piece, Debussy creates forward thrust by a series of tones that are gonglike but placed on different scalar pitches – something a traditional gamelan would not normally do – as in the five-step descent (from G♯ to the "tonic" B, almost entirely stepwise) at mm. 19–26 and a longer, octave-spanning descent (B to B) at mm. 80–98. We may be reminded of a similar descending bass line in a piece such as Mendelssohn's *Song without Words*, Op. 62, no. 1, in G major (nicknamed "May Breezes"), mm. 21–23.

The Chausson and Mendelssohn resemblances show Debussy putting to use some very traditional Western compositional techniques in order to enrich, and shape, his portrait-in-tones of a musical tradition vastly different from the one in which he grew up. In the process, Debussy makes the Javanese elements in *Pagodes* his own, adapts them to Western compositional norms, and turns them into a lasting musical work.

Are Submerged and Transcultural approaches exotic?

Is *Pagodes* exotic, in the sense of being a portrayal of Indonesia generally, not just an imitation of various procedures typical of the gamelan? A glance at some representative composers who, in the generations after Debussy, explored gamelan and other potentially exotic styles – including jazz – may help make clearer the ramifications of this question.

During the first half of the twentieth century, Submerged and Transcultural techniques became increasingly widespread options within the world of serious composition. The octatonic scale and its related harmonic options appeared in utterly non-exotic – and non-Russian-sounding – pieces by Stravinsky during his "neoclassical" period (e.g., Octet, 1923; "Dumbarton Oaks" Concerto, 1938), pieces whose primary points of reference include the concerti grossi of Bach and the symphonies of Haydn and Mozart.[74] Still, the latent exotic aura around a number of musical procedures, including octatonic and other once-unusual scales, could be quickly rekindled by a composer through a variety of framing devices, such as a title or program note. Several important pieces by Edgard Varèse were strongly influenced by Stravinsky's early ballets and announce their primitivist-exoticist intent in titles of varying geographical specificity: *Amériques* (Americas, presumably evoking the New World before European contact, but also new artistic vistas), *Ecuatorial* (lands at the Equator), and *Déserts* (desert regions, but where?). *Amériques* includes two recurring near-quotations from Stravinsky's *Le sacre du printemps*. Even a piece of Varèse's whose title suggests no place at all, *Arcana* (i.e., "secret knowledge"), begins with a plain echo of one of the ultimate primitivist-exoticist moments in early twentieth-century music, the opening of the "Infernal Dance of [the Sorcerer] Kashchei" from Stravinsky's aforementioned *Firebird*.

André Jolivet, who had studied with Varèse, likewise linked primitivism with an exoticism that extends beyond one specific geographical location. His works suggest ritualistic activities of ancient or non-Western peoples by a combination of rich harmonic vocabulary, repetitive rhythms, and incantatory melodies – and often by their titles as well.[75] The first work that brought him international attention, through performances at various new-music festivals, was *Mana*, a set of six pieces for piano (1935 – published 1946, with a preface by Olivier Messiaen). "Mana" is a Melanesian concept for the spiritual force that resides in a gift or talisman that one person has given to another.[76] Jolivet applied this concept to six objects that Varèse had given him and that he kept on his piano as what he called his "companions" and "household gods" (*fétiches familiers*). Two were pieces of European folk art, three were metal sculptures by Alexander Calder (including a rather minimalist cow made from bent wire), and one was from Bali: a princess made out of straw (purchased at the mammoth Exposition Coloniale Internationale of 1931).[77] Though pitch content in the resulting six pieces is often based on the twelve-tone method, various short phrases are repeated several times in succession, with slight variations. The impression is ritualistic, gnarled, and obsessive, as if Jolivet's extensive reading about so-called primitive religion had enabled him to explore unusually dark and violent impulses in humans of nearly any culture.[78]

Other exotically inspired works of Jolivet's are more accessible to broad audiences: for example, his Concerto for Piano and Orchestra (1949–50), which was one of a number of works commissioned by the French Radio to celebrate France's overseas territories. The composer originally entitled the work *Equatoriales* (perhaps in homage to Varèse) and intended the three movements to evoke, in turn, Africa, Southeast Asia, and Polynesia. In good modernist fashion, Jolivet finally removed all of these geographical titles, though later he did explain (in a radio talk) how the concerto genre lends itself to incorporation of the call-and-response patterns that are typical of sub-Saharan music. The work received two splendid recordings and was turned into a successful (though locale-less) ballet.[79] In recent decades the concerto has gone largely unheard. Had Jolivet left the movement titles attached, and provided an explanatory preface, perhaps this vivid work – with its unusual, ear-catching modal scales – would have remained in the repertoire, rather like his remarkable *Cinq danses rituelles* (for piano or orchestra, 1939), a work whose five movements include dances of initiation, heroism, and – nodding perhaps to *Le sacre du printemps* – abduction.

Olivier Messiaen was readier than Jolivet to explain the non-Western elements that he included in his music and what they meant to him. His astonishing song cycle *Harawi: Chant d'amour et de mort* for dramatic soprano and piano (1945) incorporates musical phrases from native Peruvian songs, as well as Quecha words and phrases whose sound appealed to him, for example "kahpipas, mahpipas." Though the Peruvian tunes are largely pentatonic, Messiaen adjusts some pitches to accord with his favored modes (octatonic, plus ones that he had invented or had taken from music treatises of ancient India).[80]

One of Messiaen's best-known pieces is the ten-movement *Turangalîla Symphony* (1949). The composer made explicit to his students and in published writings the link between the work's musical features and Hindu concepts regarding the expansive and tragic potential of human love.[81] The title "Turangalîla" – an obscure Sanskrit term for a particular short rhythm – was intended to suggest a whole complex of things: "love song, hymn to joy, time, movement, rhythm, life and death."[82] Further exotic associations are stirred by the presence of a mini-orchestra of tuned percussion (plus piano) "with a sonority recalling the gamelan of Bali."[83] Another audible reference to Indonesian music comes in movement 7 ("Turangalîla II"), where a tam-tam – like the gong in a gamelan – articulates the end of each of several cycles of rhythmic exploration. India and a mood of meditative near-stillness come particularly to mind in movement 2 ("Chant d'amour I") in four passages that unfurl a "slow, tender" melody (in unison violins and violas) over a long-held chord (in the low strings and winds). The texture amounts to a Westernized equivalent of the slow opening section (*alap*) of a *rāga* performance, in which a singer, sitar player, or other soloist tests various melody notes against a buzzing drone in the tambura. Messiaen creates a particularly toothsome dissonance just before the end of the second and fourth phrases, with a melody G against an F-sharp-major chord.[84]

In the generations after Debussy, many composers of different compositional tendencies were drawn to Indonesian and other East or South Asian musical procedures. Among the most prominent were Henry Eichheim (now largely forgotten), Francis Poulenc, Harry Partch, Henry Cowell, Colin McPhee, and Lou Harrison.[85] Their Asian-influenced works – for example, the two gamelan-inspired codas in Poulenc's Concerto for Two Pianos and Orchestra (1932; end of movements 1 and 3) and the almost documentary reenactment of a gamelan performance in McPhee's

Tabuh-Tabuhan for orchestra (1936) – evince, like *Pagodes*, what is often called a "purely musical" (i.e., Transcultural) fascination with new modes and/or timbral combinations.[86] Yet any work that evoked Asian musical styles almost inevitably also signaled the region as well. The reading public during the early to mid-twentieth century had been inundated with writings about various Asian countries, and not least about Java or Bali. In 1913, Debussy had published a particularly ecstatic description that went on to be widely quoted: the "little peoples" of Indonesia have learned to make music as "simply as one learns to breathe," taught not by "arbitrary treatises" but by "the eternal rhythm of the sea, the wind in the leaves, and the thousand small sounds that they have listened to with care."[87] Many writings about music in Java and Bali (though not Debussy's) were accompanied by enchanting line-drawings or photographs.[88] Thus, when listeners encountered a gamelan-inspired work, many of them had a ready fund of associations about the alternately peaceful and intense music-making and skillfully graceful dancing on the islands of Indonesia; about the way in which (as Debussy phrased it) "each person [there], over the centuries, has brought his or her respectful contribution" to the "very old songs mingled with dances"; and about how all this creativity – continuous with the past yet ever-renewed – was seamlessly interwoven with communal and spiritual life.[89]

American experimentalist composers were particularly drawn to East Asian musics and philosophies. It is no accident that a number of them were born on America's West (Pacific) Coast or lived there for many years. Henry Cowell regularly attended performances of Chinese opera during his formative years in San Francisco. After Cowell moved to New York, he taught courses about the world's musics and, in the 1950s and early 60s, compiled influential recorded anthologies of Asian and other musical traditions (for the Folkways label). Along the way, he willingly shared with his students (these included John Cage and Lou Harrison) his enthusiasms for such non-Western techniques as the intense glissandos or "sliding tones" used by the players of the *erhu* (Chinese two-string fiddle). In compositions such as his String Quartet No. 4 ("United," 1936), Cowell sought to draw upon "those materials common to the music of the peoples of the world, [in order] to build a new music particularly related to our own century."[90] In later years, he increasingly incorporated performance features, modes, rhythms, and even melodies from specific cultures: for example, India (Symphony No. 13, "Madras," 1958), Persia (*Hommage to Iran*, 1957), and Japan (two Concertos for Koto and Orchestra, 1962 and 1965).

240   Musical Exoticism: Images and Reflections

Figure 9.7 Harry Partch's *The Delusion of the Fury* (1965–66), Act 1, scene 3: Emergence of the Spirit [i.e., the ghost of the slain man]. Baritone Glendon Hornbrook, in makeup and costume inspired by Japanese *nōh* drama, from performances at the University of California, Los Angeles, 9–12 January 1969. (Photo by Ted Tourtelot. By permission of the Harry Partch Archive.)

Harry Partch (who, as a child, had often heard his mother singing a lullaby that she had learned in China during missionary years there) plainly modeled his inventive musical and theatrical style on aspects of Asian and other non-European musical and theatrical traditions.[91] (See Fig. 9.7.) Partch invented and hand-crafted his own instruments (Fig. 9.8), often using local raw materials (e.g., California eucalyptus wood) or even local industrial ones (e.g., glass containers that were being given away by a subatomic-particle lab at University of California, Berkeley). He tuned the instruments to scales that are likewise of his own invention. (Partch made his scales ever more refined. In his mature works, they included forty-three notes to the octave.[92]) One remarkable example is his set of *Eleven Intrusions* (1949–51) for voice, altered guitar, and a diamond-shaped marimba built out of California redwood. Intrusion No. 2 is a setting in which the vocalist – Partch himself in a recording now easily available online – half-moans and half-speaks a poem about a lonely crane by Ki no Tsurayuki (*c.* 872–945, in a translation by Arthur Waley).[93]

Exoticism in a modernist age (*c.* 1890–1960)   241

Figure 9.8 Young musicians playing the instruments that Harry Partch designed and built for use in his own compositions. The photo was taken on the set of the documentary film *The Dreamer That Remains: A Portrait of Harry Partch* (1972). At left rear: the Cloud Chamber Bowls (made from Pyrex carboys that were being given away by the subatomic-particle radiation laboratory at the University of California at Berkeley). At front right: the Gourd Tree, made from East Asian temple bells (also called *dharma* bells), each bolted by Partch to a gourd tuned to the same pitch. The gourd-bells are attached to a shapely branch from a eucalyptus tree. Two other such eucalyptus branches serve as the side-posts of the Quadrangularis Reversum (directly behind the Gourd Tree): a kind of marimba with bamboo resonators. (Photo by Betty Freeman. By permission of the Harry Partch Archive.)

As David Nicholls notes, Partch (and a somewhat analogous figure in the second half of the century, La Monte Young) "transcended the usual bounds of transethnicism by creating not merely musical works possessing non-Western or multicultural characteristics, but rather whole aesthetic worlds that are inhabited by their performers."[94] And, at least in the cases of Cowell and Lou Harrison, the frank adoption of one or another non-Western manner of composing – styles that were patently not "their own" – went hand in hand with their rejection of the principles of originality and uniqueness that had marked Western composition ever since the age of Romanticism (e.g., Beethoven, Chopin).[95] This rejection of Romantic individualism, in turn, long relegated the Transcultural works of Cowell and Harrison to a marginal place in concert life and in historical accounts (which, even today, often remain steeped in Romantic ideology).

A foreign style, though, can accumulate new associations in its new (Western) context. The late Philip Brett persuasively argued that use of gamelan style became a clandestine marker of gay and bisexual identity for a number of composers, including most of those just mentioned (Poulenc, Cowell, McPhee, Harrison, and Cage) as well as a mid-twentieth-century operatic master, Benjamin Britten.[96] In certain of Britten's stage works, gamelan style plainly signals the complex situation of homosexuals or other individuals who are not accepted within mainstream society, who are perhaps even anathematized by that society.[97] In *Peter Grimes* (1945) and *Death in Venice* (1973), especially, pentatonicism and gamelan-like sonorities evoke a realm of illicit, lustrous fascination, a realm that contrasts vividly with the prevailing style in the rest of both works, which is angst-ridden, heavily chromatic, and (in *Death in Venice*) intensified by serial techniques.[98]

Britten had been introduced to gamelan music by McPhee in 1939. With Peter Pears and two other friends, he visited McPhee in Bali in early 1957, attending performances with great fascination over several weeks. The gamelan sounds in both *Grimes* and *Death* indicate a mysterious, attractive, even lethal force coming from somewhere outside of conventional European society yet, at the same time, from deep inside the troubled (European) protagonist of each opera. Annegret Fauser might describe these as instances of "the abstract rather than picturesque engagement of alterity" – or, in the terms that I have been using, an exoticism that is Submerged (though not fully Absorbed).[99]

Or is it only half-Submerged? By that, I mean that, just as Debussy's *Faune* refers obliquely but recognizably to Russia, Central Asia, and the Middle East, so Britten's gamelan-flecked operas may bring to mind images of the peaceful collaborativeness and intense creative energy for which Bali and Java and their rich musical cultures had been widely known since Debussy's day – known in large part, that is, through Debussy's remarkable *Pagodes* and (as noted earlier) his several published descriptions of the islands' music and its local meanings and context.

The problematic richness of a (seemingly non-exotic) Transcultural approach is plainer to see in many European composers' use of styles that had come recently from America. By the 1920s, ragtime, early jazz, and also the Charleston and other syncopated dances – all largely created by and associated with African-Americans – had attracted the attention of many European musicians with strong leanings toward modernism: Debussy, Satie, Ravel, Stravinsky, Milhaud, Křenek, Schulhoff. These composers were especially intrigued by the syncopation, the blue notes, the instruments (e.g., saxophone), and associated performing styles (e.g., a trombone's glissando smears and wah-wah mute). A composer might isolate a stylistic element, lending it more significance than it actually had in the American genre (e.g., the so-called "shimmy" rhythm dear to Kurt Weill and other composers in Germany who were fascinated by American music) and then force it into a fresh-sounding mixture with complex "modernistic" chords or with more varied orchestration than the original would have offered.[100] Milhaud, exceptionally, traveled to the United States – he heard jazz in Harlem – and lived in Brazil for a year. As a result, he developed what jazz authority Gunther Schuller unhesitatingly calls a "fine understanding of jazz" (and, one might add, of highly syncopated Latin American styles). This expertise is reflected in *La création du monde* (1923), with its trombone glissandos, blue-note fugue theme (closely related to the standard twelve-bar blues chord progression), and solo "breaks" for double-bass, saxophone, and clarinet.[101] Such Transcultural uses of jazz seem straightforward expressions of admiration and delight – even kinship with a parallel stream of musical creativity.

At the same time, the Transcultural aspect of jazz "influence" was often linked to exoticist and even frankly primitivist preconceptions about African-Americans, some of which may (by today's standards) seem racist and defamatory. For example, the title of Debussy's *Golliwoggs* [sic] *Cakewalk*, the final piece from *Children's Corner* (1908, for piano), refers to a comically grotesque blackface doll that was widely distributed on the European continent and also to the cakewalk, a high-stepping procession that often ended a blackface minstrel show. (Debussy's own painting of a golliwog doll appeared on the front cover.) Milhaud's *La création*, despite its close echoes of the imaginative solo work of Sidney Bechet and other African-American jazz artists, was originally composed for performance as a ballet whose scenario retold supposed creation myths of tribal Africans. The dancers (largely Swedes) were mostly not visible. Instead they wore costumes and masks by cubist artist Fernand Léger that were based freely on sub-Saharan animals (such as monkey, antelope, and peacock) and on traditional sculptures and masks from such places as Mali, Ivory Coast, and Angola. The backdrop, likewise by Léger, featured the "gods of creation": gigantic versions of yet more African sculptures.[102] This linkage of jazz music and African myth was consistent with Milhaud's own view (clearly intended as admiring) that "Black jazz ... never loses its primitive African character; the intensity and repetitiousness of the rhythms and melodies produce a tragic, desperate effect."[103] Other prominent writers of the day made the same basic point, but gave it a more negative or at least ambivalent tilt. The composer-conductor Constant Lambert pondered whether "the barbaric and vital Negro element" in jazz and American dance music and popular song was likely to be a stimulus or threat to the art of composition.[104]

Still, there are many pieces – using gamelan, jazz, and other stylistic materials – that offer little or no concrete evidence of larger cultural assumptions: pieces that follow more or less exclusively the principle of Transcultural Composing. To what degree such pieces might also convey an exoticist attitude is, as Fauser wisely concludes, "still open for debate."[105] No doubt the answer depends on such factors as whether the composer provided verbal clues (e.g., "Blues" – the title of the second movement of Ravel's 1927 Violin Sonata), how the performers respond to such clues, and how such clues and other biographical and cultural data are developed by what literary critics call a work's "interpretive community." (For a musical work, this includes arts journalists and writers of program notes.)

Overt Exoticism in concert music and opera

The remainder of the present chapter on music during the years 1890–1960 deals with exotic works of the more Overt kind. For reasons noted earlier, Overt Exoticism largely vanished (during these years) from the output of some of the composers considered the most advanced. Stravinsky used it in his early decades – the Russian ballets; the opera *Le rossignol*, set in a legendary Chinese court; some songs on texts translated from the Japanese; and several ragtime experiments – but hardly at all thereafter. It was even less of a factor for Hindemith (one exception being his short opera *Das Nuschi-Nuschi*, 1920, for Burmese marionettes), Bartók (two exceptions being the ballet *The Miraculous Mandarin*, 1926, and, mentioned earlier, "The Isle of Bali"), and Schoenberg and his followers.

Nonetheless, many other composers of works in the standard art-music genres (e.g., symphonic works, piano music, and operas) did practice Overt Exoticism actively, often in conjunction with various Submerged-Exotic and Transcultural approaches.[106] These composers tended to fall into one of three groups, which we shall discuss in turn.

Composers from a minority group or "peripheral" culture

During these seventy years or so, many composers presented themselves to the wider musical world through use of stylistic elements from their own nation or ethnic group. They were often inspired to do so by such frankly nationalist efforts as the Norwegian-style pieces of Edvard Grieg (e.g., *Slåtter*, Op. 72, 1903), the intensely Andalusian piano pieces of Albéniz, or the many Russian works based directly or indirectly on local folk dances and songs or on Eastern Orthodox church music. The "nationalist" works of these younger composers were often received in countries outside their own as new varieties of exoticism. Or even within their own country. Constant Lambert, the composer-conductor cited earlier about the influence of jazz, frankly derided the use of English folk songs by English composers (e.g., Ralph Vaughan Williams) as "exotic and 'arty' ... The English folk song, except to a few crusted old farmhands in those rare districts which have escaped mechanization, is nothing more than a very pretty period piece."[107]

Two Jewish composers display this urge for a "national" self-expression that easily spilled over into auto-exoticization. Joseph Achron (1886–1943) was a prominent member of the Saint Petersburg Society for Jewish Folk Music before moving to the United States to write film scores and teach. His *Hebrew Melody*, Op. 33 (1911), still remains in the international violin repertoire after nearly a hundred years, no doubt reinforcing stereotypical images of Jews as habitually inclined toward soulful melancholy. Ernest Bloch used a wider range of techniques than this in Jewish and biblical works written at various times during his long career. *Baal Shem* (1923) relies primarily on melodic and rhythmic features of Eastern European Jewish music that may well have been more exotic to Bloch – who was a French-speaking native of Switzerland – than to Achron. Bloch's masterpiece *Schelomo* (for cello and orchestra, 1916), named after the Bible's King Solomon, likewise features soaring melodies in free rhythm in Eastern European manner (as at m. 72, taken up by the orchestra at m. 117). *Schelomo* also includes passages that specifically resemble cantorial chanting (with rapid wordless "declamation" on a single repeated pitch, as in the oboe at m. 142) and two chromatically keening figures of types long associated with an exotic East (one more dancelike, at m. 6, the other more declamatory, at m. 16). Bloch had originally generated some of this material for his projected opera *Jézabel*, to indicate the sensuous, corrupt pagan world against which the righteous prophet Elijah took action. In *Schelomo*, the *Jézabel* materials are shared freely by the cello solo, representing King Solomon, and by the orchestra, representing (presumably) his court and his magnificent achievements.[108] As Klára Móricz has argued, Bloch seems to have felt free to move the pagan-associated materials from *Jézabel* to a work about King Solomon because he had internalized many of the anti-Semitic stereotypes of the day, according to which Jews in Europe, despite their attempts at assimilating, were still at heart, in his own word, "barbaric."[109] One of Bloch's most prominent proponents, the music critic

Guido Gatti, frankly presented the composer as a descendant, not of the patient northern tribes of Israel, but of Judah: "Asiatic shepherds ... joyous voluptuaries of life and adorers of a warrior-god, the enemy and destroyer of all rival peoples."[110] Bloch had been inspired to write *Schelomo* by a wax statuette of Solomon by Catherine Barjansky. This statuette made the biblical king look like a dignified but world-weary sultan. Bloch himself described the sculpture as being "decorated with gold, rings, and Oriental sumptuousness."[111]

Sometimes a composer seems to have altered his exotic practices to suit the audience he was addressing. Early in his career, the Brazilian composer Heitor Villa-Lobos wrote pieces (*Amazonas* and *Uirapurú*, both 1916) that emphasized his country's vast rain forests, its native tribes (such as the Tupinambá, whose cannibalism was much reported by early travelers from Europe), and its various pre-European legends – elements that were (as with Gypsy music for Hungarians) both exotic to city-dwelling Brazilians and sources of national pride for them.[112] One Brazilian reviewer specifically welcomed, as components in a distinctively Brazilian cultural product, the "exotic effects" in a concert of Villa-Lobos's early works.[113] By contrast, Villa-Lobos encountered a more cosmopolitan musical world during the several years that he spent in Paris in the 1920s. There he seems to have discovered that pieces relating to the urban and modern sides of Brazil could have great exotic appeal for international audiences – instead of, or in addition to, evocations of the rain forest and its "Indians." One notable result was the series of over a dozen works entitled *Chôros*, which were inspired by the guitar-based street bands of Rio de Janeiro, in which Villa-Lobos had participated during his early years. The first of the *Chôros* (1920, for guitar solo) is a kind of samba; others use Brazilian-inflected versions of familiar European dances: waltz, mazurka, gavotte. Even the rather Chopinesque *Chôros* No. 5 of 1926 (subtitled "Alma brasileira" – Brazilian Soul) is attractively seasoned at times with samba-like rhythms, as is *Chôros* No. 10 of 1925 (for chorus and orchestra), even though the latter work opens with music plainly inspired by Stravinsky's *Le sacre du printemps* and with the calls of tropical forest birds. The choral forces in the up-tempo conclusion evoke images of tribal rituals through repeated syncopated phrases on vocables (nonsense phrases) such as "Jé-ki-ri-tú-mú-rútú, Jé-ki-ri-tú, Je-ki, ah!"[114] Modern life in Brazil is likewise reflected, but without admixture of primitivism, in Villa-Lobos's somewhat later "O trenzinho do Caipira" ("The Little Train of the Caipira," 1933). This tuneful crowd-pleaser wittily combines the chug-chug rhythms of a little mountainside steam engine with syncopated dance rhythms of Brazil's street bands and night clubs. Though published as the final movement of *Bachianas brasileiras* No. 2, Villa-Lobos's "Little Train" quickly took on a life of its own in the international orchestral (and pops-concert) repertoire. By contrast, certain works of Villa-Lobos that were less explicitly tied to Brazil's cities and jungles (e.g., most of the seventeen string quartets, however attractive and expertly written) have gone relatively unnoticed by the larger musical world.

Prolific Massachusetts native Alan Hovhaness (1911–2000) offers a distinctive case. Typical of the North America melting pot, his father – who taught chemistry at Tufts University – was a Turkish-born Armenian, and his mother's family was of English and Scottish origin. He devoted much of his career to exploring what he called his "Armenian and Oriental heritage."[115] (He rarely emphasized his British roots in this manner.) Among the early influences that he liked to mention were recordings of Armenian songs (in artful arrangements by Komitas Vartabed) and a 1936 Boston performance by dancers and musicians from India under the direction of Uday Shankar.[116] Over the years, Hovhaness explored the musical and spiritual traditions of other non-Western societies, notably Japanese *gagaku*. His still-astonishing Concerto for Piano and Strings (1945) is subtitled "Lousadzak." Hovhaness explained that the title is a "made-up Armenian word meaning, roughly, 'dawn of light.'" The work consists almost entirely of unison melodies and drones in various typically Middle Eastern modes, with piano figurations reminiscent of such instruments of the Middle East and Caucasus as the *tar* (lute) and *qanun* (zither).[117]

Hovhaness was a prime example of an auto-exoticizer. He also sometimes – paradoxically or not – presented himself as transcending all cultural boundaries. He insisted that his much-performed Symphony No. 2, "Mysterious Mountain" (1955), refers to mountains in general, as "symbolic meeting places between the mundane and spiritual world."[118] Maybe so, but the middle section of the first movement features long, flexible solo passages for oboe, English horn, and clarinet, using typically Middle Eastern modes and figurations. And the last movement states, again and again, a scale redolent of Indian music (a "gapped" major scale with no sixth degree and two altered notes: 1–#2–3–#4–5–7). Hovhaness's other big success, *And God Created Great Whales* ... (1970), might be called the ultimate exotic *and* anti-exotic piece. The work incorporates recorded songs of whales from around the world. It thereby has the potential for turning listeners from any and all countries into one big Us – thereby dissolving our tightly held ethnic identities – as we marvel (aurally) at magnificent, powerful creatures who are truly Other to us all.

Non-modernists

Several of the composers in the previous category overlap at least a bit with another category: composers who did not adopt (primarily, or at all) the aesthetics and techniques that were then considered "progressive" or avant-garde. Certainly Hovhaness, though he occasionally dabbled in aleatoric techniques, was ridiculed by academics, critics, and fellow composers for his accessible and tuneful (or, in their view, simplistic and predictable) style.

Two of the century's leading non-modernists were Italian: Giacomo Puccini and Ottorino Respighi. Puccini's two Asian operas were examined in Chapter 8. His *La fanciulla del West*, 1910 – set among California miners in 1849 – is arguably another exotic work – and an effective one, at least for operagoers outside the United States. (American operagoers have tended to find its portrayal of "us" bizarre.) Respighi's taste for explicit representation of extramusical reality in general, and for an easy tunefulness, is well known to concertgoers from the Roman trilogy (including *I pini di Roma* – The Pines of Rome, 1924). What could be more natural for him, then, than to offer notable examples of Overt Exoticism? His *Impressioni brasiliane* (Brazilian Impressions, 1928) begins, a bit in the spirit of Villa-Lobos's early "Amazon" pieces, by evoking the "Notte tropicale" ("Tropical Night"). Its third and last movement ("Canzone e danza" – "Song and Dance") is more analogous to Paris-era Villa-Lobos. The middle movement, "Butantan," is probably unique among exotic portrayals in music. It describes an utterly modern tourist site: the serpentarium (for developing anti-venom serums) at the Instituto Butantan, a world-renowned medical facility established between 1901 and 1914. To symbolize the potentially fatal bite of the jungle snakes, Respighi brings in the famous "Dies irae" chant from the Catholic Mass for the Dead. That a Gregorian chant can be used for exotic purposes reminds us of the value of the "All the Music in Full Context" Paradigm, for there is nothing Brazilian, jungle-like, nor even snakelike about the "Dies irae" melody. Respighi also composed a more conventionally exotic piece about the ancient Middle East: the ballet *Belkis, regina di Saba* (Belkis, Queen of Sheba – 1930), complete with throngs of dark-skinned dancing slaves. Respighi's typically fresh and varied orchestral colors freshen the otherwise too-familiar Arabian style-signals.

"Non-modernist" is too strong a term for Aaron Copland, but, during the Depression and World War II, America's once-controversial upstart did retrench substantially from some of the asperity – and, as he was beginning to see it, artistic elitism – of his works from the 1920s. Copland's fascination with the landscapes and legends of the prairies and the "Wild West" helped ground his attempt at building a more populist style, and the results surely registered as exotic to big-city audiences in America and elsewhere. (Other "way out West" works include one of the most widely performed pieces of twentieth-century orchestral music, the "On the Trail" movement from the *Grand Canyon Suite* by Ferde Grofé, 1931.[119]) Copland's ballet *Rodeo* (with choreography by Agnes de Mille, 1942) is a lightweight, tuneful entertainment (though exquisitely crafted), full of joke-y cowboy-meets-cowgirl byplay. *Billy the Kid* (1938, choreography by Eugene Loring) emphasizes a darker side of America's fabled West, in part through ironic and distorted uses of several cowboy songs (such as "Git Along Little Dogies"). The "Gun Battle" scene, in which the outlaw Billy is captured by a posse, features convulsive effects for snare drum, timpani, bass drum, and piano, plus rapid trumpet notes on a single pitch. The ballet opens and closes with a procession of frontier folk (seen in silhouette), solemnly plodding across the prairie to tonally and emotionally ambiguous harmonies built of stacked open fifths. Many mid-century urban Americans must have found this image storybook-like and very distant, yet resonant of the analogous westward trek that their own parents or grandparents had made across the Atlantic Ocean only decades earlier.[120]

Consistent with his growing desire to write music that would be found accessible by general audiences, Copland also developed an attraction to the vitality of Latin America. He cultivated friendships with composers in Mexico and South America and visited various Latin American countries several times during his life. In 1936, he composed the rhythmically virtuosic *El salón México* for orchestra, which conveyed – inevitably from a "gringo" point of view, as he confessed – his experiences at a modest but high-spirited Mexico City nightclub. It received its first performance by the Orquesta Sinfónica de México, conducted by Carlos Chávez. Copland feared that the players and audiences might resent the piece. To his delight, they welcomed it. For international audiences, *El salón México* has become the best-known aural portrait of Mexico, and the composer's words about the shy, barefoot rural patrons on one of the nightclub's three floors (which were differentiated by socio-economic class) are trotted out again and again in program notes. Copland biographer Howard Pollack also notes a quasi-political subtext to the work: the earthy authenticity of Mexico stands as "a hopeful alternative" to the social isolation in the cities of North America.[121] In 1942, Copland followed this piece with a rhythmically captivating, slinky piece for two pianos (orchestrated 1947), entitled *Danzón cubano*. Danzón is the traditional dance music of Cuba and the source for later social dances such as the *cha-cha-chá* and mambo. Another aural "postcard," Copland's piece surely reminded many mid-century (i.e., pre-Castro) concertgoers of magazine and newsreel images of Havana's raucous night clubs. But a contrasting, blues-like episode suggests that the act of conveying Latin music into the concert hall has somehow caused the composer to reflect on a very different "roots music" that he had grown up with in New York City.[122]

The Soviet era through the 1950s

The Soviet Union comprised a wide variety of ethnic groups, whose cultures the government preferred to foster (and thereby to control). A steady stream of compositions invoked regions that were, to many of the performers and listeners, distant and unfamiliar. Some Soviet composers found inspiration in the music of more than one region. Prokofiev returned to Russia in 1934, after sixteen years in the United States and Western Europe. He based his String Quartet No. 2 (1941) on folk tunes that he had encountered in the Kabardino-Balkar Autonomous SSR. (The government had moved him there for safety after the German invasion began.)

When possible, the Soviet cultural authorities preferred to nurture composers who themselves were members, by birth, of the ethnic group or republic in question.[123] The procedure, though sometimes a little forced, could produce artistically satisfying results. Aram Khachaturian (1903–78), an Armenian, had paid little attention to local musics during his childhood years in Tbilisi, Georgia. After completing his training in Moscow, he studied various Central Asian traditions in order to produce the works that were expected of him. Among his best-known pieces are two that are full of folk flavor: the Violin Concerto and the ballet *Gayaneh*. The latter includes a *lezghinka* (a dance from the Caucasus mountains) and the "Sabre Dance"; the latter became a major radio hit for the Boston Pops and, jazzed-up, for Woody Herman's band.[124] Like Liszt's pieces inspired by Hungarian-Gypsy music and like Bloch's *Schelomo*, Khachaturian's folk-derived works are at once nationalist and exotic. And they were nationalist on two levels: the pieces extolled the individual regions but thereby also promoted Soviet nationalism as a whole.

The fact that folk-derived works such as Khachaturian's were produced in accord with Stalinist cultural policy did not necessarily deprive them of sincerity or vitality. True, Western musicians complained at the time that the standardized compositional procedures taught in Soviet conservatories led to a certain sameness no matter which republic provided the themes.[125] But Khachaturian's forthright musical personality has kept a number of his exotic works ever attractive, not least as music for TV (the BBC series *The*

Onedin Line, which portrays a nineteenth-century Liverpool family engaged in international shipping), film (*The Hudsucker Proxy*, about the business world in 1950s Manhattan), and countless circus acts (in the case of "Sabre Dance"). How much the music's original exotic associations linger once the music has been placed in a non-exotic context will, as always, vary with the listener.

Overt Exoticism in popular genres

During this same period – the early to mid-twentieth century – Overt Exoticism was even more widespread in popular culture than in new works for concert hall and opera house. Many musicians – composers, songwriters, popular-music singers, and jazz musicians – who were concerned with maintaining broad audience appeal used a limited but familiar collection of exotic styles, and in a wide range of ways. Presumably they were less worried than modernist composers about being accused of lacking originality.

The present section explores, rather quickly, a number of instances, mostly grouped by genre. Some are still familiar to many people today. Others are largely forgotten. I am avoiding music that was made within the tradition of any particular ethnic or other group or marketed primarily to members of that same group: for example, Neapolitan songs (whether recorded by Italians or Italian-Americans), klezmer recordings (by Jewish musicians in Eastern Europe and North America), and what the record industry called "race records" (by African-American performers in a wide range of popular genres).

The portrayals to be explored range in tone from the sympathetic to the crass. As cultural artifacts, they prove historically revealing, whatever one may feel about the messages that they convey.

Light orchestral music and jazz

Throughout the early and mid-twentieth century, popular venues of various types gave people the simulated experience of taking a trip to distant, scarcely known places. At the Paris World's Fair of 1900, the "Mareorama" (illusionistic sea voyage) was enhanced by recorded performances from the Arab world and Turkey.[126] Light-orchestra and band concerts provided similar occasions for exotic travel, though replacing the quasi-realism of the fairground with an imaginative quasi-artistic rendering. In 1920 Albert Ketèlbey produced the most famous such piece, *In a*

Persian Market. This "intermezzo scene" may today be thought tacky, demeaning, or gratifyingly tuneful. Early in the piece, a black-note pentatonic plea for alms is sung by members of the orchestra and harmonized entirely with open fifths and octaves over a steady drumbeat. Today, the passage may sound more like stereotypical Native American music than anything Middle Eastern, but this oddity seems not to have impeded the work's decades-long success.

Jazz and popular instrumental music of the early and mid-twentieth century likewise conveyed the listener, at times, to exotic locales. George Gershwin was plainly fascinated by a wide range of "national" styles (Spanish, Irish, etc.). Perhaps the most striking of these ethnic-exotic styles was a brand of pseudo-Chinese pentatonic writing that relied upon parallel fourths or parallel inverted triads, often combined with, or in alternation with, stiff rapid repeated notes.[127] Gershwin applied this style not only to several compositions in a specifically East Asian style – such as Oscar Gardner's "Chinese Blues" (a ragtime-flavored song that had been recorded instrumentally by the Sousa Band in 1916) – but also to theater songs that have no particular reference to the faraway, such as his own "So Am I" and "Idle Dreams."[128] A lengthy, playful passage is devoted to this Chinese style in Gershwin's *Variations on "I Got Rhythm"* for piano and orchestra (1934).[129] It is hard not to suspect that the highly mechanical nature of the musical devices in question reflected some stereotype of East Asians as emotionally reserved or – the frequent denigrating adjective at the time – "inscrutable." But there is no denying the attractiveness of this unexpected spice in the *Variations*, a work that, though written for the concert hall, also got played on Rudy Vallee's radio show, with Gershwin as soloist.

During these same decades, jazz itself repeatedly discovered and rediscovered a favored Other of its own: Latin-American music. Writer and record producer Ned Sublette has recently dubbed Latin music "the Other Great Tradition" that, along with the interactions of African and European music, has shaped Western popular music over the course of the twentieth century.[130] Jazz pioneer Jelly Roll Morton would have agreed. He drew attention decades earlier to the importance of the "Spanish tinge" for the development of ragtime and early jazz.[131] Perhaps this attraction reflected a tendency of jazz musicians and listeners during those years to identify imaginatively with places (Puerto Rico, Cuba, Brazil) where racial mixing had occurred more openly than in most of North America.[132]

The Latin influence on jazz was sometimes undisguisedly exoticizing. Kitschy instances include the costumed "tropical" numbers by various American "big bands" of the 1940s. Sometimes the effect was self-exoticizing, as when the same kinds of "tropical" displays were adopted by well-known

Latin jazz and dance bands, such as those led by Pérez Prado, Xavier Cugat (in now-forgotten films), Tito Puente, or (on TV, to audiences of billions, if one counts decades of re-runs) Desi Arnaz.

By the 1950s, the fascination with travel imagery – apparent in the Ketèlbey orchestral pieces – was burgeoning in American popular culture, perhaps in part because so many American former GIs had recently been stationed abroad – in Germany, Italy, North Africa, Japan, and the Pacific Islands – but also because the economic surge of the post-War years allowed increased civilian tourism. Ever-improving film technology – and multi-channel sound in the movies – made visions of desert and rain forest more convincing and the musical styles that were considered appropriate to them more vivid. A related phenomenon, for one's LP turntable at home, was the wave of exotic pop-orchestral numbers by conductor-arrangers such as Martin Denny (including pieces in Middle Eastern, African safari, Hawaiian/Tiki, and other standard styles) and also the occasional exotic vocal number, for example by the singer of supposed "Incan" music Yma Sumac.[133] Producer Enoch Light's much-admired LP series *Persuasive Percussion* included a jazzed-up version of Ketèlbey's *In a Persian Market*, performed by an otherwise now-forgotten group of jazz musicians known as Terry Snyder's All-Stars. The number opens with peppery bongo drums calling and responding between the left and right speakers – a tribute to the wonders of audio technology; to the disposable income that, in the post-war years, produced the legendary "bachelor pad"; and (through the ringing bongos and the pervasive un-Ketèlebeyan syncopation) to a very different exotic region than Persia, namely (again) the Caribbean.

Various more sophisticated and complex attempts at integrating Latin music and jazz – and even, occasionally, styles from elsewhere – flourished throughout the middle decades of the twentieth century. "Caravan" (1937), a song by Puerto Rican-born jazz trombonist Juan Tizol, was made famous by Duke Ellington's band. The name relates primarily to the piece's main section, which contains typical features of Middle Eastern arabesque: a sinuously winding minor-mode melody over a single unchanging (in this case: diminished) chord and ending with a six-note chromatic descent. The accompaniment is syncopated in the Caribbean manner, creating a most satisfying blend. In the late 1940s, this merging of jazz and Caribbean (but without the Middle Eastern touches) became – through the work of Dizzy Gillespie and Cuban-born arranger Mario Bauzá – a recognized stream of jazz known as "Afro-Cuban."[134] Such mergings were hardly unproblematic, though. In 1947, Gillespie brought the notable African-Cuban conga drummer Chano Pozo into his band. The bassist Al McKibbon later recalled having objected at first to Pozo's playing: "Here is this guy beating this god damn drum with his hands ... Dizzy could see him in the band, I couldn't." Gillespie's arranger, Walter Fuller, tightened many of Pozo's pieces: "[They] drive you nuts because ... it just keeps going and repeats itself ad infinitum."[135]

Popular song: America and France

Most of all, it was popular song that, during the early and mid-twentieth century, served as a vehicle of vicarious travel to Other places. In England, many songs about people from Ireland and Scotland kept alive a number of ethnic-exotic stereotypes about the country's nearest neighbors. The English also continued their obsession with India, sub-Saharan Africa, Australia, and other regions largely under their control. A famous instance of this is the song "On the Road to Mandalay," about a British seaman yearning to return to the excitements of his overseas post. (The words are by Rudyard Kipling, 1892; the best-known setting is by the American composer Oley Speaks, 1907.[136])

With its waves of immigration from distant parts of the globe, America had plenty of material for wide-ranging ethnic and "racial" exoticism right at home. From the 1890s to the 1950s, American popular song and musical theatre continued and extended the nineteenth-century tradition of offering portrayals of different ethnic groups.[137] A twelve-CD anthology of all surviving recordings of songs from the New York stage during the years 1890–1920 reminds us just how stereotypical the offerings could be. Songs from operettas and vaudeville acts alike reinscribed, and sometimes tweaked at the same time, a whole raft of simplistic ethnic images. The message is at times neatly encapsulated in the title: "Just Like a Gypsy," "Why Worry? I'm an Indian," and "I Wonder Why She Kept On Saying Si Si Si Senor."[138] Performers often added to the tone of racialist caricature through, for example, mincing movements, falsetto singing, mispronunciations, parallel fourths or fifths in a second voice, and portamento or other vocal ornaments that were marked as Other.[139]

Relevant to the whole topic of exoticism yet fraught in particular ways are portrayals of Native Americans and of African-Americans – two groups that, though internal to American society, were nonetheless perceived as variously Other by the rest of the American population. "Wild West" shows that were filled with chanting and tom-tom beating toured the country. Indian characters were often written into stage shows or described in popular songs (as in the case, just mentioned, of "Why Worry?").[140]

Minstrel shows continued, most often with white performers in blackface and exaggerated lip-makeup (and sometimes cross-dressed as overweight women). But African-American performers, too, created minstrel troupes, and even used the same exaggerated style of face paint. James A. Bland (1854–1911), an African-American born in Flushing, New York, toured widely as "The World's Greatest Minstrel Man." He spent close to twenty years performing in London before returning to the United States, where he died penniless. Bland's "Carry Me Back to Old Virginny," "In the Evening by the Moonlight," and "Oh Dem Golden Slippers" quickly became known throughout the English-speaking world. At the same time, they reinforced stereotypes about the African-Americans of the American South as carefree, spontaneously sociable, and almost childishly devout. The vaudeville and Broadway stage saw the blackface minstrel tradition continue, with Bert Williams (an African-American, born in Antigua, who eventually performed his numbers in the Ziegfeld Follies) and Al Jolson (son of Jewish immigrants). Both made commercial recordings and filmed performances that at once testify to these performers' communicative power and reenact many stereotypes that today would generally be found offensive (e.g., Williams's recording of "My Little Zulu Babe," with George Walker, and Jolson's best-selling disc of Gershwin's "Swanee").

By the beginning of the twentieth century, African-American songwriters working for the mainstream theater (not minstrel shows) gave new twists to the representation of race by widening the frame of musical and textual references. Bob Cole and J. Rosamond Johnson – who created both "white" and "black" musical shows – wrote "Under the Bamboo Tree" and performed it in their own vaudeville act in 1902. Within months, it was interpolated into the musical comedy *Sally in Our Alley*, which then reached a hundred performances. The performer was the "coon shouter" (i.e., non-African-American singer of "black" songs) Marie Cahill. Decades later, *Under the Bamboo Tree* was adapted as a song-and-dance duet for Judy Garland and young Margaret O'Brien in the 1944 MGM film *Meet Me in St. Louis*.[141]

The ungrammatical words of the refrain seem hopelessly disparaging of the love-stricken Zulu:

If you lak-a-me, lak I lak-a-you
And we lak-a-both the same,
I lak-a-say, this very day,
I lak-a change your name;
'Cause I love-a-you and love-a-you true

And if you-a love-a me,
One live as two, two live as one,
Under the bamboo tree.[142]

But the music has been understandably cherished through the years, its underlying habanera-like rhythm making it one of the better examples of the "Hispanic" variety of ragtime-era syncopation. (A close relative, in style and achievement, is *Solace: A Mexican Serenade*, 1909, by another African-American composer, ragtime pioneer Scott Joplin.) Perhaps the rhythm simply signaled Elsewhere to folks in New York City and America's other urban centers, as if the Caribbean region and sub-Saharan Africa were hardly worth distinguishing.[143]

That the song may not be as demeaning of Africa as it first appears is strongly suggested by the last strophe, which proposes that the great cities of North America have a kinship with the sub-Saharan plains:

Although the scene was miles away,
Right here at home I dare to say,
You'll hear some Zulu ev'ry day,
Gush out this soft refrain ...[144]

The Cole and Johnson shows – and coon shouters – were favorites of Boston's fabulously wealthy Isabella Stewart Gardner.[145] One wonders whether white people like her, hearing about a besotted Zulu "right here at home," imagined that the singer must surely be referring to an urban African-American. But, on a 1917 recording, the wink in Marie Cahill's voice seems to suggest that the man in the song (if one looks past his dark skin and pidgin English) could just as easily be a white guy, poor or rich, trying to persuade his beloved to join her life with his.[146]

The Cole and Johnson song comes from the early years of what is sometimes called the Great Age of American Song, which more or less coincides with the chronological limits of the present chapter, namely 1890–1960. A song from the middle of the Great Age – "Weekend of a Private Secretary" (1938) – is just as multilayered as "Bamboo Tree" about the relationship between Us and Them. To witty words by Johnny Mercer, and to the orchestra's rhumba beat and maracas, a young woman recalls the quick tourist cruise she took to Cuba "to look at the natives, to study their customs, their picturesque ways." (Copland's *Danzón cubano* would come four years later, and the Havana night-club scene in *Guys and Dolls* another six years after that.) Our working-gal heroine ends up meeting a natty local man who (quite satisfyingly, it seems) "taught me the customs." Once back at the office, she announces that, when she marries, her husband will absolutely be Cuban.[147]

Exoticism took on a special glow, vitality, and occasional nastiness during the heyday of the French *chanson* (which likewise largely coincided with the 1890–1960 era). Many French citizens – soldiers, business people, educators, administrators, and vacationers – traveled to their nation's overseas territories or lived there for an extended period.[148] These territories included several distinct countries that the French lumped together as "Indochine," plus French Equatorial Africa, i.e., vast areas from Mali southward to Senegal. Much the way that Cole Porter's "Begin the Beguine" (1935) evoked the "tropical splendor" of Caribbean islands that were becoming a major vacation getaway, the French entertainment industry reflected and reinforced the nation's often blinkered fascination with territories that were increasingly seen as making up "greater France."

Tone and subject matter could vary more widely than in the American equivalents, from a straightforward Western-style march song celebrating the hundredth anniversary (1930) of France's victory over Algeria's Abd-el-Kader to a pseudo-sultry ballad (of 1932) filled with escapist blather nearly identical to that in mid-nineteenth-century opera librettos ("Nuits coloniales, nuits d'étrange volupté … , nuits de rêve, nuits d'amour!" – Colonial nights, nights of strange sensuality, dreams, and love!).[149] Some of these *chansons* may be painful to listen to today, especially one (recorded by Edith Piaf) about a sub-Saharan African man who accidentally falls asleep on a ship that heads off for Borneo; spying a palm tree across the ocean waves and thinking it must be his native land, he jumps over the railing and drowns.[150]

Perhaps because of French Indochina, East and Southeast Asian numbers were particularly plentiful in France. "Tchin Tchin Lou, fille d'Asie" (Chin-Chin-Lu, Daughter of Asia) featured stiff-sounding even-note passages on the xylophone. "Ki San Fou" (1931), a "Chinese foxtrot," has words about a silly, devil-may-care fellow. His name, appropriately, plays on the French phrase *qui s'en fout* (someone who doesn't give a damn). The members of Ray Ventura's band adorned themselves with pigtails and drooping mustaches (Fig. 9.9) for their much-loved comic Chinese numbers. One such song, "Les trois mandarins" (1935), about a baffled Frenchman in China, is filled with rhyming pseudo-Chinese words and accompanied by a tinkling celesta (played, presumably, by the band's pianist, the future film composer Paul Misraki).[151] Paris in the 1920s also gave a hearty welcome to nightclub performances by African-American singers and dancers, who were repeatedly described in newspaper accounts, and caricatured on posters, in various highly stereotypical ways (Fig. 9.10).[152]

258   Musical Exoticism: Images and Reflections

Figure 9.9 French bandleader Ray Ventura, with his "Collégiens" (college boys), perhaps in the 1930s. Over their usual outfits, the band members have donned "Chinese" costumes. From left, the singer-percussionist and future character-actor Coco Aslan (Grégoire Arslanian, an Armenian born in Turkey) attacks with a dagger; Ventura defends the guitarist-songwriter Loulou Gasté, who is dressed as a woman (with wig and high-eyebrowed mask); and unidentified band members gesture in unison. (Photo: private collection, Archives Loulou Gasté.)

Figure 9.10 Caricature of performers in the Black Birds revue at Paris's Moulin Rouge nightclub. (Newspaper cartoon from *Le quotidien*, 16 June 1929.)

One of the best-known French songs of all time is Vincent Scotto's "Petite Tonkinoise" (Girl from Tonkin, c. 1906). The refrain playfully turns the Asian place-names into quasi-nonsense: "C'est une Anna-, c'est une Anna-, une Annamite," "ma Tonkiki-, ma Tonkiki-, ma Tonkinoise." The third strophe – as found in the published sheet music and as sung in an early recording by Karl Ditan (late 1906) – becomes leeringly salacious:

Très gentille,	She's the very
C'est la fille	Nice daughter
D'un mandarin très fameux.	Of a very famous Mandarin.
C'est pour ça qu'sur sa poitrine	That's why she has on her chest
Elle a deux p'tit's mandarines.	Two little mandarins [small oranges].
Peu gourmande,	Doesn't eat much;
Ell' ne d'mande,	All she asks,
Quand nous mangeons tous les deux,	When the two of us are eating,
Qu'un' banan', c'est peu coûteux.	Is a banana. It doesn't cost much,
Moi j'y en donne autant qu'ell' veut.	So I give her as much as she wants.

In the fourth and final strophe, our French soldier – much like Puccini's Pinkerton, just around the same time – has to leave his "p'tit' reine" (little queen) for home. He closes with an altered refrain, no longer praising the charm and birdlike voice of his "p'tit' bourgeoise" (a phrase casually suggesting her housekeeping skills) but instead assuring her that he will always recall "le souvenir de nos amours" (the memory of our loving time together).[153] The music, marked "Tempo di Polka moderato," adds bouncy good humor – with no hint of Asian color – and Ditan slows just the slightest bit to give a hint (or pretense) of regret in this final, altered refrain.

But performance can make a big difference. Today, "Petite Tonkinoise" is most familiar from a 1930 recording by the African-American singer-dancer Josephine Baker. The orchestra of the Casino de Paris adds two extended passages reminiscent of a Chinese music box. (The listener suddenly encounters flute, pizzicato strings, and rapid, briefly bitonal scales on the piano.) Baker performs only the (relatively innocuous) second strophe and the refrain – no mention of bananas. She also changes the words from third to first person, so that the story is told to us by "la Tonkinoise" herself, not by her flighty French admirer.[154] Baker's innocent delivery – quite a contrast from Ditan's – must have made the song safer for wide cultural diffusion. The sense of wholesome fun is also consistent with Baker's growing determination to move away from the jungle dances and banana skirts of her earlier triumphs in Paris and to "refine" her image in song (as cultural sociologist Bennetta Jules-Rosette has expressed it).[155] If Josephine Baker could become – for a few minutes in the spotlight – Vietnamese, she could become anything: a Tunisian, or a firefly with electric lights twinkling in her wings. Or even – in a number in which Baker comments with teasing ambivalence on her own exoticness in the eyes of the Parisians – a white woman.[156] The song is "Si j'étais blanche!" (If I Were White). Baker performed it in 1932, in blond wig and with lightened skin makeup, and she also recorded it. The words, playing upon (and simultaneously reinforcing?) the age-old equation of darkness and amorous passion, reassure her lover that, even if she were white on the outside, "the flame of my heart" would "keep its color" for him.[157]

Operetta and musical

During the early and mid-twentieth century, large numbers of popular songs in Western countries were originally heard in operettas, stage musicals, and sound films. It is easy to forget this because we so often hear the songs sung on their own, or even performed instrumentally. One of the best-loved songs of the master of Viennese operetta Franz Lehár is "Dein ist mein ganzes Herz" (You Are My Heart's Delight). It was written for the great tenor Richard Tauber to sing in the leading role of Prince Sou-Chong in *Das Land des Lächelns* (The Land of Smiles, 1929). This operetta became Lehár's second most widely performed, after *Die lustige Witwe* (The Merry Widow). The show's title, and a song in Act 1, declare (demeaningly, we may tend to feel today) that the Chinese like to smile no matter what happens. Prince Sou-Chong's name is, presumably, a shallow cultural reference to the much-prized Lapsang Souchong variety of tea. But lighthearted condescension turns into derision as the plot unfurls. The operetta begins with Sou-Chong, a Chinese diplomat in Vienna, falling in love with Lisa, the pampered daughter of an Austrian count. Sou-Chong learns that he has been named to a high office in China and returns home with Lisa in tow. On native ground, Sou-Chong reverts to harshly authoritarian behavior. Lisa is horrified, and Sou-Chong, stoically, permits her to take the boat back to Europe. Comic opera or cautionary tale? Still, there are those wonderful songs. The orchestra's several passages of Chinoiserie, delightful in their own quirky way, must have given the composer, and players, a welcome escape from operetta routine. And, as one recent scholar has noted, the work's atmosphere of resignation and failed dreams was probably well suited to the mood of audiences in 1930 – a time of economic collapse and social crisis – when *Das Land des Lächelns* (in various translations) "spread across the stages of Europe in record time."[158]

Many American operettas, too, were set in some intriguing location that is far away – and sometimes also long ago. Sigmund Romberg's *The New Moon* (1929) unfurls its marvelous songs ("Softly, as in a Morning Sunrise"; "Stout-Hearted Men"; "Lover, Come Back to Me") in a plot that begins in French-owned New Orleans (in 1792) and ends on an island off the coast of Cuba. One of the most lasting successes among American operettas is Romberg's *The Desert Song* (1926), based freely on recent struggles in North Africa between French and native troops. (This may recall the trend in nineteenth-century opera to avoid portraying the colonial exploits of one's own country.[159]) An extended number containing three songs and explicitly entitled "Eastern and Western Love" contrasts the two regions' ostensibly irreconcilable attitudes toward monogamy (and, more generally, marital fidelity). But, whereas, in Rameau's *Les Indes galantes* (see Chapter 5), it was the exotic male (the Native American *sauvage*) who was unshakably faithful, that function, in the *Desert Song* number, is assigned to a Westerner. The first two of the songs are sung by Moroccan tribesmen (one being the tribe's leader). They convey the assumption that the local males are self-centered, inconstant lovers, but feel divinely fated to be so. Love, the two Moroccans sing, is "lightly granted by Allah" for male enjoyment and then "flies away." The third song in the sequence is the show's biggest hit, "One Alone." In it, the Westerner (Pierre Birabeau, momentarily belying his disguise as the Arab bandit The Red Shadow) praises the exclusive, lasting relationship that a (Western) man with a truly "worshipping soul" establishes with a woman equally capable of constancy.

This shift over two centuries' time is notable. In Enlightenment-era works (such as Rameau's *Les Indes galantes*), authors and composers could use the non-Western world as a means of critiquing and improving the West. By the 1920s, Western empires controlled vast stretches of Africa and Asia.[160] The tone, in works such as *The Desert Song*, becomes, correspondingly, smug. The non-Western world is inferior, clearly in need of correction and control (though it also is naughtily exciting). *The Desert Song* does display an initial empathy with the natives in their fight against the French colonizers. But, by the end of the show, even this flicker of empathy is sacrificed to a plot twist, so that Pierre can reveal himself as French, marry Margot, and cap the work by singing with her a reprise of his anthem of Western-style devotion, "One Alone."

Porgy and Bess (1935) can be described (though it rarely is) as an exotic work.[161] The coastal South Carolina fishing community that it describes was (somewhat) distant from the places in which the composer and his intended audience lived – and perhaps as different from their experience as were the Egyptian pyramids and "Gypsy" hideouts of previous operas and operettas. Gershwin's opera presents its African-American characters (i.e., almost the entire cast) as a series of exotic stereotypes: childlike and trusting (Porgy), naively religious (the chorus), weak-willed and sexually promiscuous (Bess), hypersexed and violent (Crown), charming and conniving (Sporting Life), and so on. The opera's singing cast is set off as dark-skinned by the brief but potent presence of two white detectives (in spoken roles). In this regard, *Porgy* echoes (unconsciously?) a number of important and widely known exotic operas structured around the distinction between white policemen (or military men) and female racial Others – operas such as *Carmen*, *Lakmé*, and *Madama Butterfly* (Chapters 7 and 8). *Porgy* also – again like some of those works – manages to convey a sense of the humanity of those characters in spite of the stereotypes.

Broadway musicals of the mid-twentieth century inherited the exotic trend, with all its possibilities – and also with all its ambivalences and possible complexities, which one may tend to forget when listening to this or that song on its own. Rodgers and Hammerstein's *The King and I* (1951) has at times a relatively straightforward, self-satisfied obsession with a polygamous Elsewhere. The show's King of Siam sings a number in which (much like the two Moroccans in *The Desert Song*) he insists on the right of a man to "fly from blossom to blossom." The substance of his words, and perhaps even more, his comic, cavalier tone, denounce him and his whole society as morally primitive, if charming.

Greater complexity is evident in other scenes.[162] In particular, the character Tuptim (who was sent to the king as a gift from the king of Burma) is parallel in certain ways to the captured slave Liù in Puccini's *Turandot* (1926). We saw in Chapter 8 that Puccini gave Liù's aria "Signore, ascolta!" a pentatonic melody line but did not restrict the harmony to the notes of the black-note pentatonic set. Richard Rodgers did accept this limitation in much of Tuptim's song "My Lord and Master," which is about the demeaning attention she receives from the King of Siam. The pentatonicism in this song is presented – and then abandoned – to good dramatic purpose. The opening music is intentionally meek, or mock-meek, as Tuptim describes how she presents herself – modest, obedient, perhaps lowering her eyes – when standing in the dominating masculine gaze of the autocratic ruler. At the point where her melodic line modulates to the subdominant (at "What does he *mean*?"), she carries her passive pentatonic persona with her to the new pitch center. (Scale-degree 8 – the "tonic" pitch B – in the original pentatonic mode now becomes scale degree 5 in the mode built on E.) All of this melodic pentatonicism is reinforced by harmonies built from the pentatonic set: harmonies that, rather than moving dynamically, statically hover.

The song's climax, breaking free of pentatonicism, boldly claims for Tuptim the right to sing the leading tone ($\hat{7}$ in the B-major scale, a high A♯) – a crucial element in Western musical style but "lacking" in music of East Asia – as she declares her true love ("He doesn't know I love an*other* man!"). Here Tuptim attains something like full humanity, as if, through her victimization by an Oriental despot, she has become analogous to a Western prisoner with a will worth respecting (e.g., Konstanze trapped by the Pasha, in Mozart's *Entführung*).

Film music

During its first half-century or so, film thrived on all sorts of exotic settings, but those settings were reinforced by music that most often bore little resemblance to actual musical practices of the region, as in the numerous imitations of Native American music for cowboy-and-Indian adventures.[163] Before the days of sound film, movies were accompanied by a pianist, organist, or even, in certain big-city "movie palaces," a full orchestra. Some studios sent out sheets of musical cues, but often the keyboard player or conductor/arranger had to turn to such anthologies as *Motion Picture Moods* (1924, edited by the respected New York City movie-theater conductor Erno Rapée). The published anthologies were divided into numerous practical categories to enable a performer to locate quickly a passage appropriate to a scene that was about to occur (or had – a bit awkwardly – just begun). The national and ethnic categories in the anthologies are inevitably simplistic. For example, the "Oriental" section in Rapée's *Motion Picture Moods* tosses vast territories – there is no separate one for India or East Asia – into a single, mostly pseudo-Arabian stew. (The five pieces include ones by Otto Langey and T. Tertius Noble bearing such titles as "In Sight of the Oasis" and featuring the familiar swirling melodies full of augmented seconds.[164]) Rapée was clearly aware of the mutability of musical association, since he included a folk-like dance from Bizet's music for Daudet's play *L'Arlésienne*, set in southern France, as one of those five options for underscoring an "Oriental" scene.[165] A few years later, a two-volume German *Handbuch* of music for silent films took to an even further extreme this principle of reassigning a piece according to what the compilers felt it might suit in silent films of the day, rather than what the composer originally intended it to portray. The two extensive subcategories of "exotic dance" ("lively" – see Fig. 9.11 – and "calm") include some pieces that

IN | Volk - Gesellschaft

Exotischer Tanz (bewegt).

2976 Massenet 21, Herodiade Ballett Nr. 3
Allegro moderato.

2977 Massenet 21, Herodiade Ballett, Finale
Allegro. Più mosso.

2978 Massenet 37, Thérèse (Tavan) S. 1
Moderato.

2979 Massenet 39, Vierge Nr. 2
Allegretto moderato quasi andno.

2980 Mascagni 5, Iris (Tavan) S. 8
Allegro moderato.

2981 Puccini 3, Mädch. a. d. gold. West. (Tavan) S. 3
Allo. Mn. mss. Robusto sost. Più vivo.
Gleiches Thema s. Puccini 2 (Gauwin) S.2. Allo. vivo.
Wild-tänzerisch. Apachentanz.

2982 Puccini 3, Mädch. a. d. gold. West. (Tavan) S. 16
Allegretto mosso.
Clarinetto solo.
dasselbe 2, (Gauwin) S. 7
M. M. = 132
Freudig-erregtes exotisches Tanzlied.

2983 Puccini 8, Tabarro (Tavan) S. 6
Allegro.
Eben Priestertanz.

2984 Puccini 8, Tabarro (Tavan) S. 10
(And.) Allegretto mosso.

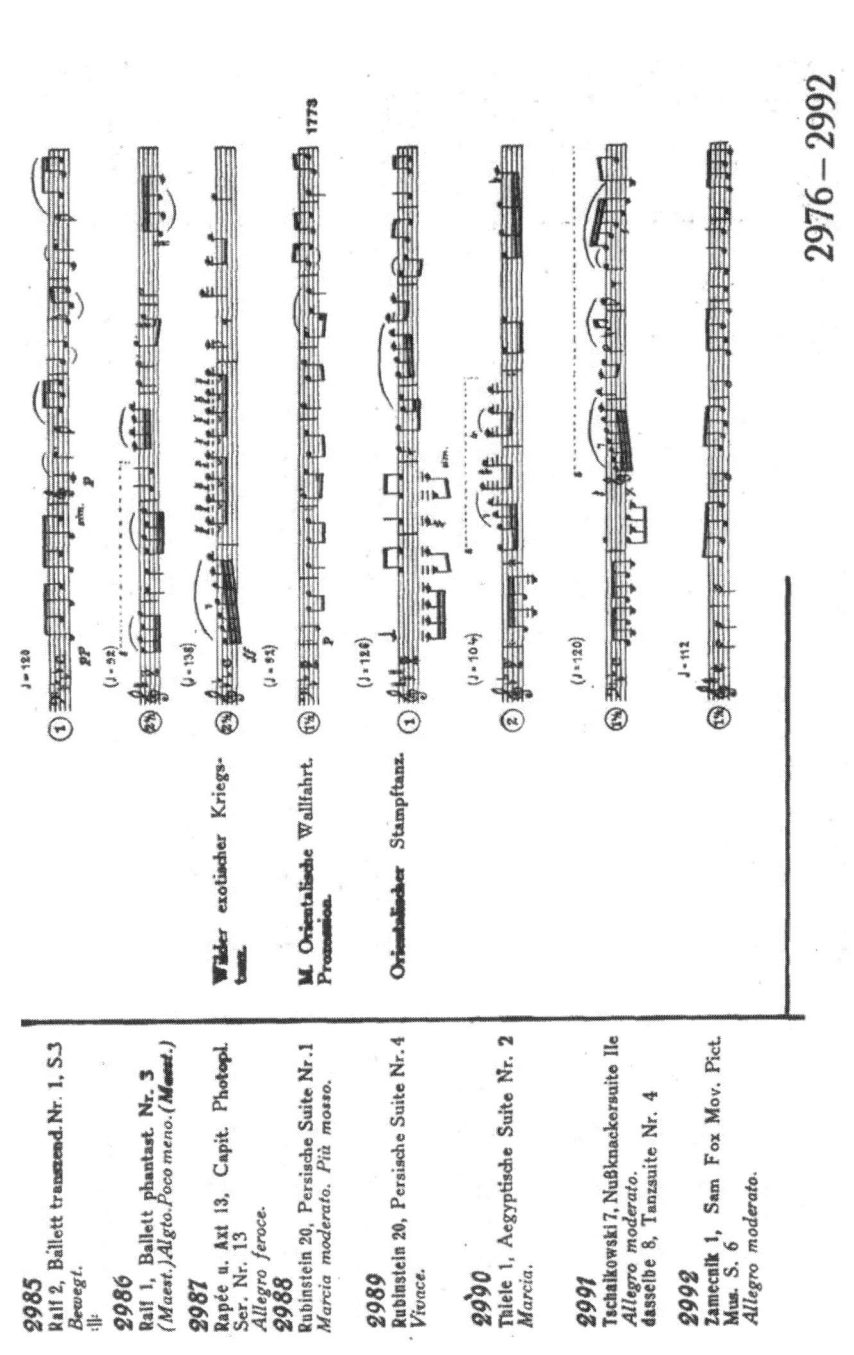

Figure 9.11 A page from the two-volume Erdmann-Becce *Allgemeines Handbuch der Film-Musik* (General Handbook of Film Music), 1927. The large heading "IN" is an abbreviation for "Inzidenz," the broad category in the *Handbuch* for scenes set in particular locations or situations. The subheading for this page reads "[Ethnic] People – Society: Exotic Dance (Lively)." The seventeen musical examples are drawn from exotic works (Rubinstein's *Persian Suite*) and also from non-exotic ones (Puccini's *Il tabarro*, set in modern-day Paris). The *Handbuch* suggests that specific musical works would be useful to accompany, respectively, a "wild Apache dance," "dance of [exotic or ancient] priests," "Oriental [i.e., Middle Eastern?] pilgrimage," and "Oriental stamping dance." The number from Tchaikovsky's *Nutcracker Suite* is, oddly, deprived of its authentic title (Chinese Dance), perhaps simply for reasons of space.

derived from works that were not about distant, less-developed societies at all: for example, two bits from Puccini's *Il tabarro* (an opera set in modern-day Paris).[166] Still, the bulk of the exotic dances in the *Handbuch* are more straightforward cases, such as dances from Delibes's *Lakmé* and from various exotic operas of Massenet.

Massenet was also on the minds of the makers of the film *Citizen Kane* when they decided to create a scene with an Eastern princess, the latter to be played by the character Susan Kane, a talentless singer who has cajoled her husband into promoting her opera career. The staging suggests extravagance and indolence – traits long associated with the ruling families of the Middle East or Central Asia – but also loneliness. A woman sits on cushions and furs, perhaps abandoned or at least waiting, and certainly wailing. All we know is that her name (because it is the opera's title on the theater marquee) is Salammbo. She launches a luscious waltz motive that is expanded ever more yearningly by composer Bernard Herrmann at each of its occurrences.[167]

Exactly where this operatic *Salammbo* takes place is not specified by sets and costumes. The princess we see and (painfully) hear could easily be located on, say, the windswept steppes of Central Asia. Even the one most plainly "exotic" passage in the scene – an interlude for high winds in unison (between the recitative and aria proper), over slowly sliding chords and a drone on the dominant – could signal any number of "Oriental" locations, from North Africa (Flaubert's novella *Salammbô* is set in ancient Carthage) to India and beyond. The passage is a fascinating facsimile of, perhaps, a snake charmer's narrow-range piping. It threatens to repeat itself endlessly, until it metamorphoses into a slower descending lament on the solo oboe – an even more standard marker of "Eastern" regions (except East Asia). The strength of Herrmann's music makes this hodgepodge-Oriental princess come alive for us even though we cannot help noticing that the high tessitura of the vocal line is bringing the singer (Susan) to the edge of despair.

In exploring the possibilities of sound film, Herrmann had good company and not-so-good. For the still-admired John Ford film *The Hurricane* (1937, starring Dorothy Lamour as a native woman), Alfred Newman provided an Oscar-winning score that vividly portrays the (fictional) South Pacific island of Manakoora and its oppressive French-colonial rulers. Other, more predictable, adventure films and "serials" set in the Amazon rain forest, the Sahara, or Malaysia have scores that are more formulaic and of interest now mainly to cultists.[168]

During World War II, numerous films portrayed the Japanese government, and even individual Japanese citizens, as authoritarian and barbaric – "subhuman," as author and film critic James Agee complained at the time – in part through use of highly stereotypical music.[169] After the war, some of the same composers who had contributed to wartime propaganda films put their efforts into lush romantic movies that sought to rehumanize the presentation of the Japanese. *Sayonara* (1957, with music by Franz Waxman) is typical of such films, in which, as W. Anthony Sheppard notes, "Japanese music [or Hollywood's adapted version thereof] served ... as a bridge to cultural understanding between American (male) and Japanese (female) lovers."[170]

All the while, exoticism continued to appear steadily in more lighthearted motion-picture entertainment. *Around the World in Eighty Days* (1956) used wide-screen techniques, much Hollywood glamour, and the musical craft of composer-arranger Victor Young and performers from different world cultures (including flamenco dancer José Greco) to make vivid a vast range of settings, not least a scene of suttee *interruptus* in India (with Shirley MacLaine as the sparkling-eyed Princess Aouda). The joking that lightens many scenes in *Around the World* had been established sixteen years earlier, in the first of Bob Hope and Bing Crosby's famous series of seven film musicals *The Road to [Exotic Place X]*. The *Road* pictures touched down in enticing and sometimes thrillingly dangerous locales, from Singapore (1940, i.e., before America's entry into World War II), Zanzibar (1941), and Morocco (1942), to Rio de Janeiro (1947) and, finally, Bali (1952) and Hong Kong (1962) – by way of Utopia (1946). The latter's title is a nice reminder of the larky unreality of the *Road* pictures.[171] The advertising tagline for *The Road to Morocco* playfully misspelled what was clearly thought a colorful foreign word: "You'll shriek at these shieks!" – those sheikhs being Hope and Crosby, two Americans trying to pass as Arabs in order to spirit Princess Shalimar (Dorothy Lamour again) out of the campsite of desert prince Mullay Kasim (Anthony Quinn). The *New York Times* reported that *The Road to Morocco* was "a lampoon of all pictures having to do with exotic romance, played by a couple of wise guys who can make a gag do everything but lay an egg." The *Road* films include musical numbers of various kinds: "African Etude" (in which Bing adds a descant – using travel-brochure lyrics – to the native-style singing of some Africans), the Brazilian "Batuque nio morro," and at least one love song that quickly became a great hit: "Moonlight Becomes You." Music helped make these road trips entertaining and (for Paramount Pictures) profitable, if also, as some reviewers complained, barely coherent.[172]

Coherent exotic works did exist in the more "popular" (or vernacular) genres of the early and mid-twentieth century, as we have noted: "The Road to Mandalay," "Under the Bamboo Tree," *Das Land des Lächelns*, "Petite Tonkinoise," *The King and I*. Such works could channel the fascination with the exotic in rich and fresh ways, producing, in the process, masterpieces of widely accessible art that could retain their cultural validity across many decades. We end this chapter by observing, in some detail, how exoticism – as a principle and as a centuries-old set of musicotheatrical traditions and practices – functions in a particularly sturdy example of mid-twentieth-century musical theatre: *West Side Story*.

West Side Story and exotic Otherness

Leonard Bernstein is not a composer whom one readily associates with "the exotic." Yet, in his writings and public presentations, Bernstein loved to observe how previous composers had found stimulus in folk and non-Western styles.[173] As a conductor, Bernstein was unsurpassed when performing music of lively ethnic or "national" profile, such as the Bacchanale from *Samson et Dalila* or syncopated Spanish or Latin American works. Bernstein had a special relationship with Copland's *El salón Mexico*: conducted it frequently, transcribed it for piano solo, and featured it on several of his television shows.

Bernstein knew the operatic repertoire well, and rose to international fame in part by conducting a run of La Scala performances with Maria Callas in the early 1950s. His own stage works contain some well-informed commentary on the habits of exotic portrayal in opera and operetta. *Wonderful Town* (1953) ends its first act with a stage-filling conga number that twits the facile habit of operatic and other theatre composers to resort to ethnic dance in order to disguise a weak spot in the plot. In *Candide* (1956), the Old Lady announces herself in one of the all-time-great "I Am" songs of Broadway: "I Am Easily Assimilated."[174] The wildly polyglot lyrics are by Bernstein and include humorously fractured Spanish lines for the back-up chorus of men to sing during the tango refrain.

Of all Bernstein's works, it is *West Side Story* that manifests tensions of race/ethnicity and concepts of exoticness (Self and Other) most extensively.[175] In this frank reworking of Shakespeare's *Romeo and Juliet*, the struggle between the two noble families of Verona is transformed into tension between Puerto Rican immigrants and what Bernstein called "self-styled 'Americans'."[176]

West Side Story is flooded with ethnic style-markers. Latin-American dance was not just a convenient symbol of Puerto Ricans but also perfect for setting Bernstein's creativity in motion.[177] Cool jazz served as an analogous marker of the white gang, which is described in the stage directions as comprising, ethnically, "an anthology of what is called 'American'": for example, Poles, Irish, Italians, and Germans. These style-markers come more or less from the "popular" realm and, when they have been discussed at all, tend to be set in opposition to the show's more "grandly operatic" elements.[178] But opera and its kissing cousin, ballet, had long thrived on stylistic tension between high and low, and between a work's (or genre's) prevailing stylistic norms and the exotic borrowings that are set in relief against those norms (see Chapters 6–8). The use of Hispanic dance rhythms within this work thus places the work firmly in the tradition of operas and operettas set in some distant and different-feeling locale. To be sure, Bernstein's work does not portray some travel-brochure location but the drugstores, modest dress-shops, and vacant schoolyards of Manhattan's lower-income neighborhoods. Nonetheless, the very act of turning Shakespeare's warring families "alike in privilege and station" (Act 1, scene 1) into two ethnic groups of distinctly unequal social position ends up making the work resemble, in important ways, the exotic operas and operettas explored earlier in this chapter and in Chapters 6, 7, and 8.

The more exotic group – the Them – is plainly the Puerto Ricans. Dark-complexioned and brightly clothed, they speak in accented dialect, are quick to dance, to taunt, to insult, and (as we see in the danced and mimed Prologue) to slash with the switchblade. The Puerto Ricans are slightly lower on the social ladder than their pale-skinned antagonists but (the spoken dialogue indicates) are encroaching, block by block and job by job. In Act 1 we get to the doorstep of (or, rather, the fire-escape just outside of) Maria's family's apartment, and hear her father calling sharply to her – in Spanish – but never encounter Tony's mother, who is presumably considered less fascinating to an audience (because she is less "colorful"). In Act 2, we even enter Maria's bedroom, with its "small shrine to the Virgin," and see Maria and her "girls" dancing away, but we still never get near Tony's home. At most, we see him at work at the drugstore.

All of this derived, directly or indirectly, from the single most crucial decision of the show's devisers, namely to turn Shakespeare's Capulets, rather than his Montagus, into Puerto Rican immigrants. This basic decision allowed the Broadway show to establish an equivalence between three crucial concepts: femininity (as represented by Maria); ethnic Otherness; and the protectiveness of interior spaces. (It is in Maria's room and bed that Tony – fleeing from the police – takes refuge in Act 2.)

Turning to specific musical numbers, we may notice that the Mambo in the gym resembles in dramatic function many opera ballets in the standard

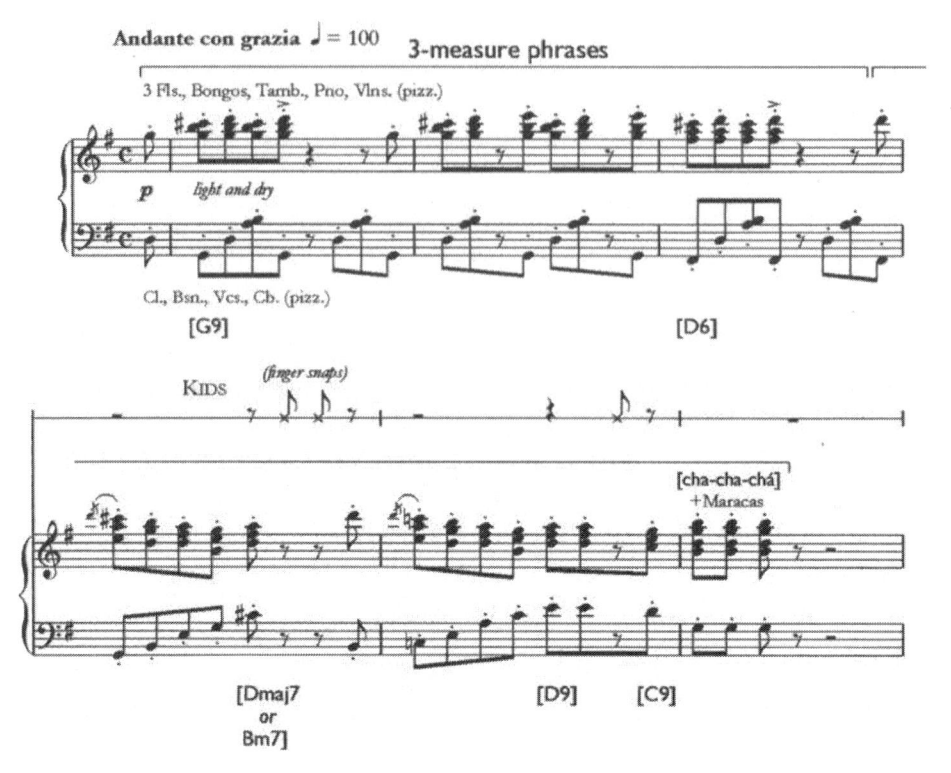

Example 9.5 Bernstein, *West Side Story*: Maria and Tony's *cha-cha-chá* (mm. 5–10), from the Act 1 "Dance at the Gym." © Copyright 1956, 1957, 1958, 1959 by Amberson Holdings, Inc. and Stephen Sondheim. Copyright renewed. Leonard Bernstein Music Publishing Company, LLC, publisher Boosey & Hawkes, Inc., sole agent. International copyright secure. Reprinted by permission.

repertoire that are filled with exotic color, such as the orgiastic Bacchanale (of the Philistines) in Saint-Saëns's *Samson et Dalila*. There is one big difference: the Mambo is danced by both ethnic groups. The delight in Latin music and Latin dance extrapolates onto all the Jets and Jet Girls the electric pull that Tony feels for Maria when – in the middle of this very dance – he spies her "across a crowded room" (as another Broadway show about love across cultural boundaries, *South Pacific*, had expressed it eight years earlier). Tony dances with Maria to a dreamlike *cha-cha-chá* with floating, three-measure phrases. (I use the dance's standard Spanish name, which is here musically more accurate, as indicated in the last measure of Ex. 9.5.) Characteristically unpredictable Caribbean cross-accents (created by rests) shift the metric placement of a given pitch in the accompaniment from a strong beat to a weak one or vice versa (first three measures of Ex. 9.5). The harmonic language, though, is spiced with elements of

Stravinskyan modernism: white-note diatonicism (e.g., the opening chord: G major plus an A) and a toying ambiguity about whether the fourth degree (C) is sharp or natural.

In the course of the whole scene at the gym, the two ethnic groups (one "exotic" group and one "mainstream" group) are portrayed by the choreographer (Jerome Robbins, both on Broadway and in the movie version) as contending with each other through music and dance and as getting their libido and aggressiveness kicked to higher and higher levels (culminating in the two gangs' challenging each other to a rumble). Still, it was very perceptive on the part of the show's creators to make that challenge-dance ensemble a mambo – Bernardo and Anita strut their stuff with special flair (Fig. 9.12) – and to have it follow upon two relatively "square" (mainstream-sounding) dance numbers.[179] White America may resent the intrusion of darker-skinned populations into its protected domain, but, on the cultural level, it absorbs elements of the Outsider, quickly domesticates and masters them. Perhaps less obviously, we in the audience are drawn into caring about these characters on stage, as we find ourselves enjoying the jolts and syncopations of Bernstein's vital and convincingly Latin music.

Certain other numbers in *West Side Story* maintain more strictly the traditional operatic alignment of exotic music with the exotic group in question and, especially, that group's women. The "America" ensemble – in *huapango* rhythm – and "I Feel Pretty" – a flamenco-flavored quick waltz, sung while Maria dresses – allows us to enjoy the spectacle of the exotic women (the Shark Girls) enjoying each other's company. Parallels in opera include the Gypsy women's dance in *Carmen* (beginning of Act 2), the Dance of the Priestesses in *Samson et Dalila*, the scene in Verdi's *Aida* in which the handmaidens sing to Amneris and dress her (Act 2, scene 1), and several moments apiece in Massenet's *Hérodiade* and *Thaïs*.[180] Such exotic numbers had also trickled down from grand and comic nineteenth-century opera into operetta and musical comedy, so Bernstein and his collaborators may have absorbed the tradition partly through operas in the standard repertoire and partly through operetta-influenced Broadway works such as *The Desert Song* (did the impetuous Riff get his name partly from the Riffs of that show?) or Rodgers and Hammerstein's *Oklahoma!* (a work that, for big-city folk, held its own exotic charms).

In addition, the ethnic tilt that the show's creative team gave to *West Side Story*, by focusing on tension between Puerto Ricans and "whites," enriches the basic plot of Shakespeare's *Romeo and Juliet* with echoes from the archetypal plot of *Madama Butterfly* and many exotic operas and operettas (see Chapter 8). As in those works, the protagonist in *West Side Story* – the

Figure 9.12 Anita and Bernardo show the native-born New Yorkers how to do the mambo with passion and style. Photo from the original Broadway production, with Chita Rivera and Ken LeRoy. (Photo, presumably 1957, by permission of the Museum of the City of New York.)

courageous yet sensitive questing Self – is set in relief early on (so as to engage our sympathy) and is a white, Western male. He is named Tony, or rather, as he tells Maria and us, Anton. He is nominally a Polish-American, but actually less an ethnic type than a blend of light-opera tenor-hero and tough kid trying to abandon his former rough life. He is also something of a dreamer, as we sense from the articulate ways in which he phrases his yearnings to Riff and from the song he sings (once he is finally left alone), "Something's Coming."

True to the archetypal exotic-opera plot, this hero intrudes, at some peril, into a forbidden, darker-skinned region, which is represented by the tender and beautiful Maria, the exotic Other, the Desired One. Tony even expresses an unconscious desire to blend with, or perhaps to absorb, her ethnic warmth by singing a song ("Maria") that is basically an elaborated repeat, with a new, samba-like accompanimental rhythm, of their *cha-cha-chá* at the gym. Verdi's *Aida* offers a direct parallel to Tony's "Maria" in Radames's "Celeste Aida," for the latter likewise contains some exotic (here "Ethiopian") music, complete with a chromatically winding solo oboe (which will also, at several later points in the opera, be associated with Radames's dark-skinned beloved and her distant land).[181]

These standard operas (and operettas) can help us notice how consistently *West Side Story* conflates ethnicity with gender: non-white with female, white with male (Fig. 9.13). For example, the Jet Girls – the women associated with the "white" male gang – are given no appealing ensemble number analogous to "America" and "I Feel Pretty" (that is, to use standard Broadway terminology, no "We Are" song, and no "Charm" song). Similarly, no single Jet Girl is presented as even remotely equivalent in dramatic or musical weight to Maria or Anita. Conversely, the Sharks (members of the Puerto Rican male gang) are not granted musical numbers analogous to the two "We Are" numbers for the "American" gang: the "Jet Song" and the disturbingly clever "Gee, Officer Krupke." The two prominent individuals among the male "Sharks" – Maria's brother (Bernardo) and intended spouse (Chino) – sing almost not at all. Chino hardly even speaks. No more convincing method could have been found to deny the Shark men a "voice" in this musical play than to keep them, literally, silent. They express themselves with weapons, not words or sung phrases, and thus grant us little sense of their feelings and thoughts.

It would be misleading to imply that exoticness inheres only in the Puerto Ricans (the Sharks). To a mainstream middle- and upper-middle-class audience in the 1950s, the Jets must have been nearly as unfamiliar, and certainly as unsavory. New York newspapers regularly reported a threatening rise of gang activity in the city's Irish and Puerto Rican communities.[182] Accordingly, in the "Tonight" ensemble (toward the end of Act 1), Bernstein seems to have taken pains to portray both the Puerto Ricans and their lighter-skinned counterparts as behaving in similarly impulsive, uncivilized ways. The two gangs sing identical music, sometimes in quick antiphonal exchanges. This particular decision was clearly Bernstein's and

274   Musical Exoticism: Images and Reflections

Figure 9.13 Anita is taunted and physically threatened by the Jets – using her own shawl – as she tries to find Tony at Doc's drugstore. Anita: "Will you let me pass?" Snowboy: "She's too dark to pass." Photo from the original Broadway production, showing Allyn Ann McLerie, who played Anita in 1960 when the show returned to Broadway after a national tour. (Reproduced by permission of the Museum of the City of New York.)

suggests his awareness of how shallow, and "constructed," ethnic difference can be. When both groups' buttons are pushed, they lash out with very similar, gut-level mechanisms of violence. Throughout *West Side Story*, ethnicity is shown – not least, musically – to be motivating the characters. Yet, at crucial moments such as the "Tonight" ensemble (another being the Rumble), ethnically coded music vanishes as a distinguishing mark.

This evenhanded portrayal of the rival ethnic groups is particularly apparent when the show is contrasted to standard exotic operas. Few such works focus as unremittingly on the search for a place of reconciliation as *West Side Story* does, especially in the "Somewhere" ballet; the end of the Maria-Anita duet; and the final, sorrowful tableau, in which the two gangs carry Tony's murdered body off the stage together. The death of exoticism – the show finally suggests – may permit the birth of a multiracial, multiethnic, mutually tolerant society. Or may exoticism itself – so evident in Tony's attraction to Maria, and in the Jets' astonished admiration for Anita and Bernardo's dancing (Fig. 9.12) – yet plant the seed of that better world?

10 | Exoticism in a global age (*c.* 1960 to today)

By the mid-twentieth century the categories of West and East were quickly losing fixed meaning. Westerners began to recognize the growing industrial economies and other hallmarks of modernization – for example, universities and public education – in Japan, Taiwan, India, and other countries.[1] One formulation, replacing the West/East divide, divided the world into industrial nations and relatively undeveloped (or "developing") ones. Another formulation spoke of two industrialized "worlds" – the Free World and the Communist World (the latter consisting of the USSR, the People's Republic of China, and their respective satellites) – and bunched the remaining countries together, despite their many differences, as the Third World.[2]

With the demise of Soviet power, a very different view of the world is becoming normative: the view that nation states are mattering less and less, as "globalization" (the current term of choice) leads to increasing contact and interconnectedness across political boundaries. This connectedness has many aspects, from the largely benign and even productive (the Internet) to the convulsive and exploitive. Vast socioeconomic and cultural differences remain between many countries and groups within the industrial world – and, even more so, between the countries of the industrial world and those of the developing world. Powerful nations continue to grow their economies at the expense of poorer nations (e.g., by using a disproportionate share of natural resources). These basic disparities have also contributed to waves of immigration: for example, Latin Americans and East and South Asians moving to North America; Pakistanis and Indians to Great Britain; Moroccans and Surinamese to the Netherlands; Algerians and Senegalese to France; and Turks and Eastern Europeans to Germany. People from the economically stronger locations – including Western Europe and North America, but also such varied countries as Japan, Australia, Saudi Arabia, and Brazil – have increasingly traveled abroad for pleasure, business, or military-governmental purposes.

Globalization – including all this migration, travel, and instant communication and access to information and images (some reliable, some misleading) – has had a major impact on music and its dissemination. Since the

1950s, billions of people have become exposed to previously unfamiliar cultures. Music of the industrialized West, and especially American popular music, has exerted a vast and varied impact on most of the world's musical cultures. Some observers within and outside a given non-Western country bemoan the resulting cultural loss, but others (including many ethnomusicologists) stress the new and creative syntheses that can result.[3]

The impact of globalization has also moved in the opposite direction: from the Rest to the West. During the 1950s–80s, the Moiseyev and other East European state folk-dance companies were a major cultural export to Western Europe and North America (and a substantial source of hard foreign currency for the troupes' home countries).[4] The National Ballet of China brought politically inspired works, such as *The Red Detachment of Women*, to audiences around the world – and to even more viewers through a widely distributed filmed version (1970).[5]

From the 1950s onward, ethnomusicologists and commercial record producers have documented and disseminated traditions from around the world, many of them so different from those of the West that they were inevitably heard and understood as strikingly exotic. Unlike in earlier decades, representative recordings now regularly appeared on commercial labels that were carried by larger record shops (e.g., Folkways, Nonesuch Explorer, and, in the case of many UNESCO recordings, Philips and Bärenreiter). Certain repertoires and specific pieces attained a cult following, for example Nonesuch's 1969 recording of the Balinese *kecak* (or "Ramayana monkey chant"). Some even attained a period of popularity on the radio, for example recordings of a folk-style Bulgarian women's chorus that were released in the UK and then the USA under the intriguing title *Le mystère des voix bulgares* (The Mystery of the Bulgarian Voices).[6]

What could be heard on recordings was not always fully traditional. The *kecak* ceremony had been created in the 1930s by Balinese musicians in collaboration with German artist Walter Spies as, in part, a tourist attraction, using elements of age-old Balinese rituals of exorcism. As for the "mysterious" Bulgarian women, they were handpicked from villages across the country by a government-paid professional conductor and then taught the traditional repertoire and trained in appropriate forms of voice production. But, whether relatively "authentic" (a problematic word, easily commodified) or heavily adjusted, a wide range of startling sounds and unfamiliar manners of musical expression were reaching the ears of the Western European and American audiences (and, of course, audiences in other industrial and post-industrial countries, such as Japan).

New compositions

These three broad developments – the complicating of the categories of West and East; population shifts (and other travel); and growing access to different music traditions – led to four specific trends regarding new exotic (or arguably exotic) compositions within the Western art-music tradition:

- More and more composers began to spring up in parts of the world that had not previously had composers (and works) in the Western sense. Some of them remained in their home country (or returned to it after study in the West), often contributing to the expansion – and Westernization/modernization – of musical life there. Others, drawn by various material and cultural advantages, moved more or less permanently to a European or North American metropolis, where they – and their works – were often treated as, to some degree, inherently exotic.
- Foreign musical traditions that Westerners were encountering for the first time often were extremely different from the West (e.g., African *mbira*, Tuvan "throat-singing," Japanese *gagaku*). Western composers could not count on listeners having as rich a fund of precise, ready-made associations with them as with, say, flamenco or Hungarian-Gypsy music.
- Even though the decades since around 1960 have sometimes been dubbed "postmodern," the ideology of modernism has continued to shape attitudes within the world of Western art music (sometimes called "serious" composition). The modernist insistence on originality and uniqueness has led many composers to avoid the more Overt forms of exoticism (see Chapter 9). The composers frequently explain (as we saw in Chapter 2) that they are interested in the deeper or more structural aspects of foreign musical traditions, rather than the more superficial or "picturesque" aspects. Often they name "exoticism" as something that they are at pains to avoid, and scholars follow suit.[7]
- The previous point is based on the expressed intentions of the composer. But the reality of a musical work and its place in its community must involve reception as well – how the work is performed, heard, and described, and how listeners and other musicians react to it. The very factor – exotic associations – that composers in recent decades have been so intent on disavowing can resurface the moment the work leaves his or her worktable and enters the push-and-pull of musical life.

The last two of these trends – the disavowal and perpetual resurgence of exoticist conceptions and discourse – have tended to play out in a variety of ways, depending on the composer's origins and situation. We may best survey these issues by encountering a diverse – and somewhat representative (or at least suggestive) – sampling of composers, some widely known and others nearly forgotten, for whom exoticism was a significant factor in their works and careers. We start with composers who worked within Western genres but came from locales (Uzbekistan/Persia, Korea, Egypt) long thought to be peripheral to the world of "classical music." Next we look at one composer from a Central Asian Soviet republic and another who lived and composed in the State of Israel during its early years. We then examine composers in the European and North American orbit (Britten, Boulez, Reich, Volans); here the question arises, as in the first half of Chapter 9, whether incorporation of foreign/exotic musical principles is necessarily an exoticizing move. We then turn our attention to Takemitsu and Tan Dun, two particularly significant composers from East Asia, a part of the world where many musicians and audience members have, in recent decades, embraced the Western classical tradition warmly.[8] We conclude the chapter by considering some manifestations of the exotic in film music and other popular media.

Composers from beyond "the Western mainstream"

Aminollah Hossein (1905–87) was born in Samarkand (Uzbekistan) to a wealthy Azeri merchant from the Caucasus and a musically talented Persian mother. Hossein lived part of his early life in Persia. He received his musical training in Moscow, Berlin (where he studied piano with Artur Schnabel), and Paris, and spent the remainder of his life in the latter city. Hossein was a proficient player of the *tar* (Persian lute). His compositions, written in a lush, audience-friendly style, include *Miniatures iraniennes*, the "Arya" Symphony (i.e., "Iranian," 1976), and songs for voice and orchestra using French versions of poems by twelfth- and thirteenth-century Persian authors Omar Khayyám and Saadi. Under the more French-sounding names André Hossein and André Gosselain, he composed extensively for film and television, including dramatic films starring notable Western actors (e.g., Geraldine Chaplin, Jean Marais, and Robert Hossein, the composer's son, who also became a prominent film director). He did compose one score for an exotic film, a 1962 *Shéhérazade*, with Danish-born Anna Karina as the tale-spinning Arab princess.

The Korean-born Isang Yun (1917–95) settled in Berlin and, in two respects, took almost the opposite path from Hossein: he was an uncompromising lifelong avant-gardist, and he consistently maintained his East

Asian identity, often emphasizing in interviews the Taoist-dualist philosophy that shaped his compositional style. Yun became headline news when abducted (along with his wife and some Korean students) by the South Korean government in 1967. He was subjected to a show trial and sentenced to prison for supposed espionage, but was released in 1969 thanks to protests from Stravinsky, Karajan, and other prominent international musicians. Yun returned to Berlin but never ceased his efforts at reuniting North and South Korea on democratic principles, or at least at helping to restore more peaceful cooperation between the two. Like certain other Asian-born composers around the same time (Chou Wen-Chung from China and José Maceda from the Philippines), Yun was among the first to carve out a space in the West for music by composers from the East, and remains much admired and appreciated by numerous composers and performers from East Asia today.

Yun's much-discussed orchestral pieces *Réak* (1966) and *Muak: Tänzerische Fantasie* (Muak: Dance Fantasy, 1978) are based on Korean ceremonial music and on principles within Korean and Chinese philosophy concerning the coexistence of opposites.[9] Many of his large-ensemble pieces include prominent parts for woodblocks (such as are repeatedly struck during Buddhist chanting) or for a Korean set of wooden platters that clack together with an effect that Yun described as a "multi-sound bull-whip." Yun's music makes frequent use of a feature of East Asian music that he called the *Hauptton* (primary sound): a note does not, as in Western tradition, maintain a fixed pitch but fluctuates by means of "decorations, grace notes, vibrato, glissandos, and changes in dynamics."[10] (Such glissandos or "sliding tones" are typical of the Korean *haegum*, Chinese *erhu*, and Mongolian *morin khuur*.) But the opposite phenomenon – use of steady, long-held tones – is likewise central to Korean musical culture, as in temple hymns.[11] The middle movement of the Quartet for Oboe and Strings (1994) sets these two tendencies in sharp juxtaposition, the strings' numerous slow slides (glissandos) against the meditative near-stasis of the oboe's long notes. The East Asian "feel" of Yun's music is so intense that critics have repeatedly expressed confusion about whether it is primarily Korean or Western, or else they have resorted to convenient but non-Taoist terms such as "blending."

Halim El-Dabh (b. 1921) is harder to pigeonhole, being at times a highly experimental modernist (like Yun) and at other times a tuneful populist (like Hossein). Born in Cairo, he moved to the United States thanks to a Fulbright grant, and became a citizen in 1961. El-Dabh has explored the possibilities of electronic music and has carried out ethnomusicological research in Africa and South America. He was a longtime member of the faculty at Kent State University (1969–91), where he established a pan-African percussion ensemble. In 1961, upon commission from the Egyptian government, El-Dabh composed and recorded a choral-orchestral score that is (even today) played nightly during the sound-and-light show at the pyramids of Giza.[12] Many of his works are inspired by texts and imagery of ancient Egypt, or use present-day instruments of the Arab world, notably the *darabuka* (goblet-shaped drum). Particularly attractive examples of his ethnically colored work, both from 2002, are *Sweet and Prickly Pear*, for violin and *darabuka*, and *The Reappearance of the Lotus Flower*, for string orchestra.[13] El-Dabh's most widely known work, *Leiyla and the Poet* (1959), was inspired by a famous medieval Arabic story generally known as *Layla and Majnun*. It uses various electronic techniques to alter pre-recorded passages in which El-Dabh himself sings phrases of the old tale, in English. Additional Middle Eastern flavor is contributed by material played on the *oud* and *nay* (Arab lute and flute).[14]

El-Dabh has been held up by Nigerian-born composer and scholar Akin Euba as a particularly distinguished practitioner of what the latter calls "intercultural" composition: "new musical idioms that reflect the blending of European and local elements." As noted in Chapter 9, interculturalism (or transculturalism, hybridity, etc.) is a potentially powerful concept, in that it no longer accepts Europe (and heavily European-derived cultures in the Western hemisphere) as Home and the local elements as Other. But one should note that the "flow" between the two musical cultures tends almost always to be in one direction, into the West from "outside." Euba frankly notes that, in El-Dabh's case, "the elements from non-Western cultures are presented in the context of Western techniques of composition." He does not suggest what the opposite might be: perhaps a traditional African ensemble improvising in its usual manner upon a Western popular tune; or (to give a South Asian example) the Madras Corporation Band performing – on Western instruments – *karnatak*-style versions of famous nineteenth-century Western orchestral pieces.[15]

Euba's words would apply just as well to the works of Hossein and Yun mentioned above as well as to many exotic works from the previous two centuries, not least Mozart's "Rondo alla turca," Liszt's and Brahms's Hungarian-Gypsy pieces, and Debussy's *Pagodes*. One wonders, again (as in Chapter 9), if there is any substantive difference between composing in an Overt Exotic(ist) manner and in an intercultural (or what I call a Transcultural) one – except, that is, in the mind of the composer, listener, or commentator. After all, audiences for much inter/Transcultural music end up being primarily Western. One suspects that these listeners find the music fascinating both for its unfamiliar sounds and for its association with a distant culture. They perceive it as surrounded, to some degree, by an exotic aura.

The later Soviet era, the State of Israel

During the final decades of Soviet control over Eastern Europe, the Union of Soviet Composers began to distance itself from its longstanding policy of promoting overtly socialist-realist works – often based on folk songs – for each people or ethnic group. Yet, as Boris Schwarz notes, this gesture toward liberalization gave little guidance about what to do instead, and composers often continued to play the ethnic card.[16]

This may help explain certain distinctive features in the life-work of Sofia Gubaïdulina (b. 1931). Born and raised in the Tatar ASSR (today Tatarstan; Tatar is a Turkic language), Gubaïdulina was one of the bolder modernists on the Soviet musical scene in the 1960s–70s. For several years, she organized and played in an experimental free-improvisation group that (perhaps partly in an attempt to be acceptable to the cultural authorities) used folk instruments.[17] *Rubaiyat* (for baritone and chamber group, 1969) sets seven classic Persian poems by Khagani Shirvani, Hafiz, and Omar Khayyám (all sung in Russian translation) to music that is, by turns, scintillating and darkly reflective. The singer's part requires various avant-garde-like vocal techniques.[18] Music critic Paul Griffiths, encountering *Rubaiyat* in a 1997 American performance, noted with evident pleasure that the work was "quite without musical orientalism, for Gubaidulina in her frankness sees through codes and conventions." Griffiths's wording here relies on the typically modernist/formalist assumption that codes and conventions somehow inhibit an artist's spontaneous and sincere self-expression.

Griffiths considers the possibility that the "catalogue of personal griefs" in the Persian poems held "an autobiographical weight" for the composer, who was "at that time ... battling official disapproval in the Soviet Union." He then adds that, more likely, the work was intended as a "portrait of the sorrowing Jesus, given a Persian disguise so as not to be recognized by the apparatchiks."[19] Either of Griffiths's two explanations, if correct, amounts to yet another instance (as during Baroque times) of an exotic portrayal – Persia was exotic in a Soviet context, if in a different way than in the West – that masked other concerns that dared not be spoken aloud.

A situation somewhat analogous to the decades-long traditions of Soviet nationalism/exoticism arose within the community of Jewish settlers in

British-mandate Palestine and (from 1948 onward) within the State of Israel. Over the decades, a number of composers arrived from Germany and Eastern Europe. Eager to create a musical voice for the young Zionist homeland – and carrying with them a typically European conception of "folk-song nationalism" (as seen in works by, say, Falla or Bartók) but applying it to a very different region – they developed what came to be known as the Mediterranean style. This style took inspiration from the musical traditions of Palestinian Arabs; of so-called *mizrahi* (Eastern or Oriental) Jews, especially Yemenite (whom many European-Jewish settlers regarded as inherently closer than they to ancient biblical traditions); and of Sephardic Jews (e.g., from Turkey and Morocco). The style also incorporated features that Israelis regularly heard on radio broadcasts from other Middle Eastern countries (such as Turkey and Egypt) and from southern Europe (notably Greece and Italy).

The most prominent exponent of the Israeli-Mediterranean style was Paul Ben-Haim (1897–1984), who was born in Munich (as Paul Frankenburger), and received his training largely in Paris. Ben-Haim settled in Jewish Palestine in 1931. Determined to achieve what he called "a new original Palestinian creation" through familiarity with "oriental folklore," he spent some ten years as accompanist and arranger to the remarkable Yemenite-Jewish singer Bracha Zephira.[20] In 1959, Ben-Haim gained international exposure through Leonard Bernstein's recording of Ben-Haim's compact, accessible *Sweet Psalmist of Israel: Three Symphonic Fragments for Orchestra*, a work based on selected biblical verses about King David. The program published in the score suggests that, in the third movement (which includes prominent passages for harp and harpsichord), David and the people of Israel sing hymns of praise as they enter the Holy Tabernacle. The procession begins at a "solemn" tempo, with a modal melody in C (it briefly slips sideways, in Prokofievan manner, but finds its way back), all over a tonic-ostinato drone in a typically Eastern Mediterranean *aksak* rhythm (which divides the eight pulses in a measure into 3 plus 3 plus 2).

Halfway through this theme-and-variations movement, a contrasting episode suddenly changes the mood to one of unbridled joy and vitality. The entire string section starts playing in the manner of a traditional-music ensemble from Istanbul or Cairo, including long passages in heterophony. The oboe – as if it were a *zurna* – sometimes offers brief two-measure replies, sometimes simultaneous commentary. Ben-Haim's good friend (and publisher) Peter Gradenwitz had originally proposed that the composer devote one section of the piece to portraying the famous incident of David dancing (ecstatically and somewhat immodestly) before the Ark of the Covenant.[21] Though the published program note does not mention the dancing-David incident, the brilliantly colored music here seems to have it in mind. Its style associates the young king with the festive rejoicing of Arabs or of "Oriental" Jews. East and West then merge musically when, in mm. 202–5, Ben-Haim adds Western triadic harmonies to the quick-twisting theme, turning David – though, again, the published program gives no hint of this – into a *hora*-dancing kibbutznik.

Composers in the West

Since the 1950s, self-defined "serious" composers who were born and raised in the United States and Europe (and who, unlike Ben-Haim, remained there) have tended to avoid straightforward evocations of the exotic. No doubt many of them regarded Overt Exoticism as inevitably linked to an outdated Romanticism and, worse, to commercial entertainment music of various kinds. This is not to say that they all have avoided influence from non-Western cultures. For example, a number of important works of modernist music theatre have drawn inspiration and energy from non-Western (and also ancient Greek and medieval) theatrical traditions and their (known or presumed) musical components.[22]

But often composers have treated non-Western influences in gingerly fashion (or highly abstract fashion), as if afraid that foreign cultural resonances might overwhelm their own musical identity – or might, worst of all, suggest that the composer was a kind of present-day Ketèlbey. For a composer from, say, Egypt, the use of non-Western music, generally, may be viewed (not least by the composer him- or herself) as a natural expressive outlet, even when the non-Western music is not his own. (El-Dabh has used Ethiopian, Yoruba, and Japanese materials.) A Westerner, by contrast, is constantly at risk of slipping into the widely derided role of imperialist plunderer or the equally derided role of a colonial settler who has, in irresponsibly carefree manner, "gone native." In Iannis Xenakis's landmark work for solo percussionist, *Rebonds* (1987–89), the performer plays three kinds of drums (bongos, tomtoms, and *tumba*) with hands only, no sticks.[23] The published score is headed with an epigraph from the French music critic Jacques Longchampt praising the work as "an immense abstract ritual, a succession of movements and hammerings without any folkloristic 'contamination.'"[24] The quotation marks around "contamination" suggest that Longchampt is quoting other critics and does not himself intend to demean certain exoticist composers whose music sounds more obviously ethnic/folkloric than Xenakis's. Nonetheless, the attitude is plain: audible cultural borrowings are somehow impure and invalidating.

Sometimes a composer himself insists that the foreign influence on the work does not extend to the musical substance, which is finally his (or hers) alone. Benjamin Britten wrote about his church parable *Curlew River*, adapted from a Japanese *nōh* play that he saw on two occasions in Tokyo in 1956: "There is nothing specifically Japanese left in the Parable that William Plomer [the librettist] and I have written, but if stage and audience can achieve half the intensity and concentration of that original drama I shall be well satisfied."[25] William Malm, Mervyn Cooke, and W. Anthony Sheppard, however, have demonstrated that *Curlew River* contains multiple echoes of Japanese theater and even of Japanese music, such as specific treatment of the organ to recall the sound of the *shō* (one of the important instruments in another Japanese court tradition: *gagaku*).[26]

Despite the tendency of many Western composers to refer to principles of Transculturalism (or equivalent terms) to explain what they are doing, even a glance at some of their work may lead one to wonder whether exoticism has not continued to play a constitutive role in it. During the 1940s and early 50s, Pierre Boulez listened intently to recordings of various non-Western musics at the Musée Guimet, Paris's remarkable repository of Asian art, and he considered joining an expedition to Southeast Asia to get to know gamelan music first-hand. Boulez admits that the instrumentation of his best-known piece, *Le marteau sans maître* (1954), for voice and small ensemble, was suggested in part by foreign instruments and the sounds and textures associated with them: the guitar, by a Japanese *koto*; the xylophone, by an African *balafon*; and the vibraphone, by the *gendèr* (a central instrument in the Balinese gamelan):

Many listeners' first impression [of *Marteau*] is primarily exotic; and in fact my use of xylophone, vibraphone, guitar and percussion is very different from the practice of Western chamber music, closer ... to the sound pictures of Far Eastern music, though the actual vocabulary used is entirely different ... Neither the style nor the actual use of these instruments has any connection with these different musical civilizations. My aim was rather to enrich the European sound vocabulary by means of non-European listening habits, some of our traditional classical sound combinations having become so charged with 'history' that we must open our windows wide in order to avoid being asphyxiated.[27]

Boulez stresses that listeners who hear exoticism in the work are responding only at a surface level. Yet the last sentence gives a sense of how crucial Boulez finds this infusion of the culturally unfamiliar – the exotic – into a Western tradition that, in his view, is at risk of suffocating under the weight of past masterpieces. Besides, a composer can only do just so much to direct and constrain reactions to his work. An early critic of *Le marteau*, Marcel

Figure 10.1 "Music of the Spheres," watercolor by Bernard Xolotl and Barbara Falconer. The painting, copyright 1977, was used by CBS Masterworks as the cover image for Terry Riley's 1978 *Shri Camel* LP album (and is used again on the Sony CD reissue). It is also repeated dozens of times (right-side-up and upside-down) as the wallpaper behind the photo of Terry Riley on the composer's official website, www.terryriley.com. The painting has been kindly adapted by Bernard Xolotl for use in the present book. Xolotl is himself also an active composer-performer working in a heavily exoticist vein: www.bernard-xolotl.com.

Schneider, complained, upon first hearing the work in performance, that the percussion made him feel that he had suddenly been transported to a "Peking opera" performance. Thirty years later, Dominique Jameux, a major French specialist in twentieth-century music, would complain that the "oriental colorings" of the work now seem to be "signals emitted by another planet" – and apparently a planet with little life on it, since Jameux concludes that "*Le marteau* belongs decidedly to History."[28]

High-modernist and avant-garde composers of the second half of the twentieth century and early twenty-first from America and other Western

Figure 10.2 Steve Reich and Musicians playing Reich's *Music for 18 Musicians*, Tokyo, 1996. (By permission of Steve Reich.)

countries have been more open than Boulez about their fascination with distant musical traditions. La Monte Young, Terry Riley, and Philip Glass have willingly addressed their creative engagement with the music (and, sometimes, musico-philosophical thought) of North India.[29] (Record companies have encouraged these associations; see Figure 10.1.) But many composers have been as wary as Boulez, especially about admitting the possible cultural implications of such borrowings. This wariness can be sensed in the music, and vividly seen in the public statements, of two composers from English-speaking countries: Steve Reich and Kevin Volans.

Steve Reich (b. 1936) has been emphatic about what world music can give a Western composer: "Non-Western music is presently the single most important source of new ideas for Western composers and musicians."[30] In his own case, he freely admits that the interlocking rhythms in West and Central African music (including for multiple drums) have deeply influenced numerous of his works, such as *Drumming* (1971), *Clapping Music* (1972), *Tehillim* (1981), and *Electric Counterpoint* (1987). Reich has named some of the sources of his knowledge of African music, for example a book (with transcriptions) by A. M. Jones. Reich studied drumming in Ghana in the summer of 1971 (until he acquired malaria and had to go home) and, soon after, Balinese gamelan at a workshop in Seattle.[31]

Like Cowell and Harrison before him, Reich has adopted standard procedures of one or another non-Western culture in many of his works. These procedures include repeated short melodies (sometimes played in overlapping fashion by different performers) over a regular pulsing accompaniment that may be pitchless or fixed on a single pitch or two. Particularly captivating examples are in movement 3 of *The Desert Music*, 1984, for chorus and orchestra, to poetic texts by William Carlos Williams. (Perhaps not by chance, one of the texts – beginning "Say to them:" – recalls the powerful formula – "Say:" – that begins dozens of verses in the Qur'an.[32])

Reich also uses non-Western techniques to enable semi-improvised group performance. As he himself explains, various patterns in *Music for 18 Musicians* (1976, Fig. 10.2) continue a flexible number of times (as is common in many primarily oral musical traditions around the world). Sometimes the result will depend on how long the performers of "breath" instruments (wind players and singers) can last before having to inhale again. Other times a new pattern is indicated to the players by a metallophone (a vibraphone with its motor turned off). Reich notes that these audible signals – rather than a conductor's gesture – resemble the way that the drummer in a Balinese gamelan or the master drummer in a West African drumming ensemble uses his instrument to call for "changes of pattern."[33] Reich is quite firm in his objection to making Western musical works *sound* African or Balinese. To him, that is what exotic normally means, and (as we saw in Chapter 2) he dismisses it even further by using the term "Chinoiserie," which is normally associated with eighteenth-century porcelain bric-à-brac.

So what led this urban Westerner and confirmed modernist (or, some would say, postmodernist), beginning in the 1960s, to seek musical roots in central Africa? Reich's statements about this emphasize that non-Western music was "the most attractive path to restoration and innovation for Western composers ... a way to reconnect with musical basics" after the (opposed yet complementary) austerities of serialism (including twelve-tone writing) and aleatoricism (chance music, as in many pieces by Cage).[34] But might it not also be relevant that Reich, like most Americans of his generation, had grown up surrounded by African-American music? Was his interest in African music (and then Balinese music) one stage in a search for cultural roots beyond the perceived blandness of Western high culture (and of much pop music as well)? If so, perhaps it formed a not unfamiliar case of searching for an expansion of the Self in the Other, a search that is often described as the central function, and motivating principle, of exoticism.[35] Surely not by chance, Reich has gone on to explore his Jewish identity, in works as varied as the aforementioned *Tehillim* (which sets verses from several psalms in Hebrew), *Different Trains*, and *The Cave*.

Kevin Volans is at once a composer fully integrated into the Western European cultural orbit and one with roots elsewhere that have helped him make his mark in the musical world. Volans was born in South Africa in 1949 to parents of European origin and received training in South Africa, Scotland, and Germany. Since 1986, he has lived in Ireland (where he is now a citizen). Four field trips during his early years resulted in works closely based on African musical traditions, especially the interlocking melodies created by groups of players of the *mbira* (sometimes, misleadingly, called the "thumb piano"). Two of these works – *White Man Sleeps* (1982–86) and *Hunting:Gathering* (1987, with no space after the colon) – became widely known through recordings by the Kronos Quartet. (His more recent works, including several concertos, make much less evident use of African materials.) Volans's African-based pieces sometimes lay substantial chunks of African or African-style music end to end, though adapted to suit Western instruments and Western concepts of what comprises a musical "work." *Hunting:Gathering*, an admittedly extreme case, consists of (the composer notes) "about 23 different pieces of music in the space of 26 minutes": pieces that Volans had transcribed from performances by Ethiopian, Malian, and Zimbabwean musicians. Perhaps as a bow to Western tradition, the work is subdivided, on the page (and by track numbers on the CD), into three movements, but the players are instructed not to pause between the movements.

Volans explains how he arranged the African bits in *Hunting:Gathering*. "To keep the fragments separate, each is written in a different key ... I wanted the different pieces to come and go in a random fashion like images or events on an unplanned journey."[36] Volans felt free to alter the fragments harmonically or melodically. Some of the segments that ended up in *Hunting:Gathering* were originally part of a collection he called *African Paraphrases*. "Paraphrases" suggests a historical parallel: Franz Liszt and other nineteenth-century composers often used that label for a piece freely based upon opera arias, folk tunes, even "Chopsticks."[37]

Volans emphasizes the Westernness of the paraphrases that comprise *Hunting:Gathering*:

Although the title and a lot of the music quoted in the piece is modelled on African music, it's not an African piece at all. When I say "modelled on," the African-ness is as relevant to it as, say, African masks are to Picasso's *Les Demoiselles D'Avignon*. The origin of that painting is undeniably African – because of the faces and so on – but the painting is nothing to do with African art. That's sort of how I feel about this piece.

African musical art is, however, undeniably central to *Hunting:Gathering*, a fact that makes the work exotic in some (largely positive) way – like a highbrow version of cultural tourism – to players and listeners alike. The middle of the second movement consists of what Volans calls "a small set of variations on the piece *muthambe* ... which was played by a famous 19th century *mbira* player and medium, Pasipamire, of the Shona people of Zimbabwe."[38]

Discussing this very passage, Martin Scherzinger poses exoticism as the one thing an African-inspired piece should strive not to convey:

[Volans places] the *mbira* tune "Mutamba" ... in the strings' most comfortable range ... [thus drawing] attention to the intricate *melodic* and *harmonic* power of "Mutamba." Challenging the Eurocentric stereotyping of African music as "rhythmic," he effectively downplays the musical exoticism of the *mbira*, and the passage in this way makes a unique aesthetic and political point.[39]

For Scherzinger, exoticism sees African music stereotypically: as rhythmic in essence (and perhaps also timbral, if one thinks of the buzzing and the complex overtones of several *mbira*s playing together). Volans, Scherzinger rightly observes, presents "Mutamba" in a way that permits us to concentrate, instead, on musical parameters that have been valued as more central, more structural, in Western music and musical aesthetics, namely melody and harmony. Melody in this passage is manifested in horizontal lines that shiftingly interlock; harmony, in implied chords that prove fascinatingly evanescent.

Perhaps, though, Volans's emphasis on melodic and harmonic features of "Mutamba" in this passage is itself exoticist – but in a sophisticated manner. One can hear, in this passage, the educated Westerner pointing out to the listener (and to the quartet's players) – as if analyzing for him or her – one and another fascinating feature of a found musical object from a tribal culture. Volans brings out the double-stops at m. 396 by having the second violinist play the passage "poco ponticello" (i.e., a bit close to the bridge, which gives a nasal effect). At m. 403, the cellist presents her syncopated duplets prominently (with only the steady double-stops as accompaniment). At m. 411, the first violinist introduces a new variation for five measures entirely alone before the other performers layer themselves back in. All of these devices help us to hear the parts separately as well as combined. The composer deconstructs the texture of "Mutamba" and then reassembles it, helping us to appreciate its dense interweavings – its artfulness. If *Hunting:Gathering* is, as I suggested, cultural tourism, the (musically enacted) commentary of our tour guide is more than usually learned and intriguing.

As the "Mutamba" variations conclude (or, rather, slowly melt away), Volans more forthrightly imposes his own compositional personality on his African sources. The instruments have been working resolutely with the white-note scale, in pan-diatonic fashion (often centered on the note E), when suddenly the second violinist adds a long high C♯ and a bit later a G♯ – notes that are conspicuously alien to the prevailing E-Phrygian sound. One reading is that Volans is not pointing out the "harmonic power" (Scherzinger's term) of "Mutamba" but, rather, its harmonic limitedness, which he feels free to transcend (before moving on to the next transcribed African snippet). Another reading might be that these alien notes comment on Volans's own sense of "apartness" from the coherent diatonic harmony of the rest of this section (and from the African musicians that made that harmony).

However we may interpret what Volans's compositional persona is trying to "say," his willingness to bring that persona frankly into the picture is very much in line with the developmental enrichment that prior composers of "exotic" works – including Mozart, Liszt, and Debussy – enact upon their found material.[40] If "Rondo alla turca," Hungarian Rhapsody No. 14, and *Pagodes* are works with a substantial exotic aura, then it is hard to see how Volans's *Hunting:Gathering* is not – especially for its audiences outside of sub-Saharan Africa (which, by the standards of new classical composition, are relatively numerous). Conversely, if some Shona musicians were to hear Volans's *Hunting:Gathering*, especially performed live, certain aspects of the work and the concert experience might well strike *them* as exotic.

A more recent attention-getting piece, Osvaldo Golijov's *Ayre* (2004), illustrates with particular clarity the problem of how adaptations of exotic materials are framed through the written word. Record critics in such unlikely venues as *The Economist* praised soprano Dawn Upshaw for singing communicatively and with stylistic acuity melodies from the Arab world, from Sephardic tradition, and from Sardinia. They also praised Golijov for working up fascinating accompaniments and arrangements to cushion, support, surround, and sometimes threaten his chameleon-like diva.

But I would propose that the piece merges all too readily the different chosen materials. In the booklet text, the composer presents this as a virtue, as if music were capable, somewhat like a food-processing machine, of smoothing out stubborn tensions between nations and peoples:

With a little bend, a melody goes from Jewish to Arab to Christian ... How connected these cultures are and how terrible it is when they don't understand each other. The grief that we are living in the world today has already happened for centuries but somehow harmony *was* possible between these civilizations.[41]

Golijov's good social intentions are undermined by a curious vagueness about the sources upon which he has drawn for this work. A taped excerpt (from a radio broadcast?) of a speaker or preacher exhorting a massive, responsive crowd in Arabic, over loudspeakers, is inserted at the end of movement No. 6 ("Wa habibi" – My Beloved). The CD booklet and Golijov's own site give no indication what all this shouting in Arabic is about. A small rubric in the published score – which, of course, almost no listeners have occasion to consult – indicates "Palestinian funeral," a brief phrase that seems to invite a variety of possible readings (sorrowful, accusatory, etc.).

As for the musical materials that are incorporated in the eleven movements of *Ayre*, Golijov is quoted as saying that "most are well-known melodies that I arranged ... but some I made up." Well known to whom? According to Golijov's website, the words of the aforementioned No. 6 are those of a "traditional Christian Arab Easter Song" and the notes of the vocal line are "based on traditional Christian Arab and Muslim Arab melodies."[42] This vocal melody has been singled out for praise by numerous reviewers and listeners as if it were a particularly splendid gem of Arab musical culture. Nobody seems to have pointed out that it is utterly typical of much eighteenth-century Western-European music in style, form, and tonal structure.[43] More notable still, the melody turns out to be identical to the tune of an eighteenth-century French song that is still published, performed, and recorded today: "Que ne suis-je la fougère" (sometimes entitled *Les souhaits*; the typically Enlightenment-era text tells of a simple shepherd's yearning to be close to his beloved shepherdess).[44] This eighteenth-century French melody had a second life, in nineteenth- and early twentieth-century France, as a Christian hymn, to the words "Jésus est la bonté même" (Jesus is kindness itself).[45] I can only assume that some Christian Arabs got to know the hymn and sang it in French (or perhaps in Arabic translation?) for several generations, long enough for the melody to have reached the ears of Golijov. To call the tune a "traditional Christian Arab melody" is thus not inaccurate: some Christian Arabs presumably did sing it, perhaps in Lebanon (long an outpost of French culture and the center of Maronite Christianity, a sect closely allied with Roman Catholicism). But Golijov's remark is, in context, utterly misleading. It obscures the fact that the tune was composed and widely published in Paris in the age of Rameau or Rousseau, to secular words (indeed, rather sexy ones implying physical contact between the two lovers), by a well-trained musician who presumably had no connection to the Arab world at all.

Takemitsu and Tan Dun

Given the increasingly large number of accomplished performers of Western classical music in East and South Asia since the 1950s – and also within Asian ethnic communities in North America and Western Europe – it is surely no surprise that the world of Western art music has seen a flourishing of composers, too, from those backgrounds. Some Asian-identified composers were born in North America, such as Alexina Louie (from Vancouver). Others arrived in the West – or at least became regularly active in the West – after having completed initial training in their homeland: Isang Yun, as described earlier, but also Chou Wen-Chung, Chen Yi, Bright Sheng, and, from Japan, Toshirō Mayuzumi (perhaps most famous for his film score to John Huston's 1966 film *The Bible: In the Beginning ...*).[46] Two who have made a particular marked impact – and who have composed works that are (or are received as) exotic – are Tōru Takemitsu (1930–96) and Tan Dun (b. 1957).

In 1958, Stravinsky, then seventy-six years old, was visiting Japan. He encountered a recent piece (*Requiem* for string orchestra) by the young, largely self-taught Takemitsu, and raved about it. American and European commissions for Takemitsu soon followed, including *Dorian Horizon* (1966, conducted by Aaron Copland). *November Steps* (1967) was written to celebrate the 125th anniversary of the New York Philharmonic. Scored for *biwa* (bowl-shaped lute), *shakuhachi* (bamboo flute with a sharp-edged mouthpiece), and symphony orchestra, it became widely known through a 1968 recording by two Japanese soloists and the Toronto Symphony under the latter's music director, Japanese-born Seiji Ozawa.

During the first part of his career, Takemitsu had rejected Japanese musical traditions, associating them with World War II-era Japanese nationalism and militarism.[47] His writings suggest that exposure to certain Western works that were at first startlingly unfamiliar (exotic?) to him – by Franck, Debussy, Messiaen, Cage – had a liberating impact on him, analogous to what Debussy felt after experiencing the music, dance, and theater of Indonesia and Vietnam in 1889.[48] Interestingly, as soon as Takemitsu began to incorporate techniques of a number of Western composers, and to compose with an international audience in mind, he began to feel free to incorporate Japanese instruments. (One thinks of Chopin and Villa-Lobos, both in Paris, penning, respectively, mazurkas and samba-like *chôros*.) *November Steps* repeatedly dramatizes the differences between the smooth, integrated sound of the Western orchestra and the *biwa* and *shakuhachi*, with their remarkable ability to give a harsh, characterful edge to a tone or vary its pitch a little – or a lot. There are questions here of cultural identification and auto-exoticization on the composer's part that are not easily disentangled.

Takemitsu was also almost systematically exoticized by the international musical community. Although only a few of Takemitsu's many pieces use Japanese instruments, those are the works that have been most performed and acclaimed around the world.[49] The composer seems to have regretted this limited view of his output. In 1975, he ruefully remarked, "I would rather be Beethoven's pupil than a pupil of a famous nineteenth-century Japanese composer like Mitsuzaki Kengyō."[50]

Tan Dun's forthright stance regarding his Asian roots offers a sharp contrast. In his early years Tan made his living as a string player and musical arranger in the People's Republic of China and studied composition at the Beijing Conservatory. In 1986 he went to New York City to complete his training at Columbia University (under Chou Wen-Chung, who had, years earlier, studied with Varèse). New York has remained his main base ever since, but the early rehearsals for his Metropolitan Opera commission *The First Emperor* (2006) took place in Shanghai, largely as a cost-saving measure. Tan Dun's most widely known work is the film score for the world-renowned martial-arts film *Crouching Tiger, Hidden Dragon* (2000), which was made in China but became a major international hit.

Numerous works by Tan cut forthrightly across the Western/Eastern divide. Sometimes (as in *Crouching Tiger*, with its Chinese instruments, solo cello, and lush symphony orchestra) the result is a smooth blending of elements. In other works, a more restless, shifting exoticism is palpable as each momentarily prevailing set of style elements becomes the listener's temporary "home," thereby heightening the Otherness of the next set of elements to arrive.

Tan's *Symphony 1997: Heaven, Earth, Mankind* was composed and performed on the occasion of the return of Hong Kong – long a British protectorate – to Chinese control. The seventy-minute-long work consists of thirteen contrasting movements that are grouped into three large sections, each labeled with one of the words in the work's subtitle. *Symphony 1997* mixes celebration with elements that, as Yu Siu Wah argues, may seem innocently "exotic" to Western audiences but are more "ominous" to those who are aware of the possible threat posed by mainland China to Hong Kong's autonomy. This autonomy is, for Yu, symbolized in the work by the Cantonese culture that Hong Kong has managed to keep alive over several generations (in the midst of a booming Western-style metropolis and financial center).[51] Movement 6 includes a two-and-a-half-minute recording of a Cantonese street-opera troupe performing a duet from a particularly tragic work, *Princess Cheungping*. This opera, Yu explains, ends with "the suicide of the princess and her husband, in defiance of the new Manchu regime." Tan adds a sense of dread by gradually introducing drones in the low strings (a minute or so into the recorded excerpt from the opera) and by having the opera recording fade away, to be replaced ("overwhelmed," Yu feels) by the striking of the famous Imperial Bells Ensemble of China. Yu proposes that these sixty-five bronze bells, buried in 433 BC and rediscovered in 1978, can be taken as referring to the imperial aims of today's mainland government.[52]

Symphony 1997 makes use also of a full symphony orchestra, a Chinese children's chorus, and ecstatic cello solos (played, like those in *Crouching Tiger*, by Yo-Yo Ma, the great American cellist whose parents were from China). The children's chorus sings melodies that, though not strictly pentatonic, often incorporate gapped melodic figures that emphasize $\hat{6}$, a pentatonic marker that strongly suggests Chinese music.

The first three movements demonstrate well the work's creative play with Chinese and Western musical traditions. In movement 1 (Song of Peace: Prelude), the children's choir sings three descending "ah"s, the second of which reaches from $\hat{5}$ to the $\hat{6}$ that lies below it (in typically pentatonic fashion), and then a hymnic melody that seems closely based on the "Ode to Joy" theme from Beethoven's Ninth. Its opening two phrases – $\hat{3}$–$\hat{3}$–$\hat{4}$–$\hat{4}$–$\hat{5}$–$\hat{5}$–$\hat{1}$–$\hat{1}$–$\hat{2}$–$\hat{2}$–$\hat{3}$–$\hat{3}$ – are identical in pitch (and very close in rhythm) to Beethoven's setting of the words "Freude, schöner Gött[erfunken]" and "Tochter aus Ely[sium]." This prelude soon incorporates material that seems more frankly Western (and entertainment-oriented): mariachi-like repeated notes in the trumpets, and a motive in the piano and high winds that moves back and forth between scale-steps 2 and 3. The latter motive is remarkably similar – except for its 5/8 meter – to the memorable accompanimental figure in Elmer Bernstein's main theme for *The Magnificent Seven* (a 1960 film based on the great Akira Kurosawa film *The Seven Samurai*).

In movement 2 (Heaven), chorus, cello, and orchestra take turns swooping down from step 6 to the tonic below it (thereby creating another "Chinese" pentatonic marker).[53] The violinist, solo cello, and children's chorus take turns stating one of the best-known Chinese tunes, "Mo-Li-Hua" (Jasmine Flower), giving it a more consistently traditional-Chinese flavor than Puccini did in *Turandot*.[54] Near the beginning of movement 3 (Dragon Dance), brass fanfares allude unmistakably to the opening of Richard Strauss's *Also sprach Zarasthustra*, or perhaps rather to the use of

296　Musical Exoticism: Images and Reflections

Figure 10.3 Tan Dun's opera *Marco Polo*, which received its first performance on 7 May 1996 at the Munich Biennale, conducted by the composer. (left to right) Thomas Young as Polo, Nina Warren as (the spirit of) Water, and Dong-Jian Gong as Kablai Khan. In the last act, Nina Warren also took the role of the Queen of China. (Photo: Regine Koerner, courtesy of Munich Biennale 1996.)

that music in Stanley Kubrick's film *2001*.[55] They are then immediately undercut by a weaker version in the oboes – as if warning us that promises of technological progress and international cooperation can be easily oversold.

Tan's opera *Marco Polo* (1996) goes even further, making no fewer than four distinct locales – medieval Venice, the Middle East (complete with the character Sheherazade), Tibet, and China – equally exotic to the audience and to each other. *Marco Polo* is structured around themes of memory and imagination. The title character is represented by two singers: Polo (a tenor) is memory, and Marco (a mezzo-soprano) makes the journey. But, since the journey is being reconstructed in memory, the aged Polo may seem more real than the Marco who travels in the tale. Concurrently, we encounter the Mongolian warrior Kublai Khan (sung by a bass), on his way to conquering China (Fig. 10.3). Various disparate musical styles (and instruments) are invoked to indicate stages along this remembered double-journey. Most striking is a scene in which Kublai Khan intones the word "Himalaya" again and again, accenting the word differently – and at the very bottom of his register, rather like the chanting of Tibetan Buddhist monks – to conjure up what the stage directions call "an atmosphere of ritual, magic, and sorcery." The two travelers' (and our) arrival in the Himalayas is then announced by noisy blasts on Tibetan ritual horns (played by the orchestra's trumpet players) and a sad, repeated three-note phrase on English horn, an instrument long associated with Eastern exotic regions.

When Marco finally reaches China, the ghost of Gustav Mahler appears, singing parts of the fifth song of *Das Lied von der Erde*. Li Po, the eighth-century author of the original Chinese poem upon which this song was distantly based, interrupts with cries of "no no" and then sings some words in Chinese that we may take to be his poem. (They are neither translated nor in any way explained in the libretto that comes with the CD recording.[56]) The part of Li Po is sung by a performer from the Beijing Opera, with characteristic wavering approach to pitch.[57]

At the very end, the librettist (Paul Griffiths) suddenly invents a Queen of China – the obligatory seductive Oriental female – to urge Marco to stay "here in peace, here in stillness." All characters on stage, including Polo (the rememberer), chant repeatedly in unison – growing scarily louder – that no corner of the globe is "beyond the rule of the Khan." Marco (the traveler) girds himself, then breaks through the Wall, presumably to return to Europe with unprecedented knowledge that will, in time, enable greater international contact and trade. But the wall-breaker could also be Tan Dun, who, in 1985, escaped from a chorus of totalitarian dictates to find his own creative voice in the West. Or it could be today's Tan Dun, who, one suspects, has sometimes needed to ponder how much to yield to the pressures and advice of self-appointed (commercial and critical) decision-makers in the Western world – perhaps wise advice, perhaps not – and how much to go his own way.[58]

The traveler Marco Polo is the exotic in China; Tan Dun is the exotic in New York; and the audience members for this opera travel the Silk Road together – thousands of miles – in company with the various historical, legendary, and symbolic characters (e.g., Water) that Tan and Griffiths have summoned up. No savvier commentary has been written on the possibilities and problems of "doing" exoticism in a postmodern, globalized era than this opera, especially its Himalayan and Chinese scenes.

Tan Dun's own comments suggest that, in *Marco Polo*, geo-cultural origins and associations are, perhaps, no longer relevant because they have been transcended by the combinative genius of the composer:

Sounds and different musical cultures guide my own development, leading me through a deeper journey before the work can reach technical refinement. From

Medieval to Mongolian chants; from Western Opera to Beijing Opera; from orchestra to sitar, pipa and Tibetan ritual horns – the fusion of musical sounds from all corners of the globe is the definition of "Marco Polo" to me. Did Marco Polo's journey actually happen? Did someone dream it up? Or did the journey imagine us?[59]

Repeatedly, in his career, Tan Dun has shied away from specifying the cultural implications that his various materials carry. Musicologist Carol J. Oja nicely sums up Tan's, at root, modernist stance:

The musics of China and the West – whether Beethoven or Meredith Monk – coexist in this symphony [i.e., *Symphony 1997*]. Tan has stationed himself at a cultural sampling board. But what term is appropriate to this process? "Integration"? "Cross-Over"? "Hybridization"? Tan himself avers, "No East anymore, no West anymore," suggesting that not only must our language change but also our geographic perception. And he puts a late-century spin on a fundamental modernist credo: "My purpose is to be flexible and freely flying around among all kinds of experience. Not to be driven by the wave of culture – fashion, trends, isms, schools – but to create my own unity."[60]

Tan seems to want to deflect the discussion away from exoticism – the very mix of estrangement and fascination that his music produces on many listeners and critics (and, no doubt, performers).

Chou Wen-Chung, the Chinese-born Columbia University professor of music composition, helped bring Tan Dun and other young composers from China to the West. By 2001, Chou (then seventy-eight years of age) was complaining in the *New York Times* that these composers incorporated Asianisms in a superficial and too easily entertaining manner. "They reflect the intellectual ambience in China today ... They are not in the habit of going to libraries, doing real research or debating issues. I'm disappointed. It's not the kind of situation I wanted. What I'm looking for is a spiritual digestion of one's legacies."[61] Ethnomusicologist Frederick Lau has recently put the point more bluntly, in terms of careerism. Lau argues that many current Asian and Asian-American composers "have knowingly or involuntarily capitalized on the Orientalized discourse for personal gain, privileging the categories [of Asian vs. Western] that they seek to transcend."

Lau concludes, though, in a more hopeful spirit. These composers may end up "contributing to a broadened, more globalized aesthetics, one that accomplishes exactly what they set out to do."[62] In short, they – and Tan Dun most prominently – are using exoticism to try to kill off exoticism, at least in the worlds of concert music and opera. They may yet succeed.

Exotic varieties of jazz

In the more frankly commercialized musical realms, exoticism is not likely to die anytime soon. There, exotic currents are numerous and powerful, and resistance is hardly to be found. In recent decades, the Afro-Cuban jazz trend of the 1950s has grown into a more varied "Latin jazz" movement. One particular stream, Brazilian-influenced jazz, developed through the interaction of musicians such as saxophonist Stan Getz and guitarist João Gilberto (notably on their international radio hit of 1963 "The Girl from Ipanema," with vocalist Astrud Gilberto) or pianist Chick Corea and percussionist Airto Moreira. North Indian classical music, too, has found many echoes in jazz, often carrying with it a range of philosophical and cultural associations. John Coltrane and his "sidemen" (e.g., bassist Jimmy Garrison) incorporated into many pieces the principles familiar from the introductory *alap* section of *rāga*-based Hindustani classical performances, such as the gradual introduction of the notes of the scale to be used, over a rhythmicized low drone or pedal point. Coltrane's half-hour-long *Om* (1965) goes further: the performers chant a passage from the *Bhagavad-Gita* in which Krishna reveals his divinity to the warrior Arjuna: "I make all things clean. I am Om-OM-OM-OM."[63] Other Westerners who have blended Indian music with jazz include Yusef Lateef, Don Ellis, Jan Garbarek, and John McLaughlin (notably the latter's Mahavishnu Orchestra, a jazz-rock fusion group, 1971–76 and 1984–87).[64]

Many jazz artists who were far from both North America and Western Europe have likewise integrated their own culture's musical traditions with those of jazz. Beginning in the mid-1970s, Japanese pianist, composer, and bandleader Toshiko Akiyoshi has occasionally incorporated into certain of her works Japanese vocal techniques (such as the slow upward-sliding cries from *nōh* drama), *tsuzumi* drum playing, and spoken texts in Japanese. Her primary collaborator, the saxophonist and flutist Lew Tabackin, has mastered a variety of techniques on the Western flute that closely recall the sounds of the *shakuhachi*. Notable Asian-inspired works of Akiyoshi include "The Long Yellow Road" (based on Akiyoshi's childhood memories of the distant haze in Manchuria, where her father was in the import/export business), "Kogun" (inspired by a news story about a Japanese soldier from World War II emerging from the jungle in the Philippines after thirty years), and "Hiroshima: Rising from the Abyss" (which features interludes by a player of the traditional Korean flute, Won Jang-Hyun).[65] As David W. Stowe argues, Akiyoshi has used her ethnic traditions to "disrupt the dominant American black/white racial binary" that marked many aspects of the jazz world in the 1960s and 70s and simultaneously to resist a different but equivalent "racial polarization" (between Japan and the West) that was being widely espoused in Japan around the same time, notably in the doctrine of *nihonjinron*.[66]

These various Asian-influenced varieties of jazz have remained something of a niche taste in the West. (The recent Akiyoshi-Tabackin recordings are available only as imports from Japan.) By contrast, within the more commercial realms of the American music business, the aforementioned stream of Latin-jazz melding has proliferated, almost becoming a *lingua franca* for many performing musicians. This became apparent in the 1960s, when a number of recordings in one or another variety of the style were widely broadcast. Among the chief exponents were Herb Alpert's Tijuana Brass and Sergio Mendes's group Brasil '66. The Tijuana Brass's 1965 LP *Whipped Cream (and Other Delights)* sold six million copies. Its famous (and much-parodied) jacket photo indulged in south-of-the-border exoticism – and played on the record's title – by featuring a dark-haired, seductively "innocent" female wearing nothing but whipped cream.

Discussion of post-1960 popular realms, of any kind, almost necessarily involves the important matter of technology. This is all the more true when questions of exoticism – hence of "the real thing," which had become recordable and easily disseminated – are at stake. It is therefore worth dwelling briefly, in the following section, on some crucial technological aspects of exoticism in the (broadly) popular musical realm before moving on, in the section after that, to film music and, in the final section, to popular music in the more usual sense (e.g., widely distributed albums and hit songs) and music for television.

With technological assistance from …

Popular instrumentalists nowadays use the techniques of electronic sampling to insert notes or passages by other performers into their own music. An early, not-quite-pop instance of this is the widely disseminated David Fanshawe LP entitled *African Sanctus* (1973), which juxtaposed African ritual musics (recorded in the field by Fanshawe) and a British chorus singing settings by Fanshawe of the Catholic Mass text.[67] Listeners will differ about whether the result is condescending or innocently engaging. To my taste, the marvelously skilled and varied African excerpts utterly outshine Fanshawe's truly primitive (in the sense of amateurish) choral compositions, though the catchiness of his tunes cannot be denied.[68]

Fanshawe's work also relates to the wide-ranging revitalization (from the 1960s onward) of Catholic and some Protestant liturgical music through contact with popular and world-music styles.[69] Whatever the benefits or losses of that much-debated general trend, it produced two fresh and stylistically coherent settings of the Mass Ordinary that have maintained a long life through recordings and performances: *Missa luba* (1965), originally using Congolese music and musicians; and *Misa criolla* (1964), an Argentine product, which was later recorded by Spanish operatic tenor José Carreras and by folk-based Argentine singer Mercedes Sosa. An instrumental arrangement of the Kyrie and Gloria from the *Misa criolla* has been recorded by klezmer clarinetist Giora Feidman.[70]

Sampling (i.e., incorporating recorded excerpts of) Western popular and non-Western popular and tribal/ritual musics, a process pioneered by Fanshawe, has continued and expanded in the commercial music scene of the West. Examples include numerous albums of what is known as World Beat music (e.g., those on the Rykodisc label, produced by Mickey Hart, former drummer of The Greatful Dead) and Paul Simon's best-selling *Graceland* CD. Some albums of this sort (though not Simon's) were released without the permission or even knowledge of the original music-makers, a practice that raises numerous ethical and legal issues.[71] Timothy D. Taylor points out, though, that the act of appropriating music for one's own creative purposes does not preclude the possibility of "attempt[ing] to put ... appropriations to positive political good."[72] Taylor arrives at this rather evenhanded conclusion after examining various instances of non-Western borrowings by such prominent artists as Peter Gabriel and the feminist rock group D'Cückoo: "Gabriel and D'Cückoo do good, and they appropriate, and there is no way around this contradiction."[73]

Elfin kingdom and other movie realms

While the technology of digital sampling has facilitated borrowing and appropriation, it has also further complicated the problem of Self and Other. A whole corps of what we might call technocomposers and techno-performers, such as Hans Zimmer (composer of the background music for the Disney film *The Lion King*) or Roy "Future Man" Wooten (synthesizer-based percussionist of Béla Fleck and the Flecktones), can now press a button and bring a specific sound or sound-mixture into play in order to evoke a region or touch the listener's nerves in some special way. This does not prevent a high-budget project from hiring a real non-Western musician to make some of the sounds. Sub-Saharan African chanting does open *The Lion King*, although – as so often when recordings of non-Western musics are incorporated into Western cultural products – no subtitles are provided. The vast bulk of the music (the main exception being a few Elton John songs written for the purpose) comes from Zimmer's chameleonlike keyboards.

The Lion King (which, with additional songs and spectacular costumes and puppetry, went on to become a successful Broadway musical) is only one of many diverse exotic portrayals that continue to flourish in the movies and also on TV. Examples include another animated Disney film, *Aladdin* (1992), and – toward the other end of the entertainment spectrum – the complex dramatic film *The English Patient* (1996, much of which is set in North Africa). Disney's 1999 animated *Tarzan*, reportedly the 48th film incarnation of one or another of Edgar Rice Burroughs's books about an Englishman who has gone extremely native, mixes typical Western-style power ballads (by Phil Collins) with African-style drumming and copious jungle noises. Episode 1 of *Star Wars* (*The Phantom Menace*, 1999) feels exoticizing in its offscreen modal choral chants, as if the distant stars themselves were making their weirdly insightful voices heard. The sounds of the Armenian *duduk* and of Nusrat Fateh Ali Khan's keening *qawwali*-style wailings create haunting effects in Peter Gabriel's score for Martin Scorsese's *The Last Temptation of Christ* (1988). Similar vocals, by Khan's nephew and chosen successor Rahat Nusrat Fateh Ali Khan, are heard at many points in *The Four Feathers* (2002), a film directed by Shekhar Kapur (born in Lahore, British India; the city is now within Pakistan) and based on a 1902 A. E. W. Mason novel about the 1898 British and Egyptian campaign against Sudan. Here, the singing is set amidst and against James Horner's orchestral wellings-up. At times, the mixture interacts intriguingly with what is being shown on screen; but, for long stretches, the elements neutralize each other, creating a deadening sameness.

The amalgam of film and music can often be quite powerful, guiding the viewer to identify a specific instrument with a specific ethnicity or exotic locale and even a specific feeling-tone. The sad playing of an Irish-style fiddle in the movie *Titanic* suggests the honest and down-to-earth attitudes of the poor immigrants from that country, huddling below decks. Through these associations, it also suggests (more generally) a feeling of vulnerability with which everyone in the audience, presumably, can identify. On a more concrete plot level, it becomes associated with the young Irish hero's touchingly brief experience of happiness and romantic fulfillment.

Or the amalgam of film and music can work more subliminally (a bit like the Submerged Exoticism of the early twentieth century), keeping short of the specifics that might lead filmgoers to identify the culture in which the instrument or style is used, yet managing to remind us of the feeling-tones and other associations that have become attached to that culture. The score for the three *Lord of the Rings* movies uses this subliminal method with great skill. For the mines of Moria, composer-conductor Howard Shore cooked up ominous background chanting by an off-screen chorus. Director Peter Jackson says that he wanted the choral singing to have the quality of a Welsh miners' chorus and something more. So, instead of Welshmen, a substantial choir of Maoris and Pacific Islanders was assembled (in a recording studio in Wellington, New Zealand) on the principle that "Polynesians ... [have] an otherworldly quality to their voice."[74] (One suspects that Polynesian voices sound very this-worldly to Polynesians!) Perhaps the moviemakers were also responding, if unconsciously, to the age-old association between darker-skinned natives – as if they were so many (off-screen) Calibans – and shadowy and, in this case literally, "underground" scenes full of menace for white intruders. At the climax, the Polynesian choir was reinforced by a bunch of hefty, mostly Caucasian (and some Maori) rugby players. As one of the athletes has explained, "They were looking for some grunty voices, and they thought that a *haka* flavor would fit in with it."[75] The *haka* is the Maori war chant that is performed – often with threatening gestures – by New Zealand's national rugby team at the beginning of every game, in the faces of their opponents. The website of the New Zealand Rugby Union explains that the *haka* "aligns with the wider Polynesian cultures of the Pacific."[76] In the *Lord of the Rings* film, these oddly assorted elements – "otherworldly" Polynesians; thick-necked white he-men making threatening noises; faint memories of Welsh miners – end up merging into a generic aural effect of nastiness and threat that, for most viewers (except perhaps for folks in the South Pacific, and rugby fans world-round), loses all association with any place on earth that we know of.

Perhaps the failure of the *haka* to communicate a specific Otherness here is all for the best. Does the world really need musical and vocal reinforcement of the already arguably racist association in these films (echoing faithfully Tolkien's novels) between the abstract principle of villainous force and visible features such as dark skin, Caribbean-like dreadlocks, Japanese samurai armor (for some of the Orcs and Orukhai), or long, Arab- or Pakistani-looking robes (for the evil Southrons, riding enormous, ground-shaking beasts)?

For the elves' kingdom (Lothlórien), by contrast, composer Shore concocted a sound that we might call Overtly Exotic, or perhaps slightly Submerged, in that it is audibly non-European and specific. "We deliberately gave it a slightly Eastern flavor," says director Jackson. This was achieved through the use of what Shore calls "very exotic African instruments playing and some East Indian instruments playing in it as well."[77] The prominent glissandos here, typical of the *sitar* or *veena*, evoke for many listeners characteristic images of India, such as a maharajah's palace, barefoot female dancers, and slowly burning joss sticks – and, for others, at least the pleasurable dreaminess often associated with such images. The music and the associations (conscious or unconscious) that it evokes reinforce the unique atmosphere of this relatively reposeful episode, in which the white-gowned elves drift about with graceful sensuality, bathed in a magical glow.[78]

Pop exotica

Within the various popular realms in industrial and post-industrial societies, exoticism functions in particularly complex ways. Musical products can now easily reach a multiethnic listenership simply by virtue of the distribution networks between different parts of the world. In addition, certain countries have, within them, a population that is culturally quite mixed. This was already the case in the United States and Canada during the early and mid-twentieth century, and has become more prevalent in many Western European countries in recent decades. The international music industry, in close cooperation with the electronic media, has tested and adopted a variety of solutions for making musical selections available to disparate groups of consumers.

How this tends to work is made dramatically clear by shifts within the popular-music industry in the United States. In the 1950s–60s, much mainstream "pop" radio in North America and Europe still attempted to appeal to a broad listenership: Elvis Presley famously alternated with Frank Sinatra and Patti Page. But these stations tended not to play much music by African-American artists – except music of the smoother sorts: for example, the Mills Brothers, Ella Fitzgerald, the Ink Spots – and next to nothing from outside the English-speaking world.

Record companies led the way in cultivating niche markets that would broaden the available material. But they did so in a hesitant manner. A record sleeve put out by Columbia Records in the mid-1960s advertises dozens of recordings, and puts them into categories to help the potential purchaser keep his or her bearings. In the midst of such straightforward categories as BROADWAY and JAZZ, one category stands out as puzzling (and interesting for the present discussion): EXOTICA. It includes seven items: a live concert by Marlene Dietrich (*Dietrich in Rio*); two albums by Yves Montand; volume 4 of *Les grandes chansons* by the now-forgotten Jacqueline François; and albums featuring guitarists: the Spanish-born flamenco specialist Sabicas, the trailblazing Puerto Rican vocal-and-guitar group Trio Los Panchos (an album of Spanish and Latin American numbers, entitled *Los favoritos de todo el mundo*: Everybody's Favorites), and an outfit of blind musicians from Madrid that was called – this was the age of bigger-is-better – One Hundred Guitars.[79] The French and German songs of Montand and Dietrich seem to have been "exotica" in the eyes of the Columbia marketing folks because, I suppose, anything sung (or indeed spoken) in a foreign language tends to be almost unbearably "Other" to most Americans – a fact that has only increased since then.[80]

There were always exceptions. Back in the 1930s–50s, mainstream radio had carried occasional hit songs that were partly or entirely in other languages.[81] Even so, two of the biggest – "Bei mir bist du schön (Means That You're Grand)" of 1938 and "Volare (Nel blu, dipinto di blu)" of 1958 – used new English lyrics after the opening line or two.[82] These songs functioned less as exotic numbers than as marks of public recognition for Jewish- and Italian-Americans, confirmations of the two ethnic groups' success at negotiating their way into the mainstream life of America's big cities. (The two songs may have seemed quite peculiar – even exotic? – to certain people in rural Iowa or Kansas who had never met a Jew or an Italian-American.[83]) By contrast, the 1963 hit song *Sukiyaki*, sung engagingly and with subtle variety by Kyu Sakamoto, was sung in Japanese throughout. This gave it more of a novelty-number charm and uniquely exotic aura for nearly the entire American listening public. *Sukiyaki* was clearly "from Japan," not a melting-pot product. The utter strangeness of the song to America is evident in the fact that the inauthentic slapped-on title is simply the name of a well-known Japanese food and has nothing to do with the lyrics, which, in any case, few listeners understood at the time. The melancholy words begin: "I look up at the sky / So that the tears won't fall, / Remembering those spring days."[84] This expression of pain may surprise those who have long enjoyed the song's bouncy and only faintly bittersweet (and entirely pentatonic, hence Japanese-sounding) main tune.

These few exceptions seem almost quaint relics today, fodder for recorded anthologies of "nostalgia" items reminding middle-aged Americans of some decade during which we were young and listening to the radio. Songs sung in other languages than English have vanished almost entirely from the mainstream airwaves in the USA in recent decades (except for the occasional Spanish number by a Latina/o artist), even while the world beyond the United States has opened its arms more and more to pop music sung in English. In that sense, the mid-1960s Columbia Records sleeve was itself inscribing a shift in American cultural values toward English-only cultural isolation, whereby Dietrich and Montand – even though singing in languages that, unlike Japanese, were somewhat familiar to many high-school-educated Americans – could now be termed EXOTICA.

Just a few years later, "exotica" gained a whole new, more expansive meaning in Western popular music. The classic case is "raga rock": the fascination with music of India on the part of pop and rock musicians. Prominent instances in the years 1965–68 included songs by the Kinks, the Yardbirds, the Beatles (including "Norwegian Wood" and "Within You Without You"), and the Rolling Stones ("Paint it Black"). On most of these songs, a guitarist either plays a sitar or else, on his usual instrument, imitates the sitar's ornaments and slides. In "Within You Without You," notes David Claman, "the use of unison violin lines recalls Indian popular film music."[85] Other prominent Indian features include extended drone tones, harmony that is mostly static, drumming rhythms reminiscent of the *tabla*, and – notably on "Within You Without You" – use of Indian-influenced melodic modes, such as the major scale with a flatted-seventh degree (equivalent to Mixolydian, and sometimes stressing the heard-as-weird tritone between $\hat{3}$ and $\flat\hat{7}$).[86] Beatles hagiography would give the impression that these efforts at incorporating Indian music derived from George Harrison's months of study in India with Ravi Shankar. In fact, the Kinks and Yardbirds songs preceded the Indian-inspired songs of the Beatles, if only by a few months. Clearly, as Jonathan Bellman concludes, something was "in the air" in the mid-1960s: romanticized attitudes toward "the East" – and India in particular – as a locus of dreamy spirituality, sexual license, and hallucinogenic drugs.[87]

Raga rock moved quickly, Bellman adds, from the "riskiness and immediacy" of songs such as the Yardbirds' emotionally complex "Heart Full of Soul" (with Jeff Beck giving out the sitar-influenced guitar lines) to The Moody Blues' *In Search of the Lost Chord* (1968), an album that alternates celestial and meditative visions, praise of drug-advocate Timothy Leary, and a long episode for sitar and tabla, the whole adding up to – in Bellman's view – a "blandly mystical constellation of mind expansion."[88] Nonetheless, the musical sophistication and superb use of recording technology keep *In Search* freshly listenable forty years later. In one song on the album, entitled "Om" ("The rain is on the roof"; "the Earth turns slowly round"), the major-pentatonic melody keeps ending its phrases by dropping to $\hat{6}$, implying the relative minor. The quasi-choral refrain on "Om" then returns us to a tonic chord, but by way of a $\hat{6}$ grace note. $\hat{6}$–$\hat{8}$ melodic cadences in Western music have long connoted the exotic, the pastoral, and/or (via the standard Amen cadence) the religious. Such cadences, in many types of twentieth-century music (such as some pieces by Debussy), create what Jeremy Day-O'Connell calls a "quintessentially Romantic sense of openness": a sense of non-resolution that – in the words of Leonard B. Meyer – "reverberate[s] in the silence of subsequent time."[89] In "Om" by The Moody Blues, exoticism thus joins hands with a wider range of musical associations, creating a mood that would have been unattainable with the more usual materials then available in rock and pop music.

Between the 1950s and today, the media gradually created separate radio stations (or separate nationwide radio networks, or, in Europe, "channels") for newer, sometimes raunchier pop styles that appealed to younger listeners, as well as for other segments of the listening audience. In the United States, these included lovers of country-western music, Hispanic listeners, "urban" (i.e., African-American) listeners, and so on.[90] New ways of reaching these many listening markets have proliferated (e.g., MP3s and iPods). Despite all this, the recent offerings of radio stations and the emphases of the pop-music market in English-speaking countries and especially the United States have largely excluded songs from the European Continent, Japan, the Philippines, Turkey, and other hotbeds of pop-music creativity.

David Byrne, a thoughtful, well-informed figure within the world of alternative pop music, bemoans this self-imposed American isolation. He touches insightfully on the problematic term "world music" by relating it to the term "exotic," which he (following a longstanding tradition within modernist circles and such) uses to indicate appropriations that are superficial and easily commodified:

In my experience, the use of the term world music is a way of dismissing artists or their music as irrelevant to one's own life. It's a way of relegating this "thing" into the realm of something exotic and therefore cute, weird but safe, because exotica is beautiful but irrelevant; they are, by definition, not like us. Maybe that's why I hate the term. It groups everything and anything that isn't "us" into "them." This grouping is a convenient way of not seeing a band or artist as a creative individual, albeit from a culture somewhat different from that seen on American television. It's a label for anything at all that is not sung in English or anything that doesn't fit into the Anglo-Western pop universe this year … It's a none too subtle way of reasserting the hegemony of Western pop culture. It ghettoizes most of the world's music.[91]

Nonetheless – and with or without Byrne's approval – an exotic fascination continues in many strands of popular music, from the thoroughgoing cross-cultural pop music of the German "Türk-Rock" group Dissidenten to certain hit songs by Fiona Apple or Joan Osborne.[92] Alanis Morrissette's "Uninvited" (from the 1998 film *City of Angels*) offers a notable sitar swoosh and a seventh degree that is sometimes lowered (and sometimes not, but emphatically insisted upon against a tonic drone, as often in traditional Indian music). The renowned English singer-songwriter Kate Bush has brought three former members of the Bulgarian State Women's Folk Choir (known as the Trio Bulgarka) into the studio to record with her on two albums.[93] A complex tangle of issues surrounds recent and current "hybrid" styles of pop music, such as the Punjabi-derived *bhangra* exemplified by the group Alaap (from Southall, a West London residential district) and the Canadian Jazzy Bains (or Jazzy B). Timothy D. Taylor points out that the concept of hybridity has tended in recent decades to replace the concept of exoticism because it provides a "marketing handle for music by Others and ... a criterion that shapes the ways musics by Others are heard by critics, fans, and listeners."[94] From the point of view of the music-makers in question, the shift from "exotic" to "hybrid" – in regard to, say, *bhangra*-based groups – thus implies a shift in what might be called authorial agency. The non-Western style elements are ones with which the musicians, to some extent, grew up – even if *where* they grew up was in West London, on the opposite side of the globe from the Indian subcontinent.

One can see David Byrne's point, though, when one surveys the relative emptiness of meaning in, for example, much New Age music of the past two decades, a kind of industrial churning-out of relatively undifferentiated quarter-hours of exotic-sounding drones and wispy or flexibly florid melodies. These melodies are often sung by a female singer with a small, rather generic-sounding voice – for example, the determinedly inexpressive Irish singer Enya, or the somewhat more colorful Lisa Gerrard (of Dead Can Dance) – in a language that she may not understand (or a made-up language) and that the CD booklet neither transcribes nor translates, except perhaps for a frustrating ten-word summary.[95] Sarah Brightman's bestselling *Harem* CD (2003) is interesting, if at all, as evidence of how homogenized and dull such an imaginary journey can become, even with a soprano whose voice does have some special qualities (in her case, an edgy thinness). Several songs on Brightman's *Harem* CD include sound clips by renowned Arab, Israeli, and Pakistani vocal artists. These insertions, often frustratingly brief or "mixed" half-inaudibly into the blend, give the album its only glimmers of intensity, making Brightman's vocal and emotional pallor all the more evident (and perhaps inadvertently reinscribing certain stereotypes regarding the greater emotional vitality of non-Westerners).

A related trend is the increasing use of world music by the advertising industry. As Taylor has noted, the music may be from a particular country or region, or written by Westerners in close imitation of such a style: Sony Music maintained for a time a website that allowed advertisers and other purchasers to select recordings in a category appropriate to the product or service being advertised, from Andean Folk and Qawwali (i.e., Pakistani religious vocals) to vague entities such as Ethnic Fusion or Tropical.[96] Increasingly often, a Westerner composes the music for an ad in a style thought of as all-purpose "primitive" and has it sung by a woman, or by a women's or children's chorus, using either a made-up language or culture-neutral vocables such as "ah." Often the vocal tone employs little or no vibrato, as is common in many traditional cultures. Such a singing style is also strikingly different from various vibrato-laden styles typical in the West, including grand opera, country-western, Broadway belting, pop crooning, and the sultrier sorts of jazz singing. Whether the snippets are from actual world music or are manufactured in some generically exotic style, the products or services to which they are linked are often ones involving travel: automobiles, airline flights, cruises. (Taylor notes that world and ethnic musics seem to have become social-class markers for well-heeled urban and suburban sophisticates, somewhat in the way that classical music was to earlier generations.[97]) For a number of years beginning in 1984, the "Viens, Malika" duet for two women's voices and orchestra from Delibes's *Lakmé* was used by British Airways for television ads (sometimes over a pop-music beat, in an arrangement – known as "Aria" – by Yanni and Malcolm McLaren). Updating the same basic approach, European Delta Airlines used the pseudo-primitive song "Adiemus" (by composer Karl Jenkins) in its television ads of 1994.[98]

Broadway, since the heyday of *Kismet* and *West Side Story*, has had oddly little success putting exoticism at the center of a show. *Bombay Dreams*, a mega-musical assembled under the aegis of Andrew Lloyd Webber (the music is by prominent Bollywood film composer A. R. Rahman), became a durable hit in London in 2002 but, despite much reworking, it "lost the better part of $14 million" in New York.[99] Television has been less enterprising in its exotic efforts but, perhaps for that reason, more reliably successful. Travelogues and nature specials were prominent during the first few decades of American network TV (before such shows migrated mainly to public TV and cable channels). These shows offered an odd mix of "information," intriguing camerawork, and entertainment. Music faintly redolent of the locale in question often helped set the scene. In somewhat similar manner, the late 1990s saw the arrival of numerous frankly exploitive and stereotyped commercial shows – such as the *Survivor* and *Great Race* "reality" game shows – that were/are set in distant and potentially intriguing places. Yet the music of *Survivor*'s opening credits offered little more than a rising fifth played on a large conch shell, and a few seconds of pseudo-Micronesian unison singing – or maybe it was not pseudo, but still too short to give more than a whiff of local color. No information was offered about the singers or the words. For better or worse, these aural snippets will be forever engraved on the memories of many viewers, linked with equally canned visual images of natural beauty (swaying palm trees) and natural dangers (toe-nibbling rats).

As we noted in Chapter 3, with regard to Algerian rap, there is another side to the exotic equation: people in countries far from America and Western Europe often adopt the styles of Western popular music, for many purposes and with varying effects. David Byrne stresses the creative aspect of this, using (interestingly) an instance in which the West is represented by music of the Caribbean: "African guitar bands were doing their level best to copy Cuban rumbas, and in their twisted failure they came up with something new."[100] (I sense some condescension – a lingering remnant of colonialist attitudes? – in Byrne's description.) What Byrne describes here may or may not be understood as an instance of exoticism. Were the musicians and their public – African, in this case – thinking of the Caribbean locale at all, or simply absorbing, and enjoying, a musical style that was, in any case, indebted in part to traditions of rhythmic syncopation that had originally come from Africa itself?

Intriguingly, almost the opposite process – a kind of self-exoticizing – was carried out in the performance from Turkey that won the 2003 Eurovision Song Contest. The singer, Sertab Erener, sang (in English) "Everyway That I Can," a song of loving devotion to her man ("nothing in the world that could stop me [from being with him], no sir"), in an enormously effective Turkish-pop style based on *aksak* rhythm. Erener and four female dancers performed the number dressed in harem costume, shimmying their shoulders with much come-on allure. At one point, the pop diva fought the other harem women off, echoing the age-old *Thousand and One Nights* motif – and ballet and opera plot – about competing to be the "sultan's favorite."[101]

Erener's first-prize win was hailed by her nation's journalists as an important step in the effort to get Turkey accepted into the European Union. It also had the oddity of being based upon a reenactment of some of the most stereotypical aspects of "Turkishness" in the Western mind. Matthew Gumpert (an American literary scholar resident in Turkey) proposes – plausibly – that Erener is here "playing ... willfully, and perhaps even ironically, the very role of the East once dictated by the West."[102]

A Turkish journalist offered a reading that was compatible with Gumpert's but broader:

Sertab Erener's first place victory at Eurovision broke the chains of the "traditional Muslim woman" who appears in Orientalist paintings, giving her her own dignity, and wings to fly towards freedom.[103]

Not the obvious reading – in a Western context, anyway – of what was, many observers felt, a slick reenactment of standard (and arguably misogynistic) Orientalist musical and visual clichés. But it is a reading that, one suspects, many Turks – including Sertab Erener herself – shared.

Clearly, exotic portrayals that involve a prominent, even predominant musical component, continue to proliferate. So will readings of them.

11 | Epilogue: exotic works of the past, today

To close, I return to my primary topic – Western classical or art music – but now shift the focus from composers to performers and listeners (including critics and scholars).[1] I concentrate on how exotic works of the past can remain alive and meaningful in our own day, considering (in the first two sections) the relationship of these works to musical performance today and then (in the final section) ways in which we think – or might think – about the works.

Performing exotic works

Musical exoticism has been one of the constitutive factors in the construction of "classical" concert life.[2] The musically exotic tends to be immediately attractive and also easy to indicate in a few words or a well-chosen visual image or typographic font. Not surprisingly, it has served regularly as an effective – some might say manipulative – device for marketing musical events and careers. A pianist from Spain surely increases his or her chances of getting hired elsewhere by offering to play Spanish works (Albéniz, Granados) that may feel more or less exotic to the target audiences though presumably not to the performer. Similarly, Fazıl Say, a Turkish pianist who has resided for some years in Berlin, included Mozart's Sonata in A Major K331 on his first commercial CD. Does the "Rondo alla turca" (the sonata's last movement) feel the opposite of exotic to him because it "belongs" to him? Does the movement become more exotic for a listener outside of Turkey – in the Netherlands, say – when it is played by Say? Actually, this Turkish pianist performs the "Rondo alla turca" – and everything else on the CD – pretty much the way other pianists do, though with a bracing freedom of tempo and dynamics (and occasional melodic embellishments) that might reflect (or be imagined as reflecting) his early exposure to a very different, more improvisatory musical tradition.[3]

One should not single out Spaniards or Turks. Throughout the Western musical world, many performers and groups add zip to their concerts through music that echoes, or in some way represents, an ethnic tradition that is *not* primarily his/her/their "own." American orchestras draw audiences nowadays by advertising their concerts under catch-phrases that are often geographical or ethnic: "Russian Jewels," "Land of the Midnight Sun," "Wonders of the East" (which can mean anything from Rimsky-Korsakov's *Sheherazade* to a rather recondite piece by Takemitsu), "Gypsy Fiddling," and, of course, "España!" or "Olé!"[4]

The place of exotic works in Western musical culture can also extend beyond the concert hall and opera house. Certain of *Carmen*'s musical numbers – and a few favorite visual images (such as a tight red and black dress, or a rose held between the teeth) – pop up in venues that make lesser aesthetic claims, such as ice-skating competitions (with the "role" of Carmen taken by female contestants from China or Germany). For many years, the children's TV show *Sesame Street* featured a stop-action animated short in which a singing orange, with big lips, long lashes (flower petals, actually), and the flair of a true diva, performed Bizet's Habanera – to great applause and cheers. The libretto of *Carmen*, and often much of the music, has been reworked by film directors of wildly different proclivities, including Peter Brook, Carlos Saura, Francesco Rosi, Robert Townsend (a "hip-hopera," starring Beyoncé Knowles), and Senegalese director Joseph Gaye (or Gaï) Ramaka.

Ketèlbey's orchestral piece *In a Persian Market* (see Chapter 9) provides an example of how a lightweight exotic piece (one that did not die away with other paraphernalia of the British Empire) has remained widely lovable. It also demonstrates the new lives that some exotic pieces can enjoy (or suffer, depending on one's taste). On a recent day, at least five video or audio versions of *Persian Market* were posted on YouTube.com. Two were videos of live concert performances by (different) harmonica orchestras in Singapore. The instruments that these harmonica-ists (students, mostly) play are of various sizes, in order to approximate the original orchestral range, from sweet high melody to tromping bass line. (Harmonica orchestras, sometimes with a hundred players, have been a distinctive phenomenon in Hong Kong and other parts of East Asia since the 1930s. Perhaps the instrument appeals to local sensibilities because of its similarity in tone production to traditional free-reed instruments, such as the Chinese *sheng*.) By the time I viewed the two *Persian Market* videos, each of them had been visited by thousands of viewers worldwide in just a few months and, as comments in the user-blog suggested, had been greatly enjoyed.[5] Ketèlbey's piece came to Singapore – perhaps in versions for military-style band – with the British, who ruled this tiny (but now economically powerful) nation from the mid-1860s to 1959.

It is hard to know to what degree the players – and YouTube viewers – associate the music of *Persian Market* with the Middle East. Ketèlbey himself intended the "black-note" pentatonic tune in the middle to be sung by a chorus (or the orchestra members), using the words "Back-sheesh, back-sheesh, Allah! Emp-shi!" ("Give alms, alms, for God's sake, and hurry it up!"). One suspects that the music in this passage feels somehow "like our own" to many of those players and audience members in Singapore. After all, many East and Southeast Asian musical traditions (e.g., village Malayan *kertok*) and many pop songs of the region make use of the same five-pitch collection. In any case, the harmonica orchestras on YouTube play the tune but do not sing; the performances thereby suppress the work's most audible reference to the Middle East.

In early 2007, Ketèlbey's *Persian Market* gained yet another life when a 1950s Latin-jazz version (mentioned in Chapter 9) was revived as background music in humorous television ads for the TomTom global positioning system for automobiles. Someone must have thought that the arrangement's prominent use of a pair of bongos (though strongly associated with Cuba) would help listeners remember the name of the product, which is of course another kind of drum from the Americas. (The name TomTom, according to the corporation's website, was chosen because Native American drums "have always been used for ... sending messages over many miles."[6]) In addition, Ketèlbey's opening tune – whose steady repeated notes he intended to indicate the steps of the camels in an approaching caravan – suits the ad's visual images of a driver winding down the road toward a nearly elusive goal.[7]

Certain exotically tinted songs and opera arias have been reworked time and time again. Mention was made (in Chapter 10) of new uses for the Flower Duet from *Lakmé* in airline ads and (a moment ago) for Bizet's Habanera. The latter, we may recall, derives from a Cuban-style song by Iradier, "El arreglito." Another Iradier song, "La paloma" (*c.* 1857) went on, without any help from Bizet, to become a permanent world-wide hit, one that gets perpetually transformed yet remains ever recognizable.[8] *La paloma* is often performed instrumentally, or sung to new words (as by Elvis Presley in the film *Blue Hawaii*, 1961, whose soundtrack album was a best-seller for over two years). Some of the original words are still widely used by Spanish-speaking musicians and by international stars such as Nana Mouskouri. The first strophe and the final one (less often heard) make clear that *La paloma* was, from the outset, an exotic song about Cuba. (The island was one of the chief holdings in what, by the nineteenth century, remained of the Spanish Empire.)

Iradier was born and lived most of his life in Spain – he taught at the Madrid Conservatory – but also traveled to Paris, London, and, in the 1850s, Cuba. He published *La paloma* in Madrid in 1857 and soon thereafter in Paris. The subtitle *canción americana* possibly indicates that Iradier was here arranging an actual Cuban song.[9] The text seems cobbled from several disparate sources. A sailor or traveler (most likely Spanish) declares his love across the open sea to his *chinita* (back in Spain, apparently), whom he hopes to marry. Iradier throws in some verbal local color by having the protagonist use a native (non-Spanish) term – common in the Caribbean and Mexico – to refer to the "lovely native woman" (*una linda guachinanga*) who attracted him as he was leaving Havana.[10] In the final strophe, he indulges in a more extensive fantasy of having a family with the Cuban woman, referring to "fifteen little native kids" (*quince guachinangitos*). The music of *La paloma* is marked throughout by the same African-derived syncopation – based on triplets against duplets and dotted rhythms – that occurs in Iradier's *El arreglito* (and hence in Bizet's Habanera).[11]

This proto-jazzy rhythm – Cuban musicians call it *tresillo* – has surely contributed to the long survival of *La paloma* and its ready adaptation by so many Western pop, rock, and jazz artists. The German firm Trikont has put out a four-volume CD anthology containing a hundred recordings of *La paloma*. Their website claims to have located more than 2,000, which is impressive even once one realizes (from the CDs) that no performance was too odd to be included. In addition to masterful performances by the operatic mezzo Conchita Supervia and by the Lecuona Cuban Boys, there are readings – tastes will differ here! – by the Paul Whiteman Orchestra (with Bing Crosby whistling rather than singing), the band of the French Garde Républicaine (*c.* 1899), a Viennese railway-workers' band (1996), an Estonian women's chorus, an unidentified harpist (female) in the Paris Métro (who sometimes sings along, wordlessly), a parrot named Jaco (from an East German television broadcast), an astonishing Finnish comedian, the darkly ironic German "alternative" group "Ich schwitze nie" ("I don't sweat") singing words of doom about shipwreck and death (they do the tune in the minor mode), and the noted Chinese *zheng* player Jiao Jin-Hai.[12]

In the highly standardized world of serious concerts, even tiny departures from the published score can help freshen a well-known exotic work. Sir Thomas Beecham's 1957 recording of Rimsky-Korsakov's *Sheherazade* is renowned for the wind players' (seemingly) spontaneous shifts of mood and pacing in their solo passages. The Royal Philharmonic's bassoonist, Gwydion Brooke, brings the *Thousand and One Nights*' beggar-prince to life in movement 2 through a lovable rhythmic quirkiness absent in more blandly literal performances.

Yet toying with agogic accents and rubato sometimes does not seem enough when a piece has become overfamiliar. The noted fortepianist Andreas Staier comments with mock despair (in the booklet to a 2004 Mozart recording):

What is one to do with a movement like the "Rondo alla turca"? It is well-nigh omnipresent, from Acapulco to Tokyo, and we can no longer say whether we really like it or not. We know it so much better than we would like to, and associate it with dreary hotel lobbies or check-in queues [at airports]. Mozart would probably have been ... shocked by the triumphal progress around the world of his little ethnic showpiece.[13]

Staier responds to the challenge with an imaginatively composed arrangement of the movement: he plays material in a different octave (and hand) than Mozart asks, adds countermelodies of his own, tweaks the harmony, and inserts a wild cadenza.

The Liszt Hungarian Rhapsodies have been repeatedly enriched in a somewhat different manner – by reconnecting them to Gypsy-derived performance traditions. Numerous Hungarian folk ensembles (e.g., Lakatos) have remade the Rhapsodies delightfully. Noted symphonic conductors Leopold Stokowski, Antal Doráti, and Ivan Fischer (the latter two were born and trained in Hungary) have made orchestral recordings in which some harp parts are transferred "back" to the cimbalom (the instrument that the harp part was meant to imitate) and certain solo passages for violin or clarinet are added or embroidered in typical Gypsy style. Such alterations are (in a broad sense) true to Liszt's own well-documented habit of playing the Rhapsodies quite differently on different occasions.

There are times where reworking a "classical" piece can spill over into serious misrepresentation. *Sacred Bridges*, a widely hailed 2005 CD by the King's Singers and Sarband (a Turkish-music group), contains sixteenth-century French and Swiss settings of biblical psalms (two by Claude Goudimel, two from the Genevan Psalter) performed in a Turkish manner, with typically Middle Eastern portamenti in the voice, accompaniment by *oud, kanun, darbuka*, and so on. (Some Hebrew psalm-settings, by the early seventeenth-century Jewish composer Salamone Rossi of Mantua, are also sung.) In the booklet essay, the founder-director of Sarband, Vladimir Ivanoff, makes proud claims for his project's historical accuracy:

For thousands of years, the biblical Psalter has been the liturgical "heart" of the three main book religions: Judaism, Christianity and Islam ... Jews, Christians and Muslims sing and listen to the same songs of lament and joy, confessions of sin, hymns of praise and adoration ... Psalm settings by composers from three religions give an example of how psalms can be ... a bridge connecting human beings.[14]

The first sentences quoted are baffling: Muslims, as is well known, have their own liturgy, based on recitations from the Qur'an.[15] The Goudimel and other Christian psalm settings are included on this recording because the performers have substituted for the French words some Turkish verse translations that were made in the seventeenth century by a Polish Huguenot, Woyciech Bobowski, living in Constantinople. Bobowski had been taken captive by Crimean Tatars and, once in the Ottoman court, had converted to Islam. In this tolerant atmosphere, Bobowski (who eventually took the Turkish name Ali Ufki) encouraged understanding between Christians and Muslims by translating into Turkish the versified psalm versions that he knew. (Another of his projects was a translation of the Bible into Turkish.)

It is not inconceivable that Bobowski's translations of the Genevan Psalter have been used at times by the (never very numerous) Protestants in Turkey. But Bobowski/Ufki surely never had any illusions that Muslims would use his psalter in their worship services, much less that biblical psalms (in any version) would become – as conductor Ivanoff misguidedly claims – "the liturgical 'heart' of ... Islam." Ivanoff's post-9/11 attempt to bring the three "religions of the book" together under the umbrella of the Psalms is, from the standpoint of the history of Islam, spectacularly ignorant, even if the performances are accomplished and intriguing.

I might note that two other international performing groups – the Pera Ensemble (consisting mainly of Turks living in Germany) and the ethnically mixed United States group Dünya – are likewise currently performing the French and Swiss psalm-settings with Bobowski's Turkish words to promote cross-cultural understanding. Both groups avoid the inflated and misleading rhetoric that surely helped Ivanoff's group receive media attention, concert dates, and a World Village record contract.

The afterlife of exotic stage works

Works for the stage (operas, musicals), whether exotic or not, are, by nature, open to the revising (and, with luck, revitalizing rather than gutting) of their premises through new sets and costumes, cuts and additions, ironic delivery, and so on. Still, sometimes very little is needed, even decades later, to make an exotic stage work "come across." (This must surely be the case in

Figure 11.1 Carmen (mezzo-soprano Miao Qing), by singing the Séguedille, persuades Don José (tenor Lin Jin Yuan) to untie the rope and let her go free. From a performance on 1 January 1982 in Beijing, only months after the Chinese Communist Party officially denounced (27 June 1981) the Great Proletarian Cultural Revolution, which had banned the performance of most Western art music. A summary of Carmen's words is projected on the side panel. (Photo source unknown; from Roy, *Bizet*.)

Epilogue: exotic works of the past, today 319

places where a work is being seen, belatedly, for the first time, as in the case of the historic 1982 performances in Beijing of Bizet's opera *Carmen* – see Fig. 11.1.) A 1996 production of the 1951 musical *The King and I* (featuring Donna Murphy and Lou Diamond Phillips) seems not to have done anything wildly different from the 1951 original or the 1956 film, yet managed to tap America's still-ongoing tension about sexual relations between people of different racial/ethnic groups. *New York Times* literary critic Margo Jefferson reported her reaction:

An ebullient polka, "Shall We Dance" heralds one of theater's most thrilling moments of East–West eros.

When the play opened in an America far more at ease with racial segregation than with any kind of miscegenation, the shock must have been overwhelming. Even now, 45 years later, the audience happily held its breath when the handsome brown-skinned Asian king placed his hand on the waist of the fair-skinned, hoop-skirted English lady.

That's the thing about "The King and I": there are so many fantasies to enter and exit from; so many characters whose skin you can move in and out of.[16]

Theater critic Vincent Canby agreed about this same duet-and-dance: "Has there ever been a polka of such sublime high spirits and emotional complexity?"[17]

There were also complaints of a type not much heard in 1951. The show's leading male role, in particular, had become problematic. Margo Jefferson continues: "The King ... [is] a virile, willful conqueror who is also naïve and at times buffoonish. He is a child's portrait of a king really, a figure meant to be looked up to and patronized simultaneously."[18] Should the performer of the role soften the portrayal of this exotic dictator? Or overdo it, as if between quotation marks? Should a director rework the whole show so that the king does not have Lun Tha executed? Should the work be relocated to some other (more recent?) situation of cultural domination? Should the work be shelved for a generation or two? This last solution might cheer some people in Thailand, where, for years at a time, the government has – I am tempted to say understandably – banned the film version (starring Yul Brynner and Deborah Kerr) as insulting to Thais and their monarchy.[19]

Behind these questions lie some more basic ones. Can one reinterpret a work, through performance, in a way that enables it to speak – even if somewhat differently than before – to audiences in an era with presumably very different assumptions about what Rudyard Kipling hailed as the "white man's burden"? Does an attempt at a "critical" performance – of works such as *The King and I* and *Madama Butterfly* – kill much of the pleasure that the work can give? Is this the only way of saving it: to interrogate its givens, so that audiences/listeners end up regarding it with historical and/or ironic distance? And, if so, is there a risk that this approach might cause the audience to feel morally superior to the work's creators and, worse, might allow them not to confront their own unspoken prejudices?

Such questions seem worth posing with regard to recent productions of many operas, exotic and non-exotic. Especially in European and certain "progressive" American opera houses (e.g., Santa Fe and Glimmerglass), stage directors have, by means of new sets, costumes, and stage action, placed the evening's work in a different location or chronological era, or made it ethnically unspecific (hence, as is often claimed, "universal" – see Fig. 11.2), and/or held its premises up to a searching critical light. Even in relatively traditional productions, a strong-willed and determined singer has sometimes put a distinctly different spin on a role. Both situations ("progressive" productions and "strong" readings of a role) clearly feel a work – or traditional approaches to it – to be outdated or noxious and in need of simultaneous commentary.[20] But precisely *what* is felt to be problematic is often not made explicit. Instead, the principle of creative freedom is usually invoked, perhaps to deflect criticism of the production's own critique.

The noted Spanish mezzo-soprano Teresa Berganza was, by contrast, admirably forthright when, in the mid-1970s, she set down her thoughts about Bizet's *Carmen*. Pernicious anti-Spanish prejudices, she felt, had distorted previous productions. Berganza insisted that Carmen is "not a prostitute: she works in a factory to earn enough to keep herself and save sufficient money to enable her to visit her mother."[21] (Actually, the sole mention of Carmen's mother in the libretto comes in the context of some outrageous lies that Carmen – in spoken dialogue, often cut – feeds Don José about being, like him, a Spaniard from the Basque country and not a Gypsy at all.) Berganza's recorded performance of the role (1978) is musically exquisite and relatively free of the usual brazenly seductive attitudes. Berganza has largely de-exoticized the role. What is left, though, is not wholly coherent. Would the hot-headed Don José have been drawn to this well-behaved, vocally refined, emotionally contained individual?

Mezzo Shirley Verrett did not write an essay, but she puts forth some fascinating readings of another exotic heroine, Dalila, in two relatively traditional videos of *Samson et Dalila* made only a year apart. Verrett's San Francisco performance (1980) follows the libretto straightforwardly. After the Philistine soldiers blind Samson, Dalila stands over her now-abject lover and raises her arms in triumph. At Covent Garden (1981), Dalila grins

Figure 11.2 American mezzo-soprano Marianne Cornetti as the imprisoned Azucena in Act 4 of San Diego Opera's 2006 production of Verdi's *Il trovatore*. The costumer has here deprived Azucena of all marks of ethnic specificity. See, by contrast, the early twentieth-century costume for Azucena in Figure 7.1. Still, the flames by which the 2006 Azucena can warm herself – a touch added by the stage director – are redolent of the Gypsy campfire in Act 2 and of the burning pyre that consumed Azucena's mother. (Photo © Ken Howard.)

maliciously as Samson begins to yield just before "Mon coeur." But, after the soldiers steal into the house and blind the Hebrew warrior, Dalila steps out of the house, throws her body against the outer wall, and averts her gaze in some combination of (we gather) exhaustion, horror, and remorse.[22] The Covent Garden interpretation goes against the grain of the text, and seems calculated to undercut standard exoticist stereotypes of "Oriental" (and especially Middle Eastern) women as manipulative and heartless. But, as with Berganza's Carmen, a larger plausibility suffers. In the final act, Dalila has to taunt Samson cruelly. Verrett does this so effectively that a viewer may well feel confused at the flip-flopping. Or the viewer may conclude that Dalila's Act 2 moment of normal human feeling (invented by Verrett and/or the stage director, Elijah Moshinsky) soon vanished, and that her essential nature as a "true" Eastern woman came to the fore in the end.

Stage directors have helped us rethink – or else have distorted, depending on one's view – a number of exotic operas. Rameau's *Les Incas du Pérou* is sensitively handled in the DVD of *Les Indes galantes* conducted by William

Christie. But, in the final *entrée* of *Les Indes* (entitled *Les sauvages*), the choreographer treats the long central number, "Forêts paisibles," in a joke-y manner. For Rameau and his librettist Fuzelier, "Forêts paisibles" was a hymn proclaiming the superiority of the simple life to the "deceitful enticements" of civilization. (The music is an elaboration of Rameau's harpsichord piece "Les sauvages" – Ex. 5.2.) But the choreography (by Spanish-born Bianca Li) combines caricaturishly exaggerated powwow stomping, awkward movements imitative of a turkey (the bird is a prominent emblem in the set design), and shoulder movements more appropriate to today's dance clubs. Such choices suggest embarrassment. Perhaps the plot premise of *Les sauvages* – that the native tribes of North America are more sincere and loving than Europeans – now strikes some people as naive and condescending. But one may wonder what is to be gained by drowning the work's own attitude – a valid, even progressive cultural view for the 1730s – with more recent and much less thoughtful exotic stereotypes (and with distracting non-exotic features, such as the 1990s dance moves).

"Turkish" operas present a particular problem nowadays. Mozart's Osmin (in *Die Entführung aus dem Serail*), for example, is unquestionably nasty, and his nastiness is understood as tied up with his adherence to real or supposed Turkish customs of the day (such as a man's forcing himself upon a woman or threatening to impale his Christian adversaries). We need to be brought to laugh at certain of his excesses and character flaws – such as his secretly enjoying wine, despite the strictures of the Qur'an – or else the opera does not work.[23] Yet to laugh at Osmin for his graceless womanizing or his religious hypocrisy smacks today of ridiculing the large cultural region and the major world religion that he so insists on representing.

The obvious and currently fashionable solution is to do something that I briefly proposed with regard to *The King and I*: change the sets and costumes of the work so that its action unfolds in some other place (or time and place) – or in a kind of universal/mythical/dreamlike space. One such solution was adopted for a production of Handel's *Orlando* that was used at Glimmerglass (where I saw it in 2003) and New York City Opera (2005). A plot that centers, in large part, on a Chinese princess (Angelica) and a Muslim warrior from Northern Africa (Medoro) lost much of its specificity when the whole opera was transferred to a place-neutral forest. The costumes became largely European. (Angelica wore a high-waisted burgundy ball gown, as if she had stepped out of a Jane Austen novel or Tolstoy's *War and Peace*.) When Orlando recovers his sanity at the end and realizes he must return to battle against the Saracens, most people in the audience probably had no idea who the Saracens were, where they had been during the rest of the opera (they had been represented – or, rather, not represented – by Medoro), nor that a centuries-old confrontation of Christianity and Islam (a "clash of civilizations," to use a problematic phrase that is much-debated today) was even being referred to.[24]

Peter Sellars is widely hailed (and derided) for the practice of relocating operas (exotic and not) to other times and places. Mozart composed about half of a Turkish-harem opera, *Zaide*, in around 1779, and then abandoned the project. In 2006, Sellars revived the work, setting it in the sweatshops of the modern industrial world. The media quoted Sellars extensively about how Mozart and his librettist were plainly opposed to unfair labor practices:

For Mr. Sellars ... the slavery in "Zaide" suggests the evils of globalization. The production's three-level set, by George Tsypin, is a group of cages where sweatshop workers toil at sewing machines [which first came into wide use in the 1840s–50s] and sleep on the floor, triple-locked in by Soliman. After the escaped slaves are captured, the staging grows darker, with Soliman and Osmin brandishing guns, and Zaide singing her "Trostlos schluchzet Philomele" aria while handcuffed to a railing.[25]

More extreme was a widely reported 2004 Berlin production of Mozart's *Die Entführung*. In the hands of Spanish stage director Calixto Bieito, the Pasha's palace becomes (predictably) a nineteenth-century European brothel. While Constanze sings one of the grandest of Mozart's arias, "Martern aller Arten" – in which she eloquently refuses to give in to the Pasha's threats – Osmin tortures one of the brothel's prostitutes in ways that the Pasha presumably has in mind for Constanze. Osmin forces the woman into sexual activity, chokes her, kills her, and cuts off her nipples and tries to hand them to Constanze, who (rather sensibly) vomits.

Objections to Bieito's production came fast and furious from critics, enraged audience members, even one corporate sponsor. The aspects most deplored were the added sexual acts and violence and the systematic removal of humor and hope. At the end, the Berlin Constanze does not take the Pasha's offer to sail to freedom in Spain with her Belmonte but instead shoots the Pasha and then herself, in utter contradiction of every word and note in the libretto and score.[26]

I might suggest a likely (and unnoted) motivation for Bieito's drastic reworking of this Mozart masterpiece. In addition to removing all Enlightenment optimism, he removed, as much as is possible without actual musical surgery, all marks of Turkishness. The sets and costumes, according to published production photos (including of the "Martern" scene) and various published reviews, showed no hint of the Middle East. Interestingly, Bieito seems not to have cut or altered Osmin's virulently Islamicist and anti-Christian/Western remarks. But, considering all the other ways in which the staging contravened the music and words, those particular lines probably passed more or less unnoticed. In a more traditional production, Osmin's remarks clash dissonantly with the work's attempts at comedy, causing the listener to think about his or her own mixed feelings about what has been presented. Which of these two approaches, I wonder, constitutes a more stimulating present-day response to a vivid, problematic work from the past?

Another solution to the challenge posed by works that are filled with exotic stereotypes now widely felt to be demeaning is one that I likewise mentioned regarding *The King and I*: refrain from performing it. Certain productions of *West Side Story* have been scuttled – or quietly discouraged from ever happening – because of the objection, or anticipated objection, that the work perpetuates largely negative stereotypes (especially in the song "America") of life in Puerto Rico and in the New York *barrio*.[27] And this is the case even though, as literary historian Frances Negrón-Muntaner reports:

I witnessed in screening *West Side Story* to young Puerto Ricans in the Philadelphia *barrio* during the mid-1990s, that teenagers repeatedly affirmed that the film was not racist, for "that's [gangs, violence, death] how it is."[28]

Negrón-Muntaner adds that *West Side Story* has, indeed, been a source of shame among "more educated AmerRicans" (i.e., Americans of Puerto Rican origin) as well as among certain public figures. Pop singer Ricky Martin, born and raised in San Juan, has repeatedly rejected suggestions that he have a role – Bernardo? – in a (largely hypothetical) new film version. "It's kicking my culture," he said in interview. "And I'm not going to feed that."[29] At the same time, notes Negrón-Muntaner, the film version gave and continues to give Puerto Ricans in America a point of reference against which to define themselves, and has even contributed to public recognition of Puerto Ricans as a "distinctly American ethnic group" with its own coherent, if conflicted, history, culture, and strivings.[30]

As for *Madama Butterfly*, an important 2003 production by the Vienna Festival was hailed for the way it "stripped away all of the traditional, stereotypical glop – fluttering fans, elaborate kimonos, cherry blossoms, simpering little 'Japanese' shuffle steps – and instead offered an intimate, intense work of conversational theater." Reportedly, the characterizations and dramatic tensions came through all the more vividly.[31] Susan McClary has recently proposed two other solutions, both more extreme than Vienna's: either shelve the work or intentionally distort and creatively misrepresent it. And not just distort it with subtle re-emphasis: "Pointing up Pinkerton's loutishness – far from undermining the story – only reinforces it ... The only way of breaking the spell this opera has cast over the West's notions of Asian women is to take it apart limb from limb."[32] McClary's solution would be to create a new work (about which she, unfortunately, offers no details) that might "speak forcefully against the patriarchal and imperialist assumptions that frame the character [of Cio-Cio-San in Puccini's opera]."[33]

Pondering exotic works as they are

I would propose that another way to keep a problematic exotic work alive, and to interact with it in a worthy manner, is not to rip it apart and rewrite it to suit our own ideas, nor to refuse to perform it, but to get to know it better, contend with its original context and messages, and think about its implications for today.

To do this, we might profitably return to a crucial hermeneutical distinction raised at various points in the book, the distinction between allegory/metaphor and representation:

- How transparent was and is the exotic veil that the composer and his/her collaborators have cast over their musical work?

The question is a crucial one, given the high cultural status that certain instrumental works and, perhaps especially, certain great operatic tragedies – for example, Verdi's *Aida* and Puccini's *Madama Butterfly* – achieved in their own day and maintain today.

One plausible answer is that exotic settings were/are often taken allegorically. Some people knew/know to read "through" the supposed setting (ancient Egypt, eighth-century Baghdad, nineteenth-century Japan, 1970s Vietnam) to more universal human issues and conflicts, or – as we noted in regard to Handel's *Belshazzar* and Verdi's *Aida* (Chapters 5 and 8) – to political debates and cultural issues contemporary with the work itself.

But another answer – as suggested above by McClary (and Ricky Martin) – is that the surface meaning of the allegory has continued to operate separately from any deeper meaning. Exotic works have created and reinforced various limited, distorted or indeed entirely fictive and self-serving (e.g., colonialist/imperialist) Western stereotypes of foreign cultures. With regard to images of gender and race in movies and television, cultural critic bell hooks notes:

> Most of us, no matter how sophisticated our strategies of critique and intervention, are usually seduced, at least for a time, by the images we see on the screen. They have power over us and we have no power over them.[34]

Many of the various stage and concert works discussed in this book, though now a century old or older, have demonstrated a continuing vitality and a lasting ability to leave an impress on the public imagination. This is particularly clear with regard to opera and other dramatic genres (musicals, films). My own conceptions of Japan remain indelibly marked by my having repeatedly seen (live or on video) and listened to – entire or in excerpts – *The Mikado* and, even more so, *Madama Butterfly*. Television news shots of skyscrapers and subway crowds in Tokyo have never succeeded in convincing me that the country is not full of (as if just outside the camera's frame) groups of tiptoeing maidens with parasols; or that, in Nagasaki today, a young woman cannot be seen awaiting, in her little house (with sliding-panel walls) that overlooks the port, the return of an unworthy American man.

I am not alone. In Nagasaki, the historic home called the "Madama Butterfly House" – actually it was owned by the influential late nineteenth-century Scottish merchant Thomas Blake Glover – is a tourist destination for visitors from the world around. Beginning in 1989 (in London's West End; 1991 on Broadway), the somewhat tired *Butterfly*-derived images of Asia and Asians in many Westerners' heads have been given new energy by *Miss Saigon*, a stage work frankly modeled on Puccini's opera in crucial respects of character, incident, and musical manner.[35] Young singers have taken to their heart this updated version of the story. Voice teachers report to me in some frustration that singers coming to audition for lessons often seem to know only the same few quasi-"legit" numbers, and that prominent among them are two from this show: one in which the Vietnamese woman Kim voices her (deluded) belief that her beloved GI, Chris, will return to her; the other in which she declares her self-sacrificial devotion to her young son.

Such an attraction to limited stereotypes of other places and peoples is perhaps inevitable. Russian soprano Marina Mescheriakova recalls her surprise at visiting the United States for the first time: "All I had known about the country came from the movies. I actually expected to see cowboys in the street."[36] Our need to be reassured by familiar images, however fallacious they may be, seems to surpass our curiosity about how things really are. Our beliefs are determined by cultural forces; but there seems to be a general tendency to cling to them even when reality is staring us in the face.[37] Besides, mythical, phantasmagoric imaginings – however inaccurate by normal standards of evidence – can be real in their own way, telling truths of a different sort.

Confronting the stereotypical images of the past may be at once (historically) honest and (for the world today) beneficial. As Michael Pisani pointed out (see Chapter 4 above), "putting a frame around [a stereotype] ... helps us understand why such stereotypes exist in the first place, and perhaps even to recognize, when we next encounter them, their effects on us and on society as a whole."[38]

How to combine all of this into a theoretically sound critique and appreciation of musical and other art works evoking the Other remains a challenge, and one worth tackling from many different angles.[39] Such a critique/appreciation of musical exoticism, to be adequate and useful, will maintain two concepts in a state of creative tension:

- On the one hand, the exotic(izing) work is essentially a Western cultural product; the work is largely irrelevant to the exotic locale being evoked, and that locale (in its actual, lived features) is largely irrelevant to the work.
- On the other hand, the exotic(izing) work has the power – through its wide dissemination, its often high cultural status, and its powerfully worked-out aesthetic features – to reflect and even shape the attitude and behavior of Westerners toward the non-Western world, of big city folk to their own domestic Others, and so on (including the reverse: America perceived abroad, rightly or wrongly, as a nation of B. F. Pinkertons). The values and images in an exotic work can be insular and damaging, but they can also sometimes push the listener/audience – directly, or through negative example – toward tolerance and a progressive spirit of cross-cultural understanding: the enlightened "cosmopolitanism" advocated by Kwame Anthony Appiah as the best alternative to the deceptive, destructive lures of provincialism and cultural chauvinism.[40]

I propose that we accept these two concepts – the autonomy, and the strong consequentiality, of musical exoticism – as irreconcilable yet equally valid. And I urge that, at the risk of intellectual messiness (or is it richness?), we take care not to privilege one over the other.

Notes

Introduction

1. Smith, "Elsewhere," 96.
2. Meyerbeer's *L'Africaine* and Ravel's *Chansons madécasses*.
3. On European perceptions of different world regions and musics, see, for example, Agawu, *Representing*; Zon, *Music*, 99–104, 179–206; Agnew, *Enlightenment*, 4–7, 73–119; and Bloechl, "Protestant" and *Native*.
4. Gluck's delightful *Le cinesi* (1754), for example, presents amorous intrigues, and much play-acting, among four young Chinese aristocrats: three women, plus a man who has recently returned from Europe.
5. See Chapters 6 and 7.
6. For reasons of space, I have not reprinted here my extended article on *Samson et Dalila* or my two on *Aida*, but do briefly summarize some of their findings.
7. See, for example, Senici, *Landscape*, and Pisani, *Imagining*.
8. Details about recordings are sometimes given if the focus is on a particular performance or if the work is less well known.
9. The Symphony Orchestra of India was founded in Mumbai (Bombay) in 2006. The Tehran Symphony Orchestra is nearly sixty years old but has been significantly challenged by recent anti-Western currents in Iran.
10. On Japanese melodies in *Madama Butterfly*, see Chapter 8.
11. Bohrer, *Orientalism*, 15–17.
12. Foucault, *Archeology*, 4–12 and (in appendix) 216, 229.
13. On individual listening and interpretation, see Cook, *Music*, 8–9, 143–52, and Abbate, "Music."
14. Botstein, "Listening," and Rabinowitz, "Chord."
15. Hepokoski, "Beethoven."
16. Kallberg, "Hearing"; Milewski, "Chopin's Mazurkas"; and Kallberg, "Arabian."
17. Scare quotes can get out of hand, but to avoid them entirely might mangle my meaning, as here.
18. Bohrer, *Orientalism*, 36. For a related argument, more broadly, about "how" (rather than "what") a piece means, see Agawu, *Playing*, 5.

1 Music, the world, and the critic

1. Said, *World*, 34–35.
2. Ibid., 35, 39. Cf. the concept of a "horizon of expectation," in Jauss, *Toward*.

3. Instrumental jazz raises similar interpretive problems.
4. Hanslick, *On the Musically Beautiful*; Stravinsky, *Poetics*; Locke, "Absolute" and "Program"; and Locke, "Doing."
5. Subotnik, *Deconstructive*, 158–59.
6. See Taruskin, "Speed."
7. It also participates in religious/social rituals in various traditional cultures, for example ceremonial drumming in sub-Saharan Africa, women's lamenting chants in Finland, and gamelan-accompanied shadow-puppet plays on the island of Bali.
8. Locke, "Doing," 344–51.
9. On other streams of music that can fairly be described as "aesthetically elaborate and demanding" (e.g., jazz or the Hindustani *rāga* tradition), see Locke, "Music," 165–66.
10. Said, *Culture*, 18–19, 32, 51, 66–68, 114, 125, 146, 194, 259, 279, 318, 336.
11. Ibid., 96.
12. Newman, *Apologia*, 15–16. Newman rocked the Church of England by converting to Catholicism in mid-career.
13. See, for example, Lane, *Arabian*.
14. The Comtesse de Gasparin (late 1840s), quoted in Gradenwitz, "Félicien David," 505; Eugène Fromentin (1848), quoted in Brancour, *Félicien David*, 110; and Joseph Reinach (1879), quoted in El Nouty, *Proche-Orient*, 149.
15. Another wide-ranging book – Oesch, *et al.*, *Europäische* – contains essays and specialist studies, some dealing with other topics than exoticism entirely.
16. For example, Whaples, *Exoticism*; Becker, *Couleur*; Fiske, *Scotland*; Schatt, *Exotik*; Schmitt, *Exotismus*; Betzwieser, *Exotismus*; Bellman, *The* style hongrois; Heidemann, *Luigi Cherubini*; Lo, *"Turandot"*; Born and Hesmondhalgh, *Western*; Sheppard, *Revealing*; Gramit, "Orientalism"; Pisani, *Imagining*; Loya, *"Verbunkos"*; and Clayton and Zon, *Music*.
17. Mandelli, "Esotismo."
18. The Turkish segment of Campra's work continued to be revived as late as 1775. Baker's recording of "Sous le ciel," with the male vocal group Comedian Harmonists, can be heard on the *Chansons coloniales et exotiques* collection, two CDs, EPM 983312. Regarding Turkey's inclusion in *Europe galante*: the Turkish region known as Rumelia has for centuries been considered part of Europe, not Asia.
19. Furthermore, influential music aestheticians and analysts, such as Eduard Hanslick (in the 1860s–80s) and Heinrich Schenker (until his death in 1935), campaigned for decades against Wagner's works or at least his categorical insistence on the supremacy of his operas over instrumental music.
20. Weber, "Beyond."
21. Taruskin, "Speed," 192.
22. There were many notable exceptions, of course – often quite different from each other (e.g., Edward Lowinsky, Georg Knepler, and the ethnomusicologist Bruno Nettl).

23. See Chapter 5.
24. Bellman, ed., *Exotic*, including chapters (e.g., by Mary Hunter, Michael Pisani, James Parakilas, and Richard Taruskin) that have gone on to be cited and used by many other scholars.
25. On Bellman's preface, see Henson review; and Head, "Musicology." See also Bellman, "'Noble'."
26. Taylor, *Beyond*, 10.
27. Especially Whaples, *Exoticism*; Betzwieser, *Exotismus*; and Born and Hesmondhalgh, *Western*.

2 Questions of value

1. Filippi, *Musica*, 365–66.
2. Tiersot, *Chanson*, 531.
3. Cooke, "'East'," 280.
4. Leprohon, "Esotismo," col. 1611.
5. de Van, "Fin de siècle," 77.
6. Dahlhaus, *Nineteenth-Century*, 306. See Locke, "Doing," 351–52.
7. Further on exoticism and nationalism, see Chapters 4 and 6.
8. Wagner, "Über die Anwendung," 182.
9. Wagner, "Über das Dichten," 148. Cf. Bellman, "'Noble'," 49–50.
10. Wagner may have had in mind certain dance-band conductors of Jewish origin, such as Johann Strauss, Jr. (who composed a fair number of Hungarian-style pieces), and Márk Rózsavölgyi (originally named Moshe – or Motek – Rosental). *Verbunkos*-style tunes by Rózsavölgyi ended up in Liszt's Hungarian Rhapsodies Nos. 8 and 12.
11. Cf. Goldmark, *Tunes*, 110–12, also 119 (*Rhapsody in Rivets*, 1941).
12. Debussy, untitled article of 1 April 1901, in *Monsieur Croche*, 26.
13. Schoenberg, "Folkloristic," 162.
14. Schenker, *Counterpoint*, 1:28–29.
15. Schoenberg, "Folkloristic," 162–63.
16. Boulez, "Oriental," 421.
17. Reich, *Writings* (2002), 70–71. I have corrected the apparent error "with own's sound."
18. *Ibid.*, 148.
19. Dahlhaus, *Nineteenth-Century*, 306 and the two-part Ex. 57.
20. *Le Moniteur universel*, 19 September 1800, cited in Bras, "Révolution," [8].
21. Monelle, "Scottish," 89–90. Monelle himself is, in other writings, a prominent advocate of research on musical semiotics.
22. Ratner, *Classic*, 1–30 (esp. 9: "characteristic figures," "subjects for musical discourse").
23. Leprohon, "Esotismo," col. 1611.
24. It "scants" them: Said, *Orientalism*, 5.

25. Said, *Orientalism*, 96: Austen's Fanny Price, a poor relation of the Bertrams, tries unsuccessfully to begin a conversation about the African slave trade with Sir Robert Bertram (who owns a plantation in Antigua) and other family members. See Austen, *Mansfield*, chapter 21 (or vol. 2, chap. 3), 135–36; see also Southam, "Silence."
26. Said, *Culture*, 131.
27. "The view of the West in Occidentalism is like the worst aspects of its counterpart, Orientalism, which strips its human targets of their humanity." Buruma and Margalit, *Occidentalism*, 10–11.
28. See MacKenzie, *Orientalism*, 1–42; Macfie, *Orientalism*; Macfie, *Orientalism: A Reader*; Irwin, *Dangerous*, 277–309; and Warraq, *Defending*.
29. MacKenzie, *Orientalism*, 71–104. Warraq similarly tracks admirative Orientalism in the arts (including music: *Defending*, 381–87).
30. Bhabha, "The Other," 66.
31. Clifford, "On Orientalism."
32. Lowe, *Critical*.
33. Loomba, *Colonialism*, 43–51; Macfie, *Orientalism: A Reader*, 217–39 (Sadik Jalal al-'Azm) and 285–98 (Aijaz Ahmad); and Bhabha, "The Other."
34. Lowe, *Critical*, 31–32; Sallis, *Sheherazade*, 13n (quoted words); Ferguson, *Subject*; and Melman, *Women's*.
35. Said, *Orientalism*, 181 (Flaubert).
36. Butler, "Orientalism," 419, 427.
37. For example, MacKenzie, *Orientalism*, 139–75.
38. Seter, "Jerusalem," 49–50.
39. Sheppard, *Revealing*, 126–41.
40. McClary, *Georges Bizet*: Carmen, 16–18, 29–43, 51–58.
41. Kramer, "Consuming."
42. Lipsitz, *Dangerous*, 61.
43. Ibid., 53.
44. "The study of world musics [including folk and popular music of Europe and America] moved out of what would nowadays be called an Orientalist stance only in the 1960s" – Slobin, *Subcultural*, 4.
45. Granade, review of Sheppard, 592, quoting Partch, *Bitter*, 252.
46. For example, McClary, "Narrative Agendas," 344.
47. Taruskin, "Speed Bumps," 191. On the electively limited and mechanical musical language(s) of *Les noces*, see Taruskin, *Stravinsky*, 2:1403 (monophony/heterophony) and 1418–20 ("rustic" anhemitonic melodies laid on top of "urbane" chromatic sliding pseudo-harmonic "automata").
48. See Keller, "Why."
49. Rosen, "From the Troubadours."
50. See Ashcroft, et al., *Empire*.
51. Appiah, *Cosmopolitanism*, p. xx.
52. Takeishi and Pacun, *Japanese*, 6, 72.

3 Exoticism with and without exotic style

1. Rosenthal, *Orientalism*, 33 (Delacroix, diary entry of 11 March 1850, regarding Mughal miniatures).
2. Scholars of visual art focus primarily on iconography (subject matter), such as wall tiles and facial features, and regularly accept that the basic style features (e.g., perspective, brushstroke) are often – though not always, as just noted – those currently prevailing in Western art. See Benjamin, *Orientalism*; on earlier art-historical studies, see Locke, "Constructing," 264, 268–69.
3. There are discussions of "satztechnische" and "harmonische Exotismen" in Korfmacher, *Exotismus*, 106–44.
4. Day-O'Connell, *Pentatonicism from the Eighteenth Century to Debussy*, 49, 48 ("musical exoticism saw only a limited practice before 1800").
5. Crispolti, "Exoticism," 297, as quoted and discussed in Bohrer, *Orientalism*, 14–18; see also Head, *Orientalism*, 88 n.49.
6. Dahlhaus, *Foundations*; Samson, "Musical"; and Taruskin, "Speed Bumps."
7. Bartoli, "Propositions," 65. See also his "L'orientalisme."
8. Bartoli, "Propositions," 67.
9. *Ibid.*, 68.
10. Bellman, "Introduction," in Bellman, *Exotic*, ix.
11. *Ibid.*
12. Betzwieser and Stegemann, "Exotismus," col. 226.
13. Huebner, review of Lindenberger, *Opera in History*, 618.
14. Other recent uses of the "Exotic Style Only" approach include Lindenberger, *Opera in History*, 160–90; Bartoli, "L'orientalisme"; Taylor, *Beyond Exoticism*, 17–72, 224–31; Head, *Orientalism*; and Scott, *From the Erotic*, 155–78, 235–39.
15. Browner, *Transposing*, 15–19.
16. Pisani, *Imagining*, 12; Browner, *Transposing*, 17–18, 133–59.
17. Bartoli, "Propositions," 65.
18. Systems of categorization other than the Peircean have been proposed. Bartoli sometimes opts for the term "figures" (a term deriving ultimately from Ciceronian rhetoric) and other times for terms from twentieth-century French semioticians (Greimas, Molinié), such as "seme" and "meaning-units" ("Propositions," 67).
19. Dahlhaus, *Nineteenth-Century*, 306.
20. I.e., identifying (to use Adorno's frequent phrase) "the state of the musical material."
21. Dahlhaus, *Nineteenth-Century*, 306.
22. On musical argument (rhetoric), see Bonds, *Wordless*, 90–118, 177–80.
23. See the lexicons of exotic stylistic features in Pisani, "Exotic," 90–100, 116–19, and (condensed) in his "'I'm an Indian'," 230–31.

24. See Day-O'Connell, *Pentatonicism*, 49–60, 84, 98, 183, and musical instances in the appendix; and Lancefield, *Hearing*, 703–39.
25. Bartoli, "Propositions," 86.
26. See, among many discussions, Head, *Orientalism*, 64–66, 117–23.
27. Hunter, "*Alla Turca*," 48–52.
28. See Kerman, *Contemplating*, 31, 59, 113–54, 225–28.
29. See the last section of Chapter 2. Among the many critiques of this bias in favor of instrumental music – which finds its extreme form in such concepts as "absolute music" and its supposedly necessary tool: "structural listening" – the following are particularly revealing: Subotnik, *Deconstructive*, 148–76, 245–52; Dell'Antonio, *Beyond*; Dahlhaus, *Idea*; Chua, *Absolute*; and, applying the critique in a practical way, Taruskin's *Oxford*.
30. Research cited and summarized in Girardi, *Puccini*, 211–20, 450–54.
31. Letter from Mozart to his father, 26 September 1781, cited in Bauman, *W. A. Mozart*, 65.
32. J. Smith, "Exoticism," 111.
33. R. L. Smith, "Elsewhere," 96.
34. Monelle, *Musical*, ix and 6–7.
35. See Locke, "Doing," 348–49.
36. On descriptive (including mimetic), expressive, and narrative techniques in word-painting and in program music, see Locke, "Program."
37. See, on Campra and Rameau, Betzwieser, *Exotismus*, 135–39, 169–70; and, on Mahler's *Das Lied* and Adler, Mitchell, *Gustav Mahler*, 62–64, 125–27, 451, 389–92, and 624–34. Betzwieser notes (*Exotismus*, 169n, 258) that the Campra tune was used even later by Favart (1742) and Gluck (1759).
38. For example, Al-Taee, "Fidelity"; Pacun, "'Thus We Cultivate'," esp. 90, 93–94; Locke, "Spanish"; and Loya, "Beyond."
39. Rimsky-Korsakov, *My Musical Life*, 292–94.
40. Some might argue that the sultan's theme is not entirely normative, given that it outlines a descending whole-tone fragment. Furthermore, its statement in bare unison might be construed as reflecting the well-known "lack of harmony" in non-European music. To these objections, one might reply that whole-tone fragments were becoming a normative option in self-consciously advanced musical style (in Liszt, and in much Russian music) and that stentorian unharmonized openings had been used non-exotically by many previous composers (e.g., Haydn, Symphony No. 104, "London," and Beethoven, Symphony No. 5). The difficulty of gaining consensus about what was (or may have been) perceived as exotic in a given time and place (and artistic context) may help explain why, as I explained in the Introduction, I define the new paradigm ("All the Music ...") as extremely broad and as *incorporating* the prevailing one ("Exotic Style Only"), not as comprising an alternative to it.

41. Rimsky-Korsakov's sea even becomes calm again (movement 4, mm. 629–40, Poco più tranquillo, beginning with *pianissimo* arpeggios in the clarinet), much as the sea does in the Third Dervish's story. Further, see Al-Taee, "Under."
42. Gramit, "Orientalism," 114. Further, see Chapter 6.
43. Betzwieser, *Exotismus*, 16–18; Betzwieser and Stegemann, "Exotismus," col. 227; Whaples, *Exoticism*, 7–9, 44–45; and Whaples, "Early," 4.
44. Hunter, "*Alla Turca* Style," 50–52.
45. A high-intensity melisma, though, tends not to be used for a text of tenderness, lament, or despair. In Baroque works – as also in Mozart, and in *primo ottocento* opera – a general distinction prevails between more-energetic and less-energetic types of melisma.
46. Schopenhauer: "Music never expresses a given phenomenon but, rather, the inner essence, the in-itself, of any phenomenon ... Words ... should never forsake [their] subordinate position in order to make themselves the chief thing, with the music becoming a mere means of expressing the [words of the] song ... No one has kept so free from this mistake as Rossini." *Wille*, 1:364–65 (in bk. 3, sect. 52).
47. Bohrer, review, 322.
48. Respectively, Bellman, "Aus alten Märchen"; and Roberts, *Images*, 35, 36–37, 68, 258–62.
49. Todd, "Mendelssohn's"; Mikusi, "Mendelssohn's."
50. Bergeron, "Lifetime." In mid-2008, the trend recurred with a CD that reached the UK top-10 pop chart: see www.chantmusicforparadise.com.
51. The first method (chronological) is sketched in Betzwieser and Stegemann, "Exotismus." The second, third, and fourth methods are combined in Betzwieser's seminal book *Exotismus*. The third method serves as the primary structural principle in Bellman, *Exotic*: each chapter deals with one "region portrayed." The fourth is exemplified by the various studies of French, Italian, and other strands of musical Orientalism mentioned in Chapter 1, n. 34. Cf. Lindenberger, *Opera*, 160–64, 311–12; and Head, "Musicology."
52. How do Algerians in France differ in this regard from Algerians in Algeria? For that matter, what about natives of various European countries: for example, non-Algerian but nonetheless rap-loving (rap-envious?), and rapping, French? Some of these issues are explored in Swedenburg, "Islamic," and Swedenburg, et al., "Arab."
53. Russell, "Race"; Hosokawa, "Blacking"; and Condry, *Hip-hop*, 24–48.
54. Further on the exotic and the national(istic), see Chapter 6.
55. See the last section of Chapter 4, and various case studies in Part II, especially Chapter 8.
56. See the Introduction.
57. De Van, "L'exotisme," 103.

4 Who is "Us"?

1. On the relationship of French symphonies to Austro-German tradition, see Holoman, "Berlioz," and Locke, "French."
2. Quoted in Prod'homme and Dandelot, *Gounod*, 1:161.
3. See Locke, "Doing."
4. Beckerman, *New*, 23–76.
5. Kallberg, *Chopin*, 3–29.
6. On these rhythmic freedoms, see Cook, "Performance."
7. See Elzbieta Wasowska, ed., *Mazurki kompozytorów polskich na fortepian: antologia ze zbiorów Biblioteki Narodewej; Piano Mazurkas of Polish Composers: Anthology from the Collection of the National Library*, 2 vols. (Warsaw: Biblioteka Narodowa, 1995); Milewski, "Chopin's," 130–35; Taruskin, *Oxford*, 3:343–63; and Goldberg, *Music*, 5, 62–63. Cf. Kallberg, "Hearing."
8. Both concertos have finales with marked Polish folk-dance elements; the other three Polish-style pieces for piano and orchestra are the Fantasy on Polish Airs, the *Krakowiak* rondo, and the *Andante spianato et grande polonaise*.
9. Parakilas, "How," 182–83, 189.
10. Beckerman, *New*, 223–24. I have corrected an apparent typo: "composer's pantheon."
11. *Ibid.*, 15–16.
12. Taruskin, "Nationalism."
13. One exception is Radice, *Concert*, 53–55.
14. Kremer, "Tango," 199.
15. Gurewitsch, "Tenor."
16. See plot summary and commentary by Marion Linhardt in Dahlhaus and Döhring, eds., *Pipers*, 5:220. A recording was once available on Urania LP set UR203, with highlights (which I have listened to) on UR8017.
17. Nine years later (1864), a theater named Bataclan would be built on the rue Voltaire and decorated in Chinese-pagoda style. Today it hosts rock and world-music concerts.
18. See the end of Chapter 2 above. Mozart's *Entführung* today feels smug, to many observers, in its portrayal of the womanizing and hypocrisy of Middle Eastern Muslim males (see Chapter 6).
19. Pisani, *Imagining*, 332.
20. One clear case of "Them" standing for "Us" is Gilbert and Sullivan's continuingly popular *The Mikado* (1885).
21. See Chapter 8.
22. On the Self/Other or I/not-I distinction in philosophical writings (Plato, Fichte, Lévinas) and musicology, see Fauser, "Alterity." On the complications of Westerners (e.g., anthropologists, ethnomusicologists, but also music historians) writing about a society that is very distant (in time and/or place) and that differs from the observer in its cultural assumptions, see Tomlinson, *Music*, 1–43.

23. Again, see Chapter 8 (Radamès and Samson).
24. To be sure, a stage work's effect can also be ruined by inept or misguided efforts from those same participants. Still, an engaged opera/theatergoer can often compensate for shortcomings in a given performance through the alchemy of his/her own imagination.
25. See Chapter 3.
26. See the final section of Chapter 1 above, and Subotnik, *Deconstructive*, 158–59 (Western music's indebtedness to "a larger cultural network of extra-musical ideas or stylistically related constructs").

5 Baroque portrayals of despots: ancient Babylon, Incan Peru

1. See the research of Edward Lowinsky, Gregory Barnett, and others, summarized in Taylor, *Beyond*, 24–29.
2. Bloechl, *Native*, 109–76, 238–44 (including natives of the New World); Winkler, *O Let*, 18–62 (witches).
3. See Alm, "Dances," 238.
4. Budasz, "Black," 5, 9. This *arromba* is performed on the CD by the ensemble Banza: *Iberian and African-Brazilian Music of the 17th Century*, Naxos 8.557969, 2006 (first released, with fuller notes, in 2004 on the Sonopress label).
5. See the entries for sarabande, chaconne, and gigue in *Grove Music Online*; and three classic articles by Stevenson: "Afro-American," "First," and "Sarabande." The last of these contains an early reference to the sarabande's serving as a couple dance among "nuestros naturales," i.e., natives of Mexico or other regions of New Spain.
6. Pruiksma, "Music," 239–40; Pruiksma goes on to explore the ways that Lully and his followers played with these associations. On the intense erotic aura of the *chacona*, *zarabanda*, and *jácara* within Spain in the seventeenth century, see Stein, "Eros," 660–61.
7. Whaples, in her dissertation, had explicitly set out to "investigate the influence ... of descriptions and quotations of all non-European musics in the available travel literature on composers of exotic stage works before 1800" ("Early Exoticism Revisited," 4). Betzwieser's definition in *MGG* allows only three conditions that might permit a work to be considered exotic: if it uses native instruments (or presumably ones similar to them or standing for them), if it uses native music (or music odd enough to be understood as standing for it), or if it stages various foreign "rites" ("Exotismus," cols. 226–27). My definition, by contrast (see Chapter 3), allows a work to be described as substantively exotic in intent and effect if the foreign characters, their customs, and their specific individual actions are portrayed in ways that differ notably from the ways in which Westerners are most often portrayed in the same genre. In a sense, I am expanding Betzwieser's third category (foreign ceremonies or rituals) to include all of human life and activity in the portrayed location. Taylor explains that he omits Handel operas and

oratorios from discussion because they do not rely upon "musical signs signifying nonwestern Others" (*Beyond*, 10). Certain studies do draw much-deserved attention to non-Westerners in specific Baroque operas: for example, two by Maehder: "Representation" and "Opfer."

8. Leopold, "Zur Szenographie," 371. A specialist on mid-eighteenth-century opera in Turin discusses operas about Montezuma, Persia, and China primarily in terms of basic plot and the desire of the Savoyard monarchy to broaden its international reputation: M. R. Butler, "Exoticism."

9. De Van, "L'exotisme," 103, 105. For Joseph Horowitz, Orientalism commenced even later: in the mid-nineteenth century, when the West began "evoking the music, legends, or landscapes" of the East through "superficial" incorporation or imitation of scraps of Arab music – "Introduction," 6. (He specifically mentions Félicien David, whose best-known "Arab" work was *Le désert*, 1844.)

10. Pontus was roughly the section of northern Anatolia along the Black Sea coast; Capadocia lay to the east and south, or it could include Pontus as well.

11. On the Christian implications – and the contemporary political implications, within England – of various aspects of the story (e.g., the Temple vessels as forerunners of the Eucharist), see R. Smith, *Handel's*, 152-53, 261-67, 304-34, 317-19; and R. Smith, "Achievements."

12. Schuhmacher, "George Friedrich Händel."

13. Smith, *Handel's*, *passim*, and "Achievements," esp. 184.

14. Bachmann, "'From Arabia's'."

15. Dean, *Handel's*, 434-59.

16. Dean, *Handel's*, 440.

17. Schuhmacher, "George Friedrich Händel," 5 ("voller Gauklertum").

18. Such arpeggiated phrases are found in other drinking songs of the era: for example, John Blow's "Tis Women Makes Us Love" (especially its opening phrase; the third line sings of drinking), which is splendidly performed by the Merry Companions on the Baltimore Consort's recording *The Art of the Bawdy Song*, Dorian CD 91055.

19. Teldec LP set 6.35326-00-501 (now rereleased on CD).

20. The *Thousand and One Nights* involve a number of tales of drunkenness and sexual debauchery. The valuable index of themes in the *Nights* by Elisséeff lists numerous instances of drunkenness, incest, couples caught *in flagrante delicto*, "pederasty" (Elisséeff finds six such instances), "feigned pederasty" (two instances), and drug-induced stupors – *Thèmes*, 85-205. For centuries, Westerners portrayed the prophet Muhammad, in particular, as lascivious – see Daniel, *Islam*, 4, 238, 274-75.

21. See Hunter, "Mozart." Cf. bk. 2, chap. 7 and bk. 4, chap. 1 (on liberality, with side-references to ambition/honor-loving): Aristotle, *Nicomachean*, 118-20 (traditional section-numbering: II:vii), 141-46 (IV:i).

22. Elias, *Court*, 68. Cf. Duindam, *Myths*, 9, 54-56, 194-95.

23. Elias, *Court*, 240.

24. Cf. Aristotle, *Nicomachean*, 122–27 (III:i-ii: children and lower animals).
25. *Ibid.*, 147 (IV:ii:13-14), cf. 209 (VIII:i:2).
26. See his letters to Edward Holdsworth, quoted in R. Smith, "Achievements," 184; also in R. Smith, "Handel's English," 108. Cf. K. Wilson, *Sense*, 84–205.
27. Isaiah 45:1.
28. R. Smith, *Handel's Oratorios*, 261–67, 304–34.
29. Further on the history of empire, see the beginning of Chapter 8.
30. Cf. Muthu, *Enlightenment*, 4.
31. Harris, "With Eyes."
32. Pitts, *Turn*; Mabilat, "Empire," 221–22; Mabilat, *Orientalism*; and Richards, *Imperialism*.
33. Several had music by Campra; see Harris-Warrick, "Staging." Other likely models included the Venetian ballets of the four corners of the world (see n. 3, above).
34. It is sung several times in the 2001 film of Marivaux's play *The Triumph of Love*, starring Ben Kingsley and Mira Sorvino.
35. Several scholarly sources, oddly, insist that none of the peoples in *Les Indes galantes*, or only the Turks, are represented by distinctive music: for example, Rice, "Representations," 63.
36. Letter of October 1727 from Rameau to Campra's frequent librettist Houdar de La Motte, in Girdlestone, *Jean-Philippe Rameau*, 9–10, also in Betzwieser, *Exotismus*, 174; see also Savage, "Rameau's," 444–46; Whaples, "Early," 16–18; Taylor, *Beyond*, 53; Pisani, *Imagining*, 37–41; and Bloechl, *Native*, 177–215, 244–50.
37. Whaples, "Early," 18.
38. Cole, *"Nature"*, 92, based in part on Betzwieser, *Exotismus*, 180–81.
39. Bouissou, "Indes," 15.
40. Girdlestone, *Jean-Philippe Rameau*, 330–31; see also Cole, *"Nature"*, 250–58.
41. Another interpretive possibility is that the back-and-forths here are a musical reflection of the verb *balancer* (literally: to weigh, in the manner of a pair of scales); one oddity with this explanation (by today's way of thinking, at least) is that Huascar is proposing that Phani *not* engage in such activity.
42. See Cole's appreciation – *"Nature"*, 262–65.
43. Fuzelier's preface, in the 1735, 1751, and 1761 libretti, as quoted in Cole, *"Nature"*, 248–49.
44. This passage is ambiguous ("our tyrants") in the booklet of the Les Arts Florissants recording. Compare Huascar's phrase "nos vainqueurs" and also, in the first *entrée*, scene 3, Emilie's "Mon tyran m'aime."
45. French and British writers of the Early Modern Era regularly portrayed the Spanish *conquistadores* as, essentially, "bad imperialists" and themselves as good ones. See Clare, *Dramas*, 235; and Maltby, *Black Legend*.
46. On the CD recording by Les Arts Florissants: Harmonia Mundi France HMC 901367.69.
47. He also admits (in the same aside) that setting off the volcano is a "barbarous procedure" (or trick) that will devastate his people's lands and lives.

48. Montesquieu (1748): "Harsh sentences are better suited to despotic government [such as those of China or the Ottoman sultans] – whose principle is terror – than they are to monarchy and republic, which have, as a driving force, honor and virtue" – *De l'esprit*, 1:79–80.
49. Cole, *"Nature"*, 261; cf. Kintzler, *Théâtre*, 192; for a seventeenth-century report (regarding Puerto Rico) of how native sorcerers practiced "[a] thousand deceptions in order to maintain those people in their blindness," see Thompson, *Music*, 8 (also 1, 10n).

6 A world of exotic styles, 1750–1880

1. Parakilas, "How," 166–69.
2. A recent exploration of the numerous performances of French *opéras-comiques* in the mid- and late eighteenth century on Saint-Domingue and other islands in the Caribbean (Camier, *Musique*) reveals some surprising trends, such as that a talented performer of African origin – the soprano known as Minette – could triumph on stage in roles that the librettist had not inherently coded as "black" (a shepherdess in love). See also Budasz, "Black."
3. Ratner, *Classic*, 1–30. Ratner tends to take Italo-Viennese traditions as the "unmarked" norm.
4. On the intertwined phenomena of exoticism and nationalism, see Chapter 4 and Taruskin, "Nationalism."
5. Or, to put it the other way around, the Exotic-Style Paradigm (see Chapter 3) fits because it was developed largely in response to these or other similar instrumental works.
6. See the final sections of Chapters 2 and 4.
7. See "Moresca" and "Todesca" in *Grove Music Online*. Several examples are included in the CD by the Ensemble Clément Janequin, Harmonia Mundi France HMC 901391 and (the *todesca* "Matona, mia cara") by the Hilliard Ensemble on EMI Classics Reflexe CDC 7 54435 2.
8. Four works entitled "Polish" by Telemann – two sonatas, a concerto, and a *Partie* [i.e., Partita] *polonoise* – are performed by Eduard Melkus and others on a Deutsche Grammophon LP: Archiv SAPM 198467 (released in 1967). Bach's Polacca is the second contrasting episode in the First Brandenburg's concluding (Minuetto) movement and features a recurring accent on the second beat (of three).
9. See *The Harpsichord or Spinnet Miscellany* (London: Robert Bremner, n.d. [c. 1765]). Facsimile edition: Williamsburg: Colonial Williamsburg Foundation, [1972].
10. Purser, *Scotland's Music*, 199–243; and Gelbart, *Invention*, 162–86, 203–19.
11. Farrell, *Indian*, 15–44, 77–78; Woodfield, *Music*, 149–80; and Cook, "Encountering."
12. Herder, *Werke*, 5:11-430 (the four volumes of *Volkslieder*, published in 1778–89 and 1807; the latter, posthumous edition is entitled *Stimmen der Völker in Liedern*); Bohlman, *Herder*; and Gelbart, *Invention*, 102–10, 197–203.

13. Excerpt from his autobiographical entry in Mattheson's *Grundlage zu einer Ehrenpforte* (1740), in Fisk, *Composers*, 26–27.
14. Gelbart, *Invention*, 11.
15. Bellman, *The* style hongrois, 24, 45.
16. Cf. Schwartz, "Cultural."
17. Betzwieser, *Exotismus*, 18 (quotation), 125–33.
18. A dialect (based on unconjugated Italian) that was practiced in port cities throughout the Mediterranean. See the *lingua franca* website of Alan D. Corré: www.uwm.edu/~corre/franca/go.html (5th edn, 2005).
19. In Molière, *Théâtre*, 4:177–83; also a recording led by Gustav Leonhardt (Deutsche Harmonia Mundi 77059-2-RG).
20. On the scene's origins, see Whaples, "Early," 11–14.
21. King, "First," 137–63. See the Qur'an 5:90–91; also 2:219 and 4:43.
22. Betzwieser, *Exotismus*, 252–58. On settings by Mozart's amanuensis Süßmayr (1799) and Friedrich Adam Hiller (1809), see Whaples, *Exoticism*, 54–55.
23. The 1726 opera, with a text by Alain-René Lesage (the author of *Gil Blas*) and D'Orneval (first name unknown), used preexisting tunes ("vaudevilles") for the musical numbers rather than newly composed music.
24. Cited in Brown, *Gluck*, 411; Zinzendorf is specifically referring to the 1726 version of the libretto.
25. See W. D. Wilson, "Turks."
26. And an optional march for the entrance of the Pasha, which can be heard in the Christopher Hogwood recording of the opera: Oiseau-Lyre CD set 30,339/341-2.
27. From Alexandre Oulibicheff's *Nouvelle biographie de Mozart* (1840, pub. 1843), as quoted in Bartha, "Mozart," 69.
28. Teldec CD set 2292-42643-2.
29. Szabolcsi, "Exoticisms," 326–28.
30. Betzwieser, *Exotismus*, 140. In Campra's day, much of Eastern Europe was under Turkish control; even today, the part of Turkey lying west of the Bosporus (i.e., Rumelia) is considered part of Europe; Anatolia, to the east, is part of Asia.
31. Betzwieser, *Exotismus*, 105–9, 140–44, 192. The *Concerto turc* shows a distinct "Turkish" feature not noted by Betzwieser: the escape-note descent in m. 10 (see Fig. 6.3 below, feature 8).
32. On the limitations of the *alla turca* style (to, primarily, a grotesque and noisy "2/4 racket, suitable for … great celebration [e.g., military], fury, or mockery"), see Bellman, *The* style hongrois, 45, 66, 68. Bellman's brief account is largely seconded by Schmitt, whose extensive discussion (*Exotismus*, 301–72, esp. 337–64) considers works of Wenzel Müller and other now-forgotten German composers.
33. M. Cole, "Monostatos."
34. Further, see M. Cole, "Monostatos"; and Scott, "Problem."
35. See also Monelle, *Musical Topic*, 117–19.
36. Hunter, "*Alla turca*," 71–73.

37. *Ibid.*, 46–47; Head, *Orientalism*, 51. Tchaikovsky later orchestrated K455 in his Suite No. 4 for Orchestra, "Mozartiana" (1887).
38. Reinhard, "Mozarts"; Bellman, *The style hongrois*, 55, 57; and Head, *Orientalism*, 11–14.
39. Similar features are found in several early examples of Hungarian-Gypsy finales – for example, the finale of Haydn's Piano Trio No. 39 in G Major, Hoboken XV/25 (1795), and Beethoven's String Quartet in C Minor, Op. 18, no. 4 (1798–1800) – and in the instrumental music by Haydn's brother Michael to Voltaire's Turkish play *Zaïre*.
40. Even so, no such list (as feature 17 in Fig. 6.3 suggests) can claim to be exhaustive. Matthew Head demonstrates that yet other all-purpose (unmarked) features – march rhythms, triple-stops in violins – could take on Turkish associations (*Orientalism*, 61–66, 78–80).
41. Perl, "Mozart," 226–27, and Betzwieser, "'Turkish'," 184–85 (also "distant tonalities from the home key," cf. 200); cf. Betzwieser, *Exotismus*, 112–14 (on G minor as "the preferred key for exotic subjects" in pieces by Lully, Rameau, and others); Bloechl, *Native*, 199–201; and Pisani, *Imagining*, 30, 33, 37-38, 40, 42, 86–87, 192, and 193 (continuing use of G minor to portray Native America in the twentieth century).
42. Cf. Signell, "Mozart."
43. Schmitt, *Exotismus*, 282.
44. Reinhard, exceptionally, does mention this ("Mozarts," 520).
45. Bauman, *W. A. Mozart*, 63. Monostatos's aria from *Magic Flute* uses the escape-note option.
46. Hunter, "Alla turca," 57–65 ("flamboyant incoherence").
47. Letter from Mozart to his father, 26 September 1781, cited in Bauman, *W. A. Mozart*, 65.
48. Hunter, "Alla turca," 48–49.
49. Sanal, *Mehter*, 121–25.
50. Szabolcsi, "Exoticisms," 326–30; cf. During, *Musique*, 30, 136, 138 (escape-note triplets).
51. On the problem of dating the work (and this movement's coda), see Head, *Orientalism*, 115–16, 120.
52. Rice, "Representations," 69.
53. Head, *Orientalism*, 87.
54. For example, the French drinking song "Il faut que l'on file doux" (possibly of folk origin) and the still-performed "Que ne suis-je la fougère" by Antoine Albanèse (an Italian-born composer and singing teacher, 1729–1800). On "Il faut," see Locke, "Music of the French Political Chanson," 435, 439, 452 (Ex. 5a). On "Que ne suis-je," see Chapter 11 below.
55. Head, *Orientalism*, 119–20; cf. Irving, *Mozart's*, 143 (ABAB' coda, with the C considered a kind of trio within the first B).
56. Such a passage was usually called a *teslim* or *mülazime*: Reinhard and Stokes, "Turkey"; see Rice, "Representations," 52, 67, 70.

57. Mozart's letter of 26 September 1781; see Hunter, "*Alla turca*," 48, 57–65, and Head, *Orientalism*, 1–10.
58. Monelle, *Musical*, ix and 6–7.
59. Clark, "Body," 129–31.
60. As so often, a single musical feature can have different meanings in different repertoires. Reverse dotting is found in much non-exotic music of early eighteenth-century Italy and is thus sometimes described at the time as "Lombardic rhythm."
61. Liszt's *Rondeau fantastique sur un thème espagnol "El contrabandista"* (1836) is recorded by Leslie Howard in *Liszt: The Complete Music for Solo Piano*, vol. 45, Hyperion CDA67145.
62. This two-chord alternation is generally termed the "Andalusian cadence" by Spanish scholars today, who thereby reconceive the two alternating chords as I and ♭II. See Manuel, "From Scarlatti," 311–36.
63. On "El arreglito" and "La paloma," respectively, see Chapters 7 and 11 below. On the two García songs and "El arreglito," see Locke, "Spanish."
64. Dahlhaus, *Between*, 80–81, 95, 97.
65. See, for example, Ringer, "On the Question"; Heartz, "Mozart's"; and Hancock, "Johannes Brahms."
66. Van der Merwe, *Roots*, 223, 248–49, 266–70, 501: see, for example, Lanner's *Steirische Tänze*, Op. 165 (1841), and Schönbrunner Walzer, Op. 200 (1842), no. 1.
67. Fiske, *Scotland*, 1–30, 55–79; Gelbart, *Invention*, 66–73, 180–86, 203–9; Pisani, *Imagining*, 161–81; Zon, *Representing*, 89, 11, 135, 148, 151, 222, 231–32, 279.
68. Arkin and Smith, "National."
69. The ballet was added for the 1869 performances at the Paris Opéra.
70. Berlioz, *Musique*, 233 ("phrases en désinence féminine," regarding Félicien David's *Le désert*).
71. See Dahlhaus, "Kategorie"; and – on "topics" – Ratner, *Classic*, 1–30, and Monelle, *Musical*.
72. See Will, *Characteristic*, and Locke, "Absolute Music" and "Program Music."
73. See Pisani, "Music."
74. Kallberg, *Chopin*, 161–214, 279–90.
75. On descriptions of various "national musics," see Gramit, *Cultivating*, 27–62.
76. Reminiscence (dating from 1844–45, recalling an event of forty years earlier) by the poet Franz Grillparzer, in Beethoven, *Letters*, 62–63.
77. See Théophile Gautier, reviews of performances by Indian dancers (*devadasi*s) in Paris (1838, 1844), in *Gautier on Dance*, 36–50, 134–37; and Berlioz, *Art*, 176 (quoted passage).
78. See Chapter 8.
79. On the (rarely noted) element of nationalism in nineteenth-century German music, see Taruskin, "Nationalism."
80. Day-O'Connell, *Pentatonicism*, 91.

81. Kallberg, "Arabian," 176–77. The Sarmatian theory is still accepted, at least in part, by some present-day scholars.
82. Kallberg, "Hearing"; and Pekacz, "Deconstructing."
83. Finson, *Voices*, 240–314; and Noske, *French Song*, 312–14.
84. Gramit, "Orientalism"; cf. Youens, "Heine."
85. Gramit, "Orientalism," 114.
86. Op. 32, no. 9 (poem by Georg Friedrich Daumer), discussed in Fehn and Thym, "Repetition."
87. Pisani, *Imagining*, 89–91, 116–25, and Pisani, "'I'm an Indian'," 224–25. See also http://IndianMusicList.vassar.edu.
88. A military band played various Hungarian (and presumably Hungarian-Gypsy) tunes to welcome Liszt back to his homeland in 1839 (Walker, *Franz Liszt*, 1:321). Liszt performed the Rákóczy March (or perhaps Hungarian Rhapsody No. 15, which is based on that march) on numerous occasions in Hungary, including one time in 1846, to a crowd of admirers who had gathered outside an open window at the private home at which he was staying (Walker, *Franz Liszt*, 1:431, also 320, 324, 330).
89. Willems, *In Search*, 1–3.
90. *Ibid.*, 14, 17, 153; cf. Goldberg, *Racial*, 98–137; Crowe, *History*, 38–40 (Czech and Slovak lands), 72–85 (Hungary), 111–25 (Romania before and after the 1855 emancipation of Rom slaves).
91. Bohlman, "Erasure," prefers "Rom" (p. 4n), but he is writing primarily about East European Roma today (and songs that they sing about their lives and history).
92. Roma in Hungary sometimes call themselves *cigányok* "to underscore their distinctiveness from purported kin outside Hungary" (Liebich, Foreword, in Crowe, *History*, x). "Gypsy" has recently been preferred by some activists because, being broader than "Rom," it can include the Sinti and other distinct groups (see catalogue of the Roma Pavilion at the Venice Biennale 2007, discussed in "Bottom of the Heap"). "Gypsy" and analogous terms remain in active use by scholars (e.g., Willems) who study exogenous images of the Roma, and even by some scholars who study various Roma groups of today or past centuries (Marsh and Strand, *Gypsies*; chapters on "the Gypsies" before 1900 in Stauber and Vago, *Roma*, esp. 5-15, 103-5, 124).
93. Sárosi, *Gypsy Music*, 23–34. Further, see Víg, "Gypsy."
94. Van der Merwe argues somewhat similarly for retaining the phrase "Hungarian Gypsy style" (in regard to Brahms, *et al.*): *Roots*, 144–49 (see 141, 216, 493, 494). See also Taruskin's review of that book.
95. On the book's authorship and its reception in Hungary, see Alan Walker, *Liszt*, 2:368–96, and K. Hamburger, "Understanding." Cf. Liszt's letter of 17 July 1847 to Marie d'Agoult, in Liszt, *Letters*, 255–56.
96. Liszt, *Des bohémiens*, 471–85; the passages that I quote below, from the second edition, are generally identical in the much shorter first edition. Evans's translation divides the book up into chapters differently. It also relocates to the end

(339–70) the sections on Bihári, Antal Csermák, Beethoven, Schubert, and Reményi.
97. Liszt, *Gipsy*, 364; here and below I adapt Evans's sometimes free or bowdlerized translation. (I sometimes render "nous" as "I.") On various traits in the music of the Gypsy-music bands – the distinctive scale and rhythms, "luxuriant" ornamentation, instruments (cimbalom), formal principles (*lassú* and *friss*), and death-defying ("*salto mortale*") shifts to unexpected chords – see Liszt, *Gipsy*, 297–309, 312–15.
98. Recorded by Leslie Howard in *Liszt: The Complete Music for Solo Piano*, vol. 32, Hyperion CDA 66954–56.
99. Liszt, *Gipsy*, 364. Further, see Bellman, *The* style hongrois, 175–77.
100. See Clegg, "Chronicle"; cf. Papp, "Quellen." Papp published a number of *verbunkos* dance tunes in vol. 7 of the scholarly series *Musicalia Danubiana* (1986).
101. Walker, *Franz Liszt*, 1:435;
102. Gárdonyi, "Chronicle," 52.
103. Walker, *Franz Liszt*, 1:335n, 434n.
104. Further, see Mayes, *Domesticating*, 167 (citing the 1859 edition of *Des bohémiens*, 163, 280, 342).
105. Liszt, *Gipsy*, 363–64.
106. See the final installment of his 1835 essay "De la situation des artistes et de leur condition dans la société," translated in Locke, "Liszt."
107. Letter to Baron Antal Augusz, 14 January 1860 (Liszt's emphasis), and see also letter to Kálmán Simonffy, 27 August 1859, in Liszt, *Selected Letters*, 493, 482. Cf. Gooley, *Virtuoso*, 117–55.
108. Liszt, *Gipsy*, 270–71; cf. Liszt, *Des bohémiens* (1859 edn), ch. 136, p. 333 (several tart sentences, not present in the 1881 edn, about bland Hungarian arrangements of Gypsy tunes).
109. *Des bohémiens*, 361–62 ("eût été menacé d'apophtose"; the last word, in science, refers to the process by which an organism kills its own unwanted cells).
110. Loya, "*Verbunkos*"; also Loya, "Beyond."
111. The orchestral Rhapsody that was at first published as No. 2 was the one based on piano No. 12, and orchestral No. 4 was based on piano No. 2. The numbers were eventually switched, presumably for convenience.
112. On pre-Liszt uses of Gypsy style, see Bellman, *The* style hongrois, 47–68, 135–73.
113. Originally composed in 1809 for viola and orchestra. A Spanish-style equivalent is the bolero-like "Rondo a l'espagnola" that concludes J. B. Cramer's Piano Concerto No. 8 in D Minor, Op. 80 (1825).
114. Liszt, *Gipsy*, 333–38.
115. Bellman, *The* style hongrois, 120–21; Loya, "*Verbunkos*," 288.
116. Bellman, *The* style hongrois, 93–130, and Loya, "*Verbunkos*", 263–68.
117. See Parakilas, *et al.*, *Piano Roles*, 133–34 (piano practice and metronomes).
118. Liszt, *Des bohémiens*, 153, 169, also 360 ("slothful," "unsociable"). Liszt's book names certain standard authorities, for example, Pott (*Des bohémiens*, 100n.).

119. Liszt, *Gipsy*, 130–31; *Des bohémiens*, 188–89.
120. Liszt, *Gipsy*, 138–39; *Des bohémiens*, 202–3.
121. The same rhythm marks the main theme of Dvořák's Symphony No. 9, movement 1 (briefly discussed earlier in this chapter).
122. Other passages of cimbalom-like tremolo are found in, for example, the opening measures of Hungarian Rhapsodies Nos. 11 and 12.
123. Gárdonyi, "Chronicle," 52. Translation slightly altered. Further on the history of *verbunkos*, see Dobszay, *History*, 96–98, 125–59, 133–37, 224–27.
124. Liszt, *Gipsy*, 307, *Des bohémiens* (1881 edn), 405: *dont les petites notes pointues et acérées viennent mordiller l'oreille*. Bellman (*The* style hongrois, 95) is misled by Evans's translation "pointed" to think that Liszt wrote or meant *pointées*, i.e., dotted notes.
125. In the *Hungarian Fantasia*, this is carried out literally: orchestral winds on the three chords, answered by the chattering piano soloist.
126. See Loya, "*Verbunkos*," 98–106 and 294–97.
127. I do not rule out the possibility that the highly modulatory passages in this work (including the *zingarese* one that I earlier called "composerly") reflected in some way the sudden unexpected key or chord that Liszt and others described hearing in Gypsy performances (see n. 97). Still, the primary compositional model in such passages seems to me the developmental procedures (e.g., *motivische Arbeit*) of Western classical tradition, such as in sonata-form movements.
128. Loya, "*Verbunkos*," 102–4, 145–48, 268; Bellman, *The* style hongrois, 122–30. Liszt indicates that the sustaining pedal is held down through eight measures of changing harmony – a clear cimbalom effect.
129. At the end of the Scherzo in C Minor, the Gypsy scale (beginning C–D♭– E) causes us to hear the tonic-major as possibly a dominant (of F minor)? (The procedure is similar to one in Andalusian-style music, noted above.) See also Bellman, *The* style hongrois, 201–13; and Daverio, *Crossing*, 192, 211–42.
130. Loya, "*Verbunkos*," 205–62.
131. A range of standard writings on the Hungarian and other Roma are surveyed in Lucassen and Willems, "Church"; and Clark, "'Severity'." The Munczi Lajos Gypsy Orchestra traveled across Europe performing such pieces as the Rákóczy March and, according to a report in a Stockholm newspaper, other "Hungarian rhapsodies" (including, presumably, at least Liszt's famous No. 2). The twenty-four-page souvenir booklet of their performances in 1887 in New York City's recently opened wax museum, Eden Musée, quotes copious passages from Liszt's book about the "sensuous softness of [Gypsy women's] lashes," the "aggressive, bitter sarcasm" and "brood[ing] over wrath" in some of the men's faces, and so on. (*Munczi*, 10–12; the passage from the *Stockholm News* is on p. 21.)
132. Anonymous jacket note for an orchestral LP entitled *Gypsy!* (Capitol P8342), [late 1950s?].

133. Sheveloff, "Dance," 165.
134. Gooley, *Virtuoso*, 147–48.
135. Salmen, *Geschichte*, 80–124.

7 Exotic operas and two Spanish Gypsies

1. On the operatic Alps, see Senici, *Landscape*.
2. Many important examples are discussed in Fiske, *Scotland*.
3. Portrayals of North Americans (including Quakers) are examined in Polzonetti, *Opera*.
4. Rosen, *Ballo*, 73–74 ("indovina di razza negra"), 114 nn. 8–10, and illustrations on 227, 238, 249.
5. Scott, "Blackface"; Pickering, *Blackface*.
6. Shaw, review of *Aida*, 29 October 1890, in *Shaw's Music*, 2:185. See also Locke, "*Aida*," 62n (Gottschalk).
7. On one other exception (a chorus with tom-tom beat), see Budden, *Operas*, 1:237.
8. See Locke, "French," 166–68. (One correction to those pages: the spoken narration for *Le désert* is not unrhymed but rather rhymes freely.)
9. Morrison, " Semiotics," 275. Morrison here refers to Kristeva, *Strangers*, 206.
10. Bobéth, *Borodin*, 47–51.
11. Dahlhaus, *Nineteenth-Century*, 302–11.
12. Another notable case is Preziosilla in Verdi's *La forza del destino*.
13. Letter to his mother, Rome, 23 June 1860 (Bizet, *Lettres*, 131); "gall" quotation: from Bizet's only published article (*Revue nationale*, 3 August 1867), in Lacombe, *Georges Bizet*, 374, and Dean, *Bizet*, 285 (whose translation is adapted here).
14. Ruiz, *Spanish*, 95, 107–8, 114, 116n, 246; and Charnon-Deutsch, *Spanish*, 36, 53, 133, 240.
15. Gould, *Fate*, 18–33; see also Seigel, *Bohemian*.
16. Budden, *Operas*, 2:72 (also noting similarity to Verdi's witches).
17. Further, see *ibid.*, 2:81–82.
18. *Ibid.*, 2:72.
19. On the development of the "second" female role in operas (the rival, the mother, etc.), see André, *Voicing*.
20. Hodgart and Bauerle, *Joyce's*, 47.
21. *Ibid.*, 91n.
22. Bauerle suggests that singing this duet was an attempt at repairing, "at a distance of time and space," the spiritual estrangement with his mother, to whom he had sung "as she lay dying, but without any reconciliation" (*James Joyce*, 100). Joyce refers to *Il trovatore* in *Finnegans Wake*. His father loved singing Manrico's aria "Ah sì, ben mio" (Hodgart and Bauerle, *Joyce's*, 91n and 5).
23. Recoing, "Azucena."

24. Deutsch, *Spanish*, 186; other writers emphasized the extreme ugliness of Gypsy women, or the fleetingness of their beauty (*ibid.*, 134).
25. Parakilas, "Soldier," 40.
26. For example, T. Cooper, "Nineteenth-Century," 29: "Bizet ... consciously avoided direct quotation."
27. Dean, *Bizet*, 228–32; and Lacombe, *Georges Bizet*, 690–701. On the Séguedille scene and the entr'acte to Act 4, see Locke, "Spanish."
28. Parakilas, "Soldier," 40.
29. On the entr'acte and its model, see Locke, "Spanish."
30. Cf. Lacombe, *Georges Bizet*, 707, 801n. Escamillo does hint at a version of the theme in Act 3 to José ("C'est une zingara, mon cher").
31. Augmented seconds are found here between the $\hat{7}$ and $\flat\hat{6}$, $\sharp\hat{4}$ and $\flat\hat{3}$, and $\flat\hat{2}$ and $\natural\hat{3}$ (i.e. the major third). See Scott, *From the Erotic*, 166–67.
32. See Wright, *Georges Bizet, Carmen*, for example 58–59 (Lauzières), 69 (Comettant).
33. Summary based on Meilhac and Halévy, *Carmen* [libretto], 10.
34. Cf. McClary, *Georges Bizet: Carmen*, 87–89.
35. On Carmen's crucial "Oui," see Locke, "What," 69–75, 86–87.
36. Parakilas, "Soldier," 40.
37. This is strongly suggested by the fact that the women's chorus in Act 3 is called "Choeur des bohémiennes" in the "Quant au douanier" ensemble in Act 3. Presumably Dancaïre and Rémendado are Gypsies, too, and all the (male-chorus) *contrebandiers*. Lilias Pastia even refers to their smuggling as *affaires d'Egypte*.
38. John, ed., *Carmen*, 65 (singing translation by Nell and John Moody).
39. Meilhac and Halévy, *Carmen*, 26.
40. *Ibid.*, 8–12.
41. Oscar Comettant, review in *Le siècle*, 8 March 1875, in Wright, *Georges Bizet, Carmen*, 67.
42. Taruskin cites numerous instances of this device (which he sometimes calls "sixthiness") in his *Defining*, 55–58, 165–72, 176–85, 242–43.
43. The men's plea, removed early on by Bizet, has been restored in some recent editions and performances.
44. The song was first published in Paris *c.* 1857, also in 1863, 1865, and 1885. For a critical edition, see *Cien años de canción lírica española (I)*, ed. Celsa Alonso = Música hispana, Serie C: Antologías 8 (Madrid: Instituto Complutense de Ciencias Musicales, 2001), 221–27. I base my translation freely on that in *Canciones de España: Songs of Nineteenth-Century Spain*, ed. Suzanne Rhodes Draayer (Lanham, Md.: Scarecrow Press, 2003), 123–24. The French words are in *Chansons espagnoles del Maëstro Yradier (avec double texte Espagnol et Français)*, with translations by Paul Bernard and D. Tagliafico (Paris: H. Heugel, [1882?]), 18–25.
45. Parakilas, "Soldier," 46.
46. Some will remember Gounod's piece as the theme music for Alfred Hitchcock's creepy TV series of 1955–62.

47. Parakilas, "Soldier," 45.
48. The only exotic moments after Act 2 are Escamillo's aforementioned "une zingara" phrase plus orchestral passages (entr'acte to Act 4, an echo of the Séguedille in the opening of Act 4, and the final appearances of the Fate theme).
49. Parakilas, "Soldier," 33.
50. In Act 1, she briefly succeeded in making José half-accept her claim of being a Basque like himself.
51. Exceptions include Dafner, *Friedrich Nietzsches*, 53–55; and Adorno, "Fantasia."
52. Lacombe, *Georges Bizet*, 710–15, 723–24, 727; also 643–44 (quotation from p. 711).
53. McClary, *George Bizet: Carmen*, 101; and Parakilas, "Soldier," 33, 45–47. See also n. 52.
54. Cf. Parakilas, "How," 166.
55. Wright, "Profiles," 66.
56. Lacombe, *Georges Bizet*, 644, also 711.
57. *Ibid.*, 711
58. McClary, *Georges Bizet: Carmen*, 101.
59. The Ponselle photo is reproduced in John, *Carmen*, 42.

8 Imperialism and "the exotic Orient"

1. MacKenzie, "Empire," 282–90.
2. Meat-avoidance among India's Brahmins influenced Western religio-moral debate, nutritional science, and diplomatic strategies – see Stuart, *Bloodless*.
3. In 1879, 16,000 British troops were overwhelmed by the massed warriors of the Zulu nation led by their king, Cetshwayo.
4. MacKenzie, "Empire," 280–82.
5. Regarding British India, see Zon, *Representing*; and Leppert, *Sight*, 91–118.
6. Also Brazil (1822) and northern Peru (Bolivia, 1825). Thus began the tense and often bloody process by which the new ruling classes in certain countries attempted to subdue a sometimes restive indigenous population and/or a restive slave population deriving (ultimately) from Africa.
7. On the pre-Verdi generation, see Izzo, "Exoticism."
8. Anonymous comment in *Le Monde artiste*, 11 March 1888, p. 191, cited in Fauser, "Hymns."
9. England seized South Africa from the Dutch in 1806, and absorbed the Transvaal at the end of the Second Boer War (1899–1902).
10. On the short-lived fashion for South African topics in the theater (and musical theater) during the early nineteenth century, see Davies, "Melodramatic."
11. On French efforts to subdue North and West Africa, see Clancy-Smith, *Rebel*.
12. On semi-colonialism or "informal empire," see Osterhammel, "Britain," 148, and Knight, "Britain," 122–26.
13. Oren, *Power*; and Duus, *Japanese*, 35 (Japanese views of American marriage), 62–72 (American views of Japan).

14. Sometimes also called "the Far East" – "far," that is, from the viewpoint of someone living near the Atlantic or Mediterranean.
15. "Orient" could also, of course, be used somewhat metaphorically, to refer to Gypsies, Jews, Slavs, or other groups understood as having originated beyond, or even in, Eastern Europe.
16. See the discussion of Said's *Orientalism* and its reception, in Chapter 2.
17. Startled by certain lurid phrases that I have just typed, I feel compelled to add that many individuals in certain non-Western countries (and some in the West, as well) hold extreme and negative images of the Western metropolis and its inhabitants, and not entirely fictive ones. Such individuals may see the West as some combination of the following: competitive, materialistic, sexually promiscuous, shameless in exposing the female body, and – in its drive to commandeer and devour other regions' natural resources while preaching moderation to those regions' inhabitants – hypocritical. (See copious instances in Buruma and Margalit, *Occidentalism*.) But those views, the extent of their factual basis, and their artistic ramifications are not the topic of the present book.
18. Comic operas raise separate questions that would complicate the chapter further.
19. Two purely orchestral pieces do frankly enact, in different ways, the imperial encounter. On Saint-Saëns's *Suite algérienne* and its concluding "Marche militaire française," see Locke, "Cutthroats," 40–41 (passage removed from the shorter version, 122–23). On Borodin's *In [the Steppes of] Central Asia*, see Taruskin, "'Entoiling," 196 and 205–7.
20. A live recording of *Il guarany* is on Sony S2K 66273. On the outlaw hero of Alencar's novel (and hence of the opera) and his roots in English gothic novels, see Serravalle de Sá, *Tropical*. Cf. Maehder, "Representation," 270–71.
21. See Chapter 7; also Parakilas, "Soldier," 34–38.
22. The composers were from, respectively, Italy, France, Brazil, and Germany; they composed the works for, respectively, Berlin, Paris, Milan, and Paris. Thus, the only direct national linkage in any of these four works is that Carlos Gomes, composer of an opera about the Portuguese in Brazil, was himself from Brazil and of Portuguese descent.
23. Henson, "Of Men," 19; cf. Cooper, "Frenchmen," 115–17, 121.
24. Newark notes this, in regard to negative operatic portrayals of church and monarchy (review of Charlton, *Cambridge Companion*, 241).
25. Conklin, *Mission*.
26. See, for example, the excerpts cited in Locke, "*Aida*," 48, 50, 53, 54, 59 (Shaw), 63, 65, and Locke, "Beyond," 105, 113 n. 28, and (further exceptions: two Arab commentators in 1901) 137–39.
27. Locke, "*Aida*," 58–59, 71–72.
28. See also Locke, "Doing."
29. Much of the chapter from this point on is based on Locke, "Reflections on Orientalism." The discussions of *Aida*, *Samson et Dalila*, and *Madama Butterfly*, though, are new or greatly expanded.

30. Brantlinger, "Victorians"; see Brantlinger, *Rule*, and Kitzan, *Victorian*, 15.
31. Cf. Sedgwick, *Between Men*.
32. Thomalla, *"Femme fragile"*; cf. Bram Dijkstra, *Idols*, 64–82, 87–93. On the association of the mezzo voice with "racial" darkness, see André, "Veiled."
33. André, "Veiled." Other examples include Azucena and Carmen (see Chapter 7). Cf. André, *Voicing*.
34. Thomalla, *"Femme fragile"*, 13–15, 60–62; Dijkstra, *Idols*, 252–53, 352–401.
35. Dijkstra, *Idols*. Cleopatra, though Greek, had, from Roman days onward, become associated with Egypt and its attractive vices – Hughes-Hallett, *Cleopatra*.
36. See Locke, "Constructing," 276–79, 289–98.
37. Said, *Culture*, 111–32; and Locke, "*Aida*," 49, 51–59, 70–71.
38. These are stages 2 and 3. Stage 1 is, of course, Turkish Captivity operas (see Chapter 6 above and Parakilas, "Soldier," 35–36).
39. Ibid., 34–38.
40. On the "prosaic" and "poetic" elements in an opera, see the end of Chapter 4 above.
41. Similarly, Bizet's *Pêcheurs* was originally to be called *Leïla*.
42. Locke, "Constructing," 294–97.
43. See Locke, "Beyond," 133–35.
44. On the Bell Song's coloratura, see Bhogal, "Lakmé's."
45. Thomalla, *"Femme fragile"*, 85–87 (referring to Maeterlinck's Mélisande, 1892).
46. But see, on female agency in *Lakmé*, Bhogal, "Lakmé's."
47. On the tendency (in criticism and some performances) to emphasize only Aida's wilting quality, see Locke, "Beyond," 126–28, 131–32, 138–39, and Locke, "*Aida*," 59.
48. On Aida's "submissiveness," for example, see Budden, *Operas*, 3:192; Locke, "Beyond," 131–32; and Locke, "*Aida*," 57–58.
49. See the music of the aria "Un bel dì vedremo" (discussed below) and of the passage containing Cio-Cio-San's nearly hopeless words, "Tu Suzuki che sei tanto buona … " (Ricordi vocal score, p. 250).
50. Reh. no. 41 (Ricordi piano-vocal score, pp. 42–43). Cf. Micznik, "Cio-Cio-San," 49.
51. D. Rosen, "Pigri," 262–67.
52. Pagannone, "Puccini," 219–22.
53. McClary, "Mounting," 25.
54. Huebner, "Thematic," 101.
55. In this pentatonic collection each of the notes can function as a "tonic" note (as ethnomusicologists rightly stress).
56. Schatt, *Exotik*, 47.
57. Ashbrook and Powers, *Puccini's*, 64, 89–100.
58. The other two *tinte* are the Middle-Eastern – for the Prince of Persia – and the dissonant (which is sometimes "bicentric") – for the crushing cruelty of "the law" in Peking.

59. The whole phrase implies a different pentatonic scale, with a lowered $\hat{6}$ and with no $\hat{2}$ or $\hat{7}$.
60. Ashbrook and Powers, *Puccini's*, 98.
61. Girardi, *Puccini*, 450–52.
62. As Ashbrook and Powers briefly hint (*Puccini's*, 17–18, 93).
63. Dahlhaus, *Nineteenth-Century*, 217–26.
64. Kandy, an independent Ceylonese/Sinhalese monarchy, fell to the British in 1818.
65. Allen, "Analysis"; and Bencheikh, "Historical."
66. The effect is ruined in performance if, as once was traditional, the tenor appropriates the succeeding phrase for English horn that brings the music to full completion on A.
67. Cf. Henson, "Victor Capoul."
68. On Ramfis and the other priests as both ancient Eastern figures and barely disguised versions of contemporary Western ones, see Locke, "Beyond," 111–19, 130, 132, 135, and Locke, "Aida," 50, 52–53, 56.
69. One exception is in Act 3 of *Aida*, when the chorus pleads for mercy toward the Ethiopian prisoners.
70. Indra permits Alim to return to earth in human form, though under conditions that ultimately prove fatal.
71. The theme is thus stated two and a half times – at least in Bizet's own (recently restored) version – and only the second time is it sung. The long-standard version, in which "Oui, c'est elle" is sung again at the end of the duet, may well not have been devised by Bizet (Lacombe, *Georges Bizet*, 306).
72. Whether such passages are considered acceptable under the Exotic-Style Paradigm therefore depends on how narrowly or broadly the observer draws the border of what "sounds exotic." In the Introduction and Chapter 3, I defined the Full-Context Paradigm as subsuming the Exotic-Style Paradigm – rather than as complementing it – precisely so as to avoid having to legislate some fixed boundary between "exotic-sounding" and "not exotic-sounding."
73. The veil is indeed nearly body-length – and blowing open to show the priestess's face and simply clad body – in one detailed rendering of the scene from the premiere – see Fig. 8.1.
74. Henson, "Of Men, Women, and Others," 36. The third statement reverses the process: it trails off, as the priestess's veil falls back down and she disappears into the crowd.
75. See Parakilas, "Soldier," 37.
76. "Oscillating" ("Pendelbewegung") is the description in Powils-Okano, *Puccinis*, 185–86.
77. On "Il sacro brando," in *Aida*, see Locke, "Beyond," 114–16. See also, in Carlos Gomes's *Il guarany*, the repeated alternation of I and iii in a chorus of native Brazilians (or perhaps vi and I, depending on which chord one regards as the tonic – Ricordi vocal score, pp. 347–48).

78. Other cases include Verdi's echoing of music from Meyerbeer's *L'Africaine* (where, oddly, it was sung by Inès, who is the Western, not exotic, female) in Aida's *romanza* "O patria mia" (as noted in Budden, *Operas*, 3:236–37); and likely echoes of Verdi's Amneris (from *Aida*) in Saint-Saëns's Dalila (in his opera *Samson et Dalila*). On *Miss Saigon*, which is modeled in close detail on *Madama Butterfly*, see Chapter 10. (On my particular adaptation of Foucault's concept of "archaeology," see the Introduction.)
79. On Abimélech, see Locke, "Constructing," 282–85.
80. On tritones, augmented triads, unresolved major sevenths, and "bicentric" harmonies in this and other execution-related numbers in the work, see Ashbrook and Powers, *Puccini's*, 16, 89–94, 100–107. A barbaric Occident is powerfully constructed in such diverse twentieth-century works as Kurt Weill's *Aufstieg und Fall der Stadt Mahagonny* and *Lost in the Stars*, Marc Blitzstein's *The Cradle Will Rock*, Sergei Prokofiev's *The Fiery Angel*, Francis Poulenc's *Les dialogues des Carmélites*, Robert Ward's *The Crucible*, Gottfried von Einem's *Der Besuch der alten Dame*, Robert Kurka's *The Good Soldier Schweik*, and the mega-musical *Les Misérables*. Perhaps the dark side of Western civilization (at home and – through colonialism, empire, and world wars – abroad) has become increasingly hard for artists, if not certain politicians, to deny or disguise.
81. Girardi, *Puccini*, 211–17, and his primary source: Powils-Okano, *Puccinis*. Groos's "Cio-Cio-San," questions whether the tune at Goro's "Ecco son giunte" (Girardi's tune A) was indebted to any one Japanese model.
82. Pacun, "'Thus'," 90, 93–94 (on harmonization of Japanese modes); also *Grove Music Online*, "Mode," pt. V, sect. 5 (the "characteristically Japanese *in* scale").
83. On this scale, and augmented triads, see discussion of "Submerged Exotic" harmonic procedures in Chapter 9.
84. These pitches exist as degrees 3–4–5–6 in two standard Western modes: ascending melodic minor and Dorian minor. This permits Puccini to harmonize them, at times, in ways that are well integrated with his own basic style but to have them stand out, at other times, as harsh, attention-grabbing markers of Japan.
85. Ricordi piano-vocal score, pp. 256 and 266; cf. Budden, "Forta," 25–27.
86. See Goro's second motive (p. 7, four measures ending at "Scivola!") and, as we saw earlier, Cio-Cio-San's "Un bel dì" and "Tu Suzuki."
87. This is the orchestration of the orchestral passage that completes Butterfly's arrival in Act 1 (discussed earlier).
88. Reh. no. 41. See J. Smith, "Musical," 113–14; and Carner, *Puccini*, 387.
89. Such as the "O Kami" chorus discussed earlier.
90. Powils-Okano, *Puccinis*, 47–62. The stage directions include "childlike" (Ricordi vocal score, pp. 185, 250); "prettily" (165); and "jumping for joy and clapping her hands" (169, cf. 144).
91. He makes fun of Suzuki, the wedding guests, and the Bonze's curses.

92. She calls both herself and Kate the "happiest maiden/woman in the world," calls Sharpless the "best man," and kisses Pinkerton's "blessed" letter (Ricordi vocal score, pp. 38, 144, 255, 165, 168). Pinkerton is (say the stage directions) "bored" – *seccato* – by Suzuki's formulaic words of wisdom (12) and later curtly rebuffs Cio-Cio-San's offer of more compliments (44–45). Prince Yamadori offers a moral maxim in place of direct emotional expression (152–53). Butterfly also uses self-deprecation or poetic images to control or disguise her feelings ("sono vecchia diggià," 50; "come passan le nuvole sur mare," 174). Immediately repeated short exclamations include Suzuki's "Chi è?" (three double statements), "Spento il sole," and "Che giova" (234–36); and Butterfly's "Tanta paura," "Lascialo giocar," and "Va, gioca" (252, 259, 265).
93. J. Smith, "Exoticism," 116.
94. An even more salon-like waltz breaks out when Cio-Cio-San serves tea to Yamadori; see Huebner, "'Addio'."
95. The futility of a full adaptation to Western norms is evident in the somewhat antipathetic portrayal of half-Westernized characters: Goro and Yamadori.
96. McClary, "Mounting," 26.
97. *Ibid.*, 26 ("increase one's disciplinary capital").
98. *Ibid.*, 27 (I have corrected an evident typo: "attacks of").
99. Is this principle a distinctive development of our own day, or inherent to classic liberalism? See Cohen, *et al.*, "Introduction," 4, and Berkowitz, review.
100. This scene may have been inspired in part by Japanese woodcuts showing the procession of a geisha and her female attendants through the Yoshiwara district. Such carefully choreographed processions helped expose a geisha to the gaze of potential clients (who, before the 1850s, would have been entirely Asian). See Greenwald, "Picturing," 251–53.
101. As early as 1906 (Paris), productions began adding, for further local color, a small bridge and sometimes also a gateway with typically Japanese concave crosspiece.
102. J. Smith, "Musical," 113.
103. Ashbrook, *Operas*, 117.
104. When the sopranos and tenors address the Cousin, "Ecco, perchè prescelta fu" (top of p. 57 in the Ricordi vocal score: a D-minor-seventh chord over an open-fifth drone on G and D).
105. See Morris, "Innocence." Representations of Japan in American popular music will be treated in Sheppard, *Extreme*.

9 Exoticism in a modernist age (*c.* 1890–1960)

1. The words are from the influential statesman Jules Ferry before the French Assembly, 28 July 1885, quoted in Revol, *Influences*, 13. Ferry spearheaded the expansion of the French Empire into Tunisia, Madagascar (December 1885), the Congo, and Indochina.

2. See Conklin, *Mission*; MacKenzie, *Imperialism*; and MacKenzie, *Propaganda*.
3. Saint-Saëns, letter of 13 July 1907. Cf. Verdi's more democratically phrased objections to empire (Chapter 8 above).
4. Even certain composers of the early twentieth century who rejected the expressive tenets of Romanticism (e.g., Satie, Stravinsky, Hindemith) tended to cling to the principle of developing an original and distinctive compositional style (or succession of exploratory styles).
5. See Debussy's intriguing complaint about composers who "put new labels on things that are as old as the hills" – such things as "the simpler sonic aspects of Javanese music" (Debussy, "Concerts Colonne," November 1912, in *Monsieur Croche*, 214; I incorporate a detail of Langham Smith's translation: *Debussy on Music*, 265).
6. Prominent instances include all of the pieces studied in some detail in Chapters 6–8, by such composers as Mozart, Liszt, Verdi, Bizet, and Puccini.
7. The "pantos," despite the name, incorporated much singing.
8. Rhodes, *Primitivism*. See also Rubin, *"Primitivism"*, and Clifford, "Histories."
9. Menninghaus, "Hummingbirds," 31. Cf. Bhogal, *Arabesque*, 34–114.
10. Potter, "Debussy," 142–43; Eigeldinger, "Debussy," 7.
11. Letter to André Poniatowski, February 1893, in *Correspondance*, 116. See also Gervais, "Notion," and Eigeldinger, "Debussy."
12. Historians of ornamental design, for example, noted the use, in many Eastern Mediterranean regions, of certain visual themes such as lotus and palmetto. See Schafter, *Order*, 45–55.
13. 20 December 1894, in *Correspondance*, 228, translation adapted from that of Austin, *Prelude*, 12.
14. Debussy, *Correspondance*, 1585 (in a diplomatically worded defense of Nijinsky's ballet).
15. Interview in *La tribuna*, 23 February 1914, in Debussy, *Correspondance*, 1585.
16. Potter, "Debussy," 144.
17. Bhogal, "Debussy's," 173.
18. See *Ibid.*, 179.
19. Debussy is known to have admired this opera greatly (Debussy, *Prelude*, ed. Austin, 8–9).
20. Debussy, "L'entretien avec M. Croche," 1 July 1901, in *Monsieur Croche*, 52. The last words ("des harmonies ignorées de vos traités") may echo Hamlet's taunt to Horatio about schoolbook philosophy (Shakespeare, *Hamlet*, Act 1, sc. 5).
21. Austin's term. The figure derives, in part, from inverting the upward triplets of m. 24.
22. See, for example, During, *Musique*, 30, 184.
23. The long note presumably derives from the very opening of the piece.
24. The poems are included in the 1970 edition of Debussy score, completed and edited by Arthur Hoérée. On the 1901 version (which was entitled *Chansons de Bilitis*), see Grayson, "Bilitis." Crotales are percussive clappers, somewhat like castanets, originally associated with ancient priestesses.

25. Pomeroy, "Debussy's," 159.
26. As Debussy's tune migrates to four muted horns, it adds two surprising degrees to its scale: ♯4 and ♭7, creating a mode rarely encountered in Western music before Debussy's day (scholars today sometimes call it the "acoustic scale") but familiar within South Indian music – Howat, "Debussy," 60; also *Grove Music Online*, s.v. "Claude Debussy," sect. 10: "Musical Language" (likewise by Howat). Debussy's familiarity with Indian music has been documented in recent years. See Howat, "Debussy," 57–69, and Debussy, *Correspondance*, 1999 (inviting Hazrat Inayat Khan and his brother to come play for him).
27. Nectoux, *Harmonie*, 191–92.
28. Debussy, untitled article, 19 January 1903, in *Monsieur Croche*, 77.
29. Grieg's works (including the music for *Peer Gynt*) were of particular fascination for late nineteenth-century French musicians; see, for example, Strasser, "Grieg," 115.
30. Baur, "Ravel's," 536–38.
31. Lesure, *Claude Debussy*, 43–47.
32. Taruskin, *Oxford*, 3:392.
33. Schimmellpenninck, *Toward*, 10.
34. Kalinowska, *Between*.
35. Examples include Pushkin's poem *Ruslan and Lyudmila* (1820), the basis of Glinka's opera, and the medieval East Slavic epic that Borodin adapted for the libretto of his opera *Prince Igor* (performed posthumously in 1890).
36. Taruskin, *Defining*, 387, 390–409; Taruskin, *Stravinsky*, 1:849–66 (quotations from the poet Aleksandr Blok, summarizing the dichotomy but not clearly endorsing it, 850), 2:1126–36, 1188–89. cf. Frolova-Walker, *Russian*, 140–60, esp. 153.
37. Taruskin, *Defining*, 409–65 (*Noces*); Taruskin, *Stravinsky*, 1:934–50 (*Sacre*).
38. McQuere, *Russian*.
39. Or, put differently, unusual harmonic devices and the scales that can be derived from them.
40. Taruskin, *Stravinsky*, 1:255–306. The octatonic scale was discovered and explored simultaneously by the amateur French composer Edmond de Polignac, who felt it particularly appropriate to portrayals of the ancient Middle East – Kahan, "Rien," and Kahan, *Search*.
41. Taruskin, *Defining*, 83–86.
42. On "sixthiness" (and sexiness), see ibid., 55–58, 165–72, 176–85, 242–43; cf. DeVoto, "Russian Submediant."
43. Fauser, *Musical*, 43 (quotation), 321–22.
44. *Ibid.*, 44 (quotation from Victor Wilder).
45. Adolphe Jullien, on Glazunov's symphonic poem *Stenka Razin*, quoted in Fauser, *Musical*, 45–46.
46. Baur, "Ravel's 'Russian' Period," 536–40.
47. Taruskin, *Stravinsky*, 2:1006–7.
48. Nice, *Prokofiev*, 110–12; Press, *Prokofiev's Ballets*, 116–37, 156–57, 170–74.

49. Russom, *Theory*, 10; Orenstein, *Ravel*, 25–26.
50. On *Voiles*, see Antokoletz, *Twentieth-Century Music*, 88–89.
51. *Pagodes* and *Soirée* are from the *Estampes* for piano; *Ibéria* is the second of the *Images* for orchestra; *Laideronnette* is from Ravel's *Ma mère l'oye*.
52. My use of the noun "composing" echoes Utz's emphasis on the composer's process and choices (e.g., in his article specifically entitled "Interkulturelles Komponieren").
53. In literary history, see Espagne, *Transferts*. Ethnomusicologists (influenced by cultural anthropology) often propose that cultural identity is fashioned through negotiation and creative appropriation. Particularly valuable for exoticist repertoires are such concepts as cultural exchange, hybridity, musical process (vs. musical product), colonial encounter, cultural encounter, intercultural contact, syncretism, reciprocity (as proposed by Bronislaw Malinowski), and transculturation (as proposed by Fernando Ortiz, with specific regard to ethnically blended musical practices in Cuba). See the studies in Kartomi and Blum, *Music-Cultures in Contact*. An exemplary (non-musical) study of cultural exchange is Bisaha, *Creating*. On the distinction between "musical process" and "musical product," see Blacking, "Study," 13, and several other essays in the volume containing that essay. There is an immense literature on present-day musical hybridity (moving from the West to the Rest, and from metropolitan centers to rural and former colonized areas, but also the reverse of each of these), and on the related question of cultural identity through the making and consumption of music. See, for example, Nettl, *Western*; Slobin, *Subcultural*; Bohlman, *Music*; and O'Connell, "In the Time."
54. Nicholls, "Transethnicism"; Utz, *Interkulturalität*, 45–47; Euba, "Foreword," xii; on "hybridity" in Bartók, see Brown, "Bartók"; Cooper, "Béla Bartók"; and Trumpener, "Béla Bartók."
55. Loya's use of the term derives from Pratt, *Imperial* (see, for example, p. 6), and MacKenzie, *Orientalism*, 21–22.
56. See my discussion of "Orientalism" in Chapter 2 above. Loya specifically contrasts the "appropriation" and "transculturation" models in "The *Verbunkos* Idiom," 111–40. On "reciprocity" (rather than unidirectional domination) in "cultural transfer," see Mittelbauer, "Kulturtransfer" (bibliography with introduction).
57. Mellers, "Final," 171.
58. Freed, booklet notes; cf. Roberts (*Images*, 156): "a deliberate transcription … heard with western ears."
59. Lesure, *Claude Debussy*, 103–6; Fauser, *Musical Encounters*, 163–215.
60. Debussy, article 15 February 1913, *Monsieur Croche*, 229.
61. The recording by Britten and McPhee of the latter's *Balinese Ceremonial Music* (1940) for two pianos is now available on Pearl GEMM CD 9177.
62. See, similarly, the discussion of Mozart's non-use of Indian raga in Locke, "Doing," 351–52.
63. McPhee, *Music*, 31–32, 36; Sorrell, *Guide*, 49–51, 55–62.

64. Further on Debussy and Indonesian music, see (among others) Watkins, *Pyramids*, 19–27, and Roberts, *Images*, 153–75, 289–92.
65. Lesure, *Claude Debussy*, 453.
66. See Chapter 3 and, with regard to Baroque works about Eastern tyrants, Chapter 5.
67. Cf. Fauser, *Musical*, 157 ("musical banality of exotic signifiers in works such as *Lakmé*"), 205.
68. Other, that is, than Vogler's weird, forgotten experiment of a century earlier. On black-note pentatonicism, see Chapters 6 and 8.
69. If this piece were transposed up a half-step (the tonic note thus becoming C), the basic pentatonic pitches would be C–D–E–G–A, the white-note version of "black-note" pentatonicism.
70. On the treatment of pitch in *Pagodes*, see, most recently, Day-O'Connell, *Pentatonicism*, 171–81.
71. Revol, *Influences*, 222–48.
72. The recurrence at m. 84 *is* underpinned with a low octave E, but still remains tonally elusive because of the A♯.
73. The accompanimental figure, characteristic of the piece's floating treatment of tonality, uses a pentatonic fragment of the three pitches 3–5–6 (no 1). A phrase resembling, but more briefly, the opening of Example 9.4 had already occurred in Debussy's early song "Il pleure dans mon coeur."
74. A. Berger, "Problems," 128–29, 141–44; van den Toorn, *Music*, 31–72, 321–66, 462–67, 492–95.
75. Conrad, "Langage."
76. For example, Mauss, *Gift*, 8, 10, 62, 75, 88n.
77. Photos in Meyer and Zimmermann, *Edgard Varèse*, 234–35.
78. Kayas, *André Jolivet*, 148–63, 190, 576–78 (Jolivet's library).
79. Ibid., 390–96, 451–55 (1958 ballet, entitled *Concerto*, about the shifting relations between a man and a woman).
80. Griffiths, *Olivier Messiaen*, 124–28; Sherlaw Johnson, *Messiaen*, 13–24.
81. Griffiths, *Olivier Messiaen*, 124–42.
82. Messiaen, "Turangalîla," 1.
83. *Ibid.*, 3.
84. For example, just before reh. no. 8.
85. Listeners tend also to link certain works of the young John Cage to Asian music (notably the Sonatas and Interludes for Prepared Piano, 1948). For Cage, though, the primary influence seems to have come from Asian philosophy rather than Asian musics.
86. Cooke, "'East'," 280.
87. Debussy, article of 15 February 1913, in *Monsieur Croche*, 229.
88. Fauser, *Musical*, 165–98; McPhee, *House*; McPhee, *Music*; Oja, *Colin McPhee*, 273–83.
89. Debussy, article of 15 February 1913, in *Monsieur Croche*, 229. Debussy's *chacun* and *son* clearly include the female dancers (hence my "his or her").

90. Cowell, "Towards Neo-Primitivism" (1933), cited in Nicholls, "Henry Cowell," 8. On contrasting views of Cowell's "United" Quartet, see Taylor, *Beyond*, 105–10.
91. See, for example, Partch, *Bitter*, 250 (*nōh* drama and Ethiopian folk play as basis for the two acts of *Delusion of the Fury*), 309 (Asian dancing and acting as the best model for stage works, including *The Bewitched: A Dance Satire*).
92. The Partch instruments are described and shown at www.newband.org and can be heard and played (from one's computer keyboard) at http:musicmavericks.publicradio.org/features/feature_partch.html#.
93. On the American-music website *Art of the States*: http://artofthestates.org/.
94. Nicholls, "Transethnicism."
95. *Ibid.*; Miller, "Lou Harrison."
96. Brett, "Queer"; and his "Eros," 238. Cf. objections in Nicholls, "Reaching," 127–28.
97. See Cooke, "'East'," 269–80; Cooke, *Britten*; and Brett, "Eros." Britten's ballet *The Prince of the Pagodas* (1957) tells a more straightforward exotic story.
98. Brett, "Eros."
99. Fauser, *Musical*, 206, with regard to echoes of Indonesian music-making and culture in *Pelléas* and other non-Asian pieces by Debussy.
100. Cook, *Opera*; Sullivan, *New World*; and Robinson, "Jazz."
101. Schuller, "Jazz."
102. Mawer, *Darius Milhaud*, 145–76, 273–76, 330–48; Watkins, *Soundings*, 276–78; Watkins, *Pyramids*, 116–21; Kramer, *Musical*, 194–215; Rosenstock, "Léger."
103. Milhaud, "The Evolution of the Jazz Band and Negro Music in North America," in Collaer, *Darius Milhaud*, 69–75 (quotation from 69); Watkins, *Pyramids*, 112–33.
104. Lambert, *Music*, 189.
105. Fauser, *Musical*, 206.
106. Many important works must be neglected in the remainder of this chapter. Three from Central Europe – all evoking, by turns, sensuality and world-weariness – are Mahler's *Das Lied von der Erde* (1909; see Lo, "Chinesische," and Draughon, "Orientalist"); Alexander Zemlinsky's *Lyrische Symphonie in sieben Gesängen* (1923, after texts by Rabindranath Tagore: "My soul goes out in a longing to touch the skirt of the dim distance"); and Karol Szymanowski's opera *Król Roger* (1926; its Act 2 evokes music of India and the Arab world).
107. Lambert, *Music*, 152–53.
108. Móricz, "Sensuous," 479–83; see also Móricz, *Jewish*, 116–52.
109. Móricz, "Ancestral," 108–14.
110. Quoted in *ibid.*, 113.
111. Móricz, "Sensuous," 477–79.
112. Peppercorn, *World*, 58; Peppercorn, *Villa-Lobos: The Music*, 82–86.
113. Peppercorn, *Villa-Lobos* (1989), 41 (concert of 17 November 1917).
114. Peppercorn, *Villa-Lobos: The Music*, 46, 50–61; the text (used without permission by Villa-Lobos) is by the poet Catullo Cearense: see S. Wright, "Villa-

Lobos." Villa-Lobos's preface to the score of *Chôros* No. 10 (Paris: Max Eschig, 1928) proposes that this series of works "synthesizes" the "different manners [*modalités*] of Brazilian, Indian, and popular music," especially rhythmic aspects and "typical" melodies.

115. Hovhaness interview, October 1983.
116. *Ibid.*
117. It can be heard at www.ArtoftheStates.org.
118. Hinako Fujihara Hovhaness, booklet notes.
119. On *Grand Canyon* and other "Western" works (William Grant Still's *The American Scene: Five Suites for Young Americans*, for orchestra, 1957: suites 3 and 4; Roy Harris's *Cimarron* overture for band, 1941), see Toliver, "Eco-ing"; Levy, *Frontier*, 183–86; and Glahn, *Sounds*, 174–208.
120. On *Billy the Kid* and *Rodeo*, see Copland and Perlis, *Copland*, 278–83, 354–64; Pollack, *Aaron Copland*, 314–25, 363–74; and Crist, *Music*, 111–12, 119–46.
121. Pollack, *Aaron Copland*, 302.
122. On *Salón* and *Danzón*, see Copland and Perlis, *Copland*, 216, 244–51, 366–67; Pollack, *Aaron Copland*, 298–303, 374–77 (including Copland's view that the blues episode creates a pan-American result); and Crist, *Music*, 43–59, 64–68.
123. Schwarz, *Music*, 132–34 (music festivals displaying each "republic"); Taruskin, *Defining*, xvi-xvii; Frolova-Walker, *Russian*, 311–38.
124. Herman's version was the no. 3 best-selling record in the USA in early May 1948.
125. Schwarz, *Music*, 317–18; see also Tomoff, *Creative*, 34–35, 43–44, 125–29, 143–44.
126. Contemporary observer Michel Corday, cited in Kramer, "Consuming," 213.
127. Nilsson, "Musical."
128. "So Am I" and "Idle Dreams": *Gershwin Plays Gershwin: The Piano Rolls*, realized on a Yamaha Disklavier by Artis Wodehouse (Nonesuch CD79287); the Gardner song is on vol. 2 of the same series (Nonesuch CD79370).
129. See Bañagale "American."
130. Sublette, *Cuba*, vii.
131. Roberts, *Latin*, 38–39; and Garrett, *Struggling*, 48–82.
132. Attitudes toward racial mixing and cultural identity are often complex among people in or from the Caribbean. Some twentieth-century Puerto Rican musicians put forth the light-skinned *jibaro* as emblematic of their island; others (after relocating to New York City) claimed to be Cuban in order to align themselves with a more intense Afro-Caribbean style of music-making (Lipsitz, *Footsteps*, 214–15, 222).
133. See Leydon, "Utopia," 45–71; and Ford, "Taboo."
134. On Latin influences in jazz, see Schuller, *Swing*, 87.
135. McKibbon and Fuller, cited in Garcia, "We Both," 13.
136. Richards, *Imperialism*, 355, 358, 514.

137. Finson, *Voices*, 270–314.
138. From *Music from the New York Stage 1890–1920*, vol. 4, three CDs, Pearl GEMM CD 9059/61.
139. Lancefield, *Hearing*, 785–91. Parallel fourths and fifths were systematically used to indicate China or Japan (791).
140. Finson, *Voices*, 240–69; Pisani, *Imagining*, 243–91.
141. In the film, the song is first given over a "jungle" rhythm, but the up-tempo finale is done in vaudeville-theater style (complete with straw "boater" hats).
142. Jasen, *Thirty-Five*, 141–43.
143. Bamboo, as the songwriters perhaps knew or suspected, is native both to the Caribbean and to sub-Saharan Africa.
144. Bob Cole and J. Rosamond Johnson, "Under the Bamboo Tree," reprinted in David A. Jasen, ed., *35 Song Hits by Great Black Songwriters* (Mineola, NY: Dover Publications, 1998), 142–43.
145. Locke, "Living," 104, 118n.
146. Recording by Marie Cahill, with male chorus, re-released on *Music from the New York Stage 1890–1920*, vol. 1 (three CDs), Pearl GEMM CDS 9050-2.
147. The music is generally attributed to Bernie Hanighen (better known as a lyricist).
148. Such postcards form the basis for the ponderings in Alloula, *Colonial*.
149. "Abd El-Kader" and "Nuits d'outremer," and the *chansons* mentioned in the following paragraphs, as well as some songs relating to the French Foreign Legion (e.g., by Piaf), are available on a two-CD collection (on the French EPM label): *Chansons coloniales et exotiques 1906–1942*, EPM983312/ADE798. The booklet reproduces travel posters, sheet-music covers, and an advertisement for the Exposition Coloniale Internationale (Paris 1931) featuring lesser-known colonies, such as Dahomey, and posing the question: "Did you know that France was so big?" The words of many of the songs are contained in Ruscio, *Que la France*, whose CD overlaps in part with the EPM CDs; Ruscio's book contains a whole section of songs praising the bravery of local (i.e., native) troops. Contemporaneous Italian songs with similar themes were gathered on an LP *c.* 1970: *Donne di terre lontane*, which was series V, no. 3 of *Fonografo italiano*, ed. Paquito Del Bosco: Cetra FC 3653.
150. "Le grand voyage du pauvre nègre," by Raymond Asso and R. Cloërec, 1937.
151. Misraki was born in Istanbul to, one presumes from the name, a Jewish family.
152. Fry, "Rethinking."
153. "Petite Tonkinoise," words by G. Villard and [Henri?] Christiné, music by Vincent Scotto, in *Premier Album 1900 Salabert pour piano et chant* (Paris: Editions Salabert, 1940), 16–17.
154. Josephine Baker, *Un message pour toi: Original Paris Recordings, 1926–1937* (Naxos Nostalgia CD 8.120630).
155. Jules-Rosette, *Josephine Baker*, 175.

156. *Ibid.*, 66, 173 (early biography by her husband Jo Bouillon).
157. *Ibid.*, 63–64.
158. Koebner, "Land," 452.
159. See the "silence" section of Chapter 8.
160. Morocco was a French protectorate from 1912 until it negotiated its independence in 1956.
161. Three exceptions: Middleton (the works uses "the nineteenth-century ... code of the picturesque" and offers "a canvas of exotic colors" – "Musical," 68, 69); a review of a performance in Vienna in 1952 ("a portrait of exotic life" – Beruth, "Ein exotisches Lebenbild"); and playwright Lorraine Hansberry ("an excursion in the 'exotic'," quoted in Pollack, *George Gershwin*, 650, 810).
162. One, involving the king, is discussed in Chapter 11 below.
163. Gorbman, "Scoring," and Pisani, *Imagining*, 292–329, 379–81.
164. Rapée, *Motion*, 496–518.
165. *Ibid.*, 519–22.
166. Erdmann, *et al.*, *Allgemeines Handbuch*, vol. 2, excerpt no. 2983: "etwa Priestertanz." This publication contains incipits of some 3,000 pieces of music by 200 composers as well as instructive essays. The more than 130 mood or style categories include other relevant headings: "exotic character dance," "Japanese/Chinese," and "exotic music – collections."
167. The aria has been recorded by (among others) Kiri Te Kanawa: RCA Victor 0707-2-RG.
168. See, for example, Maurice Baron's "Vers l'oasis (In Sight of the Oasis)," and Mort Glickman's "Arabian Tornado." The former is printed in Rapée, *Motion*, 506–9; the latter is recorded on *Music from the Serials* (The CinemaSound Orchestra, cond. James King), Cinédisc CDC1020.
169. Sheppard, "Exotic," 331n (Agee quotation).
170. *Ibid.*, 350.
171. The setting is actually the 1890s Alaskan Gold Rush.
172. Internet Movie Database (accessed 19 July 2007) and Mielke, *Road*, 38 (*Times* quotation). The musical numbers mentioned are now on *Hit the Road with Bing and Bob: From Bali to Zanzibar* (Jasmine Music two-CD set). "Batuque" is by Russo da Pandeiro and Sa Roris; the other two are credited to Johnny Burke and Jimmy Van Heusen (but they presumably did not write what the Africans sing in *Road to Zanzibar*).
173. See, for example, his remarkable senior thesis from college, "The Absorption of Race Elements into American Music," in Bernstein, *Findings*, 36–99.
174. On song categories, see Hischak, *American*, xiii–xv.
175. The remainder of the present chapter is based upon the more extensive discussion in Locke, "Border."

176. Leonard Bernstein, "Excerpts from a *West Side Story* Log," in his *Findings*, 144–47 (145).
177. As Bernstein himself noted: *Findings*, 144–47; cf. Banfield, *Sondheim's*, 103.
178. Banfield, *Sondheim's*, 37; Laurents, *Original*, 351, 348. On jazz as symbol of urban menace (especially after dark), see Ford, "Jazz."
179. These are the "Blues" – further qualified by the performance indication "rocky," i.e., play it with a rock 'n' roll swagger – and the Pasodoble, which, despite the Spanish name in the score (which means "two-step" or "double-step"), strikes the listener mainly as plodding and unsexy: an inane polka for old folks. Perhaps Bernstein was thinking of a well-known (and pompous) *pasodoble* from the classical repertoire: the Royal March from Stravinsky's *L'histoire du soldat* (1918).
180. In some of these examples (e.g., *Carmen*, beginning of Act 2), the exotic women are being watched by men, or are even dancing for them. Interestingly, in the movie version of *West Side Story*, "America" was, with Bernstein's perhaps grudging permission, turned into a debate between the male and female "Sharks." The men do not merely watch: they, too, dance. Bernstein's recording and the recent "critical edition" (1994) do not accept this both-sexes version. Cf. Banfield, *Sondheim's*, 33.
181. Also, Tony's and Radames's songs of dazzled adoration both occur early on, before the heroine has sung a note. One difference between the songs is that, in Radames's, the music is exotic only in the middle section.
182. See Wells, "*West*," and her forthcoming book *West*.

10 Exoticism in a global age (*c.* 1960 to today)

1. Japan's British-style parliament was established in 1869, the second year of the Meiji Restoration.
2. Other schemes were possible: Henry Kissinger, in 1969, divided the world into Western countries and "underdeveloped" ones that had never experienced "the impact of Newtonian thinking." Russia, in this scheme, occupied "an intermediate position," and Japan was another kind of exception (*American*, 48, 15, 165). On a different "second world" nowadays (middle-income states, such as Colombia, Libya, Ukraine, and Malaysia), see Khanna, *Second*.
3. Nettl, *Western*; Manuel, *Popular*; Stock, "Peripheries"; and Taylor, *Beyond*, 115.
4. Shay, *Choreographic*; earlier "national" performing groups in the Soviet Republics (e.g., Armenian choruses) are discussed in the various studies in Edmunds, *Soviet*.
5. Yangwen, "From *Swan Lake*."
6. *Le mystère des voix bulgares*, cond. Philip Koutev, vol. 1 (Nonesuch LP 79165-2, released 1987).
7. For example: Hiekel argues that recent efforts at "intercultural composing" avoid "an unreflective Eurocentrism, which allows anything non-European [to enter]

only as a decorative bit of exotica [*als dekoratives Exotikum*]" – *Orientierungen*, 7 (from his preface).
8. See also, in Chapter 4, the discussion of Astor Piazzolla and Henryk Górecki.
9. Yuasa, "Herausforderung," 158–89; Schalz-Laurenze, "Musikalischer Brückenbau," 233.
10. Rinser and Yun, *Verwundete*, 100 (blocks and whip), 93 (Hauptton); Revers, "Hauptton."
11. Rinser and Yun, *Verwundete*, 94.
12. Seachrist, *Musical*, 70–71, 175, 182–85. Further details at El-Dabh's website: www.halimeldabh.com.
13. Excerpts on the CD accompanying Seachrist, *Musical*.
14. The work appeared as part of a 1961 LP of music from the Columbia-Princeton Electronic Music Center (Columbia Records MS6566/ML5966).
15. Booth, "Madras."
16. Schwarz, *Music*, 324, 333–34, 488.
17. Kurtz, *Sofia Gubaidulina*, 119–23.
18. The Gubaïdulina is recorded on BMG 74321-49957-2. See Kurtz, *Sofia Gubaidulina*, 81–82, 126–28.
19. Griffiths, *Substance*, 35.
20. Ben-Haim, autobiographical sketch, 1945, transcribed in Seter, *Yuvalim*, 166, also 116 and 176.
21. Letter from Gradenwitz to Ben-Haim, 22 October 1952 (referring to 2 Samuel 6:14-23), cited in Seter, *Yuvalim*, 212–48.
22. Sheppard, *Revealing*.
23. The *tumba* is a tall, narrow Latin-American drum.
24. Jacques Longchampt, in Iannis Xenakis, *Rebonds pour percussion solo*, ed. Patrick Butin (Paris: Editions Salabert, 1991), [iv].
25. Quoted in Sheppard, *Revealing*, 127.
26. *Ibid.*, 126–43, 292–96.
27. Boulez, *Orientations*, 341.
28. Jameux, *Pierre Boulez*, 102 (Schneider quotation), 104.
29. Welch, "Meetings"; see various interviews in Lavezzoli, *Dawn*.
30. Reich, *Writings*, 70.
31. *Ibid.*, 54–63, 147–51.
32. Williams, *Desert*, 15.
33. Reich, *Writings*, 87–91; cf. Potter, *Four*, 231–33.
34. Reich, Foreword to Tenzer, *Gamelan*, xvii.
35. See the definitions by Leprohon and de Van in Chapter 3.
36. Volans, Preface, [iii].
37. The Chopsticks variations by Liszt and others are available as *Paraphrases: 24 variations et 17 petites pièces pour piano sur le théme favori et obligé*, ed. Alexandre Tcherepnin (Bonn: M. P. Belaïeff, 1959).
38. Volans, Preface, [iii].

39. Scherzinger, "'Art'," 610.
40. And also some prior composers of folk-nationalist works: for example, Grieg, in *Slåtter*, No. 4: "Halling" (chromatic middle section), and Bartók, in "Evenings in Transylvania" (dissonant "response" to folk-like opening).
41. Quoted in Guzelimian, "Counterpoint," 6.
42. www.osvaldogolijov.com/wd39t.htm
43. It is a rounded-binary, with repeated first half, in the minor mode. It briefly moves to the relative major and back.
44. The words are by Riboutté, the music probably by Antoine Albanèse (an Italian-born voice teacher based in Paris). The song has been recorded by Suzanne Mentzer (*Wayfaring Stranger*, Teldec CD 2564-61755-2, 1997) and by Mady Mesplé (*Bergerettes et pastourelles: Romances et chansons du xviiie siècle*, French EMI LP 2C069-14044; rereleased on CD, 1992). Nineteenth-century composer Ferdinand Sor wrote a set of variations on it for guitar (Op. 26), which is still available in print and occasionally performed.
45. The nineteenth-century religious version is found in *Choix*, 23–25, where reference is made to tune 13, on p. 28 of the accompanying tune collection.
46. Everett and Lau, *Locating*.
47. Burt, *Takemitsu*, 234.
48. *Ibid.*, 2, 23, 29, 31, 72, 92–97; cf. 13–19 (earlier Japanese composers' attraction to European music).
49. *Ibid.*, 111.
50. Takemitsu, "On Sawari," 204.
51. Yu, "Two." 58–59, 69–71.
52. *Ibid.*, 59.
53. Beginning at 2:30. The score is unpublished; I have therefore sometimes guessed at technical details, such as the written meter of a passage.
54. Starting at 6:00, and including decorative (*ping*) tones and prominent string portamento.
55. Beginning at 0:40; the quotation becomes explicit at 1:10.
56. David Pollack, a professor of Chinese and Japanese at the University of Rochester, kindly suggests that what Tan Dun's Li Po sings here is a poem that, though similar in meaning to the poem by the actual Li Po, was written later – in the eleventh century – by Sū Shì, also known as Su Dongpo.
57. Sony 2-CDs S2K 62912; end of CD2, track 6.
58. On Tan's collaboration with the superstar system and the "hegemonic music industry," see Lau, "Fusion," 33–34, 38.
59. Tan Dun, "On the Creation," 10.
60. Oja, "New," 6.
61. Oestreich, "Sound."
62. Lau, "Fusion," 38. Cf. Corbett, "Experimental," and Buruma, "Of Musical."
63. Porter, *John Coltrane*, 265 (the passage is from *Bhagavad-Gita*, Ch. 9.17). A year later, Coltrane's group chanted the most famous Tibetan Buddhist mantra,

"Om mani padme hum," at the start of "Reverend King" (on the LP *Cosmic Music*, which was released in 1968, after Coltrane had died).
64. Clements, "Indian," 14.
65. Stowe, "Jazz," 281–92. *Road* and *Hiroshima* are on True Life CD TLE 11000082 (2003). On *Kogun*, two Japanese musicians play different-sized *tsuzumi* drums (on *Road Time*, 1976; now a two-CD set from BMG Japan).
66. Stowe, "Jazz," 272, 282. Cf. Dale, *Myth*.
67. See Fanshawe's book *African*.
68. Two recorded performances exist: Philips 426 055-2 or D 105578; and Silva America SILKD 6003.
69. Walser, "Polka."
70. *Concert for the Klezmer*, Plane CD 88757 (1998).
71. See Feld, "Notes," "World," and "pygmy POP"; and Zemp, "Ethnomusicologist."
72. Taylor, *Global*, 112.
73. *Ibid.*, 117.
74. Jackson interview in the short documentary "Music for Middle-Earth" (2002).
75. Interview with unnamed New Zealand athlete in the short documentary "Music for Middle-Earth" (2002).
76. www.nzrugby.com/history/history_haka.asp (accessed 23 November 2003).
77. Interviews in the short documentary "Music for Middle-Earth" (2002).
78. Similarly, Jackson praises the voice of Sheila Chandra – used in the scene of Aragorn's awaking from near-death, in the second film of the trilogy – as "very exotic, almost Eastern" ("Music for Middle-Earth," 2003).
79. On Trio Los Panchos, see the entry on www.musicofpuertorico.com (accessed 14 February 2008). "One Hundred Guitars" was another name for the Orquesta Popular de Madrid de La O.N.C.E. Further on the foreign-originated Columbia releases, see www.hipwax.com/music/advent.html (accessed 14 February 2008).
80. The one obvious exception: Americans who are bilingual because of coming from an immigrant family.
81. See, for example, the listings in Whitburn, *Century*, and analogous books from *Billboard* Magazine.
82. I am referring to the recording of *Bei mir* by the Andrews Sisters (I adopt the record manufacturer's Germanized spelling of the title) and to the recording of *Volare* by Dean Martin.
83. The all-Italian recording of *Volare* by Domenico Modugno (an Italian entry to the Eurovision Song Contest in 1958) actually rose even higher on the US charts than Dean Martin's, making it a rare case of an entirely non-English (and non-Spanish) song captivating the American market.
84. For words and translation of of "Ue o muite aruk?" (the song's actual title), see www.learn-japanese.info/ueomuite.html (accessed 14 February 2008).
85. Claman, *Western*, 138; further, see Farrell, *Indian*, 182–88.
86. Bellman, "Indian," 296, 352–53n. A scale with major third degree and lowered seventh is standardly recognized within both Carnatic music theory (*melakarta*

type 28) and Hindustani (*khamāj*). Characteristic phrases can be heard, often with variable seventh degree (sometimes raised, sometimes repeatedly flatted), in the final minute of Raga Bahar (i.e., springtime) and many other tracks from the album *Indian Music: Ragas and Dances: The Original Uday Shankar Company of Hindu Musicians, Recorded During Its Historic 1937 Visit to the United States* (originally released in 1938, LP version 1968: RCA Victrola VIC-1361).

87. Bellman, "Indian," 297.
88. *Ibid.*, 302, and Reck, "Neon."
89. Day-O'Connell, *Pentatonicism*, 40 (quoting Leonard B. Meyer, *Explaining Music*, 117); cf. 4, 34, 41, 160, 162.
90. Brackett, "Politics."
91. Byrne, "I Hate."
92. For example, Osborne's "St. Teresa" (1995) and her rendition of James Taylor's "How Sweet It Is" (2002); and a snatch of the Hoochy-Cooch tune near the end of Fiona Apple's "Criminal" (1996).
93. Moy, *Kate Bush*, 51, 60, 69, 87, 104–21.
94. Taylor, *Beyond*, 141.
95. Yri, "Medievalism."
96. Taylor, *Beyond*, 171–74. The website still exists but is no longer functional; Sony did not respond to my queries.
97. *Ibid.*, 171–74.
98. The 1984 ads were arranged by Howard Blake: www.howardblake.com (accessed 5 September 2007).
99. "Bottom Line." A likely explanation is that America has had much less historical involvement with India than has Great Britain, and a far smaller proportion of its current population has come from there.
100. Byrne, "I Hate."
101. Two Middle Eastern female singers enact a similar "Tiff in the Seraglio" – using an aria from Mozart's *Entführung* and an Arab folk song – on the CD *Mozart in Egypt 2* (Virgin Classics 3-35936-2).
102. Gumpert; "Everyway," 151.
103. Ali Bukaç, in *Zaman* (a "progressive-Islamist" newspaper, according to Gumpert), 28 May 2003 (in Gumpert, "Everyway," 150–51).

11 Epilogue: exotic works of the past, today

1. On the danger of emphasizing only the composer's viewpoint, see Crawford, *American*, 39–107, and Locke and Barr, "Introduction," 3. On other ingrained habits of music-history writing, see Locke, "Music," 510–24.
2. Other factors have included (1) the cult of technical proficiency – seen in virtuosic solo playing and also in the highly coordinated large-ensemble playing that one hears today in countries around the globe – and (2) a belief (real or professed) in the uplifting powers of art.

3. Fazıl Say, Mozart Sonatas K330, 331, 332, and Variations K265, on Atlantic CD 21970-2. He has also composed "Turkish Dances" and "Variations on Mozart's Rondo Alla turca," both for piano solo.
4. For example, the CD entitled "Fiesta!" (based on a live concert) that accompanied the February 2003 issue of *BBC Music Magazine*.
5. YouTube.com (accessed on 18 July 2007). The two performances were by the Yuhua Harmonic Band and the National University of Singapore Harmonica Orchestra.
6. www.tomtom.com/about/about.php?ID=1&Language=4 (accessed 14 February 2008).
7. I have seen on YouTube.com three versions of the ad, involving characters named DougDoug, ScottScott, and SueSue.
8. Not to be confused with the Mexican song *Cucurrucucu paloma*, the slow march *La virgen de la paloma*, or the zarzuela *La verbena de la paloma*.
9. Alonso, *Cien*, xvi; the 1857 version is published on pp. 221–27, with remarkable words in dialect for the coda.
10. As an adjective, "guachinango/a" today means slimy (suave, flattering) or sharp (astute); as a masculine noun, it refers to a Caribbean fish (red snapper).
11. On some syncopation-free versions, see Baim, *Tango*, 136–37.
12. *La Paloma: One Song for All Worlds*, Trikont US-0220, -0227, -0241, and -0272; see also www.trikont.com, and Bloemeke, *Paloma*.
13. Staier, "Ornamentation," 12.
14. Ivanoff, "Sacred," 3.
15. The Qur'an does praise God's gift of the Psalms to David (4:163, 17:55).
16. Jefferson, "Culture."
17. Canby, "Once."
18. Jefferson, "Culture."
19. Klein, *Cold*, 221.
20. For a spirited defense of the reworking of literary works carrying a "high cultural cachet" (e.g., by Euripides or Shakespeare), see Forsyth, *Gadamer*.
21. Quoted and discussed in Parakilas, "How," in Bellman, *Exotic*, 163.
22. Further, see Locke, "Constructing," 289–98. Both performances are available on DVD (Kultur Video). Stage director for the 1980 video was Nicolas Joël.
23. Similarly, one has to find a way to laugh with and at Falstaff in Henry IV, Part I, not turn him into either a villain or victim.
24. Claims of a basic clash of civilizations today are laid out in Huntington, *Clash*; Warraq, *Defending*; and Buruma and Margalit, *Occidentalism*.
25. Kozinn, "Mozart's."
26. MacDonald, "Abduction," and Paulick, "Violent." These points are confirmed in excerpts from a *Financial Times* review much quoted on the Internet; see also Buschinger, "Berliner."
27. See Rubin and Melnick, *Immigration*, 99, and Denby, "Place."
28. Negrón-Muntaner, *Boricua*, 62.
29. Cited in *ibid.*, 59.

30. *Ibid.*, 60–61.
31. Lash, "Bare."
32. McClary, "Mounting," 32.
33. *Ibid.*, 26 and 34n. On *anti*-imperialism in *Butterfly*, see Chapter 8 above.
34. hooks, *Reel*, 3. (I have silently corrected in that sentence what seems a typo: "at last for a time.")
35. The quiet wedding chorus sung by the Bar-Girls ("Dju vui vai"), for example, fulfills much the same function as Puccini's wedding toast "O Kami."
36. Bernheimer, "Marina," 16.
37. hooks puts the matter more encouragingly (in her video lectures: *Cultural*, end of part 1): we, blacks and whites alike, must move toward "decolonizing our minds, so that we can both resist certain kinds of conservatizing representations and at the same time create new and exciting representations."
38. Pisani, *Imagining*, 332.
39. The present, final paragraph expands on some sentences in Locke, "Reflections," 64.
40. Appiah, *Cosmopolitanism*, p. xx (passage quoted more fully at the end of Chapter 3 above).

Bibliography

The Bibliography includes all writings cited in the notes, except for passing references to entries in *Grove Music Online* and to a few other websites (e.g., official websites of composers). It also includes some additional writings that were found helpful but are not cited in the notes. The Bibliography includes recordings whose jacket notes or CD booklets have been quoted but omits all other recordings and all scores referred to in the notes. Two valuable websites with performances are listed at the end.

Abbate, Carolyn. "Music – Drastic or Gnostic." *Critical Inquiry* 30 (2004): 505–36.

Adorno, Theodor W. "Fantasia sopra Carmen" (1955). In his *Quasi una fantasia: Essays on Modern Music*. Translated by Rodney Livingstone, 53–64. London: Verso, 1992.

Agawu, Kofi. *Playing with Signs: A Semiotic Interpretation of Classical Music*. Princeton: Princeton University Press, 1991.

Representing African Music: Postcolonial Notes, Queries, Positions. New York: Routledge, 2003.

Agnew, Vanessa. *Enlightenment Orpheus: The Power of Music in Other Worlds*. Oxford: Oxford University Press, 2008.

Alazard, Jean. *L'Orient et la peinture française au xixe siècle, d'Eugène Delacroix à Auguste Renoir*. Paris: Plon, 1930.

Al-Taee, Nasser. "Fidelity, Violence, and Fanaticism: Orientalism in Wranitzky's *Oberon, König der Elfen*." *Opera Quarterly* 17, no. 1 (2001) 43–69.

"Under the Spell of Magic: The Oriental Tale in Rimsky-Korsakov's *Scheherazade*." In Saree Makdisi and Felicity Nussbaum, eds., *The Arabian Nights in Historical context: Between East and West*, 265–96. Oxford: Oxford University Press, 2009.

"Whirling Fanatics: Orientalism, Politics, and Religious Rivalry in Western Operatic Representations of the Orient." In Baur, et al., *Musicological*, 17–30.

Allen, Ray, and George P. Cunningham. "Cultural Uplift and Double-Consciousness: African American Responses to the 1935 Opera *Porgy and Bess*." *Musical Quarterly* 88 (2005): 342–69.

Allen, Roger. "An Analysis of the 'Tale of the Three Apples' from *The Thousand and One Nights*." In Ulrich Marzolph, *The Arabian Nights Reader*, 239–48. Detroit: Wayne State University Press, 2006.

Alloula, Malek. *The Colonial Harem*. Translated by Myrna Godzich and Wlad Godzich. Minneapolis: University of Minnesota Press, 1987.

Alm, Irene. "Dances from the 'Four Corners of the Earth': Exoticism in Seventeenth-Century Venetian Opera." In Irene Alm, Alyson McLamore, and Colleen

Reardon, eds., *Musica Franca: Essays in Honor of Frank A. D'Accone*, 233–57. Stuyvesant, NY: Pendragon Press, 1996.

"Winged Feet and Mute Eloquence: Dance in Seventeenth-Century Venetian Opera." Edited by Wendy Heller and Rebecca Harris-Warrick. *Cambridge Opera Journal* 15 (2003): 216–80.

Alonso, Celsa, ed. *Cien años de canción lírica española, vol. 1: 1800–68.* Música hispana 8. Madrid: Instituto Complutense de Ciencias Musicales, 2001.

Amalfitano, Paolo, and Loretta Innocenti, eds. *L'Oriente: Storia di una figura nelle arti occidentali (1700-2000).* 2 vols. Rome: Bulzoni, 2007.

Anderson, Benedict. *Imagined Communities: Reflections on the Origin and Spread of Nationalism.* 2nd edn., rev. and extended. London: Verso, 1991. See also Sherman, "Return."

André, Naomi. "Veiled Messages and Encoded Meanings: Exoticism, Verdi and Women's Lower Voices." *Ars Lyrica* 11 (2000): 1–22.

Voicing Gender: Castrati, Travesti, and the Second Woman in Early-Nineteenth-Century Italian Opera. Bloomington: Indiana University Press, 2006.

Appiah, Kwame Anthony. *Cosmopolitanism: Ethics in a World of Strangers.* New York: W. W. Norton, 2006.

Aristotle. *Nicomachean Ethics.* Translated by Christopher Rowe. Commentary by Sarah Broadie. Oxford: Oxford University Press, 2002.

Arkin, Lisa C., and Marian Smith. "National Dance in the Romantic Ballet." In Lynn Garofala, ed., *Rethinking the Sylph: New Perspectives on the Romantic Ballet*, 11–68, 245–52. Hanover, NH: University Press of New England, 1997.

Ashbrook, William. *The Operas of Puccini.* Corrected edn, with preface by Roger Parker. Oxford: Oxford University Press, 1985.

Ashbrook, William, and Harold Powers. *Puccini's "Turandot": The End of the Great Tradition.* Princeton: Princeton University Press, 1991.

Ashcroft, Bill, Gareth Griffiths, and Helen Tiffin. *The Empire Writes Back: Theory and Practice in Post-Colonial Literatures*, 2nd edn. London: Routledge, 2002.

Austen, Jane. *Mansfield Park: A Norton Critical Edition.* Edited by Claudia L. Johnson. New York: W. W. Norton and Company, 1998.

Austin, William W., ed. *Claude Debussy: Prelude to "The Afternoon of a Faun": A Norton Critical Score.* New York: W. W. Norton, 1970.

Ayers, Brenda, ed. *The Emperor's Old Groove: Decolonizing Disney's Magic Kingdom.* New York: Peter Lang, 2003.

Bachmann, Peter. "'From Arabia's Spicy Shores': Orient in Händels Textvorlagen." *Göttinger Händel-Beiträge* 8 (2000): 1–14.

Bailyn, Evan. *Music of Puerto Rico: Know Us By the Songs We Sing.* www.musicofpuertorico.com.

Baim, Jo. *Tango: Creation of a Cultural Icon.* Bloomington: Indiana University Press, 2007.

Balardelle, Geneviève. "L'exotisme extrême-oriental en France au tournant du siècle." *Revue internationale de musique française* 6 (November 1981): 67–76.

Bañagale, Ryan Raul. "An American in Chinatown: Asian Representation in the Music of George Gershwin." MA thesis, University of Washington, 2004.

Banfield, Stephen. *Sondheim's Broadway Musicals*. Ann Arbor: University of Michigan Press, 1993.

Bartha, Dénes. "Mozart et le folklore musical de l'Europe centrale." In André Verchaly, ed., *Les Influences étrangères dans l'oeuvre de W. A. Mozart*, 157–81. Paris: Editions du Centre National de la Recherche Scientifique, 1956.

Bartoli, Jean-Pierre. "L'orientalisme dans la musique française du XIXe siècle: la *ponctuation*, la seconde augmentée et l'apparition de la modalité dans les procédures exotiques." *Revue belge de musicologie* 51 (1997): 137–70.

"Propositions pour une définition de l'exotisme musical et pour l'application en musique de la notion d'isotopie sémantique." *Musurgia* 7, no. 2 (2000): 61–71.

Basini, Laura. "Masks, Minuets and Murder: Images of Italy in Leoncavallo's *Pagliacci*." *Journal of the Royal Musical Association* 133 (2008): 32–68.

Bauerle, Ruth, ed. *The James Joyce Songbook*. New York: Da Capo Press, 1982.

Bauman, Thomas. *W. A. Mozart: Die Entführung aus dem Serail*. Cambridge: Cambridge University Press, 1987.

Baur, Steven. "Ravel's 'Russian' Period: Octatonicism in His Early Works, 1893–1908." *Journal of the American Musicological Society* 52 (1999): 531–92, and 53 (2000): 445–50 [correspondence].

Baur, Steven, Jacqueline Warwick, and Raymond Knapp, eds. *Musicological Identities: Essays in Honor of Susan McClary*. Aldershot: Ashgate, 2008.

Beaufils, Marcel. *Villa-Lobos: musicien et poète du Brésil*. 2nd edn. Preface by Pierre Vidal. Paris: EST/IHEAL, 1988.

Beaulieu, Jill, and Mary Roberts, eds. *Orientalism's Interlocutors: Painting, Architecture, Photography*. Durham, NC: Duke University Press, 2002.

Becker, Heinz, ed. *Die Couleur locale in der Opera des 19. Jahrhunderts*. Regensburg: Bosse, 1976.

Beckerman, Michael B. *New Worlds of Dvořák: Searching in America for the Composer's Inner Life*. New York: W. W. Norton, 2003.

Beirão, Christine Wassermann, Thomas Daniel Schlee, and Elmar Budde, eds. *La cité céleste: Olivier Messiaen zum Gedächtnis, Dokumentation einer Symposienreihe*. Berlin: Weidler Buchverlag, 2006.

Beethoven, Ludwig van. *Letters, Journals and Conversations*. Edited and translated by Michael Hamburger. 2nd edn. London: Cape, 1966.

Bellman, Jonathan. "Aus alten Märchen: The Chivalric Style of Schumann and Brahms." *Journal of Musicology* 13 (1995): 117–35.

"Indian Resonances in the British Invasion, 1965–1968." In Bellman, *Exotic*, 292–306, 351–54.

"Introduction." In Bellman, ed., *Exotic*, ix–xiii.

"The 'Noble Pathways of the National': Romantic and Modern Reactions to National Music." *The Pendragon Review* 1, no. 2 (Fall 2001): 45–65.

The style hongrois *in the Music of Western Europe*. Boston: Northeastern University Press, 1993.

Bellman, Jonathan, ed. *The Exotic in Western Music*. Boston: Northeastern University Press, 1998.

Bencheikh, Jamel Eddine. "Historical and Mythical Baghdad in the Tale of 'Ali b. Bakkar and Shams al-Nahar, or the Resurgence of the Imaginary." In Richard C. Hovannisian and Georges Sabagh, eds., *The Thousand and One Nights in Arabic Literature and Society*, 14–28. Cambridge: Cambridge University Press, 1997.

Benjamin, Roger. *Orientalism: Delacroix to Klee*. Sydney: Gallery of New South Wales, 1997.

Berger, Arthur. "Problems of Pitch Organization in Stravinsky." In Benjamin Boretz and Edward T. Cone, eds., *Perspectives on Schoenberg and Stravinsky*, 123–54. Princeton: Princeton University Press, 1968.

Berger, Harris M., and Michael Thomas Carroll. *Global Pop, Local Language*. Jackson: University of Mississippi Press, 2003.

Bergeron, Katherine. "A Lifetime of Chants." In Katherine Bergeron and Philip V. Bohlman, eds., *Disciplining Music: Musicology and Its Canons*, 182–96. Chicago: University of Chicago Press, 1992.

Berkowitz, Peter. Review of Okin, *Is Multiculturalism*. *The Weekly Standard*, 1 November 1999. www.peterberkowitz.com/feminismvsmulticulturalism.htm. Accessed 30 January 2007.

Berlioz, Hector. *The Art of Music and Other Essays (A travers chants)*. Translated and edited by Elizabeth Csicsery-Rónay. Bloomington: Indiana University Press, 1994.

Les musiciens et la musique. Introduction by André Hallays. Paris: Calmann-Lévy, 1903.

Bernheimer, Martin. "Marina Fortuna." *Opera News* 67, no. 1 (July 2002): 12–17.

Bernstein, Leonard. *Findings*. New York: Simon & Schuster, 1982.

Beruth, Fritzi. "Ein exotisches Lebensbild: George Gershwins Oper 'Porgy and Bess'." *Wiener Zeitung*, 9 September, no. 210, p. 3.

Betzwieser, Thomas. *Exotismus und "Türkenoper" in der französischen Musik des ancien Régime*. Laaber: Laaber, 1993.

"The 'Turkish' Language in Eighteenth Century Music: Context and Meaning." In Amalfitano and Innocenti, *L'Oriente*, 1:181–211.

Bhabha, Homi K. "The Other Question: Stereotype, Discrimination and the Discourse of Colonialism." In his *The Location of Culture*, 66–84 and 261–62. London: Routledge, 1994.

Bhogal, Gurminder Kaur. "Arabesque and Metric Dissonance in the Music of Maurice Ravel (1905–1914)." Ph.D. dissertation, University of Chicago, 2004.

"Debussy's Arabesques and Ravel's *Daphnis et Chloé*." *Twentieth-Century Music* 3 (2007): 171–99.

"Lakmé's Echoing Jewels." In *The Arts of the Prima Donna in the Long Nineteenth Century*. Edited by Hilary Poriss and Rachel Cowgill. Oxford: Oxford University Press, forthcoming.

Bisaha, Nancy. *Creating East and West: Renaissance Humanists and the Ottoman Turks*. Philadelphia: University of Pennsylvania Press, 2004.

Bizet, Georges. *Lettres (1850–1875)*. Compiled by Claude Glayman. Paris: Calmann-Lévy, 1989.

Blacking, John. "The Study of Man as Music-Maker." In John Blacking and Joann W. Keali'inohomoku, eds., *The Performing Arts: Music and Dance*, 3–16. The Hague: Mouton, 1979.

Bloechl, Olivia A. *Native American Song at the Frontiers of Early Modern Music*. Cambridge: Cambridge University Press, 2008.

"Protestant Imperialism and the Representation of Native American Song." *Musical Quarterly* 87 (2004): 44–86.

Bloemeke, Rüdiger. *La Paloma: das Jahrhundert-Lied*. Hamburg: Voodoo, 2005.

Bobéth, Marek. *Borodin und seine Opera "Fürst Igor": Geschichte – Analyse – Consequenzen*. Munich: Musikverlag Emil Katzbichler, 1982.

Bohlman, Philip. "Erasure: Displacing and Misplacing Race in Twentieth-Century Music Historiography." In Brown, *Western*, 3–23.

Herder on Music and Nationalism. Berkeley: University of California Press, in preparation.

The Music of European Nationalism: Cultural Identity and Modern History. Santa Barbara, CA: ABC-Clio, 2004.

Bohrer, Frederick N. *Orientalism and Visual Culture: Imagining Mesopotamia in Nineteenth-Century Europe*. Cambridge: Cambridge University Press, 2003.

Review of *Europa und der Orient, 800–1900* and *Exotische Welten, Europäische Phantasien* (two exhibition catalogs). *Art Bulletin* 73 (1991): 320–25.

Bonds, Mark Evan. *Wordless Rhetoric: Musical Form and the Metaphor of the Oration*. Cambridge, MA: Harvard University Press, 1991.

Booth, Gregory D. "The Madras Corporation Band: A Story of Social Change and Indigenization." *Asian Music* 28 (1996–97): 61–86.

"Musicking the Other: Orientalism in the Hindi Cinema." In Clayton and Zon, *Music*, 315–38.

Born, Georgina, and David Hesmondhalgh, eds. *Western Music and Its Others: Difference, Representation, and Appropriation in Music*. Berkeley: University of California Press, 2000.

Botstein, Leon. "Listening through Reading: Musical Literacy and the Concert Audience." *19th Century Music* 16 (1992–93): 129–45.

"Bottom Line: Let's Put on a Loser." *New York Times*, Sunday, 2 January 2005.

"Bottom of the Heap: Europe's Roma." *The Economist*, 19 June 2008.

Bouissou, Sylvie. "Les Indes galantes." In booklet of the recording of Rameau's *Les Indes galantes* by Les Arts Florissants, pp. 12–17. Harmonia Mundi France 901367.69.

Boulez, Pierre. "Existe-t-il un conflit entre la pensée européenne et non-européenne?" In Oesch, *et al.*, *Europäische Musik*, 129–45.

"Oriental Music: A Lost Paradise?" In his *Orientations: Collected Writings*, 421–24. Edited by Jean-Jacques Nattiez. Translated by Martin Cooper. London: Faber, 1986.

Bové, Paul A., ed. *Edward Said and the Work of the Critic: Speaking Truth to Power*. Durham, NC: Duke University Press, 2000.

Brackett, David. "The Politics and Practice of 'Crossover' in American Popular Music, 1963 to 1965." *Musical Quarterly* 78 (1994): 774–97.

Brancour, René. *Félicien David*. Paris: Henri Laurens, [1911].

Brantlinger, Patrick. *The Rule of Darkness: British Literature and Imperialism, 1830–1914*. Ithaca: Cornell University Press, 1988.

"Victorians and Africans: The Genealogy of the Myth of the Dark Continent." In Henry Louis Gates, Jr., ed., *"Race," Writing, and Difference*, 185–22. Chicago: University of Chicago Press, 1985.

Bras, Jean-Yves. "La Révolution souriante." Booklet essay in *La Révolution souriante* (a CD containing works by Boieldieu and Dauberval-Lazzini), [7]–[9]. Thesis CD THC 82015.

Brett, Philip. "Eros and Orientalism in Britten's Operas." In Philip Brett, Elizabeth Wood, and Gary C. Thomas, eds., *Queering the Pitch: The New Gay and Lesbian Musicology*, 235–56. New York: Routledge, 1994.

Brett, Philip. "Queer Musical Orientalism." Edited by Nadine Hubbs. Forthcoming in *ECHO: A Music-Centered Journal*, www.echo.ucla.edu.

Brown, Clive, David Cooper, and Rachel Cowgill, eds. *Art and Ideology in European Opera*. Woodbridge: Boydell, forthcoming.

Brown, Julie. "Bartók, the Gypsies, and Hybridity in Music." In Born and Hesmondhalgh, *Western Music and Its Others*, 119–42.

Brown, Julie, ed. *Western Music and Race*. Cambridge: Cambridge University Press, 2007.

Browner, Tara C. "Transposing Cultures: The Appropriation of Native North American Musics, 1890–1990." Ph.D. dissertation. University of Michigan, 1995.

Budasz, Rogério. "Black Guitar-Players and Early African-Iberian Music in Portugal and Brazil." *Early Music* 35 (2007): 3–22.

Budden, Julian. "Forta e nuova, ma non facile." In Ilaria Narici, ed., *Madama Butterfly 1904–2004*, 13–29. Milan: Ricordi, 2004.

The Operas of Verdi. 2nd edn. 3 vols. Oxford: Clarendon Press, 1992.

Buelow, George. "The 'Loci Topici' and Affect in Late Baroque Music: Heinichen's Practical Demonstration." *Music Review* 27 (1966): 161–76.

Burt, Peter. *The Music of Tōru Takemitsu*. Cambridge: Cambridge University Press, 2001.

Buruma, Ian. "Of Musical Import." [On Tan Dun.] *New York Times Magazine*, 4 May 2008. 46–51.

Buruma, Ian, and Avishai Margalit. *Occidentalism: The West in the Eyes of Its Enemies.* New York: Penguin Press, 2004.
Buschinger, Danielle. "Die Berliner Inszenienungen von Mozarts *Così Fan tutte* und *Die Entführung aus dem Serail.*" In Kühnel, "*Regietheater*," 229–38.
Butler, Margaret R. "Exoticism in 18th-Century Turinese Opera: *Motezuma* in Context." In Mara E. Parker, ed., *Music in Eighteenth-Century Life: Cities, Courts, Churches,* 105–24. Ann Arbor: Steglein, 2006.
Butler, Marilyn. "Orientalism." In *The Penguin History of Literature,* vol. 5: *The Romantic Period,* 395–447. Ed. David B. Pirie. London: Penguin Books, 1994.
Byrne, David. "I Hate World Music." *New York Times,* 3 October 1999. www.luakabop.com/david_byrne/cmp/worldmusic.html. Accessed 1 September 2007.
Camier, Bernard. "La musique coloniale et société à Saint-Domingue dans la seconde moitié du XVIIIe siècle." Thèse de doctorat, Université des Antilles-Guyane, 2004.
Camier, Bernard, and Laurent Dubois. "Voltaire et Zaïre, ou le théâtre des Lumières dans l'aire atlantique française." *Revue d'histoire moderne et contemporaine* 54, no. 4 (October–December 2007): 39–68.
Canby, Vincent. "Once Again, the Taming of a Despot." *New York Times,* 12 April 1996.
Carner, Mosco. *Puccini: A Critical Biography.* 2nd edn. London: Duckworth, 1974.
Casey, Edward S. *Representing Place: Landscape Painting and Maps.* Minneapolis: University of Minnesota Press, 2002.
Chabrier, Jean-Claude Ch. "Alphabet et langage de l'Orient emprunté." *Revue internationale de musique française* 6 (November 1981): 59–68.
Charnon-Deutsch, Lou. *The Spanish Gypsy: The History of a European Obsession.* University Park: Pennsylvania State University Press, 2004.
Choix de cantiques pour toutes les fêtes de l'année. Paris: Librairie de Mme V[euv]e Poussielgue-Rusand, 1859.
Chua, Daniel K. L. *Absolute Music and the Construction of Meaning.* Cambridge: Cambridge University Press, 1999.
Claman, David Neumann. "Western Composers and India's Music: Concepts, History, and Recent Music." PhD dissertation (Composition), Princeton University, 2002.
Clancy-Smith, Julia Ann. *Rebel and Saint: Muslim Notables, Populist Protest, Colonial Encounters (Algeria and Tunisia, 1800–1904).* Berkeley: University of California Press, 1994.
Clare, Janet, ed. *The Cruelty of the Spaniards in Peru,* in *Dramas of the English Republic 1649–60.* Manchester: Manchester University Press, 2002.
Clark, Colin. "'Severity Has Often Enraged but Never Subdued a Gypsy': The History and Making of European Romani Stereotypes." In Susan Tebbutt and Nicholas Saul, eds., *The Role of the Romanies: Images and Counter Images of "Gypsies"/Romanies in European Cultures,* 226–46. Liverpool: Liverpool University Press, 2005.

Clark, Maribeth. "The Body and the Voice in *La Muette de Portici*." *19th Century Music* 27 (2003-4): 116-31.

Clausen, Bernd. *Das Fremde als Grenze: Fremde Musik im Diskurs des 18. Jahrhunderts und der gegenwärtigen Musikpädagogik*. Augsburg: Wissner-Verlag, 2003.

Clayton, Martin, and Bennett Zon, eds. *Music and Orientalism in the British Empire, 1780s to 1940s: Portrayal of the East*. Aldershot: Ashgate, 2007.

Clegg, David. "A Chronicle of Franz Liszt's 'Hungarian Rhapsodies': Some Observations." *The Liszt Society Journal* 21 (1996): 32-34.

Clements, Carl. "Indian Concepts in the Music of John Coltrane." *Institute for Studies in American Music Newsletter* 37, no. 1 (Fall 2007): 6-7, 14-15.

Clifford, James. "Histories of the Tribal and the Modern." In Clifford, *The Predicament of Culture: Twentieth-Century Ethnography, Literature and Art*, 189-214. Cambridge, MA: Harvard University Press, 1988.

Cohen, Joshua, Michael Howard, and Martha Nussbaum. "Introduction: Feminism, Multiculturalism, and Human Equality." In Okin, et al., *Is Multiculturalism*, 3-6.

Cole, Malcolm S. "Monostatos and His 'Sister': Racial Stereotype in *Die Zauberflöte* and Its Sequel." *Opera Quarterly* 21 (2005): 2-26.

Collaer, Paul. *Darius Milhaud*. 2nd rev. edn. Revised and translated by Jane Hohfeld Galante. San Francisco: San Francisco Press, 1988.

Condry, Ian. *Hip-hop Japan: Rap and the Paths of Cultural Globalization*. Durham, NC: Duke University Press, 2006.

Conklin, Alice L. *A Mission to Civilize: The Republican Idea of Empire in France and West Africa, 1895-1930*. Stanford: Stanford University Press, 1997.

Conrad, Bridget. "Le langage musical d'Andre Jolivet." In Lucie Kayas and Laetitia Chassain-Dolliou, eds., *Andre Jolivet: Portraits*, 87-122. Arles: Actes Sud, 1994.

Cook, Nicholas. "Encountering the Other, Redefining the Self: Hindostannie Airs, Haydn's Folksongs Settings and the 'Common Practice' Style." In Clayton and Zon, *Music*, 13-37.

Music, Imagination and Culture. Oxford: Oxford University Press, 1990.

"Performance Analysis and Chopin's Mazurkas." *Musicae scientiae* 11 (2007): 183-205.

Cook, Nicholas, and Anthony Pople, eds. *The Cambridge History of Twentieth-Century Music*. Cambridge: Cambridge University Press, 2004.

Cook, Nicholas, and Mark Everist, eds. *Rethinking Music*. Oxford: Oxford University Press, 1999.

Cook, Susan C. *Opera for a New Republic: The Zeitopern of Krenek, Weill, and Hindemith*. Ann Arbor: UMI Research Press, 1987.

Cooke, Mervyn. *Britten and the Far East: Asian Influences in the Music of Benjamin Britten*. Woodbridge: Boydell, 2001.

"'The East in the West': Evocations of the Gamelan in Western Music." In Bellman, *Exotic*, 258-80, 347-50.

Cooper, David, "Béla Bartók and the Question of Race Purity in Music." In White and Murphy, *Musical*, 16-32.

Cooper, Thomas [Tom]. "'Frenchmen in Disguise': French Musical Exoticism and Empire in the Nineteenth Century." In Evans, *Empire*, 113–27.

"Nineteenth-Century Spectacle." In Smith and Potter, *French Music*, 19–52.

Copland, Aaron, and Vivian Perlis. *Copland: 1900 through 1942*. London: Faber and Faber, 1984.

Corbett, John. "Experimental Oriental: New Music and Other Others." In Born and David, *Western*, 163–86.

Corona, Ignacio, and Alejandro L. Madrid, eds. *Postnational Musical Identitites: Cultural Production, Distribution, and Consumption in a Globalized Scenario*. Lanham, MD: Lexington Books, 2008.

Cowgill, Rachel, and Julian Rushton, eds. *Europe, Empire, and Spectacle in Nineteenth-Century British Music*. Aldershot: Ashgate, 2006.

Crawford, Richard. *America's Musical Life: A History*. New York: W. W. Norton, 2001.

The American Musical Landscape. Berkeley: University of California Press, 1993.

Crist, Elizabeth Bergman. *Music for the Common Man: Aaron Copland during the Depression and War*. New York: Oxford University Press, 2005.

Crowe, David. *A History of the Gypsies of Eastern Europe and Russia*, 2nd edn. Foreword by André Liebich. New York: Palgrave Macmillan, 2007.

Csobádi, Peter, Gernot Gruber, Ulrich Müller, *et al.*, eds. *"Weine, weine, du armes Volk!": Das verführte und betrogene Volk auf der Bühne*. 2 vols. Anif/Salzburg: Müller-Speiser, 1995.

Dafner, Hugo. *Friedrich Nietzsches Randglossen zu Bizets Carmen*. Regensburg: G. Bosse, [1912].

Dahlhaus, Carl. *Between Romanticism and Modernism: Four Studies in the Music of the Later Nineteenth Century*. Translated by Mary Whittall. Berkeley: University of California Press, 1980.

Foundations of Music History. Translated by J. B[radford] Robinson. Cambridge: Cambridge University Press, 1983.

The Idea of Absolute Music. Translated by Roger Lustig. Chicago: University of Chicago Press, 1989.

"Die Kategorie des Charakeristischen in der Ästhetik des 19. Jahrhunderts." In Becker, *Couleur*, 9–22.

Nineteenth-Century Music, ed. J. Bradford Robinson. Berkeley: University of California Press, 1989.

Dahlhaus, Carl, and Sieghart Döhring, eds. *Pipers Enzyklopädie des Musiktheaters: Oper, Operette, Musical, Ballett*. 7 vols. Munich: Piper, 1986–97.

Dale, Peter N. *The Myth of Japanese Uniqueness*. Oxford: Croom Helm, 1986.

Daniel, Norman. *Islam and the West: The Making of an Image*. Edinburgh: [Edinburgh] University Press, 1960.

Daverio, John. *Crossing Paths: Schubert, Schumann, and Brahms*. Oxford: Oxford University Press, 2002.

Davies, J. Q. "Melodramatic Possessions: *The Flying Dutchman*, South Africa, and the Imperial Stage, ca. 1830." *Opera Quarterly* 21 (2005): 496–514.

Day-O'Connell, Jeremy. *Pentatonicism from the Eighteenth Century to Debussy.* Rochester: University of Rochester Press, 2007.

de Van, Gilles. "Fin de siècle Exoticism and the Meaning of the Far Away." Translated by William Ashbrook. *Opera Quarterly* 11, no. 3 (Autumn 1995): 77–94.

Dean, Winton. *Bizet*, 3rd edn. London: Dent, 1975.

Handel's Dramatic Oratorios and Masques. London: Oxford University Press, 1959.

Debussy, Claude. *Correspondance, 1872–1918.* Edited by Denis Herlin, François Lesure, and Georges Liébert. Paris: Gallimard, 2005.

Debussy on Music: The Critical Writings of the Great French Composer Claude Debussy, ed. François Lesure, trans. Richard Langham Smith. Ithaca: Cornell University Press, 1977.

Monsieur Croche et autres écrits. Edited by François Lesure. 2nd edn rev. Paris: Gallimard: 1987.

Dell'Antonio, Andrew. *Beyond Structural Listening? Postmodern Modes of Hearing.* Berkeley: University of California Press, 2004.

Denby, David. "A Place for It." *The New Yorker*, 18 September 2007.

DeVoto, Mark. "The Russian Submediant in the Nineteenth Century." *Current Musicology* 59 (1995): 48–76.

Dibbern, Mary. "Coach's Notebook: *Carmen* in Shanghai." *The Opera Journal* 30, no. 3 (September 1997). www.mary-dibbern.com/opera_journal.htm.

Dijkstra, Bram. *Idols of Perversity: Fantasies of Feminine Evil in fin-de-siècle Culture.* New York: Oxford University Press, 1986.

Dobie, Madeleine. *Foreign Bodies: Gender, Language, and Culture in French Orientalism.* Stanford: Stanford University Press, 2001.

Dobszay, László. *A History of Hungarian Music.* Translated by Mária Steiner, revised by Paul Merrick. Budapest: Corvina, 1993.

Draughon, Francesca. "The Orientalist Reflection: Temporality, Reality, and Illusion in Gustav Mahler's *Das Lied von der Erde.*" In Lee M. Roberts, ed., *Germany and the Imagined East*, 159–73. Newcastle: Cambridge Scholars Press, 2005.

Duindam, Jeroen. *Myths of Power: Norbert Elias and the Early Modern European Court.* Translated by Lorri S. Granger and Gerard T. Moran. Amsterdam: Amsterdam University Press, 1994.

During, Jean. *La musique iranienne: Tradition et évolution.* Paris: Editions Recherche sur les civilisations, 1984.

Duus, Peter, ed. *The Japanese Discovery of America: A Brief History with Documents.* Boston: Bedford Books, 1997.

Edmunds, Neil, ed. *Soviet Music and Society under Lenin and Stalin: The Baton and the Sickle.* London: Rouledge Curzon, 2004.

Eigeldinger, Jean-Jacques. "Debussy et l'idée de l'arabesque musicale." *Cahiers Debussy* 12–13 (1988–89): 5–14.

El Nouty, Hassan. *Le Proche-Orient dans la littérature française de Nerval à Barrès*. Paris: Librairie Nizet, 1958.

Elias, Norbert. *The Court Society*. Translated by Edmund Jephcott. New York: Pantheon Books, 1983.

Elisséeff, Nikita. *Thèmes et motifs des Mille et Une Nuits: Essai de classification*. Beirut: Institut Français de Damas, 1949.

Erdmann, Hans, Giuseppe Becce, and Ludwig Brav, eds. *Allgemeines Handbuch der Film-Musik*. 2 vols. Berlin-Lichterfelde: Schlesinger'sche Buch- und Musikhandlung Rob. Lienau, 1927.

Errante, Valerie. "Brahms Domesticates the Gypsy: The *Zigeunerlieder* and Their Sources." *Pendragon Review* 2, no. 1 (Fall 2003): 46–73.

Espagne, Michel. *Les transferts culturels franco-allemands*. Paris: Presses universitaires de France, 1999.

Euba, Akin, and Cynthia Tse Kimberlin. "Introduction." In Akin Euba and Cynthia Tse Kimberlin, eds., *Intercultural Music: [First International Symposium and Festival on Intercultural Music]*, 1–9. Bayreuth: E. Breitinger, 1995.

Evans, Martin, ed. *Empire and Culture: The French Experience, 1830–1940*. New York: Palgrave Macmillan, 2004.

Everett, Yayoi Uno. "Intercultural Synthesis in Postwar Western Art Music: Historical Contexts, Perspectives, and Taxonomy." In Everett and Lau, *Locating*, 1–22.

——— "'Mirrors' of West and 'Mirrors' of East: Elements of *gagaku* in Post-War Art Music." In Um, *Diasporas*, 176–203.

Everett, Yayoi Uno, and Frederick Lau, eds. *Locating East Asia in Western Art Music*. Middletown, CT: Wesleyan University Press, 2004.

Everist, Mark. "Reception Theories, Canonic Discourses, and Musical Value." In Cook and Everist, *Rethinking Music*, 378–402.

Fanshawe, David. *African Sanctus: A Story of Travel and Music*. London: Collins & Harvill Press, 1975.

Farrell, Gerry. *Indian Music and the West*. Oxford: Clarendon Press, 1997.

Fauser, Annegret. "Alterity, Nation and Identity: Some Musicological Paradoxes." *Context* 22 (Spring 2001): 5–18.

——— "'Hymns of the Future': Reading Félicien David's *Christophe Colomb* as a Saint-Simonian Symphony." *Journal of Musicological Research*, forthcoming.

——— *Musical Encounters at the 1889 Paris World's Fair*. Rochester: University of Rochester Press, 2005.

Fehn, Ann Clark, and Jürgen Thym. "Repetition as Structure in the German *Lied*: The Ghazal." *Comparative Literature* 41 (1989): 33–52. To be reprinted in Jürgen Thym, ed., *Of Poetry and Song: Approaches to the Nineteenth-Century Lied*. Rochester: University of Rochester Press, forthcoming.

Feld, Steven. "Notes on World Beat." In Feld and Keil, *Music*, 238–46.

——— "From Schizophonia to Schismogenesis: On the Discourses and Commodification Practices of 'World Music' and 'World Beat'." In Feld and Keil, *Music*, 257–89.

"pygmy POP: A Genealogy of Schizophonic Mimesis." *Yearbook for Traditional Music* 28 (1995): 1–35.

Feld, Steven, and Charles Keil. *Music Grooves: Essays and Dialogues*. Chicago: University of Chicago Press, 1994.

Ferguson, Moira. *Subject to Others: British Women Writers and Colonial Slavery, 1670–1834*. New York: Routledge, 1992.

Filippi, Filippo. *Musica e musicisti: Critiche[,] biografie ed escursioni*. Milan, 1876.

Finson, Jon. *The Voices That Are Gone: Themes in Nineteenth-Century American Popular Song*. New York: Oxford University Press, 1994.

Fisk, Josiah, ed. *Composers on Music: Eight Centuries of Writings*, 2nd edn. Consulting editor Jeff Nichols. Boston: Northeastern University Press, 1997.

Fiske, Roger. *Scotland in Music: A European Enthusiasm*. Cambridge: Cambridge University Press, 1983.

Flam, Jack, ed., with Miriam Deutsch. *Primitivism and Twentieth-Century Art: A Documentary History*. Berkeley: University of California Press, 2003.

Ford, Phil. "Jazz Exotica and the Naked City." *Journal of Musicological Research* 27 (2008): 113–33.

"Taboo: Time and Belief in Exotica." *Representations* 103 (2008): 107–35.

Forsyth, Alison. *Gadamer, History and the Classics: Fugard, Marowitz, Berkoff, and Harrison Rewrite the Theatre*. New York: Peter Lang, 2002.

Foucault, Michael. *The Archeology of Knowledge*. Translated by A. M. Sheridan Smith. Also includes "The Discourse on Language," translated by Rupert Swyer. New York: Pantheon Books, 1972.

Freed, Richard. Booklet notes to "Ivan Moravec Plays Debussy," Vox Unique CD VU9005.

Frogley, Alain. "Rewriting the Renaissance: History, Imperialism, and British Music since 1840." *Music and Letters* 84 (2003): 241–57.

Frolova-Walker, Marina. *Russian Music and Nationalism from Glinka to Stalin*. New Haven: Yale University Press, 2007.

Fry, Andy. "Beyond *Le Boeuf*: Interdisciplinary Rereadings of Jazz in France." *Journal of the Royal Music Association* 128 (2003): 137–53.

"Rethinking the *revue nègre*: Black Musical Theatre in Inter-War Paris." In Brown, *Western*, 258–75.

Galliano, Luciana. "Il contatto con il pensiero buddhista: nuove sensibilità nella ricerca musicale." In Amalfitano and Innocenti, *L'Oriente*, 2:475–86.

Garafola, Lynn. *Diaghilev's Ballets Russes*. New York: Oxford University Press, 1989.

Garcia, David F. "'We Both Speak African': Gillespie, Pozo, and the Making of Afro-Cuban Jazz." *Institute for Studies in American Music Newsletter* 37, no. 1 (Fall 2007): 1–2, 13–14.

Gardner, Kara Anne. "Edward MacDowell, Antimodernism, and 'Playing Indian' in the *Indian Suite*." *Musical Quarterly* 87 (2004): 370–422.

Gárdonyi, Zoltán. "A Chronicle of Franz Liszt's 'Hungarian Rhapsodies'." *The Liszt Society Journal* 20 (1995): 38–61.

Garrett, Charles Hiroshi. "Chinatown, Whose Chinatown? Defining America's Borders with Musical Orientalism." *Journal of the American Musicological Society* 57 (2004): 119–74.
  Struggling to Define a Nation: American Music and the Twentieth Century. Berkeley: University of California Press, 2008.
Gautier, Théophile. *Gautier on Dance*. Edited and translated by Ivor Guest. London: Dance, 1986.
Gelbart, Matthew. *The Invention of "Folk Music" and "Art Music": Emerging Categories from Ossian to Wagner*. Cambridge: Cambridge University Press, 2007.
Gerstle, C. Andrew, and Milner, Anthony, eds. *Recovering the Orient: Artists, Scholars, Appropriations*. Amsterdam: Harwood Academic Publishers, 1994.
Gervais, Françoise. "La notion de l'arabesque chez Debussy." *Revue musicale* 241 (1958): 3–23.
Ghuman, Nalini. "Elgar and the British Raj: Can the Mughals March?" In Byron Adams, eds., *Elgar and His World*, 249–85. Princeton: Princeton University Press, 2007.
Gibbs, Christopher, and Dana Gooley, eds. *Liszt and His World*. Princeton: Princeton University Press, 2006.
Girardi, Michele. *Puccini: His International Art*. Translated by Laura Basini. Chicago: University of Chicago Press, 2000.
Girdlestone, Cuthbert. *Jean-Philippe Rameau: His Life and Work*. Revised and enlarged 2nd edn. New York: Dover Publications, 1969.
Glahn, Denise von. *The Sounds of Place: Music and the American Cultural Landscape*. Boston: Northeastern University Press, 2003.
Goldberg, David Theo. *The Racial State*. Malden, MA: Blackwell Publishers, 2002.
Goldberg, Halina. *Music in Chopin's Warsaw*. New York: Oxford University Press, 2008.
Golijov, Osvaldo. Official website: www.osvaldogolijov.com.
Gooley, Dana. *The Virtuoso Liszt*. Cambridge: Cambridge University Press, 2004.
Gorbman, Claudia. "Scoring the Indian: Music in the Liberal Western." In Born and Hesmondhalgh, *Western*, 234–53.
Gould, Evlyn. *The Fate of Carmen*. Baltimore: Johns Hopkins University Press, 1996.
Gradenwitz, Peter. *Musik zwischen Orient und Okzident: Eine Kulturgeschichte der Wechselbeziehungen*. Wilhelmshaven: Heinrichshofen, 1977.
  "Félicien David (1810–1876) and French Romantic Orientalism." *Musical Quarterly* 62 (1976): 471–506.
Gramit, David. "Orientalism and the Lied: Schubert's 'Du liebst mich nicht'." *19th Century Music* 27 (2003–04): 97–115.
Granade, S. Andrew. Review of Sheppard, *Revealing*. In *American Music* 22 (2004): 591–92.
Grayson, David. "Bilitis and Tanagra: Afternoons with Nude Women." In Jane F. Fulcher, ed., *Debussy and His World*, 117–39. Princeton: Princeton University Press, 2001.

Greenwald, Helen. "Picturing Cio-Cio-San: House, Screen, and Ceremony in Puccini's *Madama Butterfly*." *Cambridge Opera Journal* 12 (2000): 237–59.

Groos, Arthur. "Cio-Cio-San and Sadayakko: Japanese Music-Theater in 'Madama Butterfly'." *Monumenta Nipponica* 54 (1999): 41–73.

Groos, Arthur, ed., with Virgilio Bernardoni, Gabriella Biagi Ravenni, and Dieter Schickling. *Madama Butterfly: Fonti e documenti della genesi*. Lucca: Centro studi Giacomo Puccini, 2005.

Gumpert, Matthew. "'Everyway That I Can': Auto-Orientalism at Eurovision 2003." In Ivan Raykoff and Robert Deam Tobin, eds., *A Song for Europe: Popular Music and Politics in the Eurovision Song Contest*, 147–57. Aldershot: Ashgate, 2007.

Gurewitsch, Matthew. "A Tenor Cashes In on His Money Notes." *New York Times*, 21 January 2007.

Guzelimian, Ara. "A Counterpoint of Cultures." Booklet essay in CD recording of Osvaldo Golijov, *Ayre*, and Luciano Berio, *Folk Songs* (1964), 4–7. Deutsche Grammophon B0004782-02.

Haddad, Emily A. *Orientalist Poetics: The Islamic Middle East in Nineteenth-Century English and French Poetry*. Aldershot: Ashgate, 2002.

Hale, Dana. "The 'Ballet blanc et noir': A Study of Racial and Cultural Identity during the 1931 Colonial Exhibition." In Evans, *Empire*, 103–12.

Hallam, Elizabeth, and Brivan V. Street, eds. *Cultural Encounters: Representing Otherness*. London: Routledge, 2000.

Hamberlin, Larry. "Visions of Salome: The Femme Fatale in American Popular Songs before 1920." *Journal of the American Musicological Society* 59 (2006): 631–96.

Hamburger, Klára. "Understanding the Hungarian Reception History of Liszt's *Des Bohémiens et de leur musique en Hongrie* (1859/1881)." *Journal of the American Liszt Society* 14–16 (2003–05): 75–84.

Hancock, Virginia. "Johannes Brahms: Volkslied/Kunstlied." In Rufus Hallmark, ed., *German Lieder in the Nineteenth Century*, 119–52. New York: Schirmer Books, 1996.

Hanslick, Eduard. *On the Musically Beautiful: A Contribution Towards the Revision of the Aesthetics of Music*. Translated by Geoffrey Payzant. Indianapolis: Hackett Publishing Company, 1986.

Harris, Ellen T. "With Eyes on the East and Ears in the West: Handel's Orientalist Operas." *Journal of Interdisciplinary History* 36 (2006): 419–43.

Harris-Warrick, Rebecca. "Lully's On-Stage Societies." In Victoria Johnson, Jane F. Fulcher, and Thomas Ertman, eds., *Opera and Society in Italy and France from Monteverdi to Bourdieu*, 53–71. Cambridge: Cambridge University Press, 2007.

———. "Staging Venice." *Cambridge Opera Journal* 15 (2003): 297–316.

Harrison, Pegram. "Music and Imperialism." *repercussions* 4, no. 1 (Spring 1995): 53–84.

Hart, Brian. "The Symphony and National Identity in Early Twentieth-Century France." In Kelly, *French*, 131–48.

Hayward, Philip, ed. *Sound Alliances: Indigenous Peoples, Cultural Politics, and Popular Music in the Pacific*. London and New York: Cassell, 1998.

Head, Matthew. "Haydn's Exoticisms: 'Difference' and the Enlightenment." In Caryl Clark, ed., *The Cambridge Companion to Haydn*, 77–94. Cambridge: Cambridge University Press, 2005.

"Musicology on Safari: Orientalism and the Spectre of Postcolonial Theory." *Music Analysis* 22 (2003): 211–30.

Orientalism, Masquerade and Mozart's Turkish Music. London: Royal Musical Association, 2000.

Heartz, Daniel. "Mozart's Sense for Nature." *19th Century Music* 15 (1991–92): 107–15.

Heidemann, Oliver. *Luigi Cherubini: Les Abencérages, ou L'Étendard de Grenade: Untersuchungen zur Operngeschichte des französischen Empire*. Münster: Waxmann, 1994.

Heister, Hanns Werner, and Walter-Wolfgang Sparrer, eds. *Der Komponist Isang Yun*. Munich: edition text + kritik, 1987.

Henson, Karen. "Of Men, Women and Others: Exotic Opera in Late Nineteenth-Century France." D.Phil. thesis. University of Oxford, 1999.

Review of Bellman, *Exotic*. *Music and Letters* 80 (1999): 144–47.

"Victor Capoul, Marguerite Olagnier's *Le Saïs*, and the Arousing of Female Desire." *Journal of the American Musicological Society* 52 (1999): 419–63.

Hepokoski, James. "Beethoven Reception: The Symphonic Tradition." In Samson, *Cambridge*, 424–59.

Herder, Johann Gottfried. *Werke*, vol. 5: *Volkslieder, Übertragungen, Dichtungen*. Edited by Ulrich Gaier. Frankfurt-am-Main: Deutscher Klassiker Verlag, 1990.

Sämmtliche Werke. Edited by Bernhard Suphan and Reinhold Steig. Berlin: Weidmann, 1877–1913.

Herrmann, Bernard. "Score for a Film" (1941). Reprinted in Ronald Gottesman, ed., *Perspectives on Citizen Kane*, 573–75. New York: G. K. Hall & Co., 1996.

Hiekel, Jörn Peter, ed. *Orientierungen: Wege im Pluralismus der Gegenwartsmusik*. Mainz: Schott, 2007.

Hirshberg, Yehoash. *Paul Ben-Haim: His Life and Works*. Translated by Nathan Friedgut. Edited by Bathja Bayer. Jerusalem: Israeli Music Publications, 1990.

Hischak, Thomas S. *The American Musical Theatre Song Encyclopedia*. Westport, CT: Greenwood Press, 1995.

Hitchcock, H. Wiley. *Music in the United States: A Historical Introduction*, 4th edn, with a final chapter by Kyle Gann. Upper Saddle River, NJ: Prentice Hall, 2000.

Hodgart, Matthew J. C., and Ruth Bauerle. *Joyce's Grand Operoar: Opera in Finnegans Wake*. Urbana: University of Illinois Press, 1997.

Hodgson, Barbara. *Dreaming of East: Western Women and the Exotic Allure of the Orient*. Vancouver: Greystone, 2005.

Holoman, D. Kern. "Berlioz." In Holoman, *Nineteenth-Century*, 108–41.

Holoman, D. Kern, ed. *The Nineteenth-Century Symphony*. New York: Schirmer Books, 1997.

hooks, bell. *Cultural Criticism and Transformation*. Video lectures (VHS and DVD). Media Education Foundation, 1997.

——— *Reel to Real: Race, Sex, and Class at the Movies*. New York: Routledge, 1996.

Horowitz, Joseph. "Introduction: Orientalism." In *East Meets West / Orientalism*. 5–7. Program book for concerts of the Chicago Symphony Orchestra and of the Brooklyn Philharmonic Orchestra festival: respectively, 8–10 and 16–17 February 1996.

Hosokawa, Shuhei. "Blacking Japanese: Experiencing Otherness from Afar." In David Hesmondhalgh and Keith Negus, eds., *Popular Music Studies*, 223–37. London: Arnold, 2002.

Hovaness, Alan. Interview by Richard Howard. October 1983. www.hovhaness.com/Interview_Howard.html. Accessed 13 February 2008.

Hovhaness, Hinako Fujihara. Booklet notes for Telarc CD-80604 (four of Hovhaness's "mountain" pieces), conducted by Gerard Schwarz.

Howat, Roy. "Debussy and the Orient." In Gerstle and Milner, *Recovering*, 45–81.

Huebner, Steven. "'Addio, fiorito asil': The Evanescent Exotic." In Arthur Groos and Virgilio Bernardoni, eds., *Madama Butterfly* (forthcoming).

——— "Thematic Recall in Late Nineteenth-Century Opera." *Studi pucciniani* 3 (2004): 77–104.

Hughes-Hallett, Lucy. *Cleopatra: Histories, Dreams and Distortions*. New York: Harper & Row, 1990.

Humbert, Jean-Michel. *L'Égyptomanie dans l'art occidental*. Courbevoie: ACR Édition Internationale, 1989.

Humbert, Jean-Michel, Michael Pantazzi, and Christiane Ziegler. *Egyptomania: Egypt in Western Art, 1730–1930*. Ottawa: National Gallery of Canada, 1994.

Hunter, Mary. "The *Alla Turca* Style in the Late Eighteenth Century: Race and Gender in the Symphony and the Seraglio." In Bellman, *Exotic in Western Music*, 43–73, 317–23.

——— "Mozart and Nobility." Forthcoming in Brown, *et al.*, *Art*.

Huntington, Samuel P. *The Clash of Civilizations and the Remaking of World Order*. New York: Simon & Schuster, 1996.

Hutnyk, John. *Critique of Exotica: Music, Politics, and the Culture Industry*. Sterling, VA: Pluto Press, 2000.

Internet Movie Database. www.imdb.com.

Irving, John. *Mozart's Piano Sonatas: Contexts, Sources, Style*. Cambridge: Cambridge University Press, 1997.

Irwin, Robert. *The Arabian Nights: A Companion*. London: Allen Lane, 1994.

——— *Dangerous Knowledge: Orientalism and Its Discontents*. Woodstock, NY: Overlook Press, 2006.

Ivanoff, Vladimir. "Sacred Bridges." In text booklet to *Sacred Bridges: The King's Singers, Sarband*, 3–4. World Village CD 68052.
Izzo, Francesco. "Exoticism, Colonialism and Oppression in Italian Early Romantic Opera." In Csobádi, *et al.*, "*Weine*," 317–26.
Jacket note for *Gypsy!* Recording by the Hollywood Bowl Symphony Orchestra, conducted by Carmen Dragon. Capitol P8342. [Late 1950s?]
Jameux, Dominique. *Pierre Boulez*. Paris: Fayard/Fondation SACEM, 1984.
Jasen, David A. *Thirty-Five Song Hits by Great Black Songwriters: Bert Williams, Eubie Blake, Ernest Hogan and Others*. Mineola, NY: Dover Publications, 1998.
Jauss, Hans Robert. *Toward an Aesthetic of Reception*. Translated by Timothy Bahti. Introduction by Paul de Man. Minneapolis: University of Minnesota Press, 1982.
Jefferson, Margo. "Culture Clashes Still Intrigue in 'King and I'." *New York Times*, 28 April 1996.
John, Nicholas, ed. *Carmen: Georges Bizet*. New York: Riverrun Press, 1982.
Jullian, Philippe. *The Orientalists: European Painters of Eastern Scenes*. Translated by Helga and Dinah Harrison. Oxford: Phaidon, 1977.
Jürgensen, Knud Arne. *The Verdi Ballets*. Parma: Istituto nazionale di studi verdiani, 1995.
Kahan, Sylvia. "'*Rien de la tonalité usuelle*': Edmond de Polignac and the Octatonic Scale in Nineteenth Century France." *19th Century Music* 29 (2004–05): 97–120.
—— *In Search of New Scales: Prince Edmond de Polignac, Octatonic Explorer*. Rochester: University of Rochester Press, 2008.
Kalinowska, Izabela. *Between East and West: Polish and Russian Nineteenth-Century Travel to the Orient*. Rochester: University of Rochester Press, 2004.
Kallberg, Jeffrey. "Arabian Nights: Chopin and Orientalism." In Irena Poniatowska, ed., *Chopin and His Work in the Context of Culture*, 171–83. 2 vols. Kraków: Polska Akademia Chopinowska, 2003.
—— *Chopin at the Boundaries: Sex, History, and Musical Genre*. Cambridge, MA: Harvard University Press, 1996.
—— "Hearing Poland: Chopin and Nationalism." In R. Larry Todd, ed., *Nineteenth-Century Piano Music*, 221–57. New York: Schirmer Books, 1989.
Kartomi, Margaret J., and Stephen Blum, eds. *Music-Cultures in Contact: Convergences and Collisions*. Sydney: Currency Press, 1994.
Kayas, Lucie. *André Jolivet*. Paris: Fayard, 2005.
Kelly, Barbara, ed. *French Music, Culture, and National Identity, 1870–1939*. Rochester: University of Rochester Press, 2008.
Kennedy, Charles A. "When Cairo Met Main Street: Little Egypt, Salome Dancers, and the World's Fair of 1893 and 1904." In Michael Saffle, ed., *Music and Culture in America, 1861–1918*, 271–98. New York: Garland Publishing, 1998.
Kerman, Joseph. *Contemplating Music: Challenges to Musicology*. Cambridge, MA: Harvard University Press, 1985.

Khanna, Parag. *The Second World: Empires and Influence in the New Global Order.* New York: Random House, 2008.
King, Richard G. "The First 'Abduction' Opera: Lewis Theobald's and John Ernest Galliard's *The Happy Captive* (1741)." *Musical Quarterly* 84 (2000): 137–63.
Kintzler, Catherine. *Théâtre et opéra à l'âge classique: une familière étrangeté.* Paris: Fayard, 2004.
Kissinger, Henry A. *American Foreign Policy.* 2nd expanded edn. New York: W. W. Norton, 1974.
Kitzan, Lawrence. *Victorian Writers and the Image of Empire: The Rose Colored Vision.* Westport, CT: Greenwood Press, 2001.
Klein, Christina. *Cold War Orientalism: Asia in the Middlebrow Imagination, 1945–1961.* Berkeley: University of California Press, 2003.
Kneif, Tibor. "Exotik im musikalischen Underground." In Oesch, et al., *Europäische,* 99–114.
Knight, Alan. "Britain and Latin America." In Porter and Low, *Oxford,* 122–45.
Koebner, Thomas. "Das Land des Lächelns." In Dahlhaus and Döhring, *Pipers,* 3: 451–53.
Korfmacher, Peter. *Exotismus in Giacomo Puccinis "Turandot".* Cologne: Verlag Dohr, 1993.
Kozinn, Allan. "Downsizing a Larger-than-Life Warlord." [On revised version of Tan Dun's *The First Emperor.*] *New York Times,* 12 May 2008, sect. B, p. 5.
——— "Mozart's Unfinished Opera 'Zaide,' with Slaves as Sweatshop Workers." *New York Times,* 11 August 2006.
Kramer, Lawrence. "Consuming the Exotic: Ravel's *Daphnis and Chloe.*" In his *Classical Music and Postmodern Knowledge,* 201–25. Berkeley: University of California Press, 1995.
——— "The Harem Threshold: Turkish Music and Greek Love in Beethoven's 'Ode to Joy.'" *19th Century Music* 22 (1998–99): 78–90.
——— *Musical Meaning: Towards a Critical History.* Berkeley: University of California Press, 2002.
Kremer, Gidon. "Tango Passion." In Kremer, *Obertöne,* 192–202. Salzburg: Residenz Verlag, 1997. Also in CD booklet to *El tango,* Nonesuch 79462 (released 1997).
Kristeva, Julia. *Strangers to Ourselves.* Translated by Leon S. Roudiez. New York: Columbia University Press, 1979.
Kühnel, Jürgen, et al. *"Regietheater": Konzeption und Praxis am Beispiel der Bühnenwerke.* Anif/Salzburg: Verlag Mueller-Speiser, 2007.
Kurtz, Michael. *Sofia Gubaidulina: A Biography.* Translated by Christoph K. Lohmann. Edited by Malcolm Hamrick Brown. Bloomington: Indiana University Press, 2007.
Lacombe, Hervé. *Georges Bizet: Naissance d'une identité créatrice.* Paris: Fayard, 2000.
Ladjili, Myriam. "La musique arabe chez les compositeurs français du xixe siècle saisis d'exotisme (1844–1914)." *International Review of the Aesthetics and Sociology of Music* 26, no. 1 (1995): 3–33.

Lambert, Constant. *Music Ho! A Study of Music in Decline*. 3rd edn. Introduction by Arthur Hutchings. New York: October House, 1967.

Lancefield, Robert Charles. "Hearing Orientality in (White) America, 1900–1930." Ph.D. dissertation, Wesleyan University, 2004.

Lane, Edward William. *Arabian Society in the Middle Ages: Studies from the Thousand and One Nights*, ed. Stanley Lane-Pool. London: Chatto and Windus, 1883. Reprinted, with a new introduction by C. E. Bosworth: London: Curzon Press, 1987.

Lash, Larry L. "Bare Necessities" [review, from 2003, of Vienna Festival productions of *Aida* and *Madama Butterfly*, in performances at Klagenfurt]. www.andante.com/article/article.cfm?id=21300. Accessed 9 December 2007.

Lau, Frederick. "Fusion or Fission: The Paradox and Politics of Contemporary Chinese Avant-Garde Music." In Everett and Lau, *Locating*, 22–39.

Lavezzoli, Peter. *The Dawn of Indian Music in the West: Bhairavi*. New York: Continuum, 2006.

Lechner, Ethan. "Composers as Ethnographers: Difference in the Imaginations of Three American Modernists." PhD dissertation. University of North Carolina, Chapel Hill, 2008.

Lemaire, Gérard-Georges. *L'Univers des orientalistes*. Paris: Éditions Place des Victoires, 2000.

Leopold, Silke. "Zur Szenographie der Türkenoper." *Analecta musicologica* 21 (1982): 370–79.

Leppert, Richard. *The Sight of Sound: Music, Representation, and the History of the Body*. Berkeley: University of California Press, 1993.

Leprohon, Pierre. "Esotismo." In *Enciclopedia dello spettacolo*, vol. 4: cols. 1611–23. Rome: Casa editrice La Maschera, 1957.

Levy, Beth Ellen. "Frontier Figures: American Music and the Mythology of the American West, 1895–1945." Ph.D. dissertation. University of California, Berkeley, 2002.

Lewis, Reina. *Gendering Orientalism: Race, Femininity and Representation*. London: Routledge, 1996.

Leydon, Rebecca. "'Ces nymphes, je les veux perpétuer': The Post-War Pastoral in Space-Age Bachelor-Pad Music." *Popular Music* 22 (2003): 159–72.

"Utopia of the Tropics – The Exotic Music of Les Baxter and Yma Sumac." In Philip Hayward, ed., *Widening the Horizon: Exoticism in Post-War Popular Music*, 45–71. Sydney: John Libbey and Co./Perfect Beat Publications, 1999.

Lindenberger, Herbert. *Opera in History: From Monteverdi to Cage*. Stanford: Stanford University Press, 1998.

Link, Dorothea. "The Fandango Scene in Mozart's *Le nozze di Figaro*." *Journal of the Royal Musical Association* 133 (2008): 69–92.

Lippmann, Friedrich. *Versificazione italiana e ritmo musicale: rapporti tra verso e musica nell'opera italiana dell'Ottocento*. Naples: Liguori, 1986.

Lipsitz, George. *Dangerous Crossroads: Popular Music, Postmodernism and the Poetics of Place*. London: Verso, 1994.
Footsteps in the Dark: The Hidden Histories of Popular Music. Minneapolis: University of Minnesota Press, 2007.

Liszt, Franz. *Des Bohémiens et de leur musique en Hongrie*. 2nd, expanded edition. Leipzig: Breitkopf und Härtel, 1881. The first edition was also consulted (Paris: A. Bourdilliat, 1859).
The Gipsy in Music. Translated (after the 1881 edition) by Edwin Evans. London: William Reeves, 1926.
Selected Letters. Translated and edited by Adrian Williams. Oxford: Clarendon Press, 1998.

Lo Kii-Ming. "China-Mythen im italienischen Opernlibretto des Settecento." In Peter Csobádi, *et al.*, eds., *Politische Mythen und nationale Identitäten im (Musik-)Theater: Vorträge und Gespräche des Salzburger Symposions 2001*, 185–202. Anif/Salzburg: Verlag Mueller-Speiser, 2003.
"Chinesische Dichtung als Text-Grundlage für Mahlers 'Lied von der Erde'." In Matthias Theodor Vogt, ed., *Das Gustav-Mahler-Fest Hamburg 1989: Bericht über den Internationalen Gustav-Mahler-Kongress*, 509–28. Kassel: Bärenreiter, 1991.
"Elements of East Asian Music as Exoticism in Twentieth-Century European Opera: The Case of Isang Yun." In Amalfitano and Innocenti, *L'Oriente*, 2:487–500.
"Turandot" auf der Opernbühne. Frankfurt am Main: P. Lang, 1996.

Locke, Ralph P. "Absolute Music." In Randel, *Harvard*, 1.
"*Aida* and Nine Readings of Empire." *Nineteenth-Century Music Review* 3 (2006): 45–72. A shortened and revised version is to appear in Roberta Montemorra Marvin and Hilary Poriss, eds., *Fashions and Legacies of Nineteenth-Century Italian Opera*. Cambridge: Cambridge University Press, forthcoming.
"Beyond the Exotic: How 'Eastern' Is *Aida*?" *Cambridge Opera Journal* 17 (2005): 105–39. Forthcoming in shortened and revised form in Brown, *et al.*, *Art*.
"The Border Territory between Classical and Broadway: A Voyage around and about *Four Saints in Three Acts* and *West Side Story*." In Paul-André Bempéchat, ed., *Liber Amicorum Isabelle Cazeaux: Symbols, Parallels and Discoveries in her Honor*, 179–226. Hillsdale, NY: Pendragon Press, 2005.
"A Broader View of Musical Exoticism." *Journal of Musicology* 24, no. 4 (Fall 2007): 477–52.
"Constructing the Oriental 'Other': Saint-Saëns's *Samson et Dalila*." *Cambridge Opera Journal* 3 (1991): 261–302.
"Cutthroats and Casbah Dancers, Muezzins and Timeless Sands: Musical Images of the Middle East." In Bellman, *Exotic*, 104–36, 326–33. A version with a fuller main text (but minus certain discursive footnotes) is in *19th Century Music* 22 (1998–99): 20–53.

"Doing the Impossible: On the Musically Exotic." *Journal of Musicological Research* 27(2008): 334–58. A shorter version appeared as "L'impossible possibilité de l'exotisme musical." Translated by Vincent Giroud. In Damien Colas, Florence Gétreau, and Malou Haine, eds., *Musique, esthétique et société en France au XIXe siècle: Liber amicorum Joël-Marie Fauquet*, 91–107. Liège: Mardaga, 2007.

"Exoticism." In Laura Macy, ed., *Grove Music Online*. www.grovemusic.com. Accessed 10 February 2008.

"Exoticism and Orientalism in Music: Problems for the Worldly Critic." In Paul A. Bové, ed., *Edward Said and the Work of the Critic: Speaking Truth to Power*, 257–81, 306–12. Durham, NC: Duke University Press, 2000.

"The French Symphony: David, Gounod, and Bizet to Saint-Saëns, Franck, and Their Followers." In Holoman, *Nineteenth-Century*, 163–94.

"Liszt on the Artist in Society." In Gibbs and Gooley, eds., *Liszt and His World*, 291–302.

"Living with Music: Isabella Stewart Gardner." In Locke and Barr, *Cultivating*, 90–121.

"Music Lovers, Patrons, and the 'Sacralization' of Culture in America." *19th Century Music* 17 (1993–94): 149–73 and (corrigendum) 18 (1994–95): 83–84.

"The Music of the French Political Chanson, 1810–50." In Peter A. Bloom, ed., *Music in Paris in the Eighteen-Thirties – La Musique à Paris dans les années 1830*, 431–56. Stuyvesant, NY: Pendragon Press, 1987.

"Musicology and/as Social Concern: Imagining the Relevant Musicologist." In Cook and Everist, *Rethinking*, 499–530.

"Orientalism." In Laura Macy, ed., *Grove Music Online*. www.grovemusic.com. Accessed 10 February 2008.

"Program Music." In Randel, *Harvard*, 680–83.

"Reflections on Art Music in America, on Stereotypes of the Woman Patron, and on Cha(lle)nges in the Present and Future." In Locke and Barr, *Cultivating*, 296–336.

"Reflections on Orientalism in Opera." *Opera Quarterly* 10, no. 1 (Autumn 1993): 48–64.

"Spanish Local Color in Bizet's *Carmen*: Unexplored Borrowings and Transformations." In *Stage Music and Cultural Transfer: Paris 1830 to 1914*, Annegret Fauser and Mark Everist, eds. Chicago: University of Chicago Press, forthcoming.

"Unacknowledged Exoticism in Debussy: The Incidental Music for *Le martyre de saint Sébastien* (1911)." Forthcoming in *Musical Quarterly* 90(2007), nos. 3–4, and (in Italian translation) in Michela Niccolai and Giuseppe Montemagno, eds., *Beyond the Stage: Musical Theatre and Performing Arts between* fin de siècle *and the* années folles.

"What Are These Women Doing in Opera?" In Corinne Blackmer and Patricia Juliana Smith, eds., *En travesti: Women, Gender Subversion, Opera*, 59–98. New York: Columbia University Press, 1995.

Locke, Ralph P., and Cyrilla Barr. "Introduction: Music Patronage as a 'Female-Centered Cultural Process'." In Locke and Barr, *Cultivating*, 1–23.

Locke, Ralph P., and Cyrilla Barr, eds. *Cultivating Music in America: Women Patrons and Activists since 1860*. Berkeley: University of California Press, 1997.

Loges, Natasha. "Exoticism, Artifice and the Supernatural in the Brahmsian Lied." *Nineteenth-Century Music Review* 3 (2007): 137–68.

Longino, Michele. *Orientalism in French Classical Drama*. Cambridge: Cambridge University Press, 2006.

Loomba, Ania. *Colonialism/Postcolonialism*. London: Routledge, 1998.

Lowe, Lisa. *Critical Terrains: French and British Orientalisms*. Ithaca: Cornell University Press, 1994.

Loya, Shay. "Beyond 'Gypsy' Stereotypes: Harmony and Structure in the *Verbunkos* Idiom." *Journal of Musicological Research* 27 (2008): 254–80.

"The *verbunkos* Idiom in Liszt's Music of the Future: Historical Issues of Reception and New Cultural and Analytical Perspectives." PhD dissertation, 2 vols., King's College, London, 2006.

Lucassen, Leo, and Wim Willems. "The Church of Knowledge: Representation of Gypsies in Encyclopaedias." In Leo Lucassen, Wim Willems, and Annemarie Cottaar, eds., *Gypsies and Other Itinerant Groups: A Socio-Historical Approach*, 35–52, 192–95. New York: St. Martin's Press, 1998.

Mabilat, Claire. "Empire and 'Orient' in Opera Libretti Set by Sir Henry Bishop and Edward Solomon." In Cowgill and Rushton, *Europe*, 221–33.

Orientalism and Representations of Music in the Nineteenth-Century British Popular Arts. Aldershot: Ashgate, forthcoming.

MacDonald, Heather. "The Abduction of Opera." *City Journal*, Summer 2007. www.city-journal.org/html/17_3_urbanities-regietheater.html. Accessed 1 September 2007.

Macdonald, Hugh. "*Les Anglais*." In his *Beethoven's Century: Essays on Composers and Themes*, 193–201. Rochester: University of Rochester Press, 2008.

Macfie, Alexander Lyon. *Orientalism*. London: Longman, 2002.

Macfie, Alexander Lyon, ed. *Orientalism: A Reader*. New York: New York University Press, 2000.

MacKenzie, John M. "Empire and Metropolitan Cultures." In Porter and Low, *Oxford*, 270–93.

Orientalism: History, Theory and the Arts. Manchester: Manchester University Press, 1995.

Propaganda and Empire: The Manipulation of British Public Opinion, 1880–1960. Manchester: Manchester University Press, 1985.

MacKenzie, John M., ed. *Imperialism and Popular Culture*. Manchester: Manchester University Press, 1986.

Maehder, Jürgen. "Non-Western Instruments in Western Twentieth-Century Music: Musical Exoticism or Globalization of Timbres?" In Amalfitano and Innocenti, *L'Oriente*, 2:441–62.

"Die Opfer der Conquista: Das Volk der Azteken auf der Opernbühne." In Peter Csobádi, *et al.*, *"Weine,"* 1:265–87.

"Orientalismo ed esotismo nel Grand Opéra francese dell'Ottocento." In Amalfitano and Innocenti, *L'Oriente*, 1:375–403.

"The Representation of the 'Discovery' on the Opera Stage." In Carol E. Robertson, ed., *Musical Repercussions of 1492: Encounters in Text and Performance*, 257–87. Washington DC: Smithsonian Institution Press, 1992.

Maehder, Jürgen, ed. *Esotismo e colore locale nell'opera di Puccini: atti del I Convegno internazionale sull'opera di Giacomo Puccini*. Pisa: Giardini, 1985.

Makdisi, Ussama. "Ottoman Orientalism." *American Historical Review* 107 (2002): 768–96.

Maltby, William S. *The Black Legend in England: The Development of Anti-Spanish Sentiment, 1558–1660*. Durham, NC: Duke University Press, 1971.

Mandelli, Alfredo. "Esotismo non esotico in Puccini." In Maehder, *Esotismo*, 229–34.

Manuel, Peter. "From Scarlatti to 'Guantanamera': Dual Tonicity in Spanish and Latin American Musics." *Journal of the American Musicological Society* 88 (2002): 311–36.

"Modal Harmony in Andalusian, Eastern European, and Turkish Syncretic Musics." *Yearbook for Traditional Musics* 21 (1989): 70–94.

Popular Musics of the Non-Western World: An Introductory Survey. New York: Oxford University Press, 1988.

McClary, Susan. *George Bizet: Carmen*. Cambridge: Cambridge University Press, 1992.

"Mounting Butterflies." In Wisenthal, *et al.*, *Vision*, 21–35.

"Narrative Agendas in 'Absolute' Music: Identity and Difference in Brahms's Third Symphony." In Ruth A. Solie, ed., *Musicology and Difference: Gender and Sexuality in Music Scholarship*, 326–44. Berkeley: University of California Press, 1993.

McClintock, Ann. *Imperial Leather: Race, Gender, and Sexuality in the Colonial Contest*. London: Routledge, 1995.

McPhee, Colin. *A House in Bali*. New York: John Day Company, 1941.

Music in Bali: A Study in Form and Instrumental Organization in Balinese Orchestral Music. New Haven: Yale University Press, 1966.

McQuere, Gordon D., ed. *Russian Theoretical Thought in Music*. Ann Arbor: UMI Research Press, 1983.

Marissen, Michael. "Rejoicing against Judaism in Handel's *Messiah*." *Journal of Musicology* 24 (2007): 167–94.

Marsh, Adrian, and Elin Strand, eds. *Gypsies and the Problem of Identities: Contextual, Contructed and Contested*. Istanbul: Swedish Research Institute in Istanbul, 2006.

Mauss, Marcel. *The Gift: The Form and Reason for Exchange in Archaic Societies* [1924]. Translated by W. D. Halls. New York: W. W. Norton, 2000.

Mawer, Deborah. *Darius Milhaud: Modality and Structure in Music of the 1920s.* Aldershot: Scolar Press, 1997.
    "Jolivet's Search for a New French Voice: Spiritual 'Otherness' in *Mana* (1935)." In Kelly, *French*, 172–93.
Mayes, Catherine. "Domesticating the Foreign: Hungarian-Gypsy Music in Vienna at the Turn of the Nineteenth Century." Ph.D. dissertation, Cornell University, 2008.
Meilhac, Henri, and Ludovic Halévy. *Carmen* [libretto]. Paris: Calmann-Lévy, n.d. [c. 1950?].
Mellers, Wilfrid. *Singing in the Wilderness: Music and Ecology in the Twentieth Century.* Urbana: University of Illinois Press, 2001.
    "The Final Works of Claude Debussy, or Pierrot fâché avec la lune." *Music and Letters* 20 (1939): 168–76.
Menninghaus, Winfried. "Hummingbirds, Shells, Picture-Frames: Kant's 'Free Beauties' and the Romantic Arabesque." In Martha B. Helfer, ed., *Rereading Romanticism*, 27–46. Amsterdam: Rodopi, 2000.
Messiaen, Olivier. "Turangalîla-Symphonie." In the booklet accompanying the recording conducted by Myun-Whun Chung. Deutsche Grammophon CD 431 781-2.
Meyer, Felix, and Heidy Zimmermann, eds. *Edgard Varèse: Composer, Sound Sculptor, Visionary.* Woodbridge: Boydell, 2006.
Micznik, Vera. "Cio-Cio-San the Geisha." In Wisenthal, *et al.*, *Vision of the Orient*, 36–58.
Middleton, Richard. "Musical Belongings: Western Music and Its Low-Other." In Born and Hesmondhalgh, *Western*, 58–85.
Mielke, Randall G. *Road to Box Office: The Seven Film Comedies of Crosby, Hope and Lamour.* Jefferson, NC: McFarland & Company, 1997.
Miki, Minoru. *Composing for Japanese Instruments.* Translated by Marty Regan. Edited by Philip Flavin. Rochester: University of Rochester Press, 2008.
Mikusi, Balázs. "Evoking the Exotic: Schumann's 'Danish' Manner." *Musical Times* vol. 149, no. 1903 (Summer 2008): 36–46.
    "Mendelssohn's 'Scottish' Tonality?" *19th Century Music* 29 (2005–6): 240–60.
Milewski, Barbara. "Chopin's Mazurkas and the Myth of the Folk." *19th Century Music* 23 (1999–2000): 113–35.
Miller, Leta. "Lou Harrison and the Aesthetics of Revision, Alteration, and Self-Borrowing." *Twentieth-Century Music* 2 (2005): 1–29.
Miller, Leta, and Frederic Lieberman. "Lou Harrison and the American Gamelan." *American Music* 17 (1999): 146–78.
Mills, Sara. *Discourses of Difference: An Analysis of Women's Travel Writing and Colonialism.* London: Routledge, 1991.
Mitchell, Donald. *Gustav Mahler, Songs and Symphonies of Life and Death: Interpretations and Annotations.* Berkeley: University of California Press, 1986.

Mitterbauer, Helga. "Kulturtransfer – Cultural Transfer – Transferts Culturels." At the Universität Graz website www-gewi.uni-graz.at/moderne/kutr.htm. Accessed 13 February 2008.

Molière, *Théâtre*, 4 vols. Edited by P.-A. Touchard. [Paris]: Club des libraires de France, [1958].

Monelle, Raymond. *The Musical Topic: Hunt, Military and Pastoral*. Bloomington: Indiana University Press, 2006.

——. "Scottish Music, Real and Spurious." In Tomi Mäkelä, ed., *Music and Nationalism in 20th-Century Great Britain and Finland*, 87–100. Hamburg: Van Bockel, 1997.

Montesquieu, Charles de Secondat, baron de. *De l'esprit des lois*. 2 vols. Paris: Librairie Garnier frères, 1927.

Móricz, Klára. "Ancestral Voices: Anti-Semitism and Ernest Bloch's Racial Conception of Art." In Brown, ed., *Western*, 102–14.

——. *Jewish Identities: Nationalism, Racism, and Utopianism in Twentieth-Century Music*. Berkeley: University of California Press, 2008.

——. "Sensuous Pagans and Righteous Jews: Changing Conceptions of Jewish Identity in Ernest Bloch's *Jézabel* and *Schelomo*." *Journal of the American Musicological Society* 54 (2001): 439–91.

Morris, Narrelle. "Innocence to Deviance: The Fetishisation of Japanese Women in Western Fiction, 1890s–1990s." *Intersections: Gender, History and Culture in the Asian Context*, 7 (March 2002). www.sshe.murdoch.edu.au/intersections/issue7/morris.html. Accessed 6 May 2007.

Morris, Robert. "Towards a 'Buddhist Music': Precursors East and West." Unpublished lecture. http://lulu.esm.rochester.edu/rdm/downloads.html.

Morrison, Simon. "The Semiotics of Symmetry, or Rimsky-Korsakov's Operatic History Lesson." *Cambridge Opera Journal* 13 (2001): 261–93.

Moy, Ron. *Kate Bush and Hounds of Love*. Aldershot: Ashgate, 2007.

Munczi Lajos and His Orchestra. New York: Eden Musée, [1887].

"Music for Middle-Earth." Short documentary films in *The Lord of the Rings*, installments 1 and 2: *The Fellowship of the Ring* and *The Two Towers*. Special extended DVD edition and appendices. New Line Home Entertainment, 2002 and 2003.

Muthu, Sankar. *Enlightenment against Empire*. Princeton: Princeton University Press, 2003.

Nectoux, Jean-Michel. *Harmonie en bleu et or: Debussy, la musique et les arts*. Paris: Fayard, 2005.

Negrón-Muntaner, Frances. *Boricua Pop: Puerto Ricans and the Latinization of American Culture from West Side Story to Jennifer Lopez*. New York: New York University Press, 2004.

Nettl, Bruno. *The Western Impact on World Music: Change, Adaptation, and Survival*. New York: Schirmer Books, 1985.

Neubauer, Eckhard. *Der Essai sur la musique orientale von Charles Fonton mit Zeichnungen von Adanson*. Frankfurt: Institute for the History of Arabic-Islamic Science, 1999.

New Zealand Rugby Union website. www.nzrugby.com.
Newark, Cormac. Review of David Charlton, ed., *Cambridge Companion to Grand Opera*. *Cambridge Opera Journal* 16 (2004): 239–47.
Newman, John Henry Cardinal. *Apologia pro vita sua: Being a History of His Religious Opinions*. Edited by Martin J. Svaglic. Oxford: Clarendon Press, 1967.
Nice, David. *Prokofiev: From Russia to the West, 1891–1935*. New Haven: Yale University Press, 2003.
Nicholls, David. *American Experimental Music, 1890–1940*. Cambridge: Cambridge University Press, 1990.
——— . "Reaching beyond the West: Asian Resonances in American Radicalism." *American Music* 17 (1999): 125–28.
——— . "Transethnicism and the American Experimental Tradition." *Musical Quarterly* 80 (1996): 569–94.
Nicholls, David, ed. "Henry Cowell: Living in the Whole World of Music." In David Nicholls, ed., *The Whole World of Music: A Henry Cowell Symposium*, 1–11. Australia: Harwood Academic Publishers, 1997.
Nilsson, Martin. "The Musical Cliché Figure Signifying the Far East: Whence, Wherefore, Whither?" http://chinoiserie.atspace.com/ Accessed 13 August 2008.
Nochlin, Linda. "The Imaginary Orient." In her *The Politics of Vision: Essays on Nineteenth-Century Art and Society*, 33–58. New York: Harper and Row, 1989.
Noske, Frits. *French Song from Berlioz to Duparc: The Origin and Development of the mélodie*. Revised by Rita Benton and Frits Noske. Translated by Rita Benton. New York: Dover, 1970.
——— . *The Signifier and the Signified: Studies in the Operas of Mozart and Verdi*. The Hague: Martinus Nijhoff, 1977.
O'Connell, John Morgan. "In the Time of *Alaturka*: Identifying Difference in Musical Discourse." *Ethnomusicology* 49 (2005): 177–205.
Oesch, Hans, Wulf Arlt, and Max Haas, eds. *Europäische Musik zwischen Nationalismus und Exotik*. Basel: Amadeus, 1984.
Oestreich, James. "The Sound of New Music Is Often Chinese: A New Contingent of American Composers." *New York Times*, 1 April 2001.
Oja, Carol J. "New Music Notes." *Institute for Studies of American Music Newsletter* 27, no. 1 (Fall 1997): 6.
Okin, Susan Moller, et al. *Is Multiculturalism Bad for Women?* Edited by Joshua Cohen, Matthew Howard, and Martha Nussbaum. Princeton: Princeton University Press, 1999.
Oren, Michael B. *Power, Faith, and Fantasy: America in the Middle East, 1776 to the Present*. New York: W. W. Norton, 2007.
Orenstein, Arbie. *Ravel: Man and Musician*. New York: Columbia University Press, 1975.
Osterhammel, Jürgen. "Britain and China, 1842–1914." In Porter and Low, *Oxford*, 146–69.

Pacun, David. "'Thus We Cultivate Our Own World, and Thus We Share It with Others': Kósçak Yamada's Visit to the United States in 1918–1919." *American Music* 24 (2006): 67–91.

Pagannone, Giorgio. "Puccini e la melodia ottocentesca: L'effetto 'barform'." *Studi pucciniani* 3 (2004): 201–23.

Papp, Géza. "Die Quellen der 'Verbunkos-Musik': Ein bibliographischer Versuch," parts 1–3. *Studia musicologica* 21 (1979): 151–217; 24 (1982): 35–97; and 26 (1984): 59–132.

Parakilas, James. "How Spain Got a Soul." In Bellman, *Exotic in Western Music*, 137–93, 333–42.

——— "The Soldier and the Exotic: Operatic Variations on a Theme of Racial Encounter." *Opera Quarterly* 10, no. 2 (1994): 33–56.

Parakilas, James, et al. *Piano Roles: Three Hundred Years of Life with the Piano*. New Haven: Yale University Press, 1999.

Partch, Harry. *Bitter Music: Collected Journals, Essays, Introductions, and Librettos*. Edited by Thomas McGeary. Urbana: University of Illinois Press, 1991.

Pasler, Jann. "Race, Orientalism, and Distinction in the Wake of the 'Yellow Peril'." In Born and Hesmondhalgh, *Western*, 86–118.

Patterson, David Wayne. "Appraising the Catchwords, c. 1942–1959: John Cage's Asian-Derived Rhetoric and the Historical Reference of Black Mountain College". PhD dissertation, Columbia University, 1996.

Paulick, Jane. "A Violent, Drug-Addled, Hooker-Filled Opera Angers Sponsors." *Deutsche Welle*, 24 June 2004. With production photos. www.dw-world.de/dw/article/0,2144,1245750,00.html. Accessed 30 May 2007.

Pekacz, Jolanta T. "Deconstructing a 'National Composer': Chopin and Polish Exiles in Paris, 1831–49." *19th Century Music* 24 (2000–01): 161–72.

Peppercorn, Lisa M. *Villa-Lobos*. Edited by Audrey Sampson. London: Omnibus, 1989.

——— *Villa-Lobos, the Music: An Analysis of His Style*. Translated by Stefan de Haan. London: Kahn & Averill, 1991.

——— *The World of Villa-Lobos in Pictures and Documents*. Aldershot: Scolar Press, 1996.

Perl, Benjamin. "Mozart in Turkey." *Cambridge Opera Journal* 12 (2000): 219–35.

Perlman, Marc. "American Gamelan in the Garden of Eden: Intonation in a Cross-Cultural Encounter." *Musical Quarterly* 78 (1994): 510–55.

Pickering, Michael. *Blackface Minstrelsy in Britain*. Aldershot: Ashgate, 2008.

Pisani, Michael V. "Exotic Sounds in the Native Land: Portrayals of North American Indians in Western Music." 2 vols. Ph.D. dissertation, University of Rochester, 1996.

——— "'I'm an Indian Too': Creating Native American Identities in Nineteenth- and Early Twentieth-Century Music." In Bellman, *Exotic*, 218–57, 343–47.

——— *Imagining Native America in Music*. New Haven: Yale University Press, 2005.

"Music for the Theatre: Style and Function in Incidental Music." In Kerry Powell, ed., *The Cambridge Companion to Victorian and Edwardian Theatre*, 70–92. Cambridge: Cambridge University Press, 2004.

Pitts, Jennifer. *A Turn to Empire: The Rise of Imperial Liberalism in Britain and France*. Princeton: Princeton University Press, 2005.

Pollack, Howard. *Aaron Copland: The Life and Work of an Uncommon Man*. New York: Henry Holt, 1999.

George Gershwin: His Life and Work. Berkeley: University of California Press, 2006.

Polzonetti, Pierpaolo. "Opera Buffa and the American Revolution." Ph.D. dissertation, Cornell University, 2003

Pomeroy, Boyd. "Debussy's Tonality: A Formal Perspective." In Trezise, *Cambridge*, 155–78.

Poovey, Mary. *A History of the Modern Fact: Problems of Knowledge in the Sciences of Wealth and Society*. Chicago: University of Chicago Press, 1998.

Porter, Andrew, and Aline Low, eds. *Oxford History of the British Empire*, vol. 3: *The Nineteenth Century*. London: Oxford University Press, 1999.

Porter, Lewis. *John Coltrane: His Life and Music*. Ann Arbor: University of Michigan Press, 2000.

Potter, Caroline. "Debussy and Nature." In Trezise, *Cambridge*, 137–51.

Potter, Keith. *Four Musical Minimalists: La Monte Young, Terry Riley, Steve Reich, Philip Glass*. Cambridge: Cambridge University Press, 2000.

Powils-Okano, Kimiyo. *Puccinis "Madama Butterfly"*. Bonn: Verlag für systematische Musikwissenschaft, 1986.

Pratt, Mary Louise. *Imperial Eyes: Travel Writing and Transculturation*. London: Routledge, 1992.

Press, Stephen D. *Prokofiev's Ballets for Diaghilev*. Aldershot: Ashgate, 2006.

Prod'homme, J.-G., and A. Dandelot. *Gounod (1818–1893): sa vie et ses oeuvres*. 2 vols. Paris: C. Delagrave, 1911.

Pruiksma, Rose A. "Music, Sex, and Ethnicity: Signification in Lully's Theatrical Chaconnes." In Todd M. Borgerding, ed., *Gender, Sexuality, and Early Music*, 227–48. New York: Routledge, 2002.

Purser, John. *Scotland's Music: A History of the Traditional and Classical Music of Scotland from Early Times to the Present Day*. Enlarged edn. Edinburgh: Mainstream Publishing, 2007.

Rabinowitz, Peter J. "Chord and Discourse: Listening through the Written Word." In Stephen Paul Scher, ed., *Music and Text: Critical Inquiries*, 38–56. Cambridge: Cambridge University Press, 1992.

Radano, Ronald, and Philip V. Bohlman. "Introduction: Music and Race, Their Past, Their Presence." In Radano and Bohlman, *Music*, 1–53.

Radano, Ronald, and Philip V. Bohlman, eds. *Music and the Racial Imagination*. Chicago: University of Chicago Press, 2000.

Radice, Mark A. *Concert Music of the Twentieth Century: Its Personalities, Institutions, and Techniques*. Upper Saddle River, NJ: Prentice-Hall, 2002.

Randel, Don Michael, ed. *Harvard Dictionary of Music*, 4th edn. Cambridge, MA: Belknap Press, 2003.

Rapée, Erno, ed. *Motion Picture Moods for Piano and Organ: A Rapid-Reference Collection of Selected Pieces Adapted to Fifty-Two Moods and Situations.* New York: G. Schirmer, 1924.

Ratner, Leonard G. *Classic Music: Expression, Form, and Style.* New York: Schirmer Books, 1980.

Reck, David R. "Beatles orientalis: Influences from Asia in a Popular Song Form." *Asian Music* 15 (1985): 83–150.

  "The Neon Electric Saraswati: Being Reflections on the Influences of Indian Music on the Contemporary Music Scene in America." *Contributions to Asian Studies* 12 (1978): 3–19.

Recoing, Eloi. "Azucena, la dette et le don." *L'Avant-Scène Opéra* 60 (February 1974): 96–98.

Reich, Steve. Foreword. In Michael Tenzer, *Gamelan gong kebyar: The Art of Twentieth-Century Balinese Music.* Chicago: University of Chicago Press, 2000.

  Writings on Music: 1965–2000. Edited by Paul Hillier. New York: Oxford University Press, 2002.

Reinhard, Kurt. "Mozarts Rezeption türkischer Musik." In Helmut Kuhn and Peter Nitsche, eds., *Bericht über den Internationalen Musikwisschenschaftlichen Kongress Berlin 1974*, 518–23. Kassel: Bärenreiter, 1980.

Reinhard, Kurt, and Martin Stokes, "Turkey," pt. 4. In Laura Macy, ed., *Grove Music Online.* www.grovemusic.com. Accessed 14 November 2006.

Revol, Patrick. *Influences de la musique indonésienne sur la musique française du XXe siècle.* Paris: L'Harmattan, 2000.

Rhodes, Colin. *Primitivism and Modern Art.* London: Thames and Hudson, 1994.

Rice, Eric. "Representations of Janissary Music (*Mehter*) as Musical Exoticism in Western Compositions, 1670–1824." *Journal of Musicological Research* 19 (1999): 41–88.

Richards, Jeffrey. *Imperialism and Music: Britain 1876–1953.* Manchester: Manchester University Press, 2001.

Riegl, Alois. *Stilfragen: Grundlegungen zu einer Geschichte der Ornamentik.* 1893. Reprint: Berlin: Richard Carl Schmidt and Co. 1923. Translated as *Problems of Style.* Translated by Evelyn Kain. Princeton: Princeton University Press, 1992.

Rimsky-Korsakov, Nikolai. *My Musical Life.* Translated by Judah A. Joffe from the 5th Russian edn. New York: Alfred A. Knopf, 1942.

Ringer, Alexander L. "Europäische Musik im Banne der Exotik." In Oesch, *et al.*, *Europäische*, 77–98.

  "On the Question of 'Exoticism' in Nineteenth-Century Music." *Studia Musicologica* 7 (1965): 115–23.

Roberts, John Storm, *The Latin Tinge: The Impact of Latin American Music on the United States.* 2nd edn. New York: Oxford University Press, 1999.

Roberts, Paul. *Images: The Piano Music of Claude Debussy*. Portland, OR: Amadeus Press, 1996.

Robinson, J. Bradford. "Jazz Reception in Weimar Germany: In Search of a Shimmy Figure." In Bryan Gilliam, ed., *Music and Performance during the Weimar Republic*, 107–34. Cambridge: Cambridge University Press, 1994.

Rosen, Charles. "From the Troubadours to Sinatra" [review of Taruskin's *Oxford History of Western Music*], parts 1 and 2. *New York Review of Books*, 23 February and 9 March 2006. www.nybooks.com/articles/18725 and /18777. Accessed 11 February 2007.

Rosen, David. "Meter and Testosterone: Preliminary Observations about Meter and Gender in Verdi's Operas." In *Una piacente estate di San Martino: studi e ricerche per Marcello Conati*, ed. Marco Capra, 180–213. Lucca: Libreria musicale italiana, 2000.

"Pigri ed obesi dei: Religion in the Operas of Puccini." In Arthur Groos, *et al.*, eds., *Madama Butterfly: l'orientalismo di fine secolo, l'approccio pucciniano, la ricezione*. Florence: Olschki, forthcoming.

Rosen, David, and Marinella Pigozzi. *Un ballo in maschera di Giuseppe Verdi*. Milan: Ricordi, 2002.

Rosenstock, Laura. "Léger: 'The Creation of the World'." In Rubin, *Primitivism*, 475–85.

Rosenthal, Donald A. *Orientalism: The Near East in French Painting 1800–1880*. Rochester: Memorial Art Gallery of the University of Rochester, 1982.

Rossi, Jérôme. "Les identités culturelles étrangères dans la musique instrumental française ide 1850 à 1900: exotisme et régénération de l'art." *Analyse musicale* 54, no. 4 (November 2006): 76–80.

Roy, Jean. *Bizet*. Paris: Seuil/Solfèges, 1983.

Rubin, Rachel, and Jeffrey Melnick, eds. *Immigration and American Popular Culture: An Introduction*. New York: New York University Press, 2007.

Rubin, William, ed. *"Primitivism" in Modern Art: Affinity of the Tribal and the Modern*. 2 vols. New York: Museum of Modern Art, 1984.

Ruiz, Teofilo F. *Spanish Society, 1400–1600*. Harlow: Longman, 2001.

Russell, John G. "Race and Reflexivity: The Black Other in Contemporary Japanese Mass Culture." In John Whittier Treat, ed., *Contemporary Japan and Popular Culture*, 17–40. Honolulu: University of Hawaii Press, 1996.

Russom, Philip Wade. "A Theory of Pitch Organization for the Early Works of Maurice Ravel." PhD dissertation, Yale University, 1985.

Said, Edward W. *Culture and Imperialism*. New York: Alfred A. Knopf, 1993.

Musical Elaborations. New York: Columbia University Press, 1991.

Orientalism. New York: Pantheon Books, 1978.

The World, the Text, and the Critic. Cambridge, MA: Harvard University Press, 1983.

Saint-Saëns, Camille. Autograph letter, signed, 13 July 1907, to "Mon cher confrère" (a composer or author?). In the catalogue of the music dealer Lisa Cox no. 55 (2007), item 99.

Salmen, Walter. *Geschichte der Rhapsodie.* Zurich: Atlantis Verlag, 1966.

Samson, Jim. "The Musical Work and Nineteenth-Century History." In Samson, *Cambridge*, 2–28.

Samson, Jim, ed. *Cambridge History of Nineteenth-Century Music.* Cambridge: Cambridge University Press, 2002.

Sanal, Haydar. *Mehter musikisi: bestekar mehterler, mehter havalari.* Istanbul: Milli Iğitim Basimevi, 1964.

Sárosi, Bálint. *Gypsy Music.* Translated by Fred Macnicol. Budapest: Corvina Press, 1978.

Savage, Roger. "Rameau's American Dancers." *Early Music* 11 (1983): 441–52.

Schafter, Deborah. *The Order of Ornament, the Structure of Style: Theoretical Foundations of Modern Art and Architecture.* Cambridge: Cambridge University Press, 2003.

Schalz-Laurenze, Ute. "Musikalischer Brückenbau: *Muak* (1978)." In Heister and Sparrer, *Komponist*, 224–33.

Schatt, Peter W. *Exotik in der Musik des 20. Jahrhunderts: Historisch-systematische Untersuchungen zur Metamorphose einer ästhetischen Fiktion.* Munich: Musikverlag E. Katzbichler, 1986.

Schenker, Heinrich. *Counterpoint: A Translation of "Kontrapunkt."* 2 vols. Originally published in 1910–12. Edited by John Rothgeb and translated by John Rothgeb and Jürgen Thym. New York: Schirmer Books, 1982.

Scherzinger, Martin. "'Art' Music in a Cross-Cultural Context: The Case of Africa." In Cook and Pople, *Cambridge*, 585–613.

Schimmelpenninck, David van der Oye. *Toward the Rising Sun: Russian Ideologies of Empire and the Path to War with Japan.* DeKalb: Northern Illinois University Press, 2001.

Schmitt, Anke. *Der Exotismus in der deutschen Oper zwischen Mozart und Spohr.* Hamburg: Verlag der Musikalienhandlung K. D. Wagner, 1988.

Schnebel, Dieter. "Neue Weltmusik." In Oesch, *et al.*, *Europäische Musik*, 115–28.

Schoenberg, Arnold. "Folkloristic Symphonies." Originally published in 1947. In *Style and Idea: Selected Writings*, 161–66. Edited by Leonard Stein. With translations by Leo Black. London: Faber, 1975.

Schopenhauer, Arthur. *Der Wille als Welt und Vorstellung*, ed. Wolfgang Frhr. von Lühneysen, vol. 1. Darmstadt: Wissenschaftliche Buchgesellschaft, 1974.

Schuhmacher, Gerhard. "George Friedrich Händel, dramatisches Oratorium Belsazar: Eine Einführung." In the booklet to the 1976 Nikolaus Harnoncourt recording, 3-5. Teldec 6.35326-00-501.

Schuller, Gunther. "Jazz and Musical Exoticism." In Bellman, *Exotic in Western Music*, 281–91.

――――. *The Swing Era: The Development of Jazz, 1930–1945.* New York: Oxford University Press, 1989.

Schwartz, Judith L. "Cultural Stereotypes and Music in the Eighteenth Century." *Studies on Voltaire and the Eighteenth Century* 155 (1976): 1989–2013.

Schwarz, Boris. *Music in Soviet Russia. Music and Musical Life in Soviet Russia.* Enlarged edition: *1917–1981*. Bloomington: Indiana University Press, 1983.

Scott, Derek B. "Blackface Minstrels, Black Minstrels, and Their Reception in England." In Cowgill and Rushton, *Europe*, 265–80.

——— *From the Erotic to the Demonic: On Critical Musicology.* Oxford: Oxford University Press, 2003.

——— "A Problem of Race in Directing *Die Zauberflöte*." In Kühnel, "*Regietheater*," 338–44.

Scott-Maxwell, Aline. "Oriental Exoticism in 1920s Australian Popular Music." *Perfect Beat: The Pacific Journal of Research into Contemporary Music and Popular Culture* 3, no. 3 (July 1997): 28–57.

Sedgwick, Eve Kosofsky. *Between Men: English Literature and Male Homosocial Desire.* With a new preface by the author. New York: Columbia University Press, 1992.

Seigel, Jerrold. *Bohemian Paris: Culture, Politics, and the Boundaries of Bourgeois Life: 1830–1930.* New York: Viking Penguin, 1986.

Senici, Emanuele. *Landscape and Gender in Italian Opera: The Alpine Virgin from Bellini to Puccini.* Cambridge: Cambridge University Press, 2005.

Serravalle de Sá, Daniel. "Tropical Gothic: The Supernatural and the Demoniac in a 19th Century Brazilian Novel." MA thesis (Studies in Fiction), University of East Anglia, Norwich, 2005. www.tropicalgothic.com. Accessed 12 January 2007.

Seter, Ronit. "Yuvalim be-Israel: Identity, Ideology and Idioms in Jewish-Israeli Art Music 1940–2000." Ph.D. dissertation, Cornell University, 2004.

——— "Jerusalem and Tel-Aviv: Different News from Israel (or, One More Step Toward Peace): Three Contemporary Music Festivals." *Tempo* 59, no. 233 (July 2005): 46–51.

Shaw, George Bernard. *Shaw's Music: The Complete Musical Criticism.* 3 vols. Edited by Dan H. Laurence. London: Max Reinhardt, the Bodley Head, 1981.

Shay, Anthony. *Choreographic Politics: State Folk Dance Companies, Representation, and Power.* Middletown, CT: Wesleyan University Press, 2002.

Sheppard, W. Anthony. "Cinematic Realism, Reflexivity and the American 'Madame Butterfly' Narratives." *Cambridge Opera Journal* 17 (2005): 59–93.

——— "Continuity in Composing the American Cross-Cultural: Eichheim, Cowell, and Japan." *Journal of the American Musicological Society* 61 (2008): 465–540.

——— "An Exotic Enemy: Anti-Japanese Musical Propaganda in World War II Hollywood." *Journal of the American Musicological Society* 54 (2001): 303–57.

——— *Extreme Exoticism: Japan in the American Musical Imagination* (in progress).

——— "Representing the Authentic: Tak Shindo's 'Exotic Sound' and Japanese American History." *ECHO: A Music-Centered Journal* 6, issue 2 (Fall 2004), www.echo.ucla.edu.

——— *Revealing Masks: Exotic Influences and Ritualized Performance in Modernist Music Theater.* Berkeley: University of California Press, 2000.

Sherman, Scott. "A Return to Java: Benedict Anderson Attempts to Reimagine Java." In Alexander Star, ed., *Quick Studies: The Best of "Lingua franca,"* 317–35. New York: Farrar, Straus, Giroux, 2002.

Sheveloff, Joel. "Dance, Gypsy, Dance!" In John Daverio and John Ogasapian, eds., *The Varieties of Musicology: Essays in Honor of Murray Lefkowitz*, 151–65. Warren, MI: Harmonie Park Press, 2000.

Signell, Karl. "Mozart and the Mehter." *The Consort* 24 (1967): 310–22.

Slobin, Mark. *Subcultural Sounds: Micromusics of the West*. Hanover, NH: Wesleyan University Press, 1993.

Smith, Julian. "Musical Exoticism in Madama Butterfly." In Maehder, *Esotismo*, 111–18.

Smith, Richard Langham, "Elsewhere and Erstwhile" [review of books by Annegret Fauser and by Katherine Ellis]. *Musical Times*, vol. 147, issue 1896 (Autumn 2006): 93–101.

Smith, Richard Langham, and Caroline Potter, eds. *French Music since Berlioz*. Aldershot and Burlington, VT: Ashgate, 2006.

Smith, Ruth. "The Achievements of Charles Jennens, 1700–73." *Music and Letters* 70 (1989): 161–90.

"Handel's English Librettists." In Donald Burrows, ed., *The Cambridge Companion to Handel*, 92–108. Cambridge: Cambridge University Press, 1997.

Handel's Oratorios and Eighteenth-Century Thought. Cambridge: Cambridge University Press, 1995.

Smith, Steven C. *A Heart at Fire's Center: The Life and Music of Bernard Herrmann*. Berkeley: University of California Press, 1991.

Solomon, Maynard. *Late Beethoven: Music, Thought, Imagination*. Berkeley: University of California Press, 2003.

Southam, Brian. "The Silence of the Bertrams." In Austen, *Mansfield*, 493–98.

Souvenir Serge de Diaghileff's Ballet[s] Russe[s], with originals by Léon Bakst and Others. New York: Metropolitan Ballet Company, 1916.

Staier, Andreas. "Ornamentation and Alteration in Mozart – Can We, Should We, Must We?" Translated by Charles Johnston. In booklet for Staier's recording of Mozart's Keyboard Sonata in A Major (K331), 11-12. Harmonia Mundi HMC 901856.

Stauber, Roni, and Raphael Vago, eds. *The Roma: A Minority in Europe: Historical, Political and Social Perspectives*. Budapest: Central European University Press, 2007.

Stein, Louise K. "Eros, Erato, Terpsichore, and the Hearing of Music in Early Modern Spain." *Musical Quarterly* 82 (1998): 654–77.

Stevens, MaryAnne, ed. *The Orientalists: Delacroix to Matisse, The Allure of North Africa and the Near East*. London: Royal Academy of Arts, 1984.

Stevenson, Robert. "The Afro-American Musical Legacy to 1800." *Musical Quarterly* 54 (1968): 475–502.

"The First Dated Mention of the Sarabande." *Journal of the American Musicological Society* 5 (1951): 29–31.

"The Sarabande: A Dance of American Descent." *Inter-American Music Bulletin* 30 (1962): 1–13.

Stock, Jonathan. "Peripheries and Interfaces: The Western Impact on Other Music." In Cook and Pople, eds., *Cambridge*, 18–39.

Stoïanova, Ivanka. "L'Orient et la musique européenne après la Deuxième guerre." In Amalfitano and Innocenti, *L'Oriente*, 2:463–74.

Stowe, David W. "'Jazz That Eats Rice': Toshiko Akiyoshi's Roots Music." In Heike Raphael-Hernandez and Shannon Steen, eds., *AfroAsian Encounters: Culture, History, Politics*, 277–94. New York: New York University Press, 2006.

Strasser, Michael. "Grieg, the Société Nationale, and the Origins of Debussy's String Quartet." In Barbara L. Kelly and Kerry Murphy, eds., *Berlioz and Debussy: Sources, Contexts, and Legacies: Essays in Honour of François Lesure*, 103–15. Aldershot: Ashgate, 2007.

Stravinsky, Igor. *The Poetics of Music in the Form of Six Lessons*. Translated by Arthur Knodel and Ingolf Dahl. Cambridge, MA: Harvard University Press, 1970.

Stuart, Tristram. *The Bloodless Revolution: A Cultural History of Vegetarianism from 1600 to Modern Times*. New York: W. W. Norton, 2007.

Sublette, Ned. *Cuba and Its Music: From the First Drums to the Mambo*. Chicago: Chicago Review Press, 2004.

Subotnik, Rose Rosengard. *Deconstructive Variations: Music and Reason in Western Society*. Minneapolis: University of Minnesota Press, 1996.

Sullivan, John. *New World Symphonies: How American Culture Changed European Music*. New Haven: Yale University Press, 1999.

Swack, Jeanne. "Anti-Semitism at the Opera: The Portrayal of Jews in the Singspiels of Reinhard Keiser." *Musical Quarterly* 84 (2000): 389–416.

Swedenburg, Ted. "Islamic Hip-Hop vs. Islamophobia: Aki Nawaz, Natacha Atlas, Akhenaton." In Tony Mitchell, ed., *Global Noise: Rap and Hip Hop outside the U.S.A*, 57–85. Middletown, CT: Wesleyan University Press, 2001.

Swedenburg, Ted, Joan Gross, and David McMurray. "Arab Noise and Ramadan Nights: Rai, Rap, and Franco-Maghrebi Identity." In Smadar Lavie and Ted Swedenburg, eds., *Displacement, Diaspora, and Geographies of Identity*, 119–55. Durham, NC: Duke University Press, 1996.

Sweeney-Turner, Steve. "The Political Parlour: Identity and Ideology in Scottish National Song." In White and Murphy, *Musical*, 212–38.

Szabolcsi, Bence. "Exoticisms in Mozart." *Music and Letters* 37 (1956): 323–32.

Takeishi, Midori. *Japanese Elements in Michio Ito's Early Period (1915–1924): Meetings of East and West in the Collaborative Works*. Edited and revised by David Pacun. Tokyo: Gendaitosho, 2005.

Takemitsu, Tōru. "On Sawari" (1975). Translated by Hugh de Ferranti and Yayoi Uno Everett. In Everett and Lau, *Locating*, 199–207, 254–55.

Tan Dun. "On the Creation of *Marco Polo*." In Tan Dun, *Marco Polo: An Opera within an Opera*. Libretto by Paul Griffiths. Pp. 10–13. Sony 2 CDs: S2K 62912.

Taruskin, Richard. *Defining Russia Musically: Historical and Hermeneutical Essays*. Princeton: Princeton University Press, 1997.

"'Entoiling the Falconet': Russian Musical Orientalism in Context." In Bellman, *Exotic*, 194–217, 342–43. Also published (without the subtitle) in Taruskin, *Defining*, 152–85.

"Nationalism." In Laura Macy, ed., *Grove Music Online*. www.grovemusic.com. Accessed 7 December 2003.

The Oxford History of Western Music, 6 vols. New York: Oxford University Press, 2005.

Review of Van der Merwe, *Roots*. *Music and Letters* 88 (2007): 134–39.

"Speed Bumps" [review of *Cambridge History of Nineteenth-Century Music* and *Cambridge History of Twentieth-Century Music*]. *19th Century Music* 29 (2005–6): 185–295.

Stravinsky and the Russian Traditions. 2 vols. Berkeley: University of California Press, 1996.

Taves, Brian. "Candidates for the National Film Registry: *The Desert Song* [1943]." www.loc.gov/film/taves8.html. Accessed 10 February 2007.

Taylor, Timothy D. *Beyond Exoticism: Western Music and the World*. Durham, NC: Duke University Press, 2007.

Global Pop: World Music, World Markets. New York: Routledge, 1997.

Tenzer, Michael. "Western Music in the Context of World Music." In Robert P. Morgan, ed., *Man and Music* [US series title: *Music and Society*], vol. 4: *Modern Times from World War I to the Present*, 388–410. London: Macmillan, 1994.

Thomalla, Ariane. *Die "femme fragile": Ein literarischer Frauentypus der Jahrhunderwende*. Düsseldorf: Bertelsmanns Universitätsverlag, 1972.

Thompson, Donald, ed. *Music in Puerto Rico: A Reader's Anthology*. Lanham, MD: Scarecrow Press, 2002.

Thompson, James. *The East: Imagined, Experienced, Remembered: Orientalist Nineteenth Century Painting*. Dublin: National Gallery of Ireland, 1988.

Tiersot, Julien. *La chanson populaire en France*. Paris: E. Plon, Nourrit, 1889.

Todd, R. Larry. "Mendelssohn's Ossianic Manner, with a New Source – *On Lena's Gloomy Heath*." In Jon W. Finson and R. Larry Todd, eds., *Mendelssohn and Schumann: Essays on Their Music and Its Context*, 137–60. Durham, NC: Duke University Press, 1984.

Todorova, Maria. *Imagining the Balkans*. New York: Oxford University Press, 1997.

Toliver, Brooks. "Eco-ing in the Canyon: Ferde Grofé's *Grand Canyon Suite* and the Transformation of Wilderness." *Journal of the American Musicological Society* 57 (2004): 325–68.

Tomlinson, Gary. *The Singing of the New World: Indigenous Voice in the Era of European Contact*. Cambridge: Cambridge University Press, 2007.

Music in Renaissance Magic: Toward a Historiography of Others. Chicago: University of Chicago Press, 1993.

Tomoff, Kiril. *Creative Union: The Professional Organization of Soviet Composers, 1939–1953*. Ithaca: Cornell University Press, 2006.

TomTom Global Positions Systems website. www.tomtom.com.

Toop, David. *Exotica: Fabricated Soundscapes in a Real World*. London: Serpent's Tail, 1999.
Trezise, Simon, ed. *The Cambridge Companion to Debussy*. Cambridge: Cambridge University Press, 2003.
Trumpener, Katie. "Béla Bartók and the Rise of Comparative Ethnomusicology: Nationalism, Race Purity, and the Legacy of the Austro-Hungarian Empire." In Radano and Bohlman, *Music*, 403–34.
Um, Hae-Kyung. *Diasporas and Interculturalism in Asian Performing Arts*. London: Routledge Curzon, 2005.
Utz, Christian. "Interkulturelles Komponieren als Herausforderung: Transformation, Bruch und Mythoskritik in Werken für die Japanische Mundorgel *shō*." In Hiekel, *Orientierungen*, 63–84.
    Neue Musik und Interkulturalität, Beihefte zum Archiv für Musikwissenschaft 51. Stuttgart: Franz Steiner, 2002.
Van, Gilles de. "L'exotisme fin de siècle et le sens du lointain." In Lorenza Guiot and Jürgen Maehder, eds., *Letteratura, musica e teatro al tempo di Ruggero Leoncavallo: Atti del 2o Convegno internazionale "Ruggero Leoncavallo nel suo tempo"*, 103–17. Milan: Casa Musicale Sonzogno, 1995. Translated by William Ashbrook as "Fin de Siècle Exoticism and the Meaning of the Far Away." *Opera Quarterly* 11, no. 3 (1995): 77–94.
Van den Toorn, Pieter C. *The Music of Igor Stravinsky*. New Haven: Yale University Press, 1983.
Van der Merwe, Peter. *Origins of the Popular Style: The Antecedents of Twentieth-Century Popular Music*. Oxford: Clarendon Press, 1989.
    Roots of the Classical: The Popular Origins of Western Music. Oxford: Oxford University Press, 2004.
Viale Ferrero, Mercedes. "'Come su ali invisibili': viaggiatori immaginari tra provincie e capitali." In Lorenz Guiot, Jürgen Maehder, and Evan Baker, eds., *Nazionalismo e cosmopolitismo nell'opera fra '800 e '900: atti del 3o Convegno internazionale "Ruggero Leoncavallo nel suo tempo": Locarno, Biblioteca cantonale, 6–7 ottobre 1995*, 229–38. Milan: Sonzogno, 1998.
    "Riflessioni sulle scenografie pucciniane." *Studi pucciniani* 1 (1998): 19–42.
Víg, Rudolf. "Gypsy Folk Songs from Hungary." Booklet notes to the 1976 2-LP set *Magyarországi népdalok*. Hungaroton SLPX 18028–29.
Volans, Kevin. Preface ("Composer's Note" and "Sources"). In *String Quartet No. 2, "Hunting: Gathering"*, [iii]. London: Chester Music, 1999.
Wagner, Richard. *Sämtliche Schriften und Dichtungen*, 10 vols. Leipzig: Breitkopf und Härtel, 1912–14.
    "Über die Anwendung der Musik auf das Drama." In Wagner, *Sämtliche*, 10:176–93.
    "Über das Dichten und Komponieren." In Wagner, *Sämtliche*, 10:137–51.
Walker, Alan. *Franz Liszt*. 3 vols. New York: Random House, 1983–96. For vol. 1, I have used the revised edition (Ithaca: Cornell University Press, 1989).

Walser, Robert. "The Polka Mass: Music of Postmodern Ethnicity." *American Music* 10 (1992): 183–202.

Warrack, John. *Carl Maria von Weber*, 2nd edn. Cambridge: Cambridge University Press, 1976.

Warraq, Ibn. *Defending the West: A Critique of Edward Said's Orientalism.* Amherst, NY: Prometheus Books, 2007.

Waters, Lindsay. "In Responses Begins Responsibility: Music and Emotion." In Bové, *Edward Said*, 97–113, 289–90.

Weber, William. "Beyond Zeitgeist: Recent Work in Music History." *Journal of Modern History* 66 (1994): 321–45.

  Music and the Middle Classes: The Social Structure of Concert Life in London, Paris and Vienna between 1830 and 1848. 2nd edn. Burlington, VT: Ashgate, 2002.

Welch, Allison. "Meetings along the Edge: *Svara* and *Tāla* in American Minimal Music." *American Music* 17 (1999): 179–99.

Wells, Elizabeth. "*West Side Story* and the Hispanic." *ECHO: A Music-Centered Journal* 2, no. 1 (2000), www.echo.ucla.edu.

  *West Side Story*s, Lanham, MD: Scarecrow Press, forthcoming.

Whaples, Miriam K. "Early Exoticism Revisited." In Bellman, ed., *Exotic in Western Music*, 3–25, 307–13.

  "Exoticism in Dramatic Music, 1600–1800." PhD dissertation, Indiana University, 1958.

Whitburn, Joel. *Joel Whitburn Presents a Century of Pop Music: Year-by-Year Top 40 Rankings of the Songs and Artists That Shaped a Century.* Menomonee Falls, WI: Record Research, 1999.

White, Harry, and Michael Murphy, eds. *Musical Constructions of Nationalism: Essays on the History and Ideology of European Musical Culture 1800–1945.* Cork: Cork University Press, 2001.

Wichmann, Siegfried, ed. *Weltkulturen und moderne Kunst; die Begegnung der europäischen Kunst und Musik im 19. und 20. Jahrhundert mit Asien, Afrika, Ozeanien, Afro-und Indo-Amerika.* Munich: Verlag Bruckmann, 1972.

Will, Richard. *The Characteristic Symphony in the Age of Haydn and Beethoven.* Cambridge: Cambridge University Press, 2002.

Willems, Wim. *In Search of the True Gypsy: From Enlightenment to Final Solution.* London: Frank Cass, 1997.

Williams, Christopher A. "Of Canons & Context: Toward a Historiography of Twentieth-Century Music." *repercussions* 2, no. 1 (Spring 1993): 31–74.

Williams, William Carlos. *Desert Music, and Other Poems.* New York: Random House, 1954.

Wilson, Kathleen. *The Sense of the People: Politics, Culture, and Imperialism in England, 1715–1785.* Cambridge: Cambridge University Press, 1995.

Wilson, W. Daniel. "Turks on the Operatic Stage and European Political, Military, and Cultural History." *Eighteenth-Century Life* 9 (1985): 79–92.

Winkler, Amanda Eubanks. "Enthusiasm and Its Discontents: Religion, Prophecy, and Madness in *Sophonisba* and *The Island Princess*." *Journal of Musicology* 23 (2006): 307–30.

   O Let Us Howle Some Heavy Note: Music for Witches, the Melancholic, and the Mad on the Seventeenth-Century English Stage. Bloomington: Indiana University Press, 2006.

Wisenthal, Jonathan, "Inventing the Orient." In Wisenthal, *et al.*, *Vision*, 3–18.

Wisenthal, Jonathan, Sherrill Grace, Melinda Boyd, Brian McIlroy, and Vera Micznik, eds. *A Vision of the Orient: Texts, Intertexts, and Contexts of Madame Butterfly*. Toronto: University of Toronto Press, 2006.

Woodfield, Ian. *Music of the Raj: A Social and Economic History of Music in Late Eighteenth-Century Anglo-Indian Society*. New York: Oxford University Press, 2000.

Wright, Lesley A. "Profiles in Courage: Two French Opera Heroines." *Fu Jen Studies: Literature and Linguistics* 30 (1997): 58–70.

Wright, Lesley A., ed. *Georges Bizet, Carmen: dossier de presse parisienne (1875)*. Weinsberg: Musik-Edition Lucie Galland, 2001.

Wright, Simon. "Villa-Lobos: Modernism in the Tropics." *Musical Times*, vol.128, no. 1729 (March 1987): 132–35.

Youens, Susan. "Heine, Liszt, and the Song of the Future." In Gibbs and Gooley, *Franz Liszt*, 39–74.

Yri, Kirsten. "Medievalism and Exoticism in the Music of Dead Can Dance." *Current Musicology* 85 (Spring 2008): 53–72.

Yu Siu[-]Wah. "Two Practices Confused in One Composition: Tan Dun's *Symphony 1997: Heaven, Earth, Man*." In Everett and Lau, *Locating*, 57–71.

Yuasa, Joji. "Herausforderung durch *Réak*." In Heister and Sparrer, *Komponist*, 158–59.

Zemp, Hugo. "The/An Ethnomusicologist and the Record Business." *Yearbook for Traditional Music* 28 (1995): 36–56.

Zheng, Yangwen. "From *Swan Lake* to *Red Girl's Regiment*: Ballet's Sinicisation." In Marion Kant, ed., *The Cambridge Companion to Ballet*, 256–62. Cambridge: Cambridge University Press, 2007.

Ziter, Edward. *The Orient on the Victorian Stage*. Cambridge: Cambridge University Press, 2003.

Zon, Bennett. *Music and Metaphor in Nineteenth-Century British Musicology*. Aldershot: Ashgate, 2000.

   Representing Non-Western Music in Nineteenth-Century Britain. Rochester: University of Rochester Press, 2007.

Websites with musical performances

http://musicmavericks.publicradio.org/features/feature_partch.html# (The instruments that composer Harry Partch created and used.)

http://www.artofthestates.org/ (Musical works by composers who were born or lived most of their lives in the United States of America.)

Index

This index includes most names and important terms in the text and in the Figure captions. Names mentioned in passing (e.g., film actors, opera companies) are omitted. To save space, works are given as sub-entries to their composer or other main creator, and they are not generally named if the discussion of that person's works is confined to a single page.

Absorbed Exoticism, *see* exoticism
Achron, Joseph, 245
Adler, Guido, 59, 65
aesthetics, cultural, 1, 24, 35, 161, 216, 218, 229, 248, 313, 327; musical, Western, 16, 21, 32, 34, 123, 124, 151, 181, 216, 217, 229, 239, 241, 248, 290, 313; musical, globalized, 298
African-American(s), 66, 106, 243, 251, 255, 256, 257, 259, 262, 288, 304, 307
Agee, James, 267
Akiyoshi, Toshiko, 299
Alaap (British group), 308
Aladdin (Disney film), 302
alap (in Indian music), 238, 299
Albéniz, Isaac, *Ibéria*, 7, 76
aleatoricism, 248, 288
Alexander II, tsar of Russia, 226
Alexander the Great, 89
Alhambra, The, 134, 218
"All the Music in Full Context" Paradigm, 3, 4, 8, 10–11, 24, 31, 42, 69, 92, 105, 248; defined, 59–65
all'ongherese/alla zingarese style, 70, 76; *see also* Hungarian-Gypsy
alla rustica, 70
alla turca, operas, 87; style(s), 43, 62, 106, 109, 110, 113, 114, 117, 118, 119, 120, 121, 122, 123, 124, 131, 156, 198, 233
Al-Nur, Salim, 37
Alpert, Herb and the Tijuana Brass, 300
Al-Rashid, Harun, 194
American Indian, *see* Native American
Andalusia, 160–66; Andalusian style, 142, 162; *see also* Spain
antiquity, 70, 71; Babylonia, 87, 89, 90, 91, 92; Greece, 37, 144, 218; Mesopotamia, 218; Rome, 65, 113
Appiah, Kwame Anthony, 41, 42, 327

Apple, Fiona, 308
Arab world (and music), *see* Egypt, Islam, Middle East, North Africa, Turkey
arabesque, 53, 54, 60, 217–22, 228, 253
Arabian Nights "pantomimes," 216
Arabian Nights, The, *see* Thousand and One Nights
"archaeology" (of knowledge), *see* Foucault
Aristotle, *Nicomachean Ethics*, 94, 95; principles, 216
Armenia(n), 88, 95, 247, 250, 302
Arnaz, Desi, 253
Around the World in Eighty Days (film), 267
arreglito, El (song), 128, 166, 168, 314, 315
arromba (Portugal), 87
Auber, Daniel-François-Esprit, 73; *Fra Diavolo*, 127; *La muette de Portici*, 127
Austen, Jane, 322; *Mansfield Park*, 18, 34
autoexoticism, 76, 78, 84, 86, 252, 310
avant-garde, 39, 248, 279, 282, 286

bacchanale, 11, 19, 215, 268, 270
Bach, J. S., Concerti grossi, 236; First Brandenburg Concerto, 109; Italian Concerto, 4, 73; *Little Notebook for Anna Magdalena Bach*, 67; *polacca*, 109
bagpipe, 67, 109, 127, 157
Baker, Josephine, 5, 20, 259, 260
Bakst, Léon, 224, 225
Bali, *see* Bartók, gamelan, Indonesia
ballet, 19, 22, 37, 64, 65, 74, 88, 89, 111, 130, 135, 222, 223, 227, 237, 243, 244, 248, 249, 250, 269, 274, 311; *see also* court ballet
Ballets Russes, 224
barcarolle, 127, 206
Barjansky, Catherine, 246
Baroque era, 5, 8, 62, 70, 87–107, 111

Bartók, Bela, "The Isle of Bali," 234, 244; *The Miraculous Mandarin*, 244
Bartoli, Jean-Pierre, 43–49, 55
Bath, Hubert, *Cornish Rhapsody*, 149
Bauzá, Mario, 253
Beatles, The, 306
Bechet, Sidney, 243
Beck, Jeff, 306
Beckerman, Michael, 75–77
Bedouins, 123
Beecham, Sir Thomas, 315
Beethoven, Ludwig van, Ninth Symphony, 122; "Ode to Joy," 295; "Rasumovsky" String Quartets, Op. 59, 132; *Ruinen von Athen, Die*, 118, 126; Symphony No. 6, "Pastoral," 131
Bei mir bist du schön (Means That You're Grand), 1938 song, 305
Bellman, Jonathan, 23–25, 45, 46, 62, 110, 306
ben Brahim, Zohra, 219
Ben-Haim, Paul, 283–84
Berganza, Teresa, 320–21
Berlioz, Hector, 130–32
Bernstein, Elmer, 295
Bernstein, Leonard, *Candide*, 268; *West Side Story*, 5, 7, 8, 214, 268–75, 270, 309, 324
Betzwieser, Thomas, 45, 46, 62, 88, 111, 114
Beyazid, sultan, 89
Béla Fleck and the Flecktones, 301
Bhabha, Homi, 35
Bhagavad-Gita, 299
bhangra, 308
Bhogal, Gurminder Kaur, 219
Bible, 88, 95, 96, 108, 150, 151, 233, 245
Bieito, Calixto, 323, 324
"big bands," 252
Bihari, Janos, 138, 139, 140, 141
binarism(s), near/far, 41, 47, 53, 67–68, 87, 132, 163, 192, 252, 261, 310; real/fictive, 68, 74; musical/extramusical signs, 69, 71, 75; Self/Other, 66, 67, 68, 72, 79, 80, 81, 82, 268, 272, 289, 301; then/now, 64, 66, 70; and stereotypes, 79, 87
Bizet, Georges, *Carmen*, 5, 7, 8, 37, 41, 46, 52, 67, 128, 150, 154, 160–72, 174, 262, 271, 313–15, 318–21; *Les pêcheurs de perles*, 80, 153, 183, 192, 194, 195, 196, 197, 198, 200; Symphony in C, 69, 131
Black Birds Revue, 258
blackface minstrel tradition, 67, 127, 151, 243, 255, 310
"black-note" pentatonicism, 57, 189, 222; *see also* pentatonic
Bland, James A., 255

Bloch, Ernest, *Jézabel*, 245; *Schelomo*, 245, 246, 250
Blomdahl, Karl Birger, *Aniara*, 68
blue notes, 242
blues, 76, 242–44, 250, 252
Bobowski, Woyciech, 317
Bohemianism, 86
bohémien, *see* Gypsy
Bohrer, Frederick N., 9, 12, 64
Boieldieu, Adrien, 32
bokázó cadences, 143
bolero, 28, 128, 168
Bolm, Adolf, 224
Borodin, Alexander Porfiryevich, *In [the Steppes of] Central Asia*, 226; "Polovetsian Dances," 152, 153, 227; *Prince Igor*, 152, 227
Boston Pops, The, 250
Bouissou, Sylvie, 100
Boulez, Pierre, 27, 30, 34, *Le marteau sans maître*, 285
Bourgault-Ducoudray, L. A., 149
Bourges, Maurice, 134
Brahms, Johannes, Hungarian Dances, 28–29, 148; "Edward" Ballade, 32, 65, 71; G-Minor Piano Quartet, 28, 32; Piano Quintet, 28, 32, 148; Violin Concerto, 28, 32; "Wie bist du, meine Königin," 135
Brazil, 7, 88, 106, 178, 243, 267; *see also* Respighi, Villa-Lobos
Bremner, Robert, 109
Brightman, Sarah, *Harem* (CD), 308
Britain, 17, 35, 41, 90, 97, 133, 149, 175, 176, 180, 215, 223, 247, 254, 276, 283, 294, 300, 302, 309, 313
British East India Company, 133
British Empire, *see* imperialism
Britten, Benjamin, *Curlew River*, 37, 38, 285; *Death in Venice*, 38, 39, 242; *Peter Grimes*, 242
Broadway musical, 1, 7, 46, 51, 52, 62, 68, 71, 214, 255, 262, 268, 269, 270, 271, 273, 302, 304, 309, 326; "belting," 309; *see also* Bernstein (Leonard), musical comedy, Rodgers and Hammerstein, Romberg
Brooke, Gwydion (bassoonist), 315
Bruch, Max, 32
Bruneau, Alfred, 227
Brynner, Yul, 319
Buddha, 210, 286
Bugs Bunny, 29
Bulgaria, 277, 308
Burroughs, Edgar Rice, 302
Buruma, Ian, 35

Bush, Kate, 308
Byrne, David, 37, 307, 308, 310
Byron, George Gordon, Lord, 36

Cage, John, 7, 239
Cahill, Marie, 255–56
cakewalk, 243
Calder, Alexander, 237
Calvé, Emma, 173–74
Cammarano, Salvatore, 151, 156
Campra, André, 20, 114; *L'Europe galante*, 20, 58, 64, 114; ballets, 94
Canteloube, Joseph, 67, 73
Caribbean, 20, 87, 253–54, 299; *see also* Hispanic, Latin America
Casella, Alfredo, 234
Cather, Willa, 37
Catholicism, 95, 113, 292; in Poland, 77, 85
Catholic(s), 36, 41, 45, 65, 77, 90, 103, 108, 113, 201, 248, 300, 301; evocation by Debussy, 65
censorship, 81, 103, 151, 153, 226
Central Asia, *see* Borodin, Gubaïdulina
Chabrier, (Alexis-)Emmanuel, *España*, 106
cha-cha-chá, 249, 270, 273
chaconne, 23, 88, 108
chanson(s), 5, 7, 257, 305; *chanson coloniale*, 20; "Chanson bohème," 168–69
chant, Mongolian, 298; modal, choral in film, 302; ritualistic, 53, 59; *see also* Gregorian chant
"characteristic" piano pieces, 22
Charlemagne, 65
Charleston, 242
Chausson, Ernest, *Poème* for violin and orchestra, 235
Chávez, Carlos, 249
China, ballet, 277; *erhu*, 280; melodies, 188; music, 59, 129, 188, 190, 200, 259, 295; music theory, 129; opera, 239; philosophy, 280, Western opera in, 318; *see also* East Asia
Chineseness, 9, 58
Chinoiserie, 30, 260, 288
Chopin, Fryderyk Franciszek, concertos, 76; mazurkas, 7, 12, 75–77, 131, 134; Nocturne in G Minor, 75
"Chopsticks," 289
chôros, 293
Chou Wen-Chung, 298
Christianity, 36, 65, 90, 96–96, 113, 122, 135, 155, 177, 180, 291, 292, 316–17, 322, 324
Christie, William, 322
Christy's Minstrels, 151
chromatic(ism), 51, 56, 87, 129, 134, 162, 167, 189, 226, 228, 242, 253

cigányok, 137
cimbalom, 54, 59, 137, 145, 146, 147, 316
Citizen Kane, 266
City of Angels (film), 308
Classic era, 111–27
"classical" concert life, 312
classical music, Western, 1, 17, 32, 106, 123, 279, 293, 299, 309
Cleopatra (1963 film), 80
codes, 2, 3, 28, 45, 46, 62, 83, 134, 216, 282
Cole, Bob, 255
Cole, Catherine, 99, 104
Coleridge, Samuel Taylor, 179
Collins, Phil, 302
colonialism, 17, 24, 34, 97, 133, 151, 162, 175, 176, 178, 179, 181, 185, 229, 261, 266, 284; anti-colonial terrorism, 100
coloratura, *see* melismatic singing
Coltrane, John, 299
comic bass character, Turkish, 121
conga, 54, 253, 268
Conrad, Joseph, 34
contredanse, 107, 124
"coon shouter," 255–56
Copland, Aaron, *Danzón cubano*, 249, 256; *El salón México Billy the Kid and Rodeo*, 249
Corea, Chick, 299
Corelli, Archangelo, 108
Corneille, Pierre, 94
Cornelius, Peter, 150
Cornetti, Marianne, 321
Corrette, Michel, 114
cosmopolitan(ism), 9, 29, 41, 45, 73, 78, 152, 160, 163, 215, 246, 327
couleur locale, 88
country-and-Western music, 307, 309
court ballet, 87
court society, 94
courtiers, Chinese, 87; in Handel's *Belshazzar*, 92; Parisian, 104
cowboy, 263, 249, 326
Cowell, Henry, 239
criticism, 181; autonomy, autonomist position, 16, 23; "contrapuntal," 18–20; literary and cultural, 34; twentieth-century, 16; "worldly," 15
Crosby, Bing, 267, 315
Crusader knights, 89
Cruz, Celia, 37, 41
csárdás, 28, 32; Tchaikovsky, 74
Cubism, 216

Cugat, Xavier, 253
cultural anthropology, 109; cultural chauvinism, 327; cultural contexts, 2, 83, 181, 215; cultural "framing," 108; cultural nationalism, 78, 133, 149; cultural tourism, 290; cultural work, 1, 11, 149

D'Alembert, Jean le Rond, 98
Da Vinci, Leonardo, 83
Dahlhaus, Carl, 27, 31, 49, 50, 128, 153, 192
dance, 20, 22, 23, 25, 28, 29, 46, 50, 52, 55, 56, 61, 65, 73–76, 87–89, 98, 99, 100, 107, 108, 114, 124–30, 134–35, 137, 143, 145, 149, 152–53, 167–69, 182, 196, 205, 222, 227, 230, 238–40, 244, 246, 249, 250, 253, 255, 259, 263, 266, 268, 269, 271, 277, 293, 319, 322
Dancourt, Louis Hurtaut, 112
Daudet, Alphonse, 263
David, Félicien, *Le désert*, 19, 25, 152, 153
Dead Can Dance (group), 308
Dean, Winton, 91–92
Debussy, Claude, 31, 33; *La cathédrale engloutie*, 65; *Children's Corner*, 243; *Cloches à travers les feuilles*, 228; *Épigraphes antiques*, 221; *Golliwoggs* [sic]*Cakewalk*, 243; *Ibéria*, 56, 229; Incidental music for Louÿs's *Chansons de Bilitis*, 219; *L'isle joyeuse*, 228; *La mer*, 221, 222; Nocturnes for orchestra, 228; *Pagodes*, 5, 6, 7, 22, 27, 56, 214, 229, 230, 232–36, 239, 242, 281, 291; *Pelléas et Mélisande*, 182; *Prélude à l'Après-midi d'un faune*, 5, 6, 218, 219, 220, 221, 228, 242; *Six épigraphes antiques*, 219; *Soirée dans Grenade*, 56, 229, 230, 232; *Trois chansons de Bilitis*, 219; *Voiles*, 228
declamation, 53, 172, 186, 196, 245
Delacroix, Eugène, 43, 44, 181
Delétré, Bernard, 101, 104
Delibes, Léo, *La source*, 130; *Lakmé*, 150, 162, 165, 182, 185, 186, 195, 196, 206, 233, 262, 266, 309, 314
De Mille, Agnes, 249
Denny, Martin, 253
Denza, Luigi, 72, 73
Diaghilev, Serge, 223, 224, 225, 227; *Cléopâtre*, 225; *L'oiseau de feu*, 223, 225; *Le sacre du printemps: Tableaux de la Russie païenne*, 225; *Shéhérazade*, 223–24
Diderot, Denis, 98
"Dies irae" chant, 248
Dietrich, Marlene, 306
Dinicu, Grigoras, 148
dioramas, 131

Dissidenten (German "Turk-Rock" group), 308
Ditan, Karl, 259
Dittersdorf, Karl Ditters von, 131
divertissement, 99, 130, 196
Donát, János, 138
Donizetti, Gaetano, 157
Doppler, Franz, 141
drone, *see* harmony
Dünya (ensemble), 317
Dvořák, Antonín, *Moravian Duets*, 77; Symphony No. 9 ("New World"), 74–77, 130

Early Modern Era, 21, 94
Egypt(ian), 5, 7, 20, 25, 65, 76, 89, 116, 132, 136, 152–53, 175, 176, 180, 183, 185, 220, 262, 279, 281, 283, 284, 302, 325; courtesans, 221
Eichheim, Henry, 238
"Ein' feste Burg ist unser Gott," 80
El-Dabh, Halim, *Sweet and Prickly Pear*, 281; *The Reappearance of the Lotus Flower*, 281
Ellington, Duke, 253
empire(s), 5, 7, 18, 34–35, 37, 41, 58, 96, 97, 133, 136, 149, 175, 176, 177, 180, 181, 202, 215, 223, 261, 313–14; *see also* imperialism
empiricism (philosophical), 43–44
Encyclopédie (Diderot, D'Alembert), 98
Enesco(u), George, *Romanian Rhapsodies*, 149
England, 34, 36, 87, 90, 94, 95, 96, 97, 108, 109, 151, 185, 202, 216, 254; social structures, 94; Stuarts, 95; Whig politics, 90, 95, 96; *see also* Britain
Enlightenment, 98, 101, 103, 261
English Patient, The (film), 302
Enya (Irish singer), 308
Erdmann-Becce, *Allgemeines Handbuch der Film-Musik*, 263–66
Erener, Sertab, 310–11
escape-note figure, 53, 59
esotismo, 26, 33, 39
Esterházy, Johann Karl, 139
Ethiopia(n), 151, 180, 202, 273, 284, 289
ethnic groups (nations), frequently portrayed/imitated, 108–10, 126–35
ethnomusicology, 147, 215–16, 229, 277; *see also* music (non-Western), musicology
Euba, Akin, 281
Eurasianism, 225–26
Eurocentrism, 1, 38, 129, 290
Eurovision Song Competition, 310
"Everyway That I Can" (winning Eurovision song, 2003), 310
Exotic Composer's Toolkit, 55, 61

"Exotic Style Only" Paradigm, 2, 3, 4, 10, 11, 20, 22, 24, 27, 31, 44, 88, 105; defined, 48–59
Exotica (popular-music genre), 305–6
exoticism, 1, 6, 12, 26, 37, 38, 40, 41, 43–48 (definitions), 49, 51, 52, 53, 57, 62, 63, 64, 68–70, 72, 74, 75, 78, 80, 83, 86; Absorbed, 217 (definition), 222, 229, 242; commercialized, 33, 37; nationalism and, 72–79, 134; negative evaluations of, 25, 27–33; positive evaluations of, 25–26; "reverse exoticism," 66, 72; Submerged, 6, 214, 217 (definition), 222, 228, 229, 236, 242, 244, 302, 303; *see also* "All the Music in Full Context" Paradigm, auto-exoticism, codes, "Exotic Style Only" Paradigm, scales, transcultural
Exotic-Style Paradigm, *see* "Exotic Style Only" Paradigm

Falconer, Barbara, 286
Falla, Manuel de, 76, 282
falso esotismo, 33, 39
Fanon, Frantz, 34
Fanshawe, David, 300
Farwell, Arthur, 48
Favart, Charles-Simon, 112
Feidman, Giora, 301
femme fatale, 182, 185
femme fragile, 182, 185, 187
Fétis, François-Joseph, 153
film, 33, 46, 61, 62, 63, 71, 79, 80, 253, 263, 266, 303; film music, 1, 7, 51, 56, 63, 69, 81, 84, 167, 245, 260, 263–68, 279, 293, 300–3, 307, 308, 313–14, 319, 320, 326; Indian, 306; silent, 263; wartime propaganda, 267
fioritura, *see* melismatic singing
flamenco, 128, 155, 157, 167, 168, 169, 267, 271, 278, 305
Flaubert, Gustave, 266
Fokine, Michel, 224–25
folk, 129, 220; instruments, 282; music, 32, 73, 75, 76, 109–10, 128, 134; style, 268; traditions, 29, 123, 133; tunes, 107, 125, 132, 250, 289; *see also* music non-Western
folklore/folklorism, 22; nationalism and, 282, 283; studies of, 109
Ford, John, 266
formalism, 83, 91, 181
Foucault, Michel, 9, 200
France, 25, 34, 36, 66, 73, 78, 88, 97, 99, 105, 108, 112, 113, 154, 160, 163, 175, 176, 179, 180, 202, 214, 215, 218, 223, 228, 237, 254, 257, 263, 276, 292; colonialism, 149, 179, 180, 261; courtiers, 111; Early Modern, 105; "greater," 257; painting in, 43; theater in, 94
François, Jacqueline, 305
Frankenburger, Paul, *see* Ben-Haim
French overture, 107
Full-Context Paradigm, *see* "All the Music in Full Context" Paradigm.
Fuller, Walter, 254
Fuzelier, Louis, 98, 99, 100, 103, 105, 322

Gabriel, Peter, 301
gagaku, 247, 278, 285
galop, 80
gamelan, 26, 30, 38, 56, 129, 132, 230–36, 238, 239, 242, 244, 285
García, Manuel, 128, 162
Gardner, Isabella Stewart, 256
Gardner, Oscar, 252
Garrison, Jimmy, 299
Gatti, Guido, 246
gavotte, 41, 246
George II, 95
German art songs (Lieder), 134–35
Gerrard, Lisa, 308
Gershwin, George, *Porgy and Bess*, 68, 261, 262; *Rhapsody in Blue*, 149; song arrangements, 252
Getz, Stan, 299
ghazāl, 135
Ghislanzoni, Antonio, 180
Gide, André, *Chansons de Bilitis*, 219; *L'immoraliste*, 33, 219; *Psyché*, 219
gigue, 88
Gilbert, Paul-César, 112
Gilbert, W. S. and Arthur Sullivan, *The Mikado*, 19, 150, 203, 326
Gilberto, Astrud, 299
Gillespie, Dizzy, 253
Giordani, Marcello, 79
"Girl from Ipanema, The," 299
"Git Along Little Dogies," 249
gitanos, 136, 154, 155, 156; *see also* Roma (in Spain), Gypsies
Glass, Philip, 287
Glinka, Mikhail Ivanovich, 45; *Jota aragonesa*, 76, 84; *Ruslan and Lyudmila*, 223, 226
glissando, 280
globalization, 6, 8, 24, 35, 276–77, 297–98, 323
Glover, Thomas Blake, 326
Gluck, Christoph Willibald Ritter von, 57, 110, 117; *La rencontre imprévue* (*Les pèlerins de la Mecque*), 123; *Orfeo ed Euridice*, 112

Gobineau, Count Joseph Arthur, 184
Golijov, Osvaldo, 291–92
Gomes, Carlos, 178
Gong Dong-Jian, 296
Górecki, Henryk, 77
Gosselain, André, *see* Hossein
Gottschalk, Louis Moreau, *La bamboula*, 106, 106; *Le banjo*, 127
Goudimel, Claude, 316
Gounod, Charles (François), *Faust*, 130; *Funeral March of a Marionette*, 167; *Mireille*, 67, 73; Symphony No. 1, 73, 81
Gradenwitz, Peter, 19, 26
Greatful Dead, The, 301
Greco, José, 267
Gregorian chant, 21, 65, 77, 85
Grétry, André-Ernest-Modeste, 113
Grieg, Edvard, 31; *Peer Gynt*, 222; *Slåtter*, Op. 72, 245
Griffes, Charles, 42
Griffiths, Paul, 282, 297
Grofé, Ferde, 249
Gubaïdulina, Sofia, 282
Guiraud, Ernest, 163
Gutiérrez, Antonio García, 156
Gypsy, 5, 8, 11, 19, 24, 28, 29, 37, 41, 46, 54, 59, 69, 70, 106, 107, 117, 126, 131, 134, 135–49, 150–74, 228, 229, 232–33, 246, 250, 262, 271, 313, 316, 320; *see also* Roma

habanera, 166, 168–69, 313–15
Hafiz, 135
haka, 303
Halévy, Fromental, 161; *La juive*, 67, 73
Handel, George Frederic, 41; *Belshazzar*, 4, 7, 62, 68, 89–97, 101, 105–6, 325; *Giulio Cesare*, 62, 64; *Orlando*, 322; *Radamisto*, 88; *Rinaldo*, 88, 89; *Solomon*, 90; *Tamerlano*, 10, 62, 68, 88, 89
Hanslick, Eduard, 25
Happy Captive, The (opera), 111
harem, 9, 12, 36, 37, 43, 98, 111, 116, 177, 310, 323
harmony, 51, 57, 208, 236, 243, 290; blues, 243; drones, 57, 63; pan-diatonic, 291; parallel, 186; Rameau and, 99; tonal, 49, 51–52, 55, 61, 63, 87, 130
Harnoncourt, Nikolaus, 92, 114
Harrison, George, 306
Harrison, Lou, 234, 238, 239, 241
Hart, Mickey, 301
Havana, 128, 168, 215, 250, 256, 315
Haydn, Franz Joseph, symphonies, 236; Symphony No. 100, "Military," 122

Head, Mathew, 37, 41
"Heart Full of Soul" (raga rock song), 306
Heifetz, Jascha, 148
Heine, Heinrich, 134
Heinichen, Johann David, 87
Henson, Karen, 179, 198
Herder, Johann Gottfried von, 109
Herman, Woody, 250
Herrmann, Bernard, 266
heterophony, 57, 63, 119, 129, 147, 148, 234, 283
Hindemith, Paul, 244
"Hindic melody," 196
Hindu, 4, 36, 73, 130, 152, 179, 180, 182, 196, 198, 233, 238; *see also satih*
hip-hop, 67, 310
Hispanic, 88, 128, 161, 174, 256, 269, 307
Hokusai, 222
Holst, Gustav, 42
Holy Roman Empire, 113
homme fragile, 194
Hope, Bob, 267
Hornbrook, Glendon, 240
Horner, James, 302
Hossein, Aminollah, 279
Hossein, André, *see* Hossein
Hovhaness, Alan, 247–48
Hudsucker Proxy, The (film), 251
Hungarian Rhapsodies, *see* Liszt
Hungarian-Gypsy music and style, 28–29, 70, 76, 137, 139, 140, 141, 142, 143, 144, 146–47, 278; *see also* Roma
Hungary, 5, 74, 82, 148, nationalism, 5, 136; *see also* Hungarian-Gypsy music, Roma
Huston, John, 293
hybridity, 229, 308; *see also* transcultural

"I Wonder Why She Kept On Saying Si Si Si Senor" (song), 254
Ibsen, Henrik, 222
"Ich schwitze nie" (German "alternative" group), 315
imperialism, 17, 18, 24, 34, 36, 38, 40–41, 65, 80, 90, 96, 133, 175, 176, 178–80, 185, 192, 203, 206, 207–8, 210–12, 215, 284, 295; British, 35, 39, 41, 45; cultural, 38, 42; French, 149, 179, 180, 261; ideologies of, 184; operatic references to, 175–213; opposition to, 17–18, 34, 185, 202–13
Incas, 97–105, 253; *see also* Peru
India, 4, 5, 17, 30, 53, 80, 89, 90, 97, 109, 130, 132, 133, 136, 153, 175–80, 222, 223, 238, 239, 247, 254, 263, 266, 267, 276, 287, 299, 304, 306

"Indochine," 257
Indonesia, 23, 26, 30, 52, 175, 176, 203, 229–36, 238–39, 293; *see also kampong,* gamelan, *tandak*
instrumental music, alleged superiority of, 21, 23; "pastoral" styles in, 108
intercultural, *see* transcultural
intermezzi (danced), 87
Iradier, Sebastián, *El arreglito* and *La paloma,* 128, 166, 168, 314, 315
Islam, Islamic, 9, 19, 40, 44, 88, 111, 112, 113, 116, 201, 217, 218, 223, 261, 313, 316, 317, 323; Islam, 43, 49; *see also* Koran, Muslims
Israel, State of, 37, 96, 201, 246, 279, 282, 283
Italy, 127, 180
Ito, Michio, 42
Ivanoff, Vladimir, 316, 317

Jackson, Peter (film director), 303, 304
Janáček, Leoš, 68
Janissary, 107, 114, 116, 118, 120, 122, 123, 125
Japan, "fragile" women in, 205; militarism, 293; music, 57, 204, 267, 285, 293; nationalism, 293; religion, 233; Steve Reich and Musicians in, 287; *nōh* drama, 240, 285; theater in, 285; vocal techniques, 299
"Japaneseness," 204, 205, 206
Japanese-sounding, 11, 12, 57, 63, 305
Java, *see* gamelan, Indonesia
jazz, 23, 76, 149, 236, 242, 243, 244, 245, 251–54, 268, 304, 309, 314, 315; Caribbean influences in, 253–54, 299–300; *see also* blues, ragtime
Jazzy B. (Jazzy Bains), 308
Jenkins, Karl, "Adiemus," 309
Jennens, Charles, 90–97
Jesus, 83, 91, 282
Jews and Judaism, 28, 29, 67, 73, 90, 94, 96, 106, 182, 245, 251, 255, 282, 283, 288, 291, 305, 316
"Jésus est la bonté même" (Christian hymn), 292
jig, 88
Jiao Jin-Hai, 315
John, Elton, 302
Johnson, J. Rosamond, 255
Jolivet, André, 237–38
Jolson, Al, 255
Jones, A. M., 287
Joplin, Scott, 256
Joyce, James, 160
Judas Iscariot, 83

Jugendstil, 218
"Just Like a Gypsy" (song), 254

kampong javanais (Paris, 1889), 230–31
Kant, Immanuel, 218
Kapur, Shekhar (film director), 302
kecak, 277
Kengyō, Mitsuzaki, 294
Ketèlbey, Albert, *In a Persian Market,* 25, 39, 43, 251, 252, 253, 284, 313, 314
Khachaturian, Aram, 250–51
Khayyám, Omar, 279
Ki no Tsurayuki (poet), 240
"Ki San Fou" ("Chinese foxtrot"), 257
King's Singers, 316
Kinks, The, 306
Kipling, Rudyard, *Kim,* 17, 34, 82, 254, 319
Kirchner, Ernst-Ludwig, 217
Kismet, 309
Klee, Paul, 217
klezmer, 251
Knowles, Beyoncé, 313
Koltói csárdás, 140, 146
Koran, *see* Qur'an
Korea, 280
koto, 285
Kremer, Gidon, 78
Krishna, 299
Kronos Quartet, 289
Kubrick, Stanley, *2001* (film), 296
Kuhnau, Johann, 131

Lacombe, Hervé, 169, 172, 174
Lakatos, 316
Lalo, Édouard, *Symphonie espagnole,* 22, 28; Symphony in G Minor, 73; *Namouna* (ballet), 222; *Rapsodie norvégienne,* 149
Lambert, Constant, 243, 245
Lamour, Dorothy, 266
Langey, Otto, 263
Lanner, Joseph, 129
Lasso, Orlando di, 41, 218
Latin America, 87, 249; music of 250, 252, 253, 268, 270, 271; *see also* Brazil, Caribbean, Hispanic
Layla and Majnun (Medieval Arabic story), 281
Lecuona Cuban Boys, 315
Lehár, Franz, *Das Land des Lächelns,* 260, 261, 268; *Die lustige Witwe,* 260
LeRoy, Ken, 272
lexicon of styles, 43, 44, 106, 107, 126, 128
Léger, Fernand, 243
Lieder, 134–35

Lion King, The (Disney film), 301, 302
Li Po, 297
Liszt, Franz, Fantasia on Hungarian Folk Melodies for Piano and Orchestra, 144; First Hungarian Rhapsody, *see* Hungarian Rhapsody No. 14; "Gypsy"-style works, 24; Hungarian Rhapsodies, 59, 65, 69–70, 75, 135–36, 139, 141, 143, 148, 229, 233, 316; Hungarian Rhapsodies, orchestral versions, 142; Hungarian Rhapsody No. 2, 29, 142–44; Hungarian Rhapsody No. 5 (Héroïde-élégiaque), 141–42; Hungarian Rhapsody No. 6, 142; Hungarian Rhapsody No. 7, 143; Hungarian Rhapsody No. 9 ("Carnival in Pesth"), 142; Hungarian Rhapsody No. 12, 142; Hungarian Rhapsody No. 14, 5, 107, 108, 140, 142, 144–48, 228, 291; *Mélodies hongroises*, 139; operatic fantasies, 289; Piano Sonata in B minor, 145; piece based on *El contrabandista*, 128; symphonic poems, 145; writings, 139, 143
Loesser, Frank, 256
London world's fair (1851), 132
Longchampt, Jacques, 284
Longfellow, Henry Wadsworth, 75
Loomba, Ania, 36
Lord of the Rings, The (film), 303
Loring, Eugene, 249
Lortzing, (Gustav) Albert, 67
Loucheur, Raymond, 149
Louis XIV, 40
Louisiana, 98
Louÿs, Pierre, 219, 221
Love Story (1944 film), 149
Loya, Shay, 141, 142, 229
Lully, Jean-Baptiste, 41, 87, 88, 94; *Le bourgeois gentilhomme*, 110–11
Lumbye, Hans Christian, 135
Luther, Martin, 80, 180

Ma, Yo-Yo, 295
Maceda, José, 280
Madagascar, 1, 73, 149, 153, 198
Maeterlinck, Maurice, *Pelléas et Mélisande*, 182
Magnificent Seven, The (film), 295
Mahavishnu Orchestra, 299
Mahler, Gustav, 58
Mahmud (sultan), 179
Mallarmé, Stéphane, 218
mambo, 249, 269, 270, 271, 273
Mannheim Rocket, 124
Marche des Janissaires, 114

Martin, Ricky, 324, 325
Mascagni, Pietro, 78, 79
Mason, A. E. W., 302
masque, 87; *see also* court ballet
Mass Ordinary, 301
Massenet, Jules, *Hériodade*, 64, 70, 152, 179, 196, 266, 271; *Le roi de Lahore*, 179, 180, 183, 196
Mattos, Gregório de, 88
Mayuzumi, Toshirō, 293
mazurkas, 7, 12, 75–76, 83, 131, 134, 246, 293; *see also* Chopin
mbira, 289–90
McClary, Susan, 37, 39, 41, 43, 164, 174, 188, 206, 212, 324, 325
McKibbon, Al, 253
McLaren, Malcolm, 309
McLerie, Allyn Ann, 274
McPhee, Colin, 234, 238–39, 242
Meck, Nadezhda von, 223
Mediterranean style, 283
Meet Me in St. Louis (film), 255
melismatic singing (coloratura), 53–54, 63–64, 92, 183, 185
melody, 53, 59, 222, 234, 237, 290
Mendelssohn, Felix, 28, 32; "Hebrides" Overture, 28, 32, 65, 71; music for *Athalie*, 64, 70; Symphony No. 3, "Scottish," 28, 32, 59, 65; *Italian* Symphony, 59, 65, 73, 81, 135; *Song without Words*, Op. 62, no. 1, in G major ("May Breezes"), 236; Symphony No. 3, "Scottish," 28, 59
Mendes, Sergio, 300
Mercer, Johnny, 256
Mercure de France, 99
Mescheriakova, Marina, 326
Messager, André, 227
Messiaen, Olivier, 217, 237; *Harawi* and *Turangalîla Symphony*, 238
Mexico, 249, 268, 315
Meyerbeer, Giacomo, 132; *L'Africaine*, 126, 153, 179, 182–84, 198; *Il crociato in Egitto*, 20; *Les huguenots*, 80, 88, 131, 165
Mérimée, Prosper, 163
microtonal inflections, 152
Middle Ages, 64–65, 71, 89
Middle East, 1, 4, 8, 9, 11, 19, 35, 38, 43, 46, 55, 61, 80, 90, 92, 106, 111, 113, 114, 121, 122–23, 127, 135, 150, 218, 220–23, 232, 233, 242, 247, 248, 252–53, 266, 276, 283, 296, 314, 324; belly dancing in, 132; music of, 53, 119, 122–23, 221
"Middle Eastern," 61, 67

Milhaud, Darius, 243
Miller, Jonathan, 62
Minkus, Ludwig (Léon), 130
minstrelsy, *see* blackface
minuet, 117
Misa criolla, 301
Misraki, Paul, 257
Miss Saigon, 326
Missa luba, 301
mode (and modal), 49, 51, 55, 57, 87, 94, 99, 118, 120, 124–26, 130, 134, 141, 145, 153, 156, 157, 162, 166, 167, 170, 185, 188, 189, 190, 194, 198, 200, 204, 232, 234, 235, 237–39, 247, 253, 262, 183, 302, 306, 315; Middle Eastern, 119
modernism, 29, 42, 49, 55, 56, 78, 216, 228, 237, 248, 251, 271, 278, 280, 282, 284, 286, 288, 298, 307
Mohammed, 112, 179
Mohammedan, *see* Muslim
Moiseyev dance company, 277
Molière, 88, 94, 110, 111
"Mo-Li-Hua" tune, 9, 190, 295
Monelle, Raymond, 32, 57–58
Mongolian fiddle, 280
monotone, 53
Monsigny, Pierre-Alexandre, 67
Montagu, Lady Mary Wortley, 36
Montand, Yves, 305, 306
Montesquieu, 111, 112
Montezuma, 89
Monti, Vittorio, 148
Moody Blues, The, 306
Moor, 116, 227
Moore, Thomas, 70
Moreira, Airto, 299
moresca, 109
Morris, William, 219
Morrison, Simon, 152
Morrissette, Alanis, 308
Morton, Jelly Roll, 252
Moshinsky, Elijah, 321
Mouskouri, Nana, 314
Mozart, Wolfgang Amadeus, *Don Giovanni*, 169; *Die Entführung aus dem Serail*, 25, 37, 57, 80, 113–14, 116, 118, 120–21, 126, 201, 263, 322–23; *Idomeneo*, 64; Keyboard Sonata in F, K533/494, 55; Piano Sonata in A K331, 123; "Rondo alla turca," 5, 7, 8, 19, 22, 28, 37, 43, 55, 67, 84, 107, 121, 123–26, 142, 228, 281, 291, 312, 316; Serenade in B-flat Major for Thirteen Wind Instruments, K361, 118; symphonies, 236; Variations for Piano K455, 117; Violin Concerto in A Major, K219, 117; Violin Concerto No. 5, 50; *Zaïde*, 323; *Die Zauberflöte*, 68, 116
multicultural, 229, 241
Murphy, Donna, 319
"musette," 41, 67
music, non-Western, 4, 5, 11, 24, 26, 30, 31, 62, 66, 100, 111, 120, 128, 142, 146, 180, 198, 213, 220–23, 229, 237–39, 241, 247, 261, 268, 277, 281, 284, 285, 287, 288, 301, 302, 308, 309, 327; increased dissemination of, 215–16, 277; scales, 120; traditions, 31, 100
musical comedy, 254–55, 268, 271; *see also* Broadway
musicology, 21, 23, 56, 215, 229
Muslim, 4, 36, 65, 89, 90, 101, 103, 116, 133, 155, 179–80, 227, 292, 311, 316, 317, 322
Musorgsky, Modest, *Boris Godunov*, 152, 223; *Pictures at an Exhibition*, 67–68

nation, *see* ethnic groups
national styles, 4, 29, 106, 107, 126, 128, 252
nationalism, 22, 27, 66, 77, 138, 244, 245, 250; cultural, 78, 133, 149; musical, 2, 4, 136, 216; Polish, 12; Soviet, 250, 282; *see also* national styles
Native American(s), 6, 48, 50, 54, 55, 56, 61, 68, 75, 81, 83, 98, 136, 254
New Age music, 308
New World, 7, 88, 89, 101
Newman, Alfred, 266
Newman, John Henry, 18
noble savage, 98, 99
Noble, T. Tertius, 263
"non-exotic exoticism," 22
"Non-Exotic Style Only" Paradigm, unhelpfulness of, 4
North Africa, 33, 66, 76, 109, 179–80, 257, 310; *see also* Egypt, Moor
North, Alex, 80
North America(n), 7, 25, 28, 66, 68, 97, 98, 127, 129, 133, 151, 152, 247, 249, 251, 252, 256, 276–79, 293, 299, 304, 322; *see also* Native American(s)
Norway and Norwegian music, 28, 31, 37, 61, 128, 135, 149, 244, 306

"Occidentalism," 35
octatonic, 6, 51, 52, 58, 152, 217, 226, 227, 236, 238

Offenbach, Jacques, 153, 154, 166, 179
  Ba-Ta-Clan, 80; *Les brigands*, 154
offensiveness, 40–41, 255
"On the Road to Mandalay," 254
One Hundred Guitars (Madrid group), 305
One Thousand and One Nights, see *Thousand and One Nights*
Onedin Line, The (television miniseries), 251
opera, 45, 46, 51, 52, 56, 61–63, 67–70, 76, 78, 79, 84, 86–89, 94, 95, 110–14, 150–213, 262, 266, 269, 271, 274, 298, 321; *alla turca*, 87; arias, 52, 53, 58–59, 64, 70, 82, 90; comic, 67, 72, 80, 88, 94, 112, 116, 150, 157, 260; French, 88, 112, 161, 163, 165, 170, 172; grand, 163, 192, 309; Orientalist, 181; staging, 317–25; tragic, 94; Venetian, 87; see also Bizet, Delibes, Handel, Meyerbeer, Mozart, Puccini, Rameau, Rossini, Saint-Saëns, Verdi
opera seria, 94, 111
opera-ballet, 114, 269
operetta, 80, 150, 179, 216, 254, 260, 261, 262, 268, 269, 271, 273
opéra-bouffe, 154, 166
opéra-comique, 80, 113, 166, 195
opéra-lyrique, 195
oratorio, 5, 7, 19, 22, 24, 38, 41, 60–64, 66–68, 70, 76, 79, 82, 87–91, 94, 96, 152, 172, 178; secular, 19; see also David (Félicien), Handel
"Orient," 5, 12, 61, 67
Orientalism, 3, 33–43, 46, 52, 61, 67, 177, 178, 181, 183, 184, 186, 192, 194, 200, 202, 208, 282, 311; applied to music, 36–38
Osborne, Joan, 308
"Other," internal, 7, 150, 156, 162; see also binarism (Self/Other)
Ottomans and Ottoman Empire, 5, 37, 41, 58, 64, 89, 90, 110, 113, 114, 122, 133, 136, 149, 177, 317; sultans, 90
Oulibicheff, *see* Ulibichev
Overt Exoticism, 6, 217, 281, 303

Palestine, 283
Parakilas, James, 76, 161, 162, 167, 168, 184
pitch, overemphasis on, 49–50
Paris, Colonial Exhibition (1931), 237; in the 1920s, 257; Opéra, 113; World's Fair (1889), 132, 227, 230–31; World's Fair (1900), 251
Partch, Harry, 38, 39, 240, 241; *Eleven Intrusions* (1949–51) for voice, altered guitar, and a diamond-shaped marimba, 240;

Delusion of the Fury, 38, 240; *Oedipus*, 38; *Revelation in the Courthouse Square*, 38
Pasipamire, 290
Paul Whiteman Orchestra, 315
Pears, Peter, 242
pedal point, 299; pedal tones, 226
Peircean semiotics, 48, 54
pentatonic(ism), 11, 20, 50, 51, 57, 63, 127, 128, 129, 134, 184, 187, 188, 189, 190, 194, 200, 203, 222, 226, 233–35, 238, 242, 252, 262–63, 295, 305, 307, 314
Pera Ensemble, 317
performance, 70, 143, 171; today, 312–17; see also opera (staging)
Perry, Commodore Mathew C., 177
Persia, 90, 97, 114
Peru, 1, 4, 87, 98, 100–5, 151
"Petite Tonkinoise" (*chanson*), 5, 7, 259, 268
Phillips, Lou Diamond, 319
phrase structure, 50, 53, 55, 63, 118, 120–21, 123; "asymmetrical," 53, 59
Piazzolla, Astor, 17, 77, 78, 79
Picasso, Pablo, 217, 289
pien tones, 129
pirates, 43, 98, 111, 177, 222
Pisani, Michael, 48, 49, 55, 81, 135, 327
Platen, August von, 134
Plomer, William, 285
Poe, Edgar Allan, 182
Poland, 12, 77, 109; see also Chopin, mazurka
polka, 128, 319
polonaise, 28, 107, 128
Ponselle, Rosa, 174
popular music, 1, 7, 252–60, 277, 300, 304, 306, 308, 300, 304, 310
Porter, Cole, 257
postmodern(ism), 278, 288, 297
Poulenard, Isabelle, 101
Poulenc, Francis, 219; Concerto for Two Pianos, 238
Pozo, Chano, 253
Prado, Pérez, 253
Pre-Raphaelitism, 216
Presley, Elvis, 304, 314
Price, Leontyne, 199
primitive, 29, 49, 55, 79, 111, 114, 122, 156, 171, 185, 198, 227, 237, 243, 262, 300, 309; religion, 237
primitivism, 37, 216, 226, 227, 237–37, 243
Princess Cheungping, 295
"progressiveness" in music, 50, 248, 320, 322, 327
Prokofiev, Serge, 227

Protestant, liturgical styles, 301
Protestant(ism), 41, 112, 301, 317
Psalter (Genevan,) 316, 317
Puccini, Giacomo, *La Bohème*, 155, 206; *La fanciulla del West*, 205, 248; *Madama Butterfly*, 1, 2, 5, 7, 8, 11, 12, 18–20, 39, 43, 44, 50, 57, 59, 150, 178, 182, 184, 186–88, 197–213, 215, 262, 271, 319, 324, 325–26; *Il tabarro*, 265, 266; *Tosca*, 20, 196, 201, 205, 206; *Turandot*, 9, 189, 190, 295
Puente, Tito, 253

"Que ne suis-je la fougère" (French song), 292
Quing Miao, 318
Quinn, Anthony, 267
Qur'an, 103, 111, 112, 233, 288, 317, 322; on wine, 113

"race records," 251
racialism, 184, 254
radio, 74, 77, 237, 250, 252, 277, 284, 292, 299, 305, 308
rāga-based music (India), 59, 238, 299, 306
raga rock, 306
ragtime, 242, 244, 252, 256
Rahman, A. R., 309
Ramaka, Joseph Gaye, 313
Rameau, Jean-Philippe, *Les Incas du Pérou*, 100, 321; *Les Indes galantes*, 4, 7, 58, 62, 64, 67, 73, 80, 97, 98, 99, 100, 101, 102, 103, 104, 105, 106, 131, 163, 261, 321, 322; *Platée*, 68, 74; *Les sauvages* (harpsichord piece), 98, 99, 322; recitative, 104
rap, 66, 72; Algerian, 310
Rapée, Erno, *Motion Picture Moods*, 263
Ravel, Maurice, *Chansons madécasses*, 53; *Boléro*, 229; *Daphnis et Chloé*, 37, 41, 64, 70, 227; "Laideronnette, impératrice des pagodes," 28, 32, 229; *Rapsodie espagnole*, 227, 229; *Tzigane*, 148; Violin Sonata, "Blues," 244; encounters with blues and jazz, 76
Rákóczi March, 141
Reich, Steve, *Clapping Music*, 287; *The Desert Music*, for chorus and orchestra, 288; *Different Trains*, 289; *Drumming*, 287; *Electric Counterpoint*, 287; *Music for 18 Musicians*, 287–88; *Tehillim*, 287, 289
Renaissance, 20, 21; polyphony, 194
Renan, Ernest, 184
repetition, 50, 53, 56, 59
Respighi, Ottorino, 248
Revalles, Flore, 224

revolution, Russian, 65, 223; Chinese, 318
rhapsody (genre), 107, 144, 149
rhythms, 20, 27, 31, 32, 49, 50, 52, 53, 54, 55, 56, 63, 83, 127, 134, 142, 152, 157, 181, 204, 219, 226, 227, 237, 239, 243, 246, 269, 287, 306, 315; "chattering," 127, 204; dissonant meter, 219; *aksak*, 310; habanera-like, 256; *huapango*, 271; irregular, 219; ostinato, 52, 58; jazzy, 315; rhumba beat, 256; rubato, 171, 316; syncopated, 127, 142, 144, 146, 149, 226, 242, 243, 246, 253, 268, 290
Rice, Eric, 123
Riley, Terry, 286
Rimsky-Korsakov, Nikolay Andreyevich, *Capriccio espagnol*, 27, 41, 50, 76, 149; *The Golden Cockerel*, 226; *Sadko*, 152, 223; *Shéhérazade* (Fokine ballet), 224–25; *Sheherazade*, 50, 59–60, 106, 221, 224–25, 313, 315; Symphony No. 2, "Antar," 227
Ring cycle (Wagner), 68, 133
ritual, 161, 166, 196, 200, 246, 277; African, 300; Tibetan Buddhist, 297; Jolivet and, 237; ritualistic exchanges, 197
Rivera, Chita, 272
Road to [Exotic Place X], The (Crosby/Hope films), 267–68
Robbins, Jerome, 271
rock music, 66, 72; *see also* raga rock
Rodgers, Richard, and Oscar Hammerstein II, *The King and I*, 262; *Oklahoma*, 271; *South Pacific*, 266, 270
Roland, tales of, 65
Rolling Stones, The, 306
Roma, 1, 7–8, 19, 29, 59, 67, 69, 70, 108, 126, 133, 136, 137, 139, 141, 143, 148, 150, 169, 229, 233; in Hungary, 1, 19, 21, 135–49; in Spain, 5, 154–57, 167; *see also* Gypsy, Hungarian-Gypsy music
Romantic(ism), 43, 216, 241, 284, 307; binary oppositions, 185; era in music, 165, 188; fulfillment, 303; ideology, 241; illusion, 205; individualism, 241; movies, 267; subjectivity, 216
romantic love triangle, 182
Romberg, Sigmund, *The Desert Song*, 261–62, 271; *The New Moon*, 261
Rossi, Salamone, 316
Rossini, Gioachino (Antonio), *Il barbiere di Siviglia*, 127; *La donna del lago*, 32, 36, 157; *L'italiana in Algeri*, 46, 70; *Mosè in Egitto*, 151; *Le siège de Corinthe*, 151
Rousseau, Jean-Jacques, *Le devin du village*, 67
rural areas, 52; music of, 109

Russia(n), 4, 6, 12, 17, 23, 27, 29, 39, 41, 66, 76, 78, 106, 113, 127, 130, 132, 133, 134, 136, 152, 177, 197, 222, 223, 225, 227, 228, 236, 242, 244, 245, 250, 282, 313; folk songs, 132
Rückert, Friedrich, 61, 70

Saadi, 279
Sabicas, 305
Said, Edward W., 4, 15, 17, 34–36, 41, 183, 200
Saint-Saëns, Camille, "Rhapsodie mauresque," 149; *Samson et Dalila*, 11, 19, 21, 82, 90, 150, 182–84, 196, 201, 215, 219–20, 268, 270, 271, 320, 321; Symphony No. 2, 73, 81; *Suite algérienne*, 149, 215; *Triptyque*, Op. 136, 215
Sakamoto, Kyu (singer), 305
Sakura (traditional Japanese song), 59, 65
saltarello, 73, 127
samba, 246, 273, 293
sarabande, 23, 88, 107, 109
Saracens, 65, 322
Sarasate, Pablo de, 148
Sarband, 316
satih (suttee), 36, 267
satire, 95, 109, 113, 154, 179
saxophone, 196, 197, 242, 243
Say, Fazıl, 312
Sayn-Wittgenstein, Princess Carolyne von, 139, 143
Sayonara (1957 film), 267
scale(s), anhemitonic, 130, 189; "black-note," 57, 129, 189, 222, 234, 252, 262, 314; chromatic, 87; chromatically altered, 51, 57; gamelan, 231; "gapped" (or "incomplete"), 49, 51, 128–30, 189, 226, 247, 295; scale(s), Japanese, 203–4; *kalindra* (Hungarian-Gypsy), 143; Messiaen and, 238; Partch's, 240; unusual, 217, 226, 236; Western, 162; whole-tone, 51, 52, 204, 217, 226, 228, 235; *see also* octatonic, pentatonic
Schenker, Heinrich, 3, 27, 30, 31, 217
Scherzinger, Martin, 290
Schnabel, Artur, 279
Schneider, Marcel, 286
Schoenberg, Arnold, 27, 29, 30; Piano Suite, 67; on folk traditions, 29; and modernism, 49
Schubert, Franz, *Divertissement à l'hongroise*, 139; "Du liebst mich nicht," 134–35; "Gretchen am Spinnrade," 58
Schumann, Robert, 134; *Arabeske*, Op. 18, 218; *Das Paradies und die Peri*, 70
Scorsese, Martin, *The Last Temptation of Christ* (film), 302

Scotland, 1, 28, 29, 32, 59, 65, 109, 110, 127, 150, 151, 157, 247, 254, 289; Scottish music and "Scottish" style, 28, 32, 109, 59, 65, 127, 157
Scott, Sir Walter, *The Lady of the Lake*, 32, 157
Scotto, Vincent, 259
Scribe, Eugène, 153
Self/Other, *see* binarism
self-exoticization, *see* autoexoticism
Seriem (*tandak* courtly dancer), 230
Sesame Street (TV show), 313
Seven Samurai, The (film), 295
Shakespeare, William, *Romeo and Juliet*, 12, 268, 269, 271
Shankar, Ravi, 306
Shankar, Uday, 247
Shaw, George Bernard, 151, 180
Sheik, The (film), 33, 37
Shelley, Percy Bysshe, 36
Sheppard, W. Anthony, 37, 267
Shore, Howard, film composer, 303, 304
Shostakovich, Dmitry, 76
siciliano, 107
signs, 75
Silk Road, 177, 297
Simon, Paul, *Graceland*, 301
Sinatra, Frank, 304
Sinbad, 60
slave trade, 18, 87
"sliding tones," 280
Smetana, Bedřich, 67
Soekia (*tandak* courtly dancer), 230
Solomon (King), 246
sonata(s), 16, 18, 21, 64, 107, 108, 125
Sondheim, Stephen, 270
song, 1, 7, 21, 22, 29, 30, 37, 51, 52, 55, 56, 58, 61, 62, 63, 69, 70, 78, 81, 109, 110, 123, 124, 128, 132, 133, 134, 135, 137, 144, 161, 167, 214, 238, 239, 244, 245, 247, 249, 251, 254, 255, 259, 261, 282, 300, 302, 305, 306, 307, 308, 314, 316; Armenian, 247; art, 21, 22, 23, 24, 61, 67; Broadway, 268, 273; folklike/"primitive," 55, 61; French, 134, 257; Neapolitan, 251; "stage" (diagetic), 167; parlor, 81, 89, 134, 216; *Sakura*, 59, 65; Western-style marching, 257; *see also* chanson, Lieder
sound-recording technology, 215, 301
"Sous le ciel d'Afrique" (song), 20–21
Soumagnas, Jean-Louis, 207
Sousa Band, 252
South America, 23, 88, 133, 151, 249, 281
Soviet Union, 250–51, 282–84

Spain, 5, 7, 22, 54, 55, 76, 103, 104, 105, 127, 128, 130, 133, 134, 136, 149–74, 222, 229, 233, 252, 268, 301, 305, 306, 312, 314, 315, 320, 322, 323; Basques in, 164; bolero, 127, 128; conquistadores, 98, 104; as exotic, 76; and maleness, 163; *see also* Gypsies, Hispanic
Speaks, Oley, 254
Spiegel, Magda, 158
Spies, Walter, 277
Spontini, Gaspare, 135; *Fernand Cortez*, 178, 184
Star Trek, 68
Star Wars (*The Phantom Menace*, film), 302
Star-Spangled Banner, The, 188
stereotype(s), 4, 5, 11, 21–22, 29, 32–36, 39, 42, 46, 49, 50, 59, 72, 78–81, 95, 104, 134, 155, 156, 160, 163, 168, 170, 177, 178, 182, 202, 245, 252, 254, 255, 262, 267, 290, 309–11, 321–24, 325, 326–27; anti-semitic, 29, 33, 100, 245; ethnic or "racial," 52; cultural, 38, 39, 40; defamatory, 43; ethnic or "racial," 46; cultural, 34, 35, 36; defamatory, 39; Enlightenment, 104
Strauss, Johann Jr., *1001 Nacht*, 80, 81; *Indigo und die vierzig Räuber*, 80; waltzes, 129; *Der Zigeunerbaron*, 150
Strauss, Richard, *Also sprach Zarasthustra*, 295; *Aus Italien*, 72, 73, 80; *Salome*, 81
Stravinsky, Igor, 39, 40, 181, 217, 223, 225, 226, 227, 236, 237, 242, 244, 246, 271, 280, 293; "Dumbarton Oaks" Concerto, 236; *L'oiseau de feu, Firebird*, 223, 225–27, 237; *Les noces*, 39, 40, 226; *Petrushka*, 227; *Le rossignol*, 244; *Le sacre du printemps*, 225, 227, 246
Streisand, Barbra, 67
styles, coded, 11, 32, 47, 48, 274; *see also* codes
style markers, 269
Submerged Exoticism, *see* exoticism
Subotnik, Rose Rosengard, 16
Sukiyaki (popular song), 305
sultan, 90, 92, 98, 110, 111, 113, 179, 180, 246, 311; Generous Sultan theme, 113
Sumac, Yma, 253
Supervia, Conchita, 315
Suppé, Franz von, 67
Survivor ("reality" game show), 310
Swabian allemande, 107
Symbolism, 216, 218
symphonic poem(s), 17, 22, 68, 107, 145
symphony, 16, 28, 29, 72, 73, 74, 107
syncopation, 134, 169, 242, 253, 256, 271, 310, 315

tableaux vivants, 131
Takemitsu, Tōru, 19; *Dorian Horizon*, 293; *November Steps* for *biwa, shakuhachi*, and orchestra, 7
Taminah (*tandak* courtly dancer), 230
Tan Dun, *Crouching Tiger*, 294, 295; *Marco Polo*, 296–98; *Symphony 1997: Heaven, Earth, Mankind*, 5, 294, 295, 298; *Marco Polo*, 5, 296, 297, 298; *The First Emperor*, 294
Tancred, tales of, 65
tandak (Javanese courtly dancers, Paris 1889): Seriem, Soekia, Taminah, Wakiem, 230
tango, 77, 78, 268
Taruskin, Richard, 3, 16, 22, 27, 39, 40, 42, 77, 223, 226
Tarzan (1999 animated film), 302
Tauber, Richard, 260
Taylor, Timothy D., 24, 301, 308, 309
Tchaikovsky, Pyotr Ilyich, 17; *Capriccio italien*, 72, 80; *Romeo and Juliet*, 12, 268; *Swan Lake*, 74; "Spanish Dance," from *The Nutcracker*, 76, 130, 265
"Tchin Tchin Lou, fille d'Asie" (popular song), 257
Tear, Robert, 92
"technologies of listening," 11
technology, 300; *see also* sound-recording technology
Teleki, Count Sandór, 140
Telemann, Georg Philipp, 109
Terry Snyder's All-Stars (jazz group), 253
tessitura, 54, 266
"textuality," 200
Thailand, 319
The Arabian Nights, see Thousand and One Nights
theater pianist, 33
"Them"; *see* binarism (Self/Other)
thematic transformation, 145
Thomas, Ambroise, *Mignon*, 28
Thousand and One Nights, The, 5, 18, 60, 69, 80, 91, 111, 150, 194, 310, 315
Tiersot, Julien, 25, 227
timbre, 20, 49, 50, 56
time, distance in, 64–65
Titanic (film), 302
Tizol, Juan, 253
todesca, 109
Tolkien, J. R. R., 303
Tolstoy, Count Leo, 322
TomTom (global positioning for autos), 314

tonality, *see* harmony, tonal
topics, or *topoi*, 32, 38, 46, 57, 58, 82, 107, 108, 121, 131, 176, 254
transcultural (and Transcultural Composing), 6, 214, 217, 222, 228, 229, 232, 233, 236, 239, 241–44 (definition), 281, 285
transethnic, 241
trepak, 130
tresillo, 315
Trio Bulgarka, 308
Trio Los Panchos, 305
Tsurayuki, Ki no (poet), 240
Tsypin, George, 323
Turkey, 3, 5, 29, 30, 36, 37, 50, 53, 56, 57, 58, 89, 98, 107–34, 152, 181, 223, 247, 251, 283, 307, 310–12, 316–17, 322–23; *see also* Janissary, Ottoman Empire, sultan
Turkish Captivity theme in literature and opera, 113
Turkish Janissary style, 107, 114, 116, 118, 120, 122, 123, 125
Turner, Bryan S., 34
Turque, La (or *Contredanse turque*), 114
Tuvan "throat-singing," 278
tyrant, Baroque operas about, 5, 10, 62, 68, 97; Eastern, 88, 95, 96, 97, 103, 104; New World, 101, 105; semi-comic Babylonian, 90, 91, 92

Ufki, Ali, *see* Bobowski
Ulibichev, Aleksandr, 113
"Under the Bamboo Tree," 255–56, 268
unison melodies, 247
usul, 123, 228
utopia, 68, 267

Valentino, Rudolph, 33
Van, Gilles de, 26, 69, 88
Varèse, Edgar, 236
Vartabed, Komitas, 247
Vasco da Gama, 153, 192, 198
vaudeville, 201, 254, 255
Vaughan Williams, Ralph, 245
Ventura, Ray, 257–58
verbunkos music, 137
Verdi, Giuseppe, *Aida*, 18, 20, 25, 26, 29, 30, 34, 38, 80, 82, 88, 90, 126, 151, 153, 180, 182–86, 192, 196, 202, 271, 273, 325; "Anvil Chorus," 156–57; cabalettas, 28, 32; *Un ballo in maschera*, 151; *Don Carlos*, 165, 196, 201; *La forza del destino*, 151; *Macbeth*, 151; *Nabucco*, 183; *Rigoletto*, 154, 157; *Simon Boccanegra*, 202; *La traviata*, 154, 160, 212; *Il trovatore*, 5, 28, 126, 150, 154, 156–60, 161, 162, 167, 188, 321
vernacularism, 22, 27
Verrett, Shirley, 153, 320–21
Villa-Lobos, Heitor, *Amazonas*, 246; early works, 246; "Notte tropicale," 248; "O trenzinho do Caipira," 246–47; string quartets, 247
Vivaldi, Antonio, concertos, Concerto in G Major for Strings and Continuo, RV 151, 70; concertos, as model for Bach, 73
vīnā, instrumental playing (India), 53
visual art, 26, 34–35, 43, 83, 91, 97, 110, 133, 176, 179, 181–83, 186, 216–17, 243, 289, 311
Vogler, Georg Joseph, Abbé, 129, 132
Volans, Kevin, *African Paraphrases*, 289; *Hunting:Gathering*, 289, 290; *White Man Sleeps*, 289
"Volare" (popular song), 305
Voltaire, 151

Wagner, Richard, 22, 27–28; *Der fliegende Holländer*, 61; *The Ring*, 68, 133
Wakiem (*tandak* courtly dancer), 230
Waley, Arthur, 240
Walker, George, 255
waltz, 80, 88, 127, 129, 192, 222, 205, 206, 266
Warren, Nina, 296
Watanabe, Yoko, 207
Waugh, Evelyn, 33
Waxman, Franz, film composer, 267
Weber, Andrew Lloyd, *Bombay Dreams*, 309
Weber, Carl Maria, 132, 142
Weill, Kurt, 243
West, the (Western portion of the United States of America), 249
West, the (Europe and America), 7, 23, 41, 95, 159, 288, 294; art music of, 2, 16, 17, 21, 27, 30, 31, 32, 54, 58, 66, 108, 110, 123, 128, 189, 214, 229, 236, 278–79, 281, 293; musical life in, 24, 78, 176; *see also* Westerner
Westerner(s), 2, 7, 8, 12, 19, 36, 56, 65, 98, 129, 175, 179, 181, 184, 188, 192, 194, 204, 222, 234, 261, 276, 278, 284, 288, 290, 299, 309, 326, 327
Westernization, 278
"Why Worry? I'm an Indian" (song), 254
"Wild West" shows, 254
Williams, Bert, 255
Williams, William Carlos, 288
witches, 87, 151
World Beat music, 301

World Columbian Exhibition (Chicago), 132
"world music," 287, 307, 309

Xolotl, Bernard, 286

Yamada, Kósçak (Kosaku), 42
Yanni, 309
Yardbirds, The, 306
Yeats, William Butler, 42
Young, La Monte, 241, 287

Young, Thomas, 296
Yun, Isang, 279–80

Zephira, Bracha (singer), 283
Ziegfeld Follies, 255
Zigeuner, 136
Zimmer, Hans (film composer), 301–2
zingarese, 145–46
zingari and *zingarelle*, 155
Zinzendorf, Count Carl von, 112

Printed in Great Britain
by Amazon